D0895607

American Diaries

American Diaries

An Annotated Bibliography of Published
American Diaries and Journals

FIRST EDITION

Volume 1:
Diaries Written from 1492 to 1844

Laura Arksey, Nancy Pries, and Marcia Reed

GALE RESEARCH COMPANY • BOOK TOWER • DETROIT, MICHIGAN 48226

Library of Congress Cataloging in Publication Data

Arksey, Laura.
    American diaries.

    Expansion and revision of a work by William
Matthews: American diaries: an annotated bibliography
of American Diaries written prior to the year 1861
        Contents: v. 1. Diaries written from 1492 to 1844 —
    Includes indexes.
        1. American diaries—Bibliography. 2. Autobio-
graphies—Bibliography. 3. United States—History,
Local—Sources—Bibliography. I. Pries, Nancy.
II. Reed, Marcia. III. Matthews, William, 1905-
American diaries. V. Title.
Z5305.U5A74 1983 [CT214] 016.92'0073 83-8860
ISBN 0-8103-1800-8 (v. 1)

Contents

Preface

A diary is a verification, proof that a person has lived and has cared enough about a life to describe it. Many have spent time on this planet, but few have made the effort to record their stay. The diarist is saying that at a particular time and place, a life has been lived and feelings have been felt and thoughts crossed a mind. The very act of recording has provided a unique attachment to surroundings and self, an opportunity to examine life. Just as Plato said, "The life which is unexamined is not worth living," one might ask, with the inveterate diarist, Emerson, "How can an unrecorded life BE examined?"

My own interest in diaries is as a collector and diarist. Both efforts go back to my ninth year. At that time I lived in a house that had a library, and the man who formed that library, my father, was a diarist. His library was in a small room at the foot of the stairs that led to my bedroom. I walked through a world of books every day of my life. I saw a person recording a life. At age nine I endeavored to record mine.

I also began collecting books on natural history. My home was on the edge of the bluff overlooking the Mississippi River in St. Paul, Minnesota, just one mile from Fort Snelling. It was a wonderful place in which to grow up and a wonderful way to live, with the downtown part of the city just a ten-minute streetcar ride and yet a relatively undisturbed wilderness out the back door. Describing nature seemed necessary.

I recorded my adventures "below the bluff" in a nature journal and also made an attempt to keep a diary that described my fourth grade experiences. I managed to keep the latter until summer vacation began, and then the days were nearly identical. There were no distinct happenings like the progress of classes, but only an idyllic swim in the river every day.

The next year I began another diary, but that, too, was not carried beyond June. The "bird journal", however, continued to receive the descriptions that nature provided. Then in my early teens, the nature journal gave way to a diary which I have kept regularly for thirty years, and my collecting of nature books, to a diary collection eventually numbering some 7000 volumes.

Although the terms tend to be used somewhat interchangeably, a diary is to me separate and distinct from a journal. A diary is for every day and tells what one did and thought, in the random, nonthematic fashion of real life. A journal is more formal, usually a book of observations on particular events, situations, or preoccupations of the writer. It may have an official purpose, such as the great exploration journals of Lewis and Clark, Zebulon Pike, and others. Of the journals dealing with particular themes or preoccupations, the nature journals of Audubon and John and William Bartram and the religious journals of Michael Wigglesworth, David Brainerd, and Mildred Ratcliff are notable.

Recordings of literary men and women often exemplify both journal and diary characteristics, with a certain thematic unity provided by the consuming interest in literature coupled with a zeal to record the welter of everyday life. Good examples are the diaries of Margaret Fuller and of Bronson Alcott, who asked:

> Was it the accident of being shown, when a boy, in the old oaken cabinet, my mother's little journal, that set me out in this chase of myself, continued almost uninterruptedly, and now fixed by habit as a part of the day, like the rising and setting of the sun? Yet it has educated me into whatever skill I possess with the pen. I know not to how much besides; has made me emulous of attaining the art of portraying my thoughts, occupations, surroundings, friendships; and could I succeed in sketching to the life a single day's doings, should esteem myself as having accomplished the chiefest feat in literature.

True diaries, especially of people who had no idea their private lives would ever be made public through the publishing of their diaries, provide an astonishing picture of the variety of human experience. Some diaries are little more than account books or records of the weather. Others are voluminous and comprehensive works of such compulsive diarists as Samuel Sewall and George Templeton Strong. Some are practical, telling of the running of a household, business, or plantation, or of labor conditions, prices, or the progress of technology and invention. Occupations of all kinds and periods are revealed through diaries. Archaeologists, farmers, whalers, teachers, doctors, missionaries, artists, and fur traders have all, either incidentally or intentionally, recorded details of their work. Leisure as well as work activities emerge through diaries. The notes of play and concert goers are entertaining and informative, as are the enthusiasms and experiences of hunters, fishermen, mountaineers, book collectors, photographers, etc. The diaries of tourists and travelers range from feeble and conventional descriptions of buildings, scenes, or countries, to the excellent and exuberant records of Francis Parkman, Richard Henry Dana, and Louisa Lord.

Some diaries have been kept for a specific duration of time in order to record significant events or circumstances. War, pioneer, and prison diaries are examples. The anonymous "Cholmley's batman" kept an outstanding account of Braddock's defeat in the French and Indian wars, while a good picture of civilian experience during war can be found in Grace Galloway's diary of Philadelphia during the Revolution. Both men and women were amazingly prolific recorders of the pioneer experience, and the diaries of Mary Richardson Walker and James Clyman are representative. Prison and prisoner-of-war diaries are of great interest, not only for their content, but for the heroic efforts often required to keep them. For example, a World War II prisoner used the pins in blackout curtains to prick words on rolls of toilet paper, which he then dropped through a grate and recovered years later. Of course, the American Revolution and Civil War provide many examples from the more distant past.

Finally, there are fascinating introspective diaries, such as Emerson's and Thoreau's, often with more attention devoted to reflections than events. Such diarists have followed Emerson's injunction to "Pay so much honor to the visits of truth to your mind as to record them." They ask, "Why am I here and what am I doing with my life?" One sees here that the search for a meaningful life becomes meaningful by reason of recording. In fact, the life and the diary may have an unusual symbiotic effect, with the diarist living a good life to record a good life.

Diaries, as primary sources, are obviously grist for the historian's mill. But they are also a too often overlooked source of enjoyment and enlightenment for the ordinary reader, for from them, we can learn so much about people, events, and ourselves. Therefore, I welcome the new *American Diaries* as a means of making published diaries more accessible to all categories of users. I, myself, shall continue to be an avid keeper, reader, and collector of diaries.

James Cummings
Stillwater, Minnesota

Introduction

American Diaries: An Annotated Bibliography of Published American Diaries and Journals to 1980 is being published in two volumes. The present volume, *Diaries Written from 1492 to 1844,* guides librarians, scholars, students, and general readers to more than 2500 published diaries and journals. Volume 2: *Diaries Written from 1845 to 1980,* scheduled for publication in 1985, will annotate another 2500 diaries and journals. Together these two volumes will supersede the previous authoritative work in this field, William Matthews' *American Diaries: An Annotated Bibliography of American Diaries Written Prior to the Year 1861* (University of California Press, 1945), providing approximately 5000 citations as compared to the earlier work's 2400, while also adding subject and geographic indexing, expanding the name indexing, and augmenting the bibliographic citations.

Need for Revision and Expansion of Matthews' Work

The bibliographic treatment of diaries as a distinct genre has a short but distinguished history. In 1923 Harriette M. Forbes published her *New England Diaries, 1602-1800.* In the same year, Arthur Ponsonby performed a similar service for English diaries with the first of his series of works combining bibliography with extensive diary extracts. In both countries, however, the prodigious activity of the late William Matthews remains unsurpassed. A professor of English linguistics, he began the study of diaries as a means of analyzing linguistic change but quickly discovered in them such antiquarian, historical, and human interest values as to claim his attention for the remainder of his life.

Matthews' work with American diaries resulted in two important bibliographies: *American Diaries: An Annotated Bibliography of American Diaries Written Prior to the Year 1861* (University of California Press, 1945) and *American Diaries in Manuscript, 1850-1954: A Descriptive Bibliography* (University of Georgia, 1974). Both are widely held in libraries and have made a substantial contribution to American historical scholarship. However, the decades that have elapsed since its 1945 publication and the original restrictions in scope of Matthews' *American Diaries* have made the need for a major revision and expansion apparent.

Interest in Personal and Local History

The decision to undertake such a project now was prompted partly by the evident interest in personal and local history among users of both public and academic libraries. People seem to want to know about others' lives; not just the lives of the famous, the individual makers of history, but the legions of unknown people who were affected by their deeds or who, engaged in a common pursuit, helped shape the events of history. Thus, readers are seeking out, through diaries and other personal narratives, the experiences of Civil War soldiers, pioneers of the westward migration, the history of a particular town, or the stories of their own immigrant forebears. At the same time, interest has not waned in the lives of the famous or infamous. However, readers are also curious about the famous as "ordinary" people, about the day-to-day events and influences surrounding the achievements for which they are known. But rather than relying entirely on the biographer or historian to select from and organize such material, some readers want to do such sifting of detail for themselves and turn to published diaries, letters, and other personal records for this purpose. Whether dealing essentially with persons or events, they would agree with William Matthews that:

> The historian can give you an orderly . . . account of major social practices and general events at particular times, but only a good diary can give you the fine detail and the wondrous confusions of daily life and the feelings and momentary reflections that reveal the living reality of the period.

Many Old Diaries Recently Reprinted

Publishing, too, both of primary and secondary works, reflects this heightened interest in the history of individuals. For while biographies proliferate, so do their primary counterparts, published auto-biographies, memoirs, letters, journals, and diaries. The first person voice is allowed to speak, not only to a historian deciphering a manuscript, but to the reading public as well. Not only are many diaries being published for the first time, many useful diaries long out of print have been reprinted or entirely reedited, many of them issued for the American Bicentennial. Although the reprint boom of recent memory has waned, it has left many libraries stocked for years to come with diaries previously held only in the largest research libraries, or at best, available in fragile old copies in rare book rooms. A major purpose of the new *American Diaries,* therefore, is to make such recently published, reprinted, or reedited diaries more widely known and easily accessible to the reader.

Present Work Covers Many Diaries Not in Matthews

Another factor prompting the decision to expand and revise Matthews' *American Diaries* was the incompleteness of some aspects of the original work. Not only have many diaries appeared since his 1945 publication, but because of his cut-off date, his work excluded an enormous body of material available to him. Thus, because Matthews carried his work only through diaries begun prior to 1861, the period of the Civil War through World War II was omitted. As he explained, "So numerous are the diaries of Americans who took part in the Civil War that when I was making my bibliography of American diaries, my courage failed me and I called a halt at 1860." Furthermore, Matthews' definition of American, while in accord with the lights of the time, dictated the omission of all Alaskan, Hawaiian and much Spanish-American material. Colonial America, to him, was largely the English-speaking eastern seaboard, and the diaries of the Spanish explorers and settlers of the Southwest, in territory once under Spanish domain, were excluded. By his own choice, he also omitted the diaries of American missionaries serving in foreign countries. The present work not only goes back to pick up diaries published during Matthews' time and omitted for the above reasons, but incorporates, as well, the results of much recent publishing of Hawaiian, Alaskan, Spanish, French, Russian, and missionary material. We do not fault the thoroughness of Matthews' coverage within his intended scope, for it was thorough indeed, but rather point out the importance of diaries which must now be included because of the addition of two new states and a long-needed recognition of American backgrounds other than English.

Subject, Geographic, and Name Indexes Included

Matthews' work was incomplete in another sense of importance to librarians and subject researchers. Although it included an index of diarists, it omitted subject and geographic indexing. His reasons are stated in the preface to his *British Diaries,* but apply equally to the American work:

> The request of several reviewers for a subject index was so much easier to make than to satisfy that I have rejected the idea ... There is danger in a subject index which by noting certain subjects and not others may suggest that others may not be dealt with. Every diary includes a multiplicity of subjects which I have been unable to note; my annotations are suggestive, not comprehensive ...

While recognizing these dangers and that no such indexing can absolutely avoid sins of omission, we have chosen to add subject and geographic indexing. As Matthews feared, the problem is one not only of indexing but of analyzing and annotating the diaries in the first place, for a detail or facet of great importance to some researcher may easily have been overlooked at that stage. For example, a user seeking descriptions of stagecoach travel will find many items cited in the subject index. Of those, some diaries will describe substantially the experience of traveling by stagecoach, while others may only mention stops along the route or even simply state that the diarist was traveling by stage. On the other hand, another long diary may contain mention of stagecoach travel entirely missed in the process of scanning for annotation and thus omitted in the indexing as well. But, should the user be denied all subject access because of this only too obvious defect? A particularly troublesome example is ship names, which we tried to glean wherever possible for annotations and indexing but which were omitted in many of Matthews' annotations. Matthews' arrangement of diaries by beginning date, without any attempt at subject indexing, while helpful for finding diaries of specific historic events or reflecting certain periods, left all other discovery up to the capricious benefits of browsing.

The present work includes, as did Matthews' work, a name index. However, his index was limited to the names of diarists, while this name index also includes names of persons mentioned prominently in diaries. The need for the addition of a geographic index seemed obvious from the start. Our geographic index includes those place-names which figure in the diary, but not diarists' birthplaces unrelated to the contents of the diary. Major place-names are given in their present form, e.g., Hawaii, rather than Sandwich Islands. Fortunately, many of the diaries themselves have excellent indexes which help the user delve further into subjects, names, and places.

Citations Are Expanded and Standardized

A final lack in Matthews is in completeness of citations. Our goal has been to make this work as useable as possible for reference and interlibrary loan purposes. Therefore, using Library of Congress catalogs we have expanded Matthews' citations wherever possible. Publishers, editors, and numbered series have been added to book citations, and in the case of periodical diaries, we have provided names of editors and titles of articles. For books and periodical articles with long titles, we have given enough of the title for easy identification. Spelling of names and place-names has been left as it appears in the original title, resulting occasionally in a variation between the spelling of a name in a title and in the annotation. We found, too, that some paging had to be expanded to include an entire article in which a diary appeared and the entry form of some periodical titles changed to conform to library practice.

In addition to completing Matthews' citations, we decided to regularize them according to library practice, using *Library of Congress Catalog, National Union Catalog, Pre-56 Imprints,* and *Union List of Serials* for this purpose. All personal names which could be so located were made to conform to entries as established at some point by the Library of Congress. Although the form of some names theoretically would be affected by recent rule changes, we decided that to stay wherever possible with the name as found in Library of Congress catalogs would simplify identification and retrieval. For periodical diaries and others involving names not established by the Library of Congress, we relied on standard biographical sources. In preparing the manuscript, book and periodical citations were arranged according to bibliographic style specified by the *Chicago Manual of Style.* The citations are, therefore, a combination of *Chicago* form and *Library of Congress* content, which should serve equally for librarians and academic researchers. A shortened form is used for collections cited more than three times. For full citation, see Frequently Cited Sources, p. xv.

Scope of This Book

We have accepted Matthews' definitions of diaries and journals as expressed in his preface to *American Diaries:*

I understand a diary to be a day-by-day record of what interested the diarist, each day's record being self-contained and written shortly after the events occurred, the style being usually free from organized exposition. Between 'diary' and 'journal' I have generally made a conventional distinction, that a diary is written for personal reasons, and that a journal, although otherwise similar to a diary, is kept as part of a job; in practice, there is often little or no difference, for journals are rarely altogether impersonal, many official journals being filled with the private opinions and affairs of the writers . . . I believe the diary to be a unique kind of writing; all other forms of writing envisage readers, and so are adapted to readers, by interpretation, order, simplification, rationalization, omission, addition, and the endless devices of exposition. Although many diaries, too, are written with readers in mind, they are in general the most immediate, truthful, and revealing documents available to the historian. A comparison of a diary with a narrative based upon it, or of letters and diaries on the same subjects, will quickly show the essential differences.

While accepting Matthews' definitions, we have tried, in our selection of diaries and journals for inclusion, to abide by them more strictly. For some reason, Matthews included considerable material which violates his own definitions, items we would consider narratives or memoirs. While we have not removed these items, we have tried not to add such material to the present work. There are admittedly borderline cases and some have been included because of their importance, especially Spanish, French, and Russian exploration journals. Our emphasis, then, is on works which record immediate experiences, events, impressions, and reflections, rather than on later reconstructions of them. Our use in annotations of the terms diary or journal is based on one of the following: the term used in the citation, the term used in Matthews' work, or the term which best fits the above definitions. Our concern has been more to exclude material which does not fit either term than to make fine distinctions between the two terms.

We have defined as American any diary or journal kept by an American, whether in America or elsewhere, or kept in America by a foreigner, or foreign diaries related to events which took place primarily on American soil or record a major event conventionally regarded as American. Thus, a British soldier's Revolutionary war diary kept at Quebec would be included, while the diary of a German soldier fighting Americans and their allies in World War II would not. We have also defined as American any area which is now part of the fifty United States, regardless of its original colonial status. We have included only diaries which are available in English, either as the original language or in translation, and only those which are published as printed books or periodical articles. Thus no manuscripts or microfilms are included. Scholars seeking manuscript diaries will find Matthews' *American Diaries in Manuscript* of continued usefulness. The premise behind the new *American Diaries* is that published diaries and journals are the province of the reading public as well as scholars; thus, our emphasis has been on published, largely loanable material of use equally to the student, the research scholar, and the ordinary reader.

Ships' logs posed a unique problem. As did Matthews, we included only those which contain diary or journal elements which go beyond the usual log entries of weather, position, etc.

Criteria Used in Annotating

Our concern in examining and annotating a diary has been to discover and call to the reader's attention whatever events, conditions, circumstances, attitudes, places, and people emerge as significant. Obviously, judgment of significance is perilously subjective, but we trust that common sense and intuition on the one hand, and our backgrounds in American history and reference librarianship on the other, did not lead us too far astray. The annotations vary in length with those of William Matthews tending to be somewhat shorter. Generally, annotations for works published before 1943 and with a beginning date prior to 1861 are from the pen of Matthews. The impossibility of doing justice in a short annotation to such monumental diaries as those of Sewall, Thoreau, Dana, or Strong must be admitted with regret. We tried in annotating to draw out the following elements.

1. Whatever the diarist emphasized heavily, e.g., religion, nature, illness, social life, even the weather.

2. Conditions of categories of persons, e.g., women, the aged, the very young, minorities, the handicapped, etc.

3. Occupations or professions

4. Historic events

5. Modes of travel

6. Religious affiliations or denominations

7. Names of specific people, places, ships, etc.

8. Customs, social milieu, etc.

9. Such broad generic categories as travel, religion, exploration, military, etc. Some annotations may exhibit a number of these emphases, while others contain only one brief reference to a historic event or place, largely depending on the length and content of the diary.

While Matthews' annotations reflect an interest in history, customs, etc., because his field was the English language, he strongly emphasized such aspects of the diary as spelling and vocabulary; hence the frequent addenda "interesting spellings" and "linguistically interesting." Although we have not removed these comments from his annotations, we have rarely included them in our own. In many diaries, the spelling is different from current practice, but as we are not linguists, we have left it up to the reader to assess the linguistic significance of such differences. For those interested in that aspect, Matthews' notes will still be useful.

We have, however, removed from Matthews' annotations such phrases as "a dull diary" and have largely avoided negative assessments in our own, again preferring to leave such judgments up to the reader. We have otherwise left Matthews' annotations as they are except for occasional changes of wording, shortening, clarifying, or in some instances, adding material.

Format of Volume

As did Matthews, we have arranged the diaries chronologically, with diaries beginning in the same year arranged alphabetically by diarist's name. By this arrangement, all published diaries of a particular diarist appear in one sequence, regardless of the time period covered. Thus, although Volume 1 cites diaries with beginning dates prior to 1845, a great deal of later material appears in diaries kept over many years or diaries or parts of diaries kept or published at later intervals. Such an arrangement makes unavoidable the presence in both volumes of diaries covering the same period or event, but use of subject indexing will ensure access to all relevant material. Although we considered alternative arrangement of diaries, particularly topical or alphabetical by name of diarist, we finally concluded that Matthews' arrangement by beginning date of diary presented the fewest problems to users, especially with the addition of indexes, while preserving the benefits of chronological browsing. It does the reader no harm to note that in 1812 while Robert Stuart was trading for furs on the Columbia, Benjamin Waterhouse was languishing in Dartmoor Prison, and Nancy Hyde was teaching school in Norwich, Connecticut. In fact, some of the amazing multiplicity of American experience emerges through this arrangement.

Other decisions made during the preparation of this volume involve the arrangement of elements in the entry, citation, and annotation. These are:

1. While Matthews included in his name headings the occupation, rank, and place of birth or residence of the diarist, we mentioned these items in the citation or annotation when applicable to the diary described.

2. We have specified months for diaries covering twelve months or less and have dropped all indication of days.

3. As in most current annotated bibliographies, citation is given first, followed by annotation, a reversal of Matthews' arrangement. When a diary or portions of it were published more than once, we have arranged them by date of publication.

4. We have eliminated the brackets that Matthews used around names to indicate assumed or disputed authorship. This situation is mentioned in the annotation instead.

Omissions From This Volume

The present work includes all of the diaries in Matthews' *American Diaries* with the exception of a few Canadian diaries containing no evidence of any American content. For these diaries, the reader is referred to Matthews' *Canadian Diaries*. However, we have retained some Canadian fur traders who may have touched on American soil but whose total wanderings were difficult to determine. We have also excluded the few foreign diaries for which we could not find English translations, as well as items cited by Forbes but which neither Matthews nor we could locate.

Are there important areas of the American experience omitted from the present work? The answer must be yes because, for various reasons, they did not lend themselves to diary keeping. The westward migration emerges strictly from the perspective of the pioneers, who kept diaries, not from that of the Indians. How illuminating it would be to have a diary of the Cherokee Removal kept by an Indian, but obviously the victims of forced marches are the participants least able to keep a record. Similarly, the subject of slavery emerges from the writings of slave traders, slave owners, visitors to the South, and abolitionists, but not, of necessity, from the slaves themselves. The student of these perspectives must seek other kinds of historical materials. No claim can be made, then, that *American Diaries* provides more than a partial, though important, access to personal narratives of the American experience. Furthermore, the prejudiced honesty of diaries must be taken as it is. Diaries reflect what their authors saw and felt, not what the hindsight of history or enlightenment indicate they should have seen and felt or how they should have interpreted their experiences. Also, because we are limited to those diaries which first have survived as manuscripts and, of these, diaries which someone has deemed worthy to publish, the puzzle of America as revealed through this medium does indeed have many gaps.

A final disclaimer must be made regarding comprehensiveness of coverage. Our attempt is to be thorough, but there are surely diaries we have missed, especially those which give no clue in the title or subtitle or do not appear on major bibliographies of important historical topics, or were overlooked in our scanning of historical and other periodicals. Nor have we attempted a complete publishing history of every diary cited.

Preparation of This Volume

Our method was similar to Matthews' but with the added advantage of computer searching unavailable to him. Our initial file was provided by the diaries in Matthews, to which we added many diaries discovered by a key word search of the Washington Library Network. More were added by the primitive but fruitful process of browsing biography sections of libraries, finding often that the bibliographies in such diaries led to further diaries. Simultaneously, we combed the bibliographies related to all aspects of Americana, as well as *Bibliographic Index* and *American Book Publishers' Record.* The Library of Congress subject subdivision—"Personal narratives" proved useful for discovering diaries of historical events in *LC Books: Subjects,* on the networks, and in the catalogs of various libraries. In addition, publishers', reprint, and dealers' catalogs yielded many citations.

The search for diaries published in periodicals involved such bibliographies and indexes as *America: History and Life, Humanities Index,* and the annuals and special bibliographies of the American Historical Association, as well as a rather laborious scanning of many historical quarterlies.

Although local libraries and interlibrary loan were a great boon, this project could not have been carried out without considerable travel to distant libraries, made possible by generous academic vacations and a sabbatical leave. These libraries include the Oregon State Library, Oregon Historical Center, University of Utah, Princeton University, Harvard University, Boston Public Library, Radcliffe College, New York Public Library, Duke University, University of North Carolina, and the Library of Congress, as well as the remarkable private library of James Cummings of Stillwater, Minnesota, containing some 7000 English-language diaries and journals. Of invaluable assistance were our own library at Seattle Pacific University and other local libraries: the University of Washington, Seattle Public Library, and the Washington State Library.

Acknowledgments

In addition, certain individuals should be singled out for acknowledgment: at Seattle Pacific University, George McDonough, Librarian, for flexible time and good advice; Ann Hill for heroic interlibrary loan service; Betty Chamberlain, Evana Marie Bloch, and Frances Glaub for manuscript typing; Robert Chamberlain and Betty Fine for help in proofreading; Jean Belch of University of Washington Library for encouragement and mentorship; and for special assistance either in person or by mail, Edwin Sanford of Boston Public Library; John Lancaster of Amherst College; Gail Petri of St. John Fisher College; Everett L. Cooley of the University of Utah; Sherri Schneider of the Iowa Historical Society; Jane Begos, author of *Annotated Bibliography of Published Women's Diaries;* Metta L. Winter, an authority on Quaker diaries, and many others who sent citations. Our thanks go, also, to friends and relatives who accommodated us during forays to distant libraries and to our families for encouragement and patience.

Frequently Cited Sources

Alvord, Clarence W. and Carter, Clarence E., eds. *The New Regime, 1765-1767.* Springfield: Illinois State Historical Library, 1916.

Beauchamp, William Martin, ed. *Moravian Journals Relating to Central New York, 1745-66.* Edited for the Onondaga Historical Association. Syracuse, N.Y.: Dehler Press, 1916. Reprint. New York: AMS Press, 1976.

Berger, Josef and Berger, Dorothy, eds. *Diary of America: The Intimate Story of Our Nation Told by 100 Diarists.* New York: Simon & Schuster, 1957.

Berger, Josef and Berger, Dorothy, eds. *Small Voices.* New York: P.S. Eriksson, 1967, c1966.

Bolton, Herbert Eugene. *Anza's California Expeditions.* Berkeley: University of California Press, 1930. 5 vols.

Calder, Isabel M., ed. *Colonial Captivities, Marches and Journeys.* Edited under the auspices of the National Society of the Colonial Dames of America. New York: Macmillan, 1935. Reprint. Port Washington, N.Y.: Kennikat Press, 1967.

Canada. Archives. *Report of the Public Archives.* Ottawa, 1882-1919.

Coffin, Charles Carleton, comp. *The History of Boscawen and Webster, N.H. from 1783 to 1878.* Concord, N.H.: Printed by the Republican Press Association, 1878.

Cook, James. *The Journals of Captain James Cook on His Voyages of Discovery.* Edited by John C. Beaglehole. Hakluyt Society Works, Extra Series, nos. 34-37. Cambridge: Published for the Hakluyt Society at the University Press, 1955-1974. 4 vols. in 5. Reprint with addenda and corrigenda. 1968-.

De Forest, Louis E., ed. *Louisbourg Journals, 1745.* New York: Committee on Historical Documents, Society of Colonial Wars in the State of New York, 1932.

Documentary History of the State of New York. Edited by Edmund B. O'Callaghan. Albany: Weed, Parsons & Co., Public Printers, 1849-1851. 4 vols.

Documents Relative to the Colonial History of the State of New York. Edited by Edmund B. O'Callaghan and Berthold Fernow. Albany: Weed, Parsons and Co., Printers, 1853-1887. 15 vols.

Dow, Charles Mason. *Anthology and Bibliography of Niagara Falls.* Albany: Published by the state of New York, J.B. Lyon Co., Printers, 1921. 2 vols.

Dow, George Francis, ed. *The Holyoke Diaries, 1709-1856.* Salem, Mass.: Essex Institute, 1911.

Drury, Clifford Merrill. *First White Women Over the Rockies; Diaries, Letters and Biographical Sketches of the Six Women of the Oregon Mission Who Made the Overland Journey in 1836 and 1838.* Glendale, Calif.: Arthur H. Clark, 1963-1966. 3 vols.

Dunaway, Philip, ed. *A Treasury of the World's Great Diaries.* Garden City, N.Y.: Doubleday, 1957.

Evans, Elizabeth. *Weathering the Storm; Women of the American Revolution.* New York: Charles Scribner's Sons, 1975.

Fries, Adelaide L., ed. *Records of the Moravians in North Carolina.* Raleigh: Edwards & Broughton Printing Co., State Printers, 1922-1969. 11 vols.

Ganong, William F., ed. *Historical-Geographical Documents, Relating to New Brunswick.* New Brunswick Historical Society Collections, vols. 2-3. Saint John: New Brunswick Historical Society, 1904-1914.

Gates, Charles M., ed. *Five Fur Traders of the Northwest*. Minneapolis: Published for the Minnesota Society of the Colonial Dames of America, University of Minnesota Press, 1933; St. Paul: Minnesota Historical Society, 1965.

Gibbes, Robert W. *Documentary History of the American Revolution: Consisting of Letters and Papers Relating to the Contest for Liberty, Chiefly in South Carolina*. New York: D. Appleton & Co., 1853-1857. 3 vols. Reprint. New York: New York Times, 1971. 3 vols. in 1. Spartenburg, S.C.: Reprint Co., 1972. 3 vols.

Hafen, Le Roy R. and Hafen, Ann W., eds. *To the Rockies and Oregon, 1839-1842*. The Far West and the Rockies Historical Series, vol. 3. Glendale, Calif.: A.H. Clark Co., 1955.

Hanna, Charles A. *The Wilderness Trail; Or, the Ventures and Adventures of the Pennsylvania Traders on the Allegheny Path*. New York and London: G.P. Putnam's Sons, 1911. 2 vols. Reprint. New York: AMS Press, 1972.

Howe, M.A. DeWolfe, ed. *The Articulate Sisters; Passages from Journals and Letters of the Daughters of President Josiah Quincy of Harvard University*. Cambridge: Harvard University Press, 1946.

Hulbert, Archer B. *Historic Highways of America*. Cleveland, Ohio: A.H. Clark Co., 1902-1905. 16 vols. Reprint. New York: AMS Press, 1971.

Hulbert, Archer B., ed. *Southwest on the Turquoise Trail; The First Diaries on the Road to Santa Fe*. Colorado Springs: The Stewart Commission of Colorado College; Denver: Public Library, 1933.

Indiana. Historical Commission. *Indiana as Seen by Early Travelers*. Selected and edited by Harlow Lindley. Indianapolis: Indiana Historical Commission, 1916.

Kagle, Steven E. *American Diary Literature, 1620-1799*. Boston: Twayne Publishers, 1979.

Knox, John. *An Historical Journal of the Campaigns in North America, for the Years 1757, 1758, 1759, and 1760*. Edited with introduction, appendix and index by Arthur G. Doughty. Toronto: The Champlain Society, 1914-1916. 3 vols. Reprint. New York: Books for Libraries, 1970

Lockwood, John Hoyt. *Westfield and Its Historic Influences, 1669-1919*. Westfield, Mass.: Printed and sold by the author, 1922. 2 vols.

Loomis, Noel M. and Nasatir, Abraham P. *Pedro Vial and the Roads to Santa Fe*. Norman: University of Oklahoma Press, 1967.

McCord, Shirley S., comp. *Travel Accounts of Indiana, 1679-1961*. Indianapolis: Indiana Historical Bureau, 1970.

Masson, Louis Francois Rodrigue. *Les Bourgeois de la Compagnie du Nord-Ouest*. Quebec: Impr. generale A. Cote, 1889-1890. 2 vols.

Mereness, Newton D., ed. *Travels in the American Colonies*. Edited under the auspices of the National Society of the Colonial Dames of America. New York: Macmillan, 1916; Antiquarian Press, 1961.

New American World: A Documentary History of North America to 1612. Edited by David Quinn. New York: Arno Press, 1979. 5 vols.

New Hampshire. *Provincial and State Papers*. Concord: Published by authority of the legislature of New Hampshire, 1867-1919.

New York State. Secretary of State. *Journals of the Military Expedition of Major General John Sullivan Against the Six Nations of Indians in 1779*. Prepared by Frederick Cook, secretary of state. Auburn, N.Y.: Knapp, Peck & Thomson, Printers, 1887.

Nolan, James Bennett. *Early Narratives of Berks County*. Reading, Pa.: Published under the auspices of the Historical Society of Berks County, 1927.

Notes and Queries: Historical, Biographical and Genealogical: Chiefly Relating to Interior Pennsylvania. Edited by William Henry Egle. Harrisburg: Telegraph Printing and Binding House, 1881-1891. 4 vols. in 3. Harrisburg Publishing Co., 1894-1901. 12 vols.

Old Eliot; A Quarterly Magazine of the History and Biography of the Upper Parish of Kittery, Now Eliot. Edited by John Lemuel Murray Willis. Eliot, Maine: Printed by A. Caldwell, 1897-1909. 9 vols. in 7.

Old Ulster; An Historical and Genealogical Magazine. Kingston, N.Y.: B.M. Brink, 1905-1914. 10 vols.

The Olden Time; A Monthly Publication, Devoted to the Preservation of Documents and Other Authentic Information in Relation to the Early Explorations, and the Settlement and Improvement of the Country Around the Head of the Ohio. Edited by Neville B. Craig. Pittsburgh: J.W. Cook; Dumars & Co., 1846-1848. 2 vols. Reprint. Cincinnati: R. Clarke, 1876.

Our First Visit in America: Early Reports from the Colony of Georgia, 1732-1740. Introduction by Trevor R. Reese. Savannah: Beehive Press, 1974.

Paine, Ralph Delahaye. *The Ships and Sailors of Old Salem.* New York: The Outing Publishing Co., 1909. New ed. Chicago: A.C. McClurg & Co., 1912. Rev. with a new preface by the author and with a new and complete index. Boston: Charles E. Lauriat Co., 1923.

Pennsylvania Archives. Philadelphia: Printed by J. Severns & Co., 1852-1856; Harrisburg, 1874-1919. Reprint. *Pennsylvania Archives, Second Series.* Edited by John B. Linn and William H. Egle. Harrisburg: C.M. Busch, State Printer, 1896-.

Phillips, Ulrich B., ed. *Plantation and Frontier Documents: 1649-1863.* Documentary History of American Industrial Society, vols. 1-2. Cleveland, Ohio: A.H. Clark Co., 1909. Reprint. New York: B. Franklin, 1969.

Roberts, Kenneth L., ed. *March to Quebec; Journals of the Members of Arnold's Expedition.* New York: Doubleday, Doran & Co., 1938. Reprinted with addition of Pierce journal. 1940, 1942, 1947.

Rupp, Israel D. *History of Northampton, Lehigh, Monroe, Carbon, and Schuylkill Counties.* Harrisburg, Pa.: Hickok & Cantine, Printers, 1845.

Society of Colonial Wars. Massachusetts. *Year Book.* Boston: The Society, 1897-1919.

Stewart, Frank H., ed. *Notes on Old Gloucester County, New Jersey.* Camden: Printed by Sinnickson Chew & Sons Co., 1917. 4 vols. Baltimore: Genealogical Publishing Co., 1977. 4 vols. in 2.

Temple, Josiah H. and Sheldon, George. *A History of the Town of Northfield, Massachusetts.* Albany, N.Y.: J. Munsell, 1875.

Thomas, Alfred B., trans. and ed. *After Coronado; Spanish Exploration Northeast of New Mexico, 1696-1727.* Norman: University of Oklahoma, 1935.

Thomas, Alfred B., trans. and ed. *Forgotten Frontiers; A Study of the Spanish Indian Policy of Don Juan Bautista de Anza Governor of New Mexico, 1777-1787.* Norman: University of Oklahoma Press, 1932. Reprint. 1969.

Thwaites, Reuben G., ed. *Early Western Travels, 1748-1846.* Cleveland, Ohio: A.H. Clark Co., 1904-1907. 32 vols. Reprint. New York: AMS Press, 1966.

United States. Naval History Division. *Naval Documents of the American Revolution.* Edited by William J. Morgan. Washington, D.C.: Government Printing Office. 1964-.

Urlsperger, Samuel, ed. *Detailed Reports on the Salzburger Emigrants Who Settled in America.* Edited with an introduction by George Fenwick Jones, translated by Hermann J. Lacher. Wormsloe Foundation Publications, nos. 9-12, 14. Athens: University of Georgia Press, 1968-1981. 6 vols.

Vanderpoel, Emily Noyes, comp. *Chronicles of a Pioneer School from 1792 to 1833, Being the History of Miss Sarah Pierce and Her Litchfield School.* Edited by Elizabeth C. Barney Buel. Cambridge, Mass.: University Press, 1903.

Van Doren, Mark, ed. *An Autobiography of America.* New York: A.&C. Boni, 1929.

Wells, Frederic P., ed. *History of Newbury, Vermont.* St. Johnsbury, Vt.: The Caledonian Co., 1902.

Williams, Samuel C., ed. *Early Travels in the Tennessee Country, 1540-1800.* Johnson City, Tenn.: Watauga Press, 1928.

American Diaries

AMERICAN DIARIES

1492

COLUMBUS, CHRISTOPHER, 1451-1506   1

THE JOURNAL OF CHRISTOPHER COLUMBUS (DURING HIS FIRST VOYAGE, 1492-93). Translated with notes and an introduction by Clements R. Markham. Hakluyt Society, 1st ser., no. 86. London: Printed for the Hakluyt Society, 1893. 259 pp. Reprint. New York: Burt Franklin, 1970.

JOURNAL OF FIRST VOYAGE TO AMERICA. Introduced by Van Wyck Brooks. New York: A. & C. Boni, 1924. 251 pp. Reprint. Freeport, N.Y.: Books for Libraries, 1971.

THE VOYAGES OF CHRISTOPHER COLUMBUS. Newly translated and edited by Cecil Jane. London: Argonaut Press, 1930. 353 pp. Reprint. Amsterdam: N. Israel; New York: Da Capo, 1971.

THE JOURNAL. Translated by Cecil Jane. Revised by L.A. Vigneras. Hakluyt Society Works, extra series, no. 38. London: Hakluyt Society, 1960. 227 pp.

JOURNALS AND OTHER DOCUMENTS ON THE LIFE AND VOYAGES OF CHRISTOPHER COLUMBUS. New York: Heritage Press, 1963. 417 pp.

ACROSS THE OCEAN SEA: A JOURNAL OF COLUMBUS' VOYAGE. Edited by George Sanderlin. New York: Harper & Row, 1966. 275 pp.

Extracts in WEST BY NORTH: NORTH AMERICA AS SEEN THROUGH THE EYES OF ITS SEAFARING DISCOVERERS, by Louis B. Wright, pp. 39-50. New York: Delacorte Press, 1971.

Extracts in DIARY OF AMERICA, edited by Josef Berger, pp. 3-12; NEW AMERICAN WORLD, edited by David Quinn, vol. 1, pp. 136-140.

> 1492-1493. Abstract by Bartolomé de las Casas of the original journal which has been lost; terrors of voyage; discovery and claiming of new lands for Spain; dealings with Indians.

1542

FERREL, BARTOLOME   2

"Translation, by Richard Stuart Evans, from the Spanish of the Account by the Pilot Ferrel of the Voyage of Cabrillo along the West Coast of North America in 1542," with introductory notes by H.W. Henshaw. In ANNUAL REPORT, by United States Geographical Surveys West of the 100th Meridian, edited by George M. Wheeler, vol. 7, pp. 299-314. Washington, D.C.: Government Printing Office, 1879.

> Jun 1542-Apr 1543. Exploration journal of sailor, and later chief pilot after the death of Juan Rodrigues Cabrillo, on a voyage to extend geographical discoveries from Navidad, Mexico, northward to present southern border of Oregon; earliest

known contact of Europeans with Indians of California; harbors, land features, water and food supply.

1566

MARTINEZ, FRANCISCO   3

Folmsbee, Stanley. "Journals of the Juan Pardo Expeditions, 1560-1567." EAST TENNESSEE HISTORICAL SOCIETY PUBLICATIONS 37 (1965):106-121. Journal, pp. 116-118.

> 1566-1567. Account of expedition, ordered by Governor Pedro Menéndez de Avilés, to secure allegiance of Indians of Florida for Spain.

PARDO, JUAN   4

Folmsbee, Stanley. "Journals of the Juan Pardo Expedition, 1560-1567." EAST TENNESSEE HISTORICAL SOCIETY PUBLICATIONS 37 (1965):106-121. Journal, pp. 112-116.

> 1566-1567. Leader's journal of Spanish expedition to counter French influence with Indians in interior of present day Florida, probably covering much of same territory as De Soto Expedition of 1539-1542; attempts to teach Indians duty to God and Spanish king received cordially by some and scoffed at by others.

VANDERA, JUAN DE LA   5

Folmsbee, Stanley. "Journals of the Juan Pardo Expeditions, 1560-1567." EAST TENNESSEE HISTORICAL SOCIETY PUBLICATIONS 37 (1965):106-121. Journal, pp. 118-121.

> 1566-1567. Descriptions of Indian towns along the route of the Juan Pardo Expedition; houses, land, agricultural products.

1582

PEREZ DE LUXAN, DIEGO   6

EXPEDITION INTO NEW MEXICO MADE BY ANTONIO DE ESPEJO. Translated by George P. Hammond. Quivira Society Publications, vol. 1. Los Angeles: Quivira Society, 1929. 143 pp. Reprint. New York: Arno Press, 1967.

"Diego Pérez de Luxán's Account of the Antonio de Espejo Expedition into New Mexico, 1582." In THE REDISCOVERY OF NEW MEXICO, 1580-1594, by George P. Hammond and Agapito Rey, pp. 153-212. Albuquerque: University of New Mexico Press, 1966. Revised translation of edition published by Quivira Society, 1929.

> Nov 1582-Sep 1583. Journey from San Bartolome into New Mexico seeking fate of two friars of the Chamuscado-Rodriquez Expedition, whom they found

had been killed; return of some of party; search by Espejo and nine others for mines; good descriptions of Indians, their pueblos, customs and gifts of food and cloth.

1587

WHITE, JOHN, fl. 1585-1593   7

"John White's Journal of His Voyage to Virginia in 1587, with Three Ships Carrying the Second Colony to the New World." In THE NEW WORLD: THE FIRST PICTURES OF AMERICA, edited by Stefan Lorant, pp. 155-166, 185-244. New York: Duell, Sloan & Pearce, 1946.

> Apr-Nov 1587. White's journal of his second trip to America to become governor of Virginia; diary itself scant, but important for watercolors he made of Indians, settlement, flora and fauna, "the first authenticated pictorial records of life in the New World." Some scholars question whether this is the same John White sent by Sir Walter Raleigh to be governor of Virginia.

1590

CASTAÑO DE SOSA, GASPAR   8

A COLONY ON THE MOVE: GASPAR CASTAÑO DE SOSA'S JOURNAL. Translated by Dan S. Matson, notes by Albert H. Schroder. Santa Fe: School of American Research, 1965. 196 pp.

"Castaño de Sosa's 'Memoria'." In THE REDISCOVERY OF NEW MEXICO, 1580-1594, by George P. Hammond and Agapito Rey, pp. 245-295. Albuquerque: University of New Mexico Press, 1966.

Extracts in NEW AMERICAN WORLD, edited by David Quinn, vol. 5, pp. 385-390.

> 1590-1591. The journal, possibly kept by a secretary, of a colonizing expedition into New Mexico; of ethnological and archeological interest for locations of pueblos; especially good description of Pecos, the people, crafts, and languages.

1602

VIZCAINO, SEBASTIAN   9

"Diary of Sebastian Vizcaino." In SPANISH EXPLORATION IN THE SOUTHWEST, 1542-1706, by Herbert E. Bolton, pp. 52-103. New York: Scribner's, 1916.

Extracts in NEW AMERICAN WORLD, edited by David Quinn, vol. 5, pp. 426-430.

> 1602-1603. Diary of the commander of an expedition ordered by viceroy of Mexico for exploration of California coast; recruitment in Mexico City; supplying ships SAN DIEGO, SANTO TOMAS and TRES REYES; departure from Acapulco; exchange of gifts and food with Indians at San Diego and Santa Catalina Island; discovery of Bay of Monterey.

1604

ESCOBAR, FRANCISCO DE   10

"Father Escobar's Diary; Fray Francisco de Escobar's Diary of the Oñate Expedition to California, 1605." In DON JUAN DE OÑATE: COLONIZER OF NEW MEXICO, 1595-1628, by George P. Hammond and Agapito Rey, pp. 1012-1031. Albuquerque: University of New Mexico Press, 1953.

> 1604-1605. Diary of Catholic priest accompanying Oñate, first governor of New Mexico, on exploration

from San Gabriel in search of the South Sea; travels west to Zuni, through Hopi pueblos, down Colorado River to Gulf of California; descriptions of Indians, pueblos, language, crops, food and mines; tales told by Indian chief of monstrous and strange nations along Buena Esperanza River.

1609

JUET, ROBERT, d. 1611   11

JUET'S JOURNAL: THE VOYAGE OF THE HALF MOON. Edited by Robert M. Lunny. Newark: New Jersey Historical Society, 1959. 37 pp.

Extracts in WEST BY NORTH: NORTH AMERICA AS SEEN THROUGH THE EYES OF ITS SEAFARING DISCOVERERS, edited by Louis B. Wright, pp. 340-344. New York: Delacorte Press, 1971.

Extracts in AMERICAN HISTORY TOLD BY CONTEMPORARIES, edited by Albert B. Hart, vol. 1, pp. 121-125; NEW AMERICAN WORLD, edited by David Quinn, vol. 3, pp. 471-488.

> Apr-Nov 1609. Exploration diary of officer on board Henry Hudson's HALF MOON during attempt to find Northwest Passage; Amsterdam to Cape Cod to coast of Virginia, then north to explore Chesapeake Bay and Hudson River; geographical features, soundings, some contacts with Indians; archaic spellings.

1629

HIGGINSON, FRANCIS, 1588-1630   12

In CHRONICLES OF THE FIRST PLANTERS OF THE COLONY OF MASSACHUSETTS BAY, FROM 1620 TO 1636, by Alexander Young, pp. 213-238. Boston: C.C. Little and J. Brown, 1846. Reprint. New York: Da Capo, 1970; Baltimore: Genealogical Publishing Co., 1975.

Extracts in A COLLECTION OF ORIGINAL PAPERS RELATIVE TO THE HISTORY OF THE COLONY OF MASSACHUSETTS BAY, edited by Thomas Hutchinson, pp. 32-46. Boston: Printed by Thomas and John Fleet, 1769.

Extracts in AMERICAN HISTORY TOLD BY CONTEMPORARIES, edited by Albert B. Hart, vol. 1, pp. 190-195.

> Apr-May 1629. Clergyman's diary of voyage of fleet from England to New England; adventures at sea; God's providences; description of New England.

1630

WINTHROP, JOHN, 1588-1649   13

A JOURNAL OF THE TRANSACTIONS AND OCCURRENCES IN THE SETTLEMENT OF MASSACHUSETTS AND OTHER NEW ENGLAND COLONIES. Hartford, Conn.: Elisha Babcock, 1790. 364 pp.

HISTORY OF NEW ENGLAND FROM 1630 TO 1649. Edited by James Savage. Boston: Little, Brown, 1853. 2 vols.

WINTHROP'S JOURNAL, "HISTORY OF NEW ENGLAND." Edited by James K. Hosmer. New York: C. Scribner's Sons, 1908. 2 vols.

Extracts in "The Journal of John Winthrop." MASSACHUSETTS HISTORICAL SOCIETY PROCEEDINGS 62 (1928-1929):325-361.

Extracts in AMERICAN HISTORY TOLD BY CONTEMPORARIES, edited by Albert B. Hart, vol. 1, pp. 412-413.

Discussed in AMERICAN DIARY LITERATURE, by Stephen E. Kagle, pp. 143-147.

1630–1649. Impersonal daily record of public events by the governor of Massachusetts.

1631

EASTON, PETER, 1622–1694　　　　　**14**

NEWPORT MERCURY, 26 December 1857 and 2 January 1858.

"Peter Easton's Notes." RHODE ISLAND HISTORICAL SOCIETY COLLECTIONS 11 (1918):78–80.

> 1631–1678. Notes about his family and settlement in New England; events in Newport history.

1634

CURLER, ARENT VAN, d. 1667　　　　　**15**

Wilson, James Grant. "Arent Van Curler and His Journal of 1634–35." AMERICAN HISTORICAL ASSOCIATION ANNUAL REPORT (1895):81–101.

> Dec 1634–Jan 1635. Travel diary of member of Rensselaerwyck colony; early journey among Iroquois; personal notes and descriptions of Indian customs and vocabulary; fairly good narrative and valuable as first account of the Iroquois. Translated from the Dutch.

HULL, JOHN, 1624–1683　　　　　**16**

"Diary of John Hull." AMERICAN ANTIQUARIAN SOCIETY TRANSACTIONS AND COLLECTIONS 3 (1857):141–164, 167–265. Reprint. Boston: J. Wilson and Son, 1857.

> 1634–1682. Prosperous Boston merchant's account of public and private occurrences in Boston and England; ships and cargoes; his trips to England; family matters, including much illness and death; examples of God's providences toward New England and himself; historic events on both sides of the Atlantic and his reactions to them; items about the Dutch and the Quakers; an interesting Puritan diary.

VAN DEN BOGAERT, HARMEN MEYNDERTSZ　　　　　**17**

In NARRATIVES OF NEW NETHERLAND, 1609–1664, edited by John F. Jameson, pp. 137–162. New York: C. Scribner's Sons, 1909.

> Dec 1634–Jan 1635. Surgeon's travel journal; journey from Fort Orange into the Mohawk country; Mohawk vocabulary. Authorship assumed; translated from the Dutch.

1635

HOBART, PETER, d. 1679　　　　　**18**

Egan, C. Edward, Jr. "The Hobart Journal." NEW ENGLAND HISTORICAL AND GENEALOGICAL REGISTER 121 (1967):3–25, 102–127, 191–216, 269–294.

Extracts in DIARY, by William Bentley, vol. 3, pp. 282–284. Gloucester, Mass.: P. Smith, 1962.

> 1635–1717. Journal kept by Peter Hobart, pastor to Hingham settlers, and continued after his death by his son, deacon David Hobart, with some random entries made after 1717 by David's children; brief entries, mostly of births, baptisms, marriages and deaths; genealogical interest.

MATHER, RICHARD, 1596–1669　　　　　**19**

In CHRONICLES OF THE FIRST PLANTERS OF THE COLONY OF MASSACHUSETTS BAY, FROM 1620 TO 1636, by Alexander Young, pp. 445–481. Boston: Little, Brown, 1846. Reprint. New York: Da Capo, 1970; Baltimore: Genealogical Publishing Co., 1975.

"Journal of Richard Mather, 1635." DORCHESTER ANTIQUARIAN AND HISTORICAL SOCIETY COLLECTIONS 3 (1850):5–32.

> Apr–Aug 1635. Account of Atlantic crossing from England to Massachusetts; life at sea, storms, hardships, etc.; good narrative.

1638

JOSSELYN, JOHN, fl. 1630–1675　　　　　**20**

AN ACCOUNT OF TWO VOYAGES TO NEW-ENGLAND. London: Printed for G. Widdows, 1674. 277 pp.; Boston: William Veazie, 1865. 211 pp.

Extracts in AMERICAN HISTORY TOLD BY CONTEMPORARIES, edited by Albert B. Hart, pp. 430–434, 496–499.

> 1638–1671. Traveler aboard NEW SUPPLY who noted weather, fish caught for food, illnesses, ships met, provisions necessary for a sea voyage; second voyage aboard SOCIETY, with long descriptions of New England plants, trees and their use as food or medicine; birds, fish, serpents, insects, etc.; Indian customs and government; disease and medicine in the colonies.

VRIES, DAVID PIETERSZ DE, fl. 1593–1655　　　　　**21**

"New Netherland in 1640." OLD SOUTH LEAFLETS 7, no. 168 (1906):1–20.

> 1638–1642. Merchant skipper's life in New Netherland; interesting but narrative type.

1639

BUTLER, NATHANIEL　　　　　**22**

In PRIVATEERING AND PIRACY IN THE COLONIAL PERIOD: ILLUSTRATIVE DOCUMENTS, edited by John F. Jameson, pp. 3–8. New York: Macmillan, 1923.

> Feb–Mar 1639. Journal of governor of Providence Island; extracts dealing with privateers off New England coast.

1640

SHEPARD, THOMAS, 1605–1649　　　　　**23**

In THREE VALUABLE PIECES, pt. 3. Boston: Printed and sold by Rogers and Fowle in Queen Street, 1747.

> 1640–1644. Minister's religious experiences and self-analysis.

1641

DE HOOGES, ANTONY　　　　　**24**

In VAN RENSSELAER BOWIER MANUSCRIPTS, by New York State Library, translated and edited by Arnold J.F. Van Laer, pp. 580–603. Albany: University of the State of New York, 1908.

> Jul–Nov 1641. Travel journal from Holland to New Netherland; a passenger's logbook; statistics. Translated from the Dutch.

1643

ELIOT, JOHN, 1604–1690　　　　　**25**

NEW ENGLAND HISTORICAL AND GENEALOGICAL REGISTER 35 (1881):21–24, 241–247.

1643-1677. Clergyman's journal; mostly church records and notes of outstanding yearly events in Roxbury, Massachusetts; weather, Indian affairs; narrative type.

1644

FISKE, JOHN, 1601-1676   26

THE NOTEBOOKS OF THE REV. JOHN FISKE, 1644-1675. Edited by Robert G. Pope. Colonial Society of Massachusetts Publications, vol. 47. Boston: Colonial Society of Massachusetts, 1974; Salem: Essex Institute, 1974. 256 pp.

1644-1675. Meticulous record of the affairs of a Puritan congregation in Wenham and Chelmsford, Massachusetts; matters of piety and polity; spiritual condition and conduct of members discussed in congregational meetings; glimpses of early New England village life and people; hard work of a conscientious pastor; a solemn but often colorful journal.

1645

WINTHROP, JOHN, 1606-1676   27

"Diary of John Winthrop, Jr." MASSACHUSETTS HISTORICAL SOCIETY PROCEEDINGS, 2d ser. 8 (1892-1894): 4-12.

Extracts translated in "Overland to Connecticut in 1645: A Travel Diary of John Winthrop, Jr.," by William R. Carleton. NEW ENGLAND QUARTERLY 13 (1940):494-510.

Nov-Dec 1645. Trip from Boston to Nameaug via Springfield and Hartford, and back along coast through Providence; brief notes of stages, travel difficulties, weather, visits. Mostly in Latin.

1649

DANFORTH, SAMUEL, 1626-1674   28

"Rev. Samuel Danforth's Records of the First Church in Roxbury, Mass." NEW ENGLAND HISTORICAL AND GENEALOGICAL REGISTER 34 (1880):84-89, 162-166, 297-301, 359-363.

1649-1674. Clergyman's journal of town and church events in Roxbury, Massachusetts.

1650

BLAND, EDWARD, d. 1653   29

THE DISCOVERY OF NEW BRITTAINE. London: Printed by T. Harper for J. Stephenson, 1651. 16 pp. Frequently reprinted; most recently, Ann Arbor: University Microfilms, 1966.

In THE FIRST EXPLORATIONS OF THE TRANS-ALLEGHENY REGION BY THE VIRGINIANS, 1650-1674, by Clarence W. Alvord and Lee Bidgood, pp. 114-130. Cleveland: Arthur H. Clark, 1912.

Aug-Sep 1650. Travel diary; long entries of a week in country and on rivers beyond Fort Henry, Virginia, in the company of Captain Abraham Woods and Elias Pennant.

1653

FLYNT, JOSIAH, 1645-1680   30

"Manuscript of Rev. Josiah Flynt, of Braintree and Dorchester." DEDHAM HISTORICAL REGISTER 10 (1899): 19-25.

1653-1674. Clergyman's journal; a few brief entries, mostly about church affairs and troubles with the deacon.

MINOR, THOMAS, 1608-1690   31

THE DIARY OF THOMAS MINOR, STONINGTON, CONNECTICUT. New London, Conn.: Press of the Day, 1899. 221 pp.

1653-1684. Brief notes of personal matters, farming, and local affairs; some linguistic interest.

WIGGLESWORTH, MICHAEL, 1631-1705   32

"The Diary of Michael Wigglesworth." COLONIAL SOCIETY OF MASSACHUSETTS PUBLICATIONS 35 (1942-1946): 311-344. Reprint. New York: Harper, 1965.

THE DIARY OF MICHAEL WIGGLESWORTH, 1653-1657; THE CONSCIENCE OF A PURITAN. Edited by Edmund S. Morgan. Gloucester, Mass.: Peter Smith, 1970. 125 pp.

Discussed in AMERICAN DIARY LITERATURE, by Steven E. Kagle, pp. 31-38.

1653-1657. Religious diary of Puritan divine and tutor at Harvard College; constant bewailing of his own and others' sins, especially of pride and lust; ill health and difficulties of preaching while ill; pastorates in Massachusetts; marriage and birth of first child.

1656

NUTON, BRIAN   33

In DOCUMENTARY HISTORY OF THE STATE OF NEW YORK, edited by E.B. O'Callaghan, vol. 3, pp. 557-559.

Dec 1656-Jan 1657. Captain's diary of four-day trip from New Amsterdam to Eastchester. Translated from the Dutch.

1659

ANON.   34

In VOYAGES OF THE SLAVERS ST. JOHN AND ARMS OF AMSTERDAM, 1659-1663; TOGETHER WITH ADDITIONAL PAPERS ILLUSTRATIVE OF THE SLAVE TRADE UNDER THE DUTCH, translated and edited by E.B. O'Callaghan, pp. 1-9. New York Colonial Tracts, no. 3. Albany: J. Munsell, 1867.

Mar-Nov 1659. Slave-ship journal; scattered entries from business journal of the slaver ST. JOHN. Translated from the Dutch.

HERMAN (or HEERMANS), AUGUSTINE   35

"Journal of the Dutch Embassy to Maryland." In DOCUMENTS RELATIVE TO THE COLONIAL HISTORY OF THE STATE OF NEW YORK, edited by E.B. O'Callaghan, vol. 2, pp. 88-98.

Revised translation in NARRATIVES OF EARLY MARYLAND, 1633-1684, edited by Clayton Colman Hall, pp. 311-333. New York: Charles Scribner's Sons, 1910.

Sep-Oct 1659. Dutch diplomatic journal; journey from New Amstel to South River; negotiations. Translated from the Dutch.

1660

GOFFE, WILLIAM, ca. 1605-ca. 1679   36

"Journal of Colonel Goffe." MASSACHUSETTS HISTORICAL SOCIETY PROCEEDINGS, 1st ser. 7 (1863-1864):280-283.

Mar–Jul 1660. Brief extract of social and religious affairs in Boston.

1661

SPOERI, FELIX CHRISTIAN, b. 1601   37

Schemel, Emma, ed. "A Swiss Surgeon Visits Rhode Island, 1661–1662." NEW ENGLAND QUARTERLY 10 (1937):536–548.

1661–1664. Extracts of travel diary of voyage from Bermuda to America; detailed description of New England, Rhode Island; whale hunt; voyage to London and Amsterdam; irregular entries, many apparently post facto. Translated from the German.

1662

BOWNE, JOHN, 1628–1695   38

"Persecution of an Early Friend or Quaker." AMERICAN HISTORICAL RECORD 1 (1872):4–8.

1662–1664. Journal of New York Quaker; persecutions by Dutch; seminarrative.

1663

ANON.   39

In VOYAGES OF THE SLAVERS ST. JOHN AND ARMS OF AMSTERDAM, 1659–1663; TOGETHER WITH ADDITIONAL PAPERS ILLUSTRATIVE OF THE SLAVE TRADE UNDER THE DUTCH. Translated and edited by E.B. O'Callaghan, pp. 89–95. New York Colonial Tracts, no. 3. Albany: J. Munsell, 1867.

Apr–Oct 1663. Slave-ship journal; scattered entries; recapture of slaver ARMS OF AMSTERDAM.

ANON.   40

In CHRONICLES OF THE CAPE FEAR RIVER, by James Sprunt, pp. 26–30. Raleigh, N.C.: Edwards & Broughton, 1914.

Sep–Nov 1663. Official exploration journal of commissioners sent from Barbados to explore the Cape Fear River.

ANON.   41

In HISTORICAL AND GENEALOGICAL MISCELLANY: DATA RELATING TO THE SETTLEMENT AND SETTLERS OF NEW YORK AND NEW JERSEY, by John Edwin Stillwell, vol. 3, pp. 248–249. New York, 1914.

Dec 1663. Voyage from Gravesend, Long Island, to the Nevesinks in search of a place to settle.

KREGIER, MARTIN   42

In THE DOCUMENTARY HISTORY OF THE STATE OF NEW YORK, edited by E.B. O'Callaghan, vol. 4, pp. 33–62.

Jul 1663–Jan 1664. Military officer's official report of second Esopus War; attack by Indians and massacre at Wildwyck, New York. Translated from the Dutch.

VAN RUYVEN, CORNELIUS   43

"Journal Kept by Cornelius van Ruyven, Burgomaster Cortlandt and John Laurence, Delegates from New Netherland to the General Assembly at Hartford." In DOCUMENTS RELATIVE TO THE COLONIAL HISTORY OF THE STATE OF NEW YORK, edited by E.B. O'Callaghan, vol. 2, pp. 385–393.

A new translation in NARRATIVES OF NEW NETHERLAND, 1609–1664, edited by John F. Jameson, pp. 385–393. New York: C. Scribner's Sons, 1909.

Oct 1663. Official journal of voyage and horseback journey of delegates; territorial dispute. Translated from the Dutch.

1664

BRADSTREET, SIMON, 1640–1683   44

"Bradstreet's Journal." NEW ENGLAND HISTORICAL AND GENEALOGICAL REGISTER 8 (1854):325–333; 9 (1855):43–51, 78–79.

1664–1683. Notes of important local happenings and providences in New London, Connecticut; fires, flood, accidents, fevers; a few fairly interesting entries each year.

1667

ADAMS, WILLIAM, 1650–1685   45

"Memoir of the Rev. William Adams of Dedham, Mass., and of the Rev. Eliphalet Adams of New London, Conn." MASSACHUSETTS HISTORICAL SOCIETY COLLECTIONS, 4th ser. 1 (1852):1–51. Diary, pp. 8–22.

1667–1682. Diary written partly while author was student at Harvard; later, brief local notes, with a good supernatural story.

1668

TAYLOR, EDWARD, 1642–1729   46

DIARY. Edited by Francis Murphy. Springfield, Mass.: Connecticut Valley Historical Museum, 1964. 40 pp. Originally published in MASSACHUSETTS HISTORICAL SOCIETY PROCEEDINGS, 1st ser. 18 (1880–1881):4–18.

In WESTFIELD AND ITS HISTORIC INFLUENCES, edited by John Lockwood, pp. 130–136.

1668–1672. Clergyman's diary of voyage from Wapping to New England; entry at Harvard, study, comments on teachers; journey through New England; an interesting document.

1669

GOULD, DANIEL, ca. 1626–1716   47

In THE GOULDS OF RHODE ISLAND, by Rebecca G. Mitchell, pp. 10–31. Providence: A.C. Greene, 1875.

1669–1693. Travel journal of Newport Quaker; brief notes of travel in Maryland, Virginia, Pennsylvania and New England; visits, meetings, distances, weather.

GRAVE, JOHN, 1633–1695   48

Maher, Annie K. "'John Grave: His Book'––The Diary of a Connecticut Citizen in 1697." CONNECTICUT MAGAZINE 10 (1906):18–24.

1669–1794. Accounts, births, deaths, family and farm memoranda at Guilford, Connecticut; kept up by his descendants; interesting spellings.

PENN, WILLIAM, 1644–1718   49

THE PAPERS OF WILLIAM PENN. Edited by Mary Maples Dunn and Richard S. Dunn. Philadelphia: University of Pennsylvania Press, 1981–(in progress). Vol. 1 contains "Irish Journal," pp. 101–143, "Journey through Kent, Sussex and Surrey," pp. 241-248, and "An Account of my Journey into Holland and Germany," pp. 425-508.

A COLLECTION OF THE WORKS OF WILLIAM PENN, TO WHICH IS PREFIXED A JOURNAL OF HIS LIFE. London: Printed and sold by the assigns of J. Sowle, 1726. 2 vols. Reprint. New York: AMS Press, 1974.

> 1669-1670. Brief entries covering trip to Ireland to renew leases with tenants on his father's estates and to encourage Quakers suffering imprisonment and other persecution.

> Sept-Oct 1672. Short missionary trip through southeastern England.

> Jul-Oct 1677. Missionary journey in Holland and Germany; companionship of George Fox and other Quaker leaders; arduous travels; prayer and preaching; examination of his spiritual state; contacts with people who would later support his Pennsylvania venture.

MY IRISH JOURNAL, 1669-1670. Edited by Isabel Brubb. London, New York: Longmans, Green, 1952. 103 pp.

"William Penn's Journal of his Second Visit to Ireland." PENNSYLVANIA MAGAZINE OF HISTORY AND BIOGRAPHY 40 (1916):46-84.

> 1669-1670.

1671

ANON.   50

In DOCUMENTS RELATIVE TO THE COLONIAL HISTORY OF THE STATE OF NEW YORK, edited by E.B. O'Callaghan, vol. 3, pp. 193-197.

> Sep 1671. Official report and travel journal, in third person; exploration in western Virginia.

BATTS, THOMAS, d. 1691   51

In DOCUMENTS RELATIVE TO THE COLONIAL HISTORY OF THE STATE OF NEW YORK, edited by E.B. O'Callaghan, pp. 193-197.

In THE OHIO RIVER IN COLONIAL DAYS, by Berthold Fernow, pp. 220-229. Albany: J. Munsell's Sons, 1890.

"Explorations Beyond the Mountains." WILLIAM AND MARY COLLEGE QUARTERLY, 1st ser. 15 (1906-1907): 234-241.

In THE FIRST EXPLORATIONS OF THE TRANS-ALLEGHENY REGION BY THE VIRGINIANS, by Clarence W. Alvord and Lee Bidgood, pp. 183-193. Cleveland: Arthur H. Clark, 1912.

In ANNALS OF SOUTHWEST VIRGINIA, 1769-1800, by Lewis P. Summers, pp. 1-7. Abingdon, Va.: L.P. Summers, 1929.

> Sep-Oct 1671. Surveying and exploring journal; from Virginia across the Appalachians; discovery of Kanawha River Falls.

FALLOWS, ARTHUR   52

Bushness, David I., Jr. "Discoveries beyond the Appalachian Mountains in September, 1671." AMERICAN ANTHROPOLOGIST, n.s. 9 (1907):45-56. Reprint. JOURNAL OF ARTHUR FALLOWS. Ann Arbor: University Microfilms, 1966.

> Sep 1671. The earliest record of crossing the Appalachian Mountains by Europeans.

1673

ANON.   53

"Journal Kept on Board of the Frigate Named ZEEHOND, Captain Cornelius Evertsen, Sailing with the Commissioners, Councillor Cornelius Steenwyck, Capt. Charles Epen Steyn, and Lieutenant Charles Quirynsen. In DOCUMENTS RELATIVE TO THE COLONIAL HISTORY OF THE STATE OF NEW YORK, edited by E.B. O'Callaghan, vol. 2, pp. 654-656.

> Oct-Nov 1673. Cruise aboard ZEEHOND, from New Orange to east end of Long Island; description of storm. Translated from the Dutch.

SEWALL, SAMUEL, 1652-1730   54

THE DIARY OF SAMUEL SEWALL. Newly edited from the ms. at the Massachusetts Historical Society by M. Halsey Thomas. New York: Farrar, Straus and Giroux, 1973. 2 vols.

DIARY OF SAMUEL SEWALL. Massachusetts Historical Society Collections, ser. 5, vols. 5-7. Boston: Massachusetts Historical Society, 1878-1882. 3 vols. Reprint. New York: Arno Press, 1972.

Abridgments. Edited by Mark Van Doren. New York: Macy-Macius, 1927; edited by Harvey Wish. New York: Putnam, 1967.

Extracts in AMERICAN HISTORY TOLD BY CONTEMPORARIES, edited by Albert B. Hart, vol. 1, pp. 512-516, vol. 2, p. 48; DIARY OF AMERICA, edited by Josef Berger, pp. 35-42; TREASURY OF THE WORLD'S GREAT DIARIES, edited by Philip Dunaway, pp. 459-464.

Discussed in AMERICAN DIARY LITERATURE, by Steven E. Kagle, pp. 147-153.

> 1673-1729. Diary beginning at Harvard and ending shortly before his death; an invaluable record of Boston life in the period of the Mathers and an intimate picture of the diarist; a great diary extracted in most anthologies of American literature.

1674

MARQUETTE, JACQUES, 1637-1675   55

"Unfinished Journal of Father Jacques Marquette, Addressed to the Reverend Father Claude Dablon, Superior of the Missions." In THE JESUIT RELATIONS AND ALLIED DOCUMENTS, edited by Reuben Thwaites, vol. 59, pp. 165-183. Cleveland: Burrows Bros., 1900.

Thompson, Joseph J., ed. "Father Marquette's Second Journey to Illinois." ILLINOIS CATHOLIC HISTORICAL REVIEW 7 (1924):144-154.

> Oct 1674-Apr 1675. Missionary journal of travel from mission of St. Francois to La Concepcion; portage, hunting, Indian traders; wintering on Lake Michigan because of illness; possibly first visit of Europeans to the site of Chicago.

1675

BOSQUE, FERNANDO DEL   56

In SPANISH EXPLORATIONS IN THE SOUTHWEST, 1542-1706, edited by Herbert E. Bolton, pp. 291-309. New York: Scribner's, 1916.

Apr–Jun 1675. Possibly first missionary expedition to cross the Rio Grande into Texas; with Father Juan Larios taking ecclesiastical possession of the country; recording and naming watering places; buffalo hunts; dealings with various Indian nations and recommendations for further mission establishments.

MATHER, INCREASE, 1639–1723   57

"Diary of Increase Mather." MASSACHUSETTS HISTORICAL SOCIETY PROCEEDINGS, 2nd ser. 13 (1899–1900):340–374, 398–411.

    1675–1676. Puritan clergyman's private diary; religious observations and self-analysis; public affairs of Boston; family matters; Indian affairs, including King Philip's War.

In SO DREADFUL A JUDGEMENT: AN ANTHOLOGY OF PURITAN RESPONSES TO KING PHILIP'S WAR, 1676–1677, edited by Richard Slotkin and James K. Folsom, pp. 81–144. Middletown, Conn.: Wesleyan University Press, 1978.

    1675–1676. Mather's frequent though not daily entries recording events of King Philip's War and his reactions and interpretations, especially his sense of war as God's punishment for Puritan backsliding; later "methodized" and published by Mather as A BRIEF HISTORY OF THE WAR WITH INDIANS IN NEW ENGLAND.

RANDOLPH, EDWARD, 1632–1703   58

Extracts in THE ANDROS TRACTS, vol. 3, pp. 214–218. Boston: Prince Society, 1874. Reprint. In EDWARD RANDOLPH: INCLUDING HIS LETTERS AND OFFICIAL PAPERS FROM THE NEW ENGLAND, MIDDLE, AND SOUTHERN COLONIES IN AMERICA. New York: B. Franklin, 1967. 7 vols.

"Randolph's Narrative." MASSACHUSETTS HISTORICAL SOCIETY PROCEEDINGS, 1st ser. 18 (1880–1881):258–261.

    1675–1700 (with gaps). Diary-letters written to Sir Robert Southwall; account of his voyage to and from New England; survey in America; travels in Virginia, Maryland, Rhode Island, Massachusetts, New Hampshire.

SCOTTOW, JOSHUA, d. 1698   59

"Soldiers in King Philip's War." NEW ENGLAND HISTORICAL · AND GENEALOGICAL REGISTER 43 (1889):64–79. Journal, pp. 68–70.

    Oct–Dec 1675. Military officer's travel journal; notes of marches and improvement of Boston soldiers.

SHEPARD, HETY, b. 1660   60

Slicer, Adeline E.H., ed. "A Puritan Maiden's Diary." NEW ENGLAND MAGAZINE 11 (1894–1895):20–25.

    1675–1677. Extracts from Rhode Island teen-ager's diary; social and family life; pleasant, personal picture of Puritan influences on feminine pleasures. The genuineness of the diary, however, has been doubted.

WILTON, DAVID, 1633–1678   61

In HISTORY OF NORTHAMPTON, MASSACHUSETTS, FROM ITS SETTLEMENT IN 1654, by James R. Trumbull, vol. 1. pp. 280–283. Northampton: Press of Gazette Printing Co., 1898.

Jun–Sep 1675. Chiefly accounts, with a few farming and social notes of Northampton, Massachusetts; interesting spellings.

1677

HAMMOND, LAWRENCE, d. 1699   62

"Diary of Lawrence Hammond." MASSACHUSETTS HISTORICAL SOCIETY PROCEEDINGS, 2d ser. 7 (1891–1892): 144–172; 2d ser. 13 (1899–1900):411.

    1677–1691. Diary and commonplace book with some dates disordered; personal and social notes, outstanding local and public events in Charlestown, Massachusetts; deaths, weather; recipes; fairly amusing antiquarian material, with some linguistic interest.

MANNING, Mr.   63

"Journal, Kept by Mr. Manning." DOCUMENTARY HISTORY OF THE STATE OF MAINE 6 (1900):179–184.

    Jul–Aug 1677. From Salem to Cape Sable aboard the ketch SUPPLY in pursuit of Indians who had stolen boats; mainly log entries; interesting spellings.

STOCKWELL, QUENTIN, d. 1714   64

Hubbard, Silas G. "Historical Address." POCUMTUCK VALLEY MEMORIAL ASSOCIATION HISTORY AND PROCEEDINGS 2 (1880–1889):451–473. Diary, pp. 462–470.

    1677–1678. Capture in Deerfield by Indians and journey to Canada; seminarrative.

WALDERNE, RICHARD, 1615?–1689   65

In THE HISTORY OF THE INDIAN WARS IN NEW ENGLAND FROM THE FIRST SETTLEMENT TO THE TERMINATION OF THE WAR WITH KING PHILIP, IN 1677, by William Hubbard, revised by Samuel G. Drake, vol. 2, pp. 212–245. Roxbury, Mass.: W.E. Woodward, 1865.

    Feb–Mar 1677. Officer's journal of expedition to Maine in King Philip's War; Arrowsic, Pemaquid, etc.

1678

PIKE, JOHN, 1653–1710   66

"Journal of the Rev. John Pike." NEW HAMPSHIRE HISTORICAL SOCIETY COLLECTIONS 3 (1832):40–67.

Quint, A.H. "Journal of the Reverend John Pike." MASSACHUSETTS HISTORICAL SOCIETY PROCEEDINGS, 1st ser. 14 (1875–1876):116–152.

"Journal of Rev. John Pike." NEW HAMPSHIRE GENEALOGICAL RECORD 3 (1905–1906):77–85, 97–104, 145–153.

    1678–1709. Brief local notes of Dover, New Hampshire; weather, providences of God; some genealogical and linguistic interest; earliest entries autobiographical.

1679

DANKERS (or DANCKAERTS), JASPER, b. 1639   67

JOURNAL OF A VOYAGE TO NEW YORK AND A TOUR IN SEVERAL OF THE AMERICAN COLONIES IN 1679–80. Translated for the Long Island Historical Society and edited by Henry C. Murphy. Brooklyn: Long Island Historical Society, 1867. 440 pp. Reprint. Ann Arbor: University Microfilms, 1966.

JOURNAL OF JASPER DANCKAERTS, 1679–1680. Edited by Bartlett B. James and John F. Jameson. New York: C. Scribner's Sons, 1913. 313 pp.

Extracts in COLLECTIONS ON THE HISTORY OF ALBANY, edited by Joel Munsell, vol. 2, pp. 358–373. Albany: J. Munsell, 1865–1871.

Extracts in AMERICAN HISTORY AS TOLD BY CONTEMPORARIES, edited by Albert B. Hart, vol. 1, pp. 197–199, 496–501; DIARY OF AMERICA, edited by Josef Berger, pp. 28–33.

> 1679–1680. Journey from Friesland to the American colonies seeking site for a Labadist settlement; travels in New York, Delaware, Maryland, Hudson River country and to Boston; return to Friesland; lengthy and valuable account of the early colonial scene.

THACHER, PETER, 1651–1727   68

In THE HISTORY OF MILTON, MASS., 1640–1887, edited by Albert K. Teele, pp. 641–657. Boston: Press of Rockwell and Churchill, 1887.

> 1679–1699 (with gap). Clergyman's diary of personal and local affairs; brief notes, partly in cipher; interesting language.

1681

MATHER, COTTON, 1663–1728   69

DIARY OF COTTON MATHER, 1681–1724. Massachusetts Historical Society Collections, ser. 7, vol. 7–8. Boston: The Society, 1911–1912. 2 vols.

THE DIARY OF COTTON MATHER. New York: F. Ungar, 1957. 2 vols.

> 1681–1724. Diary of Puritan minister and scholar, co-pastor at Boston Second Church with his father, Increase Mather; ecstasies and prophecies, as well as agonized introspections; prodigious reading and writing; charities to the poor; religious instruction of his children; reference to Harvard; brief comments on the Salem witchcraft episode; advocacy of smallpox inoculation; sense of clergy's waning temporal power.

THE DIARY OF COTTON MATHER FOR THE YEAR 1712. Edited by William Manierre II. Charlottesville: University Press of Virginia, 1964. 124 pp.

Extracts relating to the MAGNALIA in "The Light Shed Upon Cotton Mather's 'Magnalia' By His Diary." MASSACHUSETTS HISTORICAL SOCIETY PROCEEDINGS, 1st ser. 6 (1862–1863):404–414.

1682

PIERPONT, JONATHAN, 1665–1709   70

"Extracts from the Diary of Rev. Jonathan Pierpont." NEW ENGLAND HISTORICAL AND GENEALOGICAL REGISTER 13 (1859):255–258.

> 1682–1707. Brief, scattered personal and religious notes of Massachusetts clergyman.

RUSSELL, NOADIAH, 1659–1713   71

"Copy of the Diary of Noahdiah Russell, Tutor at Harvard College, Beginning Anno Dom. 1682." NEW ENGLAND HISTORICAL AND GENEALOGICAL REGISTER 7 (1853):53–59.

> 1682–1684. Miscellaneous happenings, including fire, at Harvard; supernatural incident.

DIARY OF THE REVEREND NOADIAH RUSSELL OF IPSWICH, MASS., AND MIDDLETOWN, CONN., FOR THE OLD STYLE YEAR 1687. Hartford: Connecticut Historical Society, 1934. 18 pp.

> Mar 1687–Feb 1688. Account of Andros and his taking over government of Connecticut.

1683

KNEPP, JOHN   72

In A ROUGH LIST OF A COLLECTION OF TRANSCRIPTS RELATING TO THE HISTORY OF NEW ENGLAND, by Frederick Lewis Gay, pp. 135–139. Brookline, Mass.: E.O. Cockayne, 1913.

> 1683–1684. Abstract of journey from England to Boston on H.M.S. ROSE; stay in Boston; return to England.

1684

KINO, EUSEBIO FRANCISCO, 1644–1711   73

FIRST FROM THE GULF TO THE PACIFIC: THE DIARY OF THE KINO-ATONDO PENINSULAR EXPEDITION. Translated and edited by W. Michael Mathes. Los Angeles: Dawson's Book Shop, 1969. 60 pp.

> Dec 1684–Jan 1685. Record of Father Eusebio Kino and Isidro Atondo y Antillon on an expedition which made the first crossing of the Baja California Peninsula to the Pacific Ocean; difficult travel, scarce water supply, meetings with shy and fearful Indians; landmarks and wildlife.

HISTORICAL MEMOIR OF PIMERIA ALTA; A CONTEMPORARY ACCOUNT OF THE BEGINNINGS OF CALIFORNIA, SONORA, AND ARIZONA, 1683–1711. Translated and edited by Herbert E. Bolton. Berkeley: University of California Press, 1919. 2 vols. Reprint. 1948. 2 vols. in 1.

> 1700–1706. Journeys of indefatigable missionary, explorer, geographer and ranchman on first interior explorations of southern Arizona and northern Sonora; teaching, preaching, locating mission churches and searching for land route to California.

VAUGHAN, WILLIAM, 1640–1719   74

In REMINISCENCES AND GENEALOGICAL RECORD OF THE VAUGHAN FAMILY, by George E. Hodgdon, app. I, pp. 75–91. Rochester, N.Y., 1918.

> Feb–Apr 1684. Merchant's letter-diary; trial and imprisonment at Great Island for noncompliance; details of public affairs in New England and prison life; good narrative in literary style.

1686

STORY, THOMAS, 1662–1742   75

A JOURNAL OF THE LIFE OF THOMAS STORY: CONTAINING AN ACCOUNT OF HIS CONVINCEMENT OF, AND EMBRACING THE PRINCIPLES OF TRUTH, AS HELD BY THE PEOPLE CALLED QUAKERS. Newcastle Upon Tyne: Isaac Thompson, 1747. 768 pp.

> 1686–1740 (with gap, 1705–1709). Journal kept by one of Penn's colleagues; record of spiritual and temporal journeys; explanation and defense of beliefs; Quaker meetings and work in Europe, Barbados, New England and Middle Atlantic colonies; valuable for insight into early Quaker beliefs and ministry; names of colonial Quakers.

1687

DUNLOP, Capt. 76

Webber, Mabel L. "Journall: Capt. Dunlop's Voyage to the Southward, 1687." SOUTH CAROLINA HISTORICAL AND GENEALOGICAL MAGAZINE 30 (1929):127-133.

Apr 1687. Sea journal of voyage by pirogue from Charleston to St. Catherine's Island.

1688

COIT, MEHETABEL CHANDLER, 1673-1758 77

In MEHETABEL CHANDLER COIT, HER BOOK, pp. 5-12. Norwich, Conn.: Bulletin Print., 1895.

1688-1749? Commonplace book and family notes from New London, Connecticut; of genealogical interest.

DE LEON, ALONSO 78

O'Donnell, Walter J., trans. and ed. "La Salle's Occupation of Texas." MID-AMERICA 18 (1936):96-124. Diary, pp. 103-104. Reprint. TEXAS CATHOLIC HISTORI-CAL SOCIETY PRELIMINARY STUDIES 3 (1936): 3-33. Diary, pp. 12-13.

May 1688. Brief diary of Spanish military expedi-tion to apprehend a mysterious Frenchman living with the Indians.

PYNCHON, JOHN, d. 1705 79

In HISTORY OF NORTH BROOKFIELD, MASSACHUSETTS, by Josiah H. Temple, p. 140. North Brookfield: Published by the town, 1887.

Aug-Sep 1688. Diary and account book extracts; measures against attack by Quabaug Indians.

1689

BAYARD (or BEYARD), NICHOLAS, 1644?-1707 80

In DOCUMENTS RELATIVE TO THE COLONIAL HISTORY OF THE STATE OF NEW YORK, edited by E.B. O'Callaghan, vol. 3, pp. 599-604.

Jun-Jul 1689. Military journal containing official notes of public matters, disturbances and riots in New York.

A NARRATIVE OF AN ATTEMPT MADE BY THE FRENCH OF CANADA UPON THE MOHAQUE'S COUNTRY. Boston: Printed and sold by William Bradford, 1693. 14 pp. Reprint. New York: Dodd, Mead, 1903; Boston: 1937. Also reprinted as JOURNAL OF THE LATE ACTIONS OF THE FRENCH AT CANADA. New York: J. Sabin, 1868. 55 pp.

Feb 1692. Military journal describing French at-tempt on the Mohawk country; with Charles Lodo-wick.

In DOCUMENTS RELATIVE TO THE COLONIAL HISTORY OF THE STATE OF NEW YORK, vol. 4, pp. 14-16.

Feb-Mar 1693. Brief military notes covering Gov-ernor Fletcher's expedition to New York frontier against French and Indians of Canada; with Charles Lodowick.

HOMES, WILLIAM, 1663-1746 81

"Diary of Rev. William Homes of Chilmark, Martha's Vineyard." NEW ENGLAND HISTORICAL AND GENEALOG-ICAL REGISTER 48 (1894):446-453; 49 (1895):413-416; 50 (1896):155-166.

1689-1746. Extracts from clergyman's journal; weekly entries on sermons, church affairs, mar-riages, deaths, etc.

KELSEY, HENRY, 1670?-1724? 82

THE KELSEY PAPERS. With an introduction by Arthur G. Doughty and Chester Martin. Ottawa: Public Ar-chives of Canada and Public Record Office of Northern Ireland, 1929. 128 pp.

1689-1721. Fur trader's journal; travel for Hud-son's Bay Company in Canada, and work in fur trade; some accounts of Indian superstitions and customs; considerable human interest, and valuable as account of early exploration of Hudson's Bay country; many interesting spellings and an intro-duction in verse.

NEWBERRY, BENJAMIN, 1653-1711? 83

MAGAZINE OF NEW ENGLAND HISTORY 3 (1893):203-206.

1689-1706. Extracts from Newport, Rhode Island, diary; brief notes on religion and public alarms.

1690

ANON. 84

In TWO NARRATIVES OF THE EXPEDITION AGAINST QUEBEC, A.D. 1690, UNDER SIR WILLIAM PHIPS, by John Wise, with an introduction by Samuel A. Green, pp. 27-42. Cambridge, Mass.: J. Wilson and Son, 1902.

Aug 1690. Narrative and journal of expedition against Quebec; some religious notes.

BULLIVANT, BENJAMIN 85

"Journal of Dr. Benjamin Bullivant." MASSACHUSETTS HISTORICAL SOCIETY PROCEEDINGS, 1st ser. 16 (1878): 101-108.

Feb-May 1690. Lengthy notes on public affairs in New England.

Andrews, Wayne, ed., "A Glance at New York in 1697: The Travel Diary of Dr. Benjamin Bullivant." NEW YORK HISTORICAL SOCIETY QUARTERLY 40 (1956):55-73.

Jun-Aug 1697. Prominent Boston physician's round trip from Boston to Newcastle; observations of various towns and cities along the way, including detailed descriptions of New York City and Phila-delphia.

LYNDE, BENJAMIN, 1666-1745 86

THE DIARIES OF BENJAMIN LYNDE AND OF BENJAMIN LYNDE, JR. Edited by Oliver E. Fitch. Boston: Pri-vately printed; Cambridge, Mass.: Riverside Press, 1880. 251 pp.

1690-1742. Brief notes of private affairs in Salem, Massachusetts; some interesting details of food and drink; linguistic interest.

NATSTO, JOSHUA 87

In A JOURNAL OF THE PROCEEDINGS IN THE LATE EXPEDITION TO PORT-ROYAL, pp. 3-8. Boston: Printed for Benjamin Harris at the London Coffee House, 1690. Reprint. Massachusetts Historical Society Americana Series, no. 206. Boston, 1928.

Apr-May 1690. Naval clerk's journal of voyage and proceedings in expedition against Port Royal; ship movements.

PHIPS, Sir WILLIAM, 1651-1695   88

In A JOURNAL OF THE PROCEEDINGS IN THE LATE EXPEDITION TO PORT-ROYAL. Boston: Printed for Benjamin Harris at the London Coffee House, 1690. 16 pp. Reprint. Massachusetts Historical Society Americana Series, no. 206. Boston, 1928.

    1690-1691. Sea journal; notes on expedition against Quebec.

POTTER, CUTHBERT, d. 1691   89

In GREAT BRITAIN PUBLIC RECORD OFFICE CALENDAR OF STATE PAPERS, COLONIAL SERIES (1690):341-344.

In TRAVELS IN THE AMERICAN COLONIES, edited by Newton D. Mereness, pp. 3-11.

    Jul-Sep 1690. Travel account of voyage from Virginia to New England and stay in Boston.

SCHUYLER, JOHN, 1668-1747   90

"Journal of Captain John Schuyler." NEW JERSEY HISTORICAL SOCIETY PROCEEDINGS 1 (1845):72-74.

In DOCUMENTARY HISTORY OF THE STATE OF NEW YORK, edited by E.B. O'Callaghan, vol. 2, pp. 160-162.

    Aug 1690. Military journal describing activities of volunteers fighting in Canada. Translated from the Dutch.

In DOCUMENTS RELATIVE TO THE COLONIAL HISTORY OF THE STATE OF NEW YORK, edited by E.B. O'Callaghan, vol. 4, pp. 404-406.

    Aug-Sep 1698. Journey to Canada and discussions with Frontenac.

WALLEY, JOHN, 1644-1712   91

In THE HISTORY OF THE COLONY AND PROVINCE OF MASSACHUSETTS BAY, by Thomas Hutchinson, vol. 1, app. Cambridge: Harvard University Press, 1936.

SOCIETY OF COLONIAL WARS, MASSACHUSETTS, YEARBOOK 1898, pp. 116-130.

    Sep-Oct 1690. Military journal of British officer; expedition against Quebec; long entries.

WINTHROP, FITZJOHN, 1639-1707   92

"Journal of the Expedition to Canada." MASSACHUSETTS HISTORICAL SOCIETY COLLECTIONS, 5th ser. 8 (1882):312-318.

In GREAT BRITAIN PUBLIC RECORD OFFICE CALENDAR OF STATE PAPERS, COLONIAL SERIES (1696):117.

In DOCUMENTS RELATIVE TO THE COLONIAL HISTORY OF NEW YORK, edited by E.B. O'Callaghan, vol. 4, pp. 193-196.

    Jul-Sep 1690. Major General Winthrop's march from Albany to Canada; councils with Indians.

1691

MANZANET, DAMIAN   93

Hatcher, Mattie Austin, trans., and Foik, Paul J., ed. "The Expedition of Don Domingo Terán de los Rios into Texas." TEXAS CATHOLIC HISTORICAL SOCIETY PRELIMINARY STUDIES 2 (1932):2-67. Diary, pp. 48-67.

    May-Aug 1691. Ecclesiastical leader's account of expedition to establish missions among the Texas Indians; distance covered, features of countryside, meetings with Indians, naming of rivers, etc.

SCHUYLER, PETER, 1657-1724   94

In DOCUMENTS RELATIVE TO THE COLONIAL HISTORY OF THE STATE OF NEW YORK, edited by E.B. O'Callaghan, vol. 3, pp. 800-805; vol. 4, pp. 16-19, 81-83, 347-351; vol. 5, pp. 245-249.

    Jun-Aug 1691. Military journal of expedition against Canada; march from Albany to Chambly River; interesting details of raid.

    Feb 1693. Military journal containing notes of skirmishes and pursuit of French near Schenectady.

    Jan 1694. Treaty journal covering journey to Five Nations at Schenectady and negotiations.

    May-Jun 1698. Treaty journal recording journey with Dellius and reporting negotiations in Canada; discussions at Montreal with Frontenac.

    Apr-May 1711. Treaty journal providing record of negotiations with Onondaga Indians; minutes and speeches.

TERAN DE LOS RIOS, DOMINGO DE   95

Hatcher, Mattie Austin, trans., and Paul J. Foik, ed. "The Expedition of Don Domingo Terán de Los Rios into Texas." TEXAS CATHOLIC HISTORICAL SOCIETY PRELIMINARY STUDIES 2, no. 1 (1932):2-67. Diary, pp. 10-48.

    May 1691-Mar 1692. Military leader's account of expedition to establish missions among the Texas Indians; distances covered, route, countryside; meetings with Indians of various tribes; indications of disunity of military and ecclesiastical leaders of expedition; problems with stock and provisions; journeys to explore the province of the Tejas and Cadodoches tribes.

1692

VARGAS ZAPATA Y LUJAN PONCE DE LEON, DIEGO DE   96

"Journal." In THE LEADING FACTS OF NEW MEXICAN HISTORY, by Ralph E. Twitchell, vol. 4, pp. 340-354, 403-429. Cedar Rapids, Iowa: Torch Press, 1911-1917.

    Nov-Dec 1692. Spanish explorer's journal of physical condition of the area of the Valley of Rio Grande, Santa Fe and El Paso; visits with Moqui, Acomo, Zuni Indians.

    Jun-Oct 1696. An expedition from Santa Fe to Taos to locate apostate Indians.

"Vargas' Campaign Journal and Correspondence." In FIRST EXPEDITION OF VARGAS INTO NEW MEXICO, 1692, translated by J. Manuel Espinosa, pp. 48-277. Coronado Cuarto Centennial Publications, 1540-1940, vol. 10. Albuquerque: University of New Mexico Press, 1940.

    Aug 1692-Jan 1693. First campaign of the Spanish governor of New Mexico to conquer apostate rebels; description of each pueblo, outcome of meeting with the inhabitants; notes on geography and traveling conditions; recovery of religious articles and books at Zuni; search for quicksilver mine.

"Governor Vargas' Diary of His Campaign in Pursuit of the Rebellious Picuries, 1696." In AFTER CORONADO, by Alfred B. Thomas, pp. 53-59.

    Oct-Nov 1696. Pueblo revolt of 1696; attempts to follow the trail of the Indians; sending forth spies; capture of the Indians.

1693

BARREDA, RODRIGO DE LA   97

"Journal of Friar Rodrigo de la Barreda." In SPANISH APPROACH TO PENSACOLA, by Irving A. Leonard, pp. 265-281.

> 1693. Adventurer priest with Torres y Ayala expedition to discover land route to and reconnoiter bays of Pensacola and Mobile; with Indians who prepared trail and bridges.

MILAN TAPIA, FRANCISCO   98

"Journal of Don Francisco Milán Tapia." In SPANISH APPROACH TO PENSACOLA, by Irving A. Leonard, pp. 283-303.

> Jun-Aug 1693. Captain of fishing smack which sailed from Cazina Point to Pensacola Bay to meet Torres y Ayala expedition; notes on shores, soundings, rivers; trip by dugout to explore Mobile Bay.

SIGUENZA Y GONGORA, CARLOS DE   99

"Sigüenza's Instructions and Journey." In SPANISH APPROACH TO PENSACOLA, by Irving A. Leonard, pp. 152-192.

> Apr-May 1693. Exploration of northern portions of Gulf of Mexico with an eye to claiming land for Spain.

TORRES Y AYALA, LAUREANO DE, b. 1649   100

"Journal of Governor Torres Y Ayala." In SPANISH APPROACH TO PENSACOLA, by Irving A. Leonard, pp. 228-254.

> May-Aug 1693. Expedition by governor of Province of St. Augustine of Florida to establish land route from Apalache to Pensacola Bay and Mobile Bay; slow progress with unreliable Indian guides; arrival at Pensacola Bay, but Mobile Bay reached only by Captain Milan Tapia by water route.

WESSEL, DIRK   101

In DOCUMENTS RELATIVE TO THE COLONIAL HISTORY OF THE STATE OF NEW YORK, edited by E.B. O'Callaghan, vol. 4, pp. 59-63, 372-374.

> 1693-1698. Embassy from New York to Onondaga; exchange of prisoners; festivities; negotiations with sachems of Five Nations.

1694

COTTON, JOSIAH, 1680-1756   102

"Extracts from the Diary of Josiah Cotton." COLONIAL SOCIETY OF MASSACHUSETTS PUBLICATIONS 26 (1924-1926):277-280.

> 1694-1698. Reminiscences, but partly diary at Harvard.

KELPIUS, JOHANNES, 1673-1709   103

Sachse, Julius F. "The Diarium of Magister Johannes Kelpius." PENNSYLVANIA GERMAN SOCIETY PROCEEDINGS AND ADDRESSES 25 (1917):5-28.

> Jan-Jun 1694. Travel journal of German pietist's journey to America; Pennsylvania; Germantown; religious notes.

MANGE, JUAN MATEO, fl. 1692   104

UNKNOWN ARIZONA AND SONORA, 1693-1721, FROM THE FRANCISCO FERNANDEZ DEL CASTILLO VERSION OF LUZ DE TIERRA INCOGNITA. An English translation of Part II by Harry J. Karns and Associates. Tuscon: Arizona Silhouette, 1954. 303 pp.

> 1694-1701. Daily record of military captain with Eusebio Francisco Kino; seven trips of discovery in Mexico, Arizona and westward to locate route to California; travel distances and conditions; geographic features; Indian settlements visited and population counted; notes on customs and cultivated crops; missionary activities.

SCHUYLER, ARENT   105

In DOCUMENTS RELATIVE TO THE COLONIAL HISTORY OF THE STATE OF NEW YORK, edited by E.B. O'Callaghan, vol. 4, pp. 98-99.

> Feb 1694. Brief report of journey to Minisinck country; interesting spellings.

WADSWORTH, BENJAMIN, 1670-1737   106

"Wadsworth's Journal." MASSACHUSETTS HISTORICAL SOCIETY COLLECTIONS, 4th ser. 1 (1852):102-110.

> Aug 1694. Travel journal; Boston to Albany to treat with Five Nations; pleasant descriptions of journey and conference; amusing "literary" style.

1695

PAINE, JOHN, 1660-1731   107

"Deacon John Paine's Journal." MAYFLOWER DESCENDANT 8 (1906):180-184, 227-231; 9(1907):49-51, 97-99, 136-140.

> 1695-1718. Personal and religious notes in a flowery clerical style; interesting for its doggerel verses.

PRATT, WILLIAM, 1659-1713   108

In HISTORY OF THE TOWN OF EASTON, MASSACHUSETTS, by William L. Chaffin, pp. 67-68. Cambridge, Mass.: J. Wilson and Son, 1886.

In NARRATIVES OF EARLY CAROLINA, 1650-1708, edited by Alexander S. Salley, pp. 191-200. New York: Charles Scribner's Sons, 1911.

> 1695-1701. Extracts of miscellaneous notes; two voyages to South Carolina.

1696

DICKINSON, JONATHAN, 1663-1722   109

In JONATHAN DICKINSON'S JOURNAL, OR GOD'S PROTECTING PROVIDENCE, BEING THE NARRATIVE OF A JOURNEY FROM PORT ROYAL TO PHILADELPHIA, edited by Evangeline Walker Andrews and Charles McLean Andrews, pp. 24-100. New Haven: Yale University Press, 1945.

> 1696-1697. Merchant's harrowing adventure traveling from Jamaica to Philadelphia with his wife and baby on the barkentine REFORMATION; shipwreck off Florida, capture and detention by Indians, escape to St. Augustine and Charleston under terrible conditions.

FLETCHER, BENJAMIN, 1640-1703   110

A JOURNAL OF WHAT PASSED IN THE EXPEDITION OF HIS EXCELLENCY COLL. BENJAMIN FLETCHER, CAPTAIN

GENERAL AND GOVERNOUR IN CHIEF OF THE PROVINCE OF NEW YORK, ETC. New York: W. Bradford, 1696. 11 pp.

In DOCUMENTS RELATIVE TO THE COLONIAL HISTORY OF THE STATE OF NEW YORK, edited by E.B. O'Callaghan, vol. 4, pp. 235-241.

Sep-Oct 1696. Travel and treaty journal, kept by David Jamison; brief notes of journey to Albany, negotiations for renewal of treaty with Five Nations; minutes and speeches.

GREEN, JOSEPH, 1675-1715   111

Morison, Samuel E., ed. "The Commonplace Book of Joseph Green." COLONIAL SOCIETY OF MASSACHUSETTS PUBLICATIONS 34 (1937-1942):191-253.

"Diary of Rev. Joseph Green, of Salem Village." ESSEX INSTITUTE HISTORICAL COLLECTIONS 8 (1866): 215-224; 10 (1869):73-104; 36 (1900):325-330.

1696-1715. Clergyman's diary containing notes on local, church, family and personal affairs; farming and weather; a pleasant, social diary.

RUDMAN, ANDREW JOHN, 1668-1708   112

Anderson, Luther. "Diary of Rev. Andrew Rudman." GERMAN AMERICAN ANNALS 8 (1906):282-312, 315-334, 355-376; 9 (1907):9-18.

Jul 1696-Jun 1697. Diary of journey from Stockholm to London, Virginia, Maryland; descriptions of places, religious observances, life on board ship. Swedish and English text.

1697

CARERI, GEMELLI, 1651-1725   113

In A COLLECTION OF VOYAGES AND TRAVELS, edited by Awnsham Churchill, vol. 4. London: Printed for A. and J. Churchill, 1704.

Undated extracts in "Journal of the Great Voyage from Philippines to America," by William Henry Wallace. JOURNAL OF AMERICAN HISTORY 2 (1908):579-586.

1697-1698. Travel journal of Naples physician; from Philippines to America; hardships of a voyage of "204 days and 5 hours."

MARSHALL, JOHN, 1664-1732   114

Adams, Charles F., Jr., ed. "John Marshall's Diary." MASSACHUSETTS HISTORICAL SOCIETY PROCEEDINGS, 2d ser. 1 (1884-1885):148-163; 2d ser. 14 (1900-1901): 13-34.

1697-1711. Diary extracts containing brief notes of personal, religious and local affairs of Braintree, Massachusetts; deaths, notes on Indians.

MINOR, MANASSEH, 1647-1728   115

THE DIARY OF MANASSEH MINOR, STONINGTON, CONN. Jersey City?: Published by Frank Denison Miner with the assistance of Miss Hannah Miner, 1915.

1697-1720 (with gaps). Notes of personal affairs and farming; linguistic interest.

ROBERTS, HUGH, d. 1702   116

"Hugh Roberts of Merion: His Journal and a Letter to William Penn." PENNSYLVANIA MAGAZINE OF HISTORY AND BIOGRAPHY 18 (1894):199-210.

1697-1698. Brief travel diary of voyage from Pennsylvania to England and Wales.

1699

ANON.   117

"Expedition from New London to Woodstock, Conn." MASSACHUSETTS HISTORICAL SOCIETY PROCEEDINGS, 1st ser. 9 (1866-1867):473-478.

Feb 1699. Official military journal taken down upon order of Samuel Mason; expedition from New London to settle unrest among Indians; carefully detailed.

BRATTLE, WILLIAM, 1662-1717   118

"Early Records of the First Church, Cambridge." GENEALOGICAL MAGAZINE, 4th ser. 1 (1905-1906):347-361. Diary, pp. 358-361.

1699-1748. Clergyman's diary; scattered brief notes of weather, farming and gardening.

CALLEY, ROBERT   119

"Extracts from the Diary of Robert Calley of Charlestown, Mass." NEW ENGLAND HISTORICAL AND GENEALOGICAL REGISTER 16 (1862):34-40, 129-133.

1699-1765. Abstract of genealogical matter from diary of cabinetmaker and schoolmaster; partly an earlier record of church affairs in Malden.

COOTE, RICHARD, 1636-1701   120

In GREAT BRITAIN PUBLIC RECORD OFFICE CALENDAR OF STATE PAPERS, COLONIAL SERIES 18 (1700):584-591.

Aug-Sep 1699. Journey from Boston to Rhode Island; conference with Indians at Albany.

GLEN, JOHANNES   121

In DOCUMENTS RELATIVE TO THE COLONIAL HISTORY OF THE STATE OF NEW YORK, edited by E.B. O'Callaghan, vol. 4, pp. 558-560, 562-563.

Mar-Apr 1699. Glen's and Nicholas Bleeker's treaty negotiations with Indians at Onondaga. Translated from the Dutch.

LE MOYNE D'IBERVILLE, PIERRE, 1661-1706   122

In A COMPARATIVE VIEW OF FRENCH LOUISIANA . . . THE JOURNALS OF PIERRE LE MOYNE D'IBERVILLE AND JEAN-JACQUES-BLAISE D'ABBADIE, translated and edited by Carl A. Brasseaux, pp. 1-80. University of Southwestern Louisiana History Series, no. 13. Lafayette: Center for Louisiana Studies, University of Southwestern Louisiana, 1979. Revised edition, 1981.

Jan-May 1699. French-Canadian naval officer's exploration of coastal French Louisiana and the lower Mississippi to strengthen French claim to the area; navigational details, geographical features; many contacts with Indians, who assisted him as guides for canoe and cross-country exploration; names of tribes, customs.

VIELE, ARNOUT CORNELISSE, 1640-1704?   123

In DOCUMENTS RELATIVE TO THE COLONIAL HISTORY OF THE STATE OF NEW YORK, edited by E.B. O'Callaghan, vol. 4, pp. 560-562.

Apr-May 1699. Interpreter's journal; journey from Long Island to Onondaga and Indian transactions there. Translated from the Dutch.

1700

BROWN, RICHARD, 1675-1732 124

In GENEALOGICAL HISTORY OF THE TOWN OF READING, MASS., by Lilley Eaton, pp. 53-55. Boston: A. Mudge & Son, Printers, 1874.

> 1700-1719. Extracts from clergyman's journal; religious work, reflections and introspection; earlier autobiographical notes.

BRUGH, PETER VAN 125

In DOCUMENTS RELATIVE TO THE COLONIAL HISTORY OF THE STATE OF NEW YORK, edited by E.B. O'Callaghan, vol. 4, pp. 802-807.

> Sep-Oct 1700. Journey with Hendrik Hansen to Onondaga; negotiations with Indians.

DU RU, PAUL, 1666-1741 126

JOURNAL OF PAUL DU RU. Translated, with introduction and notes, by Ruth Lapham Butler. Chicago: Printed for the Caxton Club, 1934. 74 pp.

> Feb-May 1700. Events of Jesuit's journey from Biloxi Bay up the Mississippi. Translated from the French.

LAWSON, JOHN, d. 1712 127

A NEW VOYAGE TO CAROLINA. London, 1709. 258 pp. Reprint. Ann Arbor: University Microfilms, 1966.

A NEW VOYAGE TO CAROLINA. Edited by Hugh T. Lefler. Chapel Hill: University of North Carolina Press, 1967. 305 pp.

In THE HISTORY OF CAROLINA, pp. 1-60. London: Printed for W. Taylor and J. Baker, 1714; Printed for T. Warner, 1718. Reprint. Raleigh: O.H. Perry, printed by Strother & Marcom, 1860; Charlotte: Observer Printing House, 1903; Richmond, Va.: Garrett and Massie, 1937.

> Dec 1700-Jan 1701?. Notes of journey of about a thousand miles made by surveyor general of North Carolina; along the Catawba Path; interesting descriptions of backcountry, Indians and their customs.

ROMER, Col. 128

In DOCUMENTS RELATIVE TO THE COLONIAL HISTORY OF THE STATE OF NEW YORK, edited by E.B. O'Callaghan, vol. 4, pp. 798-801.

> Sep 1700. Negotiations with Indians at Onondaga. Translated from the Dutch.

1701

BLEEKER, JOHANNES 129

In DOCUMENTS RELATIVE TO THE COLONIAL HISTORY OF THE STATE OF NEW YORK, edited by E.B. O'Callaghan, vol. 4, pp. 889-895.

> Jun 1701. Journey with David Schuyler to Onondaga; negotiations with Indians.

MAHER, JOHN 130

JOURNAL OF THE VOYAGE OF THE SLOOP MARY. With introduction and notes by E.B. O'Callaghan. Albany, N.Y.: J. Munsell, 1866. 50 pp.

> Oct-Nov 1701. Account of voyage of the sloop MARY from Quebec and her wreck off Montauk Point, Long Island. Presumably written by Maher, the mate.

MICHEL, FRANCIS LOUIS 131

Hinke, William J., trans. and ed. "Report of the Journey of Francis Louis Michel." VIRGINIA MAGAZINE OF HISTORY AND BIOGRAPHY 24 (1916):1-43, 113-141, 275-288.

> 1701-1702. Swiss traveler's report, partly in narrative form, of journey from Berne to Virginia; interesting account of travel, geographical, social and religious conditions. Translated from the German.

1702

KEITH, GEORGE 132

A JOURNAL OF TRAVELS FROM NEW-HAMPSHIRE TO CARA-TUCK. London: Printed by J. Downing for B. Aylmer, 1706. 92 pp. Reprint. "A Journal of the Travels and Ministry of the Reverend George Keith, A.M." PROTESTANT EPISCOPAL HISTORICAL SOCIETY COLLECTIONS I (1851):5-51.

> 1702-1704. English clergyman's missionary travel journal; voyage from England to Boston; travel and ministry among the Quakers, especially in New England and Pennsylvania; preaching, religious life and disputes, comments on clergymen, account of churches appended; formal style; useful view of early Quakers in New England.

SANDEL, ANDREAS 133

"Extracts from the Journal of Rev. Andreas Sandel." PENNSYLVANIA MAGAZINE OF HISTORY AND BIOGRAPHY 30 (1906):287-299, 445-452.

> 1702-1719. Journal of the pastor of "Gloria Dei" Swedish Lutheran Church in Philadelphia; church affairs and visits; an excellent ghost story. Translated from the Swedish.

1703

CAMPBELL, JOHN, 1653-1728 134

"John Campbell to Gov. Fitz John Winthrop." MASSA-CHUSETTS HISTORICAL SOCIETY PROCEEDINGS, 1st ser. 9 (1866-1867):485-501.

> Apr-Sep 1703. Rather lively diary-letters, containing news of public affairs in Boston and ship movements, written to Governor Winthrop of Connecticut.

1704

HASTINGS, THOMAS, 1679-1728 135

In A HISTORY OF HATFIELD, MASSACHUSETTS, by Daniel W. Wells and Reuben F. Wells, pp. 150-152. Springfield, Mass.: Published under the direction of F.C.H. Gibbons, 1910.

> 1704-1746. Town clerk's notes on French and Indian wars; Queen Anne's War; Father Rasle's War.

HILTON, WINTHROP, 1671-1710 136

"Journal of the March and Proceedings with the Forces under My Command." MAINE HISTORICAL SOCIETY DOCUMENTARY HISTORY OF THE STATE OF MAINE, 2d ser. 9 (1907):140-142.

Feb-Mar 1704. Military commander's account of expedition against Indians to Saco River.

KNIGHT, SARAH KEMBLE, 1666-1727 137

In THE JOURNALS OF MADAM KNIGHT AND REV. MR. BUCKINGHAM, pp. 1-70. New York: Wilder & Campbell, 1825. Frequently reprinted; recently, New York: Garrett Press, 1970.

Extracts in AMERICAN HISTORY TOLD BY CONTEMPORARIES, edited by Albert B. Hart, vol. 2, pp. 224-229; DIARY OF AMERICA, edited by Josef Berger, pp. 43-51; most American literature anthologies.

Discussed in AMERICAN DIARY LITERATURE, by Steven E. Kagle, pp. 59-63.

Oct 1704-Jan 1705. Travel diary of intrepid New England lady; journey from Boston to New York and back; remarkable for its lively descriptions, character sketches, conversation pieces, sharp-tongued wit, romanticism and literary merit.

PALMER, ESTHER, d. 1714 138

"The Journal of Susanna Freeborn and Esther Palmer." FRIENDS' HISTORICAL SOCIETY JOURNAL 6 (1909):38-40.

1704. Quaker's diary of travel from Rhode Island to Pennsylvania; some interesting spellings.

"The Journal of Esther Palmer and Mary Lawson." FRIENDS' HISTORICAL SOCIETY JOURNAL 6 (1909):63-71.

1705. From Philadelphia to Maryland, Virginia, Carolinas and back.

"The Journal of Mary Banister and Esther Palmer's Travells." FRIENDS' HISTORICAL SOCIETY JOURNAL 6 (1909):133-139.

1705. Travels in Maryland and Virginia.

SHARPE, JOHN, b. 1680 139

"Journal of Rev. John Sharpe." PENNSYLVANIA MAGAZINE OF HISTORY AND BIOGRAPHY 40 (1916):257-297, 412-425.

1704-1713. Line-a-day notes of clerical work with prior autobiographical entries.

1706

RAMIREZ, ALFEREZ JUAN MATHEO 140

"Diary of the Journey to the Land Passage to California." In KINO'S HISTORICAL MEMOIR OF PIMERIA ALTA, by Eusebio Francisco Kino, vol. 2, pp. 197-209. Cleveland: Arthur H. Clark, 1919.

Oct-Nov 1706. Account by Catholic missionary from Presidio of Santa Rosa de Corodeguachi, who joined Father Kino in visiting missions, teaching, baptizing, observing conditions of crops and cattle and searching for possible land passage to California.

ULIBARRI, JUAN DE 141

"The Diary of Juan de Ulibarri to El Cuartelejo, 1706." In AFTER CORONADO, by Alfred B. Thomas, pp. 59-77.

Jul-Sep 1706. Journey from Santa Fe to El Cuartelejo along the Arkansas River to return Picuries chief, Don Lorenzo; observations on Indian life, their cultivated land; giving of gifts and promises of aid against the French.

1707

BARNARD, JOHN, 1681-1770 142

"Autobiography of the Rev. John Barnard." MASSACHUSETTS HISTORICAL SOCIETY COLLECTIONS, 3d ser. 5 (1836):177-243. Diary, pp. 192-195.

In HISTORY OF THE COUNTY OF ANNAPOLIS, by William A. Calnek, edited and completed by Alfred W. Savary, pp. 54-58. Toronto; W. Briggs, 1897.

May-Jul 1707. Experiences with French and Indians at Port Royal.

"Autobiography of the Rev. John Barnard." MASSACHUSETTS HISTORICAL SOCIETY COLLECTIONS, 3rd ser. 5 (1836):177-243. Diary, pp. 211-212.

Aug-Nov 1710. Trip from England to Boston.

1708

MAY, JOHN, 1686-1770 143

In MY ANCESTORS, compiled by Lyman M. Paine, pp. 94-96. Chicago: Printed for private circulation, 1914.

1708-1717. Extracts from private diary; very brief notes of work, farming, building, etc.; some local items of East Woodstock, Connecticut.

1709

BALDWIN, WILLIAM, 1677-1720 144

"The Travels of William Baldwin in America, 1709." FRIENDS' HISTORICAL SOCIETY JOURNAL 15 (1918):27-30.

Mar 1709-? Abstract of English Quaker's travel diary; southern states and New England.

BYRD, WILLIAM, 1674-1744 145

THE SECRET DIARY OF WILLIAM BYRD OF WESTOVER, 1709-1712. Edited by Louis B. Wright and Marion Tinling. Richmond, Va.: Dietz Press, 1941. 622 pp. Reprint. New York: Arno, 1972.

THE GREAT AMERICAN GENTLEMAN. Edited by Louis B. Wright and Marion Tinling. New York: Putnam, 1963. 249 pp. Abridgment.

1709-1712. Detailed daily record of the life of a Virginia gentleman; manners, customs, politics, domestic affairs, and above all, his personal life; an interesting diary, sometimes almost a Virginia counterpart to Sewall's diary; kept in shorthand.

THE LONDON DIARY (1717-1721) AND OTHER WRITINGS. Edited by Louis B. Wright and Marion Tinling. New York: Oxford University Press, 1958. 647 pp. Reprint. New York: Arno, 1972.

1717-1721. Byrd's adventures as a widower in England; much emphasis on courtships and dalliances.

WILLIAM BYRD'S HISTORIES OF THE DIVIDING LINE BETWIXT VIRGINIA AND NORTH CAROLINA. Edited by William K. Boyd. Raleigh: North Carolina Historical Commission, 1929. 341 pp.

Feb-Nov 1728. Another secret journal; running the line between Virginia and North Carolina; surveying work; serious conflict between commissioners and their men from the two states; their pranks and escapades; some highly entertaining character sketches; conversations with and comments on Indians.

ANOTHER SECRET DIARY OF WILLIAM BYRD OF WEST-OVER. Edited by Maude H. Woodfin. Richmond, Va.: Dietz Press, 1942. 490 pp.

1739-1741. Routine, formalized entries of daily activities; reading, morning prayers, meals, etc.

All of Byrd's diaries are discussed in AMERICAN DIARY LITERATURE, edited by Steven E. Kagle, pp. 153-159.

DUMMER, JEREMIAH, 1681-1739   146

Cohen, Sheldon S., ed. "The Diary of Jeremiah Dummer." WILLIAM AND MARY QUARTERLY, 3d ser. 24 (1967):397-422.

1709-1711. Extracts from spiritual diary kept in London by young Puritan who, his teaching and clerical ambitions having been thwarted, had accepted assignment defending Massachusett's claim to Martha's Vineyard; qualms and agonizing as secular career blossoms; appointment as agent of Massachusetts in England.

ESPINOSA, ISIDRO FELIX DE, 1679-1755   147

Foik, Paul J., ed., and Gabriel Tous, trans. "The Espinosa-Olivares-Aguirre Expedition of 1709: Espinosa's Diary." TEXAS CATHOLIC HISTORICAL SOCIETY PRELIMINARY STUDIES 1, no. 3 (1930):1-14.

Apr 1709. Franciscan missionary's account of journey from the Mission of San Juan Bautista on the Rio Grande del Norte across what is now Texas to the Rio Colorado in unsuccessful search for the Tejas Indians; description of route, land fertility, Indian customs; meetings with several tribes.

Tous, Gabriel, trans. "Ramón Expedition: Espinosa's Diary of 1716." MID-AMERICA 12 (1930):339-361. Reprint. TEXAS CATHOLIC HISTORICAL SOCIETY PRELIMINARY STUDIES 1, no. 4 (1930):1-24.

Apr-Jul 1716. From Rio Grande into the Province of Texas to establish missions among the Indians; record of religious observances and details of formalities involved in setting up a mission; an interesting and enjoyable document revealing diarist's sense of humor and appreciation of natural beauty.

HOLYOKE, EDWARD, 1689-1769   148

In THE HOLYOKE DIARIES, with an introduction and annotations by George Francis Dow, pp. 1-30.

1709-1768. Line-a-day notes of personal, religious and Harvard matters.

SMIBERT, JOHN, 1688-1751   149

THE NOTEBOOK OF JOHN SMIBERT. Boston: Massachusetts Historical Society, 1969. 131 pp.

1709-1747. British painter's record of work and accounts for portaits painted; London, Florence and, after 1729, Boston; family vital statistics.

1710

ANON.   150

JOURNAL OF AN EXPEDITION PERFORMED BY THE FORCES OF OUR SOVEREIGN. London, 1711. 24 pp.

1710. Expedition against Port Royal under General Nicholson.

1710

ANON.   151

SOCIETY OF COLONIAL WARS, MASSACHUSETTS, YEARBOOK 1897, pp. 84-94.

Jul-Sep 1710. Expedition from Massachusetts against Port Royal; articles of capitulation.

BUCKINGHAM, THOMAS, 1671-1731   152

In THE JOURNALS OF MADAM KNIGHT AND REV. MR. BUCKINGHAM, pp. 71-129. New York: Wilder & Campbell, 1825.

In ROLL AND JOURNAL OF CONNECTICUT SERVICE IN QUEEN ANNE'S WAR, 1710-1711, pp. 12-43. Acorn Club Publications, no. 13. New Haven, Conn.: Tuttle, Morehouse & Taylor, 1916.

Oct-Nov 1710, Aug-Oct 1711. Chaplain's journal covering expeditions against Port Royal and Crown Point.

FARWELL, JOSEPH, b. 1696   153

"Memoranda by Joseph Farwell of Groton." NEW ENGLAND HISTORICAL AND GENEALOGICAL REGISTER 35 (1881):275-276.

In THE FARWELL FAMILY, by John D. Farwell, completed and compiled by Jane Harter Abbott and Lillian M. Wilson, vol. 1, pp. 72-73. Orange, Tex.: F.H. Farwell and Fanny B. Farwell, 1929.

1710-1775. A few scattered, brief notes of private, church and war matters.

NICHOLSON, Sir FRANCIS, 1660-1728   154

JOURNAL OF AN EXPEDITION PERFORMED BY THE FORCES OF OUR SOVRAIGN LADY ANNE. London: Printed for R.S. and sold by J. Morphew, 1711. 24 pp.

NOVA SCOTIA HISTORICAL SOCIETY COLLECTIONS 1 (1879):59-104.

Jul-Oct 1710. Journal, mixed with letters and orders, kept by general commanding the expedition against Port Royal; daily happenings in siege.

WEISER, CONRAD, 1696-1760   155

THE LIFE OF (JOHN) CONRAD WEISER, THE GERMAN PIONEER, PATRIOT, AND PATRON OF TWO RACES. By Clement Z. Weiser. Reading, Pa.: D. Miller, 1876. 449 pp.

THE LIFE OF CONRAD WEISER AS IT RELATES TO HIS SERVICES AS OFFICIAL INTERPRETER BETWEEN NEW YORK AND PENNSYLVANIA. Compiled and edited by William M. Beauchamp. Syracuse, N.Y.: Onondaga Historical Association, 1925. 122 pp.

Contain reprints of most of the diaries kept by this noted Indian agent and provincial interpreter.

"The Journal of Conrad Weiser." OLDE ULSTER 2 (1906):199-204, 229-235.

1710. Journal translated from the German.

Muhlenberg, Hiester H., trans. "Narrative of a Journey." PENNSYLVANIA HISTORICAL SOCIETY COLLECTIONS 1 (1853):6-22.

Feb-Oct 1737. Journey from Tulpehocken to the headquarters of the Six Nations at Onondaga.

PENNSYLVANIA COLONIAL RECORDS 4 (1841):640-646, 660-669, 680-685; 5 (1842):470-480, 541-543; 6 (1843): 150-160.

1743–1754. Various journeys to Shamokin, Onondaga and Aucquick (Auckwick?).

PENNSYLVANIA COLONIAL RECORDS 5 (1842):348–358.

In EARLY HISTORY OF WESTERN PENNSYLVANIA, by Israel D. Rupp, app., pp. 22–33. Pittsburgh: A.P. Ingram, 1848.

PENNSYLVANIA HISTORICAL SOCIETY COLLECTIONS 1 (1853):23–33.

In EARLY WESTERN TRAVELS, edited by Reuben G. Thwaites, vol. 1, pp. 21–44.

Aug–Oct 1748. Journey to the Ohio.

PENNSYLVANIA COLONIAL RECORDS 6 (1843):642–647.

In DOCUMENTS RELATIVE TO THE COLONIAL HISTORY OF THE STATE OF NEW YORK, edited by E.B. O'Callaghan, vol. 6, pp. 795–799.

Jul–Aug 1753. Journey from Heidelberg, Berks County, to Mohawks; negotiations.

PENNSYLVANIA COLONIAL RECORDS 7 (1844):33–35.

Jan 1756. Treaty journal; proceedings with Indians at John Harris' Ferry.

In PENNSYLVANIA ARCHIVES, 1st ser., vol. 3, pp. 32–33.

Nov 1756. Extracts concerning Indians at Bethlehem and Easton.

In PENNSYLVANIA ARCHIVES, 1st ser., vol. 3, pp. 66–68.

Nov 1756. Record kept at Fort Allen.

1711

BARNWELL, JOHN, d. 1724   156

"Journal of John Barnwell." VIRGINIA MAGAZINE OF HISTORY AND BIOGRAPHY 5 (1897–1898):391–402; 6 (1898–1899):42–55. Reprint. "The Tuscarora Expedition." SOUTH CAROLINA HISTORICAL AND GENEALOGICAL MAGAZINE 9 (1908):28–54.

Jan–May 1711. Scouting journal in letters describing expeditions against Tuscarora Indians.

CRANE, BENJAMIN, ca. 1656–1721   157

In THE FIELD NOTES OF BENJAMIN CRANE, BENJAMIN HAMMOND, AND SAMUEL SMITH, by Dartmouth, Massachusetts, Proprietors, pp. 1–618. New Bedford, Mass.: New Bedford Free Public Library, 1910.

1711–1721. Surveyor's journal containing surveying and statistical notes at New Bedford, Dartmouth, etc.

HEMPSTEAD, JOSHUA, 1678–1758   158

DIARY OF JOSHUA HEMPSTEAD. New London County Historical Society Collections, vol. 1. New London, Conn.: New London County Historical Society, 1901. 750 pp.

1711–1758. Primarily local, personal, business and farming notes; journey from New London to Maryland; mostly brief entries, but the time span covered and details included make it an interesting and valuable diary of farming life.

HESSELIUS, ANDREAS, 1677–1733   159

JOHNSON, Amandus, trans. and ed. "The Journal of Andreas Hesselius." DELAWARE HISTORY 2 (1947):61–118.

1711–1723. Sporadic entries by rector of Holy Trinity (Old Swedes) Church in Wilmington; voyage from Sweden via London; focus on fauna and flora; reports of Indian customs.

SPOTSWOOD, ALEXANDER, 1676–1740   160

"Journal of the Lieut. Governor's Travels and Expeditions Undertaken for the Public Service of Virginia." WILLIAM AND MARY COLLEGE QUARTERLY, 2d ser. 3 (1923):40–45.

1711–1717. Travels and expeditions in the public service; single entry for each journey; distances, statistics, etc.

VETCH, SAMUEL, 1668–1732   161

NOVA SCOTIA HISTORICAL SOCIETY COLLECTIONS 4 (1884):105–110.

Jul–Oct 1711. Expedition from Boston to Quebec in fleet commanded by Sir Hovenden Walker.

WALKER, Sir HOVENDEN, 1656?–1728   162

A JOURNAL: OR FULL ACCOUNT OF THE LATE EXPEDITION TO CANADA. London: D. Browne, 1720. 304 pp.

Apr–Oct 1711. Journal kept by admiral commanding the fleet in an expedition from Boston to Quebec; appendix containing orders, letters, etc.

1712

EDWARDS, TIMOTHY, 1669–1758   163

"From a Colonial Account Book." YALE REVIEW, n.s. 15 (1926):621–624.

1712–1724. Scattered extracts from his notebook; purchases, domestic and family notes.

SEWALL, SAMUEL, 1678–1712   164

"A Journal of Proceedings to Martha's Vineyard." NEW ENGLAND HISTORICAL AND GENEALOGICAL REGISTER 18 (1864):74–75.

Oct 1712. Trip from Boston to Martha's Vineyard; visits and stages.

"Diary of Samuel Sewall, Jr." MASSACHUSETTS HISTORICAL SOCIETY PROCEEDINGS, 2d ser. 8 (1892–1894): 221–225.

Jan–Dec 1714. Brief notes of weather, local and personal affairs in Brookline, Massachusetts.

1713

GRIFFITH, JOHN, 1713–1776   165

A JOURNAL OF THE LIFE, TRAVELS, AND LABOURS IN THE MINISTRY OF JOHN GRIFFITH. London: James Phillips, 1779; Philadelphia: Joseph Crick, 1780; New York: W. Alexander & Co., 1830. 426 pp. Reprint. FRIENDS' LIBRARY 5 (1842):329–468.

?–1770. Quaker autobiography and journal; journeys and meetings in New England and Pennsylvania.

HANSEN, HENDRIK   166

"Conference with the Five Nations at Onondaga." In DOCUMENTS RELATIVE TO THE COLONIAL HISTORY OF THE STATE OF NEW YORK, edited by E.B. O'Callaghan, vol. 5, pp. 372–376.

Sep 1713. Treaty journal covering mission with John Bleeker and Lowrens Clasen to Onondaga; journey to Oneida, negotiations, speeches. Translated from the Dutch.

MAYHEW, EXPERIENCE, 1673–1758 167

In SOME CORRESPONDENCE BETWEEN THE GOVERNORS AND TREASURERS OF THE NEW ENGLAND COMPANY IN LONDON AND THE COMMISSIONERS OF THE UNITED COLONIES OF AMERICA, by Company for Propagation of the Gospel in New England and the Parts Adjacent in America, pp. 97–127. London: Printed by Spottiswoode, 1896. Reprint. New York: Burt Franklin, 1970.

    1713–1714. Seminarrative journal describing missionary visits to Indians.

STODDARD, JOHN, 1681–1748 168

"Stoddard's Journal." NEW ENGLAND HISTORICAL AND GENEALOGICAL REGISTER 5 (1851):21–42.

    Nov 1713–Sep 1714. Negotiations with governor general of Canada; full entries of discussions and letters.

1714

FONTAINE, JOHN, b. 1693 169

THE JOURNAL OF JOHN FONTAINE: AN IRISH HUGUENOT SON IN SPAIN AND VIRGINIA, 1710–1719. Edited by Edward Porter Alexander. Williamsburg, Va.: Colonial Williamsburg Foundation, 1972. 190 pp.

In MEMOIRS OF A HUGUENOT FAMILY, translated and compiled by Jacques Fontaine, edited by Ann Maury, pp. 245–310. New York: G.P. Putnam, 1853.

Extracts in PLANTATION AND FRONTIER DOCUMENTS, edited by Ulrich B. Phillips, vol. 2, pp. 230–235.

    1714–1718. Journey from England to America; trading and travel in Virginia; notes on colonial and Indian customs, scenery, coffee houses, clubs, religious practices; rare contemporary account of Spotswood's expedition; well-written, interesting diary.

1715

CAPON, PETER 170

"Journal of Peter Capon's Voyage from Annapolis Royal to Cape Breton--1715." HISTORICAL MAGAZINE, 3d ser. 3 (1875):18–20.

    Aug–Nov 1715. Journey to investigate Indian depredations.

COOPER, WILLIAM, 1693–1743 171

"Memoranda from the Rev. William Cooper's Interleaved Almanacs." NEW ENGLAND HISTORICAL AND GENEALOGICAL REGISTER 30 (1876):435–441; 31 (1877): 49–55.

    1715–1730. Extracts from Boston clergyman's journal; church and personal affairs; notes of sermons; genealogical interest.

HURTADO, JUAN PAEZ 172

"Diary of the Campaign of Juan Páez Hurtado Against the Faraon Apache, 1715." In AFTER CORONADO, translated and edited by Alfred B. Thomas, pp. 94–98.

    Aug–Sep 1715. Campaign made under order of Governor Juan Ignacio Flores Mogollon of New Mexico; traveling conditions, geography and water supply along Mora River into Texas and return along Canadian River; evidence of but no encounters with Apaches.

MASON, JOSEPH, d. 1761 173

In GENEALOGY OF THE SAMPSON MASON FAMILY, compiled by Alverdo H. Mason, pp. 49–56. East Braintree, Mass.: Printed by A.H. Mason, 1902.

    1715–1794. Brief, erratic extracts of genealogical interest and notes of public affairs in Warren, Massachusetts; latter part by diarist's son, Marmaduke.

READING, JOHN 174

"Copy of Journal of John Reading." NEW JERSEY HISTORICAL SOCIETY PROCEEDINGS, 3d ser. 10 (1915): 35–46, 90–110, 128–133.

    Apr–Jun 1715, May–Jul 1716. Surveyor's notes and statistics while working in northern New Jersey; very good section describing surveyors' adventures.

RETIS, JUAN ANTONIO DE TRASVIÑA 175

Reindorp, Reginald C., trans. "The Founding of Missions at La Junta de Los Rios." TEXAS CATHOLIC HISTORICAL SOCIETY SUPPLEMENTARY STUDIES 1, no. 1 (1938):3–28.

    May–Jun 1715. Account by leader of escort for missionaries to west Texas; record of distances covered, route, Indian settlements, speeches made to Indians; return to San Francisco de Cuéllar.

1716

PAINE, MOSES, 1695–1764 176

"Extracts from the Diary of Moses Paine, of Truro, Mass." NEW ENGLAND HISTORICAL AND GENEALOGICAL REGISTER 54 (1900):87–88.

    1716–1719. Extracts of very brief entries about family affairs, weather, etc.

PEÑA, DIEGO 177

Boyd, Mark F., trans. "Diego Peña's Expedition to Apalachee and Apalachicolo in 1716." FLORIDA HISTORICAL QUARTERLY 28 (1949):1–27.

    Aug–Sep 1716. Spanish diplomatic mission to escort Chief Chislacasliche back to his people along the Chattahoochee River and to cement Indian allegiance to the Spanish; considerable light shed on complex, continuous struggle between Spanish and English for trade and military advantages with the Indians; effects upon Indians of warfare and tribal dislocation resulting from European incursions.

RAMON, DOMINGO 178

Foik, Paul J., trans. "Captain Don Diego Ramón's Diary of His Expedition into Texas in 1716." TEXAS CATHOLIC HISTORICAL SOCIETY PRELIMINARY STUDIES 2, no. 5 (1933):1–23.

    Feb–Jul 1716. Military commander's account of expedition marking the beginnings of permanent settlement of the Province of Texas; from Saltillo into Texas; distances covered, natural resources, mishaps, meetings with Indians, founding of four missions.

1717

BAXTER, JOSEPH, 1676–1745   179

Nason, Elias, ed. "Journal of the Rev. Joseph Baxter."
NEW ENGLAND HISTORICAL AND GENEALOGICAL REGISTER
21 (1867):45–60.

> 1717–1721. Journal kept while missionary to Indians
> at Arrowsic Island, Maine; notes on travel,
> preaching, Indians and missionary rivalry.

KNIGHT, JAMES, d. 1720?   180

In THE FOUNDING OF CHURCHILL, by James Knight,
edited by James Francis Kenney, pp. 111–189. Toronto:
J.M. Dent and Sons, 1932.

> Jul–Sep 1717. Fur trader's journal covering voyage
> from York Fort to Churchill River to found
> Hudson's Bay Company post; excellent narrative of
> dangers, hardships, daily life.

SHULTZE (or SCHULTZ), DAVID, 1717–1799   181

"David Shultze's Journal." THE PERKIOMEN REGION,
PAST AND PRESENT 2 (1900):165, 187–189; 3 (1901):
10–14, 22–24, 41–43, 60–63, 90–93, 106–110, 124–127,
140–144, 155–159, 164.

> 1717, 1752, 1756, 1757, 1759, 1768. Brief entries,
> in a mixture of English and German, recording
> work as surveyor and scrivener in Perkiomen
> Valley of Pennsylvania; weather, deaths, farm
> activities, war news, etc.

THE JOURNAL AND PAPERS OF DAVID SHULTZE. Translated and edited by Andrew S. Berky. Pennsburg,
Pa.: The Schwenkfelder Library, 1952. 2 vols.

> 1733–? Journal of German-born surveyor in western
> Pennsylvania, member of Schwenkfelders, a Protes-
> tant sect driven out of Germany by persecution;
> ocean crossing from Holland to Philadelphia; sur-
> veying, farming, deaths, marriages; reports of
> Indian massacres, preparation of a hymnal, medi-
> cinal remedies for various human and animal
> maladies.

"The David Schultz Diary." THE PERKIOMEN REGION,
PAST AND PRESENT 6 (1928):109–114; 7 (1929):8–15, 34–
47, 66–73.

> 1769, 1774, 1780, 1782.

1718

CELIZ, FRANCISCO   182

Hoffman, Fritz Leo, trans. DIARY OF THE ALARCON
EXPEDITION INTO TEXAS. Quivira Society Publications,
vol. 5. Los Angeles: Quivira Society, 1935. 124 pp.

> Apr 1718–Feb 1719. Diary of the chaplain of an
> expedition led by Martin de Alarcón from Coahuila
> into Texas to determine natural resources, convert
> Indians, establish missions and secure the terri-
> tory from the French; distances, land features,
> meetings with Indians.

FRANKLIN, BENJAMIN, 1650–1727   183

"Commonplace-Book of Benjamin Franklin (1650–1727)."
COLONIAL SOCIETY OF MASSACHUSETTS PUBLICATIONS 10
(1904–1906):191–205.

> 1718–1724. Antiquarian notes about Boston by uncle
> of Benjamin Franklin; a few almanac and common-
> place-book jottings.

HADWEN, ISAAC, 1687–1737   184

"From the Journal of Isaac Hadwen." FRIENDS' HISTOR-
ICAL ASSOCIATION BULLETIN 15 (1926):29–32.

> 1718–1719. Extracts from Quaker journal; brief,
> scattered notes of travel to and in the American
> colonies; many interesting spellings.

HARPE, BENARD DE LA   185

Smith, Ralph H., trans. and ed. "Account of the
Journey of Benard de la Harpe." SOUTHWESTERN HIS-
TORICAL QUARTERLY 62 (1958–1959):75–86, 246–259,
371–385, 525–541.

> 1718–1720. French expedition west of the Missis-
> sippi, mainly in Red River area; detailed notes on
> Indians; rather coercive missionary and diplomatic
> efforts of the French.

Smith, Ralph A., trans. and ed. "Exploration of the
Arkansas River by Benard de la Harpe, 1721–1722:
Extracts from His Journals and Instructions." ARKANSAS
HISTORICAL QUARTERLY 10 (1951):339–363.

> Dec 1721–Apr 1722. Journey to determine sites for
> French posts to protect settlements and establish
> trade; description of river, surrounding lands,
> site of present-day Little Rock; difficulties of
> expedition, including Indians' reluctance to trade.

WIEGNER, CHRISTOPHER, ca. 1712–1746   186

Kriebel, H.W. "Christopher Wiegner, the Towamencin
Diarist." HISTORICAL SOCIETY OF MONTGOMERY COUNTY
HISTORICAL SKETCHES 3 (1905):271–289.

> 1718–1739. Account of and a few extracts from
> diary of religious introspection.

1719

DES URSINS   187

Rothensteiner, John E. "Earliest History of Mine La
Motte." MISSOURI HISTORICAL REVIEW 20 (1925–1926):
199–213. Journal, pp. 205–207.

> Jun 1719. Travel journal kept by French intendant
> of the Illinois country; from Kaskaskia to lead
> mines in what is now Madison County, Missouri;
> official report and descriptions. Translated.

FISKE, SAMUEL, 1689–1770   188

"Fragment of a Diary Kept by Rev. Samuel Fiske of
Salem." ESSEX INSTITUTE HISTORICAL COLLECTIONS 51
(1915):282–289.

> 1719–1721. Extracts from clergyman's journal; notes
> of church and local affairs, preaching.

GUILLEN, CLEMENTE, 1677–1748   189

CLEMENTE GUILLEN, EXPLORER OF THE SOUTH: DIARIES
OF THE OVERLAND EXPEDITIONS TO BAHIA MAGDALENA
AND LA PAS. Translated and edited by W. Michael
Mathes. Baja California Travels Series, vol. 42. Los
Angeles: Dawson's Book Shop, 1979. 99 pp.

> Mar–Apr 1719, Nov 1720–Jan 1721. Spanish priest's
> diary of expedition to Gulf of California area of
> Baja California; masses and baptisms, dealings
> with Indians, comments on inland terrain and sea-
> coast with an eye to harbor and trade devel-
> opment.

PARKMAN, EBENEZER, 1703-1782 190

THE DIARY OF EBENEZER PARKMAN, 1703-1782. Edited by Francis G. Walett. Worcester, Mass.: American Antiquarian Society, 1974. 3 vols. in 1. First published in AMERICAN ANTIQUARIAN SOCIETY PROCEEDINGS 71-76 (1961-1966):passim.

1719-1755. Minister's unsurpassed record of small town life in colonial New England; work and concerns of a conscientious pastor; daily activities, mores, superstitions of townsfolk in Westborough, Massachusetts; illnesses, including an epidemic of "throat distemper," medical remedies; theological disputes and diarist's reactions to such divines as Jonathan Edwards and George Whitefield; Indian disputes; impact of the Great Awakening. The diary reveals a practical, compassionate, learned man of wide interests, less given to agonizing introspections than some of his colonial brethren.

THE DIARY OF REV. EBENEZER PARKMAN OF WESTBOROUGH, MASS. Edited by Harriette M. Forbes. Westborough, Mass.: Westborough Historical Society, 1899. 327 pp.

Feb-Nov 1737, 1778-1780. Local news and gossip; notes on Indians and Acadians.

VALVERDE, ANTONIO DE, b. 1671 191

"Diary of the Campaign of Governor Antonio de Valverde Against the Ute and Comanche Indians, 1719." In AFTER CORONADO, translated and edited by Alfred B. Thomas, pp. 110-133.

Sep-Oct 1719. Military campaign to subdue Ute and Comanche nations; Santa Fe to Taos and north along South Platte and Arkansas rivers; description of geography, manner of moving and providing food and water for their forces; meeting with Apaches of El Cuartelejo who were escaping the French; indication of areas occupied by various Indian tribes; return due to winter weather and lack of provisions.

1720

CLAWSON, LAWRENCE 192

In DOCUMENTS RELATIVE TO THE COLONIAL HISTORY OF THE STATE OF NEW YORK, edited by E.B. O'Callaghan, vol. 5, pp. 550-551.

Apr-May 1720. Interpreter's journal; journey to Niagara country; negotiations with Senecas.

DEXTER, SAMUEL, 1700-1755 193

"Extracts from the Diary of Rev. Samuel Dexter, of Dedham." NEW ENGLAND HISTORICAL AND GENEALOGICAL REGISTER 13 (1859):305-310; 14 (1860):35-40, 107-112, 202-205.

1720-1752. Diary of clerical life, mainly at Medford, Massachusetts; occasional entries of private and public affairs; long descriptions of deaths and an earthquake.

LORD, JOSEPH, 1690-1748 194

YARMOUTH REGISTER, 17 December 1846.

1720-1748. Extracts from clergyman's diary.

MOODY, JOSEPH, 1700-1753 195

"Extracts from the Diary of the Rev. Joseph Moody of York, Sometimes Called Handkerchief Moody." MAINE HISTORICAL SOCIETY COLLECTIONS, 2d ser. 3 (1892): 317-324.

1720-1724. Brief entries from clergyman's journal, mostly in Latin cipher; marriages, deaths; a few general entries on weather, Indians, pirates, etc.

RHODES, JOHN, b. 1658 196

"John Rhodes, Ejus Liber." NEWPORT HISTORICAL MAGAZINE 1 (1880-1881):234-235.

1720-1731. Very brief extracts of personal and public matters in Newport, Rhode Island; recipes.

SCHUYLER, MYNDERT 197

In DOCUMENTS RELATIVE TO THE COLONIAL HISTORY OF THE STATE OF NEW YORK, edited by E.B. O'Callaghan, vol. 5, pp. 542-545.

Apr-May 1720. Treaty journal covering negotiations with Senecas at Albany; minutes and speeches; with Robert Livingston.

VILLASUR, PEDRO DE, d. 1720 198

Sheldon, Addison E., trans. and ed. "The Battle at the Forks of the Loup and the Platte, August 11, 1720." NEBRASKA HISTORY 6 (1923):1-32. Diary, pp. 13-19.

"A Portion of the Diary of the Reconnaissance Expedition of Colonel Don Pedro de Villasur along the Platte River, 1720." In AFTER CORONADO, translated and edited by Alfred B. Thomas, pp. 133-137.

Aug 1720. Commander's record of expedition searching for French incursions northeast of Santa Fe; description of Platte River and Pawnee village. Found on the battlefield, the diary chronicles events leading to the massacre of the Spanish by Indians.

1721

FOTHERGILL, JOHN, 1676-1744 199

"An Account of the Life and Travels, in the Work of the Ministry, of John Fothergill." FRIENDS' LIBRARY 13 (1849):352-445. American diary, pp. 378-396, 418-425.

1721-1722, 1736-1737. English Quaker's journal of travel in most of the Atlantic states; visits to meetings.

LYNDE, BENJAMIN, 1700-1781 200

THE DIARIES OF BENJAMIN LYNDE AND OF BENJAMIN LYNDE, JR. Edited by Fitch E. Oliver. Boston: Privately printed; Cambridge, Mass.: Riverside Press, 1880. 251 pp.

1721-1780. Notes of personal affairs, apparently summarized from almanacs.

PEÑA, JUAN ANTONIO DE LA 201

Forrestal, Peter P., trans. and ed. "Peña's Diary of the Aguayo Expedition." UNITED STATES CATHOLIC HISTORICAL SOCIETY HISTORICAL RECORDS AND STUDIES 24 (1934):143-208. Reprint. TEXAS CATHOLIC HISTORICAL SOCIETY PRELIMINARY STUDIES 2, no. 7 (1935): 3-68.

1721-1722. Priest's account of expedition to curb French encroachments in east Texas; route and distances covered; natural resources, water, hardships; naming of places; meetings with Indians and negotiations with French; establishment of presidios and restoration of missions.

SMITH, THOMAS, 1702-1795   202

In JOURNALS OF THE REV. THOMAS SMITH, AND THE REV. SAMUEL DEANE, PASTORS OF THE FIRST CHURCH IN PORTLAND, edited by William Willis, pp. 39-284. Portland, Maine: J.S. Bailey, 1849.

   1721-1788. Mostly brief, impersonal notes, but its span and consistency make it a valuable New England record of foreign and domestic news, especially at Falmouth.

1722

ASHTON, PHILIP, 1703-1746   203

THE STRANGE ADVENTURES OF A CASTAWAY, PHILIP ASHTON OF MARBLEHEAD. Marblehead, Mass.: n.d. 16 pp.

ASHTON'S MEMORIAL. By John Barnard. Boston: Printed for S. Gerrish, 1725. Reprint. In THE PIRATES OF THE NEW ENGLAND COAST, 1630-1730, by George Francis Dow and John Henry Edmonds, pp. 218-269. Marine Research Society Publications, no. 2. Salem, Mass.: Marine Research Society, 1923.

Shortened version in THE SHIPS AND SAILORS OF OLD SALEM, by Ralph D. Paine, pp. 46-59.

   1722-1725. Captive's narrative with daily entries; account of capture by pirates and life on desert island; highly interesting story of unwilling pirate and new Robinson Crusoe.

BLANCHARD, JOSHUA, 1692-1748   204

Brown, Abram E. "Builder of the Old South Meeting House." NEW ENGLAND MAGAZINE, n.s. 13 (1895-1896): 390-398. Diary, pp. 396-398.

   1722-1730. Brief yearly entries of family affairs and principal public events in Boston.

BUMSTEAD, JEREMIAH, 1678-1729   205

"Diary of Jeremiah Bumstead of Boston, 1722-1727." NEW ENGLAND HISTORICAL AND GENEALOGICAL REGISTER 15 (1861):193-204, 305-315.

   1722-1727 (with gaps). Brief notes of Boston news; births, deaths, and marriages; interesting language.

COGAN, JOHN, b. 1699   206

"Capt. Cogan's Expedition to Pigwacket, 1722." NEW ENGLAND HISTORICAL AND GENEALOGICAL REGISTER 34 (1880):382-383.

   Sep-Oct 1722. Scouting journal containing brief notes of expedition in vain search for Indians.

COMER, JOHN, 1704-1734   207

THE DIARY OF JOHN COMER. Edited by C. Edwin Barrows and James W. Willmarth. Rhode Island Historical Society Collections, vol. 8. Providence: Rhode Island Historical Society, 1893. 132 pp.

   1722-1734. Brief impersonal entries of Baptist clergyman; religious and public affairs in Newport, Rhode Island; providences, preaching; inter-

esting language; includes autobiographical notes from birth.

D'ARTAGUIETTE, DIRON   208

"Journal of Diron d'Artaguiette, Inspector General of Louisiana, 1722-1723." In TRAVELS IN THE AMERICAN COLONIES, edited by Newton D. Mereness, pp. 17-92.

   1722-1723. Journey from New Orleans up the Mississippi to the Illinois country; report on conditions in the country, complaints, etc.; notes on travel difficulties and personal affairs. Translated from the French.

DELISLE, LEGARDEUR   209

Faye, Stanley, ed. "A Search for Copper on the Illinois River: the Journal of Legardeur Delisle." ILLINOIS STATE HISTORICAL SOCIETY JOURNAL 38 (1945):38-57.

   May-Jun 1722. Record kept by sublieutenant commanding the military escort; exploration of Illinois River in search of an elusive copper mine.

EDWARDS, JONATHAN, 1703-1758   210

In THE LIFE OF PRESIDENT EDWARDS, by Sereno E. Dwight, pp. 74-106. New York: G.&C.&H. Carvill, 1830.

   1722-1735. Journal of religious meditations and self-analysis, spiritual life and resolutions.

JOHNSON, SAMUEL, 1696-1772   211

In LIFE AND CORRESPONDENCE OF SAMUEL JOHNSON, P.P., MISSIONARY OF THE CHURCH OF ENGLAND IN CONNECTICUT, AND FIRST PRESIDENT OF KING'S COLLEGE, NEW YORK, by Eben E. Beardsley, pp. 18-53. New York: Hurd & Houghton, 1874.

   1722-1723. Extracts providing account of visit to England.

TAITT, DAVID   212

In TRAVELS IN THE AMERICAN COLONIES, edited by Newton D. Mereness, pp. 497-565.

   Jan-Jun 1722. Journey from Pensacola to and through the country of the Upper and Lower Creeks; arranging secession of land on Scamba River; brief travel notes; longer notes of meetings with Indians about Tuckabatchee, etc.; good descriptions of Indian ceremonies.

1723

ELIOT, JACOB, 1700-1766   213

Gillett, E.H., ed. "Diary of Rev. Jacob Eliot." HISTORICAL MAGAZINE, 2d ser. 5 (1869):33-35.

   1723-1764. Scattered extracts from clergyman's diary; weather, personal and miscellaneous affairs.

FAIRBANK, JABEZ, ca. 1674-1758   214

In THE EARLY RECORDS OF LANCASTER, MASSACHUSETTS, edited by Henry S. Nourse, pp. 218-220. Lancaster: Printed by W.J. Coulter, 1884.

   Dec 1723-Apr 1724. Scouting expeditions sent out from Lancaster by Fairbank; brief notes of movements.

HAMMOND, BENJAMIN, 1673-1747 215

In THE FIELD NOTES OF BENJAMIN CRANE, BENJAMIN HAMMOND, AND SAMUEL SMITH, edited by Dartmouth, Massachusetts, Proprietors, pp. 647-659. New Bedford, Mass.: New Bedford Free Public library, 1910.

1723-1741. Surveyor's field notes from around New Bedford.

MOULTON, JEREMIAH, b. 1688 216

"Captain Jeremiah Moulton's Scouting Expedition." MAINE HISTORICAL AND GENEALOGICAL RECORDER 1 (1884):204-207.

May-Jun 1723. Scouting journal containing brief notes of expedition to York, Maine.

PECKER, DANIEL, 1690-1750 217

In LETTERS OF COL. THOMAS WESTBROOK AND OTHERS, edited by William B. Trask, pp. 187-188. Boston: G.E. Littlefield, 1901.

Nov-Dec 1723. Scouting journal of expedition to New Hampshire; brief notes; stages of march.

SAYWARD, JOSEPH, 1684-1741 218

In THE SAYWARD FAMILY, by Charles A. Sayward, pp. 49-50. Ipswich, Mass.: Independent Press, F.G. Hall, 1890.

Nov-Dec 1723. Scouting diary containing very brief notes of expedition, under Captain Bragdon, to Salmon Falls River, Maine.

WESTBROOK, THOMAS, d. 1744 219

In LETTERS OF COL. THOMAS WESTBROOK AND OTHERS, edited by William B. Trask, pp. 16-26. Boston: G.E. Littlefield, 1901.

May-Jun 1723. Officer's journal of camp life at garrisons in Maine; work, sickness, etc.

1724

BARLOW, JONATHAN 220

Seybolt, Robert Francis, ed. "Captured by Pirates: Two Diaries of 1724-1725." NEW ENGLAND QUARTERLY 2 (1929):658-669. Diary, pp. 658-663.

Jun 1724-Jan 1725. Notes on personal affairs and adventures of sailor captured by pirates.

BROWN, ALLISON 221

In LETTERS OF COL. THOMAS WESTBROOK AND OTHERS, ed. by William B. Trask, pp. 58-59. Boston: G.E. Littlefield, 1901.

May 1724. Sergeant's brief notes of a march to Saco River and Arundel.

JEFFRY, JAMES, ca. 1706-1755 222

"James Jeffry's Journal for the Year 1724." ESSEX INSTITUTE HISTORICAL COLLECTIONS 36 (1900):331-338.

Jan-Dec 1724. Line-a-day entries of personal and local affairs in Salem; some linguistic interest.

"Extracts Copied, Some Twoscore Years Ago, from Interleaved Almanacs." ESSEX INSTITUTE HISTORICAL COLLECTIONS 2 (1860):64-67.

1727-1749. Scattered extracts of local and personal notes.

KELLOGG, JOSEPH, 1691-1756 223

In A HISTORY OF THE TOWN OF NORTHFIELD, by Josiah H. Temple and George Sheldon, p. 207.

Nov-Dec 1724. Scouting journal consisting of very brief notes of expedition stages.

SIMMONS, NICHOLAS 224

Seybolt, Robert Francis, ed. "Captured by Pirates: Two Diaries of 1724-1725." NEW ENGLAND QUARTERLY 2 (1929):658-669. Diary, pp. 663-669.

1724-Jan 1725. See Barlow, Jonathan.

SKINNER, RICHARD, ca. 1666-1727 225

"Richard Skinner of Marblehead and His Bible." NEW ENGLAND HISTORICAL AND GENEALOGICAL REGISTER 54 (1900):413-422. Diary, pp. 413-415.

1724-1725. Notes from family Bible; sermons and odd family items.

WARNER, ELEAZAR, 1687-1776 226

In HISTORY OF NORTH BROOKFIELD, MASSACHUSETTS, by Josiah H. Temple, pp. 204-205. North Brookfield: Published by the town, 1887.

1724-1725. Sergeant's very brief notes of guards and marches while serving near Brookfield.

WHEELWRIGHT, SAMUEL, b. 1692 227

In THE HISTORY OF WELLS AND KENNEBUNK, by Edward E. Bourne, p. 323. Portland, Maine: B. Thurston, 1875.

In INDIAN WARS OF NEW ENGLAND, by Herbert M. Sylvester, vol. 3, pp. 245-246. Boston: W.B. Clarke, 1910.

Nov-Dec 1724. Very brief notes of expedition to Pigwacket in search of Indians.

WRIGHT, SAMUEL, 1670-1740 228

WORCESTER SOCIETY OF ANTIQUITY PROCEEDINGS 7 (1885):53-61.

Nov 1724-Jun 1725. Brief notes on scouting expeditions around Rutland.

1725

ATKINSON, THEODORE, 1697-1779 229

In SOCIETY OF COLONIAL WARS, NEW HAMPSHIRE, REGISTER, edited by G.A. Gordon, pp. 25-53. Concord: The Society, 1907.

Jan-May 1725. Indian commissioner's account of journey from Portsmouth to Montreal; visits with Indians and captives; treaty with French Mohawks.

McAnear, Beverly, ed. "Personal Accounts of the Albany Congress of 1754." MISSISSIPPI VALLEY HISTORICAL REVIEW 39 (1953):727-746. Diary, pp. 727-739.

Jun-Jul 1754. Record kept by New Hampshire delegation's leader during the deliberations of the congress called to form a colonial union to deal with deteriorating British-Indian relations.

BLANCHARD, JOSEPH, 1704-1758   230

"Blanchard's Journal." NEW ENGLAND HISTORICAL AND GENEALOGICAL REGISTER 7 (1853):184.

Jul-Aug 1725. Scouting journal covering march from Dunstable to Penacook Falls and back in search of Indians.

CHICKEN, GEORGE   231

In TRAVELS IN THE AMERICAN COLONIES, edited by Newton D. Mereness, pp. 97-172.

Extracts in EARLY TRAVELS IN THE TENNESSEE COUNTRY, edited by Samuel C. Williams, pp. 97-104.

Jun-Oct 1725. South Carolina Indian commissioner's account of visit to the Cherokees; largely negotiations and reports of talks; letters, etc.

FITCH, TOBIAS   232

In TRAVELS IN THE AMERICAN COLONIES, edited by Newton D. Mereness, pp. 176-212.

Jun-Dec 1725. Indian commissioner's description of journey to Creek Indians in Alabama; negotiations and lengthy reports mainly in direct speech; some interesting language.

LOVEWELL, JOHN, 1691-1725   233

In THE EXPEDITIONS OF CAPT. JOHN LOVEWELL, AND HIS ENCOUNTERS WITH THE INDIANS, by Frederic Kidder. Boston: Bartlett and Halliday, 1865. 138 pp. Reprint, with slight revisions. MAGAZINE OF HISTORY, extra no. 5, 2 (1909):1-121. Journal, pp. 16-18.

Kidder, Frederic. "The Adventures of Capt. Lovewell." NEW ENGLAND HISTORICAL AND GENEALOGICAL REGISTER 7 (1853):61-70. Journal, pp. 62-63.

Jan-Feb 1725. Notes of the second campaign against the Indians.

NORRIS, ISAAC, 1701-1766   234

Parsons, William T., ed. "Journey to Rhoad Island." PENNSYLVANIA MAGAZINE OF HISTORY AND BIOGRAPHY 85 (1961):411-422.

Sep-Oct 1725. Business trip, on horseback, from Philadelphia to Boston; brief entries covering road conditions and characteristics of colonial travel; record of expenses.

"The Journal of Isaac Norris." PENNSYLVANIA MAGAZINE OF HISTORY AND BIOGRAPHY 27 (1903):20-28.

Sep-Oct 1745. Journey to Albany and treaty negotiations there.

TYNG, ELEAZAR, 1690-1782   235

Little, William, ed. "Capt. Eleazar Tyng's Scout Journal." GRANITE MONTHLY 15 (1893):183-186.

Mar-Apr 1725. Brief notes of scouting in Lovewell's War; stages about Penacook, etc.

WHITE, JOHN, 1684-1725   236

In THE EARLY RECORDS OF LANCASTER, MASSACHUSETTS, by Henry S. Nourse, pp. 230-234. Lancaster: Printed by W.J. Coulter, 1884.

Little, William, ed. "Captain John White's Scout Journal." GRANITE MONTHLY 14 (1892):205-211.

Feb-Aug 1725. Service with Lovewell; marches from Groton to Contookook, etc.; notes on weather; interesting spellings.

WILLARD, SAMUEL, 1690-1752   237

In THE EARLY RECORDS OF LANCASTER, MASSACHUSETTS, by Henry S. Nourse, pp. 237-242. Lancaster: Printed by W.J. Coulter, 1884.

Jul-Oct 1725. Scouting journal containing brief notes of distances and Indian affairs; interesting language.

WRIGHT, BENJAMIN, 1660-1743   238

In A HISTORY OF THE TOWN OF NORTHFIELD, MASSACHU-SETTS, by Josiah H. Temple and George Sheldon, pp. 210-212.

Jul-Sep 1725. Account of expedition to Lake Champlain; brief notes on marches, etc.

1726

FRANKLIN, BENJAMIN, 1706-1790   239

"Journal of a Voyage." In PAPERS, edited by Leonard W. Labaree, vol. 1, pp. 72-99. New Haven: Yale University Press, 1959-(in progress).

"Journal of Occurences in My Voyage to Philadelphia on Board the Berkshire, Henry Clark, Master, from London." In THE WRITINGS OF BENJAMIN FRANKLIN, edited by Albert H. Smyth, vol. 2, pp. 53-86. New York and London: Macmillan, 1905-1907.

Jul-Oct 1726. Descriptions of Portsmouth, Cowes, Newport, England; life at sea; observations of natural phenomena.

In FRANKLIN IN FRANCE, by Edward Everett Hale and Edward Everett Hale, Jr., pp. 246-250. Boston: Roberts Brothers, 1887-1888.

Oct 1778, Jan, Feb 1779, Jan 1780. Notes on his health in France; illnesses and treatment.

In FRANKLIN IN FRANCE, pp. 437-446.

In THE COMPLETE WORKS OF BENJAMIN FRANKLIN, edited by John Bigelow, vol. 8, pp. 345-355. New York; London: G.P. Putnam's Sons, 1887-1888.

Dec 1780-Jan 1781. Primarily notes on political activities in France; commercial entanglements.

In THE WRITINGS OF BENJAMIN FRANKLIN, vol. 8, pp. 459-560.

Mar-Jul 1782. Negotiations for peace with Great Britain; letters and documents.

"Extracts from a Private Journal." In THE WORKS OF BENJAMIN FRANKLIN, edited by Jared Sparks, vol. 1, pp. 579-591. Boston: Hilliard, Gray, 1836-1840.

Jun-Jul 1784. Notes on official business in Paris, in the court, etc.

Jul-Sep 1785. Leave taking after eight years in France; arrival in Philadelphia.

In THE COMPLETE WORKS OF BENJAMIN FRANKLIN, vol. 10, pp. 347-359; vol. 11, pp. 189-196.

Jun 1784, Jul 1785.

GODDARD, EDWARD, 1675-1754   240

Whitmore, Brewer G., ed. "Edward Goddard's Journal of the Peace Commission to the Eastern Indians, 1726." COLONIAL SOCIETY OF MASSACHUSETTS PUBLICATIONS 20 (1917-1919):128-147.

Jul-Aug 1726. Official treaty journal; peace commission to eastern Indians; journey, proceedings, treaty in Maine; some social items.

WAINWRIGHT, JOHN, 1690-1721   241

In THE HISTORY OF CONCORD, by Nathaniel Bouton, pp. 64-77. Concord, N.H.: B.W. Sanborn, 1856.

May 1726. Surveying journal covering journey from Haverhill of a committee to lay out lands in Penacook.

1727

HERBERT, JOHN   242

JOURNAL OF COLONEL JOHN HERBERT, COMMISSIONER OF INDIAN AFFAIRS FOR THE PROVINCE OF SOUTH CAROLINA. Edited by A.S. Salley. Columbia: Historical Commission of South Carolina, 1936. 34 pp.

Oct 1727-Mar 1728. Account of mission to secure assistance of Cherokees against hostile Creeks and other tribes; record of negotiations; regulation of trade with Indians; transcript of conversations with Indian leaders; speeches of diarist and chiefs.

LANE, JOSHUA, d. 1766   243

In LANE FAMILIES OF THE MASSACHUSETTS BAY COLONY, by James P. Lane, pp. 50-53. Norton, Mass.: Printed by Lane Brothers, 1886.

1727-1755. Account, with a few brief extracts, of private diary; religious activities and reflections, providences; local and family affairs at Hampton, Massachusetts.

RODENEY, CAESAR, 1707-1745   244

Hancock, Harold B., ed. "'Fare Weather and Good Helth': The Journal of Caesar Rodeney." DELAWARE HISTORY 10 (1962):33-70.

1727-1729. Fishing, hunting, dancing and merry-making with family and friends in Kent County, Delaware; rather complete account of wedding festivities; only monthly summaries for 1728.

WHIPPLE, JOSEPH, 1701-1757   245

In HISTORY OF THE TOWN OF HAMPTON FALLS, N.H., by Warren Brown, pp. 33-40. Concord, N.H.: Rumford Press, 1900.

1727-1754. Clergyman's brief notes of church events and proceedings.

1728

BUSS, STEPHEN, 1718-1790   246

In A CENTENNIAL DISCOURSE DELIVERED TO THE FIRST CONGREGATIONAL CHURCH AND SOCIETY IN LEOMINSTER, SEPTEMBER 24, 1843, by Rufus P. Stebbins, p. 90. Boston: C.C. Little & J. Brown, 1843.

1728-1762. Brief extracts concerning church affairs, necrology, local history.

WALKER, BENJAMIN   247

"Governor Burnet in the Diary of Benjamin Walker, Jr." COLONIAL SOCIETY OF MASSACHUSETTS PUBLICATIONS 28 (1930-1933):238-244.

1728-1729. Extracts from shopkeeper's diary relating to Governor Burnet; description of official ceremonies.

WHITE, TIMOTHY, 1700-1765   248

"Journal of Timothy White." NANTUCKET HISTORICAL ASSOCIATION BULLETIN 1, no. 2 (1898):15-26.

1728-1756. Very brief notes of missionary work among Indians, school accounts, etc.

WOODBRIDGE, DUDLEY, 1705-1790   249

"Diary of Dr. Dudley Woodbridge." MASSACHUSETTS HISTORICAL SOCIETY PROCEEDINGS, 1st ser. 17 (1879-1880):337-340.

Oct 1728. Long entries covering journey from Cambridge; stages and scenery.

1729

CLINTON, CHARLES   250

"Extracts from the Journal of Charles Clinton." PENNSYLVANIA MAGAZINE OF HISTORY AND BIOGRAPHY 26 (1902):112-114.

May-Oct 1729. Brief extracts concerning voyage from Ireland to Pennsylvania; list of deaths.

FESSENDEN, BENJAMIN, 1701-1746   251

"Extracts from Rev. Benjamin Fessenden's Manuscript." NEW ENGLAND HISTORICAL AND GENEALOGICAL REGISTER 13 (1859):30-33.

Jun-Oct 1729. Extracts containing brief entries, mostly about building his house.

SANFORD, WILLIAM, 1676-1760   252

"Remarks by Henry Herbert Edes, in Exhibiting a Copy of Titan's New Almanack for the Year of Christian Account 1729." COLONIAL SOCIETY OF MASSACHUSETTS PUBLICATIONS 7 (1900-1902):198-202.

Jan-Oct 1729. Very brief almanac entries; mostly necrology, births, etc.

1730

CORSE (or CROSS), JAMES, 1694-1783   253

BLACK RIVER GAZETTE (Ludlow, Vt.), 5 August 1870.

In A HISTORY OF DEERFIELD, MASSACHUSETTS, by George Sheldon. vol. 1, p. 518. Deerfield, Mass.: Press of E.A. Hall, 1895.

Charlton, Mary F. "The Crown Point Road." VERMONT HISTORICAL SOCIETY PROCEEDINGS 2 (1931):163-193. Diary, pp. 165-167.

Apr 1730. Brief account of trader's journey on the old Crown Point road; from Fort Dummer to Lake Champlain.

CUMING, Sir ALEXANDER, 1692-1775   254

"Account of the Cherrokee Indians, and of Sir Alexander Cuming's Journey amongst Them." HISTORICAL REGISTER 16, no. 61 (1731):1-18.

In EARLY TRAVELS IN THE TENNESSEE COUNTRY, edited by Samuel C. Williams, pp. 115-143.

Mar-Apr 1730. Scotsman's travel diary; from Charleston, South Carolina, to the Cherokees; an account of the Indians.

EGMONT, JOHN PERCEVAL, FIRST EARL OF, 255
1683-1748

MANUSCRIPTS OF THE EARL OF EGMONT: DIARY OF VISCOUNT PERCIVAL AFTERWARDS FIRST EARL OF EGMONT, vol. 1. London: H.M. Stationary Office, 1920.

1730-1733. Extracts from mainly British journal containing some items about Georgia and Oglethorpe's colony.

THE JOURNAL OF THE EARL OF EGMONT: ABSTRACT OF THE TRUSTEES PROCEEDINGS FOR ESTABLISHING THE COLONY OF GEORGIA, 1732-1738. Edited by Robert G. McPherson. Wormsloe Foundation Publications, no. 5. Athens: University of Georgia. 414 pp.

1732-1738. Account of weekly trustees' meeting kept by the first president of the Georgia Corporation; record of transportation of colonists just out of jail, founding of Savannah, treaty with Lower Creek Indians, difficulties with Oglethorpe, excessive expenditures, etc.; copies of communiques from Georgia settlers.

JOURNAL OF THE EARL OF EGMONT. Colonial Records of Georgia, vol. 5. Atlanta: Franklin-Turner, 1908. 783 pp.

1738-1744. Continuing his largely official and administrative minutes; much political and social interest.

"Diary of the Earl of Egmont." In DOCUMENTS ILLUSTRATIVE OF THE HISTORY OF THE SLAVE TRADE TO AMERICA, edited by Elizabeth Donnan, vol. 4, pp. 592-603. Carnegie Institution of Washington Publications, no. 409. Washington, D.C.: Carnegie Institution of Washington, 1930-1935. Reprint. New York: Octagon Books, 1965.

1739-1742. Extracts.

ROBBINS, PHILEMON, 1709-1781 256

In DICKERMAN GENEALOGY, by Edward D. Dickerman and George S. Dickerman, pp. 510-511. New Haven, Conn.: Tuttle, Morehouse & Taylor Press, 1922.

1730-1745. Clergyman's journal; a very few notes of religious and parish affairs and family matters.

1731

HALE, ROBERT, 1703-1767 257

"Journal of a Voyage to Nova Scotia Made in 1731 by Robert Hale of Beverly." ESSEX INSTITUTE HISTORICAL COLLECTIONS 41 (1906):217-244.

1731-1732 (with gaps). Sea journeys to Maine and Nova Scotia; mainly descriptions of scenery, character and habits of people, stopping places.

1732

CHRISTIE, THOMAS 258

McPherson, Robert G., ed. "The Voyage of the Anne--a Daily Record." GEORGIA HISTORICAL QUARTERLY 44 (1960):220-230.

Nov 1732-Jan 1733. Atlantic crossing of the ANNE with Governor Oglethorpe and settlers bound for Georgia; weather, food; sickness among passengers and crew.

GORDON, PETER, 1697-1740 259

THE JOURNAL OF PETER GORDON. Edited by E. Merton Coulter. Wormsloe Foundation Publications, no. 6.

Athens: University of Georgia Press, 1963. 78 pp.

1732-1734. Account by colony member who settled on the Savannah River; trip aboard the ANNE; first year of colony; critique of trustees' policies.

TUDOR, JOHN, 1709-1795 260

DEACON TUDOR'S DIARY. Edited by William Tudor. Boston: Press of W. Spooner, 1896. 110 pp.

Extracts covering the Boston Massacre in AMERICAN HISTORY TOLD BY CONTEMPORARIES, edited by Albert H. Bushnell, vol. 2, pp. 429-431; DIARY OF AMERICA, edited by Josef Berger, pp. 101-104.

1732-1793. Occasional entries of private and public affairs in Boston.

YEAMANS, JOHN, d. 1749 261

In A HISTORY OF EAST BOSTON, by William H. Sumner, pp. 724-729. Boston: J.E. Tilton, 1858.

Nov 1732-May 1733. Brief parliamentary notes on progress of sugar bill.

1733

ANON. 262

A NEW VOYAGE TO GEORGIA. 2d ed. London: Printed for J. Wilford, 1737. 62 pp. Reprint. GEORGIA HISTORICAL SOCIETY COLLECTIONS 2 (1842):37-66.

1733-1734. Seminarrative account of voyage to Georgia and travels in the Carolinas.

ANON. 263

"Narrative of the Journey of the Schwenckfelders to Pennsylvania, 1733." PENNSYLVANIA MAGAZINE OF HISTORY AND BIOGRAPHY 10 (1886):167-179.

Apr-Sep 1733. Travel from Rotterdam to Plymouth and to Philadelphia.

BOLTZIUS, JOHANN MARTIN, 1703-1765 264

"The Travel Diary of the Two Pastors Messrs. Boltzius and Gronau Which the Two Have Kept from Halle to Georgia and for Some Time after Their Arrival in That Land." In DETAILED REPORTS ON THE SALZBURGER EMIGRANTS WHO SETTLED IN AMERICA, edited by Samuel Urlsperger and George Fenwick Jones, translated by Hermann J. Lacher, vol. 1, pp. 25-107. Omitted parts appear in "Supplement: Excerpts from the Original Diary," translated by William Holton Brown, vol. 3, pp. 271-321.

Extracts in AMERICAN HISTORY TOLD BY CONTEMPORARIES, edited by Albert B. Hart, vol. 2, pp. 114-116; OUR FIRST VISIT IN AMERICA, pp. 55-80.

1733-1734. Travel diary of spiritual leader of Salzburg Lutherans and his assistant, Israel Christian Gronau; trip from Halle to Wernigerode for ordination; on to Rotterdam to join other Salzburgers for journey to Georgia supported by Trustees for Establishing a Colony in Georgia; religious life aboard ship and in first settlement at Ebenezer.

"Daily Register of the Two Pastors, Mr. Boltzius and Mr. Gronau." In DETAILED REPORTS ON THE SALZBURGER EMIGRANTS, vols. 2-5.

1734-1738. Continues two pastors' account of their ministry, both secular and spiritual, during period of worst hardships; resettlement at Red Bluff on the Savannah; problems of food and health, especially with Third Transport; dealings with Thomas Causton, keeper of the storehouse at Savannah. Portions originally deleted in Urlsperger's published report (any misbehaviors, disagreements between pastors, difficulties with British authorities, etc.) are restored in this edition.

In AN EXTRACT OF THE JOURNALS OF MR. COMMISSARY VON RECK, WHO CONDUCTED THE FIRST TRANSPORT OF SALTZBURGERS TO GEORGIA: AND OF THE REVEREND MR. BOLZIUS, ONE OF THEIR MINISTERS, by Philipp George Friedrich von Reck, pp. 17-37. London: Society for Promoting Christian Knowledge, 1734. Reprint. In TRACTS AND OTHER PAPERS, compiled by Peter Force, vol. 4, no. 5, pp. 17-37. Washington, D.C.: W.Q. Force, 1846.

Mar-May 1734. Travel diary; scenery, religious and moral observations.

"The Travel Diary of Pastor Boltzius from Ebenezer to Charleston and Back." In DETAILED REPORTS ON THE SALZBURGER EMIGRANTS WHO SETTLED IN AMERICA, vol. 1, pp. 108-115.

May-Jun 1734.

Jones, George F. "The Secret Diary of Pastor Johann Martin Boltzius." GEORGIA HISTORICAL QUARTERLY 53 (1969):78-110. Reprint. Savannah: Georgia Salzburger Society, 1975. 33 pp.

Feb-May 1736. Record of difficult times for Salzburg Lutherans settled in Ebenezer by Governor Oglethorpe; mainly Boltzius' lengthy negotiations with Oglethorpe to remove colony to healthier, more fertile location; complaints against colleagues Baron Philipp Georg Von Reck and Jean Vat.

Tresp, Lothar L. "August, September, 1748 in Georgia, from the Diary of John Martin Bolzius." GEORGIA HISTORICAL QUARTERLY 47 (1963):204-216, 320-332.

Aug-Sep 1748. Part of record kept for "Christian patrons and friends" in Germany by pastor of the Salzburg Lutherans settled in Georgia; extensive notes on climate, crops, commerce; comments about Creek Indians.

SHEFTALL, BENJAMIN, 1692-1765   265

Stern, Malcolm H. "The Sheftall Diaries: Vital Records of Savannah Jewry (1733-1808)." AMERICAN JEWISH HISTORICAL QUARTERLY 54 (1965):243-277.

1733-1808. A community record of births, deaths, marriages, arrivals of Jewish immigrants to Savannah; of genealogical interest.

1734

ANON.   266

In HISTORICAL AND GENEALOGICAL MISCELLANY; DATA RELATING TO THE SETTLEMENT AND SETTLERS OF NEW YORK AND NEW JERSEY, by John Edwin Stillwell, vol. 1, pp. 222-224. New York, 1903-1932.

Nov 1734. Six day voyage from Red Bank, New Jersey, to New York City; loading goods; return.

RECK, PHILIPP GEORG FRIEDRICH VON,   267
1710-1798

AN EXTRACT OF THE JOURNALS OF MR. COMMISSARY VON RECK, WHO CONDUCTED THE FIRST TRANSPORT OF SALTZBURGERS TO GEORGIA: AND OF THE REVEREND MR. BOLZIUS, ONE OF THEIR MINISTERS. London: Society for Promoting Christian Knowledge, 1734. 72 pp. Reprint. In TRACTS AND OTHER PAPERS, compiled by Peter Force, vol. 4, no. 5, pp. 1-16; Washington, D.C.: W.Q. Force, 1846.

Extract in OUR FIRST VISIT IN AMERICA, pp. 41-54.

Jan-May 1734. Voyage of the Salzburgers from Dover, England, to Charleston, South Carolina, and thence to Ebenezer, Georgia, to establish a settlement; notes on Indians and worship.

"Travel Diary of Commissioner Von Reck, When He Went from Ebenezer in Georgia to the Northern Regions of America and from There Back Again to England, Holland and Germany." In DETAILED REPORTS ON THE SALZBURGER EMIGRANTS WHO SETTLED IN AMERICA, edited by Samuel Urlsperger and George F. Jones, vol. 1, pp. 116-134.

Jones, George F. "Journal of Travel in Colonial America." SOCIETY FOR THE HISTORY OF THE GERMANS IN MARYLAND, 31st Report (1963):83-90.

May-Aug 1734. Travel journal of manager of secular affairs of Ebenezer Salzburgers; Savannah to Charleston and Philadelphia by boat, on to New England; description of cities and countryside, agriculture, commerce and hospitality in each area visited.

Jones, George F. "Von Reck's Second Report From Georgia." WILLIAM AND MARY QUARTERLY, 3d ser. 22 (1965):319-333.

Feb-Oct 1736. Account of travels around Georgia following arrival of Third Transport; relocation of Salzburger settlement from Ebenezer Creek to the Savannah River; relations with Indians; journey with Oglethorpe south from St. Simons Island to the St. Johns River; negotiations with Spanish; return to Ebenezer; description of fauna and flora.

SERGEANT, JOHN, 1710-1749   268

In HISTORICAL MEMOIRS, RELATING TO THE HOUSATUNNUK INDIANS, by Samuel Hopkins. Boston: Printed and sold by S. Kneeland, 1753. 182 pp. Reprint. MAGAZINE OF HISTORY, extra no. 17, 5 (1911):1-198.

1734-1739. Scattered extracts from missionary's journal; work among the Housatonic Indians.

1735

ANON.   269

In OLD NEW ENGLAND INNS, by Mary C. Crawford, pp. 55-61. Boston: L.C. Page, 1924.

Aug-Sep 1735. Official travel journal of Governor Belcher's journey to council with Indians at Deerfield, Massachusetts; mainly distances.

CHECKLEY, SAMUEL, 1696-1769   270

"Diary of the Rev. Samuel Checkley, 1735." COLONIAL SOCIETY OF MASSACHUSETTS PUBLICATIONS 12 (1908-1909):270-306.

Jan-Dec 1735. Record of church affairs, local Boston events, weather.

INGHAM, BENJAMIN   271

In OUR FIRST VISIT IN AMERICA, pp. 159-184.

Oct 1735-Apr 1736. Missionary diary of member of John Wesley's group at Oxford; Atlantic crossing and religious attitudes of those on board ship; work with Wesley on St. Simons Island, Georgia; especially interesting for material on Wesley and Governor Oglethorpe.

MORRIS, ROBERT HUNTER, 1713-1764   **272**

McAnear, Beverly, ed. "An American in London." PENNSYLVANIA MAGAZINE OF HISTORY AND BIOGRAPHY 64 (1940):164-217, 356-406.

> Apr 1735-Jan 1736. Views of London business and social life by young American on business trip with father; domestic affairs, travel, reading; lively diary with lengthy entries.

WESLEY, JOHN, 1703-1791   **273**

In THE JOURNAL OF THE REV. JOHN WESLEY, edited by Nehemiah Curnock, vol. 1. London: R. Culley, 1909-1916. Reprint. New York: Dutton, 1922-1930; London: Epworth, 1938. Wesley's journals will also appear in the new definitive WORKS undertaken by Oxford University Press.

Abridged editions include THE HEART OF JOHN WESLEY'S JOURNAL, edited by Percy L. Parker. New Canaan, Conn.: Keats, 1979. 512 pp.; THE JOURNAL OF JOHN WESLEY, edited by Percy L. Parker. Chicago: Moody Press, 1974, 419 pp.

Extracts in AMERICAN HISTORY AS TOLD BY CONTEMPORARIES, edited by Albert B. Hart, pp. 283-287; OUR FIRST VISIT IN AMERICA, pp. 185-242.

> 1735-1738. Wesley's disappointing missionary venture in Georgia; voyage to Georgia aboard the SIMONDS and return aboard the SAMUEL; preaching and teaching among passengers; his rigorous daily schedule; pastoral work in Savannah and Frederica when appeals to go and teach the Indians were denied; interactions with Oglethorpe; troubles with contentious parishioners leading to court proceedings and his departure from Georgia; an interesting portion of a monumental journal.

1736

LORING, NICHOLAS, 1711-1763   **274**

Loring, Amasa. "North Yarmouth Necrology." OLD TIMES 8 (1884):1105-1109.

> 1736-1762. Extracts from clergyman's journal; very short notes of journeys and sermons; mainly necrology.

SECCOM, THOMAS, 1711-1773   **275**

"Extracts from the Diary of Thomas Seccom of Medford." NEW ENGLAND HISTORICAL AND GENEALOGICAL REGISTER 12 (1858):267-268.

> 1736-1743. Brief notes of local news, sermons, etc., in Medford, Massachusetts.

STEPHENS, WILLIAM, 1671-1753   **276**

"Journal of William Stephens on His Mission to South Carolina in 1736 for Colonel Samuel Horsey." In THE JOURNAL OF WILLIAM STEPHENS, edited by E. Merton Coulter, vol. 1, app. A, pp. 235-260. Wormsloe Foundation Publications, no. 2. Athens: University of Georgia, 1958-1959.

> Apr-Aug 1736. Meetings with Oglethorpe; explorations and surveys in South Carolina and Georgia.

A JOURNAL OF THE PROCEEDINGS IN GEORGIA, BEGINNING OCTOBER 20, 1737. London: Printed for W. Meadows, 1742. 2 vols. Reprint. COLONIAL RECORDS OF THE STATE OF GEORGIA, vol. 4. Atlanta: Franklin Printing and Publishing Co., 1906. 698 pp. JOURNAL OF COLONEL WILLIAM STEPHENS . . . CONTAINING ALL OF HIS JOURNAL NOT EMBRACED IN VOLUME IV OF THIS COMPILATION. Colonial Records of the State of Georgia, suppl. to vol. 4. Atlanta: Franklin-Turner, 1908. 285 pp.

JOURNAL RECEIVED FEBRUARY 4, 1741 BY THE TRUSTEES . . . FROM WILLIAM STEPHENS, ESQ. . . . COMMENCING SEPTEMBER 22, 1741, AND ENDING OCTOBER 28 FOLLOWING. London: Printed for W. Meadows, 1742. 44 pp.

> 1737-1741. Official journal kept by secretary to the trustees; lengthy, detailed investigation of complaints arising from colonists' discontents with the plan of government; huge daily survey with some personal notes.

THE JOURNAL OF WILLIAM STEPHENS. Edited by E. Merton Coulter, 2 vols. Wormsloe Foundation Publications, nos. 2 and 3.

> 1741-1745. Continuing the secretary's account of events and circumstances in the colony; flavor of daily life through reporting of small, even mundane, details.

WESLEY, CHARLES, 1707-1788   **277**

THE JOURNAL OF THE REV. CHARLES WESLEY. Edited by Thomas Jackson. London: J. Mason, 1849. 2 vols. Reprint. Kansas City, Mo.: Beacon Hill Press, 1980; Grand Rapids, Mich.: Baker Book House, 1980. American journal, vol. 1.

THE JOURNAL OF THE REV. CHARLES WESLEY: THE EARLY JOURNAL, 1736-1739. New ed. Taylors, S.C.: Methodist Reprint Society, 1977. 324 pp.

> 1736-1739. Early pastoral labors at Frederica, St. Simons Island, Georgia, and in England; problems with contentious colonists who caused serious misunderstandings between Wesley and Governor Oglethorpe; details of Oglethorpe's administration; unrest between Spanish and English; return to England, with good description of Atlantic crossing and life on board ship; religious work in England with notes on John Wesley and George Whitefield.

1737

BALLANTINE, JOHN, 1716-1776   **278**

In WESTFIELD AND ITS HISTORIC INFLUENCES, 1669-1919, by John Hoyt Lockwood, pp. 380-437. Westfield, Mass.: Printed and sold by the author, 1922.

> 1737-1774. Extracts from clergyman's diary; record of domestic and family matters, work, local news, teaching; interesting, varied account.

CAUSTON, THOMAS   **279**

In OUR FIRST VISIT IN AMERICA, pp. 243-277.

> May-Jul 1737. Record of storekeeper and bailiff of Savannah, sometimes in authority when Governor Oglethorpe was away from Georgia; legal matters, administration, trade; a glimpse of John Wesley's disappointed love affair and diarist's quarrel with Wesley over the matter.

COOKE, MIDDLECOTT   **280**

"Middlecott Cooke: Journal." In THE SALTONSTALL PAPERS, 1607-1815, selected and edited by Robert Earle Moody, vol. 1, pp. 392-397. Collections of the Massachusetts Historical Society, vol. 80. Boston: Massachusetts Historical Society, 1972.

> May-Jun 1737. Sparse account of voyage on a sloop from Boston to St. Georges (now Warren, Maine) and back; mainly weather reports with few details of business.

HOLMES, JONATHAN, 1704-1778　　　281

In HISTORICAL AND GENEALOGICAL MISCELLANY; DATA RELATING TO THE SETTLEMENT AND SETTLERS OF NEW YORK AND NEW JERSEY, by John Edwin Stillwell, vol. 3, pp. 362-375. New York: 1903-1932.

　　1737-1738. A most interesting record of local affairs in Monmouth County, New Jersey; public news and local events; law, trade, farming, amusements, church; personal affairs, reading, illness.

PRINCE, THOMAS, 1687-1758　　　282

"Diary of the Rev. Thomas Prince, 1737." COLONIAL SOCIETY OF MASSACHUSETTS PUBLICATIONS 19 (1916-1917):331-364.

　　Jan-Dec 1737. Journal of pastor of Old South Church, Boston; mainly preaching and church affairs; some local and Harvard notes.

TOBLER, JOHN　　　283

Cordle, Charles G., ed. "The John Tobler Manuscripts: An Account of German-Swiss Emigrants in South Carolina, 1737." JOURNAL OF SOUTHERN HISTORY 5 (1939): 83-97.

　　Feb-Mar 1737. Diary fragment providing record of colony and journey to Fort Moore; factual details. Translated from the German.

WADSWORTH, DANIEL, 1704-1747　　　284

DIARY OF REV. DANIEL WADSWORTH, SEVENTH PASTOR OF THE FIRST CHURCH OF CHRIST IN HARTFORD. With notes by George Leon Walker. Hartford, Conn.: Press of the Case, Lockwood & Brainard Co., 1894. 149 pp.

　　1737-1747. Short notes of work, study, weather, local affairs.

WESTON, MARY, 1712-1766　　　285

In ELIOT PAPERS, compiled by Eliot Howard, pp. 93-110. London: E. Hicks, Jr., 1895.

　　1737-1752. Extracts from Quaker travel journal; notes of meetings and preaching in Rhode Island, Boston, Nantucket, Connecticut, and southern colonies in 1750-1751.

1738

ADAMS, ELIPHALET, 1677-1753　　　286

"Memoir of the Rev. William Adams of Dedham, Mass. and of the Rev. Eliphalet Adams of New London, Conn." MASSACHUSETTS HISTORICAL SOCIETY COLLECTIONS, 4th ser. 1 (1852):1-51. Diary, pp. 27, 35-36.

　　Apr-Oct 1738. Very brief memoranda of a trip among the Indians; bits of earlier diary (Aug 1699) added.

GREEN, JONATHAN, 1719-1795　　　287

In THE HISTORY OF MELROSE, COUNTY OF MIDDLESEX, MASSACHUSETTS, by Elbridge H. Goss, p. 98. Melrose: The City, 1902.

　　1738-1744. Brief extracts concerning public and local affairs.

SMITH, WILLIAM, 1702-1783　　　288

"Diaries of Rev. William Smith and Dr. Cotton Tufts, 1738-1784." MASSACHUSETTS HISTORICAL SOCIETY PROCEEDINGS 42 (1908-1909):444-478. Diary, pp. 445-470.

1738-1768 (with many gaps). Extracts of almanac notes; church work, religious introspection, some verses.

VITRY, PIERRE, 1700-1749　　　289

Delanglez, Jean, ed. "The Journal of Pierre Vitry, S.J." MID-AMERICA 28 (1946):23-30. Reprint. LOUISIANA STUDIES 3 (1964):247-315.

　　1738-1740. Chaplain's chronicle of second French campaign against the Chickasaw; journey up the Mississippi River; building of forts at St. Francis River and site of present-day Memphis; relations with and activities of various Indian allies; Indian tortures; report of attack on Chickasaw forts and subsequent negotiations summarized from journal of Chaussegros de Lery.

WHITEFIELD, GEORGE, 1714-1770　　　290

Frequently printed, but most readily available in WORKS: CONTAINING ALL HIS SERMONS AND TRACTS WITH A SELECT COLLECTION OF LETTERS, ETC., compiled by J. Gilles. London: Printed for E. and C. Dilly, 1771-1772. 6 vols.; JOURNALS. London: Banner of Truth Trust, 1960. 594 pp. JOURNALS: 1737-1741, TO WHICH IS PREFIXED HIS SHORT ACCOUNT (1746) AND FURTHER ACCOUNT (1747). Gainesville, Fla.: Scholars' Facsimiles, 1969. 515 pp.

JOURNAL OF A VOYAGE FROM LONDON TO SAVANNAH IN GEORGIA. London: Printed for Hunt and Clarke, 1826; London: Whittaker, Treacher, and Arnot, 1829. 274 pp.

In OUR FIRST VISIT IN AMERICA, pp. 281-314.

　　1738-1770. Journals of English Methodist evangelist; travels throughout the colonies during various missionary tours; meetings, sermons, etc.; exuberant and ejaculatory style. American sections deal with tour in Georgia, 1738, and more extended tours through the colonies in 1738-1741, 1744-1748, 1751-1752, 1754-1755, 1763-1764, 1769-1770.

Hancock, Harold B., ed. "Descriptions and Travel Accounts of Delaware, 1700-1740." DELAWARE HISTORY 10 (1962):115-151. Journal, pp. 149-151.

　　Oct-Dec 1739. Extracts describing travel in Delaware; preaching at Lewis Town, Wilmington, New Castle and Christian-Bridge.

Eells, Earnest Edward, ed. "An Unpublished Journal of George Whitefield." CHURCH HISTORY 7 (1938):297-345.

　　Oct 1744-Spring 1745. Tour in New England.

WILLIAMS, STEPHEN, 1693-1782　　　291

Harding, John W. "Doctor Stephen Williams." CONNECTICUT VALLEY HISTORICAL SOCIETY PAPERS AND PROCEEDINGS (1876-1881):36-61.

　　1738-1742. Clergyman's journal; quotations in biography; personal activities.

In LOUISBOURG JOURNALS, edited by Louis E. de Forest, pp. 121-169.

　　Jul 1745-Jan 1746. Chaplain at the siege of Louisbourg; military, religious, personal items; notes on suffering of men.

In PROCEEDINGS OF THE CENTENNIAL CELEBRATION OF THE INCORPORATION OF THE TOWN OF LONGMEADOW, pp. 221-229. Longmeadow, Mass.: Secretary of the Centennial Committee under Authority of the Town, 1884.

　　1754-1761. Extracts covering clerical work and local affairs; varied incidents, news, gossip, moral reflections.

In AMERICAN HISTORY TOLD BY CONTEMPORARIES, edited by Albert B. Hart, vol. 2, pp. 455-457.

1776. Pertaining to the Revolution.

1739

ANON.   292

In TRAVELS IN THE AMERICAN COLONIES, edited by Newton D. Mereness, pp. 218-236.

1739-1742. Travel journal of a ranger with General Oglethorpe; journey to Indian assembly at Coweta on Chattahoochee River; operations against St. Augustine and in defense of Georgia coast against Spaniards; scattered and impersonal entries at long intervals; some good descriptions of Indian ceremonies.

LANE, SAMUEL, 1718-1806   293

A JOURNAL FOR THE YEARS 1739-1803. Edited by Charles Lane Hanson. Concord, N.H.: New Hampshire Historical Society, 1937. 115 pp.

1739-1803. Farmer/tanner's notes of family affairs, work, reading, war; yearly notes on events of public interest; brief entries focusing on weather and farming in Stratham, New Hampshire; some interesting vocabulary.

PINCKNEY, ELIZA LUCAS, 1723-1793   294

JOURNAL AND LETTERS OF ELIZA LUCAS. Edited by Harriett P. Holbrook. Wormsloe Quartos, no. 3. Spartanburg, S.C.: Reprint Co., 1967.

Extracts in AMERICAN HISTORY TOLD BY CONTEMPORARIES, edited by Albert B. Hart, vol. 2, pp. 99-100, 238-240.

1739-1762. Diary of daughter of Lieutenant Colonel Lucas, governor of Antigua, who came with her mother to South Carolina for mother's health and almost alone managed her father's three plantations; planting of crops; observation of the productivity of various soils; introduction of indigo as a crop.

1740

BRAINERD, DAVID, 1718-1747   295

MIRABILIA DEI INTER INDICOS. Philadelphia: Printed and sold by William Bradford in Second Street, 1746. 253 pp. Often reprinted and abridged, the most accessible editions:

AN ABRIDGMENT OF MR. DAVID BRAINERD'S JOURNAL AMONG THE INDIANS. London: Printed for J. Oswald, 1748. 110 pp.

In AN ACCOUNT OF THE LIFE OF THE LATE REVEREND MR. DAVID BRAINERD, by Jonathan Edwards, pp. 321-472. Boston: Printed for and sold by D. Henchman, 1749.

DAVID BRAINERD, THE MAN OF PRAYER. Abridged and edited by Oswald J. Smith. Grand Rapids, Mich.: Zondervan, 1941. 86 pp.

THE LIFE AND DIARY OF DAVID BRAINERD, edited by Jonathan Edwards, newly edited by Philip Eugene Howard. Chicago: Moody Press, 1949. 385 pp.

Discussed in AMERICAN DIARY LITERATURE, by Steven E. Kagle, pp. 38-46.

1740-1747. Important missionary journal; youthful soul-searching and despondency over sin giving way to more mature inner confidence; work among Indians of western Massachusetts, New York, New Jersey and Pennsylvania; vignettes of converts; Indian customs; frontier life and conditions.

BRINGHURST, JOHN, 1691-1750   296

In TORTOLA, A QUAKER EXPERIMENT OF LONG AGO IN THE TROPICS, by Charles F. Jenkins, pp. 87-88. London: Friends' Bookshop, 1923.

1740-1744. Travel diary extracts containing brief and scattered notes of visit to Tortola and Barbados.

DUDLEY, PAUL, 1675-1751   297

"Diary of Paul Dudley, 1740." NEW ENGLAND HISTORICAL AND GENEALOGICAL REGISTER 35 (1881):28-31.

Jan-Dec 1740. Brief notes of weather and public affairs.

GLADDING, JOHN, 1717-1785   298

In THE GLADDING BOOK, by Henry C. Gladding, pp. 45-46. Providence, R.I., 1901.

1740-1779. A few brief extracts, mostly news of the Revolution.

HAZEN, RICHARD, 1696-1754   299

"The Boundary Line of New Hampshire and Massachusetts." NEW ENGLAND HISTORICAL AND GENEALOGICAL REGISTER 33 (1879):323-333.

Mar-Apr 1740. Surveying Massachusetts boundary at Pentucket; notes of scenery, some personal matters, and a duel.

HOPKINS, SAMUEL, 1721-1803   300

In SKETCHES OF THE LIFE OF THE LATE REV. SAMUEL HOPKINS, PASTOR OF THE FIRST CONGREGATIONAL CHURCH IN NEWPORT, pp. 43-72 passim. Hartford, Conn.: Printed by Hudson and Goodwin, 1805.

1740-1800. Religious work and meditations; some personal items; some cipher.

SALLEY, JOHN PETER, d. 1755   301

In CHRISTOPHER GIST'S JOURNALS, edited by William M. Darlington, pp. 253-260. Pittsburgh: J.R. Weldin, 1893.

Harrison, Fairfax. "The Virginians on the Ohio and the Mississippi in 1742." LOUISIANA HISTORICAL QUARTERLY 5 (1922):316-332. Journal, pp. 323-332.

1740-1744. Scattered entries and dates comprising journal and recollections; exploration on the Ohio and Mississippi; with John Howard; capture by French, imprisonment in New Orleans, escape.

SEWARD, WILLIAM   302

JOURNAL OF A VOYAGE FROM SAVANNAH TO PHILADELPHIA. London: J. Oswald, 1740. 87 pp.

Apr-Jun 1740. Voyage from Savannah to Philadelphia and then to England, accompanying George Whitefield; preaching and religious reflections.

STORER, JOHN, 1694-1768   303

Thayer, Henry O. "Fort Richmond, Maine." MAINE HISTORICAL SOCIETY COLLECTIONS, 2d ser. 5 (1894): 129-160. Journal, pp. 142-143.

Oct 1740-Jan 1741. Offical journal while acting as

government agent in building of Fort Richmond, Maine.

PORTSMOUTH JOURNAL, 6 May 1854. Reprint. In A HISTORY OF THE CUTTER FAMILY OF NEW ENGLAND, revised and enlarged by William R. Cutter, p. 310. Boston: Printed by D. Clapp & Son, 1871.

Apr 1745. Military journal giving brief details of siege of Louisburg.

1741

BONNEFOY, ANTOINE 304

In TRAVELS IN THE AMERICAN COLONIES, edited by Newton D. Mereness, pp. 241–255.

In EARLY TRAVELS IN THE TENNESSEE COUNTRY, edited by Samuel C. Williams, pp. 149–162.

Aug 1741–May 1742. Captive's seminarrative diary; capture by Cherokees while on trip from New Orleans; journey to French post.

BRYENT, WALTER, 1710–1807 305

"Journal of the Survey of the Boundary between Maine and New Hampshire, 1741." HISTORICAL MAGAZINE, 2d ser. 9 (1871):17–19.

NEW HAMPSHIRE PROVINCIAL AND STATE PAPERS 6 (1872):349–351.

Mar–Apr 1741. Surveying journal.

"Walter Bryent's Winnepesaukee Journal, 1747." NEW ENGLAND HISTORICAL AND GENEALOGICAL REGISTER 32 (1878):297–302.

Jan–Feb 1747. Military journal covering march from New Hampshire to Canada; tapping rum cask.

BURR, ESTHER EDWARDS, 1732–1758 306

ESTHER BURR'S JOURNAL. 3d ed. Edited by Jeremiah E. Rankin. Washington, D.C.: Woodward & Lothrop, 1903. 100 pp.

Extensive extracts, and criticism of earlier edition, in "The Journal of Esther Burr," by Josephine Fisher. NEW ENGLAND QUARTERLY 3 (1930):297–315.

1741 1757. Diary of Jonathan Edwards' daughter; notes on religion and religious figures (her father, Hopkins, Brainerd, etc.); household matters; later, marriage and children, one of whom was Aaron Burr.

Extracts in SMALL VOICES, by Josef and Dorothy Berger, pp. 22–27.

1741–1743. Childhood diary.

CHIRIKOV, ALEXEI ILICH, d. 1748 307

"Journal Kept on the Ship ST. PAUL in Command of Captain Alexei Chirikov." In BERING'S VOYAGES: AN ACCOUNT OF THE EFFORTS OF THE RUSSIANS TO DETERMINE THE RELATION OF ASIA AND AMERICA, by Frank A. Golder, vol. 1, pp. 283–311. American Geographical Society Research Series, no. 2. New York: American Geographical Society, 1922–1925.

Jun–Oct 1741. Expedition to explore coast of America and search for Northwest Passage; loss of fifteen men attempting to land in small boats on coast of Alaska; unsuccessful efforts to communicate and trade with Indians; return with many sick or dead from scurvy.

SMITH, JOHN, 1722–1771 308

In HANNAH LOGAN'S COURTSHIP, edited by Albert C. Myers, pp. 65–324, 326–345. Philadelphia: Ferris & Leach, 1904. Account of missing portions and a single extract in "The Diary of John Smith," by Albert C. Myers. FRIENDS' HISTORICAL SOCIETY OF PHILADELPHIA BULLETIN 12 (1923):26.

1741–1752. Charming diary of Quaker social and business life; voyage to Barbados; journey to New York; work as merchant; courtship of Hannah Logan; last years in Philadelphia.

STELLER, GEORG WILHELM, 1709–1746 309

Stejneger, Leonhard, trans. "Journal of the Sea Voyage from Kamchatka to America and Return on the Second Expedition." In BERING'S VOYAGES: AN ACCOUNT OF THE EFFORTS OF THE RUSSIANS TO DETERMINE THE RELATION OF ASIA AND AMERICA, by Frank A. Golder, vol. 2, pp. 9–187. American Geographical Society Research Series, no. 2. New York: American Geographical Society, 1925.

"Journal of Beering's Voyage of Discovery From Kamtchatka to the Coast of America." In ACCOUNT OF THE RUSSIAN DISCOVERIES BETWEEN ASIA AND AMERICA, 4th ed., by William Coxe, pp. 30–93. London: Cadell and Davies, 1803.

1741–1742. Physician and naturalist accompanying Vitus Bering on the ST. PETER; scientific observations; personal relations with officers; disabling of ship and bitter winter on Bering Island, where Bering and many others died; building of small boat with materials salvaged from wrecked ship and voyage back to Kamchatka. Translated from the German.

VEZIAN, PETER 310

In PRIVATEERING AND PIRACY IN THE COLONIAL PERIOD, by John F. Jameson, pp. 381–429. New York: Macmillan, 1923.

Extracts in "Journal of a Privateersman." ATLANTIC MONTHLY 8 (1861):353–359, 417–424.

Jun–Oct 1741. Very interesting journal of quartermaster of sloop REVENGE; cruising against pirates and Spanish privateers off the American coast.

WHEELOCK, ELEAZAR, 1711–1779 311

"Diary of Rev. Eleazar Wheelock." HISTORICAL MAGAZINE, 2d ser. 5 (1869):237–240.

Oct–Nov 1741. Long entries describing journey to Boston.

1742

ARREDONDO, ANTONIO DE 312

"Journal Kept by Don Antonio de Arrendondo, Chief Engineer of the Present Expedition." GEORGIA HISTORICAL SOCIETY COLLECTIONS 7 (1913):pt. 3, 52–64.

Jun 1742. Details of Spanish expedition against Georgia. Translated from the Spanish.

BETHLEHEM, PENNSYLVANIA, 313
MORAVIAN CONGREGATION

THE BETHLEHEM DIARY. Translated and edited by Kenneth G. Hamilton. Bethlehem, Pa.: Archives of the Moravian Church, 1971–(in progress).

1742-1744. Moravian church records chronicling church business and activities of congregation members; views of local events, frontier life, Indian relations, etc.

THE MORAVIAN, 6 and 13 July 1910. Reprint. "Extracts from the Diary of the Bethlehem Congregation." PENN GERMANIA, n.s. 2 (1913):187-193.

1756. Religious life and work. Translated.

Jordan, John W. "Bethlehem during the Revolution." PENNSYLVANIA MAGAZINE OF HISTORY AND BIOGRAPHY 12 (1888):385-406; 13 (1889):71-89.

1775-1782. Extracts relating to the Revolution.

BOWEN, NATHAN, 1697-1776   314

"Extracts from Interleaved Almanacs of Nathan Bowen, Marblehead." ESSEX INSTITUTE HISTORICAL COLLEC-TIONS 91 (1955):163-190, 266-283, 353-383.

1742-1790. Diary kept by shopkeeper/scrivener and continued, after his death, by his sons, Edward and Ashley, and his grandson, Nathan; reflection of current events (Great Awakening, Stamp Act, Revolution, Constitution, etc.); also births, marriages, deaths, ship movements. Authorship of some parts difficult to determine.

CARY, MARGARET, 1719-1762   315

In CARY LETTERS, edited by Caroline G. Curtis, pp. 59-64. Cambridge, Mass.: Printed at the Riverside Press, 1891.

Extracts in NOTES ON THE TUCKERMAN FAMILY OF MASSACHUSETTS, by Bayard Tuckerman, pp. 122-123. Boston: Privately printed, 1914.

1742-1759. Occasional entries about family, personal and religious matters.

CASINAS, MARQUESS OF   316

"Details of What Occurred in the Present Expedition, Entrusted to the Care of Brigadier Don Manuel de Montiano, from the 15th Day of June, On Which the Convoy Arrived from Havana at St. Augustine." GEORGIA HISTORICAL SOCIETY COLLECTIONS 7 (1913): pt. 3, 65-87.

Jul-Aug 1742. Account of failure of Spanish expedition against Georgia. Translated from the Spanish.

CLEAVELAND, JOHN, 1722-1799   317

Beales, Ross W., Jr., ed. "The Diary of John Cleaveland." ESSEX INSTITUTE HISTORICAL COLLECTIONS 107 (1971):143-172.

Jan-May 1742. Yale freshman's diary; vivid daily account of turmoil created, in himself and in New Haven, by the Great Awakening.

Cleaveland, Nehemiah, ed. "The Journal of the Rev. John Cleaveland." ESSEX INSTITUTE HISTORICAL COL-LECTIONS 12 (1874):85-103, 179-196; 13 (1875):53-63.

Jun-Aug 1759. Chaplain's account of the siege of Louisburg; clerical and military details.

CURTIS, PHILIP, 1717-1797   318

THE CHURCH RECORDS OF REV. PHILIP CURTIS OF SHARON. By Sharon, Massachusetts, First Congrega-tional Church, edited by John G. Phillips. Sharon Historical Society Publications, no. 5. Boston: Arakel-yan Press, 1908. 64 pp.

1742-1797. Private church records; births, mar-riages, deaths.

GOODHUE, JOSEPH, b. 1720   319

"Vital Records from the Diary of Joseph Goodhue of Newbury." ESSEX INSTITUTE HISTORICAL COLLECTIONS 67 (1931):401-407.

1742-1763. Extracts of vital records; some miscel-laneous notes.

HOLYOKE, EDWARD AUGUSTUS, 1728-1829   320

In THE HOLYOKE DIARIES, edited by George F. Dow, pp. 31-43.

1742-1744, 1746-1747. Almanac notes, partly in shorthand; brief, cryptic entries; college life at Harvard, preaching, etc.

MUHLENBERG, HENRY MELCHIOR, 1711-1787   321

THE JOURNALS OF HENRY MELCHIOR MUHLENBERG. Translated by Theodore G. Tappert and John W. Do-berstein. Philadelphia: Evangelical Lutheran Minist-erium of Pennsylvania and Adjacent States, 1942-1958. 3 vols.

NOTEBOOK OF A COLONIAL CLERGYMAN, CONDENSED FROM THE JOURNALS OF HENRY MELCHIOR MUHLENBERG. Translated and edited by Theodore G. Tappert and John W. Doberstein. Philadelphia: Muhlenberg Press, 1959. 250 pp.

Extracts in notes in THE LIFE OF MAJOR-GENERAL PETER MUHLENBERG, OF THE REVOLUTIONARY ARMY. Philadelphia: Carey and Hart, 1849.

1742-1787. Valuable record of colonial Pennsylvania and surrounding areas kept by diligent pastor sent from Germany to serve Lutheran congregations and considered founder of American Lutheranism; preaching and pastoral work, deathbed conver-sions, church business, rigors of ceaseless travel, controversies with Quakers, Moravians and others; views of the American Revolution. Although kept partly as means of reporting to his ecclesiastical superior, often personal and candid.

Muhlenberg, Heister H., trans. "Extracts from the Rev. Dr. Muhlenberg's Journals of 1776 and 1777." PENN-SYLVANIA HISTORICAL SOCIETY COLLECTIONS 1 (1853): 147-186.

1776-1777. Relating to military events.

PECKOVER, EDMUND, 1695-1767   322

"Abstract of the Journal of Edmund Peckover's Travels in North America and Barbados." FRIENDS' HISTORICAL SOCIETY JOURNAL 1 (1904):95-109.

Sep 1742-Jan 1743. English Quaker's journeys in New England, southern states, Barbados.

SOULE, CORNELIUS, 1703-1755   323

Banks, Charles E. "The Soule Family." OLD TIMES 6 (1882):861-871. Diary, pp. 862-863.

Jul 1742. Journey from Boston to eastern frontier; a few brief personal entries.

1743

BANGS, BENJAMIN, 1721-1769   324

In HISTORY AND GENEALOGY OF THE BANGS FAMILY IN AMERICA, by Dean Dudley, pp. 4-8. Montrose, Mass.: The author, 1896.

1743-1744. Brief, varied notes of daily life in Harwich, Massachusetts; fishing, local events, visits, ship movements, whaling, journeys to Boston, etc.

DOOLITTLE, BENJAMIN, 1695-1749   325

In A SHORT NARRATIVE OF MISCHIEF DONE BY THE FRENCH AND INDIAN ENEMY, pp. 1-19. Boston: Printed and sold by S. Kneeland, 1750. Reprint. In A HISTORY OF THE TOWN OF NORTHFIELD, MASSACHSUETTS, by Josiah H. Temple and George Sheldon, pp. 370-382; MAGAZINE OF HISTORY, extra no. 7, 2 (1909):199-225.

  1743-1748. Public diary giving accounts of leading events in French and Indian wars; interesting Indian episodes.

EMERSON, JOHN, 1707-1774   326

In THE IPSWICH EMERSONS, by Benjamin K. Emerson, assisted by George Augustus Gordon, pp. 424-428. Boston: D. Clapp & Son, 1900.

  Jan-Dec 1743, Jan-Dec 1754. Extracts from clergyman's journal; brief almanac entries; mostly church work, baptisms, etc.; a few notes of personal affairs.

JOHNSTON, ANDREW, 1694-1762   327

"Journals of Andrew Johnston." SOMERSET COUNTY HISTORICAL QUARTERLY 1 (1912):190-196, 262-265; 2 (1913):35-38, 120-125, 186-188, 277-280; 3 (1914):19-26, 106-109, 193-197, 261-267; 4 (1915):35-41, 113-118, 198-204.

  1743-1762. Merchant's journeys to and surveying at Peapack, New Jersey; other details concerning the Peapack patent, leases, rents, etc.; local topographical interest.

KIMBER, EDWARD, 1719-1769   328

A RELATION OR JOURNAL OF A LATE EXPEDITION TO THE GATES OF ST. AUGUSTINE. London: Printed for T. Astley, 1744. 36 pp. Reprint. With notes by Sidney A. Kimber. Boston: C.E. Goodspeed & Co., 1935; with an introduction and index by John J. Tepaske. Gainesville: University Presses of Florida, 1976.

  Feb-Mar 1743. English novelist with Oglethorpe's expedition; literary description of the campaign; defense of Oglethorpe's conduct.

MACSPARRAN, JAMES, d. 1757   329

In A LETTER BOOK AND ABSTRACT OF OUT SERVICES, edited by Daniel Goodwin, pp. 1-67. Boston: D.B. Updike, 1899.

  1743-1751. Clergyman's journal of religious and missionary services outside his parish; personal affairs at Narragansett, Rhode Island; some social notes.

MILLS, WILLIAM, b. 1718   330

In HISTORY OF NEEDHAM, MASSACHUSETTS, 1711-1911, by George Kuhn Clarke, pp. 49-51. Cambridge, Mass.: Privately printed at the University Press, 1912.

  1743-1778. Diary extracts arranged by subject; accounts, weather, family and local affairs.

POTIER, PIERRE, 1708-1781   331

Ott, E.R., trans. and ed. "Selections from the Diary and Gazette of Father Pierre Potier, S.J." MID-AMER-

ICA 18 (1936):199-202.

  1743-1747. Scattered, very brief extracts outline activities at Assumption Mission located on Bois Blanc Island below Detroit.

PRESTON, JOHN, 1717-1771   332

"Diary of John Preston of Danvers." NEW ENGLAND HISTORICAL AND GENEALOGICAL REGISTER 56 (1902): 80-83.

"Extracts from the Diary of Lieut. John Preston, of Salem Village." ESSEX INSTITUTE HISTORICAL COLLECTIONS 11 (1871):256-262.

  1743-1760. Entries of important public events, family affairs, weather, etc.

REED, SOLOMON, 1719-1785   333

In THE HISTORY OF THE CHURCH OF NORTH MIDDLEBOROUGH, MASSACHUSETTS, by Samuel H. Emery, pp. 31-32. Middleborough, Mass.: Harlow & Thatcher, Printers, 1876.

  1743-1745. Brief extracts from clergyman's journal; notes on religious work and George Whitefield's preaching.

SCHNELL, LEONARD   334

Hinke, William J. and Charles E. Kemper, eds. "Moravian Diaries of Travels through Virginia." VIRGINIA MAGAZINE OF HISTORY AND BIOGRAPHY 11 (1903-1904): 370-393; 12 (1904-1905):55-82; 11(1903-1904):113-131.

  Nov 1743-Apr 1744. Moravian presbyter's journey with Robert Hussey to Georgia; daily life and worship; social and travel notes; one of the best of the Moravian journals. Translated from the German.

  May-Jul 1747. Journey with V. Handrup to Maryland and Virginia.

  Oct-Dec 1749. With John Brandmueller from Bethlehem, Pennsylvania, to Virginia; notes on worship and brethren; some interesting German-English spellings.

WHITING, JOHN, 1716-1784   335

"Diary of John Whiting of Dedham, Mass." NEW ENGLAND HISTORICAL AND GENEALOGICAL MAGAZINE 63 (1909):185-192, 261-265.

  1743-1784. A few brief entries each year concerning weather, local affairs and public events; fires, epidemics, war news, etc.

1744

ANON.   336

In THE CLAPP MEMORIAL, by Ebenezer Clapp, pp. 377-378. Boston: D. Clapp & Son, 1876.

  1744-1756. Extracts containing brief notes on remarkable providences, prodigies and coincidences.

BLACK, WILLIAM   337

"Journal of William Black." PENNSYLVANIA MAGAZINE OF HISTORY AND BIOGRAPHY 1 (1877):117-132, 233-249, 404-419; 2 (1878):40-49, 466.

  May-Jun 1744. Journey while secretary to commissioners in Maryland and Pennsylvania; personal and social side of the trip; feasts, flirtations, ceremonies; an entertaining account in a flowery, epic style.

HAMILTON, ALEXANDER, 1712-1756   338

HAMILTON'S ITINERARIUM. Edited by Albert B. Hart. Saint Louis, Mo.: Printed for only private distribution by W.K. Bixby, 1907. 263 pp.

GENTLEMAN'S PROGRESS: THE ITINERARIUM OF DR. ALEXANDER HAMILTON. Edited by Carl Bridenbaugh. Chapel Hill, N.C.: Published for the Institute of Early American History and Culture at Williamsburg, Va., by the University of North Carolina Press, 1948. 267 pp.

> May-Sep 1744. Skeptical Scottish physician's health trip from Annapolis to New Hampshire and back; extensive and vigorous descriptions and ironical comments on social and religious life, with many excellent scenes involving medicos and sectarians; some literary matters and conversation pieces.

MACK, JOHN MARTIN, 1713?-1784?   339

Johnson, Frederick, C. "Diary of Br. John Martin Mack's and Christian Froelich's Journey to Wayomick and Hallobanck." WYOMING HISTORICAL AND GEOLOGICAL SOCIETY PROCEEDINGS AND COLLECTIONS 8 (1902-1903):149-155.

> Apr 1744. Moravian travel journal; trip with Christian Froelich from Bethlehem to Wyoming, Pennsylvania.

"Indian Famine in 1748." HISTORICAL JOURNAL 1 (1887):287-289. Appears in PENNSYLVANIA MAGAZINE OF HISTORY AND BIOGRAPHY 16 (1892):430-432, attributed to David Zeisberger.

> Jul 1748. Description of Indian famine.

In MORAVIAN JOURNALS RELATING TO CENTRAL NEW YORK, by William M. Beauchamp, pp. 112-156.

Extracts in NOTES AND QUERIES, edited by William H. Egle, 3d ser., vol. 1, pp. 345-355.

Extracts in "Rev. John Martin Mack's Narrative of a Visit to Onondaga in 1752," edited by John W. Jordan. PENNSYLVANIA MAGAZINE OF HISTORY AND BIOGRAPHY 29 (1905):343-358.

> Jul-Nov 1752. Journey to Onondaga with Zeisberger and Rundt.

Jordan, John W. "Journal of John Martin Mack." HISTORICAL JOURNAL 1 (1887):93-97.

> Aug 1753. Moravian travel journal, Bethlehem to Shamokin, Pennsylvania; missionary work.

OSBORN, SARAH, 1714-1796   340

In MEMOIRS OF THE LIFE OF MRS. SARAH OSBORN, by Samuel Hopkins, pp. 65-322. Worcester, Mass.: Printed by Leonard Worcester, 1799.

> 1744-1768. Religious diary containing God's dealings with her; self-analysis, prayers, religious reading, etc.

PEPPERELL, Sir WILLIAM, 1696-1759   341

AN ACCURATE JOURNAL AND ACCOUNT OF THE PROCEEDINGS OF THE NEW ENGLAND LAND FORCES. Exon: A. & S. Brice, 1746. 40 pp. Reprint. "The Sir William Pepperell Journal." AMERICAN ANTIQUARIAN SOCIETY PROCEEDINGS, n.s. 20 (1909-1910):139-183.

> 1744-1745. A kind of log of the siege of Louisburg; in hand of Benjamin Green, Pepperell's secretary.

In A LETTER FROM WILLIAM SHIRLEY, GOVERNOR OF MASSACHUSETTS BAY, TO HIS GRACE THE DUKE OF NEWCASTLE, pp. 17-32. London: Printed by E. Owen, 1746.

> Mar-Jun 1745. Official military journal; siege of Louisburg and other military operations in expedition against Cape Breton; full day-to-day narrative, signed by a committee.

PIERCE, DANIEL, 1709-1773   342

In RAMBLES ABOUT PORTSMOUTH: FIRST SERIES, 2d ed., by Charles W. Brewster, pp. 360-361. Portsmouth, N.H.: L.H. Brewster, 1873.

> 1744-1772. Brief scattered extracts from almanac notes; public and private events.

1745

ANON.   343

In COLONIAL CAPTIVITIES, edited by Isabel M. Calder, pp. 3-136.

> 1745-1748. British sailor's entertaining account of capture, journey to Quebec, imprisonment there, subsequent travel to the West Indies; lively details; vigorous criticism of the colonists.

ANON.   344

In DOCUMENTS RELATIVE TO THE COLONIAL HISTORY OF THE STATE OF NEW YORK, edited by E.B. O'Callaghan, vol. 10, pp. 38-75.

> 1745-1746. Frenchman's journal of military and other operations in Canada; official abstracts in form of journal; military affairs affecting the colonies, news from abroad. Translated.

ANON.   345

JOURNAL OF TRAVELS THROUGH SEVERAL TOWNS IN THE COUNTRY, AND TO BOSTON AGAIN, IN THE WINTER PAST; CONTAINING MANY STRANGE AND REMARKABLE OCCURRENCES. WHICH MAY BE OF SINGULAR ADVANTAGE TO THE PUBLIC IF RIGHLY IMPROVED IN THE PRESENT DAY. IN THE METHOD OF MR. WHITEFIELD'S JOURNAL, BUT VASTLY MORE ENTERTAINING. Boston: Printed by T. Fleet, 1745.

> 1745. Travel in New England.

ANON.   346

In LOUISBOURG JOURNALS, edited by Louis E. de Forest, pp. 67-72.

> Mar-Jun 1745. From Boston to Louisburg and the siege.

ANON.   347

In LOUISBOURG JOURNALS, edited by Louis E. de Forest, pp. 73-79.

> Mar-Jun 1745. Siege of Louisburg as seen by member of Massachusetts contingent.

ANON.   348

In LOUISBOURG JOURNALS, edited by Louis E. de Forest, pp. 80-96.

> Mar-Jul 1745. Journey from Charlestown to Louisburg with the Second Massachusetts Regiment; details of siege; interesting spellings, language and doggerel verses.

ANON.   349

A JOURNAL OF THE VOIGE IN THE SLOOP UNION, ELISHA MAYHEW, MASTER, IN AN EXPEDITION AGAINST CAPE

BRITON, 1745. By Elisha Mayhew, with an introduction by Howard M. Chapin. Providence, R.I.: E.A. Johnson Co., Printers, 1929. 26 pp.

Mar-Aug 1745. Journal of the UNION: ship movements and engagements; interesting spellings.

ANON.　　　350

In LOUISBOURG JOURNALS, edited by Louis E. de Forest, pp. 1-54.

Mar-Oct 1745. Siege of Louisburg described by member of the Fourth Massachusetts Regiment; intelligent, detailed observation; colloquial style.

ANON.　　　351

In LOUISBOURG JOURNALS, edited by Louis E. de Forest, pp. 61-66.

Aug-Sep 1745. Description of siege of Louisburg by member of the crew of the HECTOR.

ANON.　　　352

In DOCUMENTS RELATIVE TO THE COLONIAL HISTORY OF THE STATE OF NEW YORK, edited by E.B. O'Callaghan, vol. 10, pp. 32-35.

Dec 1745-Aug 1746. Military operations of French in New England and New York; brief abstracts; scalpings, etc. Translated.

BIDWELL, ADONIJAH, 1716-1784　　　353

"Expedition to Cape Breton: Journal of the Rev. Adonijah Bidwell, Chaplain of the Fleet." NEW ENGLAND HISTORICAL AND GENEALOGICAL REGISTER 27 (1873): 153-160.

Apr-Oct 1745. Brief notes of ship movements, deaths, bombardments, etc.

BRADSTREET, DUDLEY, 1708-ca. 1750　　　354

Green, Samuel A., ed. "Dudley Bradstreet's Diary." MASSACHUSETTS HISTORICAL SOCIETY PROCEEDINGS 11 (1896-1897):417-446. Diary, pp. 423-446.

In THREE MILITARY DIARIES KEPT BY GROTON SOLDIERS IN DIFFERENT WARS, edited by Samuel A. Green, pp. 3-39. Groton, Mass.: Cambridge University Press, J. Wilson and Son, 1901.

Apr 1745-Jan 1746. Colonel's description of naval and military details of siege of Louisburg; camp life, weather, private comments.

BUCHANAN, JOHN　　　355

In SMYTH COUNTY HISTORY AND TRADITIONS, by Goodridge Wilson, pp. 10-15. Kingsport, Tenn.: Kingsport Press, 1932.

Oct 1745. Journal of deputy surveyor of Augusta County, Virginia; with Peter Salley, laying claim in Smyth County, Virginia; meeting with Dunkers.

CHANDLER, SAMUEL, 1713-1775　　　356

In THE CHANDLER FAMILY, collected by George Chandler, pp. 192-198. Worcester, Mass.: Press of C. Hamilton, 1883.

1745-1764. Varied short notes from clergyman's diary; parish work in Scotland and Gloucester, Massachusetts; journeys, visits; domestic and family affairs, weather, etc.

"Extracts from the Diary of Rev. Samuel Chandler."

NEW ENGLAND HISTORICAL AND GENEALOGICAL REGISTER 17 (1863):346-354.

Extracts in COLLECTIONS ON THE HISTORY OF ALBANY, edited by Joel Munsell, vol. 2, pp. 373-375. Albany: J. Munsell, 1865-1871.

Sep 1755-Apr 1756. Account of expedition to Crown Point; scenery, estates, camp life.

CLEAVES, BENJAMIN, 1722-1808　　　357

"Benjamin Cleaves's Journal of the Expedition to Louisbourg." NEW ENGLAND HISTORICAL AND GENEALOGICAL REGISTER 66 (1912):113-124.

Mar-Jul 1745. Account of siege of Louisburg; interesting language.

CRAFT, BENJAMIN, 1706-1746　　　358

"Craft's Journal of the Siege of Louisburg." ESSEX INSTITUTE HISTORICAL COLLECTIONS 6 (1864):181-194.

Extracts in THE CRAFTS FAMILY, compiled by James Monroe Crafts and William Francis Crafts, pp. 659-670. Northampton, Mass.: Gazette Printing Co., 1893.

Apr-Nov 1745. Military journal of siege of Louisburg; short notes of camp life, religious reflections, etc.

CURWEN, SAMUEL, 1715-1802　　　359

In JOURNAL AND LETTERS OF THE LATE SAMUEL CURWEN, edited by George Atkinson Ward, pp. 12-14. New York: C.S. Francis; Boston: J.H. Francis, 1842. Reprint. New York: Da Capo, 1970; New York: AMS, 1973.

In AMERICAN HISTORY TOLD BY CONTEMPORARIES, edited by Albert B. Hart, vol. 2, pp. 346-349.

Mar-Jul 1745. Military journal extracts covering siege of Louisburg.

"Journal of a Journey from Salem to Philadelphia in 1755." ESSEX INSTITUTE HISTORICAL COLLECTIONS 52 (1916):76-83.

May-Jun 1755. Journey from Salem to Philadelphia; distances, roads, taverns.

JOURNAL OF SAMUEL CURWEN, LOYALIST. Edited by Andrew Oliver. Cambridge: Harvard University Press, for the Essex Institute, Salem, Mass., 1972. 2 vols.

Condensed version in JOURNAL AND LETTERS OF THE LATE SAMUEL CURWEN, edited by George Atkinson Ward, pp. 25-418.

Extracts in AMERICAN HISTORY TOLD BY CONTEMPORARIES, edited by Albert B. Hart, vol. 2, pp. 477-480.

1775-1784. Loyalist diary; interesting and important record of life in London with other Loyalists; travel in England.

EMERSON, JOSEPH, 1724-1775　　　360

"Emerson's Louisburg Journal." MASSACHUSETTS HISTORICAL SOCIETY PROCEEDINGS 44 (1910-1911):65-84.

Mar-Aug 1745. Naval chaplain's quite interesting account of siege of Louisburg.

"Joseph Emerson's Diary." MASSACHUSETTS HISTORICAL SOCIETY PROCEEDINGS 44 (1910-1911):262-282.

Extract in "Experiences of an American Minister from His Manuscript in 1748," by Edith March Howe. JOURNAL OF AMERICAN HISTORY 3 (1909):119-127.

Aug 1748–Apr 1749. Diary of Ralph Waldo Emerson's uncle; everyday rounds of a clergyman; quiet and pleasant details; interesting language.

GIBSON, JAMES, 1690?–1752 361

A JOURNAL OF THE LATE SIEGE. London: Printed for J. Newbery, 1745. 49 pp.

A BOSTON MERCHANT OF 1745. By one of his descendants. Boston: Redding and Co., 1847. 102 pp.

A JOURNAL OF THE SIEGE OF LOUISBURG AND CAPE BRETON, IN 1745. Washington, D.C.: Reprinted by J.B. Johnson, 1894. 35 pp.

Apr–Jul 1745. Notes of a gentleman volunteer at siege of Louisburg; clear but impersonal.

GIDDINGS, DANIEL, ca. 1704–1771 362

"Journal Kept by Lieut. Daniel Giddings of Ipswich During the Expedition against Cape Breton in 1744–5." ESSEX INSTITUTE HISTORICAL COLLECTIONS 48 (1912): 293–304.

Mar–Nov 1745. Journey to Louisburg with notes on siege, camp life, religion; interesting spellings.

GORHAM, JOHN, 1709–1746 363

Bowman, George E., ed. "Col. John Gorham's 'Wast Book' and His 'Dayly Journal.'" MAYFLOWER DESCENDANT 5 (1903):172–180.

Jun 1745. Sea journal kept during siege of Louisburg; very brief military details; some family and genealogical notes from Barnstable, Massachusetts.

HOW, NEHEMIAH, 1693–1747 364

A NARRATIVE OF THE CAPTIVITY OF NEHEMIAH HOW. Boston: Printed and sold opposite to the prison in Queen Street, 1748. 22 pp. Reprint. With introduction and notes by Victor H. Paltsits. Cleveland, Ohio: Burrows Brothers, 1904. 72 pp.

In INDIAN CAPTIVITIES, by Samuel G. Drake, pp. 127–138. Auburn: Derby, Miller, 1850.

1745–1747. Putney, Vermont, clergyman's record of capture by Indians, journey to Quebec and imprisonment there; begins as narrative; good record of captivity.

LAMB, CALEB 365

In LOUISBOURG JOURNALS, edited by Louis E. de Forest, pp. 106–108.

Nov 1745–Apr 1746. Continuation of George Mygate's diary of siege of Louisburg.

LOGAN, WILLIAM, 1718–1776 366

"William Logan's Journal of a Journey to Georgia." PENNSYLVANIA MAGAZINE OF HISTORY AND BIOGRAPHY 36 (1912):1–16, 162–186.

Sep 1745–Jan 1746. Philadelphia Quaker's business journey to Georgia; details of social life in the South; interesting spellings.

MYGATE, GEORGE, d. 1745 367

In LOUISBOURG JOURNALS, edited by Louis E. de Forest, pp. 97–106.

May–Sep 1745. Private's account of siege of Louisburg; some personal notes; interesting language. Continued by Caleb Lamb.

POMEROY, SETH, 1706–1777 368

In THE JOURNALS AND PAPERS OF SETH POMEROY, edited by Louis E. de Forest, pp. 14–51, 100–127. Society of Colonial Wars, New York, Publications, no. 38. New York: Society of Colonial Wars in the State of New York, 1926.

In HISTORY OF NORTHAMPTON, MASSACHUSETTS, by James Russell Trumbull, vol. 2, pp. 121–146, 260–280. Northampton: Press of Gazette Printing, 1898–1902.

Mar–Aug 1745, Jun–Oct 1755. Well-written and valuable accounts of the siege of Louisburg and the Lake George expedition.

POTE, WILLIAM, 1718–1755 369

THE JOURNAL OF CAPTAIN WILLIAM POTE, JR. DURING HIS CAPTIVITY IN THE FRENCH AND INDIAN WAR. Edited by J.F. Hurst. New York: Dodd, Mead, 1896. 223 pp.

1745–1747. Lively and highly personal account of capture by French and Indians off coast, journey to Quebec and imprisonment there; notes of Indian customs and barbarities, daily life in prison; interesting language.

REINCKE, ABRAHAM, 1712–1760 370

"Reincke's Journal of a Visit Among the Swedes of West Jersey." PENNSYLVANIA MAGAZINE OF HISTORY AND BIOGRAPHY 33 (1909):99–101.

Mar–Apr 1745. Swedish Moravian's visit to the Swedes of West Jersey; comments on miscegenation.

SHERBURNE, JOSEPH, b. 1694? 371

In LOUISBOURG JOURNALS, edited by Louis E. de Forest, pp. 55–60.

May–Jun 1745. Brief military details of siege of Louisburg.

SHIRLEY, WILLIAM, ca. 1693–1771 372

A LETTER FROM WILLIAM SHIRLEY, GOVERNOR OF MASSACHUSETTS BAY, TO HIS GRACE THE DUKE OF NEWCASTLE. London: Printed by E. Owen, 1746. 32 pp.

In LOUISBOURG JOURNALS, edited by Louis E. de Forest, pp. 109–120.

Mar–Jun 1745. Description of the siege of Louisburg.

SPANGENBERG, AUGUST GOTTLIEB, 1704–1792 373

"Spangenberg's Notes of Travel to Onondaga in 1745." PENNSYLVANIA MAGAZINE OF HISTORY AND BIOGRAPHY 2 (1878):424–432; 3 (1879):56–64.

In MORAVIAN JOURNALS RELATING TO CENTRAL NEW YORK, edited by William M. Beauchamp, pp. 5–16.

May–Jul 1745. Moravian's notes of travel to the Onondaga; missionary work among Indians. Translated from the German.

In RECORDS OF THE MORAVIANS IN NORTH CAROLINA, edited by Adelaide L. Fries, vol. 1, pp. 30–64.

"Extracts from Bishop Spangenberg's Journal of Travels in North Carolina." SOUTHERN HISTORICAL ASSOCIATION PUBLICATIONS 1 (1897):99–111.

Sep 1752–Jan 1753. Journey from Bethlehem, Pennsylvania, to North Carolina; topographical notes and description of government; interesting German spellings of place names. Translated from the German.

STEARNS, BENJAMIN, 1714-1755   374

"The Siege of Louisburg." MASSACHUSETTS HISTORICAL SOCIETY PROCEEDINGS 42 (1908-1909):135-144.

Clark, J.C.L., ed. "Louisburg." ACADIENSIS 8 (1908): 317-329.

> Mar-Aug 1745. Military journal of the siege of Louisburg; interesting language.

WOLCOTT, ROGER, 1679-1767   375

"Journal of Roger Wolcott at the Siege of Louisbourg." CONNECTICUT HISTORICAL SOCIETY COLLECTIONS 1 (1860):131-161.

> May-Jul 1745. Journal covering siege of Louisburg; military affairs, documents, recapitulation.

1746

ANON.   376

"A Journey from Boston to Albany in 1746." BOSTON PUBLIC LIBRARY BULLETIN, 4th ser. 4 (1922):126-133.

> Jul-Aug 1746. Official treaty journal; journey from Boston to Albany; conference of a Massachusetts commission with the Six Nations.

ANON.   377

In DOCUMENTS RELATIVE TO THE COLONIAL HISTORY OF THE STATE OF NEW YORK, edited by E.B. O'Callaghan, vol. 10, pp. 89-132.

> Nov 1746-Sep 1747. Frenchman's official military record; notes of the most interesting occurrences in Canada; military movements and foreign news. Translated from the French.

CLOUGH, ABNER, 1720-1786   378

"Abner Clough's Journal." NEW HAMPSHIRE HISTORICAL SOCIETY COLLECTIONS 4 (1834):201-214.

> Jul-Sep 1746. Military march with Captain Ladd's company to protect Rumford, New Hampshire, against Indians; good narrative of Indian skirmishes; colloquialisms.

CUSHING, JOHN, 1709-1772   379

"Items from an Interleaved Copy of AMES'S ALMANAC for 1746, Belonging to Rev. John Cushing." NEW ENGLAND HISTORICAL AND GENEALOGICAL REGISTER 19 (1865):237-241.

"Journal of Rev. John Cushing." ESSEX ANTIQUARIAN 4 (1900):155-156.

> Jan-Dec 1746. Clergyman's journal; brief notes of private and town affairs in Boxford, Massachusetts.

DE BEAUCHAMPS   380

In TRAVELS IN THE AMERICAN COLONIES, edited by Newton D. Mereness, pp. 261-297.

> Sep-Oct 1746. Journal of trip from Mobile to Choctaw Indians to settle for assassinations of Frenchmen; mainly inquiries and discussions. Translated from the French.

HEYWOOD, WILLIAM, 1728-1803   381

In HISTORY OF CHARLESTOWN, NEW HAMPSHIRE, by Henry H. Saunderson, pp. 402-406. Claremont, N.H.: The town, 1876.

> 1746-1751. Extracts of colonel's military marches through Deerfield to Fort Dummer, Canada, and Fort Massachusetts.

LEWIS, THOMAS, 1718-1790   382

In ANNALS OF AUGUSTA COUNTY, VIRGINIA, FROM 1726 TO 1871, 2d ed., rev. and enl., by Joseph A. Waddell, pp. 84-88. Staunton, Va.: C.R. Caldwell, 1902.

THE FAIRFAX LINE: THOMAS LEWIS'S JOURNAL OF 1746. With footnotes and index by John W. Wayland. New Market, Va.: Henkel Press, 1925. 97 pp.

> Sep 1746-Feb 1747. Surveying and making maps of the southwest line of the "princely domain" of Thomas, Lord Fairfax, in Augusta County.

NICHOLSON, THOMAS, 1715-1780   383

"The Journal of Thomas Nicholson." SOUTHERN HISTORICAL ASSOCIATION PUBLICATIONS 4 (1900):172-186, 233-247, 301-315.

> Apr 1746, 1749-1750, Nov-Dec 1771. Journal of Quaker of Perquimans County, North Carolina; visits to friends at Cape Fear; 2,500 miles of travel in England, visiting Quakers; visit to North Carolina Assembly.

NORTON, JOHN, 1716-1778   384

THE REDEEMED CAPTIVE: BEING A NARRATIVE OF THE TAKING AND CARRYING INTO CAPTIVITY THE REVEREND JOHN NORTON, WHEN FORT MASSACHUSETTS SURRENDERED TO A LARGE BODY OF FRENCH AND INDIANS, AUGUST 20TH 1746. Boston: Printed and sold opposite the prison by S. Kneeland, 1748. 40 pp.

NARRATIVE OF THE CAPTURE AND BURNING OF FORT MASSACHUSETTS. Edited by Samuel G. Drake. Albany: Printed for S.G. Drake of Boston, by J. Munsell, 1870. 51 pp.

In A PARTICULAR HISTORY OF THE FIVE YEARS FRENCH AND INDIAN WAR IN NEW ENGLAND AND PARTS ADJACENT, by Samuel G. Drake, pp. 253-295. Albany: J. Munsell, 1870.

> 1746-1747. Seminarrative journal describing capture of Fort Massachusetts by the French and Indians and his subsequent captivity.

PRINGLE, ROBERT, 1702-1776   385

Webber, Mabel L. "Journal of Robert Pringle." SOUTH CAROLINA HISTORICAL AND GENEALOGICAL MAGAZINE 26 (1925):21-30, 93-112.

> 1746-1747. Merchant's line-a-day notes on trade and domestic affairs around Charleston, South Carolina; accounts.

RICE, WILLIAM, 1708-1747   386

In NINE MUSTER ROLLS OF RHODE ISLAND TROOPS ENLISTED DURING THE OLD FRENCH WAR; TO WHICH IS ADDED THE JOURNAL OF CAPTAIN WILLIAM RICE IN THE EXPEDITION OF 1746, by Society of Colonial Wars, Rhode Island, pp. 45-53. Providence: Printed for the Society by the Standard Printing Co., 1915.

> May-Dec 1746. Military movements of Rhode Island company during expedition against Canada; some good details; gambling; sickness.

ROSE, ROBERT, 1704–1751   387

THE DIARY OF ROBERT ROSE: A VIEW OF VIRGINIA BY A SCOTTISH COLONIAL PARSON. Edited by Ralph E. Fall. Verona, Va.: McClure Press, 1977. 400 pp.

   1746–1751. Brief entries of Scottish Anglican clergyman, who owned land and slaves in colonial Virginia; marriages, baptisms, funerals, management of his own plantation and parish; tireless travels by horseback, canoe, etc., to bring services and consolations of the church to remote areas; weather, social life, sicknesses of family and flock, some medical treatments.

SCHLATTER, MICHAEL, 1716–1790   388

In THE LIFE OF REV. MICHAEL SCHLATTER, by Henry Harbaugh, pp. 87–234. Philadelphia: Lindsay & Blakiston, 1857.

   1746–1751. Moravian journal; pastor of First Reformed Church in Philadelphia; notes of work among Moravians in Pennsylvania, New Jersey, Maryland, Virginia; notes during French and Indian wars. Translated from the Dutch.

Hinke, William J., ed. "Diary of the Rev. Michael Schlatter." PRESBYTERIAN HISTORICAL SOCIETY JOURNAL 3 (1905–1906):105–121; 158–176.

   Jun–Dec 1746.

WALKER, TIMOTHY, 1705–1782   389

DIARIES OF REV. TIMOTHY WALKER, THE FIRST AND ONLY MINISTER OF CONCORD, N.H., FROM HIS ORDINATION NOVEMBER 18, 1730 TO SEPTEMBER 1, 1782. Edited by Joseph B. Walker. Concord, N.H.: I.C. Evans, 1889. 80 pp.

Walker, Joseph B. "Diaries of the Rev. Timothy Walker." NEW HAMPSHIRE HISTORICAL SOCIETY COLLECTIONS 9 (1889):123–191.

   1746–1780 (with gaps). Clergyman's brief notes of local and personal affairs, church work, and farming; interesting picture of life in an interior pioneer village.

WRIGHT, NOAH, 1716–1797   390

"Copy of a Journal Kept by Dea. Noah Wright." NEW ENGLAND HISTORICAL AND GENEALOGICAL REGISTER 2 (1848):208–210.

   1746–1747. Extracts giving news of Indian raids at Deerfield, Massachusetts.

1747

ANON.   391

In DOCUMENTS RELATIVE TO THE COLONIAL HISTORY OF THE STATE OF NEW YORK, edited by E.B. O'Callaghan, vol. 10, pp. 137–179.

   Nov 1747–Oct 1748. Official French journal; notes of operations of the war at Quebec. Translated.

BACKUS, ISAAC, 1724–1806   392

THE DIARY OF ISAAC BACKUS. Edited by William G. McLoughlin. Providence: Brown University Press, 1979. 3 vols.

In A MEMOIR OF THE LIFE AND TIMES OF THE REV. ISAAC BACKUS, by Alvah Hovey, pp. 73–305 passim. Boston: Gould and Lincoln; New York: Sheldon Blakeman, 1859.

   1747–1806. Diary of itinerant Baptist minister; religious and secular affairs; family life; spiritual introspections; opinions on people, religious groups, American Revolution, slavery, theological disputes of the time; an important source for early American social history, formulation of separation of church and state, Baptist history and theology.

BATCHELDER, DAVID, 1736–1811   393

In HISTORY OF THE TOWN OF HAMPTON FALLS, by Warren Brown, vol. 1, pp. 476–481. Concord, N.H.: Rumford Press, 1900.

   1747–1811. Brief scattered notes of weather, farming, etc., at Portsmouth, New Hampshire.

BOWEN, SILAS, 1722–1790   394

In THE FAMILY OF GRIFFITH BOWEN, by Daniel Bowen, pp. 188–194. Jacksonville, Fla.: Da Costa Printing, 1893.

   1747–1787. Brief extracts of births, marriages, family notes; some public items of Woodstock, Connecticut.

DE BOISHEBERT, CHARLES DESCHAMPS   395

In DOCUMENTS RELATIVE TO THE COLONIAL HISTORY OF THE STATE OF NEW YORK, edited by E.B. O'Callaghan, vol. 10, pp. 79–80.

   Jun 1747. Military journal of French and Indian expeditions against Fort Clinton. Translated from the French.

GOELET, FRANCIS   396

"Extracts from Capt. Francis Goelet's Journal, Relative to Boston, Salem and Marblehead, etc." NEW ENGLAND HISTORICAL AND GENEALOGICAL REGISTER 24 (1870): 50–63.

   1747–1754. Lively account of voyages along New England coast; social life at the ports, feasts, parties, etc.

PHILBROOK, JONATHAN, 1721–1801   397

In HISTORY OF BRUNSWICK, TOPSHAM, AND HARPSWELL, MAINE, by George A. Wheeler and Henry W. Wheeler, pp. 58–60. Boston: A. Mudge & Son, Printers, 1878.

   Mar–Apr 1747. Scouting journal; brief notes by clerk of expedition up the Kennebec River.

1748

CAMMERHOFF, JOHN CHRISTOPHER FREDERICK,   398
1721–1756

Jordan, John W. "Bishop J.C.F. Cammerhoff's Narrative of a Journey to Shamokin, Penna." PENNSYLVANIA MAGAZINE OF HISTORY AND BIOGRAPHY 29 (1905):160–179.

   Jan 1748. Bishop's travel journal and account of Moravian life and worship. Translated from the German.

In MORAVIAN JOURNALS RELATING TO CENTRAL NEW YORK, edited by William M. Beauchamp, pp. 24–112.

   May–Aug 1750. Journey with Zeisberger from Bethlehem to Onondaga; excellent full narrative; travel, religion and Indian notes. Translated from the German.

GOTTSCHALK, MATTHIAS GOTTLIEB, d. 1748   **399**

Hinke, William J. and Kemper, Charles E. "Moravian Diaries of Travels through Virginia." VIRGINIA MAGAZINE OF HISTORY AND BIOGRAPHY 12 (1904-1905):62-86. Diary, pp. 62-76.

> Mar-Apr 1748. Moravian missionary's journey through Virginia and Maryland; religious life and preaching.

HOLYOKE, JOHN, 1734-1753   **400**

In THE HOLYOKE DIARIES, edited by George F. Dow, pp. 44-46.

> Jan-Dec 1748. Brief notes of social life and study at Harvard; interesting language.

KALM, PEHR, 1716-1779   **401**

TRAVELS INTO NORTH AMERICA. Translated by John Reinhold Forster. London: Printed for the editor, 1770-1771. 3 vols. Reprint. Barre, Mass.: Imprint Society, 1972. 514 pp.

THE AMERICA OF 1750: PETER KALM'S TRAVELS IN NORTH AMERICA; THE ENGLISH VERSION OF 1770. Revised and edited by Adolph B. Benson. New York: Wilson-Erickson, 1937. 2 vols. Reprint. New York: Dover, 1966.

Extracts in AMERICAN HISTORY TOLD BY CONTEMPORARIES, edited by Albert B. Hart, vol. 2, pp. 324-326, 330-332, 352-353.

> 1748-1750. Excellent diary of Swedish traveler; detailed descriptions of places and activities.

Benson, Adolph B. "Peter Kalm's Journey to North America." AMERICAN SCANDINAVIAN REVIEW 10 (1922): 350-355.

> 1748. Travel in New York, New Jersey, Pennsylvania.

"Kalm's Journey Through New Jersey." SOMERSET COUNTY HISTORICAL QUARTERLY 5 (1916):29-33.

> 1748. Extracts relating to New Jersey.

Cadbury, Henry J. "Philadelphia Quakerism in 1749 as Seen by a Finn." FRIENDS' HISTORICAL ASSOCIATION BULLETIN 31 (1942):26-32.

> Dec 1748. Extract containing description of Quaker service, probably the Bank Meeting, and customs.

MELVEN (or MELVIN), ELEAZAR, 1703-1754   **402**

"Journal of Capt. Eleazer Melven." NEW HAMPSHIRE HISTORICAL SOCIETY COLLECTIONS 5 (1837):207-211.

Charlton, Mary F. "The Crown Point Road." VERMONT HISTORICAL SOCIETY PROCEEDINGS 2 (1931):163-193. Journal, pp. 167-168.

> May 1748. Military officer's march to Crown Point; well-written, brief notes of Indian skirmishes.

PARSONS, MOSES, 1716-1783   **403**

In THE STORY OF BYFIELD, by John L. Ewell, pp. 101-158 passim. Boston: G.E. Littlefield, 1904.

> 1748-1783. Extracts from clergyman's diary; brief notes of weather, farming, social and family affairs in Byfield, Massachusetts; longer notes on important public affairs.

ROGERS, JOHN, 1692-1773   **404**

"Diary of Rev. John Rogers." OLD ELIOT 7 (1906): 15-20.

> Feb-Jun 1748. Clergyman's journal of religious work and self-analysis; some local items of Eliot, Maine.

SPANGENBERG, JOSEPH, 1704-1792   **405**

Hinke, William J. and Kemper, Charles E. "Moravian Diaries of Travels through Virginia." VIRGINIA MAGAZINE OF HISTORY AND BIOGRAPHY 11 (1903-1904):225-242. Diary, pp. 235-242.

> Jun-Aug 1748. Extracts of Moravian travel journal; through Maryland and Virginia with Matthew Reutz; missionary work. Translated from the German.

WASHINGTON, GEORGE, 1732-1799   **406**

THE DIARIES OF GEORGE WASHINGTON. Edited by Donald Jackson and Dorothy Twohig. Charlottesville: University Press of Virginia, 1976-1980. 6 vols.

THE DIARIES OF GEORGE WASHINGTON, 1748-1799. Edited by John C. Fitzpatrick. Boston; New York: Houghton Mifflin, 1925. 4 vols. Reprint. New York: Kraus, 1971.

> 1748-1799. Diary of first president of the United States, with some gaps, especially during Revolution and presidency; mostly brief notes of farming, sport, and social life at Mount Vernon.

In GEORGE WASHINGTON IN THE OHIO VALLEY, by Hugh Cleland. Pittsburgh: University of Pittsburgh Press, 1955. 405 pp.

> 1753-1784. Includes expedition to the Ohio and separate journals for other years.

A REPRINT OF THE JOURNAL OF GEORGE WASHINGTON AND THAT OF HIS GUIDE, CHRISTOPHER GIST, RECITING THEIR EXPERIENCES ON THE HISTORIC MISSION FROM GOVERNOR DINWIDDIE, OF VIRGINIA, TO THE FRENCH COMMANDANT AT FORT LE BOEUF IN NOVEMBER-DECEMBER, 1753. Edited by Don M. Larrabee. Williamsport, Pa.: Grit Publishing, 1924. 41 pp. Reprint. 1950.

TRIAL BY WILDERNESS: THE EMERGENCE OF GEORGE WASHINGTON AS REVEALED IN HIS OWN JOURNAL, 1753-1754. Edited by Earl S. Miers. Kingsport, Tenn.: Privately printed by Kingsport Press, 1957. 59 pp.

THE JOURNAL OF MAJOR GEORGE WASHINGTON: AN ACCOUNT OF HIS FIRST OFFICIAL MISSION, MADE AS EMISSARY FROM THE GOVERNOR OF VIRGINIA TO THE COMMANDANT OF THE FRENCH FORCES ON THE OHIO, OCTOBER 1753-JANUARY 1754. Facsimile ed. Williamsburg, Va.: Colonial Williamsburg, 1959. 28 pp.

> 1753-1754. Expedition to the Ohio.

JOURNAL OF COLONEL GEORGE WASHINGTON, COMMANDING A DETACHMENT OF VIRGINIA TROOPS, SENT BY ROBERT DINWIDDIE, LIEUTENANT-GOVERNOR OF VIRGINIA, ACROSS THE ALLEGHANY MOUNTAINS, IN 1754, TO BUILD FORTS AT THE HEAD OF THE OHIO. Edited by J.M. Toner. Albany: J. Munsell's Sons, 1893. 273 pp.

THE JOURNAL OF MAJOR GEORGE WASHINGTON (1754). With an introduction by Randolph G. Adams. New York: Scholars' Facsimiles & Reprints, 1940. 28 pp.

THE JOURNAL OF MAJOR GEORGE WASHINGTON, OF HIS JOURNEY TO THE FRENCH FORCES ON OHIO. Facsimile of the Williamsburg edition, 1754, with an introduction by J. Christian Bay. Cedar Rapids, Iowa: Torch Press, 1955. 19 pp.

Kent, Donald H. "Contrecoeur's Copy of George Washington's Journal for 1754." PENNSYLVANIA HISTORY 19 (1952):1-32.

> 1754. March to the Ohio, skirmish with the French, and diplomatic negotiations with Indian allies. The Contrecoeur version appears to corrob-

orate the authenticity of the translation used by previous editors.

Rinaldi, Nicholas. "George Washington at Home in Virginia." EARLY AMERICAN LIFE 8 (1977):11–17, 69–71.

1760–1786, 1799. Extracts, most undated, describing activities of Washington, the Virginia planter.

"Diary of George Washington." COLONIAL SOCIETY OF MASSACHUSETTS PUBLICATIONS 7 (1900–1902):128–181, 341–398; 17 (1913–1914):161–205; 18 (1915–1916):28–54.

1785–1786.

DIARY OF WASHINGTON: FROM THE FIRST DAY OF OCTOBER, 1789, TO THE TENTH DAY OF MARCH, 1790. New York: Privately printed, 1858. 89 pp.

THE DIARY OF GEORGE WASHINGTON, FROM 1789 TO 1791; EMBRACING THE OPENING OF THE FIRST CONGRESS, AND HIS TOURS THROUGH NEW ENGLAND, LONG ISLAND, AND THE SOUTHERN STATES. TOGETHER WITH HIS JOURNAL OF A TOUR TO THE OHIO, IN 1753. Edited by Benson J. Lossing. New York: C.B. Richardson, 1860. 248 pp. Reprint. Freeport, N.Y.: Books for Libraries, 1972.

Oct 1789–Mar 1790.

Treville, Virginia E. de. "The First President Visits Augusta." RICHMOND COUNTY HISTORY 4 (1972):39–53. Diary, pp. 43–44.

May 1791. Brief extracts concerning the president's visit to Georgia's capital; descriptions of the town, its surroundings and formal events of the visit.

Townsend, Mary M. "Diary of President Washington." PENNSYLVANIA MAGAZINE OF HISTORY AND BIOGRAPHY 37 (1913):230–239.

Jan–Jun 1796. Daily weather reports made on a copy of THE AMERICAN REPOSITORY OF USEFUL INFORMATION CONTAINING A CALENDAR FOR THE PRESENT YEAR.

ZEISBERGER, DAVID, 1721–1808   407

"An Account of the Famine Among the Indians of the North and West Branch of the Susquehanna, in the Summer of 1748." PENNSYLVANIA MAGAZINE OF HISTORY AND BIOGRAPHY 16 (1892):430–432. Appears in HISTORICAL JOURNAL 1 (1887):287–289, attributed to John Martin Mack.

Jul 1748. Journal extract describing Indian famine.

In MORAVIAN JOURNALS RELATING TO CENTRAL NEW YORK, edited by William M. Beauchamp, pp. 156–197, 222–240.

Apr–Nov 1753. Journey to Onondaga with Henry Frey; missionary work there; notes on travel, religious life and Indians.

Oct 1766. Trip with Gottlob Senseman on mission from Friedenshuetten to Onondaga and Cayuga; Indian conferences.

Hulbert, Archer B. and Schwarze, William N. "Diary of David Zeisberger's Journey to the Ohio." OHIO ARCHEOLOGICAL AND HISTORICAL QUARTERLY 21 (1912): 8–32.

Extracts in NOTES AND QUERIES, edited by William H. Egle, 4th ser., vol. 1, pp. 351–352.

Sep–Nov 1767. Narrative in journal form; journey to the Monsey town at the mouth of Tionesta Creek on the Allegheny River; meetings, accounts of Indians, religious discussions.

Hulbert, Archer B. and Schwarze, William N. "Diary of David Zeisberger and Gottlob Zenseman." OHIO ARCHE-

OLOGICAL AND HISTORICAL QUARTERLY 21 (1912): 42–104.

May 1768–Jan 1769. Journey with Senseman to Goschgoschinck on the Ohio and their sojourn there; notes on travel, meetings, councils, topography.

SCHOENBRUNN STORY; EXCERPTS FROM THE DIARY OF THE REVEREND DAVID ZEISBERGER, 1772–1777, AT SCHOENBRUNN IN THE OHIO COUNTRY. Translated by August C. Mahr. Columbus: Ohio Historical Society, 1972. 26 pp.

1772–1777. Missionary journey to Schoenbrunn.

DIARY OF DAVID ZEISBERGER, A MORAVIAN MISSIONARY AMONG THE INDIANS OF OHIO. Translated by Eugene F. Bliss. Historical and Philosophical Society of Ohio Publications, n.s., vols. 3–4. Cincinnati: R. Clarke, 1885. 2 vols. Reprint. St. Clair Shores, Mich.: Scholarly Press, 1972.

Extracts in "David Zeisberger and His Delaware Indians," by John Morrison. ONTARIO HISTORICAL SOCIETY PAPERS AND RECORDS 12 (1914):176–198.

1781–1798. Travel and missionary journal of life and work at missions at Muskingum, Upper Sandusky, Detroit, Clinton River, Cuyahoga, Huron River, New Salem, mouth of Detroit River, and Fairfield on the Thames.

Mueller, Paul E. "David Zeisberger's Official Diary, Fairfield." MORAVIAN HISTORICAL SOCIETY TRANSACTIONS 19 (1963):5–229. Reprint. Easton, Pa.: Printed for the Society by Laros Printing, 1963. 234 pp.

1791–1795. Missionary journal at Fairfield; content similar to that of other Moravian journals.

1749

ANTHONY, SUSANNA, 1726–1791   408

THE LIFE AND CHARACTER OF MISS SUSANNA ANTHONY. Compiled by Samuel Hopkins. Worcester, Mass.: Leonard Worcester, 1796. 193 pp. passim.

1749–1769. Religious meditations of Quaker of Newport, Rhode Island.

BONNECAMPS, JOSEPH PIERRE DE, 1707–1790   409

Jarvis, N.S., trans. "An Account of a Journey down 'La Belle Riviere' (Ohio River) in 1749 by Pere Bonnecamp, S.J." MILITARY SERVICE INSTITUTION OF THE UNITED STATES JOURNAL 40 (1907):278–289.

"Account of the Voyage on the Beautiful River Made in 1749, under the Direction of Monsieur de Céloron, by Father Bonnecamps." OHIO ARCHEOLOGICAL AND HISTORICAL QUARTERLY 29 (1920):397–423.

Jun–Nov 1749. Surveyor's journal incorporated into official report; Céloron de Blainville's explorations in the Old Northwest.

BRAINERD, JOHN, 1720–1781   410

In THE LIFE OF JOHN BRAINERD, by Thomas Brainerd, pp. 160–226. Philadelphia: Presbyterian Publication Committee; New York: A.D.F. Randolph, 1865.

Aug–Nov 1749. Missionary journal of work among Indians of New Jersey; religious reflections and introspection; journeys in New Jersey; Elizabethtown, Newark, Brunswick, Gnadenhuetten; impressions of Moravians.

CELORON DE BLAINVILLE, PIERRE JOSEPH DE, 1693-1759   411

Lambing, A.A. "Céloron's Journal." OHIO ARCHEOLOG-ICAL AND HISTORICAL QUARTERLY 29 (1920):335-396.

"1749: Céloron's Expedition down the Ohio." WISCONSIN STATE HISTORICAL SOCIETY COLLECTIONS 18 (1908): 36-58.

> Jun-Nov 1749. Exploration journal; expedition from Quebec down the Allegheny and Ohio rivers; negotiations with various Indian tribes.

CHANCELLOR, WILLIAM, d. 1763   412

Wax, Darold D. "A Philadelphia Surgeon on a Slaving Voyage to Africa." PENNSYLVANIA MAGAZINE OF HISTORY AND BIOGRAPHY 92 (1968):465-493.

> 1749-1751. Extracts, arranged topically within explanatory text, from diary of physician responsible for slaves' health during middle passage; information on the mechanics of the trade; opinions and descriptions of Africa and its inhabitants.

FITCH, JABEZ, 1737-1812   413

"The Diary of Jabez Fitch, Jr." MAYFLOWER DESCENDANT 1-15 (1899-1914):passim; 27-28, 30-34 (1925-1937): passim; continued in PILGRIM NOTES AND QUERIES 2-5 (1914-1917):passim.

> 1749-1770. Lengthy, detailed diary of private affairs, in intimate and entertaining style; social life; service in French and Indian wars; interesting spellings and language.

"Diary of Jabez Fitch, Jr." MASSACHUSETTS HISTORICAL SOCIETY PROCEEDINGS 9 (1894-1895):40-91.

> Aug-Dec 1775. Extracts relating to the Revolution.

THE NEW YORK DIARY OF LIEUTENANT JABEZ FITCH OF THE 17th (CONNECTICUT) REGIMENT. Edited by W.H.W. Sabine. New York: Colburn & Tegg, 1954. 288 pp.

> 1776-1777. Taken prisoner during the Battle of Long Island; life on board prison ship MENTOR and then on parole in New York City and Long Island; eventual exchange and return home.

VERMONT HISTORICAL GAZETEER 2 (1871):638-653.

> 1787-1788. Extracts covering settlement in northern Vermont.

PHILLIPS, CATHERINE PAYTON, 1727-1794   414

MEMOIRS OF CATHERINE PHILLIPS. London: Printed and sold by J. Phillips and Son, 1797. Reprint. Philadelphia: Printed by Budd and Bartram for Robert Johnson, 1798. 384 pp.

> 1749-1785. An English Quaker's memoirs in journal form; visit to America; North Carolina, Virginia, Maryland, New York, New England; sociological and religious notes.

SEDELMAYR, JACOBO, 1703-1779   415

"Trek to the Yumas." In JACOBO SEDELMAYR; MISSIONARY, FRONTIERSMAN, EXPLORER IN ARIZONA AND SONORA: FOUR ORIGINAL MANUSCRIPT NARRATIVES, 1744-1751. Translated and annotated by Peter Masten Dunne, pp. 55-75. Great Southwest Travels Series, no. 1. Tucson: Arizona Pioneers Historical Society, 1955.

> Oct-Nov 1749. Jesuit's diary of exploration and missionary endeavor among Yuma Indians, mainly following the Gila and Colorado rivers.

STEVENS, PHINEAS, 1706-1756   416

"Journal of Capt. Phineas Stevens." NEW HAMPSHIRE HISTORICAL SOCIETY COLLECTIONS 5 (1837):199-205.

> Aug-Dec 1749. Brief official travel journal of journey to Canada, via Deerfield, Albany, Crown Point and Montreal.

In TRAVELS IN THE AMERICAN COLONIES, edited by Newton D. Mereness, pp. 302-322.

> Apr-Nov 1752. Journey to Canada to negotiate about prisoners; cryptic domestic notes.

1750

BEVERLEY, WILLIAM, 1698-1756   417

"Diary of William Beverley of 'Blandfield' during a Visit to England." VIRGINIA MAGAZINE OF HISTORY AND BIOGRAPHY 36 (1928):161-169.

> Jun-Oct 1750. Social and public details; impersonal notes of things done, seen, and places visited on trip to England.

BIRKET, JAMES   418

SOME CURSORY REMARKS MADE BY JAMES BIRKET. New Haven: Yale University Press, 1916. 74 pp.

> 1750-1751. Travel diaries; voyage from Antigua, British West Indies, to Portsmouth, New Hampshire; travels in New England, New York, Pennsylvania; long descriptions of places, people and trade.

GIST, CHRISTOPHER, ca. 1706-1759   419

CHRISTOPHER GIST'S JOURNALS WITH HISTORICAL, GEOGRAPHICAL AND ETHNOLOGICAL NOTES AND BIOGRAPHIES OF HIS CONTEMPORARIES. Edited by William M. Darlington. Pittsburgh: J.R. Weldin, 1893. 296 pp. Reprint. New York: Published for University Microfilms by Argonaut Press, 1966. Journal, pp. 31-66.

Extracts in FIRST EXPLORATIONS OF KENTUCKY, by Josiah S. Johnston, pp. 85-185. Louisville, 1898; ANNALS OF SOUTHWEST VIRGINIA, 1769-1800, by Lewis P. Summers, pp. 29-57. Abingdon, Va.: L.P. Summers, 1929; THE WILDERNESS TRAIL, by Charles A. Hanna, vol. 2, pp. 143-152.

"Christopher Gist's First and Second Journals, September 11, 1750-March 29, 1752." In GEORGE MERCER PAPERS RELATING TO THE OHIO COMPANY OF VIRGINIA, by Pittsburgh University Library, Darlington Memorial Library, edited by Lois Mulkearn, pp. 7-40. Pittsburgh: University of Pittsburgh Press, 1954.

In A TOPOGRAPHICAL DESCRIPTION OF THE DOMINIONS OF THE UNITED STATES OF AMERICA, by Thomas Pownall, pp. 171-199. Pittsburgh: University of Pittsburgh Press, 1949.

> 1750-1751. Explorer's journal; exploring for Ohio Company beyond Allegheny Mountains as far as Falls of the Ohio, searching for level lands; meetings with Indians, Indian customs; mainly official and surveying notes.

"Journal of Mr. Christopher Gist, Who Accompanied Major George Washington in His First Visit to the French Commander of the Troops on the Ohio, 1753." MASSACHUSETTS HISTORICAL SOCIETY COLLECTIONS, 3d ser. 5 (1836):101-108.

In A REPRINT OF THE JOURNAL OF GEORGE WASHINGTON AND THAT OF HIS GUIDE, CHRISTOPHER GIST, RECITING THEIR EXPERIENCES ON THE HISTORIC MISSION FROM GOVERNOR DINWIDDIE, OF VIRGINIA, TO THE FRENCH

COMMANDANT AT FORT LE BOEUF IN NOVEMBER-DECEM-
BER, 1753, by George Washington, edited by Don M.
Larrabee. Williamsport, Pa., Grit Publishing, 1924.
Reprint. 1950.

> Oct 1753-Jan 1754. Visit with George Washington to
> French forts on the Ohio.

HAZARD, THOMAS, 1720-1798   420

In THOMAS HAZARD, SON OF ROBT, CALL'D COLLEGE
TOM, by Caroline Hazard. pp. 1-324 passim. Boston:
Houghton, Mifflin, 1893.

> 1750-1790. A few farming and personal notes from
> account book and diary; Rhode Island.

JONES, SARAH   421

NEW ENGLAND FAMILY HISTORY 4 (1911-1912):577-587,
599-604.

> 1750-1766. Social life, sleighing parties, etc., in
> Falmouth and later Portland, Maine. Editor notes
> that authenticity is doubtful, as language is too
> modern.

MITTELBERGER, GOTTLIEB   422

GOTTLIEB MITTELBERGER'S JOURNEY TO PENNSYLVANIA
IN THE YEAR 1750 AND RETURN TO GERMANY IN THE
YEAR 1754. Translated by Carl T. Eben. Philadelphia:
Privately printed for J.Y. Jeanes, 1898. 129 pp.

> 1750-1754. German Moravian's diary of journey to
> Pennsylvania; Moravian religious life; topography,
> natural history and trade of Pennsylvania. Trans-
> lated from the German.

WALKER, THOMAS, 1715-1794   423

JOURNAL OF AN EXPLORATION IN THE SPRING OF THE
YEAR 1750. Edited by William C. Rives. Boston: Little,
Brown, 1888. 69 pp.

"Doctor Thomas Walker's Journal." In FIRST EXPLORA-
TIONS OF KENTUCKY, by Josiah S. Johnston, pp. 1- 84.
Louisville, Ky.: J.P. Morton, 1898.

Extracts in ANNALS OF SOUTHWEST VIRGINIA, 1769-1800,
by Lewis P. Summers, pp. 8-26. Abingdon, Va.: L.P.
Summers, 1929; HISTORIC HIGHWAYS OF AMERICA, by
Archer B. Hulbert, vol. 6, chap. 2; EARLY TRAVELS IN
THE TENNESSEE COUNTRY, edited by Samuel C.
Williams, pp. 169-174.

> Mar-Jul 1750. First exploration of Kentucky; stages
> and distances; a few descriptions of places; gener-
> ally impersonal; account of snakebite of horses;
> important in history of the frontier.

WATSON, JOHN, 1720-1761   424

Jordan, John W. "Penn Versus Baltimore." PENNSYL-
VANIA MAGAZINE OF HISTORY AND BIOGRAPHY 38 (1914):
385-406; 39 (1915):1-47.

> 1750-1751. Surveying journal; Pennsylvania-Mary-
> land boundary dispute; topographical descriptions;
> some personal notes.

WINSLOW, JOSHUA, 1727-1801   425

THE JOURNAL OF JOSHUA WINSLOW. Edited by John C.
Webster. Saint John: New Brunswick Museum, 1936. 40
pp.

> Mar-Dec 1750. Journal of paymaster of British
> forces in Nova Scotia; with Major Lawrence on two
> expeditions to Chignecto, New Brunswick; brief
> entries, mostly military and naval movements.

1751

ANON.   426

"Journal of a Visit to the Moravian Settlements in the
Forks of the Delaware in 1751." THE JERSEYMAN 3
(1895):8-11.

> Apr 1751. Travel journal from Oxford Furnace in
> the Jerseys; narrative account of Moravians and
> their settlements.

BLAIR, JOHN, 1687-1771   427

Tyler, Lyon G. "Diary of John Blair." WILLIAM AND
MARY COLLEGE QUARTERLY, 1st ser. 7 (1898-1899):
133-153; 8 (1899-1900):1-17.

> Jan-Dec 1751. Diary of the president of the Council
> of Virginia; line-a-day almanac notes on outstand-
> ing local and private items; plantation life; some
> longer political entries.

CROGHAN, GEORGE, d. 1782   428

In EARLY WESTERN TRAVELS, edited by Reuben G.
Thwaites, vol. 1, pp. 58-69.

PENNSYLVANIA COLONIAL RECORDS 5 (1842):530-536.

In EARLY HISTORY OF WESTERN PENNSYLVANIA, by
Israel D. Rupp, app., pp. 75-98. Pittsburgh: D.W.
Kauffman; Harrisburg: W.O. Hickok, 1846.

Extract in THE OLDEN TIME, edited by Neville B.
Craig, vol. 1, pp. 135-136.

> May 1751. Journals of travel and transactions with
> the Indians; mostly containing minutes and speech-
> es; treaty with the Ohio Indians.

"Journal of George Croghan." AMERICANA 10 (1915):
677-683.

> Jan-Feb 1753. At Logstown.

In EARLY WESTERN TRAVELS, vol. 1, 72 81; PENNSYL-
VANIA COLONIAL RECORDS 5 (1842):731-735; EARLY
HISTORY OF WESTERN PENNSYLVANIA, app., pp. 50-53.

> Jan 1754. Conditions on the Ohio.

"Journal of Captain George Croghan, and the Treaty at
Easton, etc., 1757." PENNSYLVANIA ARCHIVES, 2d ser.,
vol. 6, pp. 527-538.

> May-Aug 1757. Journey from Lancaster and negotia-
> tions for a treaty with Teedyuscung and other
> Indians at Easton, Pennsylvania.

PENNSYLVANIA ARCHIVES, 1st ser., vol. 3, pp. 560-
563.

> Nov-Dec 1758. From Pittsburgh to the Delaware
> Indians. Author given as Christian Frederick Post,
> but Thwaites, vol. 1, p. 101 note, identifies him
> as Croghan.

Wainwright, Nicholas B., ed. "George Croghan's Journal." PENNSYLVANIA MAGAZINE OF HISTORY AND BIOG-
RAPHY 71 (1947):303-444.

> 1759-1763. British-Indian frontier diplomacy be-
> tween the Easton Treaty of 1758 and Pontiac's
> uprising in 1763.

"Capt. Croghan's Journal to Presque Isle and Intelli-
gence Received Lately." MASSACHUSETTS HISTORICAL
SOCIETY COLLECTIONS, 4th ser. 9 (1871):283-289.

> Jul 1760. Fort Pitt to Presque Isle.

In EARLY WESTERN TRAVELS, vol. 1, pp. 100-125.

"Croghan's Journal." MASSACHUSETTS HISTORICAL SO-
CIETY COLLECTIONS, 4th ser. 9 (1871):362-379.

Oct 1760–Jan 1761. Expedition under Major Robert Rogers to secure possession of Detroit and other western posts.

In THE NEW REGIME, edited by Clarence W. Alvord and Clarence E. Carter, pp. 1–23.

PENNSYLVANIA COLONIAL RECORDS 9 (1846):250–256.

Feb–May 1765. Negotiations with Indians at Fort Pitt.

In THE NEW REGIME, pp. 38–52.

In PIONEER HISTORY, by Samuel P. Hildreth, pp. 68–85. Cincinnati: H.W. Derby; New York: A.S. Barnes, 1848.

In DOCUMENTS RELATIVE TO THE COLONIAL HISTORY OF THE STATE OF NEW YORK, edited by E.B. O'Callaghan, vol. 7, pp. 779–788.

May–Sep 1765. Official journal and report of trip down Ohio River to Shawneetown; capture by Indians and release; meeting with Pontiac; return to Detroit.

In THE NEW REGIME, pp. 23–38.

MONTHLY JOURNAL OF AMERICAN GEOLOGY 1 (1831):257–272.

In A HISTORY OF THE COMMONWEALTH OF KENTUCKY, 2d ed., rev. and enl., by Mann Butler, app. Cincinnati: J.A. James; Louisville: The author, 1836.

In THE OLDEN TIME, vol. 1, pp. 404–415.

May–Sep 1765. The personal journal of the above events, omitting meeting with Pontiac and Indian affairs; largely topographical.

In EARLY WESTERN TRAVELS, vol. 1, pp. 126–166.

May–Sep 1765. A combined version of official and personal journals.

GEORGE CROGHAN'S JOURNAL OF HIS TRIP TO DETROIT IN 1767. Edited by Howard H. Peckham. Ann Arbor: University of Michigan Press; London: H. Milford, Oxford University Press, 1939.

Oct–Dec 1767. From Fort Pitt to Detroit and return; council with Indians.

CUTHBERTSON, JOHN, 1719–1791   429

REGISTER OF MARRIAGES AND BAPTISMS PERFORMED BY REV. JOHN CUTHBERTSON. Edited by S. Helen Fields. Washington, D.C., and Lancaster, Pa.: Lancaster Press, 1934. 301 pp. Diary, pp. 69–260.

Extracts and discussion of the diary in "The Diary of John Cuthbertson, Missionary to the Covenanters of Colonial Pennsylvania," by William L. Fisk, Jr. PENNSYLVANIA MAGAZINE OF HISTORY AND BIOGRAPHY 73 (1949):441–458.

1751–1790. Covenanting minister's horseback journeys; preaching and clerical work; mostly in Pennsylvania, but also in Maryland, Delaware, Virginia, New Jersey, New York, Connecticut and Massachusetts; extracts arranged geographically and genealogically.

MASON, JONAS, 1708–1801   430

Banks, Charles E. "Almanac Notes." OLD TIMES 8 (1884):1188–1189.

Feb–Nov 1751. A few brief, miscellaneous notes of local affairs at North Yarmouth, Maine.

PICQUET, FRANCOIS, 1708–1781   431

Jezierski, John V., ed. "A 1751 Journal of Abbé François Picquet." NEW YORK HISTORICAL SOCIETY QUARTERLY 54 (1970):360–381.

Jun–Jul 1751. French Catholic priest's trip in area around Lake Ontario; gathering Indian converts to his mission; assessing the regional situation in terms of British, French and Indian relations.

WILLIS, BENJAMIN, 1686–1767   432

"Extracts from Dea. Willis's Diary." MEDFORD HISTORICAL REGISTER 5 (1902):95.

1751–1764. Brief notes of weather, sickness, prayers of deacon in Medford, Massachusetts.

1752

ANON.   433

A JOURNAL OF THE PROCEEDINGS OF JACOB WENDELL. By Massachusetts Colony Commissioners to Treat with the Eastern Indians. Boston: Printed by J. Draper, 1752. 16 pp.

Oct 1752. Treaty journal of conference held with eastern Indians at St. George's.

BALCH, EBENEZER, 1723–1808   434

In BALCH LEAFLETS; A COLLECTION OF HISTORICAL AND GENEALOGICAL NOTES, vol. 1. Salem, Mass.: Eben Putnam, 1896.

1752–1757. Religious diary; good insight into religious fervor of the time; at Wethersfield, Connecticut.

BILLING, EDWARD, 1707–1760   435

In WILLARD'S HISTORY OF GREENFIELD, by David Willard, pp. 119–122. Greenfield, Mass.: Kneeland & Eastman, 1838.

1752–1756. Clergyman's diary; a few extracts of personal and local affairs at Greenfield.

BOSOMWORTH, THOMAS   436

In DOCUMENTS RELATING TO INDIAN AFFAIRS, edited by William L. McDowell, vol. 1, pp. 268–337. Colonial Records of South Carolina. Columbia: South Carolina Archives Department, 1958.

Jul 1752–Jan 1753. Journal of the Indian agent in the Creek Nation from time of appointment at Charleston; husband of Creek Indian who played important role in continuing negotiations to maintain peace.

BUCKLES, JOHN   437

In DOCUMENTS RELATING TO INDIAN AFFAIRS, edited by William L. McDowell, vol. 1, pp. 382–385, 509–510. Colonial Records of South Carolina. Columbia: South Carolina Archives Department, 1958.

Jun 1752–May 1753. Indian agent's journal of conflicts between Chickasaw and Choctaw Indians in South Carolina.

CARTER, LANDON, 1710–1778   438

THE DIARY OF COLONEL LANDON CARTER OF SABINE HALL, 1752–1778. Edited by Jack P. Greene. Virginia Historical Society Documents, vol. 4. Charlottesville:

University Press of Virginia for the Virginia Historical Society, 1965. 2 vols.

> 1752-1778. Plantation diary of classically educated Virginian of philosophical and scientific turn of mind; much on Carter's personal and public life; detailed account of plantation management, from livestock to crops; the difficulties of agriculture based on slave labor; diseases prevalent among man and beast and the dire remedies of the time; service in the Virginia House of Burgesses, with reports on its deliberations; views on the American Revolution; a monumental diary of considerable importance as social history.

"The Diary of Col. Landon Carter." WILLIAM AND MARY COLLEGE QUARTERLY, 1st ser. 13 (1904-1905):45-53, 157-164, 219-224; 14 (1905-1906):38-44, 181-186, 246-253; 15 (1906-1907):15-20, 86-87, 205-221; 16 (1907-1908):149-156, 257-268; 17 (1908-1909):9-18; 18 (1909-1910):37-44; 20 (1910-1911):173-185; 21 (1911-1912):172-181.

Extracts in PLANTATION AND FRONTIER DOCUMENTS, edited by Ulrich B. Phillips, vol. 1, pp. 300-324, 326-328; vol. 2, pp. 33-34.

> 1770-1776.

MUELLER, JOSEPH 439

In RECORDS OF THE MORAVIANS IN NORTH CAROLINA, edited by Adelaide L. Fries, vol. 2, pp. 521-525.

> 1752-1753. Moravian travel journal; written post facto but arranged by dates; from Bethlehem, Pennsylvania, to North Carolina and return; difficulties of trip; nursing fever-stricken Brethren. Translated from the German.

RAMSOUR (or RAMSAUER), DAVID, d. 1785 440

"A Rare Old Diary." PENN GERMANIA, n.s. 2 (1913): 22-25.

> 1752 1759. Farmer's diary from Lincoln County, North Carolina; partly financial memoranda, partly record of work on plantation; very interesting language, German-English combinations.

RAVENEL, HENRY, 1729-1785 441

In RAVENEL RECORDS: A HISTORY AND GENEALOGY OF THE HUGUENOT FAMILY OF RAVENEL, OF SOUTH CAROLINA, by Henry Edmund Ravenel, pp. 212-220, 223-225. Atlanta: Franklin Printing and Publishing, 1898.

Extract in PLANTATION AND FRONTIER DOCUMENTS, edited by Ulrich B. Phillips, vol. 2, p. 91.

> 1752-1822. Domestic work, farming, weather, family affairs, local events and memoranda of births and deaths in Hanover, South Carolina. Continued by unknown diarist.

TRENT, WILLIAM, 1715-1787? 442

JOURNAL OF CAPTAIN WILLIAM TRENT, edited by Alfred T. Goodman, pp. 83-105. Cincinnati: Printed by R. Clarke for W. Dodge, 1871. 117 pp. Reprint. New York: Arno, 1971.

In THE WILDERNESS TRAIL, by Charles A. Hanna, vol. 2, pp. 291-298.

> Jul-Aug 1752. Travel journal from Wastown to Pickawillany; good account of Twightee (Miami) Indians in Ohio; largely reports of speeches, but many descriptions.

In FORT PITT AND LETTERS FROM THE FRONTIER, compiled by Mary Carson O'Hara Darlington, pp. 84-110. Pittsburgh: J.R. Weldin, 1892.

Volwiler, A.T. "William Trent's Journal at Fort Pitt, 1763." MISSISSIPPI VALLEY HISTORICAL REVIEW 11 (1924-1925):390-413.

> May-Sep 1763. Trading journal at Fort Pitt; trouble with Indians. Journal ascribed by Darlington to Captain S. Ecuyer.

1753

ANON. 443

In TRAVELS IN THE AMERICAN COLONIES, edited by Newton D. Mereness, pp. 325-356.

Hinke, William J. and Kemper, Charles E. "Moravian Diaries of Travels Through Virginia." VIRGINIA MAGAZINE OF HISTORY AND BIOGRAPHY 12 (1904-1905):134-153, 271-281.

> Oct-Nov 1753. Moravian travel journal; from Bethlehem, Pennsylvania, to Bethabara, North Carolina; extensive details of travel, services, etc.; an interesting record. Translated from the German, with some interesting German spellings of place names.

ADAMS, JOHN, 1735-1826 444

THE EARLIEST DIARY OF JOHN ADAMS: JUNE 1753-APRIL 1754, SEPTEMBER 1758-JANUARY 1759. Edited by Lyman H. Butterfield. The Adams Papers, ser. 1. Cambridge: Belknap Press of Harvard University Press, 1966. 120 pp.

DIARY AND AUTOBIOGRAPHY OF JOHN ADAMS. Edited by Lyman H. Butterfield. The Adams Papers, ser. 1. New York: Atheneum, 1965. 5 vols.

THE WORKS OF JOHN ADAMS. Edited by Charles Francis Adams. Boston: Little, Brown, 1856. 3 vols. Reprint. New York: AMS, 1971. Diary, vols. 2-3.

Extracts relating to Boston Tea Party in "Diary of John Adams." MASSACHUSETTS HISTORICAL SOCIETY PROCEEDINGS, 1st ser. 13 (1873-1875):191-192.

Extracts in AMERICAN HISTORY TOLD BY CONTEMPORARIES, edited by Albert B. Hart, pp. 220-223; DIARY OF AMERICA, edited by Josef Berger, pp. 106-109.

Discussed in AMERICAN DIARY LITERATURE, by Steven E. Kagle, pp. 179-182.

> 1753-1796. Public work, private resolutions and activities, travel abroad, residence in France and return, of second president of the United States.

"Extracts from John Adams' Diary Relating to James Putman, Esq." DANVERS HISTORICAL SOCIETY COLLECTIONS 20 (1932):58-61.

> 1756, 1758, 1771-1772. Scattered entries pertaining to Putnam, a distinguished Massachusetts lawyer in whose Worcester office Adams studied law.

BAILEY, JACOB, 1731-1808 445

In THE FRONTIER MISSIONARY, by William S. Bartlet, pp. 11-171 passim. Boston: Ide and Dutton, 1853; Protestant Episcopal Historical Society Collections, vol. 2. New York: Stanford and Swords, 1853.

> 1753-1779. Clergyman's diary; begun at Harvard, with visits and journeys to New England towns; schoolmastering at Kingston; later, mostly church affairs and records of Pownalborough, Maine.

COOPER, SAMUEL, 1725–1783   446

"Diary of Rev. Samuel Cooper." NEW ENGLAND HISTOR-ICAL AND GENEALOGICAL REGISTER 41 (1887):388–391.

"Notes from the Rev. Samuel Cooper's Interleaved Almanacs." NEW ENGLAND HISTORICAL AND GENEALOG-ICAL REGISTER 55 (1901):145–149.

"Diary of Rev. Samuel Cooper." HISTORICAL MAGAZINE 10, suppl. 2 (1866):82–84.

> 1753–1769 (with large gaps). Massachusetts clergy-man's diary; brief daily entries; baptisms, notes for sermons, some personal and public affairs.

"Diary of Samuel Cooper. AMERICAN HISTORICAL REVIEW 6 (1900–1901):301–341.

> 1775–1776. Notes relating to the Revolution; Lexing-ton, siege of Boston; travel and religious work in Massachusetts.

DAVIES, SAMUEL, 1723–1761   447

THE REVEREND SAMUEL DAVIES ABROAD: THE DIARY OF A JOURNEY TO ENGLAND AND SCOTLAND, 1753–55. Edited by George W. Pilcher. Urbana: University of Illinois Press, 1967. 176 pp.

In SKETCHES OF VIRGINIA, HISTORICAL AND BIOGRA-PHICAL, by William H. Foote, pp. 228–281. Philadel-phia: W.S. Martien, 1850–1855.

> 1753–1755. Diary of Presbyterian minister from Virginia traveling in England and Scotland to raise money for College of New Jersey (now Prince-ton University) and for Indian missions; preaching and visiting; meetings with Methodists Wesley and Whitefield, as well as Presbyterians, Baptists and other dissenters; evidence of wide reading; good literary style.

GRUBE, BERNARD ADAM, 1715–1808   448

"A Missionary's Tour to Shamokin and the West Branch of the Susquehanna, 1753." PENNSYLVANIA MAGAZINE OF HISTORY AND BIOGRAPHY 34 (1915):440–444.

> Aug 1753. Moravian missionary's tour to Shamokin and notes of Moravian affairs in Indian towns along west branch.

HAWLEY, GIDEON, 1727–1807   449

In DOCUMENTARY HISTORY OF THE STATE OF NEW YORK, edited by E.B. O'Callaghan, vol. 3, pp. 1031–1046.

> May–Jun 1753. Missionary work by a newly or-dained clergyman; journey to Oquago (now Wind-sor), New York.

MORAVIAN CONGREGATIONS, NORTH CAROLINA   450

In RECORDS OF THE MORAVIANS IN NORTH CAROLINA, edited by Adelaide L. Fries, vol. 1, 1752–1771; vol. 2, 1752–1775; vol. 3, 1776–1779; vol. 4, 1780–1783; vol. 5, 1784–1792; vol. 6, 1793–1808; vol. 7, 1809–1822; vol. 8, 1823–1837; vol. 9, 1838–1847; vol. 10, 1841–1851; vol. 11, 1852–1879.

> 1753–1879. The work and worship of the Moravian congregations in Bethania, Bethabara, Ens, Fried-berg, Friedland, Hope, Salem and Wachovia; notes of travel between the various settlements; domestic and civic life of the communities; notes on new-comers; religious observances, love-feasts; troubles with Indians; genealogical facts; the slavery question; the shift from the German lan-guage to the English; relations with churches of other denominations; occasional individual disa-greement with the authority of the church; extension of the Moravian churches.

PRINCE, JONATHAN, 1734–1759   451

"Jonathan Prince, Jr., His Book." GENEALOGICAL QUAR-TERLY MAGAZINE 2 (1901):51–53.

> Jan–Dec 1753. Massachusetts clergyman's brief notes of births, deaths, weather, visits, sickness, and local affairs in Danvers, Massachusetts.

1754

ANON.   452

A JOURNAL OF THE PROCEEDINGS AT TWO CONFERENCES. By Massachusetts Colony Governor, 1741–1757 (William Shirley). Boston: Printed by J. Draper, 1754. 27 pp.

> Jun–Jul 1754. Treaty journal covering two confer-ences held at Falmouth, Massachusetts, and later at Portland, Maine, between William Shirley and the Norridgewock Indians.

ANON.   453

In PENNSYLVANIA ARCHIVES, 1st ser., vol. 2, pp. 159–166.

> Jun–Jul 1754. Notes by officer in command at "Fort on Northkill"; trouble with marauding Indians; good frontier journal.

BARBER, JOHN, 1708–1754?   454

"Journal of Capt. Eleazer Melvin's Company." NEW ENGLAND HISTORICAL AND GENEALOGICAL REGISTER 27 (1873):281–285.

> May–Aug 1754. Military journal of Shirley's ex-pedition; scattered notes.

BROWNE, CHARLOTTE   455

In COLONIAL CAPTIVITIES, edited by Isabel M. Calder, pp. 169–200.

Harrison, Fairfax, ed. "With Braddock's Army: Mrs. Browne's Diary in Virginia and Maryland." VIRGINIA MAGAZINE OF HISTORY AND BIOGRAPHY 32 (1924):305–320.

> 1754–1756. Journal of hospital matron with British forces under Braddock during French and Indian War; entertaining record of personal affairs, hardships, illness, travel through Atlantic states.

DE LERY, JOSEPH GASPARD CHAUSSEGROS, 1721–1797   456

Keeler, Lucy E. "Old Fort Sandoski of 1754." OHIO ARCHAEOLOGICAL AND HISTORICAL QUARTERLY 17 (1908): 357–430.

> Aug 1754. Military journal of French engineer; operations around fort.

DE VILLIERS, NEYON   457

In DOCUMENTS RELATIVE TO THE COLONIAL HISTORY OF THE STATE OF NEW YORK, edited by E.B. O'Callaghan, vol. 10, pp. 261–262.

> Jul 1754. Extract from French officer's journal; defeat of English by French and Indians at the "Beautiful River." Translated.

FREDERICK, CHARLES 458

In MORAVIAN JOURNALS RELATING TO CENTRAL NEW YORK, edited by William M. Beauchamp, pp. 197-222.

1754-1755. Moravian travel journal; journey with David Zeisberger from Bethlehem, Pennsylvania, to Onondaga; residence, missionary work, and return.

Apr-May 1766. Extracts covering journey and mission to Cayuga.

FRIIS, JOHN JACOB 459

In RECORDS OF THE MORAVIANS IN NORTH CAROLINA, edited by Adelaide L. Fries, vol. 2, pp. 529-533.

Apr-Jul 1754. Letter-diary, written originally in English, of Moravian pastor; intimate glimpse of Moravian life at Bethabara.

HENDRY, ANTHONY 460

Burpee, Lawrence J. "York Factory to the Blackfeet Country." ROYAL SOCIETY OF CANADA PROCEEDINGS AND TRANSACTIONS, 3rd ser. 1 (1907):307-354.

1754-1755. Fur trader's journal; journey from York Factory of Hudson's Bay Company to the Blackfoot country, stirring up trade and off-setting French competition; 1,000 miles inland to South Saskatchewan River; important geographically, and interesting for details of Blackfoot Indians; good, simple style.

MANIGAULT, ANN, 1703-1782 461

Webber, Mabel L., ed. "Extracts from the Journal of Mrs. Ann Manigault." SOUTH CAROLINA HISTORICAL AND GENEALOGICAL MAGAZINE 20 (1919):57-63, 128-141, 204-212, 256-259; 21 (1920):10-23, 59-72, 112-120.

1754-1781. Half-line entries of social, domestic, personal and religious affairs.

PATTEN, MATTHEW, 1719-1795 462

THE DIARY OF MATTHEW PATTEN OF BEDFORD, N.H. Concord, N.H.: Rumford Printing Co., 1903. 545 pp.

1754-1788. Short entries of his everyday affairs and local events; a farmer's view of the Revolution; the length and consistency of the diary make it a valuable counterpart to the diaries of Joshua Hempstead and "Nailer" Tom Hazard.

POWERS, PETER, 1707-1757 463

In HISTORY OF THE TOWN OF BRISTOL, GRAFTON COUNTY, NEW HAMPSHIRE, by Richard W. Musgrove, vol. 1, pp. 25-26. Bristol: Printed by R.W. Musgrove, 1904.

Jun 1754. Extracts covering military expedition from Massachusetts to explore the northern country, as far as Dalton.

POWNALL, THOMAS, 1722-1805 464

In THE REMEMBRANCER, vol. 5, pp. 486-490. London: Printed for J. Almon, 1775-1784.

"Governor Thomas Pownall's Description of the Streets and the Main Roads about Philadelphia." PENNSYLVANIA MAGAZINE OF HISTORY AND BIOGRAPHY 18 (1894): 211-218.

1754. Travel journal; notes on Pennsylvania roads.

Williamson, J., ed. "Journal of the Voyage of Gov. Thomas Pownall, from Boston to the Penobscot River."

MAINE HISTORICAL SOCIETY COLLECTIONS 5 (1857): 365-387.

May 1759. Treaty journal; voyage to Penobscot; notes on negotiations with Indians, and on Fort Pownall; possibly written by Pownall's secretary, but signed by Pownall.

SEWALL, DAVID, 1735-1825 465

"Father Flynt's Journey to Portsmouth." MASSACHUSETTS HISTORICAL SOCIETY PROCEEDINGS, 1st ser. 16 (1878): 5-11.

Jun 1754. Journey with his tutor, Henry Flynt, from Harvard to Portsmouth; very entertaining.

SPICER, JACOB, d. 1765 466

"Extract from a Diary." NEW JERSEY HISTORICAL SOCIETY PROCEEDINGS 3 (1848-1849):103-104, 192-198.

CAPE MAY COUNTY HISTORICAL AND GENEALOGICAL REGISTER 1 (1933-1934); 2 (1934-1935).

1754-1764. Memorandum book; domestic affairs.

Ellis, William A., ed. "Diary of Jacob Spicer." NEW JERSEY HISTORICAL SOCIETY PROCEEDINGS 63 (1945): 37-50, 82-117, 175-188.

1755-1756. Diary of member of the Provincial Assembly and co-compiler of the laws of New Jersey in Leaming and Spicer's GRANTS AND CONCESSIONS; record of daily activities, focusing on business, legal and government affairs.

STILES, EZRA, 1727-1795 467

"Diary of Ezra Stiles." MASSACHUSETTS HISTORICAL SOCIETY PROCEEDINGS, 2d ser. 7 (1891-1892):338-345.

Sep-Oct 1754. Horseback journey from New Haven to Philadelphia and return; charming social details.

EXTRACTS FROM THE ITINERARIES AND OTHER MISCELLANIES OF EZRA STILES. Edited by Franklin B. Dexter. New Haven: Yale University Press, 1916. 620 pp.

1755-1794. Travel diaries; notes of persons and places during his many journeys in New England, etc.

THE LITERARY DIARY OF EZRA STILES. Edited by Franklin B. Dexter. New York: C. Scribner's Sons, 1901. 3 vols.

Jastrow, Morris. "References to Jews in the (Literary) Diary of Ezra Stiles." AMERICAN JEWISH HISTORICAL SOCIETY 10 (1902):5-36.

EZRA STILES AND THE JEWS: SELECTED PASSAGES FROM HIS LITERARY DIARY CONCERNING JEWS AND JUDAISM. Critical and explanatory notes by George A. Kohut. New York: P. Cowen, 1902. 155 pp.

Extracts in "The Literary Diary of Ezra Stiles," by Harrison J. Thornton. JOURNAL OF AMERICAN HISTORY 26 (1932):146-170.

1769-1795. Religious, scholarly, and literary interests of president of Yale; social news and gossip; very detailed and consistent entries; a most valuable diary.

Hill, Amelia L., ed. "The News of the Evacuation of Boston and the Declaration of Independence." NEW ENGLAND MAGAZINE 14 (1896):317-322.

Mar-Aug 1776. Extracts from LITERARY DIARY.

"Extracts from President Stiles' Diary." LONG ISLAND HISTORICAL SOCIETY MEMOIRS 2 (1869):480-481.

Aug-Sep 1776. News of military activities on Long Island.

WINSLOW, JOHN, 1703-1774   468

In MILITARY AFFAIRS IN NORTH AMERICA, 1748-1765, edited by Stanley M. Pargellis, pp. 54-58. New York and London: D. Appleton-Century, 1936.

1754. Journey to Kennebec to build forts and maintain Indian alliance.

"Journal of Colonel John Winslow, of the Provincial Troops, While Engaged in Removing the Acadian French." NOVA SCOTIA HISTORICAL SOCIETY COLLECTIONS 3 (1883):71-196.

"Journal of Colonel John Winslow, of the Provincial Troops, While Engaged in the Siege of Fort Beausejour." NOVA SCOTIA HISTORICAL SOCIETY COLLECTIONS 4 (1884):113-246.

Extracts in AMERICAN HISTORY TOLD BY CONTEMPORARIES, edited by Albert B. Hart, vol. 2, pp. 360-365.

1755. An orderly book with brief diary entries covering the siege of Fort Beausejour and deportation of French Acadians.

1755

ANON.   469

In BRADDOCK'S DEFEAT: THE JOURNALS OF CAPTAIN ROBERT CHOLMLEY'S BATMAN; THE JOURNAL OF A BRITISH OFFICER; HALKETT'S ORDERLY BOOK, edited by Charles Hamilton, pp. 5-36. Norman: University of Oklahoma Press, 1959.

Evidence of authenticity in articles by Paul E. Kopperman, WESTERN PENNSYLVANIA HISTORICAL MAGAZINE 62 (1979):197-220; 64 (1981):269-287.

Jan-Aug 1755. Batman's diary of events before, during and after the defeat of Braddock during French and Indian War; wilderness marching and camping, scrounging for food, severe military discipline; attack, chaotic action, defeat; the only known eye-witness account written immediately after the battle; interesting spellings.

ANON.   470

In HISTORIC HIGHWAYS OF AMERICA, by Archer B. Hulbert, vol. 4, pp. 83-107.

THE MORRIS JOURNAL, by Capt. Harry Gordon. London: 1854. Reprint. In THE HISTORY OF AN EXPEDITION AGAINST FORT DU QUESNE IN 1755, by Winthrop Sargent, pp. 359-389. Historical Society of Pennsylvania Memoirs, vol. 5. Philadelphia: Historical Society of Pennsylvania, 1855.

Apr-Aug 1755. Journal of one of thirty sailors with Braddock's expedition; march of Dunbar's brigade through Maryland and Virginia; military details; accounts of Indians and their customs; the battle; long and good descriptions; some notes post facto.

ANON.   471

In HISTORY OF NORTHAMPTON, LEHIGH, MONROE, CARBON, AND SCHUYLKILL COUNTIES, compiled by Israel D. Rupp, pp. 463-477.

Jun-Aug 1755? Activities at Fort North Kill; principally scouting notes.

ANON.   472

In BRADDOCK'S DEFEAT: THE JOURNALS OF CAPTAIN ROBERT CHOLMLEY'S BATMAN; THE JOURNAL OF A BRITISH OFFICER; HALKETT'S ORDERLY BOOK, edited by Charles Hamilton, pp. 39-58. Norman: University of Oklahoma Press, 1959.

Evidence of authenticity in articles by Paul E. Kopperman, WESTERN PENNSYLVANIA HISTORICAL MAGAZINE 62 (1979):197-220; 64 (1981):269-287.

Jul 1755. British officer's account, written a few weeks after, of General Braddock's defeat; wilderness marching, hauling heavy artillery over difficult terrain; hunger of the troops; utter confusion and defeat of British under Indian and French attack.

ANON.   473

In DOCUMENTS RELATIVE TO THE COLONIAL HISTORY OF THE STATE OF NEW YORK, edited by E.B. O'Callaghan, vol. 10, pp. 337-340.

In PENNSYLVANIA ARCHIVES, 3d ser., vol. 6, pp. 334-338.

Jul-Sep 1755. Official journal of operations of the French army; from Quebec to Lake Champlain, and battle there.

ANON.   474

In DOCUMENTS RELATIVE TO THE COLONIAL HISTORY OF THE STATE OF NEW YORK, edited by E.B. O'Callaghan, vol. 10, pp. 401-406.

Oct 1755-Jun 1756. Official French journal of occurrences in Canada; military details and news.

BALDWIN, JEDUTHAN   475

Calef, John H., ed. "Extracts from the Diary of a Revolutionary Patriot." MILITARY SERVICE INSTITUTION OF THE UNITED STATES JOURNAL 39 (1906):123-130.

Dec 1755-May 1756. Officer's account of expedition against Crown Point; duties and events at Fort William Henry; "scout" to Crown Point and back.

THE REVOLUTIONARY JOURNAL OF COL. JEDUTHAN BALDWIN. Edited by Thomas Williams Baldwin. Bangor: Printed for the De Burians by C.H. Glass, 1906. 164 pp. Reprint. New York: New York Times, 1971.

1775-1778. Military diary with personal notes; siege of Boston; New York campaign; expedition against Crown Point; march to Canada; Burgoyne's surrender; mostly brief entries, but some long ones; good picture of life of troops; interesting spellings.

"Baldwin's Diary." FORT TICONDEROGA MUSEUM BULLETIN 4, no. 6 (1938):10-40.

Calef, John H., ed. "Extracts from the Diary of a Revolutionary Patriot." MILITARY SERVICE INSTITUTION OF THE UNITED STATES JOURNAL 39 (1906):257-273.

1776-1777. Maneuvers around Ticonderoga.

BURK, JOHN, 1717-1784   476

In HISTORY OF THE TOWN OF BERNARDSTON, by Lucy C. Kellogg, pp. 42-46. Greenfield, Mass.: Press of E.A. Hall, 1902.

Jul-Sep 1755. Brief notes of marches, camp life; Saratoga, Crown Point.

DE MONTREUIL, Chevalier   477

In DOCUMENTS RELATIVE TO THE COLONIAL HISTORY OF THE STATE OF NEW YORK, edited by E.B. O'Callaghan, vol. 10, pp. 335-337.

Aug-Sep 1755. Account of battle of Lake George by Baron Dieskau's adjutant general. Translated from the French.

DE VAUDREUIL, M.   478

In DOCUMENTS RELATIVE TO THE COLONIAL HISTORY OF THE STATE OF NEW YORK, edited by E.B. O'Callaghan, vol. 10, pp. 297-299.

> May-Jun 1755. Abstract of sea journal; journey of fleet under De la Mothe from Brest to Quebec. Translated from the French.

DWIGHT, NATHANIEL, 1711-1784   479

Dwight, Melatiah E., ed. "The Journal of Capt. Nathaniel Dwight of Belchertown, Mass." NEW YORK GENEALOGICAL AND BIOGRAPHICAL RECORD 33 (1902):3-10, 65-70.

> Sep-Dec 1755. Battle of Lake George; Crown Point expedition; building of Fort William Henry.

FIEDMONT, LOUIS THOMAS JACAU,   480
sieur de, b. ca. 1720

THE SIEGE OF BEAUSEJOUR IN 1755; A JOURNAL OF THE ATTACK ON BEAUSEJOUR, edited by John C. Webster. Saint John: New Brunswick Museum, 1836. 42 pp.

> Mar-Jun 1755. Journal of attack on Beausejour by officer in charge of French artillery. Translated from the French.

FISHER, DANIEL   481

"Extracts from the Diary of Daniel Fisher." PENNSYLVANIA MAGAZINE OF HISTORY AND BIOGRAPHY 17 (1893):236-278.

> May-Aug 1755. Extracts of diary kept mainly at Philadelphia: long entries describing persons and places.

FLEET, MARY, b. 1729   482

"Extracts from the Diary of Miss Mary Fleet, Boston." NEW ENGLAND HISTORICAL AND GENEALOGICAL REGISTER 19 (1865):59-61.

> 1755-1803. Brief, scattered notes of social and church affairs of the Old South Church, Boston.

FRANKLAND, Sir CHARLES HENRY, 1716-1768   483

In SIR CHARLES HENRY FRANKLAND, BARONET: OR, BOSTON IN THE COLONIAL TIMES, by Elias Nason, pp. 51-97. Albany: J. Munsell, 1865.

> 1755-1767. Travel diary; stay in Lisbon; notes on business, private and social matters in New England; fashions and current events.

FROST, EDMUND, 1715?-1775   484

"Frost Diary." NEW ENGLAND HISTORICAL AND GENEALOGICAL REGISTER 55 (1901):441-442.

> 1755-1759. A few notes of outstanding family events.

GATES, JOHN, 1713-1797   485

"Stow, and John Gate's Diary." WORCESTER SOCIETY OF ANTIQUITY PROCEEDINGS (1898):267-280.

> 1755-1789. Few occasional entries, mostly on religion and public affairs in Stow, Massachusetts.

GILBERT, JAMES, b. 1730   486

MAGAZINE OF NEW ENGLAND HISTORY 3 (1893):188-195.

> Jul-Sep 1755. Military journal covering march from Albany to Lake George; skirmishes and battle; interesting spellings.

GODFREY, RICHARD, b. 1711   487

In THE PEIRCE FAMILY OF THE OLD COLONY, by Ebenezer W. Peirce, pp. 109-114. Boston: Printed for the author, D. Clapp & Son, 1870.

In HISTORY OF TAUNTON, MASSACHUSETTS, by Samuel H. Emery, pp. 419-424. Syracuse, N.Y.: D. Mason, 1893.

> Jun-Oct 1755. With Major Godfrey's company on expedition to Crown Point; Taunton, New York, Albany, Saratoga; interesting details of camp life and discontents; vigorous account of the victory; some interesting spellings.

HAWLEY, ELISHA, 1726-1755   488

In HISTORY OF NORTHAMPTON, MASSACHUSETTS, by James R. Trumbull, vol. 2, pp. 254-258. Northampton: Press of Gazette Printing Co., 1902.

> Jun-Sep 1755. Brief military details of expedition against Crown Point; Fort Lyman.

HEBRON, PENNSYLVANIA, MORAVIAN CONGREGATION   489

Heisey, John W., trans. and ed. "Extracts from the Diary of the Moravian Pastors of the Hebron Church, Lebanon." PENNSYLVANIA HISTORY 34 (1967):44-63.

> 1755-1814. Raids by hostile Indians during the French and Indian War; difficulties experienced by those who on religious grounds would neither fight nor take loyalty oaths during the Revolution; billeting of two hundred Hessian prisoners of war in the parsonage; news and rumors of the war's progress; events in the congregation and community.

In NOTES AND QUERIES, edited by William H. Egle, 4th ser., vol. 2.

"Extracts from the Records of the Moravian Congregation at Hebron, Pennsylvania." PENNSYLVANIA MAGAZINE OF HISTORY AND BIOGRAPHY 18 (1894): 449-462.

Redsecker, J.H. "The Hebron Diary During the Revolutionary Period." LEBANON COUNTY HISTORICAL SOCIETY PUBLICATIONS 1 (1898):8-16.

> 1775-1783. Life and work of Moravians at New Lebanon; some very interesting general entries; quarrels with the Hessians.

HERVEY, WILLIAM, 1732-1815   490

JOURNALS OF THE HON. WILLIAM HERVEY, IN NORTH AMERICA AND EUROPE, FROM 1755 TO 1814. Bury St. Edmunds: Paul & Matthew, 1906. 548 pp. American journals, pp. 1-17, 18-46, 47-52, 65-184.

> 1755. Brief journal of march with Shirley's regiment from Boston to Lake Ontario.

> Summer 1756. Work on roads and forts under Shirley.

> 1758. Ticonderoga campaign.

> 1760-1763. Full journal of Amherst's campaign; orderly books at Montreal.

HILL, JAMES, 1735-1811   491

Moffett, Edna V., ed. "The Diary of a Private on the First Expedition to Crown Point." NEW ENGLAND QUARTERLY 5 (1932):602-618.

> May-Dec 1755. Brief entries describing first Crown

Point expedition; battle of Lake George; interesting spellings.

JOHNSON, Sir WILLIAM, 1715–1774   492

In DOCUMENTARY HISTORY OF THE STATE OF NEW YORK, edited by E.B. O'Callaghan, vol. 4, pp. 167–185.

Sep 1755–Jul 1756. Brief reports in journal form made by Johnson's scouts; reconnoitering from Lake George to Fort Frederick and Crown Point fort, etc. Among the scouts were Robert Rogers, Israel Putnam, William Symes, James Connor, Samuel Angell, Michael Thorley, Lieutenant Waterbury.

In DOCUMENTS RELATIVE TO THE COLONIAL HISTORY OF THE STATE OF NEW YORK, edited by E.B. O'Callaghan, vol. 7, pp. 91–116, 130–161, 171–200, 229–265, 324–333, 378–394.

Extracts in PENNSYLVANIA ARCHIVES, 2d ser., vol. 6, pp. 461–515.

1756–1762. Nine journals, kept by superintendent of Indian affairs, of public conferences held with Indians at Fort Johnson, Onondaga, Canajoharie, etc.; mostly minutes and speeches, with some brief notes of ceremonials; reports to the Lords of Trade, signed by Peter Wraxall, secretary.

In THE LIFE AND TIMES OF SIR WILLIAM JOHNSON, by William Leete Stone, vol. 2, app., pp. 394–429. Albany: J. Munsell, 1865. Reprint. In AN HISTORICAL JOURNAL OF THE CAMPAIGNS IN NORTH AMERICA, by John Knox, vol. 3, app., pp. 187–232.

Jul–Oct 1759. Private diary kept at Niagara and Oswego; Indian affairs during the war; some notes on weather, hunting, entertainment, etc.

KING, TITUS, ca. 1729–1791   493

NARRATIVE OF TITUS KING OF NORTHAMPTON, MASS. Hartford: Connecticut Historical Society, 1938. 21 pp.

1755–1758. Captive's diary with some narrative; capture by Indians, journey to Canada; hardships; Indian customs; interesting spellings and language.

LAWRENCE, ELEAZER, 1708–1789   494

In HISTORICAL SKETCHES OF SOME MEMBERS OF THE LAWRENCE FAMILY, by Robert Means Lawrence, p. 33. Boston: Rand Avery Co., Printers, 1888.

Jul–Aug 1755. Scouting expedition from Lunenburg, between Connecticut River and Merrimac.

LEWIS, CHARLES, d. 1774   495

VIRGINIA HISTORICAL SOCIETY COLLECTIONS, n.s. 11 (1891):203–218.

"Journal." WEST VIRGINIA HISTORICAL MAGAZINE 4 (1904):109–116.

Oct–Dec 1755. March to Fort Cumberland after Braddock's defeat; notes on drunkenness and discipline of troops, marches, weather, Indian atrocities.

NAZARETH, PENNSYLVANIA,   496
MORAVIAN CONGREGATION

"Six Months on the Frontier of Northampton County, Penna., During the Indian War." PENNSYLVANIA MAGAZINE OF HISTORY AND BIOGRAPHY 39 (1915):345–352.

Oct 1755–May 1756. Congregational journals; details of Indian warfare on the frontier.

METCALF, SETH, b. 1735   497

DIARY AND JOURNAL (1755–1807) OF SETH METCALF. Boston: Historical Records Survey, 1939. 31 pp.

1755–1807. Scattered notes of memorable events, weather and providences, with military journal of brief notes kept at Fort Edward, April 1757 to January 1758; interesting spellings.

ORME, ROBERT, ca. 1725–1781   498

In THE HISTORY OF AN EXPEDITION AGAINST FORT DU QUESNE, edited by Winthrop Sargent, pp. 281–358. Historical Society of Pennsylvania Memoirs, vol. 5. Philadelphia: For the Historical Society of Pennsylvania, 1855, 1856.

Feb–Jul 1755. With the Coldstream Guards on Braddock's expedition; mostly military details, vicissitudes of troops, topography.

OWEN, NICHOLAS, d. 1759   499

JOURNAL OF A SLAVE DEALER. Edited by Eveline Martin. London: G. Routledge and Sons, 1930. 120 pp.

1755–1758. Begins as narrative in 1746(?) with last few entries kept by Blayney Owen; interesting account of hardships and philosophy of slave trader between Africa and America.

ROGERS, ROBERT, 1731–1795   500

JOURNALS OF MAJOR ROBERT ROGERS. London: Printed for the author and sold by J. Milan, 1765. 236 pp. Frequently reprinted; recently, New York: Corinth Books, 1961. 171 pp.; Ann Arbor: University Microfilms, 1966.

JOURNALS OF MAJOR ROBERT ROGERS. Edited by Franklin B. Hough. Albany: J. Munsell, 1883. 297 pp.

1755–1761. Scouting expedition during French and Indian War.

Paltsits, Victor H., ed. "Journal of Robert Rogers the Ranger on His Expedition for Receiving the Capitulation of Western French Posts." NEW YORK PUBLIC LIBRARY BULLETIN 37 (1933):261–276.

Oct 1760–Feb 1761. Journey to renew occupation of western French posts. Errors in previous editions corrected.

In DIARY OF THE SIEGE OF DETROIT IN THE WAR WITH PONTIAC, edited by Franklin B. Hough, pp. 121–135. Albany: J. Munsell, 1860.

May–Jul 1763. Fragment of Rogers' journal of the siege of Detroit.

Clements, William L., ed. "Rogers' Michillimackinac Journal." AMERICAN ANTIQUARIAN SOCIETY PROCEEDINGS, n.s. 28 (1918):224–273.

Sep 1766–Jul 1767. Journal kept while Rogers was officer at Fort Michillimackinac at the entrance of Lake Michigan; good picture of Indian trade.

SAUTER, JOHANN MICHAEL   501

In RECORDS OF THE MORAVIANS IN NORTH CAROLINA, edited by Adelaide L. Fries, vol. 1, pp. 140–147.

Sep–Nov 1755. Moravian's journal of travel between Bethlehem, Pennsylvania, and Wachovia, North Carolina; religious details. Translated from the German.

STACKPOLE, JOHN, 1708-1796 502

Stackpole, Everett S., ed. "An Old Journal." MAINE HISTORICAL SOCIETY COLLECTIONS, 3d ser. 2 (1906): 241-244.

Jul 1755. Lieutenant's brief notes of a march to Maine; some interesting spellings.

STUART, CHARLES 503

Bond, Beverley W., Jr., ed. "The Captivity of Charles Stuart." MISSISSIPPI VALLEY HISTORICAL REVIEW 13 (1926-1927):58-81.

1755-1757. Day-to-day narrative of captivity among Indians; apparently copy of a statement.

THOMAS, JOHN, 1724-1776 504

"Diary of John Thomas." NOVA SCOTIA HISTORICAL SOCIETY COLLECTIONS 1 (1877-1878):119-140.

"Diary of John Thomas." NEW ENGLAND HISTORICAL AND GENEALOGICAL REGISTER 33 (1879):383-398. Reprint. Boston: Press of D. Clapp & Son, 1879? 16 pp.

In JOURNALS OF BEAUSEJOUR, edited by John C. Webster, pp. 11-39. Sackville, New Brunswick: Tribune Press, 1937.

Apr-Dec 1755. Surgeon with Winslow's expedition to remove the Acadians; interesting spellings.

TRUMBULL, BENJAMIN, 1735-1820 505

Cohen, Sheldon S., ed. "The Yale College Journal of Benjamin Trumbull." HISTORY OF EDUCATION QUARTERLY 8 (1968):375-385.

Sep 1755-Mar 1756. Extracts from student's journal; sermon topics; student misdemeanors and punishments; one of his Latin declamations.

"A Concise Journal or Minutes of the Principal Movements Towards St. John's of the Siege and Surrender of the Forts There in 1755." CONNECTICUT HISTORICAL SOCIETY COLLECTIONS 7 (1899):137-173.

"The Montgomery Expedition." FORT TICONDEROGA MUSEUM BULLETIN 1, no. 1 (1927):11-18; no. 2 (1927): 26-33; no. 3 (1928):16-30; no. 4 (1928):21-35.

Jul-Nov 1775. Chaplain's account of Montgomery's march and siege of St. John's.

"Journal of the Campaign at New York." CONNECTICUT HISTORICAL SOCIETY COLLECTIONS 7 (1899):175-218.

1776-1777. Expedition near New York; battles of Long Island and White Plains; succinct and factual account.

WALTON, JOSIAH, 1736-1831 506

"Mr. Walton's Journal." NEW ENGLAND HISTORICAL AND GENEALOGICAL REGISTER 5 (1851):42.

Jun-Oct 1755. A few brief entries on the expedition to Crown Point.

WILLARD, ABIJAH, 1724-1789 507

Webster, J. Clarence, ed. "Journal of Abijah Willard of Lancaster, Mass." NEW BRUNSWICK HISTORICAL SOCIETY COLLECTIONS 13 (1930):1-75.

Extracts in "An Unwritten Chapter of 'Evangeline.'" MAGAZINE OF HISTORY 9 (1901):10-12.

Apr 1755-Jan 1756. Monckton's expedition to Nova Scotia and siege of Fort Beausejour; mainly military details, but good narrative and description

of camp life; situation of Acadians, etc.; interesting spellings.

1756

ANON. 508

In THE MILITARY HISTORY OF GREAT BRITAIN, FOR 1756, 1757, pp. 26-50. London: Printed for J. Millan, 1757.

Apr-Nov 1756. British officer's letter-diary of march from Boston to Schenectady, Oneida, Oswego; siege of Oswego; journey to Canada; description of Montreal and Quebec.

ANON. 509

In DOCUMENTARY HISTORY OF THE STATE OF NEW YORK, edited by E.B. O'Callaghan, vol. 1, pp. 315-319.

Aug 1756. Frenchman's account of the siege of Chouaguen (Fort Pepperell).

BACON, WILLIAM, 1716-1761 510

In THE DEDICATION OF A MONUMENT TO THE MEMORY OF THE MEN OF WALPOLE, by George A. Plimpton. New York?, 1901? 23 pp.

May-Dec 1756. Record of march from Dedham, Massachusetts, to Albany.

BEATTY, CHARLES, ca. 1715-1772 511

THE JOURNAL OF A TWO MONTHS TOUR. London: Printed for W. Davenhill, 1768.

Extracts in NOTES AND QUERIES, edited by William H. Egle, pt. 5. pp. 205-208.

May-Jun 1756. Clergyman's journal of missionary travel and preaching in Pennsylvania among Indians west of the Alleghenies.

BOUGAINVILLE, LOUIS ANTOINE DE, 1729-1811 512

ADVENTURE IN THE WILDERNESS: THE AMERICAN JOURNALS OF LOUIS ANTOINE DE BOUGAINVILLE. Translated and edited by Edward P. Hamilton. Norman: University of Oklahoma Press, 1964. 344 pp.

1756-1760. French army lieutenant's detailed account of the Seven Years' War; campaigns against the British with assistance of Iroquois and other tribes; European and Indian methods of warfare; Indian customs and atrocities; battles of Fort Carillon at Ticonderoga, Fort George, Oswego and others; harrowing return to France on board OUTARDE; 1759-1760 covered by short, undated summary.

BURD, JAMES, 1726-1793 513

In PENNSYLVANIA ARCHIVES, 2d ser., vol. 2, pp. 743-820.

Dec 1756-Oct 1757. Building Fort Augusta at Shamokin, Pennsylvania; some notes on Indian affairs; a few interesting spellings.

In HISTORY OF NORTHAMPTON, LEHIGH, MONROE, CARBON, AND SCHUYLKILL COUNTIES, compiled by Israel D. Rupp, app., pp. 449-459.

In PENNSYLVANIA ARCHIVES, 1st ser., vol. 3, pp. 352-357.

Feb-Mar 1758. Official journal of inspection of Pennsylvania frontier forts (Fort Henry, Fort William, Fort Hamilton).

In PENNSYLVANIA ARCHIVES, 2d ser., vol. 7, pp. 441-444, 447-456.

Feb-Mar, Jul-Nov 1760. Brief, factual notes; Indian affairs at Fort Augusta; Pittsburgh.

In PENNSYLVANIA ARCHIVES, 2d ser., vol. 7, pp. 459-484.

Jun-Dec 1763. Military journal kept at Fort Augusta; most entries signed by Colonel Burd, others by various lieutenants.

CHESNEY, ALEXANDER, b. 1756   514

THE JOURNAL OF ALEXANDER CHESNEY, A SOUTH CAROLINA LOYALIST IN THE REVOLUTION AND AFTER. Edited by E. Alfred Jones. Ohio State University Studies, Contributions in History and Political Science, no. 7. Columbus: Ohio State University, 1921. 166 pp. Journal, pp. 1-56.

Extracts in "The Battle of King's Mountain: as Seen by the British Officers," by Samuel C. Williams. TENNESSEE HISTORICAL MAGAZINE 7 (1921):51-66.

Extracts in THE KING'S MOUNTAIN MEN, by Katherine K. White, pp. 108-112. Dayton, Va.: Joseph K. Ruebush Co., 1924.

1756-1820. Vicissitudes of Carolina loyalist in the Revolution; battle of King's Mountain; early years autobiographical; last part of diary kept in Ireland.

CROSS, STEPHEN, 1731-1809   515

Milliken, Sarah E., ed. "Journal of Stephen Cross of Newburyport." ESSEX INSTITUTE HISTORICAL COLLECTIONS 75 (1939):334-357; 76 (1940):14-42.

Mar 1756-Jan 1757. Adventures of a shipwright who went to build boats at Oswego to transport a British army for the attack on Montreal and Niagara; Lake Ontario, Quebec; excellent details of hardships; imprisonment in France.

CUTTER, AMMI RUHAMAH, 1735-1820   516

In A HISTORY OF THE CUTTER FAMILY OF NEW ENGLAND, compiled by Benjamin Cutter, revised and enlarged by William R. Cutter, pp. 61-70. Boston: Printed by D. Clapp & Son, 1871.

1756-1758. Brief, businesslike entries in surgeon's military journal; with New Hampshire regiment; stages to Albany, Ticonderoga, Fort Edward; military details, casualties, etc,; in Connecticut and Massachusetts; siege of Louisburg.

FRIZZELL, JOHN, 1730-1815   517

Sturtevant, Florence H., ed. "The Diary of John Frizzell." MAGAZINE OF HISTORY 23 (1916):88-94.

1756-1760. Extracts from prisoner's journal; capture at Oswego, journey to Canada, exchange; interesting spellings.

GRAHAM, JOHN, 1694-1774   518

"The Journal of the Rev. John Graham." MAGAZINE OF AMERICAN HISTORY 8 (1882):206-213.

Jun-Aug 1756. Journal kept by chaplain with Connecticut troops during expedition against Crown Point and Fort William Henry.

HUTCHINSON, THOMAS, 1711-1780   519

THE DIARY AND LETTERS OF HIS EXCELLENCY THOMAS HUTCHINSON, CAPTAIN-GENERAL AND GOVERNOR-IN-CHIEF OF MASSACHUSETTS BAY. Compiled by Peter O. Hutchinson. London: S. Low, Marston, Searle & Rivington, 1883-1886; Boston: Houghton, Mifflin, 1884-1886. 2 vols. Reprint. New York: B. Franklin, 1971; New York: AMS, 1973.

Oct-Nov 1756. Journey to Rhode Island and Albany.

1774-1780. Extracts, combined with letters, of Massachusetts governor's efforts on both sides of the Atlantic to resolve disputes between colonists and Britain; unpopularity with colonists; dealings with leaders in England, including George III; valuable diary for its illumination of colonial affairs, American and British attitudes, and Hutchinson's personal plight.

"Extracts from the Journal of Thomas Hutchinson." MASSACHUSETTS HISTORICAL SOCIETY PROCEEDINGS, 1st ser. 15 (1876-1877):326-334.

Jul 1774. Conversation with George III.

JONES, JOHN, 1716-1801   520

BOOK OF MINUTES OF COL. JOHN JONES OF DEDHAM, MASSACHUSETTS. Notes by Amos Perry. Boston: G.E. Littlefield; Providence: Preston and Rounds, 1894. 42 pp.

1756-1767. Affairs as justice of the peace.

1762-1763. Surveying at Mount Desert.

LOWRY, JEAN   521

A JOURNAL OF THE CAPTIVITY OF JEAN LOWRY AND HER CHILDREN. Philadelphia: William Bradford, 1760. 31 pp.

Apr 1756-? Captive's journal; capture by Indians at Rocky Spring, Pennsylvania; notes of hardships; religious disputes with French.

MIRANDA Y FLORES, BERNARDO DE   522

Patten, Roderick B., trans. and ed. "Miranda's Inspection of Los Almagres: His Journal, Report and Petition." SOUTHWESTERN HISTORICAL QUARTERLY 74 (1970):223-254.

Feb-Mar 1756. Small expedition to investigate a deposit of gossan (almagre) for silver mining potential; a difficult venture which proved fruitless.

MORTON, THOMAS   523

"Morton's Diary." VIRGINIA HISTORICAL REGISTER 4 (1851):143-147.

Mar 1756. Account of expedition against Shawnee Indians; notes of movements, discipline, etc.; some interesting spellings.

POND, PETER, 1740-1807   524

"Remarkable Experiences in Early Wars of New World." CONNECTICUT MAGAZINE 10 (1906):239-259. Reprint. "1740-75: Journal of Peter Pond." WISCONSIN STATE HISTORICAL SOCIETY COLLECTIONS 18 (1908): 314-354.

In FIVE FUR TRADERS OF THE NORTHWEST, edited by Charles M. Gates, pp. 11-59.

Extracts in "Experiences in the Early Wars in America." JOURNAL OF AMERICAN HISTORY 1 (1907):89-93, 357-365.

1756-? Fur trader's autobiography and journal; a most lively and entertaining account of fur trade and travel in Old Northwest, mainly Wisconsin; details of Wisconsin Indians; vivid portrayal of himself, his life and his milieu; very interesting spellings and vocabulary.

SECCOMBE, JOSEPH, b. 1732   525

"Extracts from 'Text Books' of Dea. Joseph Seccombe." ESSEX INSTITUTE HISTORICAL COLLECTIONS 34 (1898): 23-39.

"Extracts from the 'Text Books' of Deacon Joseph Seccombe, 1762-1777." DANVERS HISTORICAL SOCIETY COLLECTIONS 9 (1921):112-115.

1756-1777. Scattered notes, in journal of Medford, Massachusetts, clergyman; sermons, births, deaths, weather, public events.

SMITH, JOHN   526

In COLONIAL CAPTIVITIES, edited by Isabel M. Calder, pp. 137-139.

1756-1757. Brief extracts from major's journal, relating to French and Indian War.

VAN ETTEN, JOHN   527

In HISTORY OF NORTHAMPTON, LEHIGH, MONROE, CARBON, AND SCHUYLKILL COUNTIES, compiled by Israel D. Rupp, app., pp. 423-445.

In PENNSYLVANIA ARCHIVES, 1st ser., vol. 3, pp. 222-235.

In REPORT OF THE COMMISSION TO LOCATE THE SITE OF THE FRONTIER FORTS OF PENNSYLVANIA, 2d ed., by Pennsylvania Indian Forts Commission, edited by Thomas L. Montgomery, vol. 1, pp. 305-321. Harrisburg: W.S. Ray, 1916.

Dec 1756-Jan 1757. Journal of commander of Fort Hyndshaw; events there and at Fort Hamilton; scouting, duties, Indian encounters; some interesting spellings.

WYMAN, ISAAC, 1725-1792   528

In ORIGINS IN WILLIAMSTOWN, 2d ed., by Arthur L. Perry, pp. 278-280. New York: C. Scribner's Sons, 1896.

May-Jul 1756. Brief notes of military activities at Fort Massachusetts; guards, etc.

YOUNG, JAMES   529

In HISTORY OF NORTHAMPTON, LEHIGH, MONROE, CARBON, AND SCHUYLKILL COUNTIES, compiled by Israel D. Rupp, app., pp. 410-420.

In PENNSYLVANIA ARCHIVES, 1st ser., vol. 2, pp. 675-681.

Jun 1756. Commissary general's journal; from Reading to forts in northern Pennsylvania (North Kill, Lebanon, etc.); descriptions and details.

1757

ANON.   530

In REPORT OF THE COMMISSION TO LOCATE THE SITE OF THE FRONTIER FORTS OF PENNSYLVANIA, 2d ed., by

Pennsylvania Indian Forts Commission, edited by Thomas L. Montgomery, vol. 1, pp. 107-117. Harrisburg: W.S. Ray, 1916.

Jun-Aug 1757. Official report of officer in command of Fort North Kill; march from Reading to the fort; Indian affairs around the fort.

ANON.   531

In DOCUMENTS RELATIVE TO THE COLONIAL HISTORY OF THE STATE OF NEW YORK, edited by E.B. O'Callaghan, vol. 10, pp. 598-605.

Jul-Aug 1757. Official French report of expedition against Fort William Henry.

BANCROFT, SAMUEL, 1715-1782   532

FAMILY RECORD OF DEA. SAMUEL BANCROFT, 1715-1782, OF READING, MASS. Introduction by Frank D. Andrews. Vineland, N.J., 1922. 24 pp.

Aug 1757. Military expedition to Brookfield.

1766-1769. Personal and religious notes; farming.

BANYAR, GOLDSBROW   533

"Diary of Goldsbrow Banyar, Deputy Secretary of the Province of New York." MAGAZINE OF AMERICAN HISTORY 1 (1877):25-33.

Aug 1757. Mostly official military business in French and Indian War; impersonal notes, orders, statistics.

CLINTON, GEORGE, 1739-1812   534

Spaulding, E. Wilder, ed. "George Clinton's Cruise on the Privateer DEFIANCE." NEW YORK HISTORY 16 (1935):89-95.

Oct 1757-Jan 1758. Brief notes made on board New York privateer during French and Indian War.

DARLING, JONATHAN, 1741-1763   535

Dodge, R.G.W., ed. "Jonathan Darling Jr.'s Journal." BANGOR HISTORICAL MAGAZINE 2 (1886-1887):76-78.

1757-1772. Mostly military items, Louisburg campaign of 1759; other notes on life in Andover, Massachusetts, and Bluehill, Maine.

ENGLE, ANDREW   536

In NOTES AND QUERIES, edited by William H. Egle, 1897, 13 pp.

Dec 1757. Lieutenant's very brief notes of stationing men around Lehigh during French and Indian War.

FREEMAN, JOSHUA, 1717-1794   537

In ANNALS OF THE TOWN OF WARREN, IN KNOX COUNTY, MAINE, 2d ed., by Cyrus Eaton, pp. 106-108. Hallowell, Maine: Masters & Livermore, 1877.

May-Jul 1757. Brief notes of march to Meduncook.

GAINE, HUGH, 1727-1807   538

THE JOURNALS OF HUGH GAINE, PRINTER. Edited by Paul Leicester Ford. New York: Dodd, Mead, 1902. 2 vols. Reprint. New York: Arno, 1970. 239 pp.

1757-1758. Notes of public occurrences, political and military.

1777–1782. News of war; short notes, mainly of naval and military movements.

1797–1798. Notes on weather, news, local affairs and gossip in New York; ship movements.

GRIDLEY, LUKE, b. 1734   539

LUKE GRIDLEY'S DIARY OF 1757 WHILE IN SERVICE IN THE FRENCH AND INDIAN WAR. Acorn Club Publications, no. 10. Hartford, Conn.: Hartford Press, Case, Lockwood & Brainerd, 1906. 64 pp.

Mar–Nov 1757. Notes of military life at Fort Edward during French and Indian War; interesting spellings.

HAYWARD, BENJAMIN   540

"Diary of Ensign Hayward of Woodstock, Conn., Kept Principally at Fort Edward in 1757." In THE FORT EDWARD BOOK, by Robert O. Bascom, pp. 89–102. Fort Edward, N.Y.: J.D. Keating, 1903.

Apr–Oct 1757. Sporadic entries with dates jumbled; march from Connecticut to Fort Edward; reports of deaths, "scrimmage" with Indians; financial records.

HERRICK, ISRAEL, 1721–1782   541

"Capt. Herrick's Journal." MAINE HISTORICAL SOCIETY COLLECTIONS, 2d ser. 2 (1891):219–224.

May–Jul 1757. Scouting journal from expedition between the Androscoggin and Kennebec rivers; mainly notes of movements; some interesting spellings.

HINCHMAN, JOSEPH   542

Mervine, William M. "The Log of Dr. Joseph Hinchman, Surgeon of the Privateer Brig PRINCE GEORGE." PENNSYLVANIA MAGAZINE OF HISTORY AND BIOGRAPHY 29 (1905):268–281.

Aug–Nov 1757. Log with many private entries; wreck, landing on Tortuga Island; interesting spellings.

KELSEY, MOSES, d. 1758   543

Thompson, Lucien, ed. "Journal of Moses Kelsey, an Officer in the Seven Years' War." GRANITE STATE MAGAZINE 2 (1906):95–101.

Jul 1757–May 1758. Brief notes of movements and discipline, mainly kept during Loudon's expedition against Louisburg; interesting spellings.

KNOX, JOHN, d. 1778   544

AN HISTORICAL JOURNAL OF THE CAMPAIGNS IN NORTH-AMERICA. London: Printed for the author and sold by W. Johnston, 1769. 2 vols. Reprint. Edited by Arthur G. Doughty. Champlain Society Publications, vol. 8–10. Toronto: The Champlain Society, 1914–1916.

1757–1760. Copious journal of campaigns in the French and Indian War; sieges of Louisburg and Quebec; many general notes and character sketches.

In OLD SOUTH LEAFLETS, vol. 3, no. 73, pp. 1–16.

Extracts in AMERICAN HISTORY TOLD BY CONTEMPORARIES, edited by Albert B. Hart, vol. 2, pp. 369–372.

Sep 1759. Extracts covering battle of Quebec.

MALARTIC, Adjt.   545

In DOCUMENTS RELATIVE TO THE COLONIAL HISTORY OF THE STATE OF NEW YORK, edited by E.B. O'Callaghan, vol. 10, pp. 721–725, 835–855.

1757–1758. Occurrences in camps occupied by the Béarn Regiment; quite interesting.

Jun–Jul 1758. French operations before Ticonderoga on frontier of Lake St. Sacrament. Translated from the French.

MONTRESOR, JOHN, 1736–1799   546

THE MONTRESOR JOURNALS. Edited and annotated by Gideon D. Scull. New York Historical Society Collections, Publication Fund Series, vol. 14. New York: Printed for the Society, 1882. 578 pp.

1757–1778. Engineer's extensive notes of journeys and campaigns; Fort Edward, Louisburg, Quebec, Bradstreet's expedition; building fortifications in New York, 1757–1759; Albany and New York, 1765; Boston, 1770; Long Island, 1771; the Revolution; an important journal.

MAINE HISTORICAL SOCIETY COLLECTIONS 1 (1865): 448–466.

In MARCH TO QUEBEC, edited by Kenneth L. Roberts, pp. 5–24.

Jun–Jul 1760. Diary of journey from Quebec to Maine, which was used as guidebook on Arnold's expedition to Quebec.

Webster, J.C. "The Life of John Montrésor." ROYAL SOCIETY OF CANADA PROCEEDINGS AND TRANSACTIONS, 3d ser. 22, sec. 2 (1928):1–31. Journal, pp. 10–29.

1763. Journal of expedition to Detroit.

Scull, G.D., ed. "Journal of Captain John Montrésor, July 1, 1777, to July 1, 1778, Chief Engineer of the British Army." PENNSYLVANIA MAGAZINE OF HISTORY AND BIOGRAPHY 5 (1881):393–417.

1777–1778. Extracts cover Brandywine, occupation and evacuation of Philadelphia.

MORGAN, JACOB, 1716–1792   547

In PENNSYLVANIA ARCHIVES, 1st ser., vol. 3, pp. 252–254.

In TALES OF THE BLUE MOUNTAINS, by David C. Henning, pp. 47–48. Historical Society of Schuylkill County Publications, vol. 3. Pottsville, Pa., 1911.

In REPORT OF THE COMMISSION TO LOCATE THE SITE OF THE FRONTIER FORTS OF PENNSYLVANIA, 2d ed., by Pennsylvania Indian Forts Commission, edited by Thomas L. Montgomery, vol. 1, pp. 129–133. Harrisburg: W.S. Ray, 1916.

Jul 1757. Notes of daily routine at Fort Lebanon, Pennsylvania.

"Life in a Frontier Fort During the Indian War." PENNSYLVANIA MAGAZINE OF HISTORY AND BIOGRAPHY 39 (1915):186–191.

Apr 1758. Fort life in Pennsylvania during French and Indian War.

OLIVER, PETER, 1741–1822   548

Extracts in THE DIARY AND LETTERS OF HIS EXCELLENCY THOMAS HUTCHINSON, by Thomas Hutchinson, compiled by Peter O. Hutchinson, pp. 68–69. London: S. Low, Marston, Searle & Rivington, 1883–1886; Boston: Houghton, Mifflin, 1884–1886. Reprint. New York: B. Franklin, 1971; AMS, 1973.

Extracts in HISTORY OF THE TOWN OF MIDDLEBORO, MASSACHUSETTS, by Thomas Weston, pp. 148-150. Boston and New York: Houghton, Mifflin, 1906.

> 1757-1821. Private diary beginning with autobiographical sketch; notes of personal affairs, life in New England and England, public affairs.

PUTNAM, RUFUS, 1738-1824   549

JOURNAL OF GEN. RUFUS PUTNAM KEPT IN NORTHERN NEW YORK DURING FOUR CAMPAIGNS. With notes and biographical sketch by Ephraim C. Dawes. Albany: J. Munsell's Sons, 1886. 115 pp.

> 1757-1760. Military movements, hardships and atrocities during French and Indian War.

In THE TWO PUTNAMS, by Israel Putnam, pp. 143-262. Hartford: Connecticut Historical Society, 1931.

> Dec 1772-Aug 1773. Reconnoitering and exploring around the Mississippi; a long and a shorter journal; interesting spellings.

REMILLY, MATTHIAS   550

In ANNALS OF THE TOWN OF WARREN, IN KNOX COUNTY, MAINE, 2d ed., by Cyrus Eaton, pp. 111-114. Hallowell, Maine: Masters & Livermore, 1877.

> May-Jun 1757. Scouting journal containing brief notes of service at Broad Bay; some interesting spellings.

WITHERSPOON, JOHN   551

NOVA SCOTIA HISTORICAL SOCIETY COLLECTIONS 2 (1879-1880):31-62.

> 1757-1759. Prisoner's account of capture by French and imprisonment at Quebec; varied events, hardships, siege, religion, etc.

WOOLMAN, JOHN, 1720-1772   552

THE JOURNAL AND MAJOR ESSAYS OF JOHN WOOLMAN. Edited by Phillips P. Moulton. New York: Oxford University Press, 1971. 336 pp.

THE WORKS OF JOHN WOOLMAN. Philadelphia: Printed by Joseph Crukshank, 1774. 436 pp. Journal, pt. 1.

THE JOURNAL OF JOHN WOOLMAN. Introduction by John Greenleaf Whittier. Glasgow: R. Smeal, 1883. 315 pp.

THE JOURNAL AND ESSAYS OF JOHN WOOLMAN. Edited by Amelia M. Gummere. New York: Macmillan, 1922. 643 pp.

JOURNAL. Edited by Janet Whitney. Chicago: H. Regnery, 1950. 233 pp.

THE JOURNAL OF JOHN WOOLMAN, AND A PLEA FOR THE POOR. The John Greenleaf Whittier edition text. Introduction by Frederick B. Tolles. New York: Corinth Books, 1961. 249 pp. Reprint. Gloucester, Mass.: P. Smith, 1971.

Extracts in AMERICAN HISTORY TOLD BY CONTEMPORARIES, edited by Albert B. Hart, vol. 2, pp. 302-308; DIARY OF AMERICA, edited by Josef Berger, pp. 71-81.

Discussed in AMERICAN DIARY LITERATURE, by Steven E. Kagle, pp. 47-51.

> 1757?-1772. Quaker journal containing dated entries within autobiography; personal life, religious reflections and reading; tireless travels and work as an itinerant "recommended minister" throughout American colonies; efforts to persuade Quakers to give up slavery and to renew emphasis on pacifism

and simple living; journey to England in 1772; descriptions of poverty of working people; a major Quaker source.

1758

ANON.   553

In THE HISTORY OF ANCIENT WETHERSFIELD, CONNECTICUT, by Sherman W. Adams, edited by Henry R. Stiles, vol. 1, p. 406. New York: Grafton Press, 1904.

> May-Jun 1758. Brief extracts from military journal concerning French and Indian War.

ANON.   554

"Diary of Gen. Jeffery Amherst's Expedition Against Louisbourg." In THE LETTERS AND PAPERS OF CADWALLADER COLDEN, by Cadwallader Colden, vol. 5, pp. 265-282. New York: Printed for the New York Historical Society, 1918-1937.

> May-Aug 1758. Notes of the expedition.

ANON.   555

Choate, Isaac B., ed. "Journal of a Provincial Officer." HISTORICAL MAGAZINE, 2d ser. 10 (1871):113-122.

> May-Nov 1758. Kept while campaigning in northern New York.

ANON.   556

AN AUTHENTIC ACCOUNT OF THE REDUCTION OF LOUISBOURG IN JUNE AND JULY, 1758. London: W. Owen, 1758. 60 pp.

> Jun-Jul 1758. Spectator's full day-to-day account of the siege of Louisburg.

ANON.   557

In DOCUMENTS RELATIVE TO THE COLONIAL HISTORY OF THE STATE OF NEW YORK, edited by E.B. O'Callaghan, vol. 10, pp. 741-744.

> Jul 1758. Official French military journal of the battle of Ticonderoga. Translated from the French.

ALEXANDER, THOMAS, 1727-1801   558

In A HISTORY OF THE TOWN OF NORTHFIELD, by Josiah H. Temple and George Sheldon, pp. 303-305.

> May-Oct 1758. Ensign's brief notes of movements and military affairs in the Ticonderoga expedition.

AMES, NATHANIEL, 1741-1822   559

JACOBIN AND JUNTO: OR, EARLY AMERICAN POLITICS AS VIEWED IN THE DIARY OF DR. NATHANIEL AMES. By Charles Warren. Cambridge: Harvard University Press, 1931. 324 pp. Reprint. New York: Blom, 1968; New York: AMS, 1970.

Calder, Edna F., ed. "Extracts from the Ames Diary." DEDHAM HISTORICAL REGISTER 1-14 (1890-1903):passim.

Extracts in AMERICAN HISTORY TOLD BY CONTEMPORARIES, edited by Albert B. Hart, vol. 2, pp. 266-272; vol. 3, pp. 336-339.

> 1758-1821. Diary of doctor and almanac-maker in Dedham, Massachusetts; extensive and sustained personal, social, local and national notes; a valuable and entertaining diary.

AMHERST, JEFFERY, 1717–1797   560

THE JOURNAL OF JEFFERY AMHERST, RECORDING THE MILITARY CAREER OF GENERAL AMHERST IN AMERICA FROM 1758–1763. Edited by J. Clarence Webster. Chicago: University of Chicago Press, 1931. 324 pp.

 1758–1763. Military affairs during the French and Indian War.

A JOURNAL OF THE LANDING OF HIS MAJESTY'S FORCES ON THE ISLAND OF CAPE-BRETON, AND OF THE SIEGE AND SURRENDER OF LOUISBOURG. Boston: Green and Russell, 1758. 22 pp.

In AN HISTORICAL JOURNAL OF THE CAMPAIGNS IN NORTH AMERICA, by John Knox, vol. 3, app., pp. 1–96.

 1758–1760. Military journal, with Colonel William Amherst, in the French and Indian War.

AMHERST, WILLIAM, 1732–1781   561

JOURNAL OF WILLIAM AMHERST IN AMERICA, 1758–1760. With an introduction by John C. Webster. London: Printed by Butler & Tanner, 1927. 82 pp.

 1758–1760. Journey to America; military affairs up to surrender of Montreal, including an important account of siege of Louisburg; military details only.

THE RECAPTURE OF ST. JOHN'S, NEWFOUNDLAND, IN 1762 AS DESCRIBED IN THE JOURNAL OF LIEUT.-COLONEL WILLIAM AMHERST, COMMANDER OF THE BRITISH EXPEDITIONARY FORCE. Edited by John C. Webster. n.p.: Privately printed, 1928. 15 pp.

 Aug–Oct 1762. Recapture of St. John's, Newfoundland.

BARROWS, ABNER, 1732–1818   562

In HISTORY OF THE TOWN OF MIDDLEBORO, MASSACHUSETTS, by Thomas Weston, pp. 95–98. Boston and New York: Houghton, Mifflin, 1906.

 Jul 1758. Extracts from military journal; service in French and Indian War; engagement at Lake George; interesting spellings.

BARTON, THOMAS, 1730–1780   563

Hunter, William A., ed. "Thomas Barton and the Forbes Expedition." PENNSYLVANIA MAGAZINE OF HISTORY AND BIOGRAPHY 95 (1971):431–483.

 Jul–Sep 1758. Military journal kept by Anglican chaplain with Forbes campaign against Fort Duquesne; details of army on the march and in camp, as well as diarist's clerical duties.

BASS, BENJAMIN   564

"Account of the Capture of Fort Frontenac." NEW YORK HISTORY 16 (1935):449–452.

 Aug–Oct 1758. Lieutenant's account of expedition under Bradstreet against Fort Frontenac; linguistically interesting.

BIGELOW, SILAS, 1739–1769   565

Crane, John C., ed. "The Diary of Rev. Silas Bigelow, the First Minister of Paxton, Mass." WORCESTER SOCIETY OF ANTIQUITY PROCEEDINGS 17 (1900):260–268.

 1758–1761. Schoolmaster's diary; short personal entries; clothes, illnesses and remedies, a startling dream.

CALLENDER, HANNAH, 1737–1801   566

Vaux, George. "Extracts from the Diary of Hannah Callender." PENNSYLVANIA MAGAZINE OF HISTORY AND BIOGRAPHY 12 (1888):432–456.

 1758–1762. Social, personal and topographical notes from Philadelphian's diary.

CARGILL, JAMES   567

Seybolt, Robert F., ed. "Hunting Indians in Massachusetts: a Scouting Journal of 1758." NEW ENGLAND QUARTERLY 3 (1930):527–531.

Extracts in DIARY OF AMERICA, edited by Josef Berger, pp. 65–67.

 1758. Matter-of-fact account of a bounty hunter's successful scalping of an Indian for a substantial fee, paid to him from the public treasury of the colony of Massachusetts.

CHAMPION, HENRY, 1723–1797   568

In THE CHAMPION GENEALOGY, by Francis B. Trowbridge, pp. 417–435. New Haven, Conn.: Printed for the author, 1891.

 Jun–Nov 1758. March from Colchester to Ticonderoga; mostly brief notes of march, camp life, discipline, military details, return home.

CHEW, COLBY   569

In LETTERS TO WASHINGTON, AND ACCOMPANYING PAPERS, edited by Stanislaus M. Hamilton, vol. 3, pp. 39–43. Boston and New York: Houghton, Mifflin, 1896–1902.

 Aug 1758. Official expedition report sent to Washington; frontier scouting methods.

COBB, ELISHA, 1736–1794   570

In HISTORY OF GORHAM, ME., by Hugh D. McLellan, compiled and edited by Katharine B. Lewis, pp. 66–68. Portland: Smith & Sale, Printers, 1903.

 May–Jul 1758. Extracts from scouting journal; with Preble's regiment in French and Indian War; notes of army movements.

COBB, SAMUEL, 1718–1790?   571

In REGISTER OF THE OFFICERS AND MEMBERS OF THE SOCIETY OF COLONIAL WARS IN THE STATE OF MAINE, by Society of Colonial Wars, Maine, pp. 90–113. Portland: Marks Printing House, 1905.

 May–Nov 1758. Shipwright's military journal; march from Falmouth to Kittery; New York, Schenectady, Ticonderoga; military details; interesting language.

DORR, MOSES   572

"A Journal of an Expedition Against Canaday." NEW YORK HISTORY 16 (1935):452–464.

 May–Oct 1758. Ensign's description of expedition against Canada in Captain Parker's company; Roxbury and Fort Stanwix; military movements; some interesting spellings.

DRINKER, ELIZABETH SANDWITH, 1734–1807   573

EXTRACTS FROM THE JOURNAL OF ELIZABETH DRINKER. Edited by Henry D. Biddle. Philadelphia: J.B. Lippincott, 1889. 423 pp.

"Extracts from the Journal of Mrs. Henry Drinker, of Philadelphia, from September 25, 1777, to July 4, 1778." PENNSYLVANIA MAGAZINE OF HISTORY AND BIOGRAPHY 13 (1889):298-308.

Extracts in EARLY NARRATIVES OF BERKS COUNTY, by James B. Nolan, pp. 54-56; WEATHERING THE STORM, by Elizabeth Evans, pp. 156-179.

> 1758-1807. Private and social life in Philadelphia; notes on the Revolution.

FOSTER, ASA, 1710-1787   574

"Diary of Capt. Asa Foster of Andover, Mass." NEW ENGLAND HISTORICAL AND GENEALOGICAL REGISTER 54 (1900):183-188.

> Jun-Oct 1758. Notes kept in New York during French and Indian War.

FULLER, ARCHELAUS, 1727-1776   575

"Journal of Col. Archelaus Fuller of Middleton, Mass." ESSEX INSTITUTE HISTORICAL COLLECTIONS 46 (1910): 209-220.

> May-Nov 1758. Expedition to Ticonderoga; sympathy toward victims; many very interesting spellings.

GLASIER, BENJAMIN, 1734?-1774   576

"French and Indian War Diary of Benjamin Glasier of Ipswich." ESSEX INSTITUTE HISTORICAL COLLECTIONS 86 (1950):65-92.

> Feb-Nov 1758, Apr-Jun 1760. Ship carpenter's diary; expedition against Oswego, Fort Edward and Fort Ticonderoga; record of army life; tasks such as building bridges; illness, executions, etc.; 1760 expedition to Lake George and Fort Edward.

GORDON, Capt.   577

NOVA SCOTIA HISTORICAL SOCIETY COLLECTIONS 5 (1886-1887):97-153.

> Apr-Aug 1758. Military journal, combined with order book, of member of Royal Artillery; siege of Louisburg; very little of nonmilitary or personal interest.

GORDON, JAMES, 1713-1768   578

"Journal of Col. James Gordon of Lancaster County, Va." WILLIAM AND MARY COLLEGE QUARTERLY, 1st ser. 11 (1902-1903):98-112, 217-236; 12 (1903-1904):1-12.

Extracts in "Chronicle of a Southern Gentleman: Life in the Old South," by Louisa C. Blair. JOURNAL OF AMERICAN HISTORY 3 (1909):81-89.

> 1758-1763. Life in Lancaster County; rather brief notes on domestic, business, local, plantation, social affairs; Presbyterian church activities and controversies.

GORDON, WILLIAM AUGUSTUS   579

"Journal of the Siege of Louisburg." ROYAL UNITED SERVICE INSTITUTION JOURNAL 60 (1915):117-152.

> Apr-Aug 1758. Military journal of member of Highland Infantry during siege of Louisburg; statistics.

GUILD, AARON, 1728-1818   580

In THE DEDICATION OF A MONUMENT TO THE MEMORY OF THE MEN OF WALPOLE, by George A. Plimpton. New York?, 1901?

> May-Jul 1758. Ensign's march with Nichol's regiment to Fort Edward.

HAYDEN, AUGUSTIN, 1740-1823   581

In RECORDS OF THE CONNECTICUT LINE OF THE HAYDEN FAMILY, by Jabez H. Hayden, pp. 120-123. Windsor Locks, Conn.: Case, Lockwood and Brainard, 1888.

> May-Nov 1758, Apr-Dec 1759. Military journal; brief notes of march from Windsor to Ticonderoga and back; activities at Fort Edward and Crown Point.

HOLT, JOSEPH, 1718-1789   582

"Journals of Joseph Holt, of Wilton, N.H." NEW ENGLAND HISTORICAL AND GENEALOGICAL REGISTER 10 (1856):307-311.

> May-Oct 1758. Brief notes of army movements in expedition to Canada.

> Jun-Jul 1676 (sic). Travel journal of voyage to Penobscot. Authorship questioned.

JEWETT, BENJAMIN   583

"The Diary of Benjamin Jewett." NATIONAL MAGAZINE 17 (1892-1893):60-64.

> Apr-Nov 1758. Expedition from Windham against Canada; interesting spellings.

KENNY, JAMES   584

Jordan, John W., ed. "Journal of James Kenny." PENNSYLVANIA MAGAZINE OF HISTORY AND BIOGRAPHY 23 (1913):1-47, 152-201, 395-449.

Extracts in DIARY OF AMERICA, edited by Josef Berger, pp. 67-71.

> 1758-1759, 1761-1763. Journey to Pittsburgh and trade there; excellent description of frontier life by a shrewd and humorous Quaker; interesting language.

West, Francis D., ed. "John Bartram's Journey to Pittsburgh in the Fall of 1761." WESTERN PENNSYLVANIA HISTORICAL MAGAZINE 38 (1955):111-115.

> Sep 1761. Extracts covering ten-day trip from Fort Pitt down the Ohio and Monongahela rivers with botanist John Bartram whose journal of this trip has not survived; notes on unusual flora and visit with Indians.

KERN, JACOB   585

In NOTES AND QUERIES, edited by William H. Egle, 3d ser., vol. 2, pp. 124-125.

> Jan-Feb 1758. Journey from Reading, Pennsylvania, to Delaware and back.

KNAP, NATHANIEL, 1736-1816   586

SOCIETY OF COLONIAL WARS, MASSACHUSETTS, YEARBOOK 1895, pp. 1-42.

Extracts in OULD NEWBURY, by John J. Currier, pp. 485-487. Boston: Damrell and Upham, 1896.

> 1758-1759. Brief military and naval notes of the siege of Louisburg.

LYON, LEMUEL, b. 1738   587

In THE MILITARY JOURNALS OF TWO PRIVATE SOLDIERS, 1758-1775, compiled by Abraham Tomlinson with notes by Benson J. Lossing, pp. 11-45. Poughkeepsie, N.Y.: A. Tomlinson, 1855. Reprint. Freeport, N.Y.: Books for

Libraries Press, 1970; New York: Da Capo, 1971.

Apr-Nov 1758. Expedition against Canada; fairly good personal and military notes, some of them amusing.

MONCKTON, ROBERT   **588**

"Report of the Proceedings of the Troops on the Expedition up St. John's River in the Bay of Fundy under the Command of Colonel Monckton." In HISTORICAL-GEOGRAPHICAL DOCUMENTS, RELATING TO NEW BRUNSWICK, edited by William F. Ganong, vol. 2, pp. 163-188.

Sep-Nov 1758. Military details of expedition up St. John's River, destroying Acadian settlements.

NOYES, JOHN, 1740-1784   **589**

"Journal of John Noyes of Newbury." ESSEX INSTITUTE HISTORICAL COLLECTIONS 45 (1909):73-77.

Apr-Nov 1758. Ticonderoga expedition; marches, distances, general notes; a few interesting spellings; some items after November 1758.

PARKMAN, WILLIAM, 1741-1832   **590**

"Journal of William Parkman." MASSACHUSETTS HISTORICAL SOCIETY PROCEEDINGS, 1st ser. 17 (1879-1880): 243-244.

Jul-Aug 1758. Extracts from military journal; a few entries relating to battle of Ticonderoga; Howe's death; capture of Putnam.

POST, CHRISTIAN FREDERICK, 1710-1785   **591**

In AN ENQUIRY INTO THE CAUSES OF THE ALIENATION OF THE DELAWARE AND SHAWANESE INDIANS FROM THE BRITISH INTEREST, by Charles Thomson, pp. 130-171. London: Printed for J. Wilkie, 1759.

In THE HISTORY OF PENNSYLVANIA, by Robert Proud, vol. 2, app., pp. 65-95. Philadelphia: Printed and sold by Zachariah Poulson, 1797-1798.

In THE OLDEN TIME, edited by Neville B. Craig, vol. 1, pp. 99-125.

In EARLY HISTORY OF WESTERN PENNSYLVANIA, by Israel D. Rupp, app., pp. 75-98. Pittsburgh: D.W. Kauffman; Harrisburg: W.O. Hickock, 1846.

In PENNSYLVANIA ARCHIVES, 1st ser., vol. 3, pp. 520-544. (This version has slight variations from the original ms.)

In EARLY WESTERN TRAVELS, edited by Reuben G. Thwaites, vol. 1, pp. 183-233.

Jul-Sep 1758. Moravian missionary's travel journals; official negotiations with Indians; language normalized from an extraordinary German-English (sample in Thwaites, pp. 183-184); tour to the Ohio Indians with Charles Thomson.

THE SECOND JOURNAL OF CHRISTIAN FREDERICK POST. London: Printed for J. Wilkie, 1759. 67 pp.

In THE HISTORY OF PENNSYLVANIA, vol. 2, app., pp. 96-132.

In THE OLDEN TIME, vol. 1, pp. 145-177.

In EARLY HISTORY OF WESTERN PENNSYLVANIA, app., pp. 99-126.

In EARLY WESTERN TRAVELS, vol. 1, pp. 234-291.

Oct 1758-Jan 1759. Second journey to the Ohio.

In PENNSYLVANIA ARCHIVES, 1st ser., vol. 4, pp. 92-98.

Jul-Aug 1762. Leading Indians from Tuscarora to Lancaster.

REA, CALEB, 1727-1760   **592**

Ray, F.M., ed. "The Journal of Dr. Caleb Rea, Written during the Expedition against Ticonderoga in 1758." ESSEX INSTITUTE HISTORICAL COLLECTIONS 18 (1881):81-120, 177-205.

May-Nov 1758. Surgeon's diary; long medical, general and personal notes; camp life.

RICHARDSON, WILLIAM, 1729-1777   **593**

Williams, Samuel C., ed. "An Account of the Presbyterian Mission to the Cherokees, 1757-1759." TENNESSEE HISTORICAL MAGAZINE, 2d ser. 1 (1931):125-138.

Nov 1758-Feb 1759. Missionary among the Overhill Cherokees; preaching and baptizing; fall of Fort Loudoun.

SHUTE, DANIEL, 1722-1802   **594**

"A Journal of the Rev. Daniel Shute, D.D., Chaplain in the Expedition to Canada in 1758." ESSEX INSTITUTE HISTORICAL COLLECTIONS 12 (1874):132-151.

May-Oct 1758. From Boston through Albany and Schuyler's Farm; religious, social, personal details.

SMITH, JOSEPH, 1735-1816   **595**

"Journal of Joseph Smith, of Groton." CONNECTICUT SOCIETY OF COLONIAL WARS IN THE STATE OF CONNECTICUT PROCEEDINGS 1 (1896):303-310.

Jun-Sep 1758. Brief notes of expedition to Ticonderoga and Crown Point; skirmishes, camp life, hardships; some spellings of interest.

SPAULDING, LEONARD   **596**

VERMONT HISTORICAL GAZETTEER 5, pt. 2 (1891):28-32.

Jul-Oct 1758. Officer's account of Crown Point expedition; marches, discipline, camp life; interesting spellings.

SPICER, ABEL, 1746-ca. 1787   **597**

In HISTORY OF THE DESCENDANTS OF PETER SPICER, compiled by Susan S. Meech and Susan B. Meech, pp. 388-408. Boston: F.H. Gilson, 1911.

Jun-Sep 1758. Enlistment, expedition with Stanton's company; New London to Lyme and New York, Tappan Bay, Albany, Fort Edward; marches, skirmishes, news from other fronts, camp life; details of Major Rogers; solid entries.

SWEAT, WILLIAM, 1730-1808   **598**

Blanchette, Paul O., ed. "Captain William Sweat's Personal Diary of the Expedition Against Ticonderoga." ESSEX INSTITUTE HISTORICAL COLLECTIONS 93 (1957): 36-57.

May-Nov 1758. Account by shipwright who enlisted for the Ticonderoga campaign; march from Salisbury, Massachusetts; camp life; working on boats for the military; march home.

THOMSON, CHARLES, 1729-1824   **599**

"Minutes of a Conference Between the Government of Pennsylvania and Teedyuscung, King of the Delaware Indians." HAZARD'S REGISTER OF PENNSYLVANIA 8

(1831):85-87, 97-98, 113-116, 129-130, 145-148.

Mar 1758. Travel journal of Chief Teedyuscung's secretary; with Christian Post on journey to northern frontiers of Pennsylvania; report of conferences with Indians.

THOMPSON, SAMUEL, 1731-1820   **600**

"Diary of Lieut. Samuel Thompson of Woburn." In THE HISTORY OF WOBURN, MIDDLESEX COUNTY, MASS., by Samuel Sewall, app. 9, pp. 547-558. Boston: Wiggin and Lunt, 1865.

May-Nov 1758. Expedition against French at Lake George; marches, camp life.

    601

TINKHAM, SETH

In THE PEIRCE FAMILY OF THE OLD COLONY, by Ebenezer W. Peirce, pp. 119-128. Boston: Printed for the author, D. Clapp & Son, 1870.

May-Sep 1758. Sergeant's military journal; march of Pratt's company to join Col. Bradstreet; Lake George and Ticonderoga; battle of Lake George; marches, camp life, casualties, hardships; some spellings of interest.

TITAMY, MOSES   **602**

"Journal of Moses Titamy and Isaac Hill to Minisinks." In PENNSYLVANIA ARCHIVES, 1st ser., vol. 3, pp. 504-508.

Jun-Jul 1758. Journey to Minisink Indians; dealings with Indians.

WHEELER, JONATHAN, 1741-1811   **603**

In HISTORY OF GRAFTON, WORCESTER COUNTY, MASSACHUSETTS, by Frederick C. Pierce, pp. 71-73. Worcester: Press of C. Hamilton, 1879.

1758-1796. A few scattered notes of weather, accidents, news of French and Indian War.

ZANE, ISAAC   **604**

Coates, Joseph H. "Journal of Isaac Zane to Wyoming." PENNSYLVANIA MAGAZINE OF HISTORY AND BIOGRAPHY 30 (1906):417-426.

May-Jun 1758. Carpenter's adventures among the Indians; journey to Wyoming, Pennsylvania, to build an Indian town; some interesting spellings.

1759

ANON.   **605**

A JOURNAL OF THE EXPEDITION UP THE RIVER ST. LAWRENCE: CONTAINING A TRUE AND MOST PARTICULAR ACCOUNT OF THE TRANSACTIONS OF THE FLEET AND ARMY UNDER THE COMMAND OF ADMIRAL SAUNDERS AND GENERAL WOLFE, FROM THE TIME OF THEIR EMBARKATION AT LOUISBOURG 'TIL AFTER THE SURRENDER OF QUEBECK. By the Serjeant-Major of Gen. Hopson's Grenadiers. Boston: Printed and sold by Fowle and Draper, 1759. 24 pp. Reprint. MAGAZINE OF HISTORY, extra no. 24, 6 (1913):487-503; Photostat Americana, ser. 2, no. 113. Boston, 1940.

1759. British account of the siege of Quebec.

ANON.   **606**

NEW YORK MERCURY, 31 December 1759. Reprint. A JOURNAL OF THE EXPEDITION UP THE RIVER ST. LAW-

RENCE. Literary and Historical Society of Quebec Manuscripts Relating to the Early History of Canada, 2d ser., no. 6. Quebec: Printed by Middleton & Dawson, 1868. 19 pp.

1759. Apparently based on the preceding journal.

ANON.   **607**

A JOURNAL OF THE SIEGE OF QUEBEC. London: 1760. 16 pp.

1759. Military journal includes plan of Quebec's environs and battle on September 13, executed by Thomas Jefferys.

ANON.   **608**

In DOCUMENTS RELATIVE TO THE COLONIAL HISTORY OF THE STATE OF NEW YORK, edited by E.B. O'Callaghan, vol. 10, pp. 993-1001.

May-Aug 1759. Fragment of official French journal of siege of Quebec; narrative with daily entries. Translated.

ANON.   **609**

A JOURNAL OF THE EXPEDITION UP THE RIVER ST. LAWRENCE. Literary and Historical Society of Quebec Manuscripts Relating to the Early History of Canada, 4th ser., no. 1. Quebec: Printed by Dawson & Co., 1875. 21 pp.

May-Sep 1759. Purely military details; found among papers of George Alsop, secretary to Wolfe's quartermaster general.

ANON.   **610**

"Extracts from 'Journal of the Particular Transactions During Siege of Quebec.'" HISTORICAL MAGAZINE 4 (1860):321-326.

Jun-Aug 1759. Detailed description of operations, possibly by officer in Fraser's regiment; siege of Quebec; at anchor opposite Isle of Orleans.

ANON.   **611**

AN ACCURATE AND AUTHENTIC JOURNAL OF THE SIEGE OF QUEBEC. London: Printed for J. Robinson, 1759. 44 pp.

In THE SIEGE OF QUEBEC AND THE BATTLE OF THE PLAINS OF ABRAHAM, by Arthur G. Doughty and George W. Parmelee, vol. 4, pp. 279-294. Quebec: Dussault & Proulx, 1901.

Jun-Sep 1759. Siege of Quebec; military and naval movements, bombardments.

ANON.   **612**

In DOCUMENTS RELATIVE TO THE COLONIAL HISTORY OF THE STATE OF NEW YORK, edited by E.B. O'Callaghan, vol. 10, pp. 1016-1046.

Jun-Sep 1759. Official French account of the French army under Montcalm before Quebec; discursive entries. Translated.

ANON.   **613**

NEW YORK MERCURY, 20 August 1759.

"Journal of the Siege of Niagara." HISTORICAL MAGAZINE, 2d ser. 5 (1869):197-199.

Jul 1759. Military journal covering siege of Niagara and British victory. Translated from the French.

BAYLEY, JACOB, 1726-1815   614

In HISTORY OF NEWBURY, VERMONT, by Frederic P. Wells, pp. 376-380.

> Jul-Oct 1759, Aug 1760. Fragments of letter-journals, describing journey to and siege of Ticonderoga, camp life at Isle aux Noix.

BOWEN, ASHLEY, 1728-1813   615

THE JOURNALS OF ASHLEY BOWEN OF MARBLEHEAD. Edited by Philip C.F. Smith. Colonial Society of Massachusetts Publications, vols. 44-45. Boston: Colonial Society of Massachusetts, 1972. 2 vols.

> 1759-1804. Journal of merchant seaman, later captain; service in Royal Navy at siege of Quebec; survey of St. Lawrence River with Captain James Cook; ambiguous loyalties during Revolution, with war news secondary to town and family events; excellent record of the day-to-day work of seamanship at all levels; shipfitting, names of ships, people, and daily events of Marblehead, Massachusetts.

"Journal Kept on the Quebec Expedition." ESSEX INSTITUTE HISTORICAL COLLECTIONS 70 (1934):227-266; 88 (1952):336-347.

> Apr-Nov 1759, Jun 1760-May 1761. Voyage from Boston to Halifax to join fleet for expedition to Quebec; military and naval details at Quebec; later expedition; movements and activities of transport schooner on the St. Lawrence River.

"Personal Diary of Ashley Bowen of Marblehead." MASSACHUSETTS MAGAZINE 1 (1908):174-176, 260-265; 2 (1909):109-114; 3 (1910):240-245; 5 (1912):29-35.

> 1773-1774. Important events at Marblehead; local affairs, ship movements, necrology.

BOYLE, JOHN, 1746-1819   616

"Boyle's Journal of Occurrences in Boston." NEW ENGLAND HISTORICAL AND GENEALOGICAL REGISTER 84 (1930):142-171, 248-272, 357-382; 85 (1931):5-28, 117-133.

> 1759-1778. Journal compiled from news items; public affairs; important for social history and genealogy.

BURNABY, ANDREW, 1734-1812   617

TRAVELS THROUGH THE MIDDLE SETTLEMENTS IN NORTH AMERICA. London: T. Payne, 1775. 106 pp.; 2d ed. London: Printed for T. Payne, 1775. 198 pp. Reprint. Ithaca, N.Y.: Great Seal Books, 1960. 154 pp.; 3d ed., rev., cor., and greatly enl. London: T. Payne, 1798. 209 pp. Reprint. BURNABY'S TRAVELS THROUGH NORTH AMERICA. With introduction and notes by Rufus R. Wilson. New York: A. Wessels, 1904. 265 pp.

> 1759-1760. English clergyman's travels through Pennsylvania, New York, Rhode Island, Massachusetts, New Hampshire, Virginia; account of the colonies; acute Tory observations on colonial politics and policies; an important sourcebook.

"Burnaby's Travels in Virginia." VIRGINIA HISTORICAL REGISTER 5 (1852):27-38, 81-93, 144-157.

> Apr-May 1759. Extracts relating to Virginia.

BURRELL (or BURNELL), JOHN, b. 1717   618

"Diary of Sergeant John Burrell." NEW ENGLAND HISTORICAL AND GENEALOGICAL REGISTER 59 (1905):352-354. Reprint. "A Soldier's Diary." ACADIENSIS 5 (1905):287-294.

"John Burnell's Diary." JOURNAL OF AMERICAN HISTORY 20 (1926):375-381.

> Aug 1759-Jul 1760. With Parke's company during French and Indian War; brief notes at St. John, New Brunswick, Fort La Tour; very interesting spellings.

CLARK, THOMAS, 1737-1809   619

In NOTES ON OLD GLOUCESTER COUNTY, NEW JERSEY, compiled and edited by Frank H. Stewart, vol 1, pp. 303-306.

> ca. 1759-1809. Summary, with obscured dates; farm life; prisoner of British; life as judge and influential citizen.

CLOUGH, GIBSON, 1738-1799   620

"Extracts from Gibson Clough's Journal." ESSEX INSTITUTE HISTORICAL COLLECTIONS 3 (1861):99-106, 195-201.

> 1759-1761. March from Salem to Louisburg; siege.

DIBBLE, EBENEZER, d. 1784   621

"Diary of Ebenezer Dibble." SOCIETY OF COLONIAL WARS IN THE STATE OF CONNECTICUT PROCEEDINGS 1 (1896):311-329.

In A HISTORY OF CORNWALL, CONNECTICUT, by Edward C. Starr, pp. 179-184. New Haven: Tuttle, Morehouse & Taylor, 1926.

> May-Dec 1759. Brief notes of marches and hardships during Amherst's campaign against Ticonderoga and Crown Point.

> May-Nov 1762. In garrison at Crown Point; very interesting spellings.

FOBES, PEREZ, 1742-1812   622

Dewey, Edward H., ed. "The Diary and Commonplace Book of Perez Fobes." NEW ENGLAND QUARTERLY 2 (1929):654-658.

> 1759-1760. Dates obscure in text; his reading, philosophical and introspective observations; extempore Latin.

FRASER, MALCOLM   623

EXTRACT FROM A MANUSCRIPT JOURNAL, RELATING TO THE SIEGE OF QUEBEC IN 1759. Literary and Historical Society of Quebec Manuscripts Relating to the Early History of Canada, 2d ser., no. 1. Quebec, 1866. 37 pp.

Alexander, R.O., ed. "The Capture of Quebec." SOCIETY FOR ARMY HISTORICAL RESEARCH JOURNAL 18 (1939):135-168.

In A CANADIAN MANOR AND ITS SEIGNEURS, by George M. Wrong, pp. 249-271. Toronto: Macmillan, 1908.

> 1759-1760. Account, by member of Fraser's Highlanders, of the siege of Quebec.

GARDNER, SAMUEL, 1740-1762   624

"Diary for the Year 1759 Kept by Samuel Gardner of Salem." ESSEX INSTITUTE HISTORICAL COLLECTIONS 49 (1913):1-22.

> Jan-Dec 1759. Begins with flippant account of Harvard life; long description of voyage to Portugal and Algiers.

HARDY, CONSTANTINE, 1737-1777   625

"Extracts from the Journal of Constantine Hardy." NEW ENGLAND HISTORICAL AND GENEALOGICAL REGISTER 60 (1906):236-238.

Apr-Sep 1759. Crown Point expedition; skirmishes; very interesting spellings.

HAWKS, JOHN, 1707-1784   626

ORDERLY BOOK AND JOURNAL OF MAJOR JOHN HAWKS ON THE TICONDEROGA-CROWN POINT CAMPAIGN. With an introduction by Hugh Hastings. Society of Colonial Wars in the State of New York Publications, no. 15. New York: Printed by H.K. Brewer, 1911. 92 pp.

1759-1760. Mostly military details and orders.

HENSHAW, WILLIAM, 1735-1820   627

"William Henshaw's Journal for the Campaign in the Year 1759." WORCESTER SOCIETY OF ANTIQUITY PROCEEDINGS 25 (1912):43-63.

May-Nov 1759. Brief notes of service at and about Ticonderoga under General Amherst.

HURLBUT, JOHN, 1730-1782   628

"The Journal of a Colonial Soldier." MAGAZINE OF AMERICAN HISTORY 29 (1893):395-396.

May-Dec 1759. Crown Point expedition; private items for 1775.

"Diary of Deacon John Hurlbut." HISTORICAL RECORD OF WYOMING VALLEY 1 (1886-1887):213-214.

May-Jun 1773. Journey from Connecticut to Wyoming Valley, Pennsylvania, and ·Delaware, to inspect lands.

LANE, DANIEL, 1740-1811   629

"Journal of Daniel Lane." NEW ENGLAND HISTORICAL AND·GENEALOGICAL REGISTER 26 (1872):236-243.

Jul-Dec 1759. Siege of Quebec; journeys to Halifax to work on fortifications.

May-Nov 1761, May-Jun 1762. Travel journals.

MACKELLAR, PATRICK, 1717-1778   630

"A Short Account of the Expedition Against Quebec." JOURNAL CORPS ROYAL ENGINEERS (1848). Reprint. In THE SIEGE OF QUEBEC AND THE BATTLE OF THE PLAINS OF ABRAHAM, by Arthur G. Doughty, vol. 5, pp. 33-58. Quebec: Dussault & Proulx, 1901.

Apr-Sep 1759. Siege of Quebec; known as "Journal of Major Moncrief."

A CORRECT JOURNAL OF THE LANDING OF HIS MAJESTY'S FORCES ON THE ISLAND OF CUBA. 2d ed. London: Printed; Boston: Reprinted and sold by Green and Russell, 1762. 19 pp. Reprint. THE CAPTURE OF HAVANA IN 1762. With introduction by Edward Everett Hale. Cambridge, Mass.: Printed at the Press of the Cooperative Printing Society, 1898. 35 pp.

Jun-Aug 1762. Military, engineering and artillery details.

MERRIMAN, SAMUEL, 1723-1803   631

In A HISTORY OF DEERFIELD, MASSACHUSETTS, by George Sheldon, vol. 1, pp. 661-668. Deerfield: Press of E.A. Hall, 1895-1896.

1759-1760. Two military journals, one official and

one personal; at Albany, Ticonderoga, Crown Point, etc.; interesting spellings.

MURRAY, JAMES, 1721-1794   632

"Journal of the Siege of Quebec." LITERARY AND HISTORICAL SOCIETY OF QUEBEC HISTORICAL DOCUMENTS, 3d ser., no. 4 (1871):1-45.

Sep 1759-May 1760. Military and political activities at Quebec after its surrender; official entries, but many items of general interest.

In AN HISTORICAL JOURNAL OF THE CAMPAIGNS IN NORTH AMERICA, by John Knox, vol. 3, app., pp. 306-334.

May-Sep 1760. Mainly notes of military and naval movements at and about Quebec and Montreal.

POUCHOT, Capt.   633

In DOCUMENTS RELATIVE TO THE COLONIAL HISTORY OF THE STATE OF NEW YORK, edited by E.B. O'Callaghan, vol. 10, pp. 977-992.

Jul 1759. Siege of Niagara. Translated from the French.

PROCTER, JONATHAN, 1739-1821   634

"Diary Kept at Louisburg." ESSEX INSTITUTE HISTORICAL COLLECTIONS 70 (1934):31-57.

1759-1760. Siege of Louisburg and return home to Massachusetts; notes on terrain and works; ship movements; weather; some personal items; very interesting language.

SHIPPEN, WILLIAM, 1736-1808   635

In WILLIAM SHIPPEN, JR., PIONEER IN AMERICAN MEDICAL EDUCATION, by Betsy C. Corner, pp. 11-49. Philadelphia: American Philosophical Society, 1951.

Jul 1759-Jan 1760. Young Philadelphian's medical studies in London, principally at Guys Hospital; lectures, dissection, treating of patients; social life, theater, contacts with such famous men as George Whitefield, David Garrick and the anatomists William and John Hunter; a good picture of medical education and London social life in the eighteenth century.

SMITH, REUBEN   636

In FARMINGTON PAPERS, by Julius Gay, pp. 146-148. Hartford, Conn.: Privately printed by Case, Lockwood & Brainard, 1929.

Apr-Nov 1759. Scattered entries in diary of soldier from Farmington, Connecticut; deaths, noteworthy events; in camp at Schenectady.

TRUE, HENRY, 1726-1782   637

JOURNAL AND LETTERS OF REV. HENRY TRUE, OF HAMPSTEAD, NEW HAMPSHIRE, WHO WAS CHAPLAIN IN THE NEW HAMPSHIRE REGIMENT OF THE PROVINCIAL ARMY IN 1759 AND 1762. Marion, Ohio: Printed for H. True, 1900. 36 pp.

Jun-Oct 1759. Chaplain's journals at Ticonderoga, Fort Edward, Crown Point.

WARNER, SAMUEL, 1708-1783   638

In AN HISTORICAL ADDRESS, DELIVERED AT THE CENTENNIAL CELEBRATION OF THE INCORPORATION OF THE TOWN OF WILBRAHAM, JUNE 15, 1863, by Rufus P.

Stebbins, pp. 208-213. Boston: G.C. Rand & Avery, 1864.

In THE HISTORY OF WILBRAHAM, MASSACHUSETTS, by Chauncey E. Peck, pp. 86-89. Wilbraham?, pref. 1914.

Jun-Nov 1759. March from Albany to Fort Edward, Lake George, and return; hardships, military details, news of war; very interesting spellings and language.

WEBSTER, ROBERT   **639**

"Robert Webster's Journal." FORT TICONDEROGA MUSEUM BULLETIN 2 (1931):120-153.

Extracts in "The Crown Point Road," edited by Mary F. Charlton. VERMONT HISTORICAL SOCIETY PROCEEDINGS 2 (1931):163-193. Journal, pp. 173-175.

Apr-Nov 1759. March of Fourth Connecticut Regiment from Woodstock in Amherst's campaign; Lake George, Crown Point, Saratoga; brief, factual details of hardships and camp life.

WOOD, LEMUEL, 1741-1819   **640**

"Diaries Kept by Lemuel Wood, of Boxford." ESSEX INSTITUTE HISTORICAL COLLECTIONS 19 (1882):61-74, 143-152, 183-192; 20 (1883):156-160, 198-208, 289-296; 21 (1884):63-68.

1759-1760. Amherst's expedition against Canada; extensive journal of march, taverns, ordinary camp life and incidents; many interesting spellings.

WOODS, JOHN, 1735-1816   **641**

"John Woods, His Book." GENEALOGICAL MAGAZINE, 4th ser. 1 (1905-1906):307-312, 339-342.

Jun-Nov 1759. March from Worcester, Massachusetts, to Lake George and Ticonderoga via Albany; military details, guards, etc.; personal details of daily camp life and work; some interesting language and spellings.

1760

ANON.   **642**

ALL CANADA IN THE HANDS OF THE ENGLISH. Boston: Printed and sold by B. Mecom, 1760. 20 pp.

Aug-Sep 1760. Historical journal of Amherst's campaign and reduction of Montreal.

BOOTH, JOSEPH, 1736-1810   **643**

In ONE BRANCH OF THE BOOTH FAMILY, by Charles Edwin Booth, pp. 142-144. New York: Privately printed, 1910.

Jul-Oct 1760. Military journal of French and Indian War.

BRADBURY, JOHN, 1736-1821   **644**

In BRADBURY MEMORIAL, compiled by William B. Lapham, pp. 261-295. Portland, Maine: Brown, Thurston, 1890.

Extracts in "Diary of John Bradbury of York." MAINE HISTORICAL SOCIETY COLLECTIONS AND PROCEEDINGS, 2d ser. 1 (1890):329-335.

1760-1762. Brief notes of war services; march from Saco to Crown Point, Lake George and Montreal, with Moulton's company; camp life, casualties, engagements, discipline, weather; return to Boston, and journey to Kittery; rather intimate and very readable; some interesting spellings.

BREHM, DIEDERICK   **645**

"Lieut. Diederick Brehm." NEW ENGLAND HISTORICAL AND GENEALOGICAL REGISTER 37 (1883):21-26.

Nov 1760-Feb 1761. Report, by member of Royal American Regiment, of journey up St. Lawrence; Niagara, Detroit, Sandusky, etc.; notes on countryside and its condition.

BUCK, ABIJAH, ca. 1742-ca. 1829   **646**

In A HISTORY OF BUCKFIELD, OXFORD COUNTY, MAINE, by Alfred Cole and Charles F. Whitman, pp. 509-512. Buckfield, 1915.

1760-1785. Scattered notes of family affairs, journeys and accounts.

COFFIN, PAUL, 1737-1821   **647**

"A Tour to Connecticut River, through the Colony of Massachusetts, from Wells." NEW ENGLAND HISTORICAL AND GENEALOGICAL REGISTER 9 (1855):340-342.

Woodman, Cyrus, ed. "Memoir and Journals of Rev. Paul Coffin." MAINE HISTORICAL SOCIETY COLLECTIONS, 1st ser. 4 (1856):235-405.

Jul-Aug 1760. Clergyman's visits to meetings and relatives.

Jul-Aug 1761. Preaching tour to Rhode Island.

Sep-Oct 1768. Ride to Pigwacket; some good stories and notes on charms of the countryside.

Oct 1795. Trip to Hanover to enter son at Dartmouth College.

Jun-Aug 1796, Aug-Nov 1797, Aug-Oct 1798, Aug-Oct 1800. Various missionary tours in Maine; sermons; comments on people and places; account of Sandy River; remarks on Methodists and Baptists.

EVANS, HENRY, 1725?-1782   **648**

In HISTORY OF THE COUNTY OF ANNAPOLIS, by William A. Calnek, edited and completed by Alfred W. Savary, pp. 148-151. Toronto: W. Briggs, 1897.

Apr-Nov 1760. Brief notes of judge's voyage from Marblehead to Halifax, and his activities there.

EYRE, JEHU, 1738-1781   **649**

Keyser, Peter D., ed. "Memorials of Col. Jehu Eyre." PENNSYLVANIA MAGAZINE OF HISTORY AND BIOGRAPHY 3 (1879):296-307.

May-Dec 1760. Brief, interesting notes of travel in the western parts of Pennsylvania, etc.

FROST, JOHN, 1738-1810   **650**

"Expedition Against Canada." OLD ELIOT 8 (1908): 109-117.

May-Nov 1760. Brief entries in lieutenant's journal; march to St. Johns and return to Crown Point; interesting spellings.

HAYS, JOHN   **651**

In PENNSYLVANIA ARCHIVES, 1st ser., vol. 3, pp. 735-741.

May-Jun 1760. Notes of Indian trouble in Wyoming, Pennsylvania.

HOLDEN, DAVID, 1738–1803   **652**

"Journal of Sergeant Holden." MASSACHUSETTS HISTOR-ICAL SOCIETY PROCEEDINGS, 2d ser. 4 (1887–1889): 384–406.

In THREE MILITARY DIARIES KEPT BY GROTON SOLDIERS IN DIFFERENT WARS, edited by Samuel A. Green, pp. 47–74. Groton, Mass.: Cambridge University Press, J. Wilson and Son, 1901.

Extracts in "The Crown Point Road," edited by Mary F. Charlton. VERMONT HISTORICAL SOCIETY PROCEED-INGS, n.s. 2 (1931):163–193. Diary, pp. 178–179.

> Feb–Nov 1760. Expedition against Canada; Crown Point, Ticonderoga; notes on campaign, camp life; interesting spellings.

HOLYOKE, MARY VIAL, 1737–1802   **653**

In THE HOLYOKE DIARIES, by George F. Dow, pp. 47–138.

> 1760–1799. Brief notes of domestic, personal, and social affairs; interesting record of a woman's life in Salem.

HUTCHINS, THOMAS, 1730–1789   **654**

"Western Pennsylvania in 1760." PENNSYLVANIA MAGA-ZINE OF HISTORY AND BIOGRAPHY 2 (1878):149–153.

> Jul 1760. Engineer's military journal; march from Fort Pitt to Venango.

In THE WILDERNESS TRAIL, by Charles A. Hanna, vol. 2, pp. 362–367.

> Apr–Sep 1762. Journey to posts on western lakes, Wabash and Scioto, to hold councils with Indians; sent by George Croghan.

JENKS, SAMUEL, 1732–1801   **655**

"Journal of Captain Jenks." MASSACHUSETTS HISTORICAL SOCIETY PROCEEDINGS, 2d ser. 5 (1889–1890):352–391.

> May–Nov 1760. Highly personal record of campaign against Canada; camp life, hardships; a vigorous and entertaining diary, with substantial entries and much linguistic interest.

KENT, JACOB, 1726–1812   **656**

In HISTORY OF NEWBURY, VERMONT, edited by Frederic P. Wells, pp. 380–382.

> 1760–1791. Scattered notes; military movements during Amherst's campaign; Burgoyne's surrender; farming.

MOODY, THOMAS   **657**

DIARY OF THOMAS MOODY: CAMPAIGN OF 1760 OF THE FRENCH AND INDIAN WAR. Edited by P.M. Woodwell. South Berwick, Maine: Chronicle Print Shop, 1976. 56 pp.

> May–Dec 1760. Diary of young lieutenant under Captain John Wentworth in the British campaign against the French in Canada; route from York, Maine, to Albany, up through Lake Champlain; skirmishes; names of casualties; ravages of sickness among soldiers; regimental membership lists.

SOELLE, GEORGE, 1709–1773   **658**

Stahl, Jasper J., ed. "Diary of a Moravian Missionary at Broad Bay, Maine." NEW ENGLAND QUARTERLY 12 (1939):747–759.

> Aug–Sep 1760. Journey with Samuel Herr, seeking site for Moravian settlement in New England; Boston to New Hampshire; long entries describing travel and religious life. Translated.

In RECORDS OF THE MORAVIANS IN NORTH CAROLINA, edited by Adelaide L. Fries, vol. 2, pp. 784–803.

> 1771–1773. Editorial compilation from diaries of pastoral tours; straightforward notes of travel, meetings, work, conveying good picture of missionary zeal.

WALKER, JAMES, d. ca. 1786   **659**

In HISTORY OF BEDFORD, NEW HAMPSHIRE, by the town of Bedford, New Hampshire, pp. 122–123. Boston: Printed by A. Mudge, 1851. Enl. ed. Concord, N.H.: Rumford Printing Co., 1903.

> Jun–Sep 1760. Brief notes of work as sutler in French and Indian War; Crown Point and Ticonderoga.

WATERMAN, ASA, b. 1743   **660**

LEAFLET. Brooklyn, N.Y.: W.F. Eddy, 1904.

HARTFORD TIMES, 24 May 1904.

BRIDGEWATER DAILY STANDARD, 13 September 1904.

> Jun–Sep 1760. March against Canada; list of casualties.

WEKQUITANK, PENNSYLVANIA, MORAVIAN INDIAN MISSION   **661**

In NOTES AND QUERIES, edited by William H. Egle, 1899, pp. 123–126, 129–132, 134–138, 140–142.

> 1760–1763. Extracts from congregational diary; particularly interesting notes on missionary work and worship.

WHITALL, ANN, 1716–1797   **662**

In JOHN M. WHITALL: THE STORY OF HIS LIFE, by Hannah Whitall Smith, pp. 14–21. Philadelphia: Printed for the family, 1879.

Extracts in NOTES ON OLD GLOUCESTER COUNTY, NEW JERSEY, edited by Frank H. Stewart, vol. 1, pp. 315–316.

> 1760–1783. Quaker's diary; notes of meetings, weather, children's pranks, overeating; quite lively.

1761

ANON.   **663**

In THE HISTORY OF NEW BEDFORD, BRISTOL COUNTY, MASSACHUSETTS, by Daniel Ricketson, pp. 62–64. New Bedford: The author, 1858.

> Aug–Sep 1761, Sep 1762. Extracts from journal of sailor on sloop BETSEY of Dartmouth; brief notes of whaling voyages from Dartmouth to Newfoundland Banks.

ANON.   **664**

Butler, Amos W., ed. "A Visit to Easton." INDIANA MAGAZINE OF HISTORY 32 (1936):266–274.

> Aug 1761. Philadelphia Quaker's travel journal; narrative with dates; Philadelphia to Easton, Pennsylvania; Indian treaty; Quaker relations with Indians.

DEANE, SAMUEL, 1733-1814   665

In JOURNALS OF THE REV. THOMAS SMITH, AND THE REV. SAMUEL DEANE, PASTORS OF THE FIRST CHURCH IN PORTLAND, 2d ed., by William Willis, pp. 301-406. Portland, Maine: J.S. Bailey, 1849.

"Extracts from the Diary of Reverend Samuel Dean." SPRAGUE'S JOURNAL OF MAINE HISTORY 2 (1914-1915): 27-28.

> 1761-1814. Extracts relating principally to local, domestic and religious affairs in Portland, Maine.

GORRELL, JAMES   666

"Lieut. James Gorrell's Journal." WISCONSIN STATE HISTORICAL SOCIETY COLLECTIONS 1 (1855, reprint 1903):24-48.

> 1761-1763. Military journal beginning at Detroit and ending at Montreal; councils with Puans, Chippewas, etc.; account of attempts of French to turn Indians against the English; Indian trade.

"Lieut. Gorrell's Journal." MARYLAND HISTORICAL MAGAZINE 4 (1909):183-187.

> Aug 1763-Jan 1764. Wilkin's expedition from Montreal; brief, scattered notes of military affairs.

GRANT, JAMES, 1720-1806   667

"Journal of Lieutenant-Colonel James Grant, Commanding an Expedition Against the Cherokee Indians." FLORIDA HISTORICAL SOCIETY QUARTERLY 12 (1933):25-36.

> Jun-Jul 1761. Report to Lord Amherst on expedition against Cherokees from Fort Prince George; purely military.

NEWTON, ROGER, 1737-1816   668

In WILLARD'S HISTORY OF GREENFIELD, by David Willard, pp. 121-130. Greenfield, Mass.: Kneeland & Eastman, 1838.

In HISTORY OF GREENFIELD, by Francis McGee Thompson, vol. 2, pp. 700-748. Greenfield, Mass.: Press of T. Morey & Son, 1904.

"Extracts from the Diary of Rev. Roger Newton, D.D. of Greenfield, Mass." NEW ENGLAND HISTORICAL AND GENEALOGICAL REGISTER 62 (1908):263-273.

> 1761-1812. Extracts from clergyman's diary; notes on personal, social and church affairs, but mainly baptisms, deaths, etc.

PIERCE, SMAUEL, 1739-1815   669

In THE HISTORY OF THE TOWN OF DORCHESTER, MASSACHUSETTS, by Dorchester Antiquarian and Historical Society, pp. 358-371, 588. Boston: E. Clapp, Jr., 1859.

> 1761-1787 (with gap). A varied, interesting diary of personal, local and public affairs in and around Dorchester; fishing, farming, religion; Boston Tea Party, burning of Charleston, troop movements around Boston; some interesting language.

SMETHURST, GAMALIEL, 1738-1826   670

"A Narrative of an Extraordinary Escape out of the Hands of the Indians, in the Gulph of St. Lawrence." In HISTORICAL-GEOGRAPHICAL DOCUMENTS, RELATING TO NEW BRUNSWICK, edited by William F. Ganong, vol. 2, pp. 362-390.

> Oct-Dec 1761, 1763-1765. Travel in Nova Scotia; fisheries in the St. Lawrence; good narrative and details of adventures.

TILESTON, JOHN, 1735-1826   671

In JOHN TILESTON'S SCHOOL, by Daniel C. Colesworthy, pp. 71-80. Boston: Antiquarian Book Store, 1887.

> 1761-1766. Meager notes on neighbors, schools, politics, expenses.

"Extracts from the Diary of Mr. John Tileston." NEW ENGLAND HISTORICAL AND GENEALOGICAL REGISTER 20 (1866):11.

> Feb-Apr 1775.

WINTHROP, JOHN, 1714-1779   672

RELATION OF A VOYAGE FROM BOSTON TO NEWFOUNDLAND, FOR THE OBSERVATION OF THE TRANSIT OF VENUS. Boston: Printed and sold by Edes and Gill, 1761. 24 pp.

> Jun 1761. Scientific travel journal of some astronomical interest.

1762

ANON.   673

In RECORDS OF THE MORAVIANS IN NORTH CAROLINA, edited by Adelaide L. Fries, vol. 1, pp. 256-263.

> Apr-Jun 1762. Moravian's journal of travel from Bethlehem, Pennsylvania, to Wachovia, North Carolina, via Philadelphia, Wilmington, Bethabara; sea, river and land journey; difficulties of voyage; mistaken for pirates.

BALDWIN, EBENEZER, 1745-1775   674

In YALE COLLEGE, A SKETCH OF ITS HISTORY, edited by William L. Kingsley, vol. 1, pp. 444-446. New York: H. Holt, 1879.

> Mar-May 1762. Yale student's brief notes; lively picture of college social life, curriculum, etc.

BERNARD, Sir FRANCIS, 1712-1779   675

"Journal of a Voyage to the Island of Mount Desart." BANGOR HISTORICAL MAGAZINE 2 (1887):185-188.

> Sep-Oct 1762. Surveying journey by governor of Massachusetts to island of Mount Desert, Maine; voyage from Boston.

BROWN, BERIAH, 1714-1792   676

"A Journey to the Susquehannah River in 1762." NARRAGANSETT HISTORICAL REGISTER 2 (1883-1884):219-221.

> Sep 1762. Horseback journey with Christopher Gardiner and Benoni Gardiner, from North Kingstown, Rhode Island, to the Susquehannah River; stages, taverns, meals, trade; some interesting spellings.

CALHOUN, WILLIAM   677

Salley, A.S., Jr., ed. "Journal of William Calhoun." SOUTHERN HISTORICAL ASSOCIATION PUBLICATIONS 8 (1904):179-195.

> 1762-1770. Mostly accounts and memoranda; some earlier and later family records in Abbeville County, South Carolina.

CHOUTEAU, AUGUSTE, 1750–1829   678

FRAGMENT OF COL. AUGUSTE CHOUTEAU'S NARRATIVE OF THE SETTLEMENT OF ST. LOUIS. St. Louis: G. Knapp, 1858. 10 pp. Reprint. "Chouteau's Journal of the Founding of St. Louis." MISSOURI HISTORICAL SOCIETY COLLECTIONS 3 (1908–1911):335–366. Journal in French, pp. 335–349; journal in English, pp. 349–366.

    1762–1764. Merchant's account of founding of St. Louis; written as recollections with a few dates.

EYRE, WILLIAM, d. 1764   679

Reece, Frances R., ed. "Colonel Eyre's Journal of His Trip from New York to Pittsburgh." WESTERN PENNSYL-VANIA HISTORICAL MAGAZINE 27 (1944):37–50.

    Feb–Apr 1762. Account of engineer sent to assess flood damage to Fort Pitt; detailed description of route through Pennsylvania; terrain, road conditions, settlements, forts.

FORBES, ELI, 1726–1804   680

"Diary of Rev. Eli Forbes." MASSACHUSETTS HISTORICAL SOCIETY PROCEEDINGS, 2d ser. 7 (1891–1892):384–399.

    Jan–Dec 1762. Brief entries of church affairs and visits in Brookfield, Massachusetts; journey to council with Tuscarora Indians in western New York.

FOULKE, SAMUEL, 1718–1797   681

"Fragments of a Journal Kept by Samuel Foulke, of Bucks County." PENNSYLVANIA MAGAZINE OF HISTORY AND BIOGRAPHY 5 (1881):60–73.

    1762–1764. Brief political notes.

GLOTTOF, STEPHEN   682

"Journal of Glottof, on Board the ANDREAN and NATA-LIA." In ACCOUNT OF THE RUSSIAN DISCOVERIES BE-TWEEN ASIA AND AMERICA, 4th ed., by William Coxe, pp. 200–208. London: Cadell and Davies, 1803.

    1762–1766. Brief entries of exploring trip from Kamchatka to Copper Island, Kodiak and Umnak, with successful trading.

GORHAM, JOSEPH, 1725–1790   683

SOCIETY OF COLONIAL WARS, MASSACHUSETTS, YEARBOOK 1899, pp. 159–161.

    Jun–Aug 1762. Expedition of corps of rangers from New York to Havana; capture of city; return; a brief general diary with personal comments on Havana, sickness, etc.

GRAHAM, JOHN, 1722–1796   684

EXTRACTS FROM THE JOURNAL OF THE REVEREND JOHN GRAHAM. Society of Colonial Wars, New York, Publications, no. 1. New York, 1896. 18 pp.

    Sep–Oct 1762. Journal of chaplain with First Connecticut Regiment during siege of Havana.

HECKEWELDER, JOHN GOTTLIEB, 1743–1823   685

THIRTY THOUSAND MILES WITH JOHN HECKEWELDER. Edited by Paul A. Wallace. Pittsburgh: University of Pittsburgh Press, 1958. 474 pp.

    1762–1813. Part memoir, part diary of German Moravian missionary to the Indians of the Ohio area; travel by horseback, canoe, Ohio River flatboat and on Indian trails of western Pennsyl-

vania and Ohio; the influx of settlers; work among Mohicans and Delawares recently displaced from the east; encyclopedic detail on customs, councils, alliances; mutual massacres by Indians and whites; diarist's captivity by British during the Revolution. Translated from the German.

Mahr, August C., trans. and ed. "A Canoe Journey from the Big Beaver to the Tuscarawes." OHIO ARCHAE-OLOGICAL AND HISTORICAL QUARTERLY 61 (1952):283–298.

    Apr–May 1773. Moravian missionary diary of journey by canoe on the Ohio and Muskingum rivers to move Indian converts farther west. Translated from the German.

"Narrative of John Heckewelder's Journey to the Wabash in 1792." PENNSYLVANIA MAGAZINE OF HISTORY AND BIOGRAPHY 11 (1887):466–475; 12 (1888):34–54, 165–184. Reprint. Philadelphia: 1888. 51 pp.

    May–Dec 1792. Journey from Bethlehem, Pennsylvania, to the Wabash on peace mission to the Indians; river route and settlements; narrative style. Translated from the German.

Jordan, John W., ed. "Notes of Travel of William Henry, John Heckewelder, John Rothrock, and Christian Clewell, to Gnadenhuetten on the Muskingum, in the Early Summer of 1797." PENNSYLVANIA MAGAZINE OF HISTORY AND BIOGRAPHY 10 (1886):125–157.

    Apr–Jul 1797. From Bethlehem to Gnadenhuetten on the Muskingum to survey lands for Christian Indians; return trip; journey and surveying described in interesting detail.

HOYT, SAMUEL, 1744–1826   686

Pease, Julius W., ed. "Adventures of an Early American Sea-Captain." CONNECTICUT MAGAZINE 10 (1906):631–646; 11 (1907):275–284.

Extracts in "Adventures of an American Seaman." JOURNAL OF AMERICAN HISTORY 1 (1907):81–88, 485–493; 2 (1908):64–73.

    1762–1800. Adventures of a sailor's life written up from journal and memory; extracts pertaining to life on a fighting ship off Havana.

JOHNSON, GUY, 1740?–1788   687

In DOCUMENTS RELATIVE TO THE COLONIAL HISTORY OF THE STATE OF NEW YORK, edited by E.B. O'Callaghan, vol. 7, pp. 511–515.

    Nov–Dec 1762. Official journal of deputy agent for Indian affairs; meeting with Indians at Onondaga to settle for murders in Seneca country; minutes and speeches.

KNIGHT, NATHANIEL   688

"Journal of Capt. Nathaniel Knight, Senior." NEW ENGLAND HISTORICAL AND GENEALOGICAL REGISTER 44 (1890):200–202.

    May–Jul 1762. Voyage from St. Martins toward Salem; captured by Spanish privateer off Puerto Rico.

MAXWELL, HUGH, 1733–1799   689

THE CHRISTIAN PATRIOT. New York: 1833.

    1762–1795. Diary extracts, partly during French and Indian War, partly during Revolution; personal experiences and reflections.

MIFFLIN, BENJAMIN, b. 1718   690

Paltsits, Victor H., ed. "Journal of Benjamin Mifflin on a Tour from Philadelphia to Delaware and Maryland." NEW YORK PUBLIC LIBRARY BULLETIN 39 (1935):423-438. Reprint. New York: New York Public Library, 1935. 18 pp.

     Jul-Aug 1762. Travel diary; some good observations on people, towns, taverns, trade.

"Journal of a Journey from Philadelphia to the Cedar Swamps and Back." PENNSYLVANIA MAGAZINE OF HISTORY AND BIOGRAPHY 52 (1928):130-140.

     Jun-Jul 1764. Vigorous comments on inns, expenses, religion.

PARK, ROSWELL, 1726-1762   691

"A Journal of the Expedition Against Cuba." UNIVERSITY OF BUFFALO STUDIES 1 (1919-1920):231-244.

     May-Aug 1762. Notes on expedition to Havana.

ROBERTSON, ARCHIBALD, ca. 1745-1813   692

ARCHIBALD ROBERTSON--HIS DIARIES AND SKETCHES IN AMERICA. Edited by Harry M. Lydenberg. New York: New York Public Library, 1930. 300 pp. Reprint. Lydenberg, Harry M., ed. "Archibald Robertson, Lieutenant-General Royal Engineers: His Diaries and Sketches in America." NEW YORK PUBLIC LIBRARY BULLETIN 37 (1933):7-37, 113-134, 181-199, 277-290, 479-503, 577-608, 660-694, 775-795, 865-901, 953-969.

     1762-1780 (with gap, 1762-1775). Five journals, mainly relating to the Revolution, Havana expedition, siege of Boston, White Plains, Danbury expedition, Cornwallis' expedition, etc.; surveying and engineering work; primarily military notes, with many interesting drawings.

SMITH, HEZEKIAH, 1737-1805   693

CHAPLAIN SMITH AND THE BAPTISTS. By Reuben A. Guild. Philadelphia: American Baptist Publication Society, 1885. 429 pp.

     1762-1805 (with gaps). Abundant brief notes of missionary work in South, experiences as chaplain in Nixon's regiment in Fourth Continental Infantry; Saratoga, Burgoyne's surrender, White Plains, etc.

STARR, WILLIAM, b. 1730   694

Myers, William S., ed. "Log of an American Marine in 1762 on a British Fighting Ship." JOURNAL OF AMERICAN HISTORY 3 (1901):113-117.

     May-Nov 1762. Expedition against Havana in British fighting ship; good picture of life on board man-o'-war.

WILKINSON, ELIZABETH, 1712-1771   695

"Extracts from the 'Journal of a Religious Visit to Friends in America, 1761-1763.'" FRIENDS' HISTORICAL ASSOCIATION BULLETIN 18 (1929):87-90.

     Mar 1762-Jan 1763. Extracts from journal of ministering English Quaker; meetings on Long Island and in Pennsylvania; some ecstatic religious entries.

1763

ANON.   696

JOURNAL OF AN OFFICER DURING THE SIEGE OF FORT DETROIT. London: 1858.

     1763-1764. Pontiac's siege.

ABBADIE, JEAN-JACQUES-BLAISE D', 1726-1765   697

In A COMPARATIVE VIEW OF FRENCH LOUISIANA . . . THE JOURNALS OF PIERRE LE MOYNE D'IBERVILLE AND JEAN-JACQUES-BLAISE D'ABBADIE, translated and edited by Carl A. Brasseaux, pp. 83-138. University of Southwestern Louisiana History Series, no. 13. Lafayette: Center for Louisiana Studies, University of Southwestern Louisiana, 1979. Rev. ed., 1981.

     1763-1764. Official journal of chief French administrator of Louisiana during critical period following Seven Years' War; responsibility for orderly transfer of territory to England and Spain according to terms of Treaty of Paris; concern for dismal condition of French settlers; extensive dealings with Indians; activities of Jesuits and Capuchins. Translated from the French.

ARMSTRONG, GEORGE   698

Wainwright, Nicholas B., ed. "Voyage to England: 2. Shipwreck of the Britannia, 1764." PENNSYLVANIA MAGAZINE OF HISTORY AND BIOGRAPHY 73 (1949):87-91.

     Dec 1763-Feb 1764. Diary, found in notebook of George Croghan, describing perils of sea voyage; shipwreck on coast of France; travel through France to England.

DYER, JOHN, d. 1811   699

"Memoranda from the Diary of John Dyer of Plumstead, Bucks Co., Pa." GENEALOGICAL SOCIETY OF PENNSYLVANIA PUBLICATIONS 3 (1906):38-72.

     1763-1805. Brief notes, mostly of births, marriages, deaths, removals; a few local affairs.

HAY, JEHU, d. 1785   700

DIARY OF THE SIEGE OF DETROIT IN THE WAR WITH PONTIAC. Edited by Franklin B. Hough. Albany: J. Munsell, 1860. 304 pp.

Extracts in "Diary of the Siege of Detroit," by W.L. Jenks. MICHIGAN HISTORY MAGAZINE 12 (1928):437-442.

     1763-1765. Daily events of siege of Detroit; full details; an extremely valuable journal of Pontiac's siege.

MASON, CHARLES   701

JOURNAL OF CHARLES MASON AND JEREMIAH DIXON. Transcribed from the original in the United States National Archives, with an introduction by A. Hughlett Mason. Philadelphia: American Philosophical Society, 1969. 231 pp.

     1763-1768. Highly technical journal by British astronomers Mason and Dixon of surveying expedition to establish the long-disputed boundary between colonies of Pennsylvania and Maryland; wealth of surveying details; rigors of carrying out the project under frontier and wilderness conditions.

NAVARRE, ROBERT 702

JOURNAL OF PONTIAC'S CONSPIRACY. Edited by M. Agnes Burton, translated by R. Clyde Ford. Detroit: Published by Clarence Monroe Burton under the auspices of the Michigan Society of the Colonial Wars, 1912. 243 pp.

1763. Journal of keeper of notorial records at Detroit; account of the conspiracy. Parallel French and English texts. Authorship not definitely established.

In THE SIEGE OF DETROIT IN 1763: THE JOURNAL OF PONTIAC'S CONSPIRACY AND JOHN RUTHERFORD'S NARRATIVE OF A CAPTIVITY, edited by Milo M. Quaife, pp. 3-215. Chicago: R.R. Donnelley, 1958.

May-Jul 1763. Siege by Ottowa chief and his Huron and Potawatomi allies against British at Detroit; disappointment of Pontiac's hopes for French alliance against British; Major Henry Gladwin's defense of fort against waves of Indian assault; Indian atrocities against captives; battle of Bloody Run. Some episodes obviously written up more fully after the siege.

PHELPS, ELIZABETH PORTER, 1747-1817 703

In UNDER A COLONIAL ROOF-TREE: FIRESIDE CHRONICLES OF EARLY NEW ENGLAND, by Arria S. Huntington, pp. 26-105. Boston and New York: Houghton, Mifflin, 1891.

1763-1812. Extracts from private diary, reflecting life in Hadley, Massachusetts, kept by daughter and wife of leading citizens; social life of family and friends; illnesses, births, marriages, deaths; notes on sermons.

Andrews, Thomas Eliot, ed. "The Diary of Elizabeth Porter Phelps." NEW ENGLAND HISTORICAL AND GENEALOGICAL REGISTER 118 (1964):3-30, 108-127, 207-236, 297-308; 119 (1965):43-59, 127-140, 205-223, 289-307; 120 (1966):57-63, 123-135, 203-214, 293-304; 121 (1967): 57-69, 95-100, 296-303; 122(1968):62-70, 115-123, 220-227, 302-309.

1763-1805.

SMITH, WILLIAM, 1728-1793 704

HISTORICAL MEMOIRS OF WILLIAM SMITH. Edited by William H.W. Sabine. New York: Colburn & Tegg, 1956-1958. 2 vols.

1763-1778. Valuable and interesting diary of lawyer, politician, historian and member of influential New York family, kept to record official events as source material for a history of New York; personal animosities and struggle for power among prominent New York families; two years of inactivity at The Hermitage on Livingston Manor; conversations with numerous relatives and news of the war as recounted by visitors of all sorts, with his voluminous critical commentaries.

THE DIARY AND SELECTED PAPERS OF CHIEF JUSTICE WILLIAM SMITH, 1784-1793. Edited by L.F.S. Upton. Toronto: The Champlain Society, 1963-1965. 2 vols.

1784-1787. Years in London as Loyalist exile; travels and theater-going; comments on political and social affairs in England; struggle to reclaim his wartime losses.

WALKER, TIMOTHY, 1737-1822 705

In HISTORY OF THE TOWN OF CANTERBURY, NEW HAMPSHIRE, 1727-1912, by James O. Lyford, vol. 1, pp. 96-97. Concord, N.H.: Rumford Press, 1912.

1763-1766 (with gaps). Judge's very brief notes of personal affairs, journeys, visits, preaching.

WISWALL, JOHN, 1731-1821 706

NOVA SCOTIA HISTORICAL SOCIETY COLLECTIONS 13 (1908):1-73 passim.

1763-1797. Clergyman's notes of private affairs in Portland, Maine, war news, journey to England; quotations.

1764

ANON. 707

"Journal of a French Traveller in the Colonies." AMERICAN HISTORICAL REVIEW 26 (1920-1921):726-747; 27 (1921-1922):70-89.

Dec 1764-Sep 1765. Voyage to West Indies; journey through southern colonies and Annapolis, Philadelphia, New York; accounts of country and its resources; notes on topography, towns, trade, agriculture, weather; written in English, with part redaction in French; a very interesting journal, with some interesting spellings in English portion.

BOUQUET, HENRY, 1719-1765 708

In THE OLDEN TIME, edited by Neville B. Craig, vol. 1, pp. 217-221, 241-260.

Aug-Oct 1764. Military journal; expedition against the Ohio Indians.

EMERSON, WILLIAM, 1743-1776 709

DIARIES AND LETTERS OF WILLIAM EMERSON, 1743-1776, MINISTER OF THE CHURCH IN CONCORD, CHAPLAIN IN THE REVOLUTIONARY ARMY. Arranged by Amelia F. Emerson. n.p., 1972. 150 pp.

1764-1776. Preaching and pastoral work in Concord, Massachusetts, and pulpit exchanges in neighboring communities; preparation of Concord for war, service as chaplain, including some sermons preached to troops; battle of Lexington and Concord.

In THE LITERATURE OF THE NINETEENTH OF APRIL, by James L. Whitney, pp. 165-173. Concord, Massachusetts, Proceedings of the Centennial Celebration of Concord Fight. Concord: Published by the town, 1876.

Apr 1775. Extract providing good description of the battle of Lexington and Concord.

GORDON, ADAM, Lord, ca. 1726-1801 710

In TRAVELS IN THE AMERICAN COLONIES, edited by Newton D. Mereness, pp. 365-453.

1764-1765. Travel diary of member of Sixty-sixth Foot Regiment; tour in West Indies and North America; Georgia, Carolina, Virginia, Maryland, New York, New England, Canada; interesting descriptions of places, persons, trade, routes, etc. Authorship assumed.

KIRKLAND, SAMUEL, 1741-1808 711

THE JOURNALS OF SAMUEL KIRKLAND; 18TH-CENTURY MISSIONARY TO THE IROQUOIS, GOVERNMENT AGENT, FATHER OF HAMILTON COLLEGE. Edited by Walter Pilkington. Clinton, N.Y.: Hamilton College, 1980. 459 pp.

1764-1807. Missionary journal of work among the Iroquois of western New York, kept by a protégé of

Eleazer Wheelock for the Society in Scotland for the Propagation of Christian Knowledge; preaching; participation in Indian councils and conferences; efforts to represent Indian cause to government officials; establishment of Hamilton-Oneida Academy; decline of Iroquois traditional culture under increase of settlement; a detailed and important diary.

In AN AUTHENTIC AND COMPREHENSIVE HISTORY OF BUFFALO, by William Ketchum, vol. 1, pp. 212-239. Buffalo: Rockwell, Baker & Hill, Printers, 1864.

Nov 1764-Apr 1765. Missionary journal of visit to Seneca Indians.

"Journal of the Reverend Samuel Kirkland." HISTORICAL MAGAZINE, 2d ser. 3 (1868):37-39.

Sep-Nov 1776. Missionary journal among Oneida Indians.

In AN AUTHENTIC AND COMPREHENSIVE HISTORY OF BUFFALO, vol. 2, pp. 97-110.

Sep-Dec 1788. Missionary travel journal; Fort Stanwix to the Five Nations.

LOFTUS, ARTHUR   712

Haffner, Gerald O., ed. "Major Arthur Loftus' Journal of the Proceedings of His Majesty's Twenty-Second Regiment up the River Mississippi in 1764." LOUISIANA HISTORY 20 (1979):325-334.

Feb-Mar 1764. Military leader's record of unsuccessful expedition to secure control of Illinois country; winds, distances covered; desertions, an execution; Indian attack 240 miles above New Orleans, retreat and abandonment of enterprise.

MITCHEL, JOHN   713

"John Mitchel's Diary and Field Book of His Survey of Passamaquoddy in 1764." In HISTORICAL-GEOGRAPHICAL DOCUMENTS, RELATING TO NEW BRUNSWICK, edited by William F. Ganong, vol. 2, pp. 175-188.

May-Jun 1764. Captain's surveying journal on Massachusetts and New Brunswick border; personal details; some interesting spellings.

MORGAN, JOHN, b. 1736   714

"A Visit to Voltaire." PENNSYLVANIA MAGAZINE OF HISTORY AND BIOGRAPHY 10 (1886):43-50.

Discussed in AMERICAN DIARY LITERATURE, by Steven E. Kagle, pp. 71-75.

Sep 1764. Travel journal of Philadelphia physician; extract concerning visit with Voltaire.

MORRIS, THOMAS, b. 1732?   715

MISCELLANIES IN PROSE AND VERSE. London: Printed for James Ridgway, 1791. 181 pp.

"Miscellanies in Prose and Verse." MAGAZINE OF HISTORY, extra no. 76, 19 (1922):165-191.

JOURNAL OF CAPTAIN THOMAS MORRIS, FROM MISCELLANIES IN PROSE AND VERSE. Ann Arbor: University Microfilms, 1966. 39 pp.

In EARLY WESTERN TRAVELS, edited by Reuben G. Thwaites, vol. 1, pp. 301-328.

Aug-Sep 1764. Military travel journal of captain of Seventeenth Infantry; journey to Miami Indians; narrative arranged as a diary; amusing account of adventures and self-glorification of an insignificant hero.

MOSLEY, JOSEPH   716

Devitt, Edward I., ed. "Letters of Father Joseph Mosley, S.J., and Some Extracts from His Diary." AMERICAN CATHOLIC HISTORICAL SOCIETY OF PHILADELPHIA RECORDS 17 (1906):180-210. Journal, pp. 196-200.

1764-1768. Brief extracts concerning period of foundation of St. Joseph's Mission, Pennsylvania.

ROGERS, JOHN, 1724-1779   717

A LOOKING GLASS FOR THE PRESBYTERIANS OF NEW-LONDON. Providence: Printed for the author, 1767.

1764-1766. Religious notes; Quaker meetings and opposition.

ROWE, JOHN, 1715-1787   718

LETTERS AND DIARY OF JOHN ROWE, BOSTON MERCHANT. Edited by Anne Rowe Cunningham. Boston: W.B. Clarke, 1903. 453 pp. Reprint. New York: New York Times, 1969.

Pierce, Edward L., ed. "Diary of John Rowe." MASSACHUSETTS HISTORICAL SOCIETY PROCEEDINGS 10 (1895): 11-108. Diary extracts, pp. 60-108.

1764-1779. Social and public life of a Boston merchant; political disturbances, dinners, clubs; impersonal, but of considerable genealogical interest.

WRANGEL, CARL MAGNUS, 1727-1786   719

Anderson, Carl M., trans. and ed. "Pastor Wrangel's Trip to the Shore." NEW JERSEY HISTORY 87 (1969): 4-31.

Oct 1764. Extract from the diary of the dean of the Swedish Evangelical Lutheran Churches in America; ten-day round trip from Philadelphia across New Jersey to Egg Harbor on the Atlantic Ocean to bring religious instruction to Swedes living there.

1765

AULD, JAMES, d. 1780   720

"The Journal of James Auld." SOUTHERN HISTORICAL ASSOCIATION PUBLICATIONS 8 (1904):253-268.

1765-1766. Journal of resident of Anson County, North Carolina; erratic notes of travel, mostly in the South; a few genealogical notes by a later writer.

BARTRAM, JOHN, 1699-1777   721

DIARY OF A JOURNAL THROUGH THE CAROLINAS, GEORGIA AND FLORIDA. Annotated by Francis Harper. American Philosophical Society Transactions, New Series, vol. 33, pt. 1. Philadelphia: American Philosophical Society, 1942. 120 pp.

Jul 1765-Apr 1766. Diary of Quaker naturalist, botanist to George III; travel notes and natural history observations; visit to Whitefield's Orphan House at Savannah; details of plan, architecture and buildings of St. Augustine.

AN ACCOUNT OF EAST FLORIDA, WITH A JOURNAL KEPT BY JOHN BARTRAM OF PHILADELPHIA. London: Sold by W. Nicoll and G. Woodfall, 1766. 70 pp.

In A DESCRIPTION OF EAST FLORIDA, WITH A JOURNAL, KEPT BY JOHN BARTRAM OF PHILADELPHIA, by William Stork, pt. 2, 35 pp. 3d ed. London: Sold by W. Nicoll, 1769.

Dec 1765–Feb 1766. Portions covering travel from St. Augustine up the Saint Johns River.

"Extract from the Journal of John Bartram, of Philadelphia." SMITHSONIAN INSTITUTION ANNUAL REPORT (1874):393.

1765–1766. Concerning antiquities of Florida.

CUTLER, MANASSEH, 1742–1823   722

LIFE, JOURNALS AND CORRESPONDENCE OF REV. MANASSEH CUTLER, LL.D. by William P. Cutler and Julia P. Cutler. Cincinnati: R. Clarke, 1888. 2 vols.

1765–1819 (with nine years missing). Private diary of Congregational minister, farm improver, scientist, western colonizer, and member of House of Representatives (1801–1805); preaching journeys; personal and local affairs in Dedham, Massachusetts, and Marietta, Ohio; notes on social life, religious work, etc.; a very good diary.

"New Jersey, Pennsylvania and Ohio, in 1787-8: Passages from the Journals of Rev. Manasseh Cutler." NEW JERSEY HISTORICAL SOCIETY PROCEEDINGS, 2d ser. 3 (1872–1874):73–96.

1787–1788. Scattered extracts relating to New Jersey, Pennsylvania and Ohio.

"Journal of Rev. Manasseh Cutler." NEW ENGLAND HISTORICAL AND GENEALOGICAL REGISTER 14 (1860): 104–106, 234–236, 364–366; 15 (1861):45–49.

Aug–Sep 1788. Ohio journey.

Newcomer, Lee N., ed. "A Long Journey Home from Congress." ESSEX INSTITUTE HISTORICAL COLLECTIONS 100 (1964):85–87.

Mar 1805. Extracts detailing the rigors of travel from Washington, D.C., to Salem, Massachusetts; by stage, packet, sloop.

FUENTE, PEDRO JOSE DE LA   723

Daniel, James M., trans. and ed. "Diary of Pedro José de la Fuente, Captain of the Presidio of El Paso del Norte." SOUTHWESTERN HISTORICAL QUARTERLY 60 (1956):260–281; 83 (1980):259–278.

Jan–Dec 1765. Diary kept for his superiors by commandant of frontier outpost; harassment by Apaches; tedious negotiations in quest of peace; co-operation of "friendly" Indians; missionary work among the Indians; commercial life in El Paso, especially trading caravans from Chihuahua, Janos and Sonora.

GREGORY, WILLIAM, 1742–1817   724

"William Gregory's Journal, from Fredericksburg, Va., to Philadelphia." WILLIAM AND MARY COLLEGE QUARTERLY, 1st ser. 13 (1904–1905):224–229.

Sep–Oct 1765. Journey from Fredericksburg to Philadelphia on business, and return.

Powell, Mary G., ed. "A Scotchman's Journey in New England in 1771." NEW ENGLAND MAGAZINE, n.s. 12 (1895):343–352.

Sep–Oct 1771. Journey in New England; Hartford, Sudbury, Cambridge, Boston, voyage to Newport, Yale; substantial and well-written entries describing towns and places, taverns and social life; a very readable diary.

HENFIELD, JOSEPH, 1743–1809   725

In ANNALS OF SALEM, by Joseph B. Felt, vol. 2, pp. 108–109, 138–139. 2d ed. Salem: W.&S.B. Ives; Boston:

J. Munroe, 1845–1849.

1765–1800. Almanac notes of weather, local affairs in Salem, Massachusetts; vital statistics.

HILTZHEIMER, JACOB, 1729–1798   726

EXTRACTS FROM THE DIARY OF JACOB HILTZHEIMER, OF PHILADELPHIA. Edited by Jacob Cox Parsons. Philadelphia: Press of W.F. Fell, 1893. 270 pp.

Extracts describing visits to Reading and General Mifflin in EARLY NARRATIVES OF BERKS COUNTY, by James B. Nolan, pp. 42–50.

1765–1798 (with gaps 1771, 1775–1776). Public affairs, private and domestic life in Philadelphia; mostly brief entries, but extent and consistency give a full picture of life in the city; plays, amusements, sports, journeys, visits, religion; a very attractive diary.

"Extracts from the Diary of Jacob Hiltzheimer." PENNSYLVANIA MAGAZINE OF HISTORY AND BIOGRAPHY 16 (1892):93–102, 160–177, 412–422.

1768–1798. Extracts concerning Philadelphia.

IZARD, RALPH, 1742–1804   727

AN ACCOUNT OF A JOURNEY TO NIAGARA, MONTREAL AND QUEBEC. New York: Printed by W. Osborn, 1846. 30 pp.

Extract in STUDIES OF THE NIAGARA FRONTIER, by Frank H. Severance, pp. 339–346. Buffalo Historical Society Publications, vol. 15. Buffalo, N.Y.: Buffalo Historical Society, 1911.

Jun 1765. Travel in upper New York; description of Niagara.

LEACH, CHRISTIANA   728

"Selections from the Diary of Christiana Leach, of Kingsessing." PENNSYLVANIA MAGAZINE OF HISTORY AND BIOGRAPHY 35 (1911):343–349.

1765–1796. Scattered notes, mostly of family matters. Translated from the German.

PORTEUS, JOHN   729

Hamil, Fred C., ed. "Schenectady to Michilimackinac, 1765 and 1766." ONTARIO HISTORICAL SOCIETY PAPERS AND RECORDS 33 (1939):75–98.

1765–1766. Merchant's diary of trading trip, chiefly by boat; weather, soil, details of travel route.

QUINCY, JOSIAH, 1744–1775   730

"Diary of Josiah Quincy, Jun." MASSACHUSETTS HISTORICAL SOCIETY PROCEEDINGS 4 (1858–1860):46–51.

Aug 1765. Extract describing Stamp Act riot on August 27.

"Journal of Josiah Quincy, Junior." MASSACHUSETTS HISTORICAL SOCIETY PROCEEDINGS 49 (1915–1916):424–481.

Feb–May 1773. Journey to South Carolina; good description of country and towns, etc.

In MEMOIR OF THE LIFE OF JOSIAH QUINCY, JR., edited by John Quincy, pp. 73–141. Boston: Cummings, Hilliard, 1825.

"Quincy's London Journal." MASSACHUSETTS HISTORICAL SOCIETY PROCEEDINGS 50 (1916–1917):433–470.

Sep 1774–Mar 1775. Voyage to England, and residence there; interesting details of social life and etiquette; amusing high-flying style.

WEBSTER, PELATIAH, 1725-1795   731

Harrison, T.P., ed. "Journal of a Voyage to Charles-town in So. Carolina." SOUTHERN HISTORICAL ASSOCIA-TION PUBLICATIONS 2 (1898):131-148.

> May-Jun 1765. Voyage from Philadelphia to Charleston, and return; mainly descriptions of Charleston and environs; interest in southern plants.

WESTON, WARREN, 1738-1799   732

Bowman, George E., ed. "Warren Weston's Journal." PILGRIM NOTES AND QUERIES 2 (1914):1-3.

> 1765-1766. Brief notes on personal affairs of a ship's carpenter; interesting spellings.

1766

CARVER, JONATHAN, 1710-1780   733

THE JOURNALS OF JONATHAN CARVER AND RELATED DOCUMENTS. Edited by John Parker. Bicentennial ed. Minnesota Historical Society Publications. St. Paul, Minn.: Minnesota Historical Society Press, 1976. 244 pp.

> 1766-1770. Exploration diary; attempt to find the Northwest Passage and to extend British fur trade in the upper Mississippi Valley and Great Lakes area; improperly authorized expedition under command of Major Robert Rogers; surveying data, geographical features, soil, plants and animals; notes taken with an eye to potential for fur trade and agriculture; extensive details on Indian customs and languages; an interesting diary.

CLARKSON, MATTHEW, 1733-1800   734

In INFORMATION RESPECTING THE HISTORY, CONDITION AND PROSPECTS OF THE INDIAN TRIBES OF THE UNITED STATES, by Henry R. Schoolcraft, vol. 4, pp. 265-278. Philadelphia: Lippincott, Grambo, 1854.

In THE NEW REGIME, edited by Clarence W. Alvord and Clarence E. Carter, pp. 349-363.

> Aug 1766-Apr 1767. Travel diary of agent for Indian traders; from Philadelphia to Fort Pitt, Fort Chartres and Kaskaskia; Indian vocabulary; fur prices; social details of frontier.

GODDARD, JAMES STANLEY II   735

Gilman, Carolyn, ed. "Journal of a Voyage." In THE JOURNALS OF JONATHAN CARVER AND RELATED DOCU-MENTS edited by John Parker, pp. 180-191. Bicenten-nial ed. Minnesota Historical Society Publications. St. Paul: Minnesota Historical Society Press, 1976.

> 1766-1767. Brief, seminarrative journal of expedi-tion under command of Captain James Tute to establish better fur trade contacts for the British among Indians of upper Mississippi Valley.

GORDON, HARRY, d. 1787   736

In THE NEW REGIME, edited by Clarence W. Alvord and Clarence E. Carter, pp. 290-311.

In TRAVELS IN THE AMERICAN COLONIES, edited by Newton D. Mereness, pp. 464-489.

Extracts in A TOPOGRAPHICAL DESCRIPTION OF SUCH PARTS OF NORTH AMERICA AS ARE CONTAINED IN THE (ANNEXED) MAP OF THE MIDDLE BRITISH COLONIES, by Thomas Pownall, app., pp. 2-5. London: J. Almon, 1776. Reprint. "Extracts from the Journal of Captain Harry Gordon." ILLINOIS STATE HISTORICAL SOCIETY JOURNAL 2 (1909-1910):55-64. Revised and enlarged edition published as A TOPOGRAPHICAL DESCRIPTION OF THE DOMINIONS OF THE UNITED STATES OF AMERICA, edited by Lois Mulkearn. Pittsburgh: University of Pittsburgh Press, 1949.

Extracts in THE WILDERNESS TRAIL, by Charles A. Hanna, vol. 2, pp. 40-55. Reprint. "Extracts from the Journal of Captain Harry Gordon." MISSOURI HIS-TORICAL SOCIETY COLLECTIONS 3 (1908-1911):437-443.

> May-Dec 1766. Surveying journal of member of Royal Engineers; trip, accompanied by George Croghan, down Ohio, Illinois and Mississippi rivers to New Orleans, and thence to Mobile and Pensacola; descriptions of places, distances, trade, weather, fur trade.

HASEY, ISAAC, 1742-1812   737

In THE IPSWICH EMERSONS, by Benjamin K. Emerson, assisted by George A. Gordon, pp. 431-432. Boston: D. Clapp & Son, 1900.

> 1766-1808. Extracts from clergyman's diary; brief, scattered notes of personal and parish affairs, and war news.

Chamberlain, George W., ed. "Abstracts Relating to the Revolutionary War from the Diaries of Rev. Isaac Hasey, First Settled Minister of the First Parish of Lebanon, Maine (1765-1812)." MAINE HISTORICAL SOC-IETY COLLECTIONS, 2d ser. 9 (1898):132-136.

> 1775-1784. Extracts pertaining to the war.

JENNINGS, JOHN, ca. 1738-1802   738

"John Jennings' Journal from Fort Pitt to Fort Chartres in the Illinois Country." PENNSYLVANIA MAGAZINE OF HISTORY AND BIOGRAPHY 31 (1907):145-156.

In THE NEW REGIME, edited by Clarence W. Alvord and Clarence E. Carter, pp. 167-177.

> Mar-Apr 1766. Trading expedition down Ohio River and up the Mississippi; descriptions of French villages.

"John Jennings' Journal at Fort Chartres, and Trip to New Orleans." PENNSYLVANIA MAGAZINE OF HISTORY AND BIOGRAPHY 31 (1907):304-310.

Extract in TRADE AND POLITICS, 1767-1769, edited by Clarence W. Alvord and Clarence E. Carter, pp. 336-339. Illinois State Historical Library Collections, vol. 16. Springfield: Illinois State Historical Library, 1921.

> May-Jul 1768. At the fort; trip down the Missis-sippi; descriptions of scenery and forts.

LAFORA, NICOLAS DE, b. ca. 1730   739

THE FRONTIERS OF NEW SPAIN: NICOLAS DE LAFORA'S DESCRIPTION. Translated and edited by Lawrence Kin-naird. Quivira Society Publications, vol. 13. Berkeley, Calif.: The Quivira Society, 1958. 243 pp.

> 1766-1768. Diarist and cartographer of an inspec-tion tour led by Marqués de Rubí to make recom-mendations for improving the defenses and admin-istration of Spanish frontier presidios; careful and detailed information on geography, population, frontier conditions, Indians, especially Apaches, in area which became Mexico-United States boundary.

LINCK, WENCESLAUS, b. 1736   740

WENCESLAUS LINCK'S DIARY OF HIS 1766 EXPEDITION TO NORTHERN BAJA CALIFORNIA. Translated into English, edited and annotated by Ernest J. Burrus. Los Angeles: Dawson's Book Shop, 1966. 115 pp.

> Feb-Apr 1766. Jesuit's missionary and geographical expedition from San Borja toward mouth of Colorado; failure to reach his goal; travel farther north than any other European, providing valuable information for later expeditions concerning water, food and the Indians' attitude toward Christianity.

MCCLURE, DAVID, 1748-1820   741

DIARY OF DAVID MCCLURE, DOCTOR OF DIVINITY. With notes by Franklin B. Dexter. New York: Privately printed, Knickerbocker Press, 1899. 219 pp.

> 1766-1819. Private diary of Presbyterian minister and missionary to Indians, principally Delawares, later pastor and schoolmaster in East Windsor, Connecticut; detailed entries of Indian affairs.

"Lancaster in 1772." LANCASTER COUNTY HISTORICAL SOCIETY PAPERS 5 (1901):106-112.

> Jul-Aug 1772. Description of Lancaster, Pennsylvania.

"Battle of Lexington and Concord." MASSACHUSETTS HISTORICAL SOCIETY PROCEEDINGS, 1st ser. 16 (1878): 155-158.

> Apr 1775. Lexington alarm.

MORGAN, GEORGE, 1743-1810   742

In THE NEW REGIME, edited by Clarence W. Alvord and Clarence E. Carter, pp. 438-447.

Extracts in EARLY TRAVELS IN THE TENNESSEE COUNTRY, edited by Samuel C. Williams, pp. 216-218.

> Nov-Dec 1766. Indian agent's account of remarkable occurrences during voyage down Mississippi from Kaskaskia village to Fort Bute; notes on forts, villages, etc.

In TRADE AND POLITICS, 1767-1769, edited by Clarence W. Alvord and Clarence E. Carter, pp. 67-71. Illinois State Historical Library Collections, vol. 16. Springfield: Illinois State Historical Library, 1921.

> Sep-Nov 1767. Journey from Philadelphia to Mingo town; trading details.

Oaks, Robert F., ed. "George Morgan's 'Memorandums': A Journey to the Illinois Country." ILLINOIS STATE HISTORICAL SOCIETY JOURNAL 69 (1976):185-200.

> Mar-Oct 1770. Trip from Fort Pitt, down the Ohio to the Mississippi, in attempt to salvage his firm's investments in the Illinois country; travel difficulties and business affairs.

OWEN, WILLIAM, d. 1778   743

Paltsits, Victor H., ed. "Narrative of American Voyages and Travels of Captain William Owen, R.N., and the Settlement of the Island of Campobello in the Bay of Fundy, 1766-1771." NEW YORK PUBLIC LIBRARY BULLETIN 35 (1931):71-98, 139-162, 263-300, 659-685, 705-758.

Ganong, W.F., ed. "The Journal of Captain William Owen, R.N., During His Residence on Campobello, 1770-71." NEW BRUNSWICK HISTORICAL SOCIETY COLLECTIONS 1 (1894):193-208; 2 (1899):8-27.

> 1766-1770, Apr-Jun 1771. Journey along Nova Scotia and Maine coasts; early history of Campobello; some interesting long entries.

PERKINS, SIMEON, 1735-1812   744

THE DIARY OF SIMEON PERKINS. Variously edited by Harold A. Innis, D.C. Harvey and C.B. Fergusson. Champlain Society Publications, nos. 29, 36, 39, 43, 50. Toronto: The Champlain Society, 1948-1978. 5 vols. Reprint. New York: Greenwood Press, 1969-(in progress).

> 1766-1812. A vast and varied diary of expatriate New Englander settled in Liverpool, Nova Scotia: mainly a merchant involved in shipping, fishing, and lumbering, but taking substantial part in civic life, religious activities, and maritime aspects of the American Revolution, Napoleonic Wars, and prelude to War of 1812; incredibly detailed account of privateering, commercial shipping, activities of the Loyalist community in Canada, Methodist and other church affairs, the influence of the Great Awakening, as well as much medical lore, including a smallpox epidemic and inoculation. Like Sewall, Perkins was a compulsive chronicler over a long period of time, and this charming and ingenuous diary abounds in names of ships, ship captains, privateers, clergymen, doctors, Loyalists.

McLeod, Robert R. "Old Times in Liverpool, N.S." ACADIENSIS 4 (1904):96-118. Diary extracts, pp. 104-111.

> 1779-1812 (with gaps). Long notes mostly of private affairs; some military and social affairs.

WADSWORTH, JOSEPH BISSELL, 1747-1784   745

YALE COLLEGE COURANT, 12 September 1868, pp. 131-133.

ALUMNI WEEKLY, 17 June 1896.

> Jan-Sep 1766. Physician's student diary; college affairs at Yale.

WOOD, SOLOMON, 1722-1766   746

"Journal of a Survey of Bridgeton, Me." NEW ENGLAND HISTORICAL AND GENEALOGICAL REGISTER 28 (1874): 63-67.

> Aug-Oct 1766. Brief notes in surveying journal.

WOODMASON, CHARLES   747

In THE CAROLINA BACKCOUNTRY ON THE EVE OF THE REVOLUTION, edited by Richard J. Hooker, pp. 3-66. Chapel Hill: University of North Carolina Press, 1953.

> 1766-1768. Diary of itinerant Anglican preacher in South Carolina backcountry; incredible rigors of travel; low state of education, manners and morals among frontier folk; problems with Presbyterians and Baptists; love and despair for his scattered flock but championing of their cause against the Charleston establishment; colorful picture of frontier life.

1767

ANON.   748

In THE DOCUMENTARY HISTORY OF THE STATE OF NEW YORK, edited by E.B. O'Callaghan, vol. 2, pp. 504-511.

> Jul-Sep 1767. Official report of transactions with Indians about stealing at Niagara.

BAILEY, ABIGAIL ABBOT, 1746-1815   749

MEMOIRS OF MRS. ABIGAIL BAILEY, WHO HAD BEEN THE WIFE OF MAJOR ASA BAILEY. Edited by Ethan Smith. Boston: Samuel T. Armstrong, 1815. 275 pp. passim.

> 1767-1792. Partly memoirs; her marriage and a lengthy account of her sufferings at the hands of a "depraved and deceitful man," with notes of Christian consolation.

GRANT, FRANCIS?   750

"Journal from New York to Canada." NEW YORK HISTORY 13 (1932):181-196, 305-322.

> Apr-Jul 1767. New York to Canada, via Albany, Schenectady, Ontario, Niagara, Montreal, Quebec: return by Lake Champlain and Lake George; long descriptions of towns, scenery; notes on maple sugar, Indians and their government, Niagara Falls.

SOLIS, GASPAR JOSE DE   751

Forrestal, Peter P., trans., and Foik, Paul J., ed. "The Solís Diary of 1767." TEXAS CATHOLIC HISTORICAL SOCIETY PRELIMINARY STUDIES 1, no. 6 (1931):1-42.

Kress, Margaret K., trans., with an introduction by Mattie A. Hatcher. "Diary of a Visit of Inspection of the Texas Missions made by Fray Gaspar José de Solís in the Year 1767-68." SOUTHWESTERN HISTORICAL QUARTERLY 35 (1931):28-76.

> Nov 1767-Oct 1768. Visitation of missions in the Province of Texas on behalf of the Council of the College of Nuestra Señora de Guadalupe of the City of Zacatecas; detailed descriptions of missions and customs, including cannibalism, of various Indian tribes; details of route, focusing on water supply, fertility, natural resources.

1768

ANON.   752

"North Carolina Interior Settlements in 1768." In PLANTATION AND FRONTIER DOCUMENTS, edited by Ulrich B. Phillips, vol. 2, pp. 236-238.

> Oct 1768. Brief diary of travel from New Bern to Salisbury, North Carolina.

CRAFT, JAMES, 1743-1808   753

"Extracts from Craft's Journal." HISTORICAL MAGAZINE 1 (1857):300-302.

> 1768-1785. Brief, scattered notes of local affairs in Burlington, New Jersey; war news; disowned by Quakers for joining Masons.

ETTWEIN, JOHN, 1721-1802   754

Hulbert, Archer B., and Schwarze, William N., ed. "Report of the Journey of John Ettwein, David Zeisberger and Gottlob Senseman to Friedenshuetten and Their Stay There." OHIO ARCHAEOLOGICAL AND HISTORICAL QUARTERLY 21 (1912):32-42.

> Apr-May 1768. Moravian travel journal; religious work, scenery.

"Rev. John Ettwein's Notes of Travel from the North Branch of the Susquehanna to the Beaver River, Pennsylvania." PENNSYLVANIA MAGAZINE OF HISTORY AND BIOGRAPHY 25 (1901):208-219.

In NOTES AND QUERIES, edited by William H. Egle, 1898, pp. 49-51, 58-59, 68-70, 77-79.

> Jun-Aug 1772. Overland journey with Christian Indians to settle at Beaver River; great suffering from illness, hunger and difficulties of travel.

GOODWIN, FRANCIS LEBARON, 1762-1816   755

In AN OLD RIVER TOWN, by Ada D. Littlefield, pp. 119-129. New York: Calkins, 1907.

> 1768-1816. Brief extracts from physician's diary; notes of local and personal affairs in Winterport, Maine.

JEWELL, BRADBURY, 1752-1828   756

THE FISHBASKET PAPERS: THE DIARIES, 1768-1823 OF BRADBURY JEWELL, ESQUIRE OF TAMWORTH, DURHAM AND SANDWICH, NEW HAMPSHIRE. Edited by Marjorie G. Harkness. Peterborough, N.H.: Richard R. Smith, 1963. 236 pp.

> 1768-1823. Diary and daybooks begun at age sixteen of rugged New Hampshire frontiersman; farming, trading, family and village life; service in the Revolution; an eleven-year period of diary destroyed by grandson; bare notes in original spellings but much illuminating editorial material.

JONES, JOEL, 1764-1845   757

In THE DESCENDANTS OF JOEL JONES, by Elbert Smith, pp. 279-291. Rutland, Vt.: Tuttle, 1925.

> 1768-1844. Mostly notes of his own activities, chief family affairs, deaths of friends, etc., in Lanesborough, Massachusetts; moral reflections; weather; genealogical interest.

LEES, JOHN   758

JOURNAL OF J.L., OF QUEBEC, MERCHANT. Detroit: Society of Colonial Wars of the State of Michigan, 1911. 55 pp.

> Apr-Oct 1768. Travel in New England, New York, Michigan, Montreal, etc.; descriptions from mercantile viewpoint; disjointed but interesting details.

PAINE, ROBERT TREAT, 1731-1814   759

In PAINE ANCESTRY: THE FAMILY OF ROBERT TREAT PAINE, SIGNER OF THE DECLARATION OF INDEPENDENCE, compiled by Sarah C. Paine, edited by Charles H. Pope, pp. 31-40. Boston: Printed for the family, 1912.

> 1768-1776. Extracts from Taunton, Massachusetts, lawyer's diary; personal affairs, war news, congressional affairs, visits, weather.

THOMAS, WILLIAM, 1725-1810   760

"Memoranda Entered by William Thomas, Father of Robert B. Thomas, Author of the Farmer's Almanac." ESSEX INSTITUTE HISTORICAL COLLECTIONS 14 (1877): 257-267.

> 1768-1769 (with gaps and a few later entries). Brief notes on farming, weather, religion; local and some public news in Lancaster, Massachusetts.

1769

ANON.   761

CASTANIEN, DONALD G., trans. and ed. "General O'Reilly's Arrival at New Orleans." MID-AMERICA 39 (1957):96-111.

> Aug 1769. Extract from either a personal diary or

official journal included in a report of the activities of the new governor of Spanish Louisiana, General Alejandro O'Reilly, dealing with the leaders of the rebellion against the former governor.

CAÑIZARES, JOSE DE   762

Thickens, Virginia E. and Mollins, Margaret, trans. and ed. "Putting a Lid on California: An Unpublished Diary of the Portolá Expedition." CALIFORNIA HISTORICAL SOCIETY QUARTERLY 31 (1952):109-124, 216-270, 343-354.

Mar-Jun 1769. Exploration diary of teen-aged pilot's mate, second in command, and official diarist of expedition to explore northward from San Diego as part of the overland Portolá Expedition; terrain, encampments, distances, constant search for water; activities of commander Fernando de Rivera y Moncada and chaplain Father Juan Crespi; sickness and death among Christian Indians of their company.

COSTANSO, MIGUEL   763

THE PORTOLA EXPEDITION OF 1769-1770; DIARY OF MIGUEL COSTANSO. Edited by Frederick J. Teggart. Academy of Pacific Coast History Publications, vol. 2, no. 4. Berkeley: University of California, 1911. 167 pp.

Jul 1769-Jan 1770. Diary of engineer with the Portolá Expedition from San Diego to San Francisco by land; search for and failure to find Monterey; return to San Diego due to lack of provisions and illness of expedition members; travel conditions; notes on geography, food supply, meeting with Indians.

CRESPI, JUAN, 1721-1782   764

FRAY JUAN CRESPI, MISSIONARY EXPLORER ON THE PACIFIC COAST, 1769-1774. By Herbert E. Bolton. Berkeley: University of California Press, 1927. 402 pp. Reprint. New York: AMS Press, 1971.

Extracts in CAPTAIN PORTOLA IN SAN LUIS OBISPO COUNTY. Cambria, Calif.: Printed at Savilla's Print Shop, 1968. 32 pp.

1769-1774. Chaplain's missionary diaries; travels in Mexico, Old and New California and a fog-plagued voyage up the Pacific Northwest coast; weather, latitude observations of coast line from Monterey, California, to north Vancouver Island; notes on coastal Indians, especially clothing and artifacts; numerous masses and novenas; charming diary of a gentle priest and competent observer.

"Diary of the First Expedition by Land for the Exploration of the Port of San Diego." In HISTORICAL MEMOIRS OF NEW CALIFORNIA, by Francisco Palou, edited by Herbert E. Bolton, vol. 2, pp. 42-104. Berkeley: University of California Press, 1926. Reprint. New York: Russell & Russell, 1966.

Mar-Jul 1769.

"Diary Kept during the Exploration That Was Made of the Harbor of Our Father San Francisco." in HISTORICAL MEMOIRS OF NEW CALIFORNIA, vol. 2, pp. 329-354.

Mar-Apr 1772.

"Diary of the Sea Expedition Made by the Frigate SANTIAGO, in Which Went the Father Preachers Fray Juan Crespi and Fray Tomás de la Pena." In HISTORICAL MEMOIRS OF NEW CALIFORNIA, vol. 3, pp. 147-207.

"Journal Kept during the Voyage of the Santiago, 1774." In DOCUMENTS FROM THE SUTRO COLLECTION, edited by George B. Griffin. Historical Society of Southern California Publications, vol. 2, pt. 1. Los Angeles: Franklin Printing, 1891.

"Journal Kept during the Voyage of the Santiago, 1774." In THE CALIFORNIA COAST: A BILINGUAL EDITION OF DOCUMENTS FROM THE SUTRO COLLECTION, edited by George B. Griffin, re-edited with an emended translation by Donald C. Cutter, pp. 204-278. Norman: University of Oklahoma Press, 1969.

Jun-Aug 1774.

HEMPSTEAD, JOHN   765

NEW LONDON COUNTY HISTORICAL SOCIETY PROCEEDINGS 1 (1901):711.

1769-1779. A few brief notes.

LEE, CHARLES, 1731-1782   766

"Fragments of a Journal." NEW YORK HISTORICAL SOCIETY COLLECTIONS 4 (1871):85-86; 7 (1874):73-75.

Jun 1769. Military diary fragment; service in Russia.

Jun 1784 (sic). Fragment, of uncertain date, from travel diary; Fredericksburg, Maryland, to Pittsburgh; itinerary and notes on taverns.

MARRETT, JOHN, 1741-1813   767

In HENRY DUNSTER AND HIS DESCENDANTS, by Samuel Dunster, pp. 81-94. Central Falls, R.I.: E.L. Freeman & Co., Printers, 1876.

1769-1812. Scattered extracts from clergyman's diary; weather, journeys, parish work in Woburn, Massachusetts, public events; Boston Massacre and Tea Party, Lexington, Bunker Hill.

PEMBERTON, JOHN, 1727-1795   768

"The Life and Travels of John Pemberton." FRIENDS' LIBRARY 6 (1842):267-380. Journal, pp. 284-374.

1769-1795. Philadelphia Quaker's interesting, and sometimes exciting, record of an active and troubled life; first part in New England and Virginia during Revolution; arrest by revolutionaries; greater part of journal devoted to ministry in England, Ireland, Scotland, Holland.

PILMORE, JOSEPH, 1739-1825   769

THE JOURNAL OF JOSEPH PILMORE, METHODIST ITINERANT. Edited by Frederick E. Maser and Howard T. Maag. Philadelphia: The Historical Society of the Philadelphia Annual Conference of the United Methodist Church, 1969. 262 pp.

1769-1774. Preaching tour of English clergyman dispatched by John Wesley to evangelize in American colonies, mainly in Philadelphia and New York areas and southern colonies; typical labors and perils of itineration, friends high and low with whom he stayed, respectful interactions with colleagues Richard Boardman and the more famous George Whitefield and Francis Asbury; contrasts with England and the English; introspections of a devout, cheerful and affectionate man, who later returned to Anglican communion.

PORTOLA, GASPAR, b. 1723   770

DIARY OF GASPAR DE PORTOLA DURING THE CALIFORNIA EXPEDITION OF 1769-1770. Edited by Donald Eugene

Smith and Frederick J. Teggart. Academy of Pacific Coast History Publications, vol. 1, no. 3. Berkeley: University of California, 1909. 51 pp.

> May 1769–Jan 1770. Commander in chief's diary of a land expedition from Santa Maria to San Diego, accompanied by soldiers and Fathers Junipero Serra and Miguel Campa; condition of roads, availability of water and pasture; earthquakes and illness; meeting with ships SAN CARLOS and SAN ANTONIO at San Diego; unsuccessful search for Monterey; return to San Diego due to illness of soldiers and diminished provisions.

SERRA, JUNIPERO, 1713–1784   771

"Diary by Serra of the Expedition from Loreto to San Diego." In WRITINGS OF JUNIPERO SERRA, edited by Antoine Tibesar, vol. 1, pp. 39–123. Academy of American Franciscan History Publications, Documentary Series. Washington, D.C.: Academy of American Franciscan History, 1955.

> Mar–Jul 1769. Account of the first Franciscan Presidente of the Missions of California, accompanying Don José de Galvez, who had orders to occupy Alta California, on an expedition to locate sites for three missions, San Diego, Monterey and one in between; notes on preparation of the expedition, by land and by sea; missions where he preached, received provisions and stayed to recover from a badly infected leg; appearance and behavior of Indians; route followed; water, trees, plants and animals observed. Spanish text and English translation on facing pages.

SMITH, ELIZABETH MURRAY, 1726–1786   772

In LETTERS OF JAMES MURRAY, LOYALIST, edited by Nina M. Tiffany, assisted by Susan I. Lesley, pp. 124–131. Boston, 1901.

> Oct 1769–Jul 1770. Brief notes of journey to England from Boston.

SMITH, RICHARD, 1735–1803   773

A TOUR OF FOUR GREAT RIVERS: THE HUDSON, MOHAWK, SUSQUEHANNA AND DELAWARE IN 1769. Edited by Francis W. Halsey. New York: C. Scribner's Sons, 1906. 102 pp. Reprint. Empire State Historical Publications, 30. Port Washington, N.Y.: I.J. Friedman, 1964.

Extracts in THE WILDERNESS TRAIL, by Charles A. Hanna, pp. 61–64.

> May–Jun 1769. Surveying lands from Burlington to Otsego Lake; topographical descriptions.

"Diary of Richard Smith in the Continental Congress." AMERICAN HISTORICAL REVIEW 1 (1895–1896):288–310, 493–516.

> Sep 1775–Mar 1776. Diary kept while member of Congress from New Jersey; political and war news.

VILA, VICENTE   774

THE PORTOLA EXPEDITION OF 1769–1770: DIARY OF VICENTE VILA. Edited by Robert Selden Rose. Academy of Pacific Coast History Publications, vol. 2, no. 1. Berkeley: University of California Press, 1911. 119 pp.

> Jan–May 1769, Aug 1770. The log-book of the commander of the SAN CARLOS, supply ship for the Portolá Expedition; sailing conditions, positions; some notes on supplies and Indians.

1770

ALLEN, JAMES, 1742–1778   775

"Diary of James Allen, Esq., of Philadelphia, Counsellor-at-Law." PENNSYLVANIA MAGAZINE OF HISTORY AND BIOGRAPHY 9 (1885):176–196, 278–296, 424–441.

Discussed in AMERICAN DIARY LITERATURE, by Steven E. Kagle, pp. 135–138.

> 1770–1778. Personal and political notes of member of Congress.

AMBLER, MARY CARY   776

"Diary of M. Ambler." VIRGINIA MAGAZINE OF HISTORY AND BIOGRAPHY 45 (1937):152–170.

> Sep–Oct 1770. Journey by chaise with her two children from Fauquier County, Virginia, to Baltimore to secure smallpox inoculations; extended stay in Baltimore when several inoculations failed; daily entries record visits, dinner menus, medical treatment.

BALDWIN, BETHIAH, b. 1743   777

Baldwin, Simeon E. "A Ride Across Connecticut Before the Revolution." NEW HAVEN COLONY HISTORICAL SOCIETY PAPERS 9 (1918):161–169.

> Sep–Oct 1770. Extracts from travel diary; lively notes on rigors of horseback journey from Norwich to Danbury.

COLLIN, NICHOLAS, 1746–1831   778

JOURNAL AND BIOGRAPHY. Translated by Amandus Johnson, with an introduction by Frank H. Stewart. Philadelphia?: American Swedish Historical Museum?, 1936. 368 pp. Journal, pp. 207–296.

> 1770–1786. Scattered entries in Moravian journal kept by pastor of the Swedish mission at Raccoon, New Jersey; religious and personal notes, with a few passages about the Revolution. Translated from the Swedish.

FAGES, PEDRO, fl. 1767–1796   779

EXPEDITION TO SAN FRANCISCO BAY IN 1770, DIARY OF PEDRO FAGES. Edited by Herbert E. Bolton. Academy of Pacific Coast History, vol. 2, no. 3. Berkeley: University of California, 1911. 19 pp.

> Nov 1770–Jun 1771. Inland exploration from Monterey to Santa Clara Valley to point not far from Alameda; distances traveled, trees, water. Spanish and English texts on opposite pages.

Treutlein, Theodore E. "Fages as Explorer, 1769–1772." CALIFORNIA HISTORICAL QUARTERLY 51 (1972):338–356.

> Mar–Apr 1772. Exploration of San Francisco Bay area as military commander in company with Father Juan Crespi; description of Golden Gate and main islands; terrain, distances; notes on Indians. Translated from the Spanish.

THE COLORADO RIVER CAMPAIGN, 1781–1782; DIARY OF PEDRO FAGES. Edited by Herbert I. Priestley. Academy of Pacific Coast History Publications, vol. 3, no. 2. Berkeley: University of California, 1913. 101 pp.

> Sep 1781–Apr 1782. Diary kept while commanding expedition against Yuma Indians to rescue survivors of massacre; march from Pitic, Sonora, to Yuma; negotiations for captives; retreat to Sonora and rest; return for second attack and attempt to recover bodies of massacred priests; through the

mountains to Mission San Gabriel; record of travel conditions, distances, food and water supply; descriptions of Indians, smallpox epidemic, burial of martyred missionaries, condition of land. Translated from the Spanish.

Extracts in "Retracing the Route of the Fages Expedition of 1781," edited by Ronald L. Ives. ARIZONA AND THE WEST 8 (1966):49-70, 157-170.

Sep-Dec 1781.

Extracts in "From Pitic to San Gabriel in 1782: The Journey of Don Pedro Fages," edited by Ronald L. Ives. JOURNAL OF ARIZONA HISTORY 9 (1968):222-244.

Feb-Apr 1782.

Ives, Ronald L., ed. "Retracing Fages' Route from San Gabriel to Yuma." ARIZONA AND THE WEST 17 (1975): 141-160.

Apr 1782.

HUNT, JOHN   **780**

"John Hunt's Diary." NEW JERSEY HISTORICAL SOCIETY PROCEEDINGS 52 (1934):177-193, 223-239; 53 (1935):26-43, 111-128, 194-209, 251-262.

1770-1800. Scattered notes of ministering Quaker in New Jersey; religious work and worship; civil and domestic life; excellent cumulative picture of Quaker life; intimate and revealing; many interesting spellings.

MEASE, EDWARD   **781**

"Narrative of a Journey through Several Parts of the Province of West Florida in the Years 1770 and 1771." MISSISSIPPI HISTORICAL SOCIETY PUBLICATIONS, centenary ser. 5 (1925):58-90.

Nov 1770-Apr 1771. Official travel journal; through West Florida from Pensacola; topography; notes on population and economy.

PARKER, JAMES, 1744-1830   **782**

"Extracts from the Diary of James Parker of Shirley, Mass." NEW ENGLAND HISTORICAL AND GENEALOGICAL REGISTER 69 (1915):117-127, 211-224, 294-308; 70 (1916):9-24, 137-146, 210-220, 294-308.

1770-1829. Personal and local affairs at Shirley and Groton; farming, weather, visits, preaching, law, neighbors; a few notes on military events at Lexington, etc.; a few brief entries for each month, presenting an excellent picture of New England country life and a portrait of a shrewd Yankee farmer; linguistically interesting.

POWELL, WILLIAM DUMMER, 1726-1805   **783**

Quincy, Eliza S. "Notices of the Powell Family, and Extracts from Manuscripts of T.D. Powell." MAINE HISTORICAL SOCIETY COLLECTIONS, 1st ser. 7 (1876): 231-238.

1770-1782. Brief notes of Boston affairs and journeys in the area; death of Whitefield.

RUSSELL, BARNABAS, 1745-1812   **784**

In THE HISTORY OF NEW BEDFORD, BRISTOL COUNTY, MASSACHUSETTS, by Daniel Ricketson, pp. 197-198. New Bedford: The author, 1858.

Aug-Sep 1770. Brief notes kept in London; sightseeing, visits to coffee houses, etc.

1771

ANON.   **785**

Bartlett, Ellen S., ed. "Bits from Great-Grandmother's Journal." CONNECTICUT QUARTERLY 1 (1895):265-270.

1771-1785. Extracts depicting social and farming life in Connecticut; building of meetinghouse; war news.

ASBURY, FRANCIS, 1745-1816   **786**

THE JOURNAL OF THE REV. FRANCIS ASBURY. New York: N. Bangs and T. Mason, 1821. 3 vols.

THE JOURNAL AND LETTERS OF FRANCIS ASBURY. Edited by Elmer T. Clark and others. London: Epworth Press; Nashville: Abingdon Press, 1958. 3 vols.

THE HEART OF ASBURY'S JOURNAL. Edited by Ezra S. Tipple. New York: Eaton & Mains; Cincinnati: Jennings & Graham, 1904. 720 pp.

Extracts relating to Tennessee in EARLY TRAVELS IN THE TENNESSEE COUNTRY, edited by Samuel C. Williams, pp. 291-313.

Discussed in AMERICAN DIARY LITERATURE, by Steven E. Kagle, pp. 52-54.

1771-1815. The endless travels of a Methodist minister, bishop and superintendent of Methodism in America; preaching tours over the whole country east of the Mississippi; notes religious and personal, meetings and work, the people he met and his entertainment; perhaps the best record of early Methodism in America.

Posey, Walter B., ed. "Bishop Asbury Visits Tennessee." TENNESSEE HISTORICAL QUARTERLY 15 (1956): 253-268.

1788-1815. Extracts covering many trips through Tennessee, but representing only half the journal entries made while there.

Posey, Walter B., ed. "Kentucky, 1790-1815: As Seen by Bishop Francis Asbury." FILSON CLUB HISTORY QUARTERLY 31 (1957):333-348.

1790-1815. Extracts revealing the hazards and hardships of frontier travel; life in Kentucky settlements; Indian troubles; tireless work for the cause of Methodism.

COTTEN, JOHN, 1745-1811   **787**

Matlock, J.W.L. "John Cotten: Reluctant Pioneer." TENNESSEE HISTORICAL QUARTERLY 27 (1968):277-286.

1771-1772. Extracts from journal describing involvement in rebellion of the Regulators, immigration to Tennessee and establishment of Watauga Association. Authenticity of journal questioned.

Matlock, J.W.L., ed. "The Battle of the Bluffs: from the Journal of John Cotten." TENNESSEE HISTORICAL QUARTERLY 18 (1959):252-265.

Apr 1781. Participant's account of successful defense of early settlement, which would become Nashville, against Indian attack; well-written, moving description of battle and its aftermath. Unfortunately, the journal's authenticity is questioned.

Folmsbee, Stanley J. "The Journal of John Cotten, the 'Reluctant Pioneer'--Evidences of Its Unreliability." TENNESSEE HISTORICAL QUARTERLY 28 (1969):84-94.

FAIRFAX, SALLY CARY   788

"Diary of a Little Colonial Girl." VIRGINIA MAGAZINE OF HISTORY AND BIOGRAPHY 11 (1903-1904):212-214.

In SALLY CARY: A LONG HIDDEN ROMANCE OF WASHINGTON'S LIFE, by Wilson M. Cary, pp. 59-65. New York: Privately printed, DeVinne Press, 1916.

Dec 1771-Jan 1772. Amusing domestic notes of a spirited Virginia child; interesting spellings.

HELFRICH, JOHN HENRY, 1739-1810   789

Hinke, William J., trans. "Diary of the Rev. John Henry Helffrich." PENNSYLVANIA MAGAZINE OF HISTORY AND BIOGRAPHY 38 (1914):65-82.

Sep 1771-Jan 1772. Journey from Amsterdam to New York; storms, etc.; work as German Reformed minister in Pennsylvania. Translated.

HUBBARD, JOSHUA, 1744?-1807   790

"A Hundred Years Ago: Gleanings from the Minute Books of Joshua Hubbard, Esq., Eliot." OLD ELIOT 8 (1908):22-28.

1771-1779. Personal and business affairs in Eliot, Maine; journeys.

MUHLENBERG, FREDERICK AUGUSTUS CONRAD,   791
1750-1801

Snyder, Charles F., ed. "The Journal of Frederick A.C. Muhlenberg on His Trip to the Shamokin Region in 1771." NORTHUMBERLAND COUNTY HISTORICAL SOCIETY PROCEEDINGS AND ADDRESSES 9 (1937):208-226.

Jun-Jul 1771. Journey of young minister; descriptions of scenery, towns, etc.; life of Irish Lutheran assembly.

NEALE, SAMUEL, 1729-1792   792

"Some Account of the Life and Religious Labours of Samuel Neale." FRIENDS' LIBRARY 11 (1847):1-72. American journal, pp. 49-61.

1771-1772. Ministering Quaker from Ireland, visiting Friends' meetings in southern and New England states; Salem, Philadelphia, Oswego, etc.; meeting with John Woolman.

PARKER, SAMUEL, 1744-1804   793

Lacy, Harriet S., ed. "An Eighteenth-Century Diarist Identified: Samuel Parker's Journal for 1771." HISTORICAL NEW HAMPSHIRE 25, no. 2 (1970):2-44.

Jan-Dec 1771. Very brief entries record business and social activities of teacher/lawyer in Greenland and Portsmouth.

ROBERTS, EPHRAIM, 1756-1835   794

Lacy, Harriet S., ed. "Ephraim Roberts--Memorandum Book." HISTORICAL NEW HAMPSHIRE 24, no. 3 (1969): 20-33.

1771-1776. Sporadic entries, dates jumbled at times; mainly record of farm tasks in what is now Alton, New Hampshire.

WIGHT, Sergt.   795

In COLONIAL CAPTIVITIES, edited by Isabel M. Calder, pp. 236-243.

Nov-Dec 1771. Journey from Pensacola to the Upper Creek Indians; stages; notes on Creek customs.

WILLARD, JOSEPH, 1741-1828   796

"Extracts from Mr. Willard's Diary." WORCESTER SOCIETY OF ANTIQUITY PROCEEDINGS 14 (1895):161-164.

1771-1783. Extracts from clergyman's journal; scattered notes of sermons, ordinations, church affairs in Mendon, Massachusetts.

WINSLOW, ANNA GREEN, 1759-1779   797

DIARY OF ANNA GREEN WINSLOW, A BOSTON SCHOOL GIRL OF 1771, edited by Alice M. Earle. Boston and New York: Houghton, Mifflin, 1894. 121 pp. Reprint. Detroit: Singing Tree Press, 1970; Williamstown, Mass.: Corner House, 1974.

Extracts in DIARY OF AMERICA, by Josef Berger, pp. 81-87.

Extracts in SMALL VOICES, by Josef and Dorothy Berger, pp. 223-234. New York: Paul S. Eriksson, 1966.

1771-1773. Girl's record of domestic life; naive, but vivid details; excellent picture of the social life of the Old South Church congregation.

1772

ANON.   798

In THE CLAPP MEMORIAL, by Ebenezer Clapp, pp. 376-377. Boston: D. Clapp & Son, 1876.

1772-1785. Diary extracts concerning local affairs in Dorchester, Massachusetts; some personal items; extraordinary spellings.

ANDREWS, JOHN, 1743-ca. 1822   799

"Letters of John Andrews, Esq., of Boston." MASSACHUSETTS HISTORICAL SOCIETY PROCEEDINGS 8 (1864-1865):316-412.

Extracts concerning the Boston Tea Party in AMERICAN HISTORY TOLD BY CONTEMPORARIES, edited by Albert B. Hart, vol. 2, pp. 431-433.

1772-1775. Journal-letters reflecting Boston life and public affairs.

COCKING, MATTHEW   800

Burpee, Lawrence J., ed. "An Adventurer from Hudson Bay." ROYAL SOCIETY OF CANADA PROCEEDINGS AND TRANSACTIONS, 3d ser. 2 (1908):sec. 2, 89-121.

1772-1773. Fur trading and travel journal kept by Hudson's Bay Company's second factor at Fort York; journey from York Factory to the Blackfoot country to the southwest, stirring up trade; stages; details of Indians.

In DOCUMENTS RELATING TO THE NORTH WEST COMPANY, edited by W. Stewart Wallace, pp. 44-47. Champlain Society Publications, 22. Toronto: The Champlain Society, 1934.

1776-1777. Extracts, with criticism of Burpee's version.

CONDICT, JEMIMA, 1754-1779   801

JEMIMA CONDICT, HER BOOK. Newark, N.J.: Carteret Book Club, 1930. 73 pp.

Extracts in WEATHERING THE STORM, by Elizabeth Evans, pp. 36-51.

1772-1779. Personal, family and local affairs in Essex County, New Jersey; a very attractive journal of the conflict of love and religion in a Puritan society; interesting language.

DILLWYN, WILLIAM 802

Salley, A.S., ed. "Diary of William Dillwyn During a Visit to Charles Town in 1772." SOUTH CAROLINA HISTORICAL AND GENEALOGICAL MAGAZINE 36 (1935): 1-6, 29-35, 73-78, 107-110.

Oct 1772-Jan 1773. Diary of visit to Charleston from Burlington, New Jersey.

EVE, SARAH, 1759-1774 803

"Extracts from the Journal of Miss Sarah Eve." PENN-SYLVANIA MAGAZINE OF HISTORY AND BIOGRAPHY 5 (1881):19-36, 191-205.

1772-1773. Personal, family and social affairs near Philadelphia; visits; an intimate, genteel diary; well-written and attractive.

HEARNE, SAMUEL, 1745-1792 804

Chandler, Elizabeth W. "Journey to the Northern Regions Before the American Republic." JOURNAL OF AMERICAN HISTORY 5 (1911):76-80.

1772. Journey to northern regions by explorer employed by Hudson's Bay Company; Indian affairs.

In JOURNALS OF SAMUEL HEARNE AND PHILIP TURNOR, edited by Joseph B. Tyrrell, pp. 95-194. Champlain Society Publications, 21. Toronto: The Champlain Society, 1934.

1774-1775. Inland journey from Fort York toward Basquiau; interesting details of travel, fur trade, Indians, weather, etc.; some linguistic interest.

Jul-Oct 1775. Remarkable transactions and occurrences on journey from and to Fort York and at Cumberland House.

HORTON, SAMUEL, 1731?-1808 805

"Extracts from the Diary of Samuel Horton of Newburyport." ESSEX INSTITUTE HISTORICAL COLLECTIONS 43 (1907):285-286.

1772-1781. Brief entries about ship movements, etc.

JONES, DAVID, 1736-1820 806

A JOURNAL OF TWO VISITS MADE TO SOME NATIONS OF INDIANS ON THE WEST SIDE OF THE RIVER OHIO. Burlington, N.J.: 1774. 97 pp. Reprint. New York: Arno, 1971. New York: J. Sabin, 1865. 127 pp. Reprint. Fairfield, Wash.: Ye Galleon Press, 1973.

May 1772-Apr 1773. Missionary journal of Freehold, New Jersey, minister; journeys to Shawnee Indians on Ohio and Scioto rivers; narrative of his work with some concluding poems.

MOULTRIE, WILLIAM, 1730-1805 807

Davis, Charles S., ed. "The Journal of William Moultrie While a Commissioner on the North and South Carolina Boundary Survey." JOURNAL OF SOUTHERN HISTORY 8 (1942):549-555.

May-Jun 1772. Account kept by one of the South Carolina commissioners of surveying party's work and his own acquisition of some choice land along the way.

PUTNAM, ISRAEL, 1718-1790 808

In THE TWO PUTNAMS, ISRAEL AND RUFUS, pp. 113-138. Hartford: Connecticut Historical Society, 1931.

Dec 1772-Mar 1773. Voyage from New York to the Natchez; entertaining journal of cruise around West Indies; interesting spellings and language.

ROTH, JOHANNES 809

Mahr, August C., trans. and ed. "Diary of a Moravian Indian Mission Migration across Pennsylvania in 1772." OHIO STATE ARCHAEOLOGICAL AND HISTORICAL QUARTERLY 62 (1953):247-270.

Jun-Aug 1772. Detailed account of canoe travel to join Johannes Ettwein conducting Indian converts from Susquehanna to Beaver River, Pennsylvania; Friedenshuetten to Muncy Creek; great suffering of Indians from hunger, illness, hazards of travel.

SWEAT, SAMUEL, 1744-1792 810

Lacy, Harriet S. "Samuel Sweat's Diary." HISTORICAL NEW HAMPSHIRE 30 (1975):221-230.

1772-1774. Summary of diary's contents with extracts providing view of joiner's life and work in Kingston, New Hampshire; trips on foot to Keene, New Hampshire, and Maine; comments on land; work orders; encounter of local Sons of Freedom with peddler who was forced to burn his tea.

THACHER, PETER, 1752-1802 811

"Life in the Old Parsonage." MALDEN HISTORICAL SOCIETY REGISTER, no. 1 (1910-1911), pp. 38-59.

1772-1785 (with large gaps). Extracts from clergyman's journal; notes of domestic and social life; weather, work and studies, visits, journeys; pleasant record of a quiet life in Malden and Boston, Massachusetts.

THURSTON, EDWARD, 1729-1782 812

"Extracts from Edward Thurston, Jr.'s Almanac." NEWPORT HISTORICAL MAGAZINE 1 (1880-1881):125-126.

Feb-Nov 1772. Brief almanac notes of personal and local affairs in Newport, Rhode Island.

TUFTS, COTTON, 1732-1815 813

"Diaries of Rev. William Smith and Dr. Cotton Tufts." MASSACHUSETTS HISTORICAL SOCIETY PROCEEDINGS 42 (1908-1909):444-478. Diary, pp. 470-478.

Jan-Dec 1772, Jan-Dec 1784. Brief notes, at first largely of weather and some social affairs; later, mainly local affairs in Weymouth, Massachusetts.

1773

ANON. 814

"A Summer Jaunt in 1773." PENNSYLVANIA MAGAZINE OF HISTORY AND BIOGRAPHY 10 (1886):205-213.

In EARLY NARRATIVES OF BERKS COUNTY, by James B. Nolan, pp. 38-42.

Aug 1773. Tour through Pennsylvania; from Philadelphia to Bethlehem, Nazareth, Allentown, Lancaster; summer jaunt, seeing how Moravians lived; notes on inns, sights, etc.

BARTRAM, WILLIAM, 1739-1823   815

TRAVELS THROUGH NORTH & SOUTH CAROLINA, GEORGIA, EAST & WEST FLORIDA. Philadelphia: Printed by James & Johnson, 1791. 522 pp. Reprint. Savannah, Georgia: Beehive, 1973.

THE TRAVELS OF WILLIAM BARTRAM. Edited by Mark Van Doren. New York: Macy-Masius, 1928. 414 pp. Reprint. New York: Facsimile Library, Barnes & Noble, 1940; New York: Dover, 1955.

TRAVELS. Edited by Francis Harper. Naturalist's ed. New Haven: Yale University Press, 1958. 727 pp. Reprint. Layton, Utah: Peregrine Smith, 1980.

> 1773. Travels in search of natural history specimens; Philadelphia to Florida, west Carolina, and Georgia; a valuable and entertaining record of the country, manners and customs of Indians.

CHALKER, STEPHEN, 1707-1783   816

Stark, Bruce, ed. "Journal of the General Assembly 1773." CONNECTICUT HISTORICAL SOCIETY BULLETIN 38 (1973):91-96.

> May-Jun, Oct-Nov 1773. Brief journal reflecting normal activities of the Connecticut colonial legislature, as observed by one of Saybrook's representatives in the lower house.

CHANDLER, SAMUEL, 1753-1786   817

Mulliken, S.E. "Harvard on the Eve of the Revolution." HARVARD GRADUATES' MAGAZINE 10 (1901-1902): 376-381, 529-535.

> 1773-1774. A student's year at Harvard College; notes on reading, studies, student life, fires; some interesting spellings.

DUNBAR, ASA, 1745-1787   818

Russell, E. Harlow. "Thoreau's Maternal Grandfather Asa Dunbar: Fragments from His Diary and Commonplace Book." AMERICAN ANTIQUARIAN SOCIETY PROCEEDINGS 19 (1908-1909):66-76.

> 1773-1776. Brief notes of his journeys; a poem.

FINLAY, HUGH, ca. 1731-1801   819

JOURNAL KEPT BY HUGH FINLAY. Edited by Frank H. Norton. Brooklyn: F.H. Norton, 1867. 94 pp. Reprint. THE HUGH FINLAY JOURNAL. n.p.: U.S. Philatelic Classics Society, 1975.

Extracts in HISTORIC HIGHWAYS OF AMERICA, by Archer B. Hulbert, vol. 7, pp. 112-115.

> Sep 1773-May 1774. Journal kept by surveyor of post roads; surveying journeys between Portsmouth and Savannah; mainly in Canada and New England; quite impersonal, but some pleasant topographical descriptions.

FISH, THOMAS, 1743-1782   820

In NOTES, HISTORICAL, DESCRIPTIVE, AND PERSONAL OF LIVERMORE, IN ANDROSCOGGIN (FORMERLY IN OXFORD) COUNTY, MAINE, app. D, pp. 132-141. Portland: Bailey & Noyes, 1874.

> Apr 1773-May 1774. Surveyor's journal; journeys from Oxford to Androscoggin River, Falmouth, Port Royal; camping and travel experiences; very useful linguistically.

FITHIAN, PHILIP VICKERS, 1747-1776   821

In PHILIP VICKERS FITHIAN, JOURNAL AND LETTERS, 1767-1774, STUDENT AT PRINCETON COLLEGE, 1770-72, TUTOR AT NOMINI HALL IN VIRGINIA, 1773-74, edited by John R. Williams, vol. 1, pp. 47-274. Princeton, N.J.: University Library, 1900-1934.

JOURNAL & LETTERS OF PHILIP VICKERS FITHIAN, 1773-1774; A PLANTATION TUTOR OF THE OLD DOMINION. Edited by Hunter D. Farish. Williamsburg Restoration Historical Studies, no. 3. Williamsburg, Va.: Colonial Williamsburg, 1943. 323 pp. New ed., 1957. 270 pp. Reprint. 1968.

> 1773-1774. Diary of young tutor from Greenwich, New Jersey, in the Carter family of Virginia; first-rate account of plantation and social life in the great southern family; dinners, balls, foxhunts; disapproval of slavery.

PHILIP VICKERS FITHIAN, JOURNAL AND LETTERS, vol. 2, pp. 1-258.

Extracts in "Fithian's Journal," edited by John B. Linn. HISTORICAL REGISTER 1 (1883):91-94, 177-181, 285-288; 2 (1884):13-18, 99-119, 194-201, 241-247.

> 1774-1776. Religious and military diary; duties as Presbyterian minister; preaching in New Jersey; missionary work on Virginia-Pennsylvania frontier; details of backcountry poverty; chaplaincy with Continental Army in New York.

Extracts in AMERICAN HISTORY TOLD BY CONTEMPORARIES, edited by Albert B. Hart, vol. 3, pp. 49-52; DIARY OF AMERICA, edited by Josef Berger, pp. 87-89.

Discussed in AMERICAN DIARY LITERATURE, by Steven E. Kagle, pp. 67-71.

FRISBIE, JUDAH, 1744-1829   822

In HISTORY OF THE TOWN OF WOLCOTT (CONNECTICUT), by Samuel Orcutt, pp. 306-310. Waterbury, Conn.: Press of the American Printing Co., 1874.

> Apr-Dec 1773, May-Sep 1776. Weather notes; march to New York; Ticonderoga; brief notes of marches and military affairs.

GNADENHUETTEN MORAVIAN CONGREGATION   823

Hulbert, Archer B. "The Moravian Records." OHIO ARCHAEOLOGICAL AND HISTORICAL QUARTERLY 18 (1909): 199-226. Journal, pp. 203-207.

> Jan-Oct 1773, May-Aug 1776. Extracts, selected to show character of the records of Moravian congregation in what would become Ohio; Moravian work and life.

HARROWER, JOHN   824

"Diary of John Harrower." AMERICAN HISTORICAL REVIEW 6 (1900-1901):65-107.

THE JOURNAL OF JOHN HARROWER, AN INDENTURED SERVANT IN THE COLONY OF VIRGINIA. Edited by Edward Miles Riley. Williamsburg, Va.: Colonial Williamsburg, 1963. 202 pp.

Extracts in DIARY OF AMERICA, edited by Josef Berger, pp. 89-92; PLANTATION AND FRONTIER DOCUMENTS, edited by Ulrich B. Phillips, vol. 1, pp. 188-189, 329, 366-371.

> 1773-1776. Matter-of-fact diary of Scottish merchant indentured as school teacher for children of Virginia plantation owner; unsuccessful attempts to find work in England; Atlantic passage on ship

full of indentured servants; plantation agriculture, teaching successes, ripples of impending revolution; little comment on slavery; letters to wife, poems and prayers; unaltered spellings.

HITE, ISAAC, 1753?–1794   825

Hall, Virginius C., ed. "Journal of Isaac Hite." HISTORICAL AND PHILOSOPHICAL SOCIETY OF OHIO BULLETIN 12 (1954):263–281. Journal, pp. 276–281.

Jul–Oct 1773. Journal kept by member of Thomas Bullitt's expedition organized to establish land claims along the Kentucky side of the Ohio River for colonial officers and soldiers who had fought in the French and Indian War; brief entries reporting travels, hunting, surveying operations, including marking lots at site that was to become Louisville.

KEMBLE, STEPHEN, 1740–1829   826

In THE KEMBLE PAPERS, vol. 1, pp. 1–247. New York Historical Society Collections, Publication Fund Series, vols. 16–17. New York: Printed for the Society, 1884–1885.

1773–1779, 1784–1789. Military journals of Loyalist officer; siege of Boston; social and political life in London and English counties; military affairs during the Revolution.

In THE KEMBLE PAPERS, vol. 2, pp. 1–64.

1780–1781. Expedition from New York to Nicaragua.

KENNEDY, PATRICK   827

In A TOPOGRAPHICAL DESCRIPTION OF VIRGINIA, by Thomas Hutchins, pp. 51–64. London: Printed for the author and sold by J. Almon, 1778; edited by Frederick C. Hicks, pp. 122–134. Cleveland: Burrows Brothers, 1904.

1773. Journal of travel from Kaskaskia village in the Illinois country to the head of the Illinois River in search of copper mines; topographical notes.

LACEY, JOHN, 1755–1814   828

"Papers of General John Lacey." HISTORICAL MAGAZINE, 2d ser. 7 (1870):103–107.

Jul–Sep 1773. Quaker missionary journal; from Pennsylvania to the Indians of the Ohio.

MCAFEE, JAMES, 1736–1811   829

In THE WOODS–MCAFEE MEMORIAL, by Neander M. Woods, app. A. Louisville, Ky.: Courier Journal Job Printing Co., 1905.

Jun–Aug 1773. Exploring and surveying journal; from Botetourt County, Virginia, to Ohio River, Kentucky River, through wilderness of Kentucky, to Salt River; notes on topography, soil, prospects, timber, rivers, weather; notes for settlers; impersonal.

MCAFEE, ROBERT, 1745–1795   830

In THE WOODS–MCAFEE MEMORIAL, by Neander M. Woods, app. A. Louisville, Ky.: Courier Journal Job Printing Co., 1905.

May–Aug 1773. Impersonal, plain, practical pioneer journal; notes on Indians; content similar to account by James McAfee.

NEWELL, THOMAS, b. 1749   831

"Diary for 1773 to the End of 1774, of Mr. Thomas Newell, Boston." MASSACHUSETTS HISTORICAL SOCIETY PROCEEDINGS, 1st ser. 15 (1876–1877):334–363.

1773–1774. Brief notes, mostly weather, deaths, public affairs.

"Extracts from an Original Diary by Thomas Newell." MASSACHUSETTS HISTORICAL SOCIETY PROCEEDINGS, 1st ser. 4 (1858–1860):216–224.

1773–1774. Extracts relating to Boston Tea Party, etc.

PARRISH, JOHN   832

"Extracts from the Journal of John Parrish." PENNSYLVANIA MAGAZINE OF HISTORY AND BIOGRAPHY 16 (1892): 443–448.

Jul–Sep 1773. Quaker missionary journey from Lancaster down the Ohio, around Pittsburgh, and return; mostly stages and visits, but also notes on Indian council and some well-known Indians.

WHITELAW, JAMES, 1748–1829   833

"Journal of General James Whitelaw, Surveyor-General of Vermont." VERMONT HISTORICAL SOCIETY PROCEEDINGS (1905–1906):119–157.

1773–1783 (with a few later notes). Journeys to Nova Scotia, New York, Pennsylvania, Maryland, North Carolina, Virginia, etc.; descriptions of places and people; notes on settlement of Ryegate, Vermont.

1774

ANON.   834

Kimball, Herbert W., ed. "A British Officer in Boston in 1775." MAGAZINE OF HISTORY 18 (1914):1–15.

1774–1776. Military journal, possibly kept by Lieutenant Thorne or Lieutenant Hamilton, of Fourth ("King's Own") Regiment; siege of Boston; military affairs, general news, riots; strong feeling against Yankees; description of engagements.

ANZA, JUAN BAUTISTA, 1735–1788   835

"Anza's Complete Diary." In ANZA'S CALIFORNIA EXPEDITIONS, by Herbert E. Bolton, vol. 2, pp. 1–130.

Jan–May 1774. Anza's first land expedition to break a trail from Tubac to Monterey via Colorado River, and return; distances traveled, natural features of land, watering places; actions and movements of Indian tribes; Indian villages and agriculture; mines and missions.

"Anza's Diary of the Second Anza Expedition." In ANZA'S CALIFORNIA EXPEDITIONS, vol. 3, pp. 3–60 passim.

Extracts in THE FRONTIER EXPERIENCE: READINGS IN THE TRANS-MISSISSIPPI WEST, by Robert V. Hine, pp. 124–127. Belmont, Calif.: Wadsworth, 1963.

Sep 1775–Jun 1776. A second expedition to California coast with goal to colonize San Francisco.

"Diary of the Expedition Which the Undersigned Lieutenant-Colonel, Governor and Commander of New Mexico Is Setting Out to Effect Against the Comanche Nation." In FORGOTTEN FRONTIERS, by Alfred B. Thomas, pp. 122–139.

Aug–Sep 1779. Direction and distances of march of campaign against the Comanches, joined by Utes and Apaches, in area around Santa Fe; checking abandoned pueblo as possible site for presidio; battle with the Comanches and death of their chief, Cuerno Verde; news of defeat at pueblo of Taos.

COLONEL JUAN BAUTISTA DE ANZA, GOVERNOR OF NEW MEXICO: DIARY OF HIS EXPEDITION TO THE MOQUIS IN 1780. Edited by Ralph E. Twitchell. New Mexico Historical Society Publications, no. 21. Santa Fe: Historical Society of New Mexico, 1918. 417 pp.

"Diary of the Expedition Which the Undersigned Lieutenant-Colonel and Commander of New Mexico Is Making to the Province of Moqui." In FORGOTTEN FRONTIERS, by Alfred B. Thomas, pp. 228–239.

Sep–Oct 1780. Expedition from Santa Fe to Moqui Indians at Oraibi to conduct a colony desiring to settle in New Mexico; visiting Zuni and discovering serious drought; murder of forty families by Apaches on trip to New Mexico; meeting with chief at Oraibi, declaring protection and seeking his allegiance to God and the King of Spain; effects of 1780 drought.

"Diary of the Expedition Which the Undersigned Lieutenant-Colonel Governor and Commander of the Province of New Mexico Made from That to the Province of Sonora for the Purpose of Opening a Route for Communication and Commerce from One to the Other." In FORGOTTEN FRONTIERS, by Alfred B. Thomas, pp. 195–205.

Nov–Dec 1780. Expedition from Santa Fe to Arizpe; direction of march each day, condition of trail, sources of water and Indians encountered.

ASHLEY, ELIHU, 1750–1817   836

In A HISTORY OF DEERFIELD, MASSACHUSETTS, by George Sheldon, vol. 2, pp. 686–691. Deerfield: Press of E.A. Hall, 1895–1896.

Sep 1774. Medical student's brief but entertaining social notes at Deerfield; some political notes.

BARKER, JOHN   837

THE BRITISH IN BOSTON, BEING THE DIARY OF LIEUTENANT JOHN BARKER OF THE KING'S OWN REGIMENT. With notes by Elizabeth Ellery Dana. Cambridge: Harvard University Press, 1924. 73 pp. Reprint. "The Diary of Lieutenant John Barker." SOCIETY FOR ARMY HISTORICAL RESEARCH JOURNAL 7 (1928):81–109, 145–174; THE BRITISH IN BOSTON: THE DIARY OF LT. JOHN BARKER. New York: New York Times, 1969.

Extracts in "A British Officer in Boston in 1775," by Richard H. Dana, Jr. ATLANTIC MONTHLY 39 (1877): 389–401, 544–554.

1774–1776. Valuable account from British side by officer stationed at Boston; military and political affairs; anti-Yankee sentiment; good narrative.

BELKNAP, JEREMY, 1744–1798   838

JEREMY BELKNAP'S JOURNEY TO DARTMOUTH IN 1774. Edited by Edward C. Lathem. Hanover, N.H.: Dartmouth Publications, 1950. 25 pp.

Aug 1774. Clergyman's diary of horseback trip to Dartmouth to visit President Eleazar Wheelock; sights along the way, people visited, accommodations, churches and preaching; facilities and educational practices of early Dartmouth; examination of Indian candidate for the ministry.

"Journal of My Tour to the Camp, and the Observations I Made There." MASSACHUSETTS HISTORICAL SOCIETY PROCEEDINGS, 1st ser. 4 (1858–1860):77–86.

Oct 1775. Tour to camp at Cambridge, Massachusetts; siege of Boston; some interesting details of sufferings of soldiers.

JOURNAL OF A TOUR TO THE WHITE MOUNTAINS, edited by Charles Deane. Boston: Massachusetts Historical Society, 1876. 21 pp.

Jul 1784. Touring the White Mountains.

"Dr. Belknap's Tour to Oneida." MASSACHUSETTS HISTORICAL SOCIETY PROCEEDINGS, 1st ser. 19 (1881–1882):393–423.

Jun–Jul 1796. From Boston to the Oneidas to examine Hamilton Oneida Academy; interesting travel details, scenery, hardships, Indian life.

CARPENTER, JONATHAN, 1757–1837   839

Alexander, John K., ed. "Jonathan Carpenter and the American Revolution: The Journal of an American Naval Prisoner of War and Vermont Indian Fighter." VERMONT HISTORY 36 (1968):74–90.

Extracts in "Diary of Jonathan Carpenter," by Charles Reed. VERMONT HISTORICAL SOCIETY PROCEEDINGS (1872):vii–xi.

1774–1780. Privateersman captured by British while aboard the REPRISAL; kept prisoner on prison ship CLIBBORN and at Forton Prison in England during 1778–1779; exchanged in France; account of military operations against Indians in Vermont in 1780. There is evidence of plagiarism in the account of Forton Prison.

CRESSWELL, NICHOLAS, 1750–1804   840

THE JOURNAL OF NICHOLAS CRESSWELL. New York: I. MacVeagh, Dial Press, 1924. 287 pp. Reprint. Port Washington, N.Y.: Kennikat Press, 1968.

Extracts in "The Journal of a Gentleman Emigrant." NATIONAL REVIEW 90 (1927):122–132.

Extracts in AN AUTOBIOGRAPHY OF AMERICA, edited by Mark Van Doren, pp. 108–121. New York: A.& C. Boni, 1929.

Extracts in DIARY OF AMERICA, edited by Josef Berger, pp. 92–98.

1774–1777. Voyage to Virginia; travel there and in Kentucky, Pennsylvania, New York; unsuccessful attempt to settle; unsuccessful trading trip along Ohio; misadventures in the Revolution; vigorous abuse of revolutionaries and propaganda; some good observations on places and people by a disillusioned young Englishman; a very good diary.

DEANE, SILAS, 1737–1789   841

Collier, Christopher, ed. "Silas Deane Reports on the Continental Congress; A Diary Fragment." CONNECTICUT HISTORICAL SOCIETY BULLETIN 29 (1964):1–8.

Oct 1774. Portion of lawyer's diary kept while representing Connecticut's Committee of Safety at the First Continental Congress.

Collier, Christopher, ed. "Inside the American Revolution; A Silas Deane Diary Fragment." CONNECTICUT HISTORICAL SOCIETY BULLETIN 29 (1964):86–96A.

Apr–Oct 1775 Brief entries reporting personal activities, debates in the Second Continental Congress, and news of early events of the Revolution.

DIAZ, JUAN, 1736-1781   842

In ANZA'S CALIFORNIA EXPEDITIONS, by Herbert E. Bolton, vol. 2, pp. 245-306.

Jan-May 1774. Detailed, well-written account by one of the missionaries accompanying Juan Bautista Anza on his first expedition from Tubac to San Gabriel; fertility of land; curious Indians, their clothing and desire for missionaries.

EVANS, DAVID   843

"Excerpts from the Day-Books of David Evans." PENNSYLVANIA MAGAZINE OF HISTORY AND BIOGRAPHY 27 (1903):49-55.

1774-1810. Brief business notes of Philadelphia cabinetmaker.

FITCH, EBENEZER, 1756-1833   844

In SKETCH OF THE LATE REV. EBENEZER FITCH, D.D., FIRST PRESIDENT OF WILLIAMS COLLEGE, by Calvin Durfee, pp. 20-33. Boston: Massachusetts Sabbath School Society, 1865.

1774-1777. Student's diary noting chief events of each day; college life at Yale; the war.

FOBES, TIMOTHY, 1740-1803   845

"Timothy Fobes His Book." PILGRIM NOTES AND QUERIES 2 (1914):152-154.

1774-1786. Brief notes of births, deaths, local affairs in Bridgewater, Massachusetts; genealogical interest.

FRISBIE, LEVI, 1748-1806   846

In A CONTINUATION OF THE NARRATIVE OF THE INDIAN CHARITY SCHOOL, by Eleazar Wheelock, app., pp. 44-68. Hartford, 1773. Reprint. ROCHESTER REPRINTS 8. Rochester, N.Y., 1910.

Jun-Sep 1774. Treaty journal describing mission to Quebec Indians to recover boy prisoners.

GARCES, FRANCISCO HERMENEGILDO, 1738-1781   847

In ANZA'S CALIFORNIA EXPEDITIONS, by Herbert E. Bolton, vol. 2, pp. 307-392.

Jan-Apr 1774. One of the missionaries with Juan Bautista Anza on his first expedition; exploration to establish land route from Tubac to San Gabriel; traveling conditions, sources of water, land quality, possible sites for missions; Indians; lack of interpreters.

In ON THE TRAIL OF A SPANISH PIONEER; THE DIARY AND ITINERARY OF FRANCISCO GARCES, translated and edited by Elliott Coues, vol. 2, pp. 557-608. New York: Francis P. Harper, 1900.

A RECORD OF TRAVELS IN ARIZONA AND CALIFORNIA, 1775-1776. A new translation edited by John Galvin. San Francisco: John Howell Books, 1965. 113 pp.

Oct 1775-Sep 1776. Journey from Tubac to Gila River, up the Colorado River and down to its mouth; to San Gabriel Mission, Tulare, Mojave, Yuma, and back to his mission at San Xavier del Bac; details of Indians, giving and receiving gifts; assessing Indians' readiness for Christian instruction; latitude observations and notes about landmarks.

HANSON, (THOMAS?)   848

In DOCUMENTARY HISTORY OF DUNMORE'S WAR, 1774, edited by Reuben G. Thwaites, pp. 110-133. Madison: Wisconsin Historical Society, 1905.

Apr-Aug 1774. Extract from journal kept by member of John Floyd's surveying party; exploring lands along the Ohio in what is now Kentucky; route, mileage, Indian menace, work activities.

HARE, ROBERT   849

"Memoranda on a Tour through a Part of North America in Company with Mr. William Allen." PENNSYLVANIA HISTORICAL SOCIETY COLLECTIONS 1 (1853):363-376.

May-Jul 1774. Philadelphian's trip to Canada and back, via Massachusetts; notes on places and people, Indians, Canadian Jesuits.

HARVEY, ALEXANDER, 1747-1809   850

"Journal of Colonel Alexander Harvey of Scotland and Barnet, Vermont." VERMONT HISTORICAL SOCIETY PROCEEDINGS (1921-1923):199-262.

1774-1775. Business journal kept by agent of Scottish company of farmers; journey with emigrants from Scotland; survey of site and development of community at Barnet; good picture of growth of an early settlement; interesting spellings.

LITCHFIELD, ISRAEL, 1753-1840   851

Johnson, Richard B., ed. "The Diary of Israel Litchfield." NEW ENGLAND HISTORICAL AND GENEALOGICAL REGISTER 129 (1975):150-171, 250-269, 361-378.

Extracts in THE LITCHFIELD FAMILY IN AMERICA, by Wilford J. Litchfield, pt. 1, no. 5, pp. 313-351. Southbridge, Mass.: W.J. Litchfield, 1901-1906.

1774-1775. Early days of the Revolution reflected in diary of young clocksmith and tanner; pleasant details of everyday life in Scituate, Massachusetts; religion, work, amusement, weather, militia training and movements, reports of clashes with British; journeys to Boston; some doggerel verses; linguistic interest.

LITTLE, ENOCH, 1763-1848   852

In THE HISTORY OF BOSCAWEN AND WEBSTER, compiled by Charles C. Coffin, pp. 403-406.

1774-1819. Brief scattered entries of resident of Boscawen, New Hampshire; begins as autobiography; many entries in verse form.

LOTT, ABRAHAM   853

"Journal of a Voyage to Albany, Etc." HISTORICAL MAGAZINE, 2d ser. 8 (1870):65-74.

Jun-Jul 1774. Journal kept by treasurer of the colony of New York while traveling from New York City to Albany.

MCKEE, ALEXANDER   854

In DOCUMENTS RELATIVE TO THE COLONIAL HISTORY OF THE STATE OF NEW YORK, edited by E.B. O'Callaghan, vol. 8, pp. 461-467.

In THE OLDEN TIME, edited by Neville B. Craig, vol. 2, pp. 13-26.

Mar–May 1774. Journal of Sir William Johnson's resident on the Ohio; meetings with Indians; news of Indian disturbances.

MCMILLAN, JOHN, 1752–1833   855

Bennett, D.M. "Concerning the Life and Work of the Rev. John McMillan, D.D." PRESBYTERIAN HISTORICAL SOCIETY JOURNAL 15 (1932–1933):217–248. Journal, pp. 222–238.

1774–1776. Activities of first Presbyterian minister in western Pennsylvania; notes on frontier life.

M'ROBERT, PATRICK   856

Bridenbaugh, Carl, ed. "Patrick M'Robert's TOUR THROUGH PART OF THE NORTH PROVINCES OF AMERICA." PENNSYLVANIA MAGAZINE OF HISTORY AND BIOGRAPHY 61 (1935):134–180. Reprint. PENNSYLVANIA HISTORICAL SOCIETY PAMPHLET SERIES, NARRATIVES AND DOCUMENTS, no. 1 (1935), pp. 1–47.

Aug 1774–May 1775. Journal-letters of a visiting Scotsman; acute and judicious observations based on actual experience; farming, industry, commerce; general social observations; one of the best travel books of the period.

MARSHALL, CHRISTOPHER, 1709–1797   857

EXTRACTS FROM THE DIARY OF CHRISTOPHER MARSHALL, KEPT IN PHILADELPHIA AND LANCASTER, DURING THE AMERICAN REVOLUTION. Edited by William Duane. Albany: J. Munsell, 1877. 330 pp. Reprint. New York: New York Times, 1969.

Extracts in GREAT MOMENTS IN PHARMACY, by George A. Bender, pp. 80–83. Detroit: Northwood Institute Press, 1966.

1774–1781. Philadelphia patriot's record of political and public affairs; historically valuable but impersonal jottings of newspaper kind.

PASSAGES FROM THE REMEMBRANCER OF CHRISTOPHER MARSHALL. Edited by William Duane. Philadelphia: Printed by J. Crissy, 1839. 124 pp.

1774–1776. Extracts.

PASSAGES FROM THE DIARY OF CHRISTOPHER MARSHALL. Edited by William Duane. Philadelphia: Hazard & Mitchell, 1849. 174 pp.

1774–1777. Extracts.

NEWELL, JAMES   858

"Orderly Book and Journal of James Newell." VIRGINIA MAGAZINE OF HISTORY AND BIOGRAPHY 11 (1903–1904): 242–253.

Sep–Oct 1774. Fragment describing the Point Pleasant campaign; a poem.

PALOU, FRANCISCO, 1723–1789   859

In HISTORICAL MEMOIRS OF NEW CALIFORNIA, translated and edited by Herbert E. Bolton, vol. 3, pp. 248–308. Berkeley: University of California Press, 1926. Reprint. New York: Russell & Russell, 1966.

In ANZA'S CALIFORNIA EXPEDITIONS, by Herbert E. Bolton, vol. 2, pp. 393–456.

Nov–Dec 1774. Priest from Mission San Carlos with exploring expedition from Monterey to San Francisco Bay, searching for suitable locations for missions; details of the route, travel conditions,

water, weather, exchanges with Indians and a report of six possible mission sites.

PEÑA, TOMAS DE LA   860

"Diary of Fray Tomás de la Peña Kept during the Voyage of the SANTIAGO." In THE CALIFORNIA COAST; A BILINGUAL EDITION OF DOCUMENTS FROM THE SUTRO COLLECTION, edited by George B. Griffin, re-edited with an emended translation by Donald C. Cutter, pp. 136–201. Norman: University of Oklahoma Press, 1969.

Aug 1774. Official diarist, Franciscan missionary and chaplain of voyage from Monterey north along the coast; navigational and weather information; notes on northwest coastal Indians who visited the ship by canoe; masses; scurvy among the crew; burials at sea; failure to claim or explore any land because of fog and unfavorable winds; similar to diary of Juan Crespi.

PREVOST, AUGUSTINE, 1725–1786   861

Wainwright, Nicholas B. "Turmoil at Pittsburgh: Diary of Augustine Prévost." PENNSYLVANIA MAGAZINE OF HISTORY AND BIOGRAPHY 85 (1961):111–162. Diary, pp. 119–144.

Apr–Sep 1774. Diary of British soldier from Jamaica; journey by sea and land to recruit for British army and unravel financial entanglements with his father-in-law, George Croghan; account of sojourn in Pittsburgh, reflecting the confusion of conflicting Pennsylvania and Virginia land claims combined with hostile Indian reaction to encroaching settlement.

Jones, Charles E., trans. "Journal of the Siege of Savannah in 1779." SOUTHERN HISTORICAL ASSOCIATION PUBLICATIONS 1 (1897):259–268.

Sep 1779. Journal kept while in command of British forces at the siege of Savannah; purely military details. Translated from the French.

RIVERA Y MONCADA, FERNANDO JAVIER DE   862

Brown, Alan K., trans. "Rivera at San Francisco: a Journal of Exploration." CALIFORNIA HISTORICAL SOCIETY QUARTERLY 41 (1962):325–341.

Nov–Dec 1774. Veteran Spanish captain's exploration of San Francisco Bay area; advice against future establishment of presidio and mission at Golden Gate because of lack of timber and grazing land; observations on Indians; activities of Father Francisco Palóu.

SANGER, ABNER   863

REPERTORY 1 (1926); 2 (1927).

1774–1776. Private diary of one of the early settlers of Keene, New Hampshire.

SCHAW, JANET, ca. 1731–ca. 1801   864

JOURNAL OF A LADY OF QUALITY: BEING THE NARRATIVE OF A JOURNEY FROM SCOTLAND TO THE WEST INDIES, NORTH CAROLINA, AND PORTUGAL. Edited by Evangeline Walker Andrews in collaboration with Charles McLean Andrews. New Haven: Yale University Press, 1921. 341 pp. Reprint. 1934, 1939; Spartanburg, S.C.: Reprint Co., 1971.

1774–1776. Traveler's journey to and sojourn in North Carolina; valuable description of pre-revolutionary life in area around Wilmington; views of Loyalists, plantation life, aggressive actions of "patriots," food and fun; engaging literary style.

STORRS, EXPERIENCE, 1734–1801   865

Hagelin, Wladimir and Brown, Ralph A., eds. "Connecticut Farmers at Bunker Hill: The Diary of Colonel Experience Storrs." NEW ENGLAND QUARTERLY 28 (1955): 72–93.

> Nov 1774–Jun 1775. Diary kept by farmer and town leader, reflecting the march towards war; activities of local militia; meeting of Connecticut Assembly at which he was appointed lieutenant colonel of his regiment; battle of Bunker Hill during which he was second in command of all Connecticut troops.

"From Diary of Lieut. Col. Exp. Storrs, of Mansfield, Cn." MASSACHUSETTS HISTORICAL SOCIETY PROCEEDINGS, 1st ser. 14 (1875–1876):84–87.

"Bunker Hill and the Siege of Boston." MAGAZINE OF AMERICAN HISTORY 8 (1882):124.

> Jun 1775. Extracts concerning siege of Boston, Bunker Hill, etc.

WARD, SAMUEL, 1725–1776   866

"Diary of Governor Samuel Ward, Delegate from Rhode Island in Continental Congress." MAGAZINE OF AMERICAN HISTORY 1 (1887):438–442, 503–506, 549–561.

> 1774–1776. Notes of politics, activities of First and Second Continental Congress; war news.

WATSON, ELKANAH, 1758–1842   867

MEN AND TIMES OF THE REVOLUTION; OR MEMOIRS OF ELKANAH WATSON, INCLUDING JOURNALS OF TRAVELS. Edited by Winslow C. Watson. New York: Dana, 1856. 460 pp.

Extracts in "Memoir of Elkanah Watson," by William R. Deane. NEW ENGLAND HISTORICAL AND GENEALOGICAL REGISTER 17 (1863):97–105.

> 1774–1784. Quaker travel journal; march to Lexington; journeys to the South.

A TOUR IN HOLLAND. Worcester, Mass.: Printed by Isaiah Thomas, 1790. 191 pp.

> May–Jun 1784. Travel journal in letter form.

In AMERICAN HISTORY TOLD BY CONTEMPORARIES, edited by Albert B. Hart, vol. 3, pp. 57–62.

> Sep 1791. Travels on western New York frontier, mostly by boat; description of terrain and settlements; prospects for canal building.

WETMORE, WILLIAM, 1749–1830   868

"Extracts from the Interleaved Almanacs of William Wetmore of Salem." ESSEX INSTITUTE HISTORICAL COLLECTIONS 43 (1907):115–120.

> 1774–1778. Diary extracts; brief notes, war news, etc.

WHITE, JOHN, b. 1729   869

"Extracts from Interleaved Almanacs Kept by John White of Salem." ESSEX INSTITUTE HISTORICAL COLLECTIONS 49 (1913):92–94.

> 1774–1789 (with large gaps). Weather, domestic and public affairs.

1775

ANON.   870

"The PRESTON's Journal in Boston Harbor." MASSACHUSETTS HISTORICAL SOCIETY PROCEEDINGS 5 (1860–1862):53–55.

> Apr–Oct 1775. British sailor's journal kept while PRESTON was in Boston harbor; account of incidents occurring about the time of Bunker Hill.

ANON.   871

In THE REMEMBRANCER, pp. 1–34. London: Printed for J. Almon, 1775–1784. Reprinted in HISTORY OF CANADA, by William Smith. Quebec: Printed for the author by J. Neilson, 1815; NEW YORK HISTORICAL SOCIETY COLLECTIONS (1880):173–236.

> Nov 1775–May 1776. British garrison officer's lively narrative of incidents of siege of Quebec.

ANON.   872

LITERARY AND HISTORICAL SOCIETY OF QUEBEC HISTORICAL DOCUMENTS, 7th ser. (1905):93–154.

> Nov 1775–May 1776. British military journal; apparently adapted from Thomas Ainslie's journal; Quebec after Arnold appeared before the town.

ANON.   873

LITERARY AND HISTORICAL SOCIETY OF QUEBEC HISTORICAL DOCUMENTS, 8th ser. (1906):11–53.

> Dec 1775–May 1776. Notes on artillery activities by a British officer during siege of Quebec.

ADAIR, WILLIAM   874

Hancock, Harold B., ed. "The Revolutionary War Diary of William Adair." DELAWARE HISTORY 13 (1968): 154–165.

> 1775–1783. Brief entries made by inhabitant of Lewes, Delaware; reflections of patriot-loyalist conflicts in Sussex County.

AINSLIE, THOMAS   875

LITERARY AND HISTORICAL SOCIETY OF QUEBEC HISTORICAL DOCUMENTS, 7th ser. (1905):11–89.

CANADA PRESERVED: THE JOURNAL OF CAPTAIN THOMAS AINSLIE. Edited by Sheldon S. Cohen. New York: New York University Press, 1968. 106 pp.

> Jun 1775–May 1776. Entertaining notes on the siege of Quebec from the British side, by the collector of customs at Quebec; good narrative and interesting details.

ALLINE, HENRY, 1748–1784   876

THE LIFE AND JOURNAL OF THE REV. MR. HENRY ALLINE. Boston: Printed by Gilbert and Dean, 1806. 180 pp.

> 1775–1783. Missionary diary; travel from Newport, Rhode Island; religious introspection.

AMORY, KATHARINE GREENE, 1731–1777   877

THE JOURNAL OF MRS. JOHN AMORY (KATHARINE GREENE). Edited by Martha C. Codman. Boston: Privately printed, 1923. 101 pp. Journal, pp. 3–56.

1775–1777. Private journal of Boston woman's passage to London; interesting notes of a Loyalist in London; social, religious, theatrical remarks.

ARNOLD, BENEDICT, 1741–1801   878

"Benedict Arnold's Regimental Memorandum Book." PENNSYLVANIA MAGAZINE OF HISTORY AND BIOGRAPHY 8 (1884):363–376.

May–Jun 1775. Military movements, etc., while at Ticonderoga and Crown Point.

In ARNOLD'S MARCH FROM CAMBRIDGE TO QUEBEC, by Justin Harvey Smith, pp. 467–483.

In MARCH TO QUEBEC, edited by Kenneth L. Roberts, pp. 45–61.

1775–1776. Expedition against Quebec.

AVERY, DAVID, 1746–1818   879

"A Chaplain in the American Revolution." AMERICAN MONTHLY MAGAZINE 17 (1900):342–347.

"The Siege of Boston." AMERICAN MONTHLY MAGAZINE 18 (1901):113–117.

"The Northern Campaign." AMERICAN MONTHLY MAGAZINE 18 (1901):235–240; 19 (1901):20–23, 151–156, 260–262, 375–378.

1775–1776 (with gaps). Brief notes of chaplain in Paterson's regiment during the northern campaign; siege of Boston; battle of Trenton; services, visits to sick, marches, hardships.

BARLOW, AARON, b. 1750   880

Todd, Charles B. "The March to Montreal and Quebec." AMERICAN HISTORICAL REGISTER 2 (1895):641–649.

Jun–Dec 1775. Military expedition of Schuyler and Montgomery against Montreal and Quebec; march from Redding to Stamford to join Connecticut regiment; Ticonderoga, Lake Champlain, St. Johns, etc.; military details; hardships; daily life of a common soldier.

BARWICK, ROBERT   881

"The Journal of Robert Barwick during the Canadian Campaign." In NAVAL DOCUMENTS OF THE AMERICAN REVOLUTION, by United States Naval History Division, edited by William J. Morgan, vol. 2, pp. 1387–1400.

Aug–Dec 1775. Military journal of march to Quebec; military operations on Lake Champlain and St. Lawrence River; battle and defeat at Quebec where he was taken prisoner.

BEDINGER, HENRY, 1753–1843   882

In HISTORIC SHEPHERDSTOWN, by Danske B. Dandridge, pp. 97–144. Charlottesville, Va.: Michie, 1910.

Jul 1775–Jun 1776. Military journal of march to Roxbury; in camp there and at Staten Island; movements, engagements, news.

BIXBY, SAMUEL, b. 1755   883

"Diary of Samuel Bixby." MASSACHUSETTS HISTORICAL SOCIETY PROCEEDINGS, 1st ser. 14 (1875–1876):285–298.

May 1775–Jan 1776. Account of the siege of Boston.

BOARDMAN, BENJAMIN, 1731–1802   884

"Diary of Rev. Benjamin Boardman." MASSACHUSETTS HISTORICAL SOCIETY PROCEEDINGS, 2d ser. 7 (1891–1892):400–413.

Jul–Nov 1775. Journal of chaplain with Second Connecticut Regiment; siege of Boston; news, casualties, camp life; dinner with Washington and Franklin.

BOUDINOT, ELIAS, 1740–1821   885

JOURNAL OF HISTORICAL RECOLLECTIONS OF AMERICAN EVENTS DURING THE REVOLUTIONARY WAR. Philadelphia: F. Bourquin, 1894. 97 pp. Reprint. New York: New York Times, 1968; New York: Arno, 1968.

Baker, William S. "Exchange of Major-General Charles Lee." PENNSYLVANIA MAGAZINE OF HISTORY AND BIOGRAPHY 15 (1891):26–34.

"Colonel Elias Boudinot in New York City, February, 1778." PENNSYLVANIA MAGAZINE OF HISTORY AND BIOGRAPHY 24 (1900):453–466.

1775–1789. Memoirs of the Revolution and extracts from private journal.

ELIAS BOUDINOT'S JOURNEY TO BOSTON IN 1809. Edited by Milton H. Thomas. Princeton, N.J.: Princeton University Press, 1955. 97 pp.

Jun–Oct 1809. Seventy-year-old statesman's trip from Burlington, New Jersey, to Boston; scenes and incidents of travel; taverns and inns; visits with leading ministers, his former colleagues in Continental Congress, and faculty at Harvard; comments on morals and mores of Bostonians; condition of education and religion; heavy social schedule occasionally impeded by gout.

BROWN, MOSES, 1738–1836   886

Thompson, Mack E., ed. "Moses Brown's 'Account of a Journey to Distribute Donations 12th Month 1775.'" RHODE ISLAND HISTORY 15 (1956):97–121. Journal, pp. 112–121.

Dec 1775–Jan 1776. Noted Quaker reformer's distribution of donations sent by Pennsylvania and New Jersey Friends to the New England Meeting for Sufferings to those affected by siege of Boston; negotiations with Washington, Nathanael Greene, others; journey through towns around Boston, an expedition setting precedent for organized, large scale, non-partisan aid to war victims.

BULL, EPAPHRAS   887

"Journal of Epaphras Bull." FORT TICONDEROGA MUSEUM BULLETIN 8 (July 1948):38–46.

May 1775. Military journal; journey from Stockbridge, Massachusetts; preparation for attack and capture of Fort Ticonderoga; return to Connecticut with prisoners of war; financial accounts.

BURTON, JONATHAN, 1741–1811   888

In NEW HAMPSHIRE PROVINCIAL AND STATE PAPERS, vol. 14, pp. 667–702.

Dec 1775–Nov 1776. Brief entries of encampment at Winter Hill; personal entries and record of Canada expedition route.

BUTLER, RICHARD, 1743–1791   889

William, Edward G., ed. "The Journal of Richard Butler, 1775: Continental Congress' Envoy to the Western Indians." WESTERN PENNSYLVANIA HISTORICAL MAGAZINE 46 (1963):381–395; 47 (1964):31–46, 141–156.

> Aug–Sep 1775. Continental Congress' Indian agent at Pittsburgh; transactions of diplomatic journey through the Ohio country; visiting important Indian towns and meeting with Indian leaders; many Indian speeches recorded.

VIRGINIA HISTORICAL MAGAZINE 8 (1864):102–112.

> Sep–Oct 1781. Details of strategic operations during siege of Yorktown with Fifth Pennsylvania Regiment.

In THE OLDEN TIME, edited by Neville B. Craig, vol. 2, pp. 433–464, 481–525, 529–531.

> Sep 1785–Feb 1786. Military journal kept during expedition from Carlisle, Pennsylvania, to hold treaty with the Miami Indians at Fort McIntosh; substantial descriptive notes of journey and treaty proceedings.

CALK, WILLIAM, b. 1740   890

Kilpatrick, Lewis H. "The Journal of William Calk, Kentucky Pioneer." MISSISSIPPI VALLEY HISTORICAL REVIEW 7 (1920–1921):363–377.

In THE WILDERNESS ROAD, by Thomas Speed, pp. 34–38. Louisville: J.P. Morton, 1886.

In HISTORIC HIGHWAYS OF AMERICA, by Archer B. Hulbert, vol. 6, pp. 107–117.

In A HISTORY OF TRAVEL IN AMERICA, by Seymour Dunbar, vol. 1, pp. 142–146. Indianapolis: Bobbs-Merrill, 1915.

> Mar–May 1775. Interesting details of hardships of a pioneer; journey from Prince William County, Virginia, to Boonesboro, Kentucky; settlement there; interesting language.

CAMPA, MIGUEL DE LA, b. 1719   891

A JOURNAL OF EXPLORATIONS NORTHWARD ALONG THE COAST FROM MONTEREY IN THE YEAR 1775. Edited by John Galvin. San Francisco: John Howell Books, 1964. 67 pp.

> May–Nov 1775. Journal of chaplain aboard SANTIAGO, commanded by Bruno Hezeta, on expedition to explore coast north from Monterey, California, as far as Washington State; latitude, weather, wind and coastal observations; descriptions of Indian huts and clothing; exchange of gifts and food; ceremonies of claiming the land. Similar to diary by Benito de la Sierra, chaplain aboard SONORA on the same expedition.

CHANDLER, THOMAS BRADBURY, 1726–1790   892

Gavin, Frank. "The Rev. Thomas Bradbury Chandler in the Light of His (Unpublished) Diary." CHURCH HISTORY 1 (1932):90–106.

> 1775–1786. Extracts of his missionary work in New Jersey.

CHEEVER, WILLIAM, 1752–1786   893

"William Cheever's Diary." MASSACHUSETTS HISTORICAL SOCIETY PROCEEDINGS 60 (1926–1927):91–97.

> May 1775–Mar 1776. Military journal of battle of Bunker Hill; evacuation of Boston.

CRAFT, BENJAMIN, 1738–1823   894

"Craft's Journal of the Siege of Boston." ESSEX INSTITUTE HISTORICAL COLLECTIONS 3 (1861):51–57, 133–140, 167–174, 219–220.

> Jun–Nov 1775. Siege of Boston; brief but lively notes of camp life and personal details.

CRUGER, HENRY, d. 1780   895

"Diary and Memoranda of Henry Cruger." MAGAZINE OF AMERICAN HISTORY 7 (1881):358–363.

> Aug 1775. Diary extracts concerning his life in England; opinions of Burke and North about settlement with colonies.

DANFORD, JACOB   896

Roche, John F., ed. "Quebec under Siege, 1775–1776: The 'Memorandums' of Jacob Danford." CANADIAN HISTORICAL REVIEW 50 (1969):68–85.

> Nov 1775–May 1776. War diary of civilian employee of Quebec's Board of Ordnance, serving with British militia; detailed account of use of artillery by both sides; numbers of casualties and prisoners.

DEARBORN, HENRY, 1751–1829   897

REVOLUTIONARY WAR JOURNALS OF HENRY DEARBORN. Edited by Lloyd A. Brown and Howard H. Peckham. Chicago: The Caxton Club, 1939. 264 pp. Reprint. Freeport, N.Y.: Books for Libraries, 1969; New York: Da Capo, 1971.

> 1775–1783. Military details of Arnold's expedition to Quebec; some personal items; detailed account of siege of Quebec; other campaigns in which he was engaged.

"Arnold Expedition to Quebec." MASSACHUSETTS HISTORICAL SOCIETY PROCEEDINGS, 2d ser. 2 (1885–1886): 275–305.

JOURNAL OF CAPTAIN HENRY DEARBORN IN THE QUEBEC EXPEDITION. Cambridge, Mass.: J. Wilson and Son, 1886. 33 pp.

"A Journal Kept by Capt. Henry Dearborn." MAGAZINE OF HISTORY, extra no. 135, 34 (1928):113–153.

In MARCH TO QUEBEC, edited by Kenneth L. Roberts, pp. 129–168.

> Sep 1775–Jul 1776.

"March of Colonel Dearborn along the West Side of Cayuga Lake." CAYUGA COUNTY HISTORICAL SOCIETY COLLECTIONS 1 (1879):76–81.

"Journal of Henry Dearborn." MASSACHUSETTS HISTORICAL PROCEEDINGS, 2d ser. 3 (1886–1887):102–133.

In JOURNALS OF THE MILITARY EXPEDITION OF MAJOR GENERAL JOHN SULLIVAN by New York State Secretary of State, Frederick Cook, pp. 62–79.

> 1776–1783.

DEMING, SARAH WINSLOW, 1722–1788   898

"Journal of Sarah Winslow Deming." AMERICAN MONTHLY MAGAZINE 4 (1894):45–49; 5 (1894):67–70.

> Apr 1775. Letter-diary of adventures on retreat from Boston to Providence.

EDES, PETER, 1756-1840 899

A DIARY OF PETER EDES. Bangor: S.S. Smith, Printer, 1837. 24 pp.

In PETER EDES, PIONEER PRINTER IN MAINE, edited by Samuel L. Boardman, pp. 93-109. Bangor: Printed for the De Burians, 1901.

>Jun 1775-Jan 1776. Diary of imprisonment in Boston by British after Bunker Hill; notes about his schoolhouse; simple straightforward style.

EIXARCH, THOMAS, b. 1742? 900

In ANZA'S CALIFORNIA EXPEDITIONS, by Herbert E. Bolton, vol. 3, pp. 309-381.

>Dec 1775-May 1776. Missionary experiences of a winter on the Colorado River with Yuma and related Indian tribes until the return of Juan Bautista Anza and Father Pedro Font on second Anza expedition; observations about the river; reception as a missionary; customs, food and agriculture of the Yumas; trip to the mission at Caborca on the Altar River to spend Holy Week.

EMERSON, DANIEL, 1716-1801 901

In THE IPSWICH EMERSONS, by Benjamin K. Emerson, pp. 86-91. Boston: D. Clapp & Son, 1900.

>Jul-Sep 1775. Chaplain's journal at Crown Point; march, services, prayers, religious reflections.

EWING, GEORGE, 1754-1824 902

In GEORGE EWING, GENTLEMAN, edited by Thomas Ewing, pp. 1-54. Yonkers, N.Y.: Privately printed, 1928.

"Journal of George Ewing, a Revolutionary Soldier, of Greenwich, New Jersey." AMERICAN MONTHLY MAGAZINE 37 (1910):471-473; 38 (1911):5-8, 50-53.

>1775-1778. Account of army life; Canadian expedition to reinforce Arnold's siege of Quebec; Valley Forge.

FARNSWORTH, AMOS, 1754-1847 903

In THREE MILITARY DIARIES, edited by Samuel A. Green, pp. 77-113. Groton, Mass.: Cambridge University Press, J. Wilson and Son, 1901.

Green, Samuel A., ed. "Amos Farnsworth's Diary." MASSACHUSETTS HISTORICAL SOCIETY PROCEEDINGS, 2d ser. 12 (1897-1899):74-107.

>1775-1779 (with gaps). Notes on camp life and events of the war; Concord, Lexington, siege of Boston, Bunker Hill; much religious self-analysis; more personal than the usual military journal.

FASSETT, JOHN, 1743-1803 904

In THE FOLLETT-DEWEY FASSETT-SAFFORD ANCESTRY, by Harry P. Ward, pp. 215-243. Columbus, Ohio: Champlin Printing, 1896.

>Sep-Dec 1775. March of the Green Mountain Boys to Canada and return; Montgomery's campaign; full entries and good narrative of hardships and adventures.

FINLAY, HUGH 905

JOURNAL OF THE SIEGE AND BLOCKADE OF QUEBEC BY THE AMERICAN REBELS, IN AUTUMN 1775 AND WINTER 1776. Literary and Historical Society of Quebec Manuscripts Relating to the Early History of Canada, 4th ser., no. 4. Quebec: Printed by Dawson, 1875. 25 pp.

>Nov 1775-May 1776. Siege and blockade of Quebec; nontechnical military details. Authorship assumed.

FISHER, ELIJAH, b. 1758 906

ELIJAH FISHER'S JOURNAL. Augusta, Maine: Press of Badger & Manley, 1880. 19 pp. Reprint. MAGAZINE OF HISTORY, extra no. 6, 2 (1909):123-198.

>1775-1785. Military diary and notes of a laborer during the Revolution and later; siege of Boston; Burgoyne's campaign; captivity; matter-of-fact attitude towards hardships and adventures; later, farming in Maine.

FISHER, JOHN, 1756-1840 907

"John Fisher's Reminiscences of the Revolution." MAGAZINE OF HISTORY 13 (1911):184-186.

>Jul-Oct 1775, Jun-Jul 1777. Brief notes of New York campaign, battle of Long Island, and in Connecticut; some interesting spellings.

FOBES, SIMON, 1756-1840 908

"Simon Fobes." HISTORICAL COLLECTIONS OF THE MAHONING VALLEY 1 (1876):345-394. Reprint. MAGAZINE OF HISTORY, extra no. 130, 33 (1927):61-111.

Extracts in MARCH TO QUEBEC, edited by Kenneth L. Roberts, pp. 575-613.

>1775-1780. Mainly devoted to a narrative of Bunker Hill and Arnold's expedition against Quebec.

FOGG, JEREMIAH, 1749-1808 909

JOURNAL OF MAJOR JEREMIAH FOGG. Exeter, N.H.: News-letter Press, 1879. 24 pp.

>1775-1776. Military journal.

In JOURNALS OF THE MILITARY EXPEDITION OF MAJOR GENERAL JOHN SULLIVAN, by New York State Secretary of State, Frederick Cook, pp. 92-101.

>Aug-Sep 1779. Long entries of Sullivan's campaign.

FONT, PEDRO, 1738-1781 910

"Font's Complete Diary of the Second Anza Expedition." In ANZA'S CALIFORNIA EXPEDITIONS, by Herbert E. Bolton, vol. 4.

>Sep 1775-Jun 1776. The complete private diary of the chaplain of Juan Bautista de Anza's second expedition to colonize San Francisco; names of all members, the equipment, animals, order of march and gossip of the trail; traveling conditions, distances, astronomical observations; measurements and details of La Casa Grande and Indian fables relating to it; abstracts of sermons. Translated from the Spanish.

THE ANZA EXPEDITION OF 1775-1776; DIARY OF PEDRO FONT. Edited by Frederick J. Teggart. Academy of Pacific Coast History Publications, vol. 3, no. 1. Berkeley: University of California, 1913. 131 pp.

"Font's Short Diary." In ANZA'S CALIFORNIA EXPEDITIONS, vol. 3, pp. 201-307.

Extracts in FIRST ANNUAL OF THE TERRITORIAL PIONEERS OF CALIFORNIA, by Territorial Pioneers of California, pp. 81-107. San Francisco: Printed by W.M. Hinton, 1877.

Sep 1775–Jun 1776. The version included in his official report.

FULLER, DANIEL, 1740–1829   911

THE DIARY OF THE REV. DANIEL FULLER. Edited by Daniel F. Appleton. New York: Imprinted for private distribution at the De Vinne Press, 1894. 49 pp.

1775–1797. Clergyman's journal and notes on journeys, public affairs; Charlestown and Boston during the Revolution; domestic, parish, and personal affairs in Gloucester, Massachusetts.

GERRISH, HENRY, b. 1742   912

In THE HISTORY OF BOSCAWEN AND WEBSTER, edited by Charles C. Coffin, pp. 247, 265.

1775–1777. Extracts of march to Cambridge; auction at which plunder from Fort Edward was sold.

GREENMAN, JEREMIAH, 1758–1828   913

DIARY OF A COMMON SOLDIER IN THE AMERICAN RE-VOLUTION. Edited by Robert C. Bray and Paul E. Bushnell. DeKalb: Northern Illinois University Press, 1978. 333 pp.

1775–1783. Brief entries begun at age seventeen; enlistment in the Rhode Island Continentals; Quebec campaign, during which he was taken prisoner; repatriation and re-enlistment; defense of the Delaware, battles of Valley Forge, Monmouth and Rhode Island; daily grind of marching, fighting and waiting; cold, hunger, military discipline; interesting spellings.

HALE, NATHAN, 1755–1776   914

In NATHAN HALE, 1776, by Henry Phelps Johnston, pp. 240–257. New York: De Vinne Press, 1901. Rev. ed. New Haven: Yale University Press, 1914.

In DOCUMENTARY LIFE OF NATHAN HALE, by George D. Seymour, pp. 173–199. New Haven: Privately printed, 1941.

Sep 1775–Aug 1776. Brief entries of military events.

HAMILTON, Sir J.   915

JOURNAL OF THE PRINCIPAL OCCURRENCES DURING THE SIEGE OF QUEBEC. Edited by W.T.P. Short. London: Sold by Simpkin and Co., 1824. 111 pp. Reprint. LITERARY AND HISTORICAL SOCIETY OF QUEBEC HISTOR-ICAL DOCUMENTS, 8th ser. (1906):55–126.

In BLOCKADE OF QUEBEC IN 1775–1776, edited by Frederic C. Wurtele, vol. 1, pp. 55–101. Quebec: Daily Telegraph Job Printing House, 1906.

Dec 1775–May 1776. Good British military journal of principal events of siege of Quebec; some personal details; literary style with poetical quotations. Presumed to have been written by Sir J. Hamilton, Captain of H.M.S. LIZARD.

HASKELL, CALEB, b. 1723   916

NEWBURYPORT HERALD, 1881.

"Caleb Haskell's Diary." MAGAZINE OF HISTORY, extra no. 86, 2 (1922):57–110.

In MARCH TO QUEBEC, edited by Kenneth L. Roberts, pp. 459–499.

1775–1776. Arnold's expedition; siege of Boston; hardships of soldiers.

HASLEWOOD, JOHN   917

Kellogg, Louise P., ed. "Journal of a British Officer during the American Revolution." MISSISSIPPI VALLEY HISTORICAL REVIEW 7 (1920–1921):51–58.

1775–1778. Brief military details in diary of captain of Sixty-third British Infantry; from Cork to Boston; notes on campaigns, Charlestown, Long Island, Rhode Island, New York; Bunker Hill, siege of Boston; some interesting spellings and vocabulary.

HAWS (or HAWES), SAMUEL, 1743–1780?   918

In THE MILITARY JOURNALS OF TWO PRIVATE SOLDIERS, 1758–1775, compiled by Abraham Tomlinson with notes by Benson J. Lossing, pp. 49–90. Poughkeepsie: A. Tomlinson, 1855. Reprint. Freeport, N.Y., Books for Libraries, 1970; New York: Da Capo, 1971.

Johnson, Richard Brigham, ed. "The Journal of Samuel Hawes." NEW ENGLAND HISTORICAL AND GENEALOGICAL REGISTER 130 (1976):208–219, 273–283; 131 (1977):40–50. Corrects some errors in Lossing's notes.

1775–1776. Ordinary soldier's daily life in early days of Revolution; siege of Boston.

HEATH, WILLIAM, 1737–1814   919

MEMOIRS OF MAJOR-GENERAL HEATH. Boston: Printed by I. Thomas and E.T. Andrews, 1798. 388 pp. Reprint. New York: W. Abbatt, 1901.

Extract regarding siege of Boston in "Journal of Some Occurrences in the Camp at Roxbury." MASSACHUSETTS HISTORICAL SOCIETY PROCEEDINGS, 1st ser. 4 (1858–1860):294–296.

1775–1803. Valuable source book of military affairs during the Revolution.

HENDERSON, RICHARD, 1735–1785   920

In BOONESBOROUGH: ITS FOUNDING, PIONEER STRUG-GLES, INDIAN EXPERIENCES, TRANSYLVANIA DAYS AND REVOLUTIONARY ANNALS, by George W. Ranck, pp. 169–180. Louisville, Ky.: J.P. Morton & Co., Printers, 1901.

Extracts in HISTORIC HIGHWAYS OF AMERICA, edited by Albert B. Hulbert, vol. 6, pp. 101–107; PLANTATION AND FRONTIER DOCUMENTS, edited by Ulrich B. Phillips, vol. 2, pp. 219–229.

Mar–Jul 1775. Trip from Hanover County, Virginia, to Kentucky; events in settlement of Boonesboro; details of frontier life.

HENDRICKS, WILLIAM, d. 1776   921

A JOURNAL OF THE MARCH OF A PARTY OF PROVINCIALS FROM CARLISLE TO BOSTON. Glasgow, 1776. 36 pp. Reprint. "Journal of Captain William Hendricks from Carlisle to Boston, Thence to Quebec." PENNSYLVANIA ARCHIVES, 2d ser., vol. 15, pp. 21–58.

Jul–Dec 1775. Arnold's march to Quebec; siege of Quebec; notes of hardships. Authorship uncertain; may have been commenced by Hendricks and completed by Sergeant William McCoy.

HENRY, JOHN JOSEPH, 1758–1811   922

AN ACCURATE AND INTERESTING ACCOUNT OF THE HARD-SHIPS AND SUFFERINGS OF THAT BAND OF HEROES, WHO TRAVERSED THE WILDERNESS IN THE CAMPAIGN AGAINST QUEBEC IN 1775. Lancaster, Pa.: Printed by William

Green, 1812. 221 pp. Reprint. "Journal of the Campaign Against Quebec." PENNSYLVANIA ARCHIVES, 2d ser., vol. 15, pp. 59-191.

CAMPAIGN AGAINST QUEBEC. Rev. ed. Watertown, N.Y.: Knowlton & Rice, 1844. 212 pp.

ACCOUNT OF ARNOLD'S CAMPAIGN AGAINST QUEBEC. Albany: J. Munsell, 1877. 198 pp.

In MARCH TO QUEBEC, edited by Kenneth L. Roberts, pp. 299-429.

> 1775-1776. Arnold's campaign against Quebec; author's military career; captivity; very detailed and perhaps the most extensive journal of Arnold's campaign. Written up for his children in a literary and occasionally heroic style.

HONYMAN, ROBERT, 1747-1824　　923

COLONIAL PANORAMA, 1775: DR. ROBERT HONYMAN'S JOURNAL FOR MARCH AND APRIL. Edited by Philip Padelford. San Marino, Calif.: Huntington Library, 1939. 86 pp.

> Mar-Apr 1775. Long entries during visit from Virginia to the northern colonies; touristic descriptions; economic and social conditions; a very pleasant diary.

MacMaster, Richard K., ed. "News of the Yorktown Campaign: The Journal of Dr. Robert Honyman." VIRGINIA MAGAZINE OF HISTORY AND BIOGRAPHY 79 (1971): 387-426.

> Apr-Nov 1781. Hanover County physician's private journal; news of military movements in Virginia; comments on behavior of British troops and officers; problems of provisions for army; visit to the siege of Yorktown; terms of surrender.

HOSMER, LUCY BARNES, 1742-1818　　924

Lupton, Mary Hosmer. "Journal of Lucy Barnes Hosmer: Tuesday 18 April-Wednesday 19 April 1775, Concord, Massachusetts." DAUGHTERS OF THE AMERICAN REVOLUTION MAGAZINE 114 (1980):14-17.

> Apr 1775. The anxiety of preparing for war; receiving word from companion of Paul Revere that British troops had left Boston; gathering of Minutemen on the green and battle of Concord.

HOW, DAVID, 1758-1842　　925

DIARY OF DAVID HOW. Edited by George W. Chase and Henry B. Dawson. Morrisania, N.Y.; Cambridge, Mass.: Printed by H.O. Houghton, 1865. 51 pp.

> 1775-1777. Siege of Boston, Harlem Heights, Trenton, White Plains; details of ordinary camp life of private soldier; march to Fort Edward and return to Methuen.

HOWE, JOHN　　926

A JOURNAL KEPT BY MR. JOHN HOWE, WHILE HE WAS EMPLOYED AS A BRITISH SPY, DURING THE REVOLUTIONARY WAR: ALSO, WHILE HE WAS ENGAGED IN THE SMUGGLING BUSINESS, DURING THE LATE WAR. Concord, N.H.: L. Roby, Printer, 1827. 44 pp. Reprint. MAGAZINE OF HISTORY, extra no. 132, 33 (1927):157-190; Photostat Americana, 2d ser., no. 82. Boston, 1939.

Stout, Niel R., ed. "Excerpts from John Howe's 'Smuggler's Journal.'" VERMONT HISTORY 40 (1972):262-270.

> Apr 1775, Nov 1812-Apr 1813. Adventures of British

spy in New England during Revolution; smuggler's experiences during War of 1812.

HUMPHREY, WILLIAM　　927

"A Journal Kept by William Humphrey." MAGAZINE OF HISTORY, extra no. 166, 42 (1931):83-122.

> Sep 1775-Aug 1776. Military journal of lieutenant in Thayer's company; Arnold's campaign against Quebec; largely weather notes and accounts of hard marches.

INGALLS, PHINEAS, 1758-1844　　928

"Revolutionary War Journal, Kept by Phineas Ingalls of Andover, Mass." ESSEX INSTITUTE HISTORICAL COLLECTIONS 53 (1917):81-92.

> 1775-1776 (with gap). Military journal covering siege of Boston, army movements and camp life in Cambridge, Lake Champlain campaign, Ticonderoga, Saratoga.

JEFFRY, JAMES, 1733-1807　　929

Smith, William, ed. "Journal Kept in Quebec in 1775 by James Jeffry." ESSEX INSTITUTE HISTORICAL COLLECTIONS 50 (1914):97-150.

> Jan-Oct 1775. Long entries of war news at Quebec, where diarist was postmaster.

KIMBALL, MOSES　　930

In MARCH TO QUEBEC, edited by Kenneth L. Roberts, pp. 435-454.

> 1775-1776. Arnold's campaign against Quebec; extracts published as footnotes to James Melvin's journal.

KNOX, HENRY, 1750-1806　　931

"Knox's Diary during His Ticonderoga Expedition." NEW ENGLAND HISTORICAL AND GENEALOGICAL REGISTER 30 (1876):321-326.

> Nov 1775-Jan 1776. Military journal covering journey to Stillwater, transferring ordnance; description of Niagara and the frozen Cohoos Falls.

LEACH, JOHN, ca. 1724-1799　　932

"A Journal Kept by John Leach, during His Confinement by the British." NEW ENGLAND HISTORICAL AND GENEALOGICAL REGISTER 29 (1865):255-263.

In PETER EDES, PIONEER PRINTER IN MAINE, edited by Samuel L. Boardman, pp. 115-125. Bangor: Printed for the De Burians, 1901.

> Jun-Oct 1775. Prison diary of civilian prisoner of British; a good account of life in Boston Jail.

LEMPRIERE, CLEMENT　　933

In DOCUMENTARY HISTORY OF THE AMERICAN REVOLUTION, by Robert W. Gibbes, vol. 1, pp. 121-123.

> Jul-Aug 1775. Captain's log notes of voyage of the sloop COMMERCE toward New Orleans.

LINDSAY, WILLIAM　　934

CANADIAN REVIEW 2-3 (1826), incomplete.

> Sep-Dec 1775. British militia officer's notes of siege and blockade of Quebec.

LITCHFIELD, PAUL, 1752-1827 935

"Diary of Paul Litchfield." MASSACHUSETTS HISTORICAL SOCIETY PROCEEDINGS, 1st ser. 29 (1881-1882):376-379.

Mar-Jul 1775. College diary kept while student at Harvard: mostly war news at Scituate.

LITITZ, PENNSYLVANIA, MORAVIAN CONGREGATION 936

Beck, Abraham R., trans. "Extracts from the Brethren's House and Congregation Diaries of the Moravian Church at Lititz, Pa., Relating to the Revolutionary War." PENN GERMANIA, n.s. 1 (1912):849-862.

1775-1786. Congregational journals; items relating to the Revolution, life and work of the congregation. Translated.

Beck, Herbert H., ed. "The Military Hospital at Lititz." LANCASTER COUNTY HISTORICAL SOCIETY PAPERS 23 (1919):5-14.

1777-1778.

LIVINGSTON, HENRY, 1748-1828 937

Hunt, Gaillard. "Journal of Major Henry Livingston, of the Third New York Continental Line." PENNSYLVANIA MAGAZINE OF HISTORY AND BIOGRAPHY 22 (1898):9-33.

Aug-Dec 1775. Soldier's journal of Montgomery's expedition against Canada; some independent descriptions and observations.

LUKENS, JESSE, 1748-1776 938

"Incidents of the Siege of Boston." AMERICAN HISTORICAL RECORD 1 (1872):546-550.

"Boston in 1775, a Letter from Jesse Lukens to John Shaw, Jr." BOSTON PUBLIC LIBRARY MONTHLY BULLETIN 5 (1900):23-29.

Sep 1775. Letter-diary of incidents during siege of Boston and Arnold's departure for Quebec.

LUNT, PAUL, 1747-1824 939

"Paul Lunt's Book." MASSACHUSETTS HISTORICAL SOCIETY PROCEEDINGS, 1st ser. 12 (1871-1873):192-206.

May-Dec 1775. Military journal covering travel to camp at Cambridge; notes on camp life.

LYMAN, SIMEON, 1754-1780 940

"Journal of Simeon Lyman of Sharon." CONNECTICUT HISTORICAL SOCIETY COLLECTIONS 7 (1899):111-134.

Aug-Dec 1775. Private's journal of march to Boston, siege, return to Sharon; lively, amusing record of common soldier's life; mostly personal details.

MCCURTIN, DANIEL 941

In PAPERS RELATING CHIEFLY TO THE MARYLAND LINE, edited by Thomas Balch, pp. 1-41. Philadelphia: Printed for the Seventy-Six Society, 1857.

Jul 1775-May 1776. Private's journal of siege of Boston, camp at Cambridge and Roxbury; details, but some amusing general observations and adventures.

MACKENZIE, FREDERICK, d. 1824 942

DIARY OF FREDERICK MACKENZIE, GIVING A DAILY NARRATIVE OF HIS MILITARY SERVICE AS AN OFFICER OF THE REGIMENT OF ROYAL WELCH FUSILIERS. Cam-

bridge: Harvard University Press, 1930. 2 vols. Reprint. New York: New York Times, 1968.

Covell, Elizabeth. "Newport Harbor and Lower Narragansett Bay, Rhode Island, during the American Revolution." NEWPORT HISTORICAL SOCIETY BULLETIN 86 (1933):3-37.

Covell, Elizabeth. "Military Events on Rhode Island from the Diary of a British Officer." NEWPORT HISTORICAL SOCIETY BULLETIN 93 (1934):3-31.

1775-1781. British officer's daily narrative of his service during the Revolution; campaigns in Massachusetts, Rhode Island, New York; vivid account of burning of New York; a most valuable journal from the British side.

A BRITISH FUSILIER IN REVOLUTIONARY BOSTON. Edited by Allen French. Cambridge: Harvard University Press, 1926. 83 pp. Reprint. New York: Books for Libraries, 1969.

Jan-Apr 1775. Extract describing Lexington and Concord.

"Description of the Battle of Lexington." MASSACHUSETTS HISTORICAL SOCIETY PROCEEDINGS, 2d ser. 5 (1889-1890):391-396.

Apr 1775. Extract covering the clash at Lexington and the retreat of the British troops back to Boston; British officer's perplexity and frustration over American rebels' refusal to "form a line"; numbers and names of British casualties.

MEIGS, RETURN JONATHAN, 1740-1823 943

"A Journal of Occurrences." MASSACHUSETTS HISTORICAL SOCIETY COLLECTIONS, 2d ser. 2 (1814):227-247.

JOURNAL OF THE EXPEDITION AGAINST QUEBEC, IN THE YEAR 1775, UNDER THE COMMAND OF COLONEL BENEDICT ARNOLD. With introduction and notes by Charles I. Bushnell. Crumbs for Antiquarians, vol. 1, no. 6. New York: Privately printed, 1864. 57 pp.

Green, Mrs. Melvin, ed. "Journal of Major Return Jonathan Meigs." WINCHESTER, VIRGINIA, HISTORICAL SOCIETY ANNUAL PAPERS 1 (1931):119-155.

Extracts in MARCH TO QUEBEC, edited by Kenneth L. Roberts, pp. 173-192; THE REMEMBRANCER, vol. 3, pp. 295-301. London: Printed for J. Almon, 1776.

Sep 1775-Jan 1776. Military journal of Arnold's expedition against Quebec; some descriptions of Montgomery and other leaders.

MELVIN, JAMES, b. 1754 944

JOURNAL OF THE EXPEDITION TO QUEBEC IN THE YEAR 1775, UNDER THE COMMAND OF COLONEL BENEDICT ARNOLD. Philadelphia: Printed for the Franklin Club, 1864. 34 pp.

JOURNAL OF JAMES MELVIN, PRIVATE SOLDIER IN ARNOLD'S EXPEDITION AGAINST QUEBEC. Notes and introduction by Andrew A. Melvin. Portland, Maine: H.W. Bryant, 1902. 90 pp.

Extracts in MARCH TO QUEBEC, edited by Kenneth L. Roberts, pp. 435-454.

Sep 1775-Aug 1776. Private's journal of Arnold's expedition against Quebec; first part covering imprisonment, then mostly weather notes.

MORGAN, NATHANIEL, b. 1717 945

"Journal of Ensign Nathaniel Morgan, April 21 to Dec. 11, 1775; Items of the Siege of Boston from the Roxbury Side." CONNECTICUT HISTORICAL SOCIETY COLLECTIONS 7 (1899):97-110.

Apr–Dec 1775. Military journal of Lexington alarm and siege of Boston.

MORISON, GEORGE   946

"An Interesting Journal of Occurrences during the Expedition to Quebec." MAGAZINE OF HISTORY, extra no. 52, 13 (1916):253–296. Reprint. Tarrytown, N.Y.: W. Abbatt, 1916. 44 pp.

Extracts in MARCH TO QUEBEC, edited by Kenneth L. Roberts, pp. 505–539; PENNSYLVANIA MAGAZINE OF HISTORY AND BIOGRAPHY 14 (1890):434–439.

> 1775–1776. Military journal; Arnold's expedition against Quebec; Bunker Hill; notes on camp life.

MOURELLE, FRANCISCO ANTONIO, 1755–1820   947

In MISCELLANIES, by Daines Barrington, pp. 471–519. London: Printed by J. Nichols and sold by B. White, 1781.
VOYAGE OF THE SONORA IN THE SECOND BUCARELI EXPEDITION TO EXPLORE THE NORTHWEST COAST, SURVEY THE PORT OF SAN FRANCISCO AND FOUND FRANCISCAN MISSIONS AND A PRESIDIO AND PUEBLO AT THAT PORT. Translated by Daines Barrington. San Francisco: Thomas C. Russell, 1920. 100 pp.

> 1775. Observations by a member of Spanish expedition aboard the schooner SONORA while exploring the coast line of California; attention to flora and fauna; the port of San Francisco and desirability of establishing a mission there.

NEWELL, TIMOTHY, 1718–1799   948

"A Journal Kept during the Time that Boston was Shut Up in 1775–6." MASSACHUSETTS HISTORICAL SOCIETY COLLECTIONS, 4th ser. 1 (1852):261–276.

> Apr 1775–Mar 1776. Deacon's journal of siege of Boston; good, vivid descriptions of misfortunes of inhabitants after the siege, pillage, etc.

NICHOLS, FRANCIS, d. 1812   949

"Diary of Lieutenant Francis Nichols, of Colonel William Thompson's Battalion of Pennsylvania Riflemen." PENNSYLVANIA MAGAZINE OF HISTORY AND BIOGRAPHY 20 (1896):504–514.

> Dec 1775–Sep 1776. Military diary of expedition against Quebec; imprisonment; scattered brief entries.

NOURSE, JAMES, 1731–1784   950

"Journey to Kentucky in 1775." JOURNAL OF AMERICAN HISTORY 19 (1925):121–138, 251–260, 351–364.

> Apr–Jul 1775. Journey from Virginia to Kentucky, partly by flatboat on the Ohio River.

OGDEN, MATTHIAS, b. 1754   951

"Journal of Major Matthias Ogden." NEW JERSEY HISTORICAL SOCIETY PROCEEDINGS, n.s. 13 (1928):17–30.

> Oct–Nov 1775. Officer's journal of Arnold's campaign against Quebec; failure to take Heights of Abraham; hardships of campaign; good style.

OSWALD, ELEAZER, 1755–1795   952

In AMERICAN ARCHIVES, by Peter Force, 4th ser. vol. 3, pp. 1058–1062. Captain's journal of Washington: 1837–1853.

Sep–Oct 1775. Arnold's expedition; similar to Arnold's own, and called "the missing pages of Arnold's journal."

OXNARD, EDWARD, 1747–1803   953

"Edward Oxnard." NEW ENGLAND HISTORICAL AND GENEALOGICAL REGISTER 26 (1872):3–10, 115–121, 254–259.

> 1775–1785. Extracts from Loyalist diary; a very good account of social and public life in England as an exile; meetings with public and literary figures, notes on London sights, theaters, etc.; allusions to public affairs in New England.

PIERCE, JOHN, 1745?–1808   954

In MARCH TO QUEBEC, edited by Kenneth L. Roberts, pp. 651–711.

> Sep 1775–Jan 1776. Journal of surveyor who preceded Arnold's troops on the Quebec campaign; weather, camps, food, dissatisfaction of troops, illness and dwindling supplies; French farms and equipment; names of companies determined not to attack Quebec.

PORTERFIELD, CHARLES, 1750–1780   955

"Journal of Charles Porterfield." SOUTHERN HISTORICAL ASSOCIATION PUBLICATIONS 6 (1902):113–131, 199–209, 295–303, 400–407.

Extracts in "Memorable Attack on Quebec, December 21, 1775." MAGAZINE OF AMERICAN HISTORY 21 (1889): 318–319.

Extracts in "Diary of a Prisoner of War at Quebec, 1776." VIRGINIA MAGAZINE OF HISTORY AND BIOGRAPHY 9 (1901–1902):144–152.

> Dec 1775–Jul 1776. Prison diary of soldier captured during Arnold's attack on Quebec; imprisonment there; full entries on the daily life of the prisoners; news, food, etc.

PREBLE, JEDIDIAH, 1707–1784   956

In GENEALOGICAL SKETCH OF THE FIRST THREE GENERATIONS OF PREBLES IN AMERICA, by George H. Preble, pp. 61–91. Boston: Printed for family circulation, D. Clapp & Son, 1868.

> 1775–1782. Notes of campaigns; Roxbury, Boston, etc.; a few social entries.

PRICE, EZEKIEL, 1728–1802   957

"Diary of Ezekiel Price." MASSACHUSETTS HISTORICAL SOCIETY PROCEEDINGS, 1st ser. 7 (1863–1864):185–262.

> 1775–1776. Long and detailed notes on siege of Boston and author's personal affairs; quite interesting.

Pattee, William S., ed. "Items from an Interleaved Boston Almanac for 1778." NEW ENGLAND HISTORICAL AND GENEALOGICAL REGISTER 19 (1865):329–338.

> Dec 1777–Nov 1778. War news, mainly about the French in Rhode Island.

RITZEMA, RUDOLPHUS, d. 1803   958

"Journal of Col. Rudolphus Ritzema of the New York Regiment." MAGAZINE OF AMERICAN HISTORY 1 (1877): 98–107.

> Aug 1775–Mar 1776. Montgomery's expedition against Canada; visit to Congress.

SCHAUKIRK (or SHEWKIRK), EWALD GUSTAV, 1725-1805 — 959

"Occupation of New York City by the British." PENN-SYLVANIA MAGAZINE OF HISTORY AND BIOGRAPHY 10 (1886):418-445.

1775-1783. Extracts from journal of New York Moravian congregation, kept by the bishop; British occupation of New York, war news, life and work of the congregation.

"Diary of Rev. Mr. Shewkirk, Pastor of the Moravian Church, New York." LONG ISLAND HISTORICAL SOCIETY MEMOIRS 3, pt. 2 (1878):101-127.

1775-1777. Entries reflecting impact of war on city and congregation; successful struggle to avoid housing American prisoners-of-war in church during British occupation.

SENTER, ISAAC, 1753-1799 — 960

THE JOURNAL OF ISAAC SENTER, PHYSICIAN AND SURGEON TO THE TROOPS. Philadelphia: Historical Society of Pennsylvania, 1846. 40 pp. Reprint. Tarrytown, N.Y.: Abbatt, 1915. 60 pp.; "The Journal of Isaac Senter, M.D., On a Secret Expedition Against Quebec, 1775." MAGAZINE OF HISTORY, extra no. 42, 11 (1916):85-144.

In MARCH TO QUEBEC, edited by Kenneth L. Roberts, pp. 197-241.

Sep 1775-Jun 1776. Surgeon's journal kept during Arnold's campaign against Quebec; long and well-written entries about camp life, his own work and progress of the campaign.

SHAW, THOMAS, b. 1753 — 961

In A DOWN-EAST YANKEE FROM THE DISTRICT OF MAINE, by Windsor P. Daggett, pp. 58-61. Portland, Maine: A.J. Huston, 1920.

GRANITE MONTHLY (1887). Reprint. Choate, Isaac Bassett. "Thomas Shaw of Standish, 'A Down-East Homer.'" MAGAZINE OF HISTORY, extra no. 116, 29 (1926):195-212.

1775-1837. Private and military diary; scattered notes; recollections of his youth; service at Boston, Ticonderoga, Lake George.

SIERRA, BENITO DE LA — 962

Baker, A.J., trans., and Wagner, Henry R., ed. "Fray Benito de la Sierra's Account of the Hezeta Expedition to the Northwest Coast in 1775." CALIFORNIA HISTORICAL SOCIETY QUARTERLY 9 (1930):201-242.

Mar-Nov 1775. Chaplain aboard SONORA, commanded by Juan Francisco Bodega y Quadra, on Hezeta Expedition to explore coast north from Monterey, California, to Washington; deaths of expedition members by drowning and at hands of Indians; much of the diary identical to that of Miguel de la Campa.

SQUIER, EPHRAIM, 1748-1841 — 963

"The Diary of Ephraim Squier, of Arnold's Expedition to Quebec." MAGAZINE OF HISTORY, extra no. 160, 40 (1930):203-214.

In MARCH TO QUEBEC, edited by Kenneth L. Roberts, pp. 619-628.

Sep-Nov 1775. Expedition against Quebec.

Squier, Frank. "Diary of Ephraim Squier, Sergeant in the Connecticut Line of the Continental Army."

MAGAZINE OF AMERICAN HISTORY 2 (1878):685-694.

Sep-Nov 1775, Sep-Nov 1777. Expedition against Quebec; march to Albany; Stillwater; Burgoyne's surrender.

STEVENS, JAMES, 1749-1834 — 964

"The Revolutionary Journal of James Stevens of Andover, Mass." ESSEX INSTITUTE HISTORICAL COLLECTIONS 48 (1912):41-71.

Extracts in HISTORY OF JAFFREY (MIDDLE MONADOCK) NEW HAMPSHIRE, by Albert Annett and Alice Lehtinen, vol. 1, pp. 826-840. Jaffrey, N.H.: Published by the town, 1937.

1775-1776. Military journal covering marches around Boston and Andover; notes on camp life, personal matters; some linguistic value.

STOCKING, ABNER, b. 1753 — 965

"An Interesting Journal of Abner Stocking of Chatham, Connecticut." MAGAZINE OF HISTORY, extra no. 75, 19 (1921):127-162. Reprint. Tarrytown, N.Y.: W. Abbatt, 1921. 36 pp.

In MARCH TO QUEBEC, edited by Kenneth L. Roberts, pp. 545-569.

1775-1776. Arnold's campaign; capture at Quebec; interesting, but written up after the events.

SULLIVAN, THOMAS — 966

Bradford, S. Sydney, ed. "The Common British Soldier--from the Journal of Thomas Sullivan, 49th Regiment of Foot." MARYLAND HISTORICAL MAGAZINE 62 (1967):219-253.

1775-1776. Extract from journal of British enlisted man; description of the battle of Bunker Hill, the city of Boston; details of feeding and paying the British soldiers; the siege of Boston and Howe's eventual evacuation of the city.

"The Battle of Princeton." PENNSYLVANIA MAGAZINE OF HISTORY AND BIOGRAPHY 32 (1908):54-57.

Jan 1777. Battle of Princeton and list of British casualties; description of college; mention of Hessian troops being advised to take no rebel prisoners.

"Before and After the Battle of Brandywine." PENNSYLVANIA MAGAZINE OF HISTORY AND BIOGRAPHY 31 (1907): 406-418.

"From Brandywine to Philadelphia." PENNSYLVANIA MAGAZINE OF HISTORY AND BIOGRAPHY 34 (1910):229-232.

Jul-Sep 1777. Extracts of incidents before and after the battle.

TENNENT, WILLIAM, 1740-1777 — 967

In DOCUMENTARY HISTORY OF THE AMERICAN REVOLUTION, by Robert W. Gibbes, vol. 1, pp. 225-239.

Aug-Sep 1775. Presbyterian minister's journey to South Carolina to persuade Tories to join the Revolution; travel, religious work, propaganda, military affairs around Charleston; varied and interesting.

THACHER, JAMES, 1754-1844 — 968

A MILITARY JOURNAL DURING THE AMERICAN REVOLUTIONARY WAR. Boston: Richardson & Lord, 1823. 603 pp. Reprint. Hartford, Conn.: Hurlbut, Williams, 1862. 538 pp. New York: New York Times, 1969.

Extracts in DIARY OF AMERICA, edited by Josef Berger, pp. 132-134.

Discussed in AMERICAN DIARY LITERATURE, by Steven E. Kagle, pp. 121-127.

1775-1783. Military journal dealing mainly with the revolutionary war; good picture of army life and hardships; detailed description of men and events.

THAYER, SIMEON, 1737-1800   969

"Journal." RHODE ISLAND HISTORICAL SOCIETY COLLECTIONS 6 (1867):1-45.

In MARCH TO QUEBEC, edited by Kenneth L. Roberts, pp. 247-294.

1775-1776. Arnold's expedition; brief prison notes.

TILGHMAN, TENCH, 1744-1786   970

In MEMOIR OF LIEUT. COL. TENCH TILGHMAN, SECRETARY AND AID TO WASHINGTON, TOGETHER WITH AN APPENDIX, CONTAINING REVOLUTIONARY JOURNALS AND LETTERS, by Samuel A. Harrison, pp. 81-101, 103-107. Albany: J. Munsell, 1876.

Aug-Sep 1775. Treaty journal kept by secretary of Indian commission sent to treat with Six Nations at German Flats, New York; largely social aspects of ceremonies.

Sep-Oct 1781. Military details of siege of Yorktown.

TOLMAN, EBENEZER, 1748-1838   971

"Expedition Against Quebec." NEW ENGLAND HISTORICAL AND GENEALOGICAL REGISTER 6 (1852):129-145. Reprint. MAGAZINE OF HISTORY, extra no. 134, 34 (1927):69-99; JOURNAL OF AN EXPEDITION AGAINST QUEBEC, IN 1775, UNDER COL. BENEDICT ARNOLD. By Joseph Ware. Boston: Thomas Prince, Printer, 1852. 24 pp. (Incorrectly ascribed to Joseph Ware.)

"Arnold's Expedition to Quebec." MASSACHUSETTS HISTORICAL SOCIETY PROCEEDINGS, 2d ser. 2 (1885-1886): 265-275. Reprint. MAGAZINE OF HISTORY, extra no. 134, 34 (1927):101-111; ARNOLD'S EXPEDITION AGAINST QUEBEC, 1775-1776. THE DIARY OF EBENEZER WILD, WITH A LIST OF SUCH DIARIES. By Justin Winsor. Cambridge, Mass.: J. Wilson and Son, 1886. 12 pp. (Incorrectly ascribed to Ebenezer Wild.)

Authorship discussed in ARNOLD'S MARCH FROM CAMBRIDGE TO QUEBEC: A CRITICAL STUDY, by Justin H. Smith, pp. 44-51. New York and London: G.P. Putnam's sons, 1903.

1775-1776. Military journal of Arnold's march from Cambridge, Massachusetts, to Quebec. Authorship uncertain, variously attributed to Tolman, Ware and Wild.

TOPHAM, JOHN, 1743-1792   972

SONS OF THE AMERICAN REVOLUTION, RHODE ISLAND SOCIETY PUBLICATIONS, 1902.

"The Journal of Captain John Topham." MAGAZINE OF HISTORY, extra no. 50, 13 (1916):87-132.

Sep 1775-May 1776. Arnold's expedition against Quebec; sufferings and imprisonment; some interesting spellings.

TREVETT, JOHN, 1747-1823   973

"Journal of John Trevett, U.S.N." RHODE ISLAND HISTORICAL MAGAZINE 6 (1885-1886):72-74, 106-110, 194-199, 271-278; 7 (1886-1887):38-45, 151-160, 205-208.

1775-1778. Naval officer's sea journals on board sloops CATEA and PROVIDENCE and brig ANDREW DORIA during the Revolution; engagements off New England; cruise to New Providence and Fort Nassau; some personal notes; full and well-written.

TULLY, SAMUEL, 1750-1827   974

In HISTORY OF MIDDLESEX COUNTY, CONNECTICUT, pp. 458, 467-468. New York: J.B. Beers, 1884.

1775-1815. Scattered notes of war news, local events at Saybrook, weather, and some personal affairs.

VON WALDEN, FREDERICK HERMAN   975

Johnson, E. Gustav, ed. "Two Swedes under the Union Jack." SWEDISH PIONEER HISTORICAL QUARTERLY 7 (1956):83-120.

1775-1776. Military journal kept by Frederick Herman von Walden and Hans Frederick Wachtmeister, two Swedish naval officers serving as midshipmen aboard the PHOENIX; support of British military operations, primarily in the struggle to capture New York; straightforward record of activities followed by informative commentary supplied by the journalists, reflecting on what events taught them.

WARREN, JOHN, 1753-1815   976

In GENEALOGY OF WARREN, by John C. Warren, pp. 85-98. Boston: Printed by J. Wilson and Sons, 1854.

1775-1776. Surgeon's journal of Lexington, Bunker Hill, etc.; military and camp details, war news.

WELLS, BAYZE, 1744-1814   977

"Journal of Bayze Wells of Farmington, May, 1775-February, 1777, at the Northward and in Canada." CONNECTICUT HISTORICAL SOCIETY COLLECTIONS 7 (1899):239-296.

1775-1777. March to Ticonderoga and Canada; naval operations on Lake Champlain; brief entries, with good narrative; interesting spellings.

WILLIAMS, ENNION   978

"Journal of Major Ennion Williams." PENNSYLVANIA ARCHIVES, 2d ser., vol. 15, pp. 7-20.

Oct 1775. Officer's journal of journey to camp at Cambridge, via Connecticut; some social notes and skirmishes.

"Ensign Williams' Visit to Essex County." ESSEX INSTITUTE HISTORICAL COLLECTIONS 83 (1947):143-145.

Oct 1775. Brief account by soldier from Philadelphia of a visit to Essex County; descriptions of Salem and Marblehead and effects of the war there.

WOOD, JAMES   979

In THE REVOLUTION ON THE UPPER OHIO, 1775-1777, edited by Reuben G. Thwaites and Louise P. Kellogg, pp. 34-66. Madison: Wisconsin Society of the Sons of the American Revolution, 1908. Reprint. Port Washington, N.Y.: Kennikat Press, 1970.

In THE GEORGE ROGERS CLARK ADVENTURE IN THE ILLINOIS AND SELECTED DOCUMENTS OF THE AMERICAN REVOLUTION AT THE FRONTIER POSTS, by Kathrine W. Seineke, pp. 159-161. New Orleans: Polyanthos, 1981.

Jun-Sep 1775. Indian commissioner's diary of a treaty expedition dispatched by George Washington and others to the Delaware, Mingo and other Indians of the upper Ohio River region; conversations with various chiefs, speeches of the diarist; travels from tribe to tribe, often in considerable danger.

WRIGHT, AARON   980

"Revolutionary Journal of Aaron Wright." HISTORICAL MAGAZINE 6 (1862):208-212.

BOSTON TRANSCRIPT, 11 April 1862.

 1775-1776. Private's journal of siege of Boston, Cambridge; notes on camp life.

1776

ANON.   981

"Camp Life in 1776--Siege of Boston." HISTORICAL MAGAZINE 8 (1864):326-332.

 Jan-Apr 1776. Extracts from journal of lieutenant in Connecticut regiment; evacuation of Boston by British; camp life, minute details.

ANON.   982

"A Diary of the Weather, Kept at Quebec in the Year of the Siege by the Americans in 1776." LITERARY AND HISTORICAL SOCIETY OF QUEBEC TRANSACTIONS 22 (1898):45-49.

 Apr-May 1776. Weather diary kept at Quebec during the siege; some general notes of the siege.

ANON.   983

"Diary of a Voyage from Stade in Hanover to Quebec in America of the Second Division of Ducal Brunswick Mercenaries." NEW YORK STATE HISTORICAL ASSOCIA- TION QUARTERLY JOURNAL 8 (1927):323-351.

 May-Sep 1776. Voyage from Hanover to Quebec of officer in Specht's regiment; except for a few days at Portsmouth, kept entirely at sea; long entries and good narrative. Translated from the German.

ANON.   984

"Journal of a Revolutionary Soldier in 1776." HISTOR- ICAL MAGAZINE 7 (1863):367-369.

 Jul-Dec 1776. Private's journal of operations a- round New York; brief and scattered notes; inter- esting spellings and vocabulary.

ANON.   985

"Journal of a Pennsylvania Soldier." NEW YORK PUBLIC LIBRARY BULLETIN 8 (1904):547-549.

 Jul-Dec 1776. Campaign around New York and retreat through New Jersey; lively account of engagements; interesting spellings.

ALLEN, DANIEL, 1744-1777   986

In A HISTORY OF CORNWALL, CONNECTICUT, by Edward C. Starr, pp. 252-254. New Haven, Conn.: Tuttle, Morehouse & Taylor, 1926.

 Aug? 1776-Jan 1777. Military and prison diary; brief notes of marches; tailoring for soldiers; interesting spellings.

ANGELIS, PASCAL CHARLES JOSEPH DE, 1763-1839   987

Snyder, Charles M. "With Benedict Arnold at Valcour Island." VERMONT HISTORY 42 (1974):195-200.

 Aug-Oct 1776. Account of battle of Valcour Island in Lake Champlain by a thirteen-year-old seaman on one of Arnold's row-galleys.

ATLEE, SAMUEL JOHN   988

In PENNSYLVANIA ARCHIVES, 2d ser., vol. 1, pp. 509-516.

 Aug 1776. Military journal extract; battle of Long Island.

BAMFORD, WILLIAM, b. 1727 or 1728   989

"Bamford's Diary." MARYLAND HISTORICAL MAGAZINE 27 (1932):240-259, 296-314; 28 (1933):9-26.

 Jan-Dec 1776. British captain's diary kept at Boston and during New York campaign; brief notes, largely of military movements.

BANGS, ISAAC, 1752-1780   990

JOURNAL OF LIEUTENANT ISAAC BANGS. Edited by Edward Bangs. Cambridge, Mass.: J. Wilson and Son, 1890. 70 pp.

"Extract from the Journal of Isaac Bangs." NEW JERSEY HISTORICAL SOCIETY PROCEEDINGS 8 (1856-1859):120- 125.

"New York in 1776." HISTORICAL MAGAZINE, 2d ser. 4 (1868):305-306.

 Apr-Jul 1776. Army surgeon's journal; siege of Boston and New York campaign; notes of army movements; description of towns and estates, Dutch and Jewish customs; visits to Schuyler family; notes of his own affairs.

BARBER, DANIEL, 1756-1834   991

THE HISTORY OF MY OWN TIMES. Washington City: Printed for the author, by S.C. Ustick, 1827-1832. 3 vols.

 1776. Clergyman's journal of the siege of Boston and description of officers in Humphrey's company of Connecticut regiment.

BAURMEISTER, CARL LEOPOLD, 1734-1803   992

REVOLUTION IN AMERICA: CONFIDENTIAL LETTERS AND JOURNALS 1776-1784 OF ADJUTANT GENERAL MAJOR BAURMEISTER OF THE HESSIAN FORCES. Translated and edited by Bernard A. Ulendorf. New Brunswick, N.J.: Rutgers University Press, 1957. 640 pp. Reprint. Westport, Conn.: Greenwood, 1973.

 1776-1784. Diary-letters from a general staff officer of the Hessian mercenary forces to his commanding officer; criticism of British actions; description of American social and economic conditions; Washing- ton, his officers, Congress and their relations; attempts to recognize truth and hearsay and to intercede for his fellow officers.

BAYLEY, FRYE, 1749-1787   993

In HISTORY OF NEWBURY, VERMONT, by Frederic P. Wells, pp. 382-384.

 1776-1783. Brief notes during campaign against Quebec and a few later entries.

BEATTY, WILLIAM 1758–1781 994

"The Journal of Captain William Beatty." HISTORICAL MAGAZINE, 2d ser. 1 (1867):79–85.

"Journal of Capt. William Beatty." MARYLAND HISTORICAL MAGAZINE 3 (1908):104–119.

> 1776–1781. Military journal covering activities in New York, Valley Forge, southern campaign.

BEEBE, LEWIS, 1749–1816 995

Kirkland, Frederic R., ed. "Journal of a Physician on the Expedition against Canada." PENNSYLVANIA MAGAZINE OF HISTORY AND BIOGRAPHY 59 (1935):321–361. Reprint. New York: New York Times, 1971.

Discussed in AMERICAN DIARY LITERATURE, by Steven E. Kagle, pp. 101–108.

> Apr 1776–Jan 1777. Surgeon's military journal; lively account of Arnold's campaign; vigorous notes on failings of officers, hatred for Arnold; good description of smallpox epidemics and bad conditions.

BERRY, JOSHUA, 1755–1826 996

MAGAZINE OF NEW ENGLAND HISTORY 2 (1892):192–193.

> Nov 1776. Extract from military journal; journey from Portsmouth to Albany with munitions; brief notes.

BIGELOW, JOHN 997

AMERICAN HISTORICAL RECORD 1 (1872):438–440.

> Jul–Aug 1776. Abstract of military journal; Ticonderoga to St. Johns with message from Continental Congress to Burgoyne; report.

BLAKE, HENRY, 1755–1833 998

WORCESTER SPY, 25 October 1903.

> Mar–Oct 1776. March through Connecticut and New York; Ticonderoga, Crown Point, Chamblée, Sorel; return to Castleton, Vermont.

BOARDMAN, FRANCIS 999

"Journal of Francis Boardman, Sloop ADVENTURE." In NAVAL DOCUMENTS OF THE AMERICAN REVOLUTION, by United States Naval History Division, edited by William J. Morgan, vol. 4, pp. 1485–1488.

> Jan–Jun 1776. Account by master of ship ADVENTURE captured by British ship FALCON; rough treatment of prisoners, escape by swimming to shore at Charleston.

BROWN, OBADIAH 1000

WESTCHESTER COUNTY HISTORICAL SOCIETY QUARTERLY BULLETIN 4 (1928):67–72; 5 (1929):10–20.

> 1776–1777. Military journal of action around Boston and New York; battle of Bunker Hill; movements, fatigue and guard duties; weather; linguistic interest.

CARROLL, CHARLES, 1737–1832 1001

JOURNAL OF CHARLES CARROLL OF CARROLLTON, DURING HIS VISIT TO CANADA IN 1776. Maryland Historical Society Publications, vol. 1, no. 4. Baltimore: Printed by J. Murphy, 1845, 1876. 84 pp. Reprint. New York: New York Times, 1969. 110 pp.

In THE LIFE OF CHARLES CARROLL OF CARROLLTON, by Kate M. Rowland, vol. 1, app., pp. 363–400. New York and London: G.P. Putnam's Sons, 1898.

In LIFE OF CHARLES CARROLL OF CARROLLTON, by Lewis A. Leonard, pp. 277–313. New York: Moffat, Yard, 1918.

> Apr–Jun 1776. Official travel journal; visit to Canada as commissioner from Congress; New York to Montreal; notes on scenery of Hudson, etc.

CHANDLER, ABIEL, 1760–1833 1002

"Revolutionary Journal kept by Abiel Chandler of Andover." ESSEX INSTITUTE HISTORICAL COLLECTIONS 47 (1911):181–186.

> Dec 1776–Apr 1777. Service as fifer in New York State; interesting linguistically.

CLAP, CALEB, 1752–1812 1003

"Diary of Ensign Caleb Clap, of Colonel Baldwin's Regiment, Massachusetts Line." HISTORICAL MAGAZINE, 3d ser. 3 (1874–1875):133–137, 247–251.

> Mar–Oct 1776. Service with Baldwin's regiment; siege of Boston; New York campaign.

CLARK, GEORGE ROGERS, 1752–1818 1004

In GEORGE ROGERS CLARK PAPERS, 1771–1781. Edited by James Alton James, pp. 20–28, 164–168. Illinois State Historical Library Collections, vol. 8. Springfield: Trustees of the Illinois State Historical Library, 1912.

"Intercepted Letters and Journal of George Rogers Clark, 1778, 1779." AMERICAN HISTORICAL REVIEW 1 (1895):90–94.

> 1776–1778, Feb 1779. Brief scattered notes of Indian skirmishes, general news; march to Kaskaskia; activities in the Illinois country.

"Clark's Account of the Capture in Vincennes and the Articles of Capitulation of Ft. Sackville." In THE GEORGE ROGERS CLARK ADVENTURE IN THE ILLINOIS AND SELECTED DOCUMENTS OF THE AMERICAN REVOLUTION AT THE FRONTIER POSTS, by Kathrine W. Seineke, pp. 350–353. New Orleans: Polyanthos, 1981.

> Feb 1779. Extract of Clark's Vincennes journal describing his defeat of Henry Hamilton.

"The Conquest of the Illinois Country." In AMERICAN HISTORY TOLD BY CONTEMPORARIES, by Albert B. Hart, pp. 579–583.

> 1779.

CLITHERALL, JAMES 1005

"Extracts from the Diary of Dr. James Clitherall." PENNSYLVANIA MAGAZINE OF HISTORY AND BIOGRAPHY 22 (1898):468–474.

> May–Jul 1776. Travel diary; journey from South Carolina to Philadelphia and New York.

COLLIER, Sir GEORGE, 1738–1795 1006

Tucker, Louis L., ed. "'To My Inexpressible Astonishment'; Admiral Sir George Collier's Observations on the Battle of Long Island." NEW YORK HISTORICAL SOCIETY QUARTERLY 48 (1964):293–305. Reprint. In NARRATIVES OF THE REVOLUTION IN NEW YORK, pp. 80–90. New York: New York Historical Society, 1975.

> Aug–Sep 1776. British admiral's letter-diary of battle of Long Island; diarist's dismay and astonishment at Sir William Howe's failure to pursue

his advantage against outnumbered Americans; numbers of British troops, lists of casualties and activities of supporting naval units.

COOKE, SILAS, d. 1792   1007

Brayton, Susan S. "Silas Cooke--a Victim of the Revolution." RHODE ISLAND HISTORICAL SOCIETY COLLECTIONS 31 (1938):108-121.

> 1776-1779. Merchant's memoranda relating to his sufferings during British occupation of Newport; interesting spellings.

CORBETT, ICHABOD, 1756-1829   1008

"Diary of a Revolutionary Soldier." WORCESTER SOCIETY OF ANTIQUITY PROCEEDINGS 19 (1903):170-183.

> Dec 1776-Mar 1777. March to Providence; very brief notes of army work; some private items.

> Jan-Apr 1778. March with Craggin's company and return; list of payments; doggerel poem on revolutionary generals.

CUTLER, SAMUEL, 1752-1832   1009

"Prison Ships and the 'Old Mill Prison,' Plymouth, England." NEW ENGLAND HISTORICAL AND GENEALOGICAL REGISTER 32 (1878):42-44, 184-188, 305-308, 395-398.

> 1776-1777. Prison diary of American in Old Mill Prison at Plymouth, England.

DANFORTH, JOSHUA, 1759-1837   1010

"Extracts from a Diary Kept by Joshua Danforth, an Officer in the Revolutionary Army." AMERICAN MONTHLY MAGAZINE 1 (1892):619-620.

> Mar-Oct 1776. Brief extracts relating to war events.

DAVIS, MOSES, 1743-1824   1011

"Extracts from the Diary of Moses Davis, J.P., of Edgecomb, Me." NEW ENGLAND HISTORICAL AND GENEALOGICAL REGISTER 83 (1929):414-421.

> 1776-1823. Judge's private diary; marriages, deaths, funerals, etc.; genealogical interest.

DE KRAFFT, JOHN CHARLES PHILIP, 1752-1804   1012

JOURNAL OF LT. JOHN CHARLES PHILIP VON KRAFFT. Edited by Thomas H. Edsall. New York Historical Society Collections for the Year 1832, Publication Fund Series, vol. 15. New York: New York Historical Society, 1883. 200 pp.

> 1776-1784. Hessian military journal; detailed and extensive account of service during the whole war, first as corporal with Von Donop's regiment and, from December 1783, in Von Bose's regiment; personal affairs during the war. Translated from the German.

DEWEY, JOHN, 1754-1821   1013

In LIFE OF GEORGE DEWEY, by Adelbert M. Dewey, pp. 278-281. Westfield, Mass.: Dewey Publishing Co., 1898.

> Apr 1776-Feb 1777. Private's journal of service with Third Massachusetts Regiment; march from Roxbury and campaign in New York; battle of Trenton; brief notes of marches, etc.

DEWEY, RUSSELL, 1755-1827   1014

In LIFE OF GEORGE DEWEY, by Adelbert M. Dewey, pp. 266-271. Westfield, Mass.: Dewey Publishing Co., 1898.

In WESTFIELD AND ITS HISTORIC INFLUENCES, by John H. Lockwood, pp. 590-596.

> Jan-Apr 1776. March with Porter's regiment on expedition against Canada; Ticonderoga, Crown Point; military details, camp life, sickness, news; interesting spellings.

DIGBY, WILLIAM, fl. 1776   1015

THE BRITISH INVASION FROM THE NORTH. Illustrated with historical notes by James Phinney Baxter. Albany: J. Munsell's Sons, 1887. 412 pp. Reprint. New York: Da Capo, 1970.

> 1776-1777. British officer's account of voyage to Canada and narrative of campaigns of 1776 and 1777 with Carleton and Burgoyne; battle of Hilberton.

DODGE, NATHANIEL BROWN   1016

Dodge, O.J., ed. "A Letter and Diary of 1776." VERMONT QUARTERLY 21 (1953):29-35.

> Mar? 1776. Very short daily entries charting soldier's movements in Lake Champlain area; Fort Ticonderoga, St. Johns, Crown Point, Fort George; military activities, illness, deaths.

DUNCAN, HENRY, 1735-1814   1017

"Journals of Henry Duncan, Captain, Royal Navy." In THE NAVAL MISCELLANY, edited by John K. Laughton, pp. 105-219. Navy Records Society Publications, vol. 20. London, 1902.

> 1776-1782. British naval journals; early portions concerning operations around New York.

DU ROI, AUGUSTUS WILHELM   1018

JOURNAL OF DU ROI THE ELDER, LIEUTENANT AND ADJUTANT, IN THE SERVICE OF THE DUKE OF BRUNSWICK, 1776-1778. Translated by Charlotte S.J. Epping. Philadelphia: University of Pennsylvania; New York: D. Appleton, 1911. 189 pp.

Epping, Charlotte S.J., trans. "Journal of Du Roi the Elder." GERMAN-AMERICAN ANNALS 13 (1911):40-64, 77-128, 131-239.

> 1776-1779. Hessian military journal; service with British forces in North America; notes on topography, military affairs, social life and customs in Virginia.

EDUARDO, MIGUEL ANTONIO   1019

"Diary of Miguel Antonio Eduardo," translated by F. Taylor Peck. In NAVAL DOCUMENTS OF THE AMERICAN REVOLUTION, by United States Naval History Division, ed. by William J. Morgan, vol 5, pp. 1339-1351.

> May-Oct 1776. Diary kept aboard Spanish packet boat SANTA BARBARA of the Royal Agency for Negroes in America bound for Island of Dominica from Havana; redirected to Philadelphia to get news of war between the English and Americans; detained and searched by British ship LIVERPOOL under Captain Henry Bellow; report on success of Americans and poor show by British.

ELMER, EBENEZER, 1752-1843   1020

"Journal Kept during an Expedition to Canada in 1776." NEW JERSEY HISTORICAL SOCIETY PROCEEDINGS 2 (1846-1847):95-146.

"Journal of Lieutenant Ebenezer Elmer." NEW JERSEY HISTORICAL SOCIETY PROCEEDINGS 3 (1848-1849):21-56, 90-102.

"The Lost Pages of Elmer's Revolutionary Journal." NEW JERSEY HISTORICAL SOCIETY PROCEEDINGS, n.s. 10 (1925):410-424.

> 1776-1783. Narrative of expedition against Canada.

"Extracts from the Journal of Surgeon Ebenezer Elmer of the New Jersey Continental Line." PENNSYLVANIA MAGAZINE OF HISTORY AND BIOGRAPHY 35 (1911):103-107.

> Sep 1777. Surgeon's account of the battle of Brandywine.

"Extracts from a Journal Kept by Doctor Ebenezer Elmer during General Sullivan's Expedition." NEW JERSEY HISTORICAL SOCIETY PROCEEDINGS 2 (1846-1847):43-50.

In JOURNALS OF THE MILITARY EXPEDITION OF MAJOR GENERAL JOHN SULLIVAN, by New York State Secretary of State, Frederick Cook, pp. 80-85.

> Jun-Aug 1779. Lengthy and detailed notes on Sullivan's expedition.

ENYS, JOHN, 1757-1818   1021

THE AMERICAN JOURNALS OF LT. JOHN ENYS. Edited by Elizabeth Cometti. Syracuse: The Adirondack Museum, Syracuse University Press, 1976. 377 pp.

> 1776-1788. English officer's journals of military duty and private travel in Canada and United States; action on New York and Vermont fronts during the Revolution, garrison duty in Canada after the war; visit to Niagara Falls; a tour from Montreal through New England to Virginia, incuding a visit with Washington at Mount Vernon.

In CANADA ARCHIVES REPORT, pp. ccxxvi-ccxxxiii. Ottawa, 1887.

In ANTHOLOGY AND BIBLIOGRAPHY OF NIAGARA FALLS, by Charles M. Dow, vol. 1, pp. 74-89.

> Jul 1787. Visit to Niagara Falls; long description.

EWALD, JOHANN VON, 1744-1813   1022

DIARY OF THE AMERICAN WAR: A HESSIAN JOURNAL. Translated and edited by Joseph P. Tustin. New Haven, Conn.: Yale University Press, 1979. 467 pp.

> 1776-1784. Hessian military journal covering campaigns of the Revolution; details of American and British armies, Hesse-Cassel forces, and the Jäger Corps; maps sketched in the field.

In THE SIEGE OF CHARLESTON, translated and edited by Bernhard A. Uhlendorf, pp. 30-101. Ann Arbor: University of Michigan Press, 1938. Reprint. New York: New York Times, 1968.

> Mar-Jun 1780. Expedition to Charleston and siege. German text with English translation.

"A Hessian Visits the Victor." AMERICAN HERITAGE 30 (1979):97-103.

> Oct 1783. Extracts covering trip from New York City to West Point after the war; comments on accommodations, attitudes of citizenry and soldiers, fortifications at West Point, etc.

FISHER, SARAH LOGAN, 1751?-1796   1023

Wainwright, Nicholas B., ed. "'A Diary of Trifling Occurrences': Philadelphia, 1776-1778." PENNSYLVANIA MAGAZINE OF HISTORY AND BIOGRAPHY 82 (1958):411-465.

> 1776-1778. Personal diary of member of Quaker elite kept prior to and during British occupation of Philadelphia; description of events of war from a Loyalist point of view which seemed to override official Quaker neutrality; details of everyday life among upper class Philadelphia Quakers; many names.

FLANDERS, JOHN, 1752-1827   1024

In HISTORY OF BOSCAWEN AND WEBSTER, N.H., compiled by Charles C. Coffin, pp. 250-251.

> Jan-Apr 1776. Prison diary; imprisonment in Quebec; notes mainly on weather; some interesting spellings.

FRENCH, CHRISTOPHER   1025

"Major French's Journal." CONNECTICUT HISTORICAL SOCIETY COLLECTIONS 1 (1860):189-225.

> Jan-Sep 1776. Prison diary of British major of Twenty-second Regiment kept while author was prisoner in Hartford Jail; a lively and amusing record, with long entries.

GANNETT, CALEB, 1745-1818   1026

Armstrong, Maurice W., ed. "The Diary of Caleb Gannett for the Year 1776." WILLIAM AND MARY QUARTERLY, 3d ser. 3 (1946):117-122.

> 1776. Extracts from diary of mathematics and philosophy tutor at Harvard; college affairs; military and political events; Boston's celebration of Declaration of Independence.

GAY, FISHER, 1733-1776   1027

"Diary of Lt. Colonel Fisher Gay." MAGAZINE OF AMERICAN HISTORY 8 (1882):127-129.

> Feb-Mar 1776. Brief extracts from military journal; march to Boston.

GERRISH, JACOB, 1739?-1817   1028

Toppan, Robert N. "Col. Jacob Gerrish of Newbury." PUTNAM'S MONTHLY HISTORICAL MAGAZINE 3 (1895): 220-223.

> Aug-Nov 1776. Military journal dealing with Flatbush and White Plains, New York; brief notes.

GOODWIN, JOHN, 1745?-1828   1029

"Military Journal Kept in 1777, during the Rhode Island Expedition, by John Goodwin of Marblehead, Mass." ESSEX INSTITUTE HISTORICAL COLLECTIONS 45 (1909):205-211.

> Dec 1776-Mar 1777. Expedition in Rhode Island; visits to taverns; brief notes of military details; interesting spellings.

GRAVES, DANIEL, 1757-1828   1030

WESTCHESTER COUNTY HISTORICAL SOCIETY BULLETIN 10 (1934):45-48.

> Dec 1776-Mar 1777. Military journal of service with Foster's company; campaign around New York;

Tarrytown, White Plains, Chatham; brief entries; interesting spellings.

GUILD, JOSEPH, 1735-1794   1031

Fisher, Mrs. George P., ed. "Captain Joseph Guild." DEDHAM HISTORICAL REGISTER 7 (1896):43-47.

   1776-1777. Extracts covering march from Cambridge to Ticonderoga; movements; smallpox epidemic.

HADDEN, JAMES MURRAY, d. 1817   1032

HADDEN'S JOURNAL AND ORDERLY BOOKS. Edited by Horatio Rogers. Albany: J. Munsell's Sons, 1884. 581 pp. Journal, pp. 1-166.

   1776-1777. Military journal kept during Burgoyne's campaign; lengthy and interesting notes.

HAGEN, EDMUND, 1732-1777   1033

"Diary of Dr. Edmund Hagen." AMERICAN MONTHLY MAGAZINE 24 (1904):14-16, 110-111.

   Oct-Dec 1776. Extracts from prison diary; voyage on privateer, capture, and subsequent imprisonment on prison ship BOULOGNE.

HASBROUCK, ABRAHAM   1034

"The Hasbrouck Diary." OLDE ULSTER 4 (1908):147-149.

   1776-1777. Diary extracts covering fire at his house; burning of farm buildings by British.

HASKINS, JONATHAN, 1755-1802   1035

Coan, Marion S., ed. "A Revolutionary Prison Diary: The Journal of Dr. Jonathan Haskins." NEW ENGLAND QUARTERLY 17 (1944):290-309, 424-442.

   1776-1779. Physician's diary of his imprisonment at Old Mill Prison in Plymouth, England; almost daily record of life, conditions, events, rations, sickness, deaths, escapes, punishments, help received from British individuals and charitable organizations, etc.

HETH, WILLIAM, 1750-1807   1036

Flickinger, B. Floyd, ed. "The Diary of Lieutenant William Heth while a Prisoner in Quebec." WINCHESTER, VIRGINIA, HISTORICAL SOCIETY ANNUAL PAPERS 1 (1931):27-118.

   Jan-Aug 1776. March from Winchester, Virginia, to Quebec; capture and imprisonment; military details and personal items; full and lively entries, mostly written in prison; interesting spellings.

HILDRETH, MICAH, 1749-1826   1037

In HISTORY OF DRACUT, MASSACHUSETTS, by Silas R. Coburn, pp. 147-152. Lowell, Mass.: Press of the Courier-Citizen, 1922.

   Aug-Oct 1776. March to Ticonderoga; details of smallpox epidemic; food; military notes.

HOZEY, PELEG   1038

"Privateer Sloop INDEPENDENT: A Journal Kept by Peleg Hozey, Master." RHODE ISLAND HISTORICAL SOCIETY COLLECTIONS 31 (1938):82-89, 122-123.

   Jul-Aug 1776. Log details of cruise off Rhode Island; interesting spellings and language.

IRVINE, WILLIAM, 1741-1804   1039

"General Irvine's Journal of the Canadian Campaign." HISTORICAL MAGAZINE 6 (1862):115-117.

   May-Jun 1776. Brief notes of expedition to Canada and capture.

JAMES, BARTHOLOMEW, 1752-1828   1040

JOURNAL OF REAR-ADMIRAL BARTHOLOMEW JAMES. Edited by John Knox Laughton. Navy Records Society Publications, 4. London: Navy Records Society, 1896. 402 pp.

   1776-1798. British military journal, with earlier autobiographical notes; written up from memoranda; in Boston and Rhode Island; surrender at Yorktown; Portland Harbor, and on the Kennebec in 1791; activities of British army.

Fleming, Thomas J. "'We Was Amazingly Fortunate' --or--Through the American Revolution with Pluck and Cheek." AMERICAN HERITAGE 16 (1965):32-35, 106-111.

   1776-1781. Extracts of lively adventures of British midshipman during the Revolution.

JAMISON, JOHN   1041

"Revolutionary Records." AMERICAN MONTHLY MAGAZINE 23 (1903):12-13.

   1776-1779. Brief military notes.

JOSIAH, JAMES   1042

"A Journal of a Cruise in the Brig ANDREW DORIA, Nicholas Biddle Commander, from the Port of Philadelphia, Begun January 4th 1776." In NAVAL DOCUMENTS OF THE AMERICAN REVOLUTION, by United States Naval History Division, edited by William J. Morgan, vol 4, pp. 1489-1503.

   Jan-Jun 1776. Facsimile of manuscript journal; naval operations and capture by British ship CRAWFORD.

KIMBALL, PETER, 1739-1811   1043

Coffin, Charles C., ed. "Diary of Capt. Peter Kimball." GRANITE MONTHLY 4 (1881):230-233.

   Sep-Dec 1776. Marches from New Hampshire to New York; notes on camp life; interesting spellings.

In HISTORY OF BOSCAWEN AND WEBSTER, N.H., compiled by Charles C. Coffin, pp. 261-264.

   Jul-Sep 1777. Brief notes of military movements.

LAMB, ROGER, 1756-1830   1044

AN ORIGINAL AND AUTHENTIC JOURNAL OF OCCURRENCES DURING THE LATE AMERICAN WAR. Dublin: Wilkinson & Courtney, 1809. 438 pp.

   1776-1784. British military journal; voyage from Cork to Quebec; Burgoyne's campaign and surrender; surrender of Cornwallis; battle of Hubbardton; descriptions of New England towns; imprisonment at Rutland; interesting details of life of British soldiers.

LENOIR, WILLIAM, 1751-1839   1045

Hamilton, J.G. de Roulhac, ed. "Revolutionary Diary of William Lenoir." JOURNAL OF SOUTHERN HISTORY 6 (1940):247-257. Diary, pp. 253-257.

   Aug-Oct 1776. Rutherford's campaign against Cherokee Indian towns; bare details; interesting spellings.

LINCOLN, RUFUS, 1751-1838   1046

THE PAPERS OF CAPTAIN RUFUS LINCOLN, OF WAREHAM, MASS. Compiled by James M. Lincoln. Cambridge, Mass.: Riverside Press, 1904. 272 pp. Journal, pp. 3-115.

> 1776-1780. Journal of prisoner on parole in Long Island; camp life in New York; siege of Charleston; battle of Long Island; Jersey campaign; Saratoga; Burgoyne's surrender; actions of Congress; interesting spellings.

LOXLEY, BENJAMIN   1047

"A Journal of the Campaign to Amboy, and Other Parts of the Jerseys." PENNSYLVANIA HISTORICAL SOCIETY COLLECTIONS 1 (1853):223-236.

> Jul-Aug 1776. Captain's journal of service in Pennsylvania and New Jersey.

MCCARTY, THOMAS   1048

Lobdell, Jared C., ed. "The Revolutionary War Journal of Sergeant Thomas McCarty." NEW JERSEY HISTORICAL SOCIETY PROCEEDINGS 82 (1964):29-46.

> Aug-Sep 1776, Nov 1776-Feb 1777. Journal reflecting army life on the march from Virginia to New Jersey; several military engagements.

MCMICHAEL, JAMES   1049

"Diary of Lieutenant James McMichael, of the Pennsylvania Line." PENNSYLVANIA MAGAZINE OF HISTORY AND BIOGRAPHY 16 (1892):129-159.

In PENNSYLVANIA ARCHIVES, 2d ser., vol. 15, pp. 195-218.

Extracts in "Where the Stars and Stripes Were First Shown in Battle," by Henry C. Conrad. MAGAZINE OF HISTORY 6 (1907):206-220. Diary, pp. 210-211, 218.

> 1776-1778. Military journal of service in Pennsylvania, Delaware, New Jersey, New York; Valley Forge; some verses.

MCPHERSON, WILLIAM   1050

"Extracts from the Journal of Lieut. William McPherson." LONG ISLAND HISTORICAL SOCIETY MEMOIRS 3 (1878):pt. 2, 168-169.

> 1776. Brief notes of campaign around New York and Brooklyn.

MARSTON, BENJAMIN, 1730-1792   1051

"Diary of Sheriff Marston." NEW BRUNSWICK HISTORICAL SOCIETY COLLECTIONS 2, no. 4 (1899):95-108.

"Benjamin Marston of Marblehead, Loyalist, His Trials and Tribulations during the American Revolution." NEW BRUNSWICK HISTORICAL SOCIETY COLLECTIONS 3, no. 7 (1907):79-112.

Raymond, W.O. "The Founding of Shelburne; Benjamin Marston at Halifax, Sherburne and Miramichi." NEW BRUNSWICK HISTORICAL SOCIETY COLLECTIONS 3, no. 8 (1909):204-277.

> 1776-1787. Loyalist diary; fragmentary notes, partly biography, partly diary selections; descriptions of New England; hardships endured by diarist in America, Nova Scotia and New Brunswick; verses; entertaining.

Vesey, Maud M. "Benjamin Marston, Loyalist." NEW ENGLAND QUARTERLY 15 (1942):622-651.

> 1776-1787. Extracts within biographical sketch.

MELSHEIMER, FREDERICK VALENTINE, 1749-1814   1052

"Journal of the Voyage of the Brunswick Auxiliaries from Wolfenbüttel to Quebec." LITERARY AND HISTORICAL SOCIETY OF QUEBEC TRANSACTIONS 20 (1891):133-178.

> Feb-Aug 1776. Hessian chaplain's journal; voyage to Quebec; descriptions of the city and environs. Translated from the German.

MERRICK, SAMUEL FISK, 1751-1835   1053

Davis, David B. "Medicine in the Canadian Campaign of the Revolutionary War: The Journal of Doctor Samuel Fisk Merrick." BULLETIN OF THE HISTORY OF MEDICINE 44 (1970):461-473.

> May-Sep 1776. Journal of surgeon's mate during Quebec campaign; retreat to Ticonderoga; life in camp; caring for soldiers ill with smallpox and diarrhea; his own illness; lack of provisions and medicine; desertions.

In AN HISTORICAL ADDRESS, DELIVERED AT THE CENTENNIAL CELEBRATION OF THE INCORPORATION OF THE TOWN OF WILBRAHAM, June 15, 1863, by Rufus P. Stebbins, pp. 238-240. Boston: G.C. Rand & Avery, 1864.

In THE HISTORY OF WILBRAHAM, MASSACHUSETTS, by Chauncey E. Peck, pp. 136-138. Wilbraham?: pref. 1914.

> Sep-Oct 1777. Brief notes of service at Saratoga and surrender of Burgoyne.

MIDDLETON, CHARLES S.   1054

In DOCUMENTARY HISTORY OF THE AMERICAN REVOLUTION, by Robert W. Gibbes, vol. 2, pp. 47-54.

> Dec 1776-Jan 1777. Military activities of southern troops in South Carolina and Georgia; substantial entries.

MINER, THOMAS   1055

In NEW HAMPSHIRE PROVINCIAL AND STATE PAPERS, vol. 17, pp. 69-71.

> Jul-Aug 1776. Scouting journal kept by Thomas Miner and Ezekiel Wheeler; expedition from the lower Cohoos to Cohoos Falls, under orders of John Hurd; brief surveying notes.

MORRIS, MARGARET, 1737-1816   1056

PRIVATE JOURNAL, KEPT DURING A PORTION OF THE REVOLUTIONARY WAR, FOR THE AMUSEMENT OF A SISTER. Philadelphia: Privately printed, 1836. Reprint. New York: Privately printed, 1865; New York: New York Times, 1969. 36 pp.

MARGARET MORRIS, HER JOURNAL. Biographical sketch and notes by John W. Jackson. Philadelphia: G.S. MacManus, 1949. 132 pp.

"The Revolutionary Journal of Margaret Morris, of Burlington, N.J." FRIENDS' HISTORICAL SOCIETY OF PHILADELPHIA BULLETIN 9 (1919):2-14, 65-75, 103-114.

In LETTERS OF DOCTOR RICHARD HILL AND HIS CHILDREN, collected and arranged by John Jay Smith. Philadelphia: Privately printed, 1854. Reprint. New York: Arno, 1969.

Extracts in WEATHERING THE STORM, by Elizabeth Evans, pp. 77-106.

Discussed in AMERICAN DIARY LITERATURE, by Steven E. Kagle, pp. 131-135.

1776–1778. Quaker diary; long serious descriptions and reflections on events of war at Burlington, New Jersey; some exciting personal adventures.

MUDGE, SIMON, 1748–1799   1057

In MEMORIALS: BEING A GENEALOGICAL, BIOGRAPHICAL AND HISTORICAL ACCOUNT OF THE NAME OF MUDGE IN AMERICA, by Alfred Mudge, pp. 204–205. Boston: Printed by A. Mudge & Son, 1868.

"Diary of Simon Mudge." DANVERS HISTORICAL SOCIETY COLLECTIONS 27 (1939):40–43.

     Jul–Nov 1776. Military diary of march to Ticonderoga and camp there; linguistic interest.

MUENCHHAUSEN, FRIEDRICH ERNST VON,   1058
1753–1795

AT GENERAL HOWE'S SIDE, 1776–1778: THE DIARY OF GENERAL WILLIAM HOWE'S AIDE DE CAMP. Translated by Ernst Kipping and annotated by Samuel Smith. Monmouth Beach, N.J.: Philip Freneau Press, 1974. 84 pp.

     1776–1778. Day by day account of activities in General Howe's headquarters; orders, movements of troops, battles.

NASH, SOLOMON, 1753–1778   1059

JOURNAL OF SOLOMON NASH, A SOLDIER OF THE REVOLUTION. With introduction and notes by Charles I. Bushnell. Crumbs for Antiquarians, vol. 1, no. 3. New York: Privately printed, 1861. 65 pp. Reprint. 1864.

     1776–1777. Brief military notes; weather, camp life, personal matters; siege of Boston; Roxbury, Cambridge, White Plains; interesting spellings.

NEW YORK CITY MORAVIAN CONGREGATION   1060

"Occupation of New York City by the British." PENNSYLVANIA MAGAZINE OF HISTORY AND BIOGRAPHY 1 (1877):133–148, 250–262.

     1776. Extracts from Moravian congregational journal; some good passages describing naval and military engagements around New York and a good account of the fire.

NICE, JOHN, 1739–1806   1061

"Extracts from the Diary of Captain John Nice, of the Pennsylvania Line." PENNSYLVANIA MAGAZINE OF HISTORY AND BIOGRAPHY 16 (1892):399–411.

     Aug–Dec 1776, Jun 1778. Service with Thirteenth Pennsylvania Regiment; battle of Long Island, Valley Forge; imprisonment.

PAINE, SAMUEL   1062

In NEW HAMPSHIRE PROVINCIAL AND STATE PAPERS, vol. 17, p. 72.

     Jul–Aug 1776. Scouting journal; expedition under John Hurd from the lower Cohoos to Cohoos Falls; brief surveying notes.

PARKER, BENJAMIN, b. 1743   1063

"Benjamin Parker's Mem'd'm Journal." OLD ELIOT 6 (1903):148–151.

     Dec 1776–Mar 1777. Brief notes of march from Kittery, Maine, to Kingsbridge, New York; interesting language.

PAUSCH, GEORG, d. 1796?   1064

JOURNAL OF CAPTAIN PAUSCH, CHIEF OF THE HANAU ARTILLERY DURING THE BURGOYNE CAMPAIGN. Translated and annotated by William L. Stone. Albany: J. Munsell's Sons, 1886. 185 pp.

Extracts in AMERICAN HISTORY TOLD BY CONTEMPORARIES, by Albert B. Hart, pp. 504–507; SOURCE BOOK OF AMERICAN HISTORY, edited by Albert B. Hart, pp. 154–157. New York: Macmillan, 1925.

     1776–1777. Hessian military journal; journey from Hanau to America; military life in Canada; Burgoyne's campaign; battle of Bennington; naval action on Lake Champlain; personal ill-treatment by British soldiers.

PEALE, CHARLES WILSON, 1741–1827   1065

Sellers, Horace W. "Charles Willson Peale, Artist-Soldier." PENNSYLVANIA MAGAZINE OF HISTORY AND BIOGRAPHY 38 (1914):257–286. Journal pp. 271–286.

     Dec 1776–Jan 1777. Service in militia at Philadelphia; New York campaign; life on the march; some personal notes.

PELL, JOSHUA   1066

"Diary of Joshua Pell, Junior, an Officer of the British Army in America." MAGAZINE OF AMERICAN HISTORY 2 (1878):43–47, 107–112.

     1776–1777. Military notes at Crown Point, Ticonderoga, Saratoga, etc.

PORTER, ELISHA, 1742–1796   1067

"Diary of Mr. Elisha Porter of Hadley." MAGAZINE OF AMERICAN HISTORY 30 (1893):187–206.

     Jan–Aug 1776. March to relief of forces besieging Quebec.

POST, LYDIA MINTURN   1068

PERSONAL RECOLLECTION OF THE AMERICAN REVOLUTION, A PRIVATE JOURNAL. Edited by Sidney Barclay (pseud.). New York: Rudd and Carleton, 1859. 203 pp. Reprint. Port Washington, N.Y.: Kennikat, 1970.

GRACE BARCLAY'S DIARY, OR, PERSONAL RECOLLECTIONS OF THE AMERICAN REVOLUTION. 2d ed. Edited by Sidney Barclay (pseud.). New York: D.F. Randolph, 1866. 251 pp.

     1776–1783. Diary kept by revolutionary officer's wife; difficulties and events on Long Island while her husband was away at war; sympathy toward Loyalist position of her father, an Anglican minister; pacifist Quaker neighbors; her care of a wounded enemy officer; vandalism by Hessian soldiers.

PYNCHON, WILLIAM, 1723–1789   1069

THE DIARY OF WILLIAM PYNCHON OF SALEM. Edited by Fitch E. Oliver. Boston and New York: Houghton, Mifflin, 1890. 349 pp.

     1776–1789 (with gap). Valuable account of social and political affairs in Salem; gossip, meals, war news, etc.

QUINCY, SAMUEL, 1735–1787   1070

"Diary of Samuel Quincy." MASSACHUSETTS HISTORICAL SOCIETY PROCEEDINGS, 1st ser. 19 (1881–1882):211–223.

     Oct 1776–Mar 1777. Fragment of a diary kept in

London; notes on social, artistic and political affairs; musical notes especially interesting.

RAINSFORD, CHARLES 1071

"Commissary Rainsford's Journal of Transactions, etc." NEW YORK HISTORICAL SOCIETY COLLECTIONS 12 (1879):317-334.

Feb-Apr 1776. British military journal; in Holland raising troops to fight in America; some social notes.

ROBBINS, AMMI RUHAMAH, 1740-1813 1072

JOURNAL OF THE REV. AMMI R. ROBBINS, A CHAPLAIN IN THE AMERICAN ARMY. New Haven, Conn.: Printed by B.L. Hamlen, 1850. 48 pp.

In HISTORY OF NORFOLK, LITCHFIELD COUNTY, CONNECTICUT, compiled by Theron W. Crissey, pp. 97-121. Everett, Mass.: Massachusetts Publishing Co., 1900.

Mar-Oct 1776. Chaplain's journal; northern campaign against Canada; Chambly, Lake George, retreat; notes on services, personal affairs, army movements, weather, hospital visits and comforting the sick; interesting reading.

ROBERTS, ALGERNON 1073

"A Journal of a Campaign from Philadelphia to Paulus Hook." PENNSYLVANIA MAGAZINE OF HISTORY AND BIOGRAPHY 7 (1883):456-463.

Aug-Sep 1776. Campaign from Philadelphia to Paulus Hook; interesting spellings.

RODNEY, THOMAS, 1744-1811 1074

DIARY OF CAPTAIN THOMAS RODNEY. With an introduction by Caesar A. Rodney. Delaware Historical Society Papers, no. 8. Wilmington: Delaware Historical Society, 1888. 53 pp. Diary, pp. 11-50. Reprint. New York: Da Capo, 1974.

Extracts in THE CAMPAIGN OF 1776 AROUND NEW YORK AND BROOKLYN. Long Island Historical Society Memoirs, vol. 3, pt. 2, pp. 158-162. Brooklyn: Long Island Historical Society, 1878.

Dec 1776-Jan 1777. Campaign around New York and Brooklyn; battles of Princeton, Morristown; substantial entries.

Merwin, M.M., ed. "Thomas Rodney's Diary of a Journey by Carriage from Delaware to New York City." DELAWARE HISTORY 17 (1977):199-213.

Jun 1790. Journey from near Dover through Wilmington, Philadelphia, across New Jersey on the Old York Road to New York City; sights, accommodations, expenses; road conditions; people whom he met, including Martha Washington; evidence of hard times in New Jersey.

Harrell, Laura D.S. "Diary of Thomas Rodney." JOURNAL OF MISSISSIPPI HISTORY 7 (1945):111-116.

Sep 1804. United States judge's journey through the Natchez country on horseback; visits with prominent persons of the Mississippi Territory; descriptions of land, accommodations, etc.

ROGERS, WILLIAM, 1751-1824 1075

"A Journal of My Visit to Rhode Island." RHODE ISLAND HISTORICAL SOCIETY COLLECTIONS 32 (1939):117-128.

Apr-Jun 1776. Clergyman's travel journal; visits from Philadelphia to Rhode Island; travel notes,

preaching, social life, weather, etc.

THE JOURNAL OF A BRIGADE CHAPLAIN IN THE CAMPAIGN OF 1779 AGAINST THE SIX NATIONS UNDER COMMAND OF MAJOR-GENERAL JOHN SULLIVAN. With introductions and notes by the publisher. Rhode Island Historical Tracts, 1st ser., no. 7. Providence: S.S. Rider, 1879. 136 pp.

Extracts in AMERICAN UNIVERSAL MAGAZINE 1 (1797): 390-399; 2 (1797):86-91, 200-206; JOURNALS OF THE EXPEDITION OF MAJOR GENERAL JOHN SULLIVAN, by New York State Secretary of State, Frederick Cook, pp. 246-265; PENNSYLVANIA ARCHIVES, 2d ser. vol. 15, pp. 255-262.

Jul-Sep 1779. Service as chaplain with Hand's brigade during Sullivan's expedition; solid entries of clerical and military affairs.

"Journal of My Visit to the Eastward." RHODE ISLAND HISTORICAL SOCIETY COLLECTIONS 33 (1940):39-44, 65-72.

Aug-Oct 1781. Preaching tour in Connecticut and Massachusetts.

SELLERS, NATHAN 1076

"Extracts from the Diary of Nathan Sellers." PENNSYLVANIA MAGAZINE OF HISTORY AND BIOGRAPHY 16 (1892):191-196.

1776-1778. Quaker's diary of war in Pennsylvania, New Jersey, Long Island, North Carolina.

SERLE, AMBROSE, 1742-1812 1077

THE AMERICAN JOURNAL OF AMBROSE SERLE. Edited by E.H. Tatum. San Marino, Calif.: Huntington Library, 1940. 369 pp.

1776-1778. Journal of Lord Howe's secretary; talks with Loyalists and comments on the war; a valuable civilian journal of the Revolution.

SEWALL, HENRY, 1752-1845 1078

A MAINE FARMER. Augusta, 1872.

Extracts in "Diary of Captain Henry Sewall." HISTORICAL MAGAZINE, 2d ser. 10 (1871):128-137.

1776-1783. Siege of Boston, Newburg, Saratoga, Valley Forge; campaigns in New England and New York; notes on camp life.

SHEPARD, SAMUEL 1079

Shepard, William, ed. "Some Buckingham County Letters." WILLIAM AND MARY COLLEGE QUARTERLY, 2d ser. 15 (1935):406-412.

1776, 1777, 1784, 1785. Extracts of Loyalist diary; return from Europe to Virginia; trouble at public meetings.

SLADE, WILLIAM, 1753-1826 1080

In AMERICAN PRISONERS OF THE REVOLUTION, by Danske B. Dandridge, pp. 494-501. Charlottesville, Va.: Michie Co., Printers, 1911.

Nov 1776-Jan 1777. Prison diary kept while author was on prison ship GROSVENOR; notes of daily life, hardships; interesting spellings.

SMITH, JOHN 1081

Rau, Louise, ed. "Sergeant John Smith's Diary of 1776." MISSISSIPPI VALLEY HISTORICAL REVIEW 20 (1932-1934):247-270.

Extracts in DIARY OF AMERICA, edited by Josef Berger, pp. 119-128.

> Sep?-Dec 1776. Diary of an ordinary soldier with Colonel Lippitt's company under Washington; New York and retreat through New Jersey; excellent picture of life of a resourceful and humorous soldier; hardships, thieving, adventures; colloquial style.

STEVENS, BENJAMIN, 1754-1838   1082

"Diary of Benjamin Stevens, of Canaan, Conn." DAUGHTERS OF THE AMERICAN REVOLUTION MAGAZINE 45 (1914):137-140.

> Feb-May 1776. Diary of private in Burrall's regiment on Arnold's expedition; march via Albany, Saratoga, etc.; imprisonment and miserable treatment; diary ends abruptly.

STIMSON, JEREMY, 1751-1821   1083

"Dr. Stimson's Diary." MASSACHUSETTS HISTORICAL SOCIETY PROCEEDINGS 46 (1912-1913):250-252.

> Sep-Oct 1776. Surgeon's military journal; White Plains, Horseneck, etc.; brief notes on sick and wounded.

STIRKE, HENRY   1084

Bradford, S. Sydney, ed. "A British Officer's Revolutionary War Journal." MARYLAND HISTORICAL MAGAZINE 56 (1961):150-175.

> 1776-1777. Journal of lieutenant in the light infantry with Howe's army; military events including British victories on Long Island and at Germantown.

STONE, ENOS, 1744-1822   1085

"Capt. Enos Stone's Journal." NEW ENGLAND HISTORICAL AND GENEALOGICAL REGISTER 15 (1861):299-304.

> 1776-1777. Expedition against Canada; Ticonderoga, Lake Champlain, battle of Hubbardton; long but scattered entries; interesting spellings.

TEN BROECK, ABRAHAM, 1734-1810   1086

Barry, J. Neilson. "A Diary of 1776." AMERICANA 18 (1924):169-173.

> 1776. Journal of New York colonial assemblyman and patriot; miscellaneous jottings; account with quotations.

TOMPSON, NATHANIEL   1087

"A Journall Kept by Nathaniel Tompson." MAINE HISTORICAL AND GENEALOGICAL RECORDER 1 (1884):41-42.

> Oct 1776. Brief account of capture of a schooner; interesting spellings.

VELEZ DE ESCALANTE, SILVESTRE, fl. 1768-1779   1088

In THE CATHOLIC CHURCH IN UTAH, by W.R. Harris, pp. 123-242. Salt Lake City: Intermountain Catholic Press, 1909.

Auerbach, Herbert S., trans. "Father Escalante's Journal." UTAH HISTORICAL QUARTERLY 11 (1943):27-113.

In PAGEANT IN THE WILDERNESS; THE STORY OF THE ESCALANTE EXPEDITION TO THE INTERIOR BASIN, translated and edited by Herbert E. Bolton, pp. 133-239. Utah Historical Quarterly, vol. 18. Salt Lake City:

Utah State Historical Society, 1950.

DOMINGUEZ-ESCALANTE JOURNAL: THEIR EXPEDITION THROUGH COLORADO, UTAH, ARIZONA AND NEW MEXICO IN 1776. Edited by T.J. Warner, translated by F.A. Chavez. Provo, Utah: Brigham Young University Press, 1976. 203 pp.

> Jul 1776-Jan 1777. Exploration journal; Spanish Franciscan missionaries' unsuccessful attempt to establish overland route from Santa Fe to Monterey; side trips to investigate new mission possibilities in Utah, Colorado, New Mexico and Arizona; severe winter and abandonment of project; important geographically and as a record of Spanish missionary endeavor among Indians of the Southwest.

VERNON, THOMAS, 1718-1784   1089

THE DIARY OF THOMAS VERNON, A LOYALIST, BANISHED FROM NEWPORT BY THE RHODE ISLAND GENERAL ASSEMBLY IN 1776. With notes by Sidney S. Rider. Rhode Island Historical Tracts, no. 13. Providence: S.S. Rider, 1881. 150 pp. Diary, pp. 1-116.

> Jun-Oct 1776. Loyalist diary; notes of country life kept while author was in exile; some political comments, but mostly notes of eating, gardening, walks, etc.

VOSE, JOSEPH, 1738-1816   1090

Cunningham, Henry W., ed. "Journal of Lieutenant-Colonel Joseph Vose." COLONIAL SOCIETY OF MASSACHUSETTS PUBLICATIONS 7 (1900-1902):248-262.

> Apr-Jul 1776. Letter-diary addressed to his wife; expedition from Cambridge to reinforce Montgomery's troops in Canada; details of movements and camp life; linguistic interest.

WALDECK, PHILIPP   1091

Calhoun, Gertrude L., trans. "Excerpts from Philipp Waldeck's Diary of the American Revolution." UNION COUNTY HISTORICAL SOCIETY PROCEEDINGS 2 (1934):137-143.

> 1776-1778. Diary of Hessian chaplain with Third Waldeck Regiment; journey from Germany to America; account of campaigns; a frank, direct account of army life on frontier outpost.

WEBB, SAMUEL BLACHLEY, 1753-1807   1092

CORRESPONDENCE AND JOURNALS OF SAMUEL BLACHLEY WEBB. Collected and edited by Worthington C. Ford. New York and Lancaster, Pa.: Wickersham Press, 1893. 3 vols.

Extracts in "Journal of a Member of Washington's Staff." AMERICAN HISTORICAL RECORD 1 (1872):445-448.

> 1776-1778 (with gaps). Military journals of aide to Washington; activities in New York; in camp at Cambridge; bombardment of Boston; military affairs at New Haven, Fort Montgomery and Staten Island; journeys to New Haven, Boston and New York; earlier part military, later part inclined to politics.

WHEELER, RUFUS   1093

"Journal of Lieut. Rufus Wheeler of Rowley." ESSEX INSTITUTE HISTORICAL COLLECTIONS 68 (1932):371-377.

> Jul-Dec 1776. March from Boxford to Ticonderoga; military events there; march back; interesting spellings.

WHATCOMBE, BENJAMIN, 1755-1828 1094

"Incidents of the Revolution." AMERICAN HISTORICAL RECORD 1 (1872):437-438.

Jul 1776. Short scouting expedition from Crown Point to St. Johns, Chambly, etc.; his shooting of General Gordon.

WHITTALL, JOB, 1743-1797 1095

In NOTES ON OLD GLOUCESTER COUNTY, NEW JERSEY, edited by Frank H. Stewart, vol. 1, pp. 255-261.

1776-1777. Summary and extracts of notes on activities of British and American soldiers in neighborhood, and his differences with them.

WIEDERHOLD, ANDREAS, b. ca. 1752 1096

"The Capture of Fort Washington, New York, Described by Captain Andreas Wiederhold." PENNSYLVANIA MAGAZINE OF HISTORY AND BIOGRAPHY 23 (1899):95-97.

Nov 1776. Journal of Hessian soldier with Knyphausen Regiment; capture of Fort Washington, New York.

Walker, Ralph S., ed. "'Trenton . . . I Shall Never Forget': Excerpts from a Hessian Officer's Diary." AMERICAN HISTORY ILLUSTRATED 11 (December 1976): 43-49.

1776-1777. Hessian prison diary; battle of Trenton and capture; observations of the American scene while a prisoner of war; descriptions of American soldiers, unusual fauna ("horn snack"), slavery in Virginia, a meeting with Washington, storm at sea.

WIGGLESWORTH, EDWARD, 1742-1826 1097

In HISTORY OF NEWBURYPORT, by Euphemia V. Blake, pp. 357-359. Newburyport and Boston: Press of Damrell and Moore, 1854.

Oct-Nov 1776. Extracts of a journal kept by officer with Arnold's fleet; near Schuyler's Island; engagement on Lake Champlain; Ticonderoga and Crown Point.

WILD, EBENEZER, 1758-1794 1098

"Journal of Ebenezer Wild." MASSACHUSETTS HISTORICAL SOCIETY PROCEEDINGS, 2d ser. 6 (1890-1891):78-160.

1776-1781. Corporal's journal of Ticonderoga campaign against Burgoyne, Rhode Island campaign, Yorktown; military affairs and personal items; a good, varied record; interesting linguistically.

WILLIAMS, ELISHA, 1757-1845 1099

"Elisha Williams' Diary of 1776." PENNSYLVANIA MAGAZINE OF HISTORY AND BIOGRAPHY 48 (1924):334-353; 49 (1925):44-60.

Sep-Nov 1776. Journal, mostly orderly book, of service with Ward's regiment in Washington's army; New York, Harlem.

YOUNG, WILLIAM 1100

"Journal of Sergeant William Young." PENNSYLVANIA MAGAZINE OF HISTORY AND BIOGRAPHY 8 (1884):255-278.

Dec 1776-Jan 1777. New Jersey campaign; interesting account of military life, hardships, etc.

1777

ANON. 1101

Seybolt, Robert F. "A Contemporary British Account of General Sir William Howe's Military Operations in 1777." AMERICAN ANTIQUARIAN SOCIETY PROCEEDINGS, n.s. 40 (1930):69-92.

1777. Detailed eyewitness account of Howe's proceedings, apparently by an officer of the British general staff.

ANON. 1102

"Journal of a Cruise in 1777 in the Privateer Brig OLIVER CROMWELL." ESSEX INSTITUTE HISTORICAL COLLECTIONS 45 (1909):245-255.

1777. Loglike details of cruise and engagement of privateer OLIVER CROMWELL under Captain Thomas Simmonds, of Beverly, Massachusetts.

ANON. 1103

Reid, W. Max, ed. "A Diary of the Siege of Fort Schuyler." MAGAZINE OF HISTORY 3 (1906):90-104.

Apr-Aug 1777. Journal of officer in Colonel Gansevoort's regiment; events leading to and siege of Fort Schuyler; Indian atrocities; some interesting spellings.

ANON. 1104

EXILES IN VIRGINIA: WITH OBSERVATIONS ON THE CONDUCT OF THE SOCIETY OF FRIENDS DURING THE REVOLUTIONARY WAR. Edited by Thomas Gilpin. Philadelphia: C. Sherman, Printer, 1848. 302 pp.

Sep-Dec 1777. Journal kept by a group of Quakers removed to Virginia by the revolutionary government in Philadelphia for refusal to join in war against British; arrest and imprisonment; journey to Winchester, Virginia, and life in detention there; activities, visitors, war news, meetings for worship, etc.

ALLAN, JOHN, 1746-1805 1105

In MILITARY OPERATIONS IN EASTERN MAINE AND NOVA SCOTIA DURING THE REVOLUTION, by Frederic Kidder, pp. 91-163. Albany: J. Munsell, 1867.

May 1777-Jan 1778. Official military journal of superintendent of Indians in Maine; expedition to St. John's River against Indians of Maine; military movements; return.

ALLEN, THOMAS, 1743-1810 1106

In HISTORY OF PITTSFIELD, BERKSHIRE COUNTY, MASSACHUSETTS, compiled by Joseph Edward A. Smith, vol. 1, pp. 470-475. Boston: Lee and Shepard, 1869.

1777-1780. Clergyman's diary; brief notes of domestic life, prices, etc., during the Revolution.

ANDRE, JOHN, 1751-1780 1107

ANDRE'S JOURNAL: AN AUTHENTIC RECORD OF THE MOVEMENTS AND ENGAGEMENTS OF THE BRITISH ARMY IN AMERICA. Edited by Henry Cabot Lodge. Boston: Issued by the Bibliophile Society, 1903. 2 vols.

MAJOR ANDRE'S JOURNAL: OPERATIONS OF THE BRITISH ARMY UNDER LIEUTENANT GENERALS SIR WILLIAM HOWE AND SIR HENRY CLINTON. By C. De W. Wilcox. Tarrytown, N.Y.: W. Abbatt, 1930. 128 pp.

1777-1778. Movements and engagements of the British army under Howe and Clinton.

AUSTIN, JONATHAN LORING, 1748-1826   1108

In FRANKLIN IN FRANCE, by Edward Everett Hale and Edward Everett Hale, Jr., vol. 1, pp. 156-164. Boston: Roberts Brothers, 1887.

"Diary of Col. J.L. Austin." COLLECTOR 21 (1908):123-125; 22 (1909):3-4.

Oct-Nov 1777. Extracts from travel journal; carrying dispatches from America to France with news of Burgoyne's surrender.

BACKUS, ELIJAH, b. 1759   1109

Larned, Ellen D., ed. "Yale Boys of the Last Century." CONNECTICUT QUARTERLY 1 (1895):355-361.

Jan-Dec 1777. Interesting short diary of a Yale student; social life and study; verses.

BARTLETT, ISRAEL, 1748-1837   1110

In HISTORY OF HAVERHILL, MASSACHUSETTS, by George Wingate Chase, pp. 401-402. Haverhill: Published by the author, 1861.

Oct-Nov 1777. Brief notes on troop movements; Burgoyne's surrender.

BATES, AMBROSE, 1758-1833   1111

In A NARRATIVE HISTORY OF THE TOWN OF COHASSET, MASSACHUSETTS, by Edwin V. Bigelow, pp. 299-303. Boston: Press of S. Usher, 1898.

Aug-Dec 1777. Burgoyne's surrender; brief notes of prisoners and march; interesting spellings.

BLAKE, THOMAS, 1752-1840   1112

In JOURNALS OF THE MILITARY EXPEDITION OF MAJOR GENERAL JOHN SULLIVAN, by New York State Secretary of State, Frederick Cook, pp. 38-41.

In HISTORY OF THE FIRST NEW HAMPSHIRE REGIMENT IN THE WAR OF THE REVOLUTION, by Frederic Kidder, pp. 25-56. Albany: J. Munsell, 1868.

1777-1780. Military journal covering Sullivan's expedition, Ticonderoga, Burgoyne's campaign, Hudson campaign.

BOARDMAN, OLIVER, 1758-1826   1113

"Journal of Oliver Boardman of Middletown, 1777: Burgoyne's Surrender." CONNECTICUT HISTORICAL SOCIETY COLLECTIONS 7 (1899):221-237.

Sep-Oct 1777. Interesting journal of Sullivan's campaign; Saratoga, Burgoyne's surrender.

BRIGHAM, PAUL, 1746-1824   1114

Hoyt, Edward A., ed. "A Revolutionary Diary of Captain Paul Brigham." VERMONT HISTORY 34 (1966):2-30.

1777-1778. Terse entries on movements and activities of Eighth Connecticut Regiment; routine events of army life; drills, musters, courts martial, illnesses, punishments; later very brief notes on Valley Forge and battle of Monmouth.

CALFE, JOHN   1115

In A MEMORIAL OF THE TOWN OF HAMPSTEAD, NEW HAMPSHIRE, compiled by Harriette E. Noyes, vol. 1, pp. 288-294. Boston: G.B. Reed, 1899.

Feb-Aug 1777. Military details at Ticonderoga; marches, excursions, etc.

CHILTON, JOHN, d. 1777   1116

"The Old Virginia Line in the Middle States during the American Revolution." TYLER'S QUARTERLY HISTORICAL AND GENEALOGICAL MAGAZINE 12 (1930-1931):283-289.

Jan-Sep 1777. Captain's journal of service with Third Virginia Regiment; movements, camp life, some personal items.

CLARK, JOSEPH, 1751-1813   1117

"Diary of Joseph Clark." NEW JERSEY HISTORICAL SOCIETY PROCEEDINGS 7 (1853-1855):93-110.

1777-1778. Activities of New Jersey militia in New Jersey, Pennsylvania, New York, Valley Forge, Brandywine.

COLBRAITH, WILLIAM   1118

In THE STORY OF OLD FORT JOHNSON, by William Maxwell Reid, pp. 87-99. New York: Putnam's Sons, 1906.

Apr-Aug 1777. Diary of a soldier at Fort Schuyler; account of the siege.

CONNER, TIMOTHY, 1748-1823   1119

"A Yankee Privateersman in Prison in England." NEW ENGLAND HISTORICAL AND GENEALOGICAL REGISTER 30 (1876):174-177, 343-352; 31 (1877):18-20, 212-213, 284-288; 32 (1878):70-73, 165-168, 280-286.

1777-1779. Prison diary; capture on brigantine RISING STATES, imprisonment in Forton Prison, England; excellent details of hardships, attempted escapes, food, etc.; colloquial and humorous.

CORNELIUS, ELIAS, 1758-1823   1120

JOURNAL OF DR. ELIAS CORNELIUS, A REVOLUTIONARY SURGEON. Washington, D.C.: C.M. Tompkins and C.T. Sherman, 1903. 27 pp. Diary, pp. 3-14.

Aug 1777-Mar 1778. Surgeon's journal of service with Angell's Long Island regiment; capture and imprisonment in New York; escape to Norwalk; verses.

COWAN, JOHN   1121

In TALES OF THE DARK AND BLOODY GROUND, by Willard R. Jillson, pp. 63-68. Louisville, Ky.: C.T. Dearing Printing Co., 1930.

Mar-Sep 1777. Brief notes on Indian affairs and skirmishes in Kentucky.

CRAFT, ELEAZER, 1743-1793   1122

"Journal of Eleazer Craft." ESSEX INSTITUTE HISTORICAL COLLECTIONS 7 (1864):194-198.

In THE CRAFTS FAMILY, compiled by James M. Crafts and William F. Crafts, app., pp. 689-693. Northampton, Mass.: Gazette Printing Co., 1893.

Sep-Dec 1777. March from Manchester, Massachusetts, to the Hudson, and return to Worthington; account of Burgoyne's surrender; stages of march.

CROSS, RALPH, 1738-1881   1123

"The Journal of Ralph Cross." HISTORICAL MAGAZINE, 2d ser. 7 (1870):8-11.

Aug-Dec 1777. Officer's journal of service with Essex Regiment; Bemis Heights, Saratoga, Burgoyne's surrender.

CROWNINGSHIELD, BENJAMIN   1124

"Extracts from the Journal of Benjamin Crowningshield." NEW HAMPSHIRE GENEALOGICAL RECORD 4 (1907):37.

Jul 1777. Account of fight of the BOSTON with the FOX, kept by a seaman on the BOSTON.

DEMERE, RAYMOND, 1752-1829   1125

Lawrence, Alexander A., ed. "Journal of Major Raymond Demere." GEORGIA HISTORICAL QUARTERLY 52 (1968):337-347.

May-Jun 1777. Georgia officer's journey north to join the Continental army; land and people along the way; assumption of command of Georgia troops near Philadelphia; privations and military discipline, including execution of a deserter upon Demere's orders; good descriptions of fighting and military strategy.

ELLERY, WILLIAM, 1727-1820   1126

"Diary of the Honorable William Ellery, of Rhode Island, October 20 to November 15, 1777." PENNSYLVANIA MAGAZINE OF HISTORY AND BIOGRAPHY 11 (1887): 318-329, 476-481.

"Journal of Route and Occurrences in a Journey to Philadelphia from Dighton, Begun October 24th, 1778." PENNSYLVANIA MAGAZINE OF HISTORY AND BIOGRAPHY 12 (1888):190-199.

Oct-Nov 1777, Jun-Jul 1778, Oct-Nov 1778, Jul 1779. Entertaining notes kept on various horseback journeys in Massachusetts, Connecticut, New York, New Jersey, Pennsylvania; mostly on way to and from Congress; notes on taverns, persons seen, political events and famous political figures.

FELL, JOHN, 1721-1798   1127

In AMERICAN PRISONERS OF THE REVOLUTION, by Danske B. Dandridge, pp. 112-122. Charlottesville, Va.: Michie Co., Printers, 1911.

1777-1778. Prison diary kept in Provost Jail, New York City.

"Original Documents: Full of the Most Important and Unpublished Historical Material." MAGAZINE OF HISTORY 21 (1915):257-260.

DELEGATE FROM NEW JERSEY: THE JOURNAL OF JOHN FELL. Edited by Donald W. Whisenhut. Port Washington, N.Y.: Kennikat Press, 1973. 212 pp.

1778-1779. Activities of Continental Congress, especially of Commercial Committee, of which diarist was a member; debates, votes and correspondence on many matters; dispatches and decisions relating to the Revolution.

FITTS, ABRAHAM, 1736-1808   1128

In HISTORY OF THE TOWN OF CANDIA, ROCKINGHAM COUNTY, N.H., by Jacob B. Moore, pp. 81-84. Manchester, N.H.: G.W. Browne, 1893.

Sep-Nov 1777. Brief notes of march from Candia to Saratoga; battles of Stillwater and Saratoga, and Burgoyne's surrender; interesting spellings.

FORSTER, J. GEORGE A., 1754-1794   1129

Kahn, Robert L., ed. "An Account of a Meeting with Benjamin Franklin at Passy on October 9, 1777." WILLIAM AND MARY QUARTERLY 12 (1955):472-474.

Oct 1777. Brief description by German author and scientist of Benjamin Franklin at a dinner party in Passy, France.

GARRETTSON, FREEBORN, 1752-1827   1130

THE EXPERIENCE AND TRAVELS OF MR. FREEBORN GARRETTSON, MINISTER OF THE METHODIST-EPISCOPAL CHURCH IN NORTH AMERICA. Philadelphia: Printed by Joseph Crukshank, and sold by John Dickins, 1791.

1777-? Clergyman's journal, kept at the request of Wesley; his experiences as an itinerant Methodist preacher in the South, Nova Scotia and New England; religious reflection and self-criticism; emotional appeal of his religion; animosity among sects.

GREEN, EZRA, 1746-1847   1131

"Diary of Dr. Ezra Green." NEW ENGLAND HISTORICAL AND GENEALOGICAL REGISTER 29 (1875):13-24.

DIARY OF EZRA GREEN, M.D., with historical notes by George Henry Preble. Boston: D. Clapp & Son, Printers, for private distribution, 1875. 28 pp. Reprint. New York: Arno, 1971.

Extracts in DIARY OF AMERICA, edited by Josef Berger, pp. 128-132.

Nov 1777-Sep 1778. Naval surgeon's journal; bare details of naval actions during the Revolution; aboard the RANGER, under John Paul Jones; engagement with British sloop; cruise to Belle Isle, Quiberon, Brest and Ireland.

GREENE, FLEET S., b. 1753   1132

"Newport in the Hands of the British." HISTORICAL MAGAZINE 4 (1860):1-4, 34-38, 69-72, 105-107, 134-137, 172-173.

1777-1779. American's notes on British occupation of Newport; daily events and news; good descriptions of state of the people. Authorship assumed.

HAZARD, EBENEZER, 1744-1817   1133

Shelley, Fred S., ed. "Ebenezer Hazard's Travels through Maryland in 1777." MARYLAND HISTORICAL MAGAZINE 46 (1951):44-54.

May, Jul, Nov 1777. Extracts from accounts by surveyor for the post office; three horseback journeys through Maryland during tours to inspect postal service in the South; evaluation of roads, accommodations; description of various communities, particularly Annapolis; conditions of slavery; notes on fauna and flora; gossip.

Shelley, Fred, ed. "The Journal of Ebenezer Hazard in Virginia, 1777." VIRGINIA MAGAZINE OF HISTORY AND BIOGRAPHY 62 (1954):400-423.

May-Jul, Nov-Dec 1777. Notes on Virginia; description of countryside; observations on the character of Virginians; Williamsburg.

Johnston, Hugh Buckner, ed. "The Journal of Ebenezer Hazard in North Carolina, 1777 and 1778." NORTH CAROLINA HISTORICAL REVIEW 36 (1959):358-381.

Jun 1777, Dec 1777-Jan 1778. Further journeys to inspect postal route; road conditions, accommodations, weather; comments on fauna and flora, agriculture, slavery and political events.

Shelley, Fred, ed. "Ebenezer Hazard's Diary: New Jersey during the Revolution." NEW JERSEY HISTORY 90 (1972):169–180.

Aug 1777. Ten-day trip from Philadelphia to Elizabeth and Newark, recording the destruction caused by war in New Jersey.

Shelley, Fred, ed. "Ebenezer Hazard in Pennsylvania, 1777." PENNSYLVANIA MAGAZINE OF HISTORY AND BIOGRAPHY 81 (1957):83–86.

Oct–Nov 1777. Extracts covering trip to Lancaster and York; descriptions of those towns; victory celebration for the battle of Saratoga.

Merrens, H. Roy, ed. "A View of Coastal South Carolina in 1778." SOUTH CAROLINA HISTORICAL MAGAZINE 73 (1972):177–193.

Jan–Mar 1778. Tour through the South to inspect post roads; description of roads, settlements and accommodations; observations on southern speech and character; slavery; dispute over South Carolina's constitution; description of Savannah, Georgia.

Shelley, Fred, ed. "The Journal of Ebenezer Hazard in Georgia, 1778." GEORGIA HISTORICAL QUARTERLY 41 (1957):316–319.

Feb 1778. Extracts from postmaster's account of travels in Georgia; mostly wining and dining with gentry, some of whom he did not admire; harsh words on slavery.

HERBERT, CHARLES, 1757–1808   1134

A RELIC OF THE REVOLUTION, CONTAINING A FULL AND PARTICULAR ACCOUNT OF THE SUFFERINGS AND PRIVATIONS OF ALL THE AMERICAN PRISONERS CAPTURED ON THE HIGH SEAS, AND CARRIED INTO PLYMOUTH, ENGLAND, DURING THE REVOLUTION OF 1776. Boston: C.H. Peirce, 1847. 258 pp.

THE PRISONERS OF 1776. By Richard Livesey. Boston: G.C. Rand, 1854. 264 pp.

Discussed in AMERICAN DIARY LITERATURE, by Steven E. Kagle, pp. 114–121.

1777–1780. Prison diary; capture at sea, transfer to Old Mill Prison, England; a most detailed and interesting record of prison life during the Revolution; vivid picture of diarist and his companions, hardships, illnesses, endless attempted escapes, hopes and despairs, news, etc.

HITCHCOCK, ENOS, 1744–1803   1135

Weeden, William B., ed. "Diary of Enos Hitchcock, D.D." RHODE ISLAND HISTORICAL SOCIETY PUBLICATIONS, n.s. 7 (1899):86–134, 147–194, 207–231. Diary begins p. 106.

1777–1780. Chaplain's diary; detailed notes of military events and news; Massachusetts, Vermont, Burgoyne's campaign, New York campaign; Arnold's treason and execution of André.

HUGHES, THOMAS, 1759 or 1760–1790   1136

A JOURNAL BY THOS. HUGHES FOR HIS AMUSEMENT & DESIGNED ONLY FOR HIS PERUSAL BY THE TIME HE ATTAINS THE AGE OF 50 OR IF HE LIVES SO LONG. With an introduction by Ernest A. Benians. Cambridge: University Press, 1947. 187 pp. Reprint. Port Washington, N.Y.: Kennikat, 1970.

1777–1789. Journal of British ensign with Burgoyne; capture at Ticonderoga; personal experiences, places through which he passed, behavior of fellow prisoners, daily life and treatment, amusements that brightened the routine. Journal begun anew after first one lost when diarist taken prisoner.

JENNISON, WILLIAM, 1757–1843   1137

Collum, Richard S. "Extracts from the Journal of William Jennison, Jr., Lieutenant of Marines in the Continental Navy." PENNSYLVANIA MAGAZINE OF HISTORY AND BIOGRAPHY 15 (1891):101–108.

1777–1780. Naval journal; brief notes of a marine during the Revolution.

JOSLIN, JOSEPH, b. 1759   1138

"Journal of Joseph Joslin, Jr. of South Killingly: A Teamster in the Continental Service." CONNECTICUT HISTORICAL SOCIETY COLLECTIONS 7 (1899):297–369.

Extracts in "A Teamster Boy in the Revolution," edited by Ellen D. Larned. CONNECTICUT QUARTERLY 2 (1896):50–51.

1777–1778. Life as a teamster in the revolutionary army; Connecticut and Rhode Island; very little of army affairs, but a quaint and entertaining diary of country life.

LAWSON, THOMAS, 1727–1804   1139

Extracts in HISTORY OF UNION, CONN., founded on material gathered by Charles Hammond, p. 125. New Haven, Conn.: Press of Price, Lee & Adkins, 1893.

Oct 1777. March from Tolland, Connecticut, to Stillwater; second battle of Stillwater.

LEE, ANDREW   1140

"Sullivan's Expedition to Staten Island in 1777." PENNSYLVANIA MAGAZINE OF HISTORY AND BIOGRAPHY 3 (1879):167–173.

Aug–Dec 1777. Brief military details of Sullivan's expedition.

MCKENDRY, WILLIAM, 1751?–1798   1141

"Journal of William McKendry." MASSACHUSETTS HISTORICAL SOCIETY PROCEEDINGS, 2d ser. 2 (1885–1886):442–478.

In JOURNALS OF THE MILITARY EXPEDITION OF MAJOR GENERAL JOHN SULLIVAN, by New York State Secretary of State, Frederick Cook, pp. 198–212.

1777–1780. Brief military and personal notes covering New York campaign, Cherry Valley Massacre, Sullivan's expedition; some topographical description and account of Moravian life.

MORTON, ROBERT   1142

"The Diary of Robert Morton." PENNSYLVANIA MAGAZINE OF HISTORY AND BIOGRAPHY 1 (1877):1–39.

Sep–Dec 1777. Civilian's account of the occupation of Philadelphia by the British.

NAPIER, FRANCIS, 1758–1833?   1143

Bradford, S. Sydney, ed. "Lord Francis Napier's Journal of the Burgoyne Campaign." MARYLAND HISTORICAL MAGAZINE 57 (1962):285–333.

May–Nov 1777, Apr–May 1778. Journal of a British lieutenant in light infantry company; detailed account of Burgoyne's invasion of New York and surrender at Saratoga; later entries made while diarist awaiting return to England; summary of a British raid on Warren and Bristol, Rhode Island.

NORTON, GEORGE, b. 1739   1144

"Revolutionary Diary Kept by George Norton of Ipswich." ESSEX INSTITUTE HISTORICAL COLLECTIONS 74 (1938):337-349.

> 1777-1780. Brief notes of marches, weather, expenses; a few interesting spellings.

OLMSTED, GIDEON, 1749-1845   1145

THE JOURNAL OF GIDEON OLMSTED, ADVENTURES OF A SEA CAPTAIN DURING THE AMERICAN REVOLUTION. Introduction by Gerard W. Gawalt, coda by Charles W. Kreidler. Washington, D.C.: Library of Congress, 1978. 129 pp.

> 1777-1778. Sea diary of young merchant ship captain and privateer; trading voyage to Guadalupe and back interrupted by capture of diarist's ship SEAFLOWER by British warship WEIR; imprisonment and torture aboard British ships and in Haiti; successful mutiny and capture of British ship ACTIVE; subsequent legal battle to gain prize money resulting from sale of cargo; patronage of Benedict Arnold; an exciting diary in seminarrative style.

PARKMAN, ANNA SOPHIA, 1755-1783   1146

Extracts in THE HUNDREDTH TOWN, by Harriette M. Forbes, pp. 83-89. Boston: Press of Rockwell and Churchill, 1889.

> Nov 1777-Jul 1778. Private diary; notes of social life in Westborough, Massachusetts; domestic affairs and visits; a pleasant picture of life in a clergyman's home.

PAWLING, HENRY   1147

"Journal of Henry Pawling." OLDE ULSTER 1 (1905): 335-338, 361-365; 2 (1906):18-25.

> Oct 1777-Feb 1778. Prison diary; capture by British at King's Ferry; life aboard a prison ship; food, treatment by British; well written and amusing.

PEMBERTON, JAMES   1148

"Journal of the Friends in Exile in Virginia. Taken from the Diary of James Pemberton." In EXILES IN VIRGINIA: WITH OBSERVATIONS ON THE CONDUCT OF THE SOCIETY OF FRIENDS DURING THE REVOLUTIONARY WAR, edited by Thomas Gilpin, pp. 197-233. Philadelphia: C. Sherman, Printer, 1848.

> 1777-1778. Journal kept by Philadelphia Quaker while exiled in Winchester, Virginia, by order of the revolutionary government; visitors, treatment, weather, deaths of two members, etc.; journey back to Pennsylvania.

PERCIVAL, BENJAMIN, 1752-1817   1149

Bowman, George Ernest, ed. "Birth, Marriage and Death Records from Benjamin Percival's Diary." PILGRIM NOTES AND QUERIES 1 (1913):53-56, 73-76, 87-89, 112-113; 2 (1914):27-29, 36-40.

Fawsett, Marisse. "Godspeed to the Plough." NEW ENGLAND GALAXY 17, no. 4 (1976):46-52.

> 1777-1817. Extracts, mainly of genealogical interest, but some personal, farming and local notes of

farmer in Sandwich, Massachusetts; work and leisure activities; involvement in the Revolution.

POPP, STEPHEN, b. 1755?   1150

Rosengarten, Joseph G. "Popp's Journal." PENNSYLVANIA MAGAZINE OF HISTORY AND BIOGRAPHY 26 (1902): 25-41, 245-254.

> 1777-1783. Hessian military journal; record of military services of Bayreuth Regiment during the Revolution.

RIEDESEL, FRIEDERIKE CHARLOTTE LOUISE   1151
VON MASSOW, Baroness, 1746-1808

LETTERS AND MEMOIRS RELATING TO THE WAR OF AMERICAN INDEPENDENCE, AND THE CAPTURE OF THE GERMAN TROOPS AT SARATOGA. New York: G.& C. Carvill, 1827. 323 pp.

LETTERS AND JOURNALS RELATING TO THE WAR OF THE AMERICAN REVOLUTION, AND THE CAPTURE OF THE GERMAN TROOPS AT SARATOGA. Translated by William L. Stone. Albany: J. Munsell, 1867. 285 pp.

BARONESS VON RIEDESEL AND THE AMERICAN REVOLUTION: JOURNAL AND CORRESPONDENCE OF A TOUR OF DUTY. A revised translation with introduction, notes, by Marvin L. Brown, Jr., with Marta Huth. Chapel Hill: Published for the Institute of Early American History and Culture at Williamsburg, Va. at the University of North Carolina Press, 1965. 222 pp.

Extract in AN AUTOBIOGRAPHY OF AMERICA, edited by Mark Van Doren, pp. 122-136.

> 1777-1783. Private diary; narrative and day-to-day entries, and some letters; social and army life in Canada and New England with her husband, who was with Burgoyne's army; a very readable and enlightening diary. Translated from the German.

SMITH, JACOB, 1756-1844   1152

Heathcote, Charles W., ed. "Diary of Jacob Smith-- American Born." PENNSYLVANIA MAGAZINE OF HISTORY AND BIOGRAPHY 56 (1932):260-264.

> 1777-1785. Brief and scattered notes of an American-born Swede serving with the British Army.

SMYTH, JOHN FERDINAND DALZIEL   1153

A TOUR IN THE UNITED STATES OF AMERICA. London: For G. Robinson; Dublin: Price, Moncrieffe, etc., 1784. 2 vols. Reprint. New York: New York Times, 1968.

"Narrative or Journal of Capt. John Ferdinand Dalziel Smyth, of the Queen's Rangers." PENNSYLVANIA MAGAZINE OF HISTORY AND BIOGRAPHY 34 (1915):143-169.

> 1777. Loyalist journal of captain of the Queen's Rangers; adventures, escapes from rebels, imprisonment at Philadelphia; in southern Maryland, Mississippi, Philadelphia, Baltimore, New York.

STEVENS, ELISHA, 1752-1813   1154

ELISHA STEVENS, FRAGMENTS OF MEMORANDA. Meriden, Conn.: 1922. 22 leaves.

> Oct 1777-Aug 1778. Military diary covering Brandywine, Germantown, Valley Forge; personal accounts; poem by Wigglesworth; some interesting spellings.

STEVENS, ENOS, 1739-1808   1155

Bolton, Charles K. ed. "A Fragment of the Diary of Lieutenant Enos Stevens, Tory." NEW ENGLAND QUAR-

TERLY 11 (1938):374–388.

1777–1785. Diary of Loyalist serving with the British; war news, personal affairs, expedition up West River to Fort Massachusetts; interesting spellings.

THOMPSON, GEORGE   1156

"Diary of George Thompson of Newburyport, Kept at Forton Prison, England." ESSEX INSTITUTE HISTORICAL COLLECTIONS 76 (1940):221–242.

1777–1781. Diary kept by American seaman while a prisoner of war and after; arrivals, escapes, recaptures and punishments; rules for seamen held at Forton Prison; the diarist's eventual escape, with route to London and the continent; return to Massachusetts and privateering.

TUCKER, ST. GEORGE, 1752–1828   1157

"The Tucker Papers: Journey to Charleston." BERMUDA HISTORICAL QUARTERLY 6 (1949):20–22, 135–143.

Mar–May 1777. Letter-journal of voyage to Charleston and Williamsburg; rigors of travel, enjoyment of society, balls, plays; a shocking description of runaway slaves burned at the stake; some histrionics over disappointed love.

Riley, Edward M., ed. "St. George Tucker's Journal of the Siege of Yorktown." WILLIAM AND MARY QUARTERLY 5 (1948):375–395.

Extracts in ST. GEORGE TUCKER, CITIZEN OF NO MEAN CITY, by Mary H.B. Coleman, pp. 72–87. Richmond, Va.: Dietz Press, 1938.

Sep–Oct 1781. Williamsburg officer's very precise and detailed account of military actions, sorties, bombardments, casualties, British surrender.

"Tucker Papers." BERMUDA HISTORICAL QUARTERLY 7 (1950):16–23, 106–119, 142–150.

Jul–Aug 1786. Letter-journal of stay at Norfolk and journey to New York; mostly social life; very lively and chatty.

VANDERSLICE, HENRY, 1726–1797   1158

In VAN DER SLICE AND ALLIED FAMILIES, compiled by Howard Vanderslice and Howard N. Monnett, pp. 140–161. Los Angeles: Printed by the Neuner Corp., 1931.

1777–1778. Wagon master's military journal of expenses, purchases of supplies, destruction of war; service with Washington during New York campaign; interesting spellings and language.

VARNUM, JOHN, 1705–1785   1159

Extracts in THE VARNUMS OF DRACUTT, compiled by John M. Varnum, pp. 54–64. Boston: D. Clapp & Son, Printers, 1907.

Extracts in HISTORY OF DRACUT, MASSACHUSETTS, by Silas E. Coburn, pp. 327–328. Lowell, Mass.: Press of the Courier-Citizen Co., 1922.

1777–1781. Brief notes of personal and social affairs at Dracut, Massachusetts; fishing, weather, war news.

VAUGHAN, ZEBULON, 1744–1824   1160

Wood, Virginia S. "The Journal of Private Zebulon Vaughan: Revolutionary Soldier." DAUGHTERS OF THE AMERICAN REVOLUTION MAGAZINE 113 (1979):100–114, 256–257, 320–331, 478–485, 487.

1777–1780. Daily entries of foot soldier in service with Fifth Massachusetts Regiment under Colonel Rufus Putnam; unflagging loyalty even under miserable camp conditions, smallpox epidemic, meager provisions; the battle of Bemis Heights near Saratoga and surrender of Burgoyne.

WALDO, ALBIGENCE, 1750–1794   1161

"Diary Kept at Valley Forge." HISTORICAL MAGAZINE 5 (1861):129–134, 169–172.

"Valley Forge, 1777–1778: Diary of Surgeon Albigence Waldo, of the Connecticut Line." PENNSYLVANIA MAGAZINE OF HISTORY AND BIOGRAPHY 21 (1897):299–323.

Thoms, Herbert. "Albigence Waldo, Surgeon: His Diary Written at Valley Forge." ANNALS OF MEDICAL HISTORY 10 (1928):486–497.

Extracts in AMERICAN HISTORY TOLD BY CONTEMPORARIES, edited by Albert B. Hart, vol. 2, pp. 568–573.

Discussed in AMERICAN DIARY LITERATURE, by Steven E. Kagle, pp. 108–114.

Nov 1777–Jan 1778. Surgeon's diary kept at Valley Forge; long entries, with vivid description of hardships and yearnings of troops; of interest as much for diarist's pungent comments as for direct observation of events and conditions; a fine diary.

WARREN, BENJAMIN, 1740–1825   1162

"Diary of Captain Benjamin Warren." JOURNAL OF AMERICAN HISTORY 3 (1909):202–216, 378–384.

Jul–Oct 1777, Jul–Nov 1778. Military diaries; Saratoga campaign and battle; Cherry Valley massacre; vivid and well told.

WEARE, NATHAN, 1747–1798   1163

In HISTORY OF THE TOWN OF HAMPTON FALLS, by Warren Brown, vol. 1, pp. 244–249. Concord, N.H.: Rumford Press, 1900.

Apr–Jun 1777. Military officer's journal; Ticonderoga and retreat; marches, camp life, discipline; some personal notes.

WEBB, NATHANIEL   1164

In JOURNALS OF THE MILITARY EXPEDITION OF MAJOR GENERAL JOHN SULLIVAN, by New York State Secretary of State, Frederick Cook, pp. 285–287; completed in NEW YORK STATE HISTORICAL ASSOCIATION PROCEEDINGS 6 (1906):87–93.

Extracts in "Diary Entry Covering Burning of Kingston in 1777." OLDE ULSTER 10 (1914):209–212.

1777–1779. Diary kept by sergeant of Second New York Regiment; burning of Kingston; Sullivan's expedition.

WHEELER, BENNETT, d. 1806   1165

RHODE ISLAND HISTORICAL SOCIETY PUBLICATIONS, n.s. 6 (1898):91.

1777. Extract from military journal concerning British in Rhode Island.

WHIPPLE, WILLIAM, 1730–1785   1166

"William Whipple's Notes of a Journey from Philadelphia to New Hampshire." PENNSYLVANIA MAGAZINE OF HISTORY AND BIOGRAPHY 10 (1886):366–374.

1777–1779 (with gaps). Diary covering journey between Dighton, Massachusetts, and Philadelphia, accompanying William Ellery; notes on places and people, including congressmen.

WISTER, SALLY, 1761–1804   1167

"Journal of Miss Sally Wister." PENNSYLVANIA MAGAZINE OF HISTORY AND BIOGRAPHY 9 (1885):318–333, 463–478; 10 (1886):51–60.

In HISTORICAL COLLECTIONS RELATING TO GWYNEDD, by Howard M. Jenkins, pp. 312–348. Philadelphia: The author, 1897.

SALLY WISTER'S JOURNAL. Edited by Albert C. Myers. Philadelphia: Ferris & Leach, 1902. 224 pp. Reprint. New York: New York Times, 1969.

Extracts in WEATHERING THE STORM, by Elizabeth Evans, pp. 114–148.

Discussed in AMERICAN DIARY LITERATURE, by Steven E. Kagle, pp. 86–92.

> Sep 1777–Jun 1778. Lively diary of Quaker girl living on a farm near Valley Forge; flirtations with officers of the revolutionary army; social life; only occasional intrusions of the seriousness of war; witty, with many excellent conversation pieces; a few poems.

1778

ADYE, STEPHEN PAYNE, d. 1794   1168

Ritchie, Carson I.A., ed. "A New York Diary of the Revolutionary War." NEW YORK HISTORICAL SOCIETY QUARTERLY 50 (1966):221–280, 401–416. Diary, pp. 255–280, 401–416. Reprint. In NARRATIVES OF THE REVOLUTION IN NEW YORK: A COLLECTION OF ARTICLES FROM THE NEW YORK HISTORICAL SOCIETY QUARTERLY, pp. 206–303. New York: New York Historical Society, 1975.

> 1778–1779. Military diary of officer in Royal Artillery, secretary to Brigadier General James Pattison; the evacuation of Philadelphia, retreat across New Jersey, engagements at Newport and elsewhere, the occupation of New York; matter-of-fact account of battles, casualties, movements of troops and warships, relocation of refugees, exchanges of prisoners, even amateur theatricals by officers; names of officers, ships, places. Earlier attributed to Pattison.

AIKMAN, LOUISA SUSANNAH WELLS, 1755?–1831   1169

THE JOURNAL OF A VOYAGE FROM CHARLESTOWN, S.C., TO LONDON. New York: Printed for the New York Historical Society, 1906. 121 pp. Reprint. New York: New York Times, 1968.

> May–Aug 1778. Loyalist travel diary; daily notes of a voyage from Charleston to London; really written up in the following year, but follows day-to-day pattern.

ALMY, MARY GOULD, 1735–1808   1170

"Mrs. Almy's Journal." NEWPORT HISTORICAL MAGAZINE 1 (1880–1881):17–36.

Extracts in WEATHERING THE STORM, by Elizabeth Evans, pp. 251–265.

> Jul–Aug 1778. Diary kept by a British sympathizer while her husband was away with the rebel army; bombardment of Newport by the French fleet; fears for her family and herself.

ANDERSON, WILLIAM, d. 1778   1171

In THE JOURNALS OF CAPTAIN JAMES COOK ON HIS VOYAGES OF DISCOVERY, edited by John C. Beaglehole, vol. 3, pt. 2, app. 2, pp. 721–986.

> 1778–1779. Journal of surgeon and naturalist aboard the RESOLUTION during Cook's third voyage; extensive notes on natural history of Hawaii, northwest and Alaskan coastal areas; identification of birds, fish, plants, rocks, etc.; anthropological and linguistic notes on Hawaiians.

ANGELL, ISRAEL, 1740–1832   1172

DIARY OF COLONEL ISRAEL ANGELL. Notes by Edward Field. Providence, R.I.: Preston and Rounds, 1899. 149 pp. Reprint. New York: New York Times, 1971.

> 1778–1781. Diary of commander of Second Rhode Island Regiment; siege of Boston; Peekskill, Brandywine, Red Bank, Valley Forge, Monmouth, Springfield; mainly notes of his own activities and general affairs of military life.

Smith, Dwight L., ed. "Israel Angell and the West in 1788." RHODE ISLAND HISTORY 22 (1963):1–15, 39–50.

> Aug–Oct 1788. Business journey to look into his investment in the Ohio Company; from Rhode Island by horseback to Wheeling and by boat down the Ohio to Marietta; conditions of travel, accommodations; comments on Marietta, Indians, the work of the Mound Builders, richness of land.

BELL, ANDREW   1173

"Copy of a Journal." NEW JERSEY HISTORICAL SOCIETY PROCEEDINGS 6 (1851–1853):15–19.

> Jun–Jul 1778. Military journal kept by the secretary to General Clinton; march of British army through New Jersey; mostly statistics.

BENJAMIN, SAMUEL, 1753–1824   1174

In GENEALOGY OF THE FAMILY OF LIEUT. SAMUEL BENJAMIN AND TABITHA LIVERMORE, HIS WIFE, compiled by Mary L. Benjamin, pp. 24–38. Winthrop, Maine: 1900.

> 1778–1781. Brief record of campaigns in New York, New Jersey and Maryland.

BERKENHOUT, JOHN, 1730?–1791   1175

Peckham, Howard, ed. "Dr. Berkenhout's Journal." PENNSYLVANIA MAGAZINE OF HISTORY AND BIOGRAPHY 65 (1941):79–92.

In TRAVELS IN THE AMERICAN COLONIES, edited by Newton D. Mereness, pp. 574–582.

> Aug–Sep 1778. British physician's diary of travel from New York to Philadelphia, as member of peace delegation; conversations with congressmen; notes on revolutionary forces; arrest and imprisonment by Pennsylvania Supreme Council.

BOARDMAN, TIMOTHY, 1754–1838   1176

LOG-BOOK OF TIMOTHY BOARDMAN. By Samuel W. Boardman. Albany: J. Munsell's Sons, 1885. 85 pp.

> Apr 1778, Jul–Sep 1778. Journals kept on board the privateer OLIVER CROMWELL; cruising from New London to Charleston, South Carolina; return and skirmish with a British ship.

BURNEY, JAMES, 1750-1821   1177

Extracts in THE JOURNALS OF CAPTAIN JAMES COOK ON HIS VOYAGES OF DISCOVERY, edited by John C. Beaglehole, vol. 3, pt. 1, pp. 697-701; pt. 2, app. 3, pp. 1340-1341.

In MY FRIEND THE ADMIRAL: THE LIFE, LETTERS AND JOURNALS OF REAR-ADMIRAL JAMES BURNEY, by George E. Manwaring. London: Geo. Routledge, 1931. 314 pp. passim.

> 1778-1779. Journal of an officer aboard the DISCOVERY and RESOLUTION during Cook's third voyage; Cook's death in Hawaii; Burney's subsequent command of the DISCOVERY.

CARLETON, CHRISTOPHER, b. 1749   1178

In CARLETON'S RAID, by Ida H. and Paul A. Washington, pp. 85-92. Canaan, N.H.: Phoenix Publishing Co., 1977.

> Oct-Nov 1778. Leader's account of raid by Canadian and Indian troops on American civilians settled in Lake Champlain area; destruction of boats and provisions; the taking of prisoners.

CARPENTER, BENJAMIN   1179

"Excerpts from the Diary of Benjamin Carpenter, Gloucester County, New Jersey." PENNSYLVANIA MAGAZINE OF HISTORY AND BIOGRAPHY 27 (1903):507-508.

> Nov 1778-Jan 1779. A clergyman's account of a prisoner's "Christian courage and fortitude" as he goes to execution.

CLERKE, CHARLES, 1741-1779   1180

Extracts in THE JOURNALS OF CAPTAIN JAMES COOK ON HIS VOYAGES OF DISCOVERY, edited by John C. Beaglehole, vol. 3, pt. 1, pp. 531-697 passim; pt. 2, app. 3, pp. 1301-1339.

> 1778-1779. Journal of commander of Cook's ship DISCOVERY during the third voyage; events in Hawaii and at Nootka Sound, with extensive notes on inhabitants of both; contact with Russians; observation of Cook's death and aftermath; assumption of command of expedition until his own death from tuberculosis.

COOK, JAMES, 1728-1779   1181

A VOYAGE TO THE PACIFIC OCEAN. Edited by John Douglas. London: G. Nicol and T. Cadell, 1784. 3 vols. Philadelphia: Robert Desilver, J. Maxwell, Printer, 1818. 2 vols.

CAPTAIN COOK'S THIRD AND LAST VOYAGE TO THE PACIFIC OCEAN. Faithfully abridged from the quarto edition. New York: Printed by Mott and Hurtin for Benjamin Gomez, 1795. 144 pp.

Extracts in THE VOYAGES OF CAPTAIN JAMES COOK ROUND THE WORLD, selected and edited by Christopher Lloyd. London: Cresset Press, 1949. 383 pp.

In THE JOURNALS OF CAPTAIN JAMES COOK ON HIS VOYAGES OF DISCOVERY, edited by John C. Beaglehole, vol. 3, pt. 1.

Extracts in THE EXPLORATIONS OF CAPTAIN JAMES COOK IN THE PACIFIC AS TOLD BY SELECTIONS OF HIS OWN JOURNALS, edited by Archibald Grenfell Price. New York: Limited Editions Club, 1957. 296 pp. New York: Heritage Press; Melbourne: Georgian House, 1958. 292 pp. Reprint. Sydney: Angus and Robertson, 1969; New York: Dover, 1971.

> 1778-1779. American portion of Cook's monumental journal; of third voyage, on board the RESOLUTION and DISCOVERY, in search of the Northwest Passage; activities of various officers, including William Bligh; landings on Hawaiian Islands; brief period of trading and fixing positions of islands; to coast of present Oregon and Washington and on to Nootka Sound; trade with Indians for furs; description of their appearance, garb and customs; northward to Kayak Island, Prince William Sound, Cook Inlet, Aleutians, Unalaska; notes on Indians, Eskimos and Aleuts; determination that Alaska was not an island; contact with Russians; return to Hawaii, where Cook was received royally; detailed notes on Hawaiians and natural history of the islands; quarrels between Hawaiians and Cook's men, leading to murder of Cook.

Elliott, T.C., ed. "Captain Cook's Approach to Oregon." OREGON HISTORICAL QUARTERLY 29 (1928):265-277.

> Feb 1778. Extract; description of Oregon coast.

DENNIS, JOSEPH, 1759-1807   1182

"Copy of Part of a Journal Kept at Portsmouth, R.I." NEWPORT HISTORICAL MAGAZINE 2 (1881):46-52.

> May-Aug 1778. Fragment of Quaker diary; visits, social life, amusements, farming; the British at Portsmouth.

EDGAR, THOMAS   1183

Extracts in THE JOURNALS OF CAPTAIN JAMES COOK ON HIS VOYAGES OF DISCOVERY, edited by John C. Beaglehole, vol. 3, pt. 1, pp. 701-709; pt. 2, pp. 1351-1360.

> 1778-1779. Journal of captain of the DISCOVERY during Cook's third voyage; notes on Russians in Alaska area; account of Cook's death in Hawaii.

FOOT, CALEB, 1750-1787   1184

"Reminiscences of the Revolution; Prison Letters and Sea Journal of Caleb Foot." ESSEX INSTITUTE HISTORICAL COLLECTIONS 26 (1889):90-122. Diary, pp. 104-119.

> 1778-1782. Two journeys, one to Canada and another to Europe; imprisonment in England, escape to Holland; seminarrative style.

GALLOWAY, GRACE GROWDEN, d. 1789   1185

Werner, Raymond C., ed. "Diary of Grace Growden Galloway." PENNSYLVANIA MAGAZINE OF HISTORY AND BIOGRAPHY 55 (1931):32-94; 58 (1934):152-189. Reprint. New York: New York Times, 1971.

Extracts in "Grace Growden Galloway: Survival of a Loyalist," by Beverly Baxter. FRONTIERS 3 (1978): 62-67.

Extracts in WEATHERING THE STORM, by Elizabeth Evans, pp. 190-244.

> 1778-1779. Loyalist diary kept in Philadelphia during the Revolution; her own actions and difficulties; suffering over separation from family and loss of property; illness and exhaustion; society of a few faithful friends; a good diary with long detailed entries.

GIBBS, CALEB   1186

"Part of a Diary of Major Gibbs." In PENNSYLVANIA ARCHIVES, 1st ser., vol. 6, pp. 734-736.

Aug 1778. Military diary kept at Providence and Newport.

GILBERT, BENJAMIN, 1755-1828   1187

A CITIZEN-SOLDIER IN THE AMERICAN REVOLUTION: THE DIARY OF BENJAMIN GILBERT IN MASSACHUSETTS AND NEW YORK. Edited by Rebecca D. Symmes. New York State Historical Association Monographic Studies, no. 2. Cooperstown: New York State Historical Association, 1980. 93 pp.

1778-1782. Diary of an ordinary soldier; service in Massachusetts and New York; hardships, illness, day-to-day duties; a gregarious social life while off duty.

GILE, EZEKIEL, 1743-1828   1188

BOSTON TRANSCRIPT, 4 December 1905.

1778-1780. Brief entries of military affairs in Rhode Island; interesting spellings.

GOODWIN, ICHABOD, b. 1743   1189

Goodwin, William A., ed. "The Military Journal of Colonel Ichabod Goodwin." MAINE HISTORICAL SOCIETY COLLECTIONS, 2d ser. 5 (1894):33-71.

Apr-Jun 1778. Combination of orderly book and notes of military affairs kept at Boston; discipline, etc.

GREENE, WILLIAM   1190

"Diary of William Greene." MASSACHUSETTS HISTORICAL SOCIETY PROCEEDINGS 54 (1920-1921):84-138.

Mar-Sep 1778. Diary of an American in London and Paris, apparently a prisoner released on exchange; London, Brighton, Dieppe, Rouen, Paris; accounts of his family and life; meeting with Franklin and others; social life in Paris; journey to America on man-of-war; carefully written in great detail.

GRIMKE, JOHN FOUCHERAUD, 1752-1819   1191

"Journal of the Campaign to the Southward." SOUTH CAROLINA HISTORICAL AND GENEALOGICAL MAGAZINE 12 (1911):60-69, 118-134, 190-206.

May-Jul 1778. Expedition against the British in Florida; some topographical notes; partly written by his clerk.

HAMILTON, HENRY, d. 1796   1192

In HENRY HAMILTON AND GEORGE ROGERS CLARK IN THE AMERICAN REVOLUTION, edited by John D. Barnhart, pp. 102-205. Crawfordsville, Ind.: R.E. Banta, 1951.

Aug 1778-Jun 1779. Military diary of controversial British officer and lieutenant governor of Detroit, notorious for inciting Indians against colonists, allegedly offering bounties for scalps; much on Indian customs, British dealings with various tribes, some Indian speeches; capture of Vincennes and defeat of Hamilton by George Rogers Clark; forced march to Williamsburg, Virginia, and imprisonment there under brutal conditions; release upon order of George Washington.

Extracts in THE GEORGE ROGERS CLARK ADVENTURE IN THE ILLINOIS AND SELECTED DOCUMENTS OF THE AMERICAN REVOLUTION AT THE FRONTIER POSTS, by Kathrine W. Seineke, pp. 219-236. New Orleans: Polyanthos, 1981.

Oct-Dec 1778. Journey of British troops from Detroit to Vincennes in campaign against George Rogers Clark; difficult boat travel on Wabash River route; councils with Indians along the way; military discipline.

Extracts in HISTORIC HIGHWAYS OF AMERICA, by Archer B. Hulbert, vol. 7, pp. 170-175.

Oct-Nov 1778. Journey along Wabash route toward Vincennes.

HAZARD, THOMAS BENJAMIN, 1756-1845   1193

NAILER TOM'S DIARY; OTHERWISE, THE JOURNAL OF THOMAS B. HAZARD OF KINGSTOWN, RHODE ISLAND. Introduced by Caroline Hazard. Boston: Merrymount, 1930. 808 pp.

Extracts in NARRAGANSETT HISTORICAL REGISTER 1 (1882-1883):28-41, 91-106, 167-179, 277-285.

1778-1840. Farming diary; brief notes of personal, local, social, farming matters; because of its enormous length, persistency and detail, a valuable record of local New England life; interesting linguistically.

HOLTEN, SAMUEL, 1738-1816   1194

"Journal of Samuel Holten, M.D." ESSEX INSTITUTE HISTORICAL COLLECTIONS 55 (1919):161-176, 249-256; 56 (1920):24-32, 88-97.

"Journal of Doctor Samuel Holten." DANVERS HISTORICAL SOCIETY COLLECTIONS 7 (1919):59-67; 8 (1920):97-130.

Extracts in "Remarks by Hon. Mellen Chamberlain." MASSACHUSETTS HISTORICAL SOCIETY PROCEEDINGS, 2d ser. 10 (1895-1896):463.

1778-1780. Journal of congressman from Danvers, Massachusetts; activities of Congress, news, social affairs, journeys.

JENKINS, JOHN, 1751-1827   1195

In JOURNALS OF THE MILITARY EXPEDITION OF MAJOR GENERAL JOHN SULLIVAN, by New York State Secretary of State, Frederick Cook, pp. 169-177.

1778-1781. Sullivan's campaign; battle of Newtown.

KING, JAMES, 1750-1784   1196

Extracts in THE JOURNALS OF CAPTAIN JAMES COOK ON HIS VOYAGES OF DISCOVERY, edited by John C. Beaglehole, vol. 3, pt. 1, pp. 495-678 passim; pt. 2, app. 3, pp. 1361-1456.

1778-1779. Journal of officer aboard RESOLUTION and DISCOVERY during Cook's third voyage; events at Hawaii, with extensive notes on Hawaiian customs, religion, language, etc,; activities at Nootka Sound; notes on Eskimos; account of Cook's death in Hawaii.

THE DEATH OF CAPTAIN COOK. Book Club of California, Pacific Adventures, no. 6. San Francisco: Book Club of California, 1940. 14 pp.

Feb 1779.

MCCREADY, ROBERT   1197

Williams, Edward G., ed. "A Revolutionary Journal and Orderly Book of General Lachlan McIntosh's Expedition." WESTERN PENNSYLVANIA HISTORICAL MAGAZINE 43 (1960):1-17.

Nov 1778. Adjutant's description of march from Fort McIntosh (on Ohio River at what is now Beaver, Pennsylvania) to the Muskingum River where Fort Laurens was to be built; distances, camp locations, contacts with hostile and friendly Indians.

MACLEOD, NORMAND 1198

DETROIT TO SACKVILLE, 1778-1779, THE JOURNAL OF NORMAND MACLEOD. Edited by William A. Evans. Detroit: Wayne State University Press, 1978. 134 pp.

Sep 1778-Jan 1779. Revolutionary war journal of British officer and frontiersman under Henry Hamilton; arduous march from Detroit to Vincennes in advance of Hamilton to clear way for his larger force; amicable dealings with Indians in preparation for Hamilton's recruitment of them against the Americans; ingenious solutions to problems of transporting troops and equipment by river and overland.

MIX, JONATHAN, 1753-1817 1199

In A BRIEF ACCOUNT OF THE LIFE AND PATRIOTIC SERVICES OF JONATHAN MIX OF NEW HAVEN, by William Phipps Blake, pp. 32-40. New Haven, Conn.: Printed by Tuttle, Morehouse & Taylor, 1886.

Sep-Dec 1778. Journal of captain on board MARLBOROUGH, pursuing Jamaica fleet; log items.

NEISSER, GEORGE 1200

"Incidents in the History of York, Pennsylvania." PENNSYLVANIA MAGAZINE OF HISTORY AND BIOGRAPHY 16 (1892):433-438.

Jan-Dec 1778. Moravian clergyman's journal; religious work and life in York, Pennsylvania.

NUTTING, WILLIAM, 1752-1832 1201

"William Nutting's Diary." In GROTON HISTORICAL SERIES, by Samuel A. Green, vol. 3, pp. 383-399. Groton, Mass., 1887-1899.

1778-1783. Extracts containing notes relating to the Revolution, references to Groton Library, funerals.

PASLEY, Sir THOMAS, 1734-1808 1202

PRIVATE SEA JOURNALS, 1778-1782, KEPT BY ADMIRAL SIR THOMAS PASLEY. Edited by Rodney M.S. Pasley. London and Toronto: J.M. Dent and Sons, 1931. 319 pp.

1778-1782. British admiral's record of naval service during American Revolution; voyages in ships GLASGOW, SYBIL and JUPITER.

SAMWELL, DAVID, d. 1799 1203

In THE JOURNALS OF CAPTAIN JAMES COOK ON HIS VOYAGES OF DISCOVERY, edited by John C. Beaglehole, vol. 3, pt. 2, app. 2, pp. 987-1295.

1778-1779. Journal of surgeon's mate aboard the RESOLUTION, later surgeon aboard the DISCOVERY, during Cook's third voyage; anthropological notes on Hawaiians and northwest coast Indians; account of Cook's death.

A NARRATIVE OF THE DEATH OF CAPTAIN JAMES COOK. London: Printed for G.C.J. and J. Robinson, 1786. 26 pp. Hawaiian Historical Society Reprints, no. 2. Honolulu, 1917.

CAPTAIN COOK AND HAWAII, A NARRATIVE. Introduction by Maurice Holmes. San Francisco: D. Magee, 1957. 42 pp.

Feb 1779.

SHARPE, ROBERT 1743-1798 1204

"The Sharp Papers in the Brookline Public Library." BROOKLINE HISTORICAL PUBLICATION SOCIETY PUBLICATIONS, 1st ser. no. 2 (1895):7-14. Journal, pp. 12-13.

Apr-Aug 1778. Farming journal; mostly accounts and farm details.

SPROAT, JAMES, 1772-1793 1205

Jordan, John W. "Extracts from the Journal of Rev. James Sproat, Hospital Chaplain of the Middle Department." PENNSYLVANIA MAGAZINE OF HISTORY AND BIOGRAPHY 27 (1903):441-445, 505-506.

Apr-Oct 1778. Brief notes of visits as hospital chaplain in Philadelphia.

STONE, STEPHEN, 1761-1782 1206

In THE FAMILY OF JOHN STONE, ONE OF THE FIRST SETTLERS OF GUILDFORD, CONN., by William Leete Stone, pp. 30-33. Albany: J. Munsell & Sons, 1888.

1778-1781. Brief notes of his military career; White Plains, Peekskill, etc.; partly domestic notes.

TURNOR, PHILIP, b. ca. 1752 1207

In JOURNALS OF SAMUEL HEARNE AND PHILIP TURNOR, edited by Joseph B. Tyrrell, pp. 195-491, 557-577. Champlain Society Publications, vol. 21. Toronto: The Champlain Society, 1934.

1778-1781. Travel journals of Hudson's Bay Company surveyor; surveying trips from York Fort to Cumberland House, Albany and Moose Forts, and travel around the forts; in these journals and the rest, mostly details of topography, navigation, etc., with occasional notes on his daily life and adventures, Indians, weather.

1790-1792. With Mitchel Oman; occurrences at Cumberland House; travel from Cumberland House toward the Athapiscow country and back to York Factory; from York Factory to Port Nelson River (North River).

VAILL, JOSEPH, 1751-1838 1208

MEMOIR OF REV. JOSEPH VAILL. By Isaac Parsons. New York: Taylor and Dodd, 1839. 286 pp. Diary, pp. 86-156 passim.

1778-1823. Hadlyme, Connecticut, clergyman's diary; religious meditations, reform, revivals, etc.; interesting.

VAN SCHAACK, PETER, 1747-1832 1209

Extracts in THE LIFE OF PETER VAN SCHAACK, by Henry C. Van Schaack, pp. 132-277 passim. New York: D. Appleton, 1842.

1778-1782. Voyage from New York to England and exile there; travels about England, with touristic and antiquarian notes on churches, buildings, etc.; comment on Fielding; political speculations, reading, surgical operations.

WEEKS, JOSHUA WINGATE, 1738-1806 1210

"Journal of Rev. Joshua Wingate Weeks, Loyalist Rector of St. Michael's Church, Marblehead." ESSEX INSTITUTE HISTORICAL COLLECTIONS 52 (1916):1-16, 161-176, 197-208, 345-356.

Jun 1778–May 1779. Loyalist clergyman's escape from Marblehead, Massachusetts, to Newport; bombardment of Newport; journey to New York and then to London; scandals and excitements of voyage; social life in London; very lively and entertaining.

WILLIAMSON, JOHN   1211

Extracts in THE JOURNALS OF CAPTAIN JAMES COOK ON HIS VOYAGES OF DISCOVERY, edited by John C. Beaglehole, vol. 3, pt. 2, app. 3, pp. 1342–1350.

1778–1779. Journal of an officer aboard the DISCOVERY and RESOLUTION during Cook's third voyage; brief notes on Hawaii and Nootka Sound.

1779

ANON.   1212

Hill's NEW HAMPSHIRE PATRIOT, 16 September 1843.

1779. Military journal describing western expedition.

ANON.   1213

In THE SIEGE OF SAVANNAH IN 1779, AS DESCRIBED IN TWO CONTEMPORANEOUS JOURNALS OF FRENCH OFFICERS IN THE FLEET OF COUNT D'ESTAING, translated and edited by Charles Colcock Jones, pp. 9–52. Albany: J. Munsell, 1874.

Jul–Nov 1779. Siege of Savannah; movements of fleets and troops, bombardments, gains and losses; observations at the conclusion.

ANON.   1214

"Operations in Maine in 1779." HISTORICAL MAGAZINE 8 (1864):51–54.

Jul–Aug 1779. Long and fairly detailed notes of Penobscot expedition; cruise from Nantasket; military operations in Maine.

ANON.   1215

Williamson, Joseph. "Journal of the Attack of the Rebels on His Majesty's Ships and Troops." MAINE HISTORICAL SOCIETY COLLECTIONS, 1st ser. 7 (1876): 121–126.

Jul–Aug 1779. Rebel attack on British ships and troops under command of Brigadier General McLean and Captain Henry Mowatt in Penobscot Bay; details of bombardment.

ANON.   1216

"An English Journal of the Siege of Savannah." HISTORICAL MAGAZINE 8 (1864):12–16.

Nov–Oct (sic) 1779. British naval officer's account of siege of Savannah.

ANON.   1217

"Extract from a Pocket Diary by One of the Officers of H.M.S. RESOLUTION." HONOLULU MERCURY 2 (1930): 375–382.

Feb 1779. The murder of Captain Cook, including events leading up to the attack; British efforts to retrieve the body and subsequent attacks on the Hawaiians.

ADAMS, JOHN QUINCY, 1767–1848   1218

DIARY OF JOHN QUINCY ADAMS. Edited by Robert J. Taylor. The Adams Papers, ser. 1, vol. 1–2. Cambridge: Harvard University Press, 1982–(in progress).

1779–1788. Beginning with youthful diary of twelve-year-old; maturing teen-ager; experiences as student at Harvard; good picture of American life.

"Diary of John Quincy Adams." MASSACHUSETTS HISTORICAL SOCIETY PROCEEDINGS, 2d ser. 16 (1902):291–464.

LIFE IN A NEW ENGLAND TOWN. Boston: Little, Brown, 1903. 204 pp.

1787–1789. Social life and student experiences in the office of Theophilus Parsons at Newburyport; notes on some journeys.

"Extracts from the Diary of John Quincy Adams Pertaining to Samuel Putnam." DANVERS HISTORICAL SOCIETY COLLECTIONS 28 (1940):37–45.

1787–1789. Extract of diary regarding fellow student at Harvard who was reading law at Newburyport at the same time as Adams but not in the same office.

MEMOIRS OF JOHN QUINCY ADAMS. Edited by Charles Francis Adams. Philadelphia: J.B. Lippincott, 1874–1877. 12 vols. Reprint. Freeport, N.Y.: Books for Libraries, 1969.

1794–1848. Extensive and invaluable record of life at Braintree, Massachusetts, and political affairs of sixth president of the United States.

Abridgment. THE DIARY OF JOHN QUINCY ADAMS, 1794–1845; AMERICAN POLITICAL, SOCIAL AND INTELLECTUAL LIFE FROM WASHINGTON TO POLK, Edited by Allan Nevins. New York: Longmans, Green, 1928. 586 pp. Reprint. New York: Scribner, 1951; New York: F. Ungar, 1969.

Extracts in DIARY OF AMERICA, edited by Josef Berger, pp. 383–391.

1794–1845.

THE RUSSIAN MEMOIRS OF JOHN QUINCY ADAMS. New York: Arno, 1970. 602 pp.

JOHN QUINCY ADAMS IN RUSSIA. New York: Praeger, 1970. 662 pp.

1809–1814. Reprint editions of vol. 2 of MEMOIRS OF JOHN QUINCY ADAMS.

BARR, JOHN   1219

In ORDERLY BOOKS OF THE FOURTH NEW YORK REGIMENT, by New York Infantry, prepared for publication by Almon W. Lauber, pp. 787–865. Albany: University of the State of New York, 1932.

1779–1782. Brief notes of marches and military affairs.

BARTON, WILLIAM   1220

"Journal of Lieutenant William Barton of Maxwell's Brigade." NEW JERSEY HISTORICAL SOCIETY PROCEEDINGS 2 (1846):22–42.

In JOURNALS OF THE MILITARY EXPEDITION OF MAJOR GENERAL JOHN SULLIVAN, by New York State Secretary of State, Frederick Cook, pp. 3–14.

Jun–Oct 1779. Extracts from military journal covering Maxwell's New Jersey brigade on Sullivan's expedition.

BEATTY, ERKURIES, 1759-1823   1221

"Journal of Lieut. Erkuries Beatty in the Expedition against the Six Nations under General Sullivan." In PENNSYLVANIA ARCHIVES, 2d ser., vol. 15, pp. 219-253.

"General Clinton's March down the Susquehanna." CAYUGA COUNTY HISTORICAL SOCIETY COLLECTIONS 1 (1879):60-68.

In JOURNALS OF THE MILITARY EXPEDITION OF MAJOR GENERAL JOHN SULLIVAN, by New York State Secretary of State, Frederick Cook, pp. 18-37.

    Jun-Oct 1779. Sullivan's expedition and Clinton's march.

"Diary of Major Erkuries Beatty, Paymaster of the Western Army." MAGAZINE OF AMERICAN HISTORY 1 (1877):175-179, 235-243, 309-315, 380-384, 432-438.

    1786-1787. Journey of the Western Army to Kentucky and Ohio; notes on Indian affairs, town and pioneer life; paymaster's travels to Philadelphia and New York on official business; return journey.

BEEKMAN, TJERCK   1222

"Journal of Lieutenant Tjerck Beekman, 1779, of the Military Expedition of Major John Sullivan against the Six Nations of Indians." MAGAZINE OF AMERICAN HISTORY 20 (1888):127-136.

    May-Sep 1779. Sullivan's expedition; Pennsylvania and New York.

BOWEN, EDWARD, b. 1755   1223

In THE HISTORY AND TRADITIONS OF MARBLEHEAD, by Samuel Roads, p. 391. Boston: Houghton, Osgood, 1880.

    Sep 1779-Feb 1780. Brief notes of weather and shipping at Marblehead, Massachusetts.

BOWMAN, JOSEPH, 1752-1782   1224

In GEORGE ROGERS CLARK PAPERS, 1771-1781, edited by James Alton James, pp. 155-164. Illinois Historical Society Collections, vol. 8. Springfield: Trustees of the Illinois State Historical Library, 1912.

In COL. GEORGE ROGERS CLARK'S SKETCH OF HIS CAMPAIGN IN THE ILLINOIS, introduction by Henry Pirtle, pp. 82-94. Cincinnati: R. Clarke, 1869.

    Jan-Mar 1779. News of capture of Vincennes and Clark's march on the post.

BURROWES, JOHN   1225

In JOURNALS OF THE MILITARY EXPEDITION OF MAJOR GENERAL JOHN SULLIVAN, by New York State Secretary of State, Frederick Cook, pp. 43-51.

    Aug-Oct 1779. Brief notes on Sullivan's expedition by a captain in Fifth New Jersey Regiment.

BUTLER, WALTER N., ca. 1750-1781   1226

Cruikshank, Ernest, ed. "The Journal of Captain Walter Butler." ROYAL CANADIAN INSTITUTE TRANSACTIONS 4 (1892-1893):279-283.

CANADIAN HISTORICAL REVIEW 1 (1920):386-391.

    Mar 1779. Military travel journal of American with British corps of rangers; march along northern shore of Lake Ontario from Niagara; brief topographical notes.

CALEF, JOHN, 1726-1812   1227

THE SIEGE OF PENOBSCOT BY THE REBELS. London: Printed for G. Kearsley, 1781. 55 pp. Reprint. New York: W. Abbatt, 1910; Goold, Nathan, ed. "The Siege of Penobscot by the Rebels." MAGAZINE OF HISTORY, extra no. 11, 3 (1910):303-321.

In HISTORY OF CASTINE, PENOBSCOT, AND BROOKSVILLE, MAINE, by George A. Wheeler, pp. 290-303. Bangor, Maine: Burr & Robinson, 1875.

    Jun-Aug 1779. British account of siege of Penobscot; notes written up as a journal.

CAMPFIELD, JABEZ   1228

"Diary of Dr. Jabez Campfield, Surgeon in 'Spencer's Regiment'." NEW JERSEY HISTORICAL SOCIETY PROCEEDINGS, 2d ser. 3 (1872-1874):115-136.

WYOMING COUNTY DEMOCRAT, 31 December 1873; 28 January 1874.

In JOURNALS OF THE MILITARY EXPEDITION OF MAJOR GENERAL JOHN SULLIVAN, by New York State Secretary of State, Frederick Cook, pp. 52-61.

    May-Oct 1779. Surgeon's military diary kept during Sullivan's expedition; descriptions of country and Indian towns; activities of Fifth New Jersey Regiment.

CRUGER, JOHN HARRIS   1229

"The Siege of Savannah." MAGAZINE OF AMERICAN HISTORY 2 (1878):489-492.

    Sep-Oct 1779. Brief account of the siege.

DONELSON, JOHN, 1718-1785   1230

In EARLY TRAVELS IN THE TENNESSEE COUNTRY, edited by Samuel C. Williams, pp. 233-242. Johnson City, Tenn.: Watauga, 1928.

In WHO'S WHO ON THE OHIO RIVER, by Ethel C. Leahy, pp. 21-27. Cincinnati: E.C. Leahy Pub. Co., 1931.

In THREE PIONEER TENNESSEE DOCUMENTS, pp. 1-10. Nashville: Tennessee State Historical Commission, 1964.

"Journal of a Voyage, Intended by God's Permission, in the Good Boat ADVENTURE, from Fort Patrick Henry on Holston River, to the French Salt Springs on Cumberland River." In THE ANNALS OF TENNESSEE TO THE END OF THE 18TH CENTURY, by James G.M. Ramsey, pp. 197-202. Charleston: Walker and James; Philadelphia: Lippincott, Grambo, 1853; Kingsport, Tenn.: Kingsport Press, 1926.

    Dec 1779-Apr 1780. Extracts from diary covering river voyage to north Alabama or Tennessee with a group of settlers; hazards of river travel, boat mishaps, Indian attacks, hunger, deaths.

Extracts in THE KEELBOAT AGE ON WESTERN WATERS, by Leland D. Baldwin, pp. 149-153. Pittsburgh: University of Pittsburgh Press, 1941.

    Mar 1780. Harrowing account of keelboat pioneers traveling the Holston, Tennessee, and Cumberland rivers; hunger, fatigue, battles with Indians, loss of people and boats in rapids.

ELD, GEORGE, d. 1793   1231

"Diary of Lieutenant-Colonel Eld." MASSACHUSETTS HISTORICAL SOCIETY PROCEEDINGS, 1st ser. 18 (1880-1881):69-79. Diary pp. 73-79.

May 1779–Mar 1780. Extracts from diary of member of the Coldstream Guards; activities of his regiment, especially in the Jerseys, and some personal notes.

FAIRLIE, JAMES   1232

In THE SULLIVAN-CLINTON CAMPAIGN IN 1779, by New York (State) State Historian, pp. 175–178. Albany: University of the State of New York, 1929.

Aug–Sep 1779. Sullivan's Indian expedition; brief notes of the campaign, kept by lieutenant in the Second New York Regiment.

FELLOWS, MOSES, 1755–1846   1233

In JOURNALS OF THE MILITARY EXPEDITION OF MAJOR GENERAL JOHN SULLIVAN, by New York State Secretary of State, Frederick Cook, pp. 86–91.

Jun–Sep 1779. Account of Sullivan's expedition.

FISHER, SAMUEL ROWLAND, 1745–1834   1234

"Journal of Samuel Rowland Fisher of Philadelphia." PENNSYLVANIA MAGAZINE OF HISTORY AND BIOGRAPHY 41 (1917):145–197, 274–333, 399–457.

Discussed in AMERICAN DIARY LITERATURE, edited by Steven E. Kagle, pp. 138–141.

1779–1781. Prison diary; trial for espionage, life in prison; good, substantial entries.

FLEMING, WILLIAM, 1729–1795   1235

In TRAVELS IN THE AMERICAN COLONIES, by Newton D. Mereness, pp. 619–655, 661–674.

Nov 1779–May 1780. Travel to Kentucky on commission to adjust land claims; notes on topography, natural history, trade; some personal details, illness, hunting, persons met, etc.

Jan–Apr 1783. Diary kept in Kentucky.

GOOKIN, DANIEL, 1756–1831   1236

"Revolutionary Journal of Daniel Gookin." NEW ENGLAND HISTORICAL AND GENEALOGICAL REGISTER 16 (1862):27–33.

In JOURNALS OF THE MILITARY EXPEDITION OF MAJOR GENERAL JOHN SULLIVAN, by New York State Secretary of State, Frederick Cook, pp. 102–106.

May–Sep 1779. Sullivan's expedition.

GORE, OBADIAH, 1744–1821   1237

Martin, Asa E., ed. "The Diary of Obadiah Gore in the Sullivan Expedition." WYOMING HISTORICAL AND GENEALOGICAL SOCIETY PROCEEDINGS AND COLLECTIONS 19 (1926):219–235.

In THE SULLIVAN-CLINTON CAMPAIGN IN 1779, by New York (State) State Historian, pp. 179–188. Albany: University of the State of New York, 1929.

Vail, R.W.G., ed. "Diary of Lieut. Obadiah Gore, Jr., in the Sullivan-Clinton Campaign." NEW YORK PUBLIC LIBRARY BULLETIN 33 (1929):711–742.

Jul–Sep 1779. Sullivan's expedition; march to Genesee River; military details and some notes on camp life.

GRANT, GEORGE   1238

"March of Sullivan's Army in 1779." HAZARD'S REGISTER 14 (1834):72 76.

In JOURNALS OF THE MILITARY EXPEDITION OF MAJOR GENERAL JOHN SULLIVAN, by New York State Secretary of State, Frederick Cook, pp. 107–114.

"Expedition against the Cayugas." CAYUGA COUNTY HISTORICAL SOCIETY COLLECTIONS 1 (1879):69–75. Diary extract pp. 73–75.

May–Dec 1779. Account of Sullivan's campaign, kept by member of Third New Jersey Regiment; Butler's march along Lake Cayuga.

GRANT, THOMAS   1239

"Gen. Sullivan's Expedition to the Genesee Country." HISTORICAL MAGAZINE 6 (1862):233–237, 273–276.

In JOURNALS OF THE MILITARY EXPEDITION OF MAJOR GENERAL JOHN SULLIVAN, by New York State Secretary of State, Frederick Cook, pp. 137–144.

"Expedition against the Cayugas." CAYUGA COUNTY HISTORICAL SOCIETY COLLECTIONS 1 (1879):69–75. Diary extract pp. 70–73.

Jul–Sep 1779. Surveyor's journal kept during Sullivan's expedition; surveying route from Easton, Pennsylvania, to Genesee River.

GREELE, THOMAS   1240

In HISTORY OF NEWBURYPORT, MASS., 1764–1909, by John J. Currier, vol. 1, pp. 631–632. Newburyport, Mass.: The author, 1906.

Mar–Jun 1779. Ship captain's very brief notes of cruise of the GENERAL ARNOLD; engagements with British ships.

HALSEY, ZEPHANIAH   1241

PATHFINDER MAGAZINE (Washington), September 8, 15, 22, 29, 1894.

1779–1782. Military journal kept by Zephaniah Halsey and Archibald Ramsey, quartermasters in charge of horses; New Jersey, Hudson River, New York, Yorktown, etc.

HARDENBURGH (or HARDENBERGH), JOHN L.   1242

"The Journal of Lieut. John L. Hardenbergh." CAYUGA COUNTY HISTORICAL SOCIETY COLLECTIONS 1 (1879): 7–59. Journal pp. 23–59.

In JOURNALS OF THE MILITARY EXPEDITION OF MAJOR GENERAL JOHN SULLIVAN, by New York State Secretary of State, Frederick Cook, pp. 116–136.

May–Oct 1779. Military details of Sullivan's expedition.

HARDY, JOSEPH   1243

In SETH HARDING, MARINER; A NAVAL PICTURE OF THE REVOLUTION, by James L. Howard, pp. 213–277. New Haven, Conn.: Yale University Press; London: H. Milford, Oxford University Press, 1930.

Dec 1779–Feb 1780. Military journal of captain in command of marines on frigate CONFEDERACY; cruise off New England coast; nautical, personal and social details.

HINRICHS, JOHANN   1244

In THE SIEGE OF CHARLESTON, translated and edited by Bernard A. Uhlendorf, pp. 104–363. Ann Arbor: University of Michigan Press, 1938. Reprint. New York: New York Times, 1968.

Dec 1779–Jun 1780. Military journal of engineer in

the Hessian Jäger Corps; voyage from New York to Georgia; some description of Georgia; expedition to South Carolina; landing in North Edisto; siege and reduction of Charleston; voyage to Phillipsburgh; descriptions and comments on South Carolina. Extracts from German text, with English translation.

HUBLEY, ADAM, 1740-1793   1245

Jordan, John W. "Adm Hubley, Jr., Lt Colo. Comdt 11th Penna Regt, His Journal." PENNSYLVANIA MAGAZINE OF HISTORY AND BIOGRAPHY 33 (1909):129-146, 279-302, 409-422. Reprint. Philadelphia: Printed by J.B. Lippincott, 1909. 57 pp.

> 1779. Military journal of lieutenant with Eleventh Pennsylvania Regiment; military notes and topography of Wyoming, Pennsylvania.

In HISTORY OF WYOMING, by Charles Miner, app., pp. 82-104. Philadelphia: J. Crissy, 1845.

In JOURNALS OF THE MILITARY EXPEDITION OF MAJOR GENERAL JOHN SULLIVAN, by New York Secretary of State, Frederick Cook, pp. 145-167.

In A NEW HAMPSHIRE LAWYER IN GENERAL WASHINGTON'S ARMY, by Oscar E. Rising, pp. 43-95. Geneva, N.Y.: W.F. Humphrey, 1915.

> Jul-Oct 1779. Journal of Sullivan's campaign.

LAWRENCE, WILLIAM, d. 1845   1246

In HISTORY OF CASTINE, PENOBSCOT, AND BROOKS-VILLE, MAINE, by George A. Wheeler, pp. 314-320. Bangor, Maine: Burr & Robinson, 1875.

> Jul-Aug 1779. Account of Penobscot expedition and siege of Majabiguaduce by soldier fighting on the British side.

LIVERMORE, DANIEL, 1749-1798   1247

"A Journal of the March of Gen. Poor's Brigade." NEW HAMPSHIRE HISTORICAL SOCIETY COLLECTIONS 6 (1850):308-335.

Extracts in JOURNALS OF THE MILITARY EXPEDITION OF MAJOR GENERAL JOHN SULLIVAN, by New York State Secretary of State, Frederick Cook, pp. 178-191.

> May-Dec 1779. Officer's account of Sullivan's campaign; military details, engagements; interesting spellings.

LOVELL, SOLOMON, 1732-1801   1248

In THE ORIGINAL JOURNAL OF GEN. SOLOMON LOVELL, by Gilbert Nash, pp. 93-105. Weymouth Historical Society Publications, no. 1. Boston: Weymouth Historical Society, 1881.

> Jul-Aug 1779. Penobscot expedition; notes on cruise and military details.

MACHIN, THOMAS   1249

"Journal of March from Fort Schuyler, Expedition against the Onondagas." MAGAZINE OF AMERICAN HISTORY 3 (1879):688-689.

In JOURNALS OF THE MILITARY EXPEDITION OF MAJOR GENERAL JOHN SULLIVAN, by New York State Secretary of State, Frederick Cook, pp. 192-194.

> Apr 1779. Van Schaick's expedition against the Onondagas; brief notes kept by a captain of the Second New York Artillery.

MCNEILL, SAMUEL, 1753-1817   1250

In PENNSYLVANIA ARCHIVES, 2d ser., vol. 15, pp. 753-759.

> Aug-Sep 1779. Sullivan's expedition; mostly an orderly book kept by quartermaster of Hand's brigade.

MANNING, JAMES, 1738-1791   1251

In LIFE, TIMES, AND CORRESPONDENCE OF JAMES MANNING, by Reuben A. Guild, pp. 266-286. Boston: Gould and Lincoln; New York: Sheldon, 1864.

> Apr-Sep 1779. Travel diary of Baptist clergyman, first president of Rhode Island College (Brown University); trip to New York, New Jersey, Philadelphia; observations on estates, taverns, scenery, crops, historical incidents, social and private matters; terse but copious.

MATHEW, GEORGE   1252

Balch, Thomas, ed. "Mathew's Narrative." HISTORICAL MAGAZINE 1 (1857):102-106.

> 1779-1781. Welshman's voyage to New York; notes on hardships of military life; account of the André-Arnold affair; monthly post facto entries.

MOODY, WILLIAM, 1756-1821   1253

Goold, Nathan. "Colonel Jonathan Mitchell's Cumberland County Regiment. Bagaduce Expedition." MAINE HISTORICAL SOCIETY COLLECTIONS, 2d ser. 10 (1899): 143-174. Diary, pp. 144-148.

> Jul-Aug 1779. Brief notes kept by a carpenter during the Bagaduce expedition; military details, movements, etc.

NORRIS, JAMES, 1739-1816   1254

"Major Norris' Journal of Sullivan's Expedition." BUFFALO HISTORICAL SOCIETY PUBLICATIONS 1 (1879): 217-252.

In JOURNALS OF THE MILITARY EXPEDITION OF MAJOR GENERAL JOHN SULLIVAN, by New York State Secretary of State, Frederick Cook, pp. 223-239.

> Jun-Oct 1779. Military journal of officer with the Third New Hampshire Regiment during Sullivan's expedition; long entries and good descriptions; some interesting spellings.

NOURSE, JAMES, 1758-1799   1255

Hammon, Neal O., ed. "The Journal of James Nourse, Jr." FILSON CLUB HISTORY QUARTERLY 47 (1973):258-266.

> Dec 1779-Feb 1780. Young Virginian's journey to Kentucky to acquire land; difficult travel by wagon and horseback along the Wilderness Road; camping and hunting, terrain, prospects for agriculture and settlement; extremely cold weather.

NUKERCK, CHARLES   1256

In JOURNALS OF THE MILITARY EXPEDITION OF MAJOR GENERAL JOHN SULLIVAN, by New York State Secretary of State, Frederick Cook, pp. 214-222.

> 1779-1780. Sullivan's expedition as recorded by an officer with the Second New York Regiment; campaign around Hudson River.

PAGE, SAMUEL, 1753–1814 1257

"Journal of Capt. Samuel Page, in the Campaign of 1779." ESSEX INSTITUTE HISTORICAL COLLECTIONS 4 (1862):241–249; 5 (1863):1–9.

Feb–Jun 1779. Military journal; details of camp life with Eleventh Massachusetts Regiment; orders, etc.

PARKER, ROBERT, d. 1788 1258

"Journal of Lieutenant Robert Parker, of the Second Continental Artillery." PENNSYLVANIA MAGAZINE OF HISTORY AND BIOGRAPHY 27 (1903):404–420; 28 (1904): 12–25.

In THE SULLIVAN-CLINTON CAMPAIGN IN 1779, by New York (State) State Historian, pp. 188–210. Albany: University of the State of New York, 1929.

Jun–Dec 1779. Military details of Sullivan's expedition; notes on scenery, camp life, etc.; a poem.

PITMAN, JOHN, 1751–1820 1259

Earle, Alice Morse. "A Baptist Preacher and Soldier of the Last Century." NEW ENGLAND MAGAZINE, n.s. 12 (1895):407–414.

1779–1822. Brief, but interesting, extracts from clergyman's diary; personal affairs, preaching tours, accidents, unusual sights at Providence, Rhode Island.

REIDHEAD, WILLIAM, 1757–1811 1260

Wardwell, Hosea B., ed. "William Reidhead's Journal." BANGOR HISTORICAL MAGAZINE 5 (1889–1890):226–231.

Jul–Aug 1779. The siege of Majabiguaduce and British defense; some linguistic interest.

ROBERTS, THOMAS 1261

In JOURNALS OF THE MILITARY EXPEDITION OF MAJOR GENERAL JOHN SULLIVAN, by New York State Secretary of State, Frederick Cook, pp. 240–245.

May–Sep 1779. Account of march from Elizabethtown and Sullivan's expedition by a soldier of the Fifth New Jersey Regiment.

RUSSELL, PETER, d. 1808 1262

Bain, James, Jr. "The Siege of Charleston: Journal of Capt. Peter Russell." AMERICAN HISTORICAL REVIEW 4 (1898–1899):478–501.

Dec 1779–May 1780. Siege of Charleston; mainly statistical and technical notes kept by officer with the British Sixty-fourth Foot Regiment.

RUSSELL, WILLIAM, 1748–1784 1263

In THE SHIPS AND SAILORS OF OLD SALEM, by Ralph D. Paine, pp. 124–174.

1779–1782. Prison diary kept in Old Mill Prison, England; an interesting record of prison life.

SCUDDER, WILLIAM 1264

JOURNAL OF WILLIAM SCUDDER. New York, 1794. 250 pp.

1779–1782. Prison diary; campaigns with New York Line; capture at Fort Stanwix; daily prison life in Canada.

SHUTE, SAMUEL MOORE 1265

In JOURNALS OF THE MILITARY EXPEDITION OF MAJOR GENERAL JOHN SULLIVAN, by New York State Secretary of State, Frederick Cook, pp. 267–274.

May–Nov 1779. Details of Sullivan's expedition, by officer of the Second New Jersey Regiment.

SMITH, DANIEL, 1748–1818 1266

Sioussat, St. George L., ed. "The Journal of Daniel Smith." TENNESSEE HISTORICAL MAGAZINE 1 (1915):40–65.

Aug 1779–Jul 1780. Surveying journal of member of commission running boundary line of Tennessee between North Carolina and Virginia, Tennessee and Kentucky; topographical notes of Tennessee-Cumberland region; some personal items.

SPROULE, MOSES, 1749–1819 1267

Vail, R.W.G., ed. "The Western Campaign of 1779: The Diary of Quartermaster Sergeant Moses Sproule." NEW YORK HISTORICAL SOCIETY QUARTERLY 41 (1957):35–69.

May–Oct 1779. New Jersey soldier's description of Sullivan's campaign against British and Iroquois on the northwest frontier of New York and Pennsylvania; military details; Indian torture of prisoners.

VAN HOVENBURGH, RUDOLPHUS 1268

In JOURNALS OF THE MILITARY EXPEDITION OF MAJOR GENERAL JOHN SULLIVAN, by New York State Secretary of State, Frederick Cook, pp. 275–284.

Jun–Dec 1779. Military journal kept on Sullivan's expedition and on march to Pompton, New Jersey, by member of the Fourth New York Regiment.

VON HUYN, JOHANN CHRISTOPH, 1720–1780 1269

In THE SIEGE OF CHARLESTON, translated and edited by Bernhard A. Uhlendorf, pp. 367–397. Ann Arbor: University of Michigan Press, 1938. Reprint. New York: New York Times, 1968.

Dec 1779–May 1780. Hessian military journal; expedition to South Carolina and siege of Charleston. German text with English translation.

ZIMMERMAN, HEINRICH 1270

ZIMMERMAN'S CAPTAIN COOK: AN ACCOUNT OF THE THIRD VOYAGE OF CAPTAIN COOK AROUND THE WORLD, 1776–1780. Translated by Elsa Michaelis and Cecil French, edited by F.W. Howay. Toronto: Ryerson Press, 1930. 120 pp. Hawaiian journal, pp. 85–98.

Jan–Feb 1779. Details of the murder and burial of Captain Cook in Hawaii.

1780

ANON. 1271

Nichols, James R., ed. "The Doughboy of 1780: Pages from a Revolutionary Diary." ATLANTIC MONTHLY 134 (1924):459–463.

Aug 1780–May 1781. Extracts from the diary of a common soldier; notes on patriotism, discipline, religion, personal items, camp life.

ANON. 1272

McCown, Mary Hardin. "A King's Mountain Diary." EAST TENNESSEE HISTORICAL SOCIETY PUBLICATIONS 14 (1942):102–105.

Sep–Oct 1780. Diary, probably of a British soldier, of events preceding battle of King's Mountain; fragmentary notes of retreat.

ALLAIRE, ANTHONY, 1755–1838 1273

In KING'S MOUNTAIN AND ITS HEROES: HISTORY OF THE BATTLE OF KING'S MOUNTAIN, by Lyman C. Draper, pp. 484–515. Cincinnati: P.G. Thomson, 1881.

Williams, Samuel C. "The Battle of King's Mountain: As Seen by British Officers." TENNESSEE HISTORICAL MAGAZINE 7 (1921):104–110.

DIARY OF LIEUT. ANTHONY ALLAIRE. New York: New York Times, 1968. 36 pp.

Mar–Nov 1780. British military journal; campaign in South Carolina; personal and military details; good, lively record with full entries.

ANDERSON, THOMAS 1274

"Journal of Lieutenant Thomas Anderson of the Delaware Regiment." HISTORICAL MAGAZINE, 2d ser. 1 (1867):207–211.

1780–1782. Extracts from military journal covering southern campaign; Delaware, Virginia, South Carolina; some interesting language.

BALDWIN, SAMUEL, b. 1754 1275

"Diary of Events in Charleston, S.C." NEW JERSEY HISTORICAL SOCIETY PROCEEDINGS 2 (1846–1847):77–86.

Mar–Apr 1780. Schoolmaster's diary of the siege of Charleston; mainly military details.

BERTHIER, LOUIS ALEXANDRE, 1753–1815 1276

In THE AMERICAN CAMPAIGNS OF ROCHAMBEAU'S ARMY, translated and edited by Howard C. Rice and Anne S.K. Brown, vol. 1, pp. 221–282. Princeton, N.J.: Princeton University Press, 1972.

1780–1783. Journal in the form of letters kept by Rochambeau's aide-de-camp; French activities at Newport; military plans and movements; personal matters; American customs and institutions; public buildings, hospitals, orphanages, porcelain factories and art galleries; notes on George Washington.

Morgan, Marshall, ed. "Alexandre Berthier's Journal of the American Campaign: The Rhode Island Sections." RHODE ISLAND HISTORY 24 (1965):77–88.

1780–1781.

BLANCHARD, CLAUDE, 1742–1802 1277

THE JOURNAL OF CLAUDE BLANCHARD, COMMISSARY OF THE FRENCH AUXILIARY ARMY SENT TO THE UNITED STATES DURING THE AMERICAN REVOLUTION. Translated by William Duane, edited by Thomas Balch. Albany: J. Munsell, 1876. 207 pp.

1780–1783. French military journal; military, social and political affairs during the Revolution; description of Washington and other outstanding figures; notes on American customs and characteristics; an interesting and important journal.

CARPENTER, JOHN 1278

In HISTORY OF BARNARD, VERMONT, WITH FAMILY GENEALOGIES, 1761–1927, by William M. Newton, vol. 2, pp. 71–72. Montpelier: Vermont Historical Society, 1928.

1780. Extracts from scouting journal; trip from Barnard through Middlesex, Brookfield, Deerfield and Northfield.

CASTRIES, ARMAND CHARLES AUGUSTIN DE LA CROIX, duc de, 1756–1842 1279

A MIDDLE PASSAGE; THE JOURNAL OF ARMAND-CHARLES AUGUSTIN DE LA CROIX DE CASTRIES, DUC DE CASTRIES, COMTE DE CHARLUS AND BARON CASTRIES. Edited by Sydney W. Jackman. Boston: The Boston Athenaeum, 1970. 113 pp.

Apr–Sep 1780. Atlantic crossing on the "troop ship" JASON of young French officer under Rochambeau, enroute to aid American colonial troops against the British; concern at poor equipment, outfitting of troops and lack of discipline; much about General Rochambeau and fellow officers; daily life on board ship, conversations, attitudes, quarrels; an interesting diary. Translated from the French.

Echeverria, Durand, ed. "The Iroquois Visit Rochambeau at Newport in 1780: Excerpts from the Unpublished Journal of the Comte de Charlus." RHODE ISLAND HISTORY 11 (1952):73–81.

Jul–Sep 1780. Extract regarding visit of Indian tribal representatives; French entertainments and diplomacy and Indian response; arrival of French army in Newport, reception by townspeople; meeting of Washington and Rochambeau.

CHASTELLUX, FRANCOIS JEAN, Marquis de, 1734–1788 1280

TRAVELS IN NORTH-AMERICA IN THE YEARS 1780, 1781 AND 1782 BY THE MARQUIS DE CHASTELLUX. Translated from the French by George Grieve. London: G.G.J. and J. Robinson, 1787. 2 vols. Reprint. New York: White, Gallaher & White, 1827; New York: A.M. Kelley, 1970.

TRAVELS IN NORTH AMERICA IN THE YEARS 1780, 1781 AND 1782 BY THE MARQUIS DE CHASTELLUX. A revised translation with introduction and notes by Howard C. Rice. Chapel Hill: Published for the Institute of Early American History and Culture at Williamsburg, Virginia, by the University of North Carolina Press, 1963. 2 vols. Diary, vol. 2, pp. 661–688.

Extracts in AMERICAN HISTORY TOLD BY CONTEMPORARIES, edited by Albert B. Hart, vol. 2, pp. 392–393, 495–497.

1780–1782. Diary of one of three major generals who accompanied French expeditionary forces to America; journeys between campaigns; views on America and American culture; major cities such as Newport, Philadelphia and Boston; the Moravian settlements at Hope and Bethlehem; travel accommodations; meetings with prominent American military and political figures.

CLERMONT-CREVECOEUR, JEAN FRANCOIS LOUIS, comte de, 1752–1824? 1281

In THE AMERICAN CAMPAIGNS OF ROCHAMBEAU'S ARMY, translated and edited by Howard C. Rice and Anne S.K. Brown, vol. 1, pp. 15–99. Princeton, N.J.: Princeton University Press, 1972.

1780–1783. French army officer's journal of trip from Brest on PLUVIER to Chesapeake Bay and

Newport; remarks on Indians, American customs, religion, especially Quakers and Presbyterians; political system, military operations, troop movements; Philadelphia and its cultural climate, Virginia society, Baltimore and Boston. Journal formerly erroneously attributed to Louis Jean Baptiste Sylvestre Robernier (or Robertnier).

CLINTON, Sir HENRY, 1730-1795   1282

Bulger, William T., ed. "Sir Henry Clinton's 'Journal of the Siege of Charleston, 1780.'" SOUTH CAROLINA HISTORICAL MAGAZINE 66 (1965):147-174.

    Apr-May 1780. Journal kept by commander of British forces laying siege to Charleston; progression of siege; alternative tactics considered and those pursued; Clinton's conflicts with Cornwallis, his second-in-command, and with Admiral Arbuthnot, commander-in-chief of the Royal Navy.

CLOSEN, LUDWIG, Baron von, b. ca. 1752-1830   1283

THE REVOLUTIONARY JOURNAL OF BARON LUDWIG VON CLOSEN, 1780-1783. Translated and edited by Evelyn M. Acomb. Chapel Hill: Published for the Institute of Early American History and Culture by the University of North Carolina Press, 1958. 392 pp.

    1780-1783. Detailed military journal with much written up later and incorporating other sources, kept by German-born officer fighting with French allies of American revolutionists; ocean crossings; observations on American ways, battles, siege of Yorktown; association with George Washington; travels from New England through southern colonies to West Indies.

Acomb, Evelyn M., ed. "The Journal of Baron Von Closen." WILLIAM AND MARY QUARTERLY, 3d ser. 10 (1953):196-236.

    1781-1782. Extract with minor deletions, covering the Yorktown campaign and its aftermath.

COWDREY, NATHANIEL, 1759-1841   1284

Moulton, Mary A. Stimpson, ed. "Nathaniel Cowdrey, of Reading, Mass." AMERICAN MONTHLY MAGAZINE 4 (1894):409-416.

    Jul-Dec 1780. Military journal kept at West Point and King's Ferry; bald military details; some bad verses; interesting spellings.

DE BRAHM   1285

In DOCUMENTARY HISTORY OF THE AMERICAN REVOLUTION, by Robert W. Gibbes, vol. 2, pp. 124-128.

    Feb-May 1780. French engineer's journal of the siege of Charleston; engineering and artillery notes. Translated.

DEUX-PONTS, GUILLAUME, comte de   1286

MY CAMPAIGNS IN AMERICA: A JOURNAL KEPT BY COUNT WILLIAM DE DEUX-PONTS. Translated from the French by Samuel A. Green. Boston: J.K. Wiggin & W.P. Lunt, 1868. 176 pp.

    1780-1781. French nobleman's military journal, kept mostly in New England; long description of revolutionary affairs. French text and English translation.

DROWNE, SOLOMON, 1753-1834   1287

JOURNAL OF A CRUISE IN THE FALL OF 1780 IN THE PRIVATE-SLOOP OF WAR, HOPE. With notes by Henry T. Drowne. New York: Printed by C.L. Moreau, 1872. 27 leaves.

"Dr. Solomon Drowne's Journal on the Privateer HOPE," by Maurice B. Gordon. In BOOK OF THE DESCENDANTS OF DR. BENJAMIN LEE AND DOROTHY GORDON, contributors, Gordon Philo Baker and others, pp. 95-125. Ventnor, N.J.: Ventnor Publishers, 1972.

Extracts in "Journal of a Cruise in the Fall of 1780," edited by Henry T. Drowne. RHODE ISLAND HISTORICAL MAGAZINE 5 (1884-1885):1-11.

Extracts in A HISTORY OF AMERICAN PRIVATEERS, by Edgar S. Maclay, pp. 167-176. New York: D. Appleton, 1924. Reprint. New York: Burt Franklin, 1968; Freeport, N.Y.: Books for Libraries, 1970.

Extracts in AMERICAN HISTORY TOLD BY CONTEMPORARIES, edited by Albert B. Hart, vol. 2, pp. 497-499.

    Oct 1780. Sea diary of young doctor on cruise from Providence on the privateer HOPE; weather, seasickness, capture of a British ship; lively, but flowery style; poetical quotations and literary effusions.

"Treaty at Fort Harmar." MAGAZINE OF AMERICAN HISTORY 9 (1883):285-286.

    Nov 1788-Jun 1789. Journal kept at Marietta, Ohio; description of ceremonies at Indian treaty of Fort Harmar.

GALVEZ, BERNARDO DE, 1746-1786   1288

YO SOLO: THE BATTLE JOURNAL OF BERNARDO DE GALVEZ DURING THE AMERICAN REVOLUTION. Translated by E.A. Montemayor, introduction by Eric Beerman. New Orleans: Polyanthos Press, 1978. 59 pp.

"Bernardo de Gálvez Diary of the Operations against Pensacola." LOUISIANA HISTORICAL QUARTERLY 1 (1917):44-84.

    Oct 1780-May 1781. Spanish commander's report of operations against British-held Pensacola; land and naval engagements; desertion of some British troops to Spanish side; graphic details of preparation for and storming of the fort.

Baker, Maury and Haas, Margaret B., eds. "Bernardo de Gálvez's Combat Diary for the Battle of Pensacola." FLORIDA HISTORICAL QUARTERLY 56 (1977):176-199.

    Mar-May 1781.

HAWES, MATTHIAS, 1754-1828   1289

In A HISTORY OF THE TOWN OF UNION, IN THE COUNTY OF LINCOLN, MAINE, by John L. Sibley, pp. 7, 50, 51, 58, 107, 161. Boston: R.B. Mussey, 1851.

    1780-1786. Extracts covering weather, personal items, local affairs.

HECKEWELDER, CHRISTIAN   1290

In TRAVELS IN THE AMERICAN COLONIES, by Newton D. Mereness, pp. 603-613.

    Oct 1780. Moravian travel journal; accompanying Bishop Reichel and his wife from Salem to Lititz. Authorship assumed.

HOPKINS, THOMAS   1291

"Journal of Thomas Hopkins of the Friendship Salt Company, New Jersey." PENNSYLVANIA MAGAZINE OF HISTORY AND BIOGRAPHY 42 (1918):46-61.

    Aug 1780. Brief business notes kept while author

was employed by the Friendship Salt Company; personal and war matters.

HUBLEY, JOHN   1292

In PENNSYLVANIA ARCHIVES, 1st ser., vol. 8, p. 401.

> Jul 1780. Extract giving statistics on volunteers from Pennsylvania.

KIRKWOOD, ROBERT, d. 1791   1293

THE JOURNAL AND ORDER BOOK OF CAPTAIN ROBERT KIRKWOOD OF THE DELAWARE REGIMENT OF THE CONTINENTAL LINE. Edited by Joseph Brown Turner. Historical Society of Delaware Papers, 56. Wilmington: Historical Society of Delaware, 1910. 277 pp. Reprint. Port Washington, N.Y.: Kennikat, 1970.

> 1780-1782. Service with Delaware Regiment in southern campaign; Charleston, Delaware, Maryland, Virginia, Carolinas; military details.

LEE, JESSE, 1758-1816   1294

MEMOIR OF THE REV. JESSE LEE. WITH EXTRACTS FROM HIS JOURNALS. By Minton Thrift. New York: N. Bangs and T. Mason, for the Methodist Episcopal Church, 1823. 360 pp. Reprint. New York: Arno, 1969.

> 1780-1815. Clergyman's diary; scattered notes of service in army and work as itinerant Methodist minister; forming Methodist societies in Connecticut, Maine, Massachusetts; travel and preaching notes.

MCCLELLAN, JOSEPH   1295

In PENNSYLVANIA ARCHIVES, 2d ser. vol. 11, pp. 599-614, 657-706, 707-762.

> 1780-1782 (with gaps). Military journal of officer with Ninth Pennsylvania Regiment; campaigns in New York and the South; revolt of the Pennsylvania Line. Most of last part kept by William Feltman.

MANIGAULT, GABRIEL, 1758-1809   1296

Crouse, Maurice A., ed. "Papers of Gabriel Manigault." SOUTH CAROLINA HISTORICAL MAGAZINE 64 (1963):1-12. Diary, pp. 8-12.

> 1780-1782. Diary extracts chiefly covering the siege of Charleston during which the diarist was a member of the defending forces.

MARTINEZ, FRANCISCO   1297

"Diary of Captain Martínez from Carrizal into Southern New Mexico and Return." In FORGOTTEN FRONTIERS: A STUDY OF THE SPANISH INDIAN POLICY OF DON JUAN BAUTISTA DE ANZA, translated and edited by Alfred B. Thomas, pp. 216-220. Norman: University of Oklahoma Press, 1932. Reprint. 1969.

> Nov 1780. Record of officer sent with troops to provide additional protection for the Anza expedition to Sonora; attacks on Indians.

"Diary of Captain Martínez Against the Gilas in Southern New Mexico." In FORGOTTEN FRONTIERS, pp. 279-285.

> Nov-Dec 1785. Trip from presidio of Janos to Carrizal to reconnoiter and subdue Gilas; route and encounter with Indians.

PENNINGTON, WILLIAM SANDFORD, 1757-1826   1298

Pennington, A.C.M., ed. "Our Camp Chest." MILITARY SERVICE INSTITUTION OF THE UNITED STATES JOURNAL 4 (1883):314-329.

Ellis, William A., ed. "The Diary of William Pennington." NEW JERSEY HISTORICAL SOCIETY PROCEEDINGS 63 (1945):199-218; 64 (1946):31-42, 109.

> May 1780-Mar 1781. Diary of officer of Second Continental Artillery under Knox; campaigns in New Jersey and New York; military and social notes.

PICKMAN, BENJAMIN, 1740-1819   1299

THE DIARY AND LETTERS OF BENJAMIN PICKMAN OF SALEM, MASSACHUSETTS. Newport, R.I., 1928. 230 pp. Diary, pp. 147-213.

> 1780-1818. Personal diary of New England merchant, begun during ten-year sojourn in England; sight-seeing and social activities in England; after return to Salem in 1785, brief, sporadic entries on social life, family and community news, deaths.

REICHEL, JOHANN FRIEDRICH   1300

In TRAVELS IN THE AMERICAN COLONIES, by Newton D. Mereness, pp. 586-599; RECORDS OF THE MORAVIANS IN NORTH CAROLINA, edited by Adelaide L. Fries, vol. 4, pp. 1893-1895.

> May-Oct 1780. Moravian travel journal; from Lititz to Salem and return; travel and religious notes.

SCUDDER, BENJAMIN, 1732-1822   1301

Hutchinson, Elmer T., ed. "Marginal Jottings from the Almanacs of the Scudder Family." NEW JERSEY HISTORICAL SOCIETY PROCEEDINGS 63 (1945):150-175, 219-236; 64 (1946):20-31, 100-109, 168-171, 219-225; 65 (1947):47-50, 104-107, 152-159, 198-209.

> 1780-1858. Almanac annotations begun by Benjamin Scudder of Springfield, New Jersey, and continued sporadically after his death by several members of his family; farm life and community events; births, marriages and deaths; entries after 1821 mainly of genealogical interest.

SEYMOUR, WILLIAM   1302

"A Journal of the Southern Expedition." PENNSYLVANIA MAGAZINE OF HISTORY AND BIOGRAPHY 7 (1883):286-298, 377-394.

A JOURNAL OF THE SOUTHERN EXPEDITION. Historical Society of Delaware Papers, 15. Wilmington: Historical Society of Delaware, 1896. 42 pp.

> 1780-1783. Military journal kept by officer of Delaware Regiment; southern campaign, New Jersey, North Carolina, South Carolina, Maryland.

SHERWOOD, JUSTUS, 1752-1836   1303

Wardner, H.S., ed. "Journal of a Loyalist Spy." VERMONTER 28 (1923):60-64, 76-82. Journal, pp. 76-81.

> Oct-Dec 1780. Account by Vermont Loyalist of mission to obtain Vermont's allegiance to Britain; meeting with Ethan Allen; return to Quebec.

SMITH, JOSIAH, 1731-1826   1304

Webber, Mabel L., ed. "Josiah Smith's Diary." SOUTH CAROLINA HISTORICAL AND GENEALOGICAL MAGAZINE 33 (1932):1-28, 79-116, 197-207, 281-289; 34 (1933):31-39, 67-84, 138-148, 194-210.

1780–1782. Prison diary of Charleston merchant; surrender of Charleston; life as a civilian on board prison ship; exile at St. Augustine; exchanged and sent to Philadelphia; a good diary.

TALLMADGE, SAMUEL, 1755–1825   1305

In ORDERLY BOOKS OF THE FOURTH NEW YORK REGIMENT, by New York Infantry, prepared for publication by Almon W. Lauber, pp. 739–785. Albany: University of the State of New York, 1932.

     1780–1782. Campaigns of the Fourth New York Regiment; mostly brief notes of military activities, weather, personal items; some poems.

VILDOSOLA, JOSEPH ANTONIO   1306

"Diary of Captain Vildosola from Nutrias into Southern Arizona and New Mexico and Return." In FORGOTTEN FRONTIERS: A STUDY OF THE SPANISH INDIAN POLICY OF DON JUAN BAUTISTA DE ANZA, translated and edited by Alfred B. Thomas, pp. 207–215. Norman: University of Oklahoma Press, 1932. Reprint. 1969.

     Nov–Dec 1780. Diary of commander at Las Nutrias assigned to provide Anza's Sonora expedition with additional protection from the Apaches; travel through Apache Territory to Sierra de las Mimbres; attacks upon Indians and looting of their goods at several rancherias.

WATERMAN, ZURIEL, 1756–1786   1307

Collins, Clarkson A., III, ed. "Captains Carousing in Providence." RHODE ISLAND HISTORY 21 (1962):136–137.

     Jan 1780. Detailed report by ship's surgeon of the "celebration" he and his shipmates enjoyed on their return to Providence from a cruise on the privateer ARGO; types, cost and amount of liquor consumed; search for amusements, entertainment, etc.

WEARE, JEREMIAH, 1757–1845   1308

"Diary of Jeremiah Weare, Jr. of York, Me." NEW ENGLAND HISTORICAL AND GENEALOGICAL REGISTER 55 (1901):55–58; 63 (1909):296–297; 64 (1910):180–182; 66 (1912):77–79, 155–160, 261–265, 311–315.

     1780–1817 (with gaps). Mostly notes on births, deaths, etc., with some general notes on weather, farming and personal affairs; interesting spellings.

WHEELER, WILLIAM, 1762–1845   1309

In BLACK ROCK, SEAPORT OF OLD FAIRFIELD, CONNECTICUT, 1644–1870, by Cornelia Penfield Lathrop, pp. 21–125. New Haven, Conn.: Tuttle, Morehouse & Taylor, 1930.

     1780–1844. Farmer's diary; experiences at Yale College and as school teacher in Connecticut; years of farming; many entries on births, marriages, illnesses, deaths; weather and harbor activities.

WILSON, JOHN   1310

Waring, Joseph I., ed. "Lieutenant John Wilson's 'Journal of the Siege of Charleston.'" SOUTH CAROLINA HISTORICAL MAGAZINE 66 (1965):175–182.

     Feb–May 1780. Officer's record of activities of the British Engineers, commanded by Captain James Moncrieff, during siege of Charleston.

1781

ANON.   1311

"Itinerary of the Pennsylvania Line from Pennsylvania to South Carolina." PENNSYLVANIA MAGAZINE OF HISTORY AND BIOGRAPHY 36 (1912):273–292.

     1781–1782. Itinerary kept by a soldier of Wayne's force; mostly bare details of marches and hardships.

ANON.   1312

"Journal of the Siege of York in Virginia." MAGAZINE OF AMERICAN HISTORY 4 (1880):449–452.

     Sep–Oct 1781. French engineer's journal of siege; tactical and statistical details; added to Cromot DuBourg's journal. Translated.

ANON.   1313

"Journal of the Siege of York in Virginia by a Chaplain in the American Army." MASSACHUSETTS HISTORICAL SOCIETY COLLECTIONS 9 (1804):102–108.

     Sep–Oct 1781. Chaplain's journal; journey from Elk River; siege of York; general military details; description of Williamsburg.

ALLEN, IRA, 1751–1814   1314

"Substance of What Passed, and Conversation with Colonel Ira Allen." VERMONT HISTORICAL SOCIETY COLLECTIONS 2 (1871):109–119.

     May 1781. Official journal; report of conference with British about union between Vermont and Canada.

"The Journal of Gen. Ira Allen." THE VERMONTER 10 (1904):207–212, 239–243.

     Dec 1795–Aug 1796. Journey to England; negotiations for trade treaty between Vermont and Canada.

ANDERSON, ISAAC, 1758–1839   1315

In PIONEER BIOGRAPHY; SKETCHES OF THE LIVES OF SOME OF THE EARLY SETTLERS OF BUTLER COUNTY, OHIO, by James McBride, vol. 1, pp. 278–285. Ohio Valley Historical Series, no. 4. Cincinnati: R. Clark, 1869.

"Journal of Lieut. Isaac Anderson." OHIO ARCHAEOLOGICAL AND HISTORICAL SOCIETY PUBLICATIONS 6 (1898):389–392.

In PENNSYLVANIA ARCHIVES, 2d ser., vol. 14, pp. 699–704.

     Aug 1781–Jul 1782. Mainly an account of Lochry's expedition into Ohio; Indian ambush; captivity; list of prisoners; bare details.

ATKINS, JOSIAH, d. 1781   1316

In THE TOWN AND CITY OF WATERBURY, CONNECTICUT, edited by Joseph Anderson, vol. 1, pp. 472–480. New Haven, Conn.: Price & Lee, 1896.

THE DIARY OF JOSIAH ATKINS, edited by Steven E. Kagle. New York: Arno Press, 1975. 64 pp.

Discussed in AMERICAN DIARY LITERATURE, by Steven E. Kagle, pp. 127–130.

     Jan–Oct 1781. Extracts from an interesting and detailed revolutionary war diary; enlistment, service in Philadelphia, New York and Maryland; discharge; criticism of Continental Army; comments on leaders, social and camp conditions and intersectional rivalries; poetical quotations.

BROWN, JOHN, 1724-1791   1317

In A NARRATIVE HISTORY OF THE TOWN OF COHASSET, MASSACHUSETTS, by Edgar V. Bigelow, p. 312. Boston: Press of S. Usher, 1898.

Oct-Dec 1781. Clergyman's brief notes, mainly personal and clerical items, funerals, etc.

CHURCHMAN, GEORGE, 1730-1814   1318

Cadbury, Henry J. "A Quaker Travelling in the Wake of War." NEW ENGLAND QUARTERLY 23 (1950):396-400.

May-Jul 1781. A few extracts within article; journal of Quaker living on Pennsylvania-Maryland border; trip to attend yearly meetings in New York and Rhode Island; difficult journey through the lines of the contending armies; destruction of war; Quaker peace testimony.

Cadbury, Henry J., ed. "An Off-Islander's Impressions." NANTUCKET HISTORICAL ASSOCIATION PROCEEDINGS, 56th annual meeting (1949):47-50.

Jun 1781. Maryland Quaker's account of visit to Nantucket; description of island and its inhabitants; tales illustrating the dangers of whaling.

CLIFFORD, ANNA RAWLE, 1758-1828   1319

In WEATHERING THE STORM, by Elizabeth Evans, pp. 290-298.

Feb-Oct 1781. Record of events in Philadelphia, kept for her Loyalist parents who had fled to New York; reading, French studies, gossip about social events; destruction of homes and possessions of suspected British sympathizers.

"A Loyalist's Account of Certain Occurrences in Philadelphia after Cornwallis's Surrender at Yorktown." PENNSYLVANIA MAGAZINE OF HISTORY AND BIOGRAPHY 16 (1892):103-107.

Oct 1781. Extracts describing wild rejoicing in Philadelphia after Cornwallis' surrender.

COBB, DAVID, 1748-1830   1320

"Before York Town, Virginia." MASSACHUSETTS HISTORICAL SOCIETY PROCEEDINGS 19 (1881-1882):67-72.

Oct-Nov 1781. Officer's account of Yorktown campaign; Maryland, Pennsylvania, New Jersey, New York; brief military notes.

In WILLIAM BINGHAM'S MAINE LANDS, 1790-1820, edited by Frederick S. Allis, vol. 1, pp. 386-499. Colonial Society of Massachusetts Publications, vol. 36. Boston: Colonial Society of Massachusetts, 1954.

Mar-Jun 1794. Term in Congress as a Federalist from Maine.

"Leaves from a Diary of General David Cobb, of Gouldsborough, Me., and Taunton, Mass." BANGOR HISTORICAL MAGAZINE 5 (1889-1890):49-57, 69-76, 116-120, 134-139.

1795-1797. Diary of social life in military and political circles; visits to Penobscot, Machias, Boston; many notes about building, farming and other work on his estate.

CROMOT DUBOURG, MARIE FRANCOIS JOSEPH   1321
MAXIME, baron, 1756-1836

"Diary of a French Officer." MAGAZINE OF AMERICAN HISTORY 4 (1880):205-214, 293-308, 376-385, 441-449.

Mar-Nov 1781. Diary of an aide to Rochambeau; voyage to America; travel in Rhode Island, Pennsylvania, New York and Maryland; interesting comments on people and places. Translated.

DAVIS, JOHN, d. 1827   1322

"The Yorktown Campaign." PENNSYLVANIA MAGAZINE OF HISTORY AND BIOGRAPHY 5 (1881):290-311.

"Diary of Capt. John Davis, of the Pennsylvania Line." VIRGINIA MAGAZINE OF HISTORY AND BIOGRAPHY 1 (1893):2-16.

May 1781-Jan 1782. Diary of officer in First Pennsylvania Regiment; service in Pennsylvania and at siege of Yorktown.

DE LANCEY, OLIVER, 1749-1822   1323

"Oliver De Lancy's Journal of the Pennsylvania Mutiny." In MUTINY IN JANUARY: THE STORY OF A CRISIS IN THE CONTINENTAL ARMY, by Carl Van Doren, pp. 243-249. New York: Viking, 1943.

Jan 1781. Account by Clinton's chief of secret service of messages received regarding mutiny of Pennsylvania army; soldiers' demands for back pay, clothing and provisions.

DENNY, EBENEZER, 1761-1822   1324

MILITARY JOURNAL OF MAJOR EBENEZER DENNY, AN OFFICER IN THE REVOLUTIONARY AND INDIAN WARS. With an introductory memoir by W.H. Denny. Philadelphia: Historical Society of Pennsylvania, 1859. 288 pp. Reprint. New York: New York Times, 1971.

Denny, William H. "Military Journal of Major Ebenezer Denny, an Officer in the Revolutionary and Indian Wars." PENNSYLVANIA HISTORICAL SOCIETY MEMOIRS 7 (1860):237-257.

1781-1783. Service with Fourth Pennsylvania Regiment; Yorktown campaign; southern campaign.

Meek, Basil, ed. "General Harmar's Expedition." OHIO ARCHAEOLOGICAL AND HISTORICAL SOCIETY PUBLICATIONS 20 (1911):74-108. Journal, pp. 102-108.

Jul-Oct 1791. Military letter-journal; report to Major General Butler, president of Court of Inquiry, concerning Harmar's unsuccessful expedition against Indians in Ohio country; careful analysis and valuable account.

DOEHLA, JOHANN CONRAD, 1750-1820   1325

Tilden, Robert J., trans. and ed. "The Doehla Journal." WILLIAM AND MARY COLLEGE QUARTERLY, 2d ser. 22 (1942):229-274.

Jan-Dec 1781. German soldier's rank-and-file view of the British campaign culminating at Yorktown; general war news; camp life in New York and Chesapeake Bay area; siege and surrender of Yorktown; march of prisoners to Winchester, Virginia, and conditions there; a readable and interesting account with historical inaccuracies (dates, numbers of troops) corrected in footnotes.

DUNCAN, JAMES, 1756-1844   1326

In NOTES AND QUERIES, edited by William H. Egle, ser. 3, vol. 3, pp. 368-372, 376-380.

In OLD NORTHWEST GENEALOGICAL QUARTERLY 7 (1904): 152-159.

Boogher, W.F., ed. "Captain James Duncan's Diary of the Siege of Yorktown." MAGAZINE OF HISTORY 2 (1905):408-416.

"Diary of Captain James Duncan, of Colonel Moses Hazen's Regiment, in the Yorktown Campaign," in PENNSYLVANIA ARCHIVES, 2d ser., vol. 15, pp. 743-752.

> Oct 1781. Military officer's account of the siege of Yorktown; army movements, firing, etc.

Phillips, Stephen and Phillips, James Duncan, eds. "Journal Kept by James Duncan, Jr. of Haverhill, Mass., while on a Journey to Gilmanton, Warren, Haverhill and Lebanon, N.H." ESSEX INSTITUTE HISTORICAL COLLECTIONS 79 (1943):1-18.

> Oct-Nov 1806. Travel journal of merchant's business trip; settlement of business affairs and land holdings after his brother's death; travel conditions and business practices of the time.

FARMAR, ROBERT ADOLPHUS, d. 1804   1327

"The Siege of Pensacola in 1781." HISTORICAL MAGAZINE 4 (1860):166-172.

In A HISTORY OF THOMAS AND ANNE BILLOPP FARMAR, by Charles F. Billopp, pp. 110-114. New York: Grafton Press, 1907.

Padgett, James A., ed. "Bernardo de Galvez's Siege of Pensacola in 1781." LOUISIANA HISTORICAL QUARTERLY 26 (1943):311-329.

> Mar-Jun 1781. Loyalist military journal; service with Sixth Regiment of Royal Americans; fall of Pensacola; military and naval actions; graphic and detailed account.

FELTMAN, WILLIAM   1328

THE JOURNAL OF LIEUT. WILLIAM FELTMAN, OF THE FIRST PENNSYLVANIA REGIMENT. Philadelphia: Published for the Historical Society of Pennsylvania by H.C. Baird, 1853. 48 pp.

"The Journal of Lieut. William Feltman of the First Pennsylvania Regiment." PENNSYLVANIA HISTORICAL SOCIETY COLLECTIONS 1 (1853):303-348.

In PENNSYLVANIA ARCHIVES, 2d ser., vol. 11, pp. 707-762.

> May 1781-Apr 1782. Journey from Pennsylvania to siege of Yorktown; southern campaign.

AMERICAN HISTORICAL RECORD 1 (1872):254-256.

> Oct 1781. Extract concerning battle of Yorktown.

GALLATIN, GASPARD GABRIEL DE, 1758-1838   1329

JOURNAL OF THE SIEGE OF YORK-TOWN IN 1781 OPERATED BY THE GENERAL STAFF OF THE FRENCH ARMY. Translated by the French Department of the College of William and Mary. 71st Congress, 3rd Session, Senate Document, No. 322. Washington: Government Printing Office, 1931. 48 pp.

> Oct 1781. Account by Swiss nobleman in Rochambeau's first brigade; day-by-day work in the trenches; fortifications, daily casualties, troops and property captured; text of terms of surrender and Washington's general order congratulating the army. Translated from the French.

HARROW, ALEXANDER   1330

"Visits to the Shipyard." BURTON HISTORICAL COLLECTION LEAFLET 2 (1924):26-29.

> Aug-Nov 1781. Extracts from the journal of the captain of ANGELICA and DUNMORE: visits to the king's shipyard at Detroit.

JOHNSON, THOMAS, 1742-1819   1331

In HISTORY OF NEWBURY, VERMONT, by Frederic P. Wells, pp. 384-393.

> Mar-Oct 1781. Prison diary; capture and imprisonment in Canada; release and journey home; interesting brief notes.

MCDOWELL, WILLIAM   1332

In PENNSYLVANIA ARCHIVES, 2d ser., vol. 15, pp. 297-340.

> 1781-1782. Southern campaign and siege of Yorktown by an officer in the First Pennsylvania Regiment; notes of distances.

MATHIS, SAMUEL, 1760-1823   1333

In HISTORIC CAMDEN, by Thomas J. Kirkland and Robert M. Kennedy, vol. 1, pp. 400-403. Columbia, S.C.: The State Co., 1905.

> Mar-Aug 1781. Brief notes of public and private affairs at Camden, South Carolina; campaign with Colonel Marion.

MENONVILLE, M. DE   1334

"Journal of the Siege of York." MAGAZINE OF AMERICAN HISTORY 7 (1881):283-288.

> Oct 1781. Brief notes on tactics and statistics of the siege; added to Cromot Du Bourg's journal. Translated.

MIRANDA, FRANCISCO DE, 1750-1816   1335

Worcester, Donald E., trans. "Miranda's Diary of the Siege of Pensacola." FLORIDA HISTORICAL QUARTERLY 29 (1951):163-196.

> Apr-May 1781. Officer's account of Spanish siege and capture of British forts at Pensacola; tactics and maneuvers during sailing of fleet from Havana; problems with cumbersome ships and unskilled seamen; digging trenches; almost continuous bombardment on both sides; references to commander Bernardo de Gálvez.

THE NEW DEMOCRACY IN AMERICA: TRAVELS OF FRANCISCO DE MIRANDA IN THE UNITED STATES. Translated by Judson P. Wood, edited by John S. Ezell. Norman: University of Oklahoma Press, 1963. 213 pp.

FRAGMENTS FROM AN XVIIITH CENTURY DIARY: THE TRAVELS AND ADVENTURES OF DON FRANCISCO DE MIRANDA. Compiled and translated by Jordan H. Stabler. Caracas: Tipografia La Nación, 1931. 196 pp.

> 1783-1784. Diary of cosmopolitan Venezuelan, early instigator of movement toward independence from Spain, world traveler, and fascinated observer of American democracy, life and institutions; travels from Carolinas to New Hampshire; visits to major American cities where he met and commented upon almost everyone of intellectual or political importance; a charming and informative diary somewhat in de Tocqueville manner.

Riaño, Juan de, trans. "A Spaniard's Visit to Newport in 1784." NEWPORT HISTORICAL SOCIETY BULLETIN, no. 85 (1932):1–15.

Schuller, Rudolf, trans. "The Sojourn of Francisco de Miranda in Massachusetts and New Hampshire." OLD-TIME NEW ENGLAND 26 (1935):3–17, 41–54.

> 1784. Descriptions of New England people, institutions and mores; travel by stage and on horseback between Boston and Portsmouth, New Hampshire.

MORRIS, ROBERT, 1734–1806   **1336**

THE PAPERS OF ROBERT MORRIS. Edited by E. James Ferguson. Pittsburgh: University of Pittsburgh Press, 1973–(in progress).

Schnappes, Morris U. "Excerpts from Robert Morris' Diaries in the Office of Finance, 1781–1784, Referring to Haym Salomon and Other Jews." AMERICAN JEWISH HISTORICAL QUARTERLY 67 (1977):9–49, 140–161.

> 1781–1784. Diaries contained within the extensive papers of wealthy Philadelphia merchant, leading revolutionary war figure, member of Continental Congress and superintendent of finance; wide ranging financial activities for the war effort and operation of government; procurement of food, supplies, ships, etc; dealings with Benjamin Franklin, John Jay, George Washington; negotiations with foreign governments; diary obviously essential to Morris' keeping track of his own staggeringly varied and complex activities and responsibilities.

ROBIN, CLAUDE C., b. ca. 1750   **1337**

NEW TRAVELS THROUGH NORTH-AMERICA. Translated by Philip M. Freneau. Philadelphia: Printed and sold by Robert Bell, 1783. 112 pp. Boston: Printed by E.E. Powars and N. Willis for F. Battelle, 1784. 95 pp.

Extracts in "Journal of Abbé Robin, Chaplain of Count Rochambeau's Army," by George W. Nesmith. GRANITE MONTHLY 4 (1881):424–428.

Extracts in TRAVELS IN VIRGINIA IN REVOLUTIONARY TIMES, edited by Alfred J. Morrison, pp. 31–37. Lynchburg, Va.: J.P. Bell, 1922.

> Jun–Nov 1781. Letter-diary of chaplain to the French army in America; campaign from Rhode Island to Virginia; travel in Rhode Island, Connecticut, Pennsylvania, Maryland, Virginia; details about American troops and domestic life in Connecticut.

SANDERSON, REUBEN, 1755–1822   **1338**

In THE YORKTOWN CAMPAIGN AND THE SURRENDER OF CORNWALLIS, by Henry P. Johnston, pp. 170–173. New York: Harper & Brothers, 1881.

> Jul–Dec 1781. Extracts covering camp life and march from Hudson River to Yorktown and return.

SHUTE, DANIEL, 1756–1829   **1339**

"The Journal of Dr. Daniel Shute, Surgeon in the Revolution." NEW ENGLAND HISTORICAL AND GENEALOGICAL REGISTER 84 (1930):383–389.

> Aug 1781–Apr 1782. Brief notes, mainly about his movements with the army.

TILDEN, JOHN BELL, 1761–1838   **1340**

"Extracts from the Journal of Lieutenant John Bell Tilden, Second Pennsylvania Line." PENNSYLVANIA MAGAZINE OF HISTORY AND BIOGRAPHY 19 (1895):51–63, 208–233.

> 1781–1782. Journal of young soldier with the Second Pennsylvania Regiment; southern campaign, Virginia, Yorktown, North and South Carolina, Maryland, Pennsylvania.

TRUMBULL, JONATHAN, 1710–1785   **1341**

In LIFE OF JONATHAN TRUMBULL, SEN., GOVERNOR OF CONNECTICUT, by Isaac W. Stuart, pp. 528–562 passim. Boston: Crocker and Brewster, 1859.

> 1781–1782. Extracts; scattered brief notes; consultation with Washington; journey to Danbury with his family; war news; work at Assembly.

TRUMBULL, JOHATHAN, 1740–1809   **1342**

"Minutes of Occurrences Respecting the Siege and Capture of York in Virginia, Extracted from the Journal of Colonel Jonathan Trumbull, Secretary to the General." MASSACHUSETTS HISTORICAL SOCIETY PROCEEDINGS 14 (1875–1876):331–338.

> Aug–Oct 1781. Almost daily record kept by Washington's private secretary; movements of Washington and his troops preparing to confront the British at Yorktown; the siege; surrender of Cornwallis.

VERGER, JEAN BAPTISTE ANTOINE DE, 1762–1851   **1343**

In THE AMERICAN CAMPAIGNS OF ROCHAMBEAU'S ARMY, translated and edited by Howard C. Rice and Anne S.K. Brown, vol. 1, pp. 117–188. Princeton, N.J.: Princeton University Press, 1972.

> 1781–1784. Journal of young officer in Royal Deux-Ponts Regiment; travel aboard the COMTESSE DE NOAILLES; notes of troop movements, conditions and battles, particularly battle of Yorktown; descriptions of Chesapeake Bay, Newport, Jamestown, Baltimore, etc.; comments on Indians.

WIDGER, WILLIAM, 1748–1823   **1344**

"Diary of William Widger of Marblehead, Kept at Mill Prison." ESSEX INSTITUTE HISTORICAL COLLECTIONS 73 (1937):311–347; 74 (1938):142–158.

> Jan–Dec 1781. Seaman's prison diary kept at Old Mill Prison, England; notes on food, escapes, news from home, etc.; interesting language.

1782

ANON.   **1345**

Paltsits, Victor H., ed. "Journal of an Irishman in New York at the Close of the American Revolution." NEW YORK PUBLIC LIBRARY BULLETIN 27 (1923):891–895.

> Oct 1782–Feb 1783. Scattered but interesting notes on voyage to America; touristic comments on New York City, its people and social amenities.

BALDWIN, SIMEON, 1761–1851   **1346**

Baldwin, Simeon E., ed. "A Young Man's Journal of a Hundred Years Ago." NEW HAVEN COLONY HISTORICAL SOCIETY PAPERS 4 (1888):193–208.

Extracts in LIFE AND LETTERS OF SIMEON BALDWIN, by Simeon E. Baldwin, pp. 22–231 passim. New Haven, Conn.: Tuttle, Morehouse & Taylor, 1918.

> 1782–1785. Journey of a recent Yale graduate to Albany to take up teaching post; picture of Albany

and its inhabitants, Dutch customs, social life; tutoring at Yale; reading, taverns, journeys; an interesting diary.

FAIRBANKS, JOHN, 1755–1796   1347

Harris, Herbert, ed. "John Fairbanks--His Journal." MAINE HISTORICAL SOCIETY COLLECTIONS, 2d ser. 6 (1895):139–144.

> Jul–Sep 1782. Movements and engagements of the privateer WASP off coast of Maine; interesting linguistically.

INMAN, GEORGE, 1755–1789   1348

Gozzaldi, Mrs. S.M. "Lieutenant George Inman." CAMBRIDGE HISTORICAL SOCIETY PUBLICATIONS 19 (1926): 46–79. Diary, pp. 61–77.

> 1782–1789. Extracts from diary of a Tory; life in Massachusetts after the Revolution.

JAY, JOHN, 1745–1829   1349

THE DIARY OF JOHN JAY DURING THE PEACE NEGOTIATIONS OF 1782. With an introduction by Frank Monaghan. New Haven: Printed at the Bibliographical Press, 1934. 17 pp.

> Jun–Dec 1782. Diplomatic diary kept during the peace negotiations in Paris.

ORR, LUCINDA LEE   1350

JOURNAL OF A YOUNG LADY OF VIRGINIA. Baltimore: J. Murphy, 1871. 56 pp. Reprint. Richmond: Whittet and Shepperson, 1976.

Extracts in AMERICAN HISTORY TOLD BY CONTEMPORARIES, edited by Albert B. Hart, vol. 3, pp. 27–31.

> Sep–Nov 1782. Journal kept on a visit to relatives, the Lees, the Washingtons, and other families of lower Virginia; daily rounds of walks, rides, teas, parties, dances, visitors and dressing for each; constant praise of friendship; descriptions of relatives and friends; reading.

RIDLEY, MATTHEW, b. ca. 1749   1351

Klingelhofer, Herbert E., ed. "Matthew Ridley's Diary during the Peace Negotiations of 1782." WILLIAM AND MARY QUARTERLY, 3d ser. 20 (1963):95–133.

> Aug–Dec 1782. Personal diary covering negotiations leading up to the signing of the Treaty of Paris; detailed account of developments kept while diarist, who was well acquainted with Adams, Jay and Franklin, was in Europe to procure loans and supplies for Maryland.

ROSENTHAL, Baron ("John Rose"), d. ca. 1830   1352

"Journal of a Volunteer Expedition to Sandusky." PENNSYLVANIA MAGAZINE OF HISTORY AND BIOGRAPHY 18 (1894):129–157, 293–328.

> May–Jun 1782. Account of an unfortunate military expedition to Sandusky.

SCATTERGOOD, THOMAS, 1748–1814   1353

"Memoirs of the Life and Religious Labours of Thomas Scattergood." FRIENDS' LIBRARY 8 (1844):1–225.

> 1782–1813. Extracts of Quaker journal; notes of experiences, travels and work in most of the Quaker settlements in New England and the Atlantic and southern states; journey to England and

Scotland; a good deal of personal and social matter, with some literary allusions to Cowper, etc.

SMITH, JOHN COTTON   1354

"Diary of John Cotton Smith While a Student at Yale." CONNECTICUT HISTORICAL SOCIETY BULLETIN 19 (1954): 26–28.

> Nov 1782. Extracts from student's diary; opinions and feelings about his reading, instrumental music, and certain young ladies.

THOMAS, ISAIAH, 1749–1831   1355

Nichols, Charles L., ed. "Extracts from the Diaries and Accounts of Isaiah Thomas from the Year 1782 to 1804 and His Diary for 1808." AMERICAN ANTIQUARIAN SOCIETY PROCEEDINGS, n.s. 26 (1916):58–79.

> 1782–1804, 1808. Mostly notes of expenses.

THE DIARY OF ISAIAH THOMAS. Edited by Benjamin T. Hill. American Antiquarian Society Transactions and Collections, vol. 9–10. Worcester, Mass.: American Antiquarian Society, 1909. 2 vols.

> 1805–1828 (with gap 1808 and a few notes 1796–1797). Extensive notes on social and domestic life and local affairs at Worcester, Massachusetts; clubs and societies; journeys in New England; scholarly and antiquarian interests.

WALTERS, MICHAEL, 1760–1818   1356

MacLean, J.P., ed. "Journal of Michael Walters." WESTERN RESERVE HISTORICAL SOCIETY TRACTS, no. 89 (1899), pp. 177–188.

> May–Oct 1782. Sandusky expedition; capture by Indians; only brief notes of distances.

1783

BRONSON, ISAAC, 1761–1845   1357

Extracts in HISTORY OF THE TOWN OF WOLCOTT (CONNECTICUT), by Samuel Orcutt, pp. 289–291. Waterbury, Conn.: Press of the American Printing Co., 1874.

> 1783–1802. Deacon's religious diary; introspections; some original hymns and poems.

CHIPMAN, WARD, 1754–1824   1358

Berry, Joseph B., ed. "Ward Chipman Diary: A Loyalist's Return to New England." ESSEX INSTITUTE HISTORICAL COLLECTIONS 87 (1951):211–241.

> Sep–Oct 1783. Diary of Loyalist's round trip from New York to Boston, Salem and Marblehead, for reunion with family and friends before leaving for England; lively account of problems of travel; bad roads, indifferent accommodations; breakdowns of horses and vehicles; Loyalists' fears and their treatment in communities through which they passed.

CONSTANT, SILAS, 1750–1825   1359

THE JOURNAL OF THE REVEREND SILAS CONSTANT, PASTOR OF THE PRESBYTERIAN CHURCH AT YORKTOWN, NEW YORK. By Emily W. Roebling, edited by Josiah G. Leach. Philadelphia: Printed for private circulation by J.B. Lippincott, 1903. 561 pp.

> 1783–1801. Clergyman's journal; notes of religious work, personal and parish matters, chiefly at Blooming Grove, New York.

FRANCIS, JOHN, 1763-1796   1360

Skillin, Glenn B., ed. "In Search of Cahoone, the 1790 Diary of John Francis." OLD-TIME NEW ENGLAND 60 (1969):55-71.

> 1783-1792. Account of a business trip from Providence to Boston and on to what is now Dummerston, Vermont, in September, 1790; business affairs; accommodations, towns along route, and colorful characters encountered; very brief extracts from diaries before and after this event.

FROST, SARAH, 1754-1817   1361

In THE FROST GENEALOGY, by Josephine C. Frost, pp. 396-397. New York: F.H. Hitchcock, 1912.

> May-Jun 1783. Loyalist journal of voyage to Nova Scotia aboard the TWO SISTERS; hardships.

HALLOCK, JEREMIAH, 1758-1826   1362

In THE GODLY PASTOR: LIFE OF THE REV. JEREMIAH HALLOCK, OF CANTON, CONN., by Cyrus Yale, pp. 31-301 passim. New York and Boston: American Tract Society, 1854?

> 1783-1826. Clergyman's diary; personal reflections and social affairs; two missions to Vermont; visits, sermons, prayers, fasting, reading.

HEATH, BETSEY, 1769-1853   1363

In THE CRAFTS FAMILY, compiled by James M. Crafts and William F. Crafts, pp. 694-699. Northampton, Mass.: Gazette Printing Co., 1893.

> May-Dec 1783, Dec 1790-Jan 1791. Entertaining diary of family, social and personal affairs; parties, dresses, meals, junketings; celebrations at her brother's wedding.

KOEHLER, JOHN DANIEL   1364

In RECORDS OF THE MORAVIANS IN NORTH CAROLINA, edited by Adelaide L. Fries, vol. 5, pp. 1964-1975.

> Sep 1783-Jun 1784. Moravian travel diary; a short account of the voyage from Amsterdam to America and shipwreck of the SINGLE BRETHREN; storm, shipwreck off West Indies, refuge in Barbados; journey to Philadelphia, Wilmington and Bethlehem.

LEWIS, JOSEPH   1365

"Diary or Memorandum Book Kept by Joseph Lewis of Morristown." NEW JERSEY HISTORICAL SOCIETY PROCEEDINGS 59 (1941):155-173, 263-282; 60 (1942):58-66, 124-137, 199-209, 254-269; 61 (1943):47-56, 115-129, 194-200; 62 (1944):35-53, 106-117, 167-180, 217-236.

> 1783-1795. Notes of business, legal and farming affairs at Morristown, New Jersey; some comments on weather, social and family matters.

LIVINGSTON, ANNE HOME SHIPPEN, 1763-1841   1366

NANCY SHIPPEN, HER JOURNAL BOOK: THE INTERNATIONAL ROMANCE OF A YOUNG LADY OF FASHION OF COLONIAL PHILADELPHIA. Compiled and edited by Ethel M. Armes. Philadelphia and London: J.B. Lippincott, 1935. 348 pp. Reprint. New York: B. Blom, 1968.

Discussed in AMERICAN DIARY LITERATURE, by Steven E. Kagle, pp. 92-97.

> 1783-1791 (with gaps). Excellent lively record of social life, romances and tragic marriage of a belle of Philadelphia; tyranny of first her father and then her husband; grief over separation from her child.

MACAULAY, ALEXANDER, d. 1798   1367

"Journal of Alexander Macaulay." WILLIAM AND MARY COLLEGE QUARTERLY, 1st ser. 11 (1902-1903):180-191.

> Feb-Mar 1783. Private diary kept at Yorktown, Virginia; an interesting, flippant account of life in the South.

MCCULLY, GEORGE, d. 1793   1368

Burton, Clarence M. "Ephraim Douglas and His Times, a Fragment of History, with the Journal of George McCully." MAGAZINE OF HISTORY, extra no. 10, 3 (1910):214-288. Journal, pp. 253-263.

> Jun-Jul 1783. Journal fragment showing itinerary of Ephraim Douglas to Detroit; council with Indians.

SCHNEIDER, MARTIN, 1756-1806   1369

In EARLY TRAVELS IN THE TENNESSEE COUNTRY, by Samuel C. Williams, pp. 250-265.

In RECORDS OF THE MORAVIANS IN NORTH CAROLINA, edited by Adelaide L. Fries, vol. 5, pp. 1976-1988.

> Dec 1783-Jan 1784. Moravian travel journal; to the Upper Cherokee towns on the Tennessee River; notes on travel difficulties, companions, religion, Indians and their customs.

SCHOEPF, JOHANN DAVID, 1752-1800   1370

TRAVELS IN THE CONFEDERATION. Translated and edited by Alfred J. Morrison. Philadelphia: W.J. Campbell, 1911. 2 vols.

> 1783-1784. Travel in the Confederation as far as Pittsburgh and thence to Florida; narrative and scenery notes. Translated from the German.

SMITH, JAMES, 1757-1800   1371

Morrow, Josiah, ed. "Tours into Kentucky and the Northwest Territory; Three Journals by the Rev. James Smith of Powhatan County, Va." OHIO ARCHAEOLOGICAL AND HISTORICAL QUARTERLY 16 (1907):348-401.

> Oct-Dec 1783. Travel from Powhatan County to Kentucky with his brother George; notes on scenery, hazards, sickness, disappointment over Kentucky, antislavery sentiment.

> Oct-Dec 1795. Through Kentucky and the Old Northwest; Gallipolis, Blue Licks, Lexington, Cincinnati, Great Miami, Frankfort, Cumberland Gap; many notes on scenery and natural phenomena; some character sketches and interesting details of minor adventures.

> Aug-Nov 1797. Pleasant descriptions of travel into Kentucky and the Old Northwest; Ohio, Plainfield, Little Miami, Columbia, Chillicothe, Deerfield, Lexington.

1784

ANON.   1372

Woodhouse, Samuel W., Jr., ed. "Log and Journal of the Ship UNITED STATES on a Voyage to China in 1784." PENNSYLVANIA MAGAZINE OF HISTORY AND BIOGRAPHY 55 (1931):255-258.

Snyder, James W., Jr., ed. "The First American Voyage to India, Being Excerpts from the Log of the Ship UNITED STATES from Philadelphia to Pondicherry." AMERICANA 32 (1938):284-304.

> Mar-Sep 1784. Voyage of UNITED STATES under Captain Thomas Bell from Philadelphia to India and China; descriptions of Sumatra, Pondicherry, etc.; natural history; more general notes than in usual log entries.

ADAMS, ABIGAIL, 1765-1813   1373

JOURNAL AND CORRESPONDENCE OF MISS ADAMS. Edited by her daughter. New York: Wiley and Putnam, 1841. 247 pp. Journal, pp. 1-96.

Extracts in AN AUTOBIOGRAPHY OF AMERICA, edited by Mark Van Doren, pp. 188-191. New York: A.&C. Boni, 1929.

> 1784-1787. Travels and social life in France and England; a very pleasant feminine journal.

BABCOCK, JOSIAH, 1752-1831   1374

In HISTORY OF THE TOWN OF ANDOVER, NEW HAMP-SHIRE, 1751-1906, prepared by John R. Eastman, pp. 313-314. Concord, N.H.: Printed by the Rumford Printing Co., 1910.

> 1784-1818. Clergyman's diary; brief scattered notes of local, family, church and personal matters in Andover, New Hampshire.

BUTLER, SAMUEL EDWARD   1375

Herndon, G. Melvin, ed. "The Diary of Samuel Edward Butler." GEORGIA HISTORICAL QUARTERLY 52 (1968):203-220.

> 1784-1786. Journey by horseback of Virginian in search of land to acquire in Georgia; route, conditions and costs of travel, including horses, equipment, meals and lodging; agricultural notes and an inventory and evaluation of every item of his property, from utensils to slaves.

COKE, THOMAS, 1747-1814   1376

EXTRACTS OF THE JOURNALS OF THE REV. DR. COKE'S THREE VISITS TO AMERICA. London: Wesley's Preaching House, 1790. 120 pp.

EXTRACTS OF THE JOURNALS OF THE REV. DR. COKE'S FIVE VISITS TO AMERICA. London: Printed by G. Paramore and sold by G. Whitfield, 1793. 195 pp.

EXTRACTS OF THE JOURNALS OF THE LATE REV. THOMAS COKE. Dublin: Printed by R. Napper, 1816. 271 pp.

> 1784-1790. Travel journals of Methodist bishop; travel and Methodist meetings in New England and Atlantic states; five visits to America, although second, third and fifth were to West Indies.

COWDIN, THOMAS, 1720-1792   1377

"Captain Thomas Cowdin's Journal." FITCHBURG HISTORICAL SOCIETY PROCEEDINGS 1 (1892-1894):135-146.

> May-Jun 1784. Legal journal; attendance at the General Court and notes of proceedings; interesting spellings.

EVANS, GRIFFITH, 1760-1845   1378

Raup, Hallock F., ed. "Journal of Griffith Evans." PENNSYLVANIA MAGAZINE OF HISTORY AND BIOGRAPHY 65 (1941):202-233.

> Sep 1784-Jan 1785. Extract of treaty journal kept

by clerk to the Pennsylvania commissioners at Fort Stanwix and Fort McIntosh; making treaties with Indians; notes on travel, private matters, places, people, etc.; full and good entries.

EWING, JOHN, 1732-1802   1379

In PENNSYLVANIA ARCHIVES, 6th ser., vol. 14, pp. 3-20.

> May-Jul 1784. Travel journal and memorandum book of Presbyterian minister and provost of University of Pennsylvania; journey with commission to settle Pennsylvania boundary; surveying and topographical notes.

GREEN, JOHN   1380

Clark, William Bell, ed. "Journal of the Ship EMPRESS OF CHINA." AMERICAN NEPTUNE 10 (1950):83-107, 220-229, 288-297; 11 (1951):59-71, 134-143.

> Feb 1784-Jan 1785. Captain's journal of voyage of first ship to open lucrative China trade to Americans; terse, but more than a log, covering all kinds of tasks aboard ship, storms and discipline of crew; notes on Samuel Shaw, first American consul at Canton, who was on board; phonetic spellings.

GUEST, MOSES, b. 1755   1381

In POEMS ON SEVERAL OCCASIONS; TO WHICH ARE ANNEXED EXTRACTS FROM A JOURNAL, pp. 83-160. Cincinnati: Looker & Reynolds, Printers, 1823; 2d ed., 1824.

> 1784-1817. Travel in West Indies, Bermuda, etc.; journey from New Jersey to Montreal and Quebec; notes on scenery and towns; description of trade, etc., of Cincinnati.

LAWRENCE, LOVE, 1754-1803   1382

Linn, Edith W. "Letters of an American Woman Sailing for England in 1784." JOURNAL OF AMERICAN HISTORY 3 (1909):441-446.

> Jul 1784. Letter-journal written during trip to England; good picture of ocean voyage.

LEADBEATER, MARY, 1758-1826   1383

Grubb, Isabel, ed. "American Visitors in Ireland." FRIENDS' HISTORICAL SOCIETY JOURNAL 37 (1940):25-30.

> 1784-1820. Brief scattered extracts and personal notes covering American's visits to Quakers in Ireland.

LEE, ARTHUR, 1740-1792   1384

In LIFE OF ARTHUR LEE, LL. D., JOINT COMMISSIONER OF THE UNITED STATES TO THE COURT OF FRANCE, by Richard Henry Lee, vol. 2, pp. 377-399. Boston: Wells and Lilly, 1829.

In THE OLDEN TIME, edited by Neville B. Craig, vol. 2, pp. 334-344.

> Nov-Dec 1784. Treaty journal; journey from Carlisle to Pittsburgh to treat with Indians; account of treaty; literary style, with quotations from Milton and Pope.

LIPSCOMB, JOHN   1385

In EARLY TRAVELS IN THE TENNESSEE COUNTRY, edited by Samuel C. Williams, pp. 272-279.

> Jun-Aug 1784. Merchant's travel journal; from

Halifax, Nova Scotia, to Cumberland County, North Carolina; lively notes; interesting language.

MINOT, GEORGE RICHARDS, 1758-1802　　　　1386

"Character of the Hon. George Richards Minot." MASSA-CHUSETTS HISTORICAL SOCIETY COLLECTIONS, 1st ser. 8 (1802):86-109. Diary, pp. 98-105.

1784-1800. Extracts from diary of a Boston judge; Shays' Rebellion and public affairs.

MUHLENBERG, JOHN PETER GABRIEL, 1746-1807　　　1387

In THE LIFE OF MAJOR-GENERAL PETER MUHLENBERG, OF THE REVOLUTIONARY ARMY, by Henry A. Muhlenberg, app., pp. 425-453. Philadelphia: Carey and Hart, 1849.

Feb-Jun 1784. Trip to Kentucky to look after bounty lands belonging to himself and friends; notes on travel, towns, topography, weather.

ROBERTSON, DANIEL　　　　1388

"Trip from Michilimackinac to Lake Superior." MICHIGAN PIONEER COLLECTIONS 9 (1886):643-646.

Jun 1784. Travel journal of captain in the Forty-eighth Regiment.

RUSH, BENJAMIN, 1745-1813　　　　1389

Butterfield, Lyman H., ed. "Dr. Benjamin Rush's Journal of a Trip to Carlisle in 1784." PENNSYLVANIA MAGAZINE OF HISTORY AND BIOGRAPHY 74 (1950):443-456.

Apr 1784. Travel journal covering trip on horseback from Philadelphia to Carlisle, Pennsylvania, for first meeting of Board of Trustees of Dickinson College; brief description of college; characteristics of German and Scotch-Irish inhabitants of the area; comments on current Pennsylvania political controversies.

THE AUTOBIOGRAPHY OF BENJAMIN RUSH. Edited by George W. Corner. American Philosophical Society Memoirs, vol. 25. Princeton, N.J.: Published for the American Philosophical Society by Princeton University Press, 1948. 399 pp. Journal, pp. 171-360. Reprint. Westport, Conn.: Greenwood, 1970.

1789-1813. Entertaining commonplace book of Philadelphia statesman and physician; conversations with and anecdotes about ordinary and illustrious people, including Washington, Jefferson and Franklin, whose death is described; odd snippets of fact and lore; reports of travelers and explorers returned from exotic places; politics; social life of Philadelphia; medical practice and notes from his medical lectures; philosophical musing about love, solitude, evil, slavery, religion, etc; a wealth of names, births and deaths.

A MEMORIAL CONTAINING TRAVELS THROUGH LIFE. Philadelphia: Published privately by Louis A. Biddle, Made at the Sign of the Ivy Leaf, 1905. 262 pp. Journal, pp. 133-215.

1792-1813. Notes of public affairs and public business; visits and social matters; meetings with various eminent scientists, including Priestly; short biographies; a useful record.

SAILLY, PETER, 1754-1826　　　　1390

Bixley, George S. "Peter Sailly, a Pioneer of the Champlain Valley." NEW YORK STATE LIBRARY HISTORY BULLETIN, no. 12 (1919), pp. 58-70.

May-Aug 1784. Travel diary; Philadelphia, Albany, Johnstown, Fort Stanwix, Lake Schuyler, Fort Edward, Crown Point, Isle aux Noix, St. John; notes on scenery, visits, fishing, etc.

SARGENT, WINTHROP, 1753-1820　　　　1391

"Journal of the General Meeting of the Cincinnati in 1784." PENNSYLVANIA HISTORICAL SOCIETY MEMOIRS 6 (1858):57-115.

1784. Minutes of the general meeting, Society of the Cincinnati.

DIARY OF COL. WINTHROP SARGENT. Wormsloe Quartos, no. 4. Wormsloe, Ga., 1851. 58 pp. Reprint. In "Winthrop Sargent's Diary while with General Arthur St. Clair's Expedition against the Indians." OHIO ARCHAEOLOGICAL AND HISTORICAL QUARTERLY 33 (1924):237-273.

Oct-Dec 1791. Full and very critical notes on St. Clair's disastrous expedition against the Indians; lengthy account of the defeat.

"Extracts from Winthrop Sargent's Journal." OHIO ARCHAEOLOGICAL AND HISTORICAL QUARTERLY 33 (1924): 273-282.

1793-1795. Items of general interest; weather, social life, etc.; visit to Washington at Mount Vernon and to Philadelphia; notes on Indian hostilities and difficulties at Cincinnati; horticultural notes.

SCOTT, JOB, 1751-1793　　　　1392

JOURNAL OF THE LIFE, TRAVELS AND GOSPEL LABOURS OF THAT FAITHFUL SERVANT AND MINISTER OF CHRIST, JOB SCOTT. New York: Printed and sold by Isaac Collins, 1798. 360 pp. Journal, pp. 93-268. Mount Pleasant, Ohio: E. Bates, 1820. 303 pp.

1784-1793. Quaker missionary journal; religious reflections and self-criticism; visits to Friends in New York State, Pennsylvania and New Jersey; trials and illnesses; visits to southern states; wife's sickness; visit to Connecticut; tour in England and Ireland.

SHAW, SAMUEL, 1754-1794　　　　1393

THE JOURNALS OF MAJOR SAMUEL SHAW, THE FIRST AMERICAN CONSUL AT CANTON. Boston: W. Crosby and H.P. Nichols, 1847. 360 pp. Journal, pp. 131-334.

1784-1780. Consular journal; voyage to Canton aboard the EMPRESS OF CHINA; visit to Bengal, return to Canton, and voyage home; valuable details of American commerce with China and the East; a good picture of Chinese life; partly diary, partly narrative.

SHOEMAKER, SAMUEL, d. 1800　　　　1394

"A Pennsylvania Loyalist's Interview with George III." PENNSYLVANIA MAGAZINE OF HISTORY AND BIOGRAPHY 2 (1878):35-39.

Oct 1784. Extract of a Loyalist's conversation with the king on October 10.

WASHINGTON, ELIZABETH FOOTE　　　　1395

In WEATHERING THE STORM, by Elizabeth Evans, pp. 342-357.

1784-1792. Private thoughts of the wife of Lund Washington, relative of George Washington and manager of his estate and business during war years; the rules she set down for conducting herself and her servants when she could go to housekeeping in her own home; religious commitment; education of her servants; births and deaths of her children.

WHITE, NANCY, 1768-1832   1396

THE SAGAMORE (Brookline High School) 1 (n.d.):21-24, 53-56, 87-90, 123-126, 157-160, 191-194; 2 (n.d.):22-25, 53-56, 87-90.

1784-1785. Schoolgirl's diary; notes of social life and school work at Brookline, Massachusetts.

1785

ALLING, JEREMIAH, 1763-1830   1397

A REGISTER OF THE WEATHER. New Haven, Conn.: Printed by O. Steele, 1810. 84 pp.

1785-1811. Weather journal; brief notes, mainly of weather at Hamden, Connecticut.

BACHE, BENJAMIN FRANKLIN   1398

Jenkins, Charles F. "Franklin Returns from France." AMERICAN PHILOSOPHICAL SOCIETY PROCEEDINGS 92 (1948):417-432. Diary, pp. 426-429.

Jul-Sep 1785. Diaries, with entries interspersed, of young Temple Franklin and Benjamin Franklin Bache on board the LONDON PACKET on which their relative, Benjamin Franklin, was a passenger.

BALLARD, MARTHA MOORE, 1735-1812   1399

In THE HISTORY OF AUGUSTA, MAINE, edited by Charles E. Nash, pp. 229-464. Augusta, Maine: Charles Nash and Sons, 1904.

1785-1812. Short entries of daily life; tasks such as making candles and clothes; weather, illness, births and deaths of neighbors; work as midwife attending births of 996 children, often making trips at night and during stormy weather; medical remedies; interesting language.

BENTLEY, WILLIAM, 1759-1819   1400

THE DIARY OF WILLIAM BENTLEY, D.D., PASTOR OF THE EAST CHURCH, SALEM, MASSACHUSETTS. Salem, Mass.: Essex Institute, 1905-14. 4 vols. Reprint. Gloucester, Mass.: P. Smith, 1962.

1785-1819. Clergyman's diary; extensive and varied notes on his life in Salem, Massachusetts; personal affairs, reading, weather, social life, shipping, etc.; a valuable and interesting diary.

"Extracts from Dr. William Bentley's Diary." DANVERS HISTORICAL SOCIETY COLLECTIONS 3 (1915):114-115; 5 (1917):48; 7 (1919):94-96; 11 (1923): 83-91; 12 (1924): 69-71; 13 (1925):83-90; 14 (1926):35- 40; 15 (1927):46-48; 16 (1928):113-121; 17 (1929):13-19; 18 (1930):47-57.

1785-1819. Extracts relating to Danvers, Massachusetts.

"Extracts from the Diary of Rev. William Bentley." TOPSFIELD HISTORICAL SOCIETY COLLECTIONS 20 (1915):49-66.

1785-1819. Extracts relating to Topsfield, Massachusetts.

BUELL, JOSEPH, d. 1812   1401

In PIONEER HISTORY, by Samuel P. Hildreth, pp. 140-164. Historical and Philosophical Society of Ohio

Publications, vol. 1. Cincinnati: H.W. Derby; New York: A.S. Barnes, 1848.

1785-1787. Brief notes of military movements and happenings on the frontier, in region from Fort McIntosh to Post Vincent on the Wabash.

CATHCART, JAMES LEANDER, 1767-1843   1402

THE CAPTIVES, BY JAMES LEANDER CATHCART, ELEVEN YEARS A PRISONER IN ALGIERS. Compiled by his daughter, Jane B. Newkirk. La Porte, Ind.: Herald Print, 1899. 312 pp.

Extracts in "Cathcart's Travels or a Day in the Life of an American Sailor," by Liva Baker. AMERICAN HERITAGE 26 (1975):52-60, 82-85.

1785-1795. Journal of American sailor captured by pirates and held as a slave in Algiers; rise to position of chief Christian secretary to the dey of Algiers; assistance in negotiating the 1795 peace treaty between the United States and Algiers; description of a slave's life and developments during peace negotiations.

"The Diplomatic Journal and Letter Book of James Leander Cathcart." AMERICAN ANTIQUARIAN SOCIETY PROCEEDINGS 64 (1954):304-436.

1788-1796. Official journal of American captive of Barbary pirates, secretary to the dey and advisor to Americans negotiating peace treaty. Subsequent revising by Cathcart's descendants has lessened reliability of this account.

Prichard, Walter, Kniffen, Fred B., and Brown, Clair A., eds. "Southern Louisiana and Southern Alabama in 1819: The Journal of James Leander Cathcart." LOUISIANA HISTORICAL QUARTERLY 28 (1945):735-921. Journal, pp. 742-880.

Dec 1818-May 1819. Record kept by navy agent in charge of expedition to survey public lands having timber suitable for use in naval construction; sea voyage from Bahamas to New Orleans, and return to Baltimore aboard NONESUCH; travel through southern Louisiana and Alabama, with detailed description of land and its inhabitants, including Choctaw and other Indians.

CORDERO, ANTONIO   1403

In FORGOTTEN FRONTIERS; A STUDY OF THE SPANISH INDIAN POLICY OF DON JUAN BAUTISTA DE ANZA, translated and edited by Alfred B. Thomas, pp. 285-290.

Nov-Dec 1785. Diary of a captain during campaign against the Gila Indians from the presidio of Janos; line of march in southern New Mexico and Arizona; searching for and killing Indians; hindrance by snow, lack of water and supplies.

CRANCH, ELIZABETH   1404

Mason, Lizzie Norton and Phillips, James D., eds. "The Journal of Elizabeth Cranch." ESSEX INSTITUTE HISTORICAL COLLECTIONS 80 (1944):1-36.

Oct 1785-Mar 1786. Personal diary of a cousin of John Quincy Adams whose social circle she describes; youthful philosophical ruminations; details of amusements, reading, etc.; visit to friends in Haverhill, Massachusetts.

FISH, ELISHA, 1762-1833   1405

"Notes from the Diary of Elisha Fish." NEW ENGLAND HISTORICAL AND GENEALOGICAL REGISTER 56 (1902):121-132.

1785-1799. Quaker diary; brief scattered notes, mainly of visits to Friends' meetings; Quaker affairs at Newport and other Rhode Island towns; necrology.

FORD, TIMOTHY, 1762-1830   1406

Barnwell, Joseph W., ed. "Diary of Timothy Ford." SOUTH CAROLINA HISTORICAL AND GENEALOGICAL MAGAZINE 13 (1912):132-147, 181-204.

> 1785-1786. Extracts of travel diary describing journey from New York to South Carolina; group notes for October 1785, then scattered notes describing the South.

HADFIELD, JOSEPH, 1759-1851   1407

AN ENGLISHMAN IN AMERICA. Edited by Douglas S. Robertson. Toronto: Hunter-Rose, 1933. 232 pp.

> Jun-Oct 1785. English tourist's journal; trip from New York to Canada, Montreal, Niagara, Quebec; return to Boston; meetings with distinguished people.

HAYNES, LEMUEL, 1753-1833   1408

In SKETCHES OF THE LIFE AND CHARACTER OF THE REV. LEMUEL HAYNES, A.M., FOR MANY YEARS PASTOR OF A CHURCH IN RUTLAND, VT., AND LATER IN GRANVILLE, NEW YORK, by Timothy M. Cooley, pp. 73-76. New York: Harper & Brothers, 1837; J.S. Taylor, 1839.

> Jul-Aug 1785. Clergyman's diary of travel in Vermont; preaching and visits.

HEART, JONATHAN, 1748-1791   1409

JOURNAL OF CAPT. JONATHAN HEART ON THE MARCH WITH HIS COMPANY FROM CONNECTICUT TO FORT PITT. Edited by Consul W. Butterfield. Albany: J. Munsell's Sons, 1885. 94 pp. Journal, pp. 1-26.

> Sep-Oct 1785. March from New Windsor, New York, to Fort Pitt via Easton, Reading, Carlisle, Bedford, etc.; mainly notes of marches.

HUNTER, JOHN   1410

"A Account of a Visit Made to Washington at Mount Vernon, by an English Gentleman." PENNSYLVANIA MAGAZINE OF HISTORY AND BIOGRAPHY 17 (1893):76-82.

> Nov 1785. Travel diary extract of Englishman's visit with Washington.

HUNTER, ROBERT, 1764-1843   1411

QUEBEC TO CAROLINA IN 1785-1786; BEING THE TRAVEL DIARY AND OBSERVATIONS OF ROBERT HUNTER, JR., A YOUNG MERCHANT OF LONDON. Edited by Louis B. Wright and Marion Tinling. San Marino, Calif.: Huntington Library, 1943. 393 pp.

> 1785-1786. Young Englishman's journey through maritime Canada, New England and Middle Atlantic states to collect delinquent accounts for his merchant father and to see sights of the New World; Atlantic crossing on the LONDON during which he suffered from seasickness and the absence of young ladies; life among Loyalist refugees, British, Scotch and French in Canada; travel to Niagara Falls, New York, Boston and Philadelphia, where he enjoyed best of society, and to Mount Vernon to meet George Washington.

LA PEROUSE, JEAN FRANCOIS DE GALAUP,   1412
comte de, 1741-1788

THE VOYAGE OF LA PEROUSE ROUND THE WORLD. London: Printed for John Stockdale, 1798. 2 vols. Reprint. Bibliotheca Australiana, nos. 27-29. Amsterdam: N. Israel; New York: Da Capo, 1969. 3 vols.

> 1785-1788. Narrative style journal; round the world expedition with two ships, the BOUSSOLE and the ASTROLABE, searching for a northwest passage from the Pacific side; visiting Hawaiian Islands, coast of America to Alaska; details of harbors; coastal observations; products; customs of Indians; effects of conversion; reception of expedition at mission of San Carlos. Translated from the French.

THE FIRST FRENCH EXPEDITION TO CALIFORNIA; LA-PEROUSE IN 1786. Translated by Charles N. Rudkin. Early California Travel Series, vol. 46. Los Angeles: Glen Dawson, 1959. 145 pp.

> 1786. Extract of journal relating to California.

MONTGOMERY, SAMUEL   1413

Bushnell, David I., Jr., ed. "A Journey through the Indian Country beyond the Ohio." MISSISSIPPI VALLEY HISTORICAL REVIEW 2 (1915-1916):261-273.

> Aug-Oct 1785. Travels of a government agent; impersonal and formal notes.

OCCOM, SAMSON, 1723-1792   1414

In SAMSON OCCOM AND THE CHRISTIAN INDIANS OF NEW ENGLAND, by William De Loss Love, pp. 249-275. Boston and Chicago: Pilgrim Press, 1899.

> 1785-1787. Extracts of travel and missionary work among Oneida and Connecticut Indians; journeys, meetings, sermons, etc.; interesting spellings.

PORTER, ANDREW, 1743-1813   1415

Porter, William A. "A Sketch of the Life of General Andrew Porter." PENNSYLVANIA MAGAZINE OF HISTORY AND BIOGRAPHY 4 (1880):261-285.

> May-Sep 1785, Jul-Sep 1786. Extracts from surveying journal; fixing western boundary of Pennsylvania.

PORTLOCK, NATHANIEL, 1748?-1817   1416

A VOYAGE AROUND THE WORLD; BUT MORE PARTICULARLY TO THE NORTH-WEST COAST OF AMERICA. London: Printed for John Stockdale and George Goulding, 1789. 384 pp. Reprint. Bibliotheca Australiana, no. 43. Amsterdam: N. Israel; New York: Da Capo, 1968.

> 1785-1788. Detailed, well written private journal by the commander of the KING GEORGE, a ship sailing with the QUEEN CHARLOTTE; around Cape Horn to Hawaii and northwest coast of America; description of Hawaii and its inhabitants; meeting, procuring supplies from and trading with northwest coast Indians.

RAVENEL, RENE, 1762-1822   1417

In RAVENEL RECORDS, A HISTORY AND GENEALOGY OF THE HUGUENOT FAMILY OF RAVENEL, OF SOUTH CAROLINA, by Henry E. Ravenel, pp. 225-251. Atlanta: Franklin Printing and Publishing, 1898.

> 1785-1821. Brief notes of journeys, visits, family affairs, deaths, work, education of children, etc.

SARYCHEV, GAVRIIL ANDREEVICH, 1763–1831   **1418**

ACCOUNT OF A VOYAGE OF DISCOVERY TO THE NORTH-EAST OF SIBERIA, THE FROZEN OCEAN, AND THE NORTH-EAST SEA. London: Printed for Richard Phillips, 1806–1807. 2 vols. Reprint. Bibliotheca Australiana, no. 64. Amsterdam: N. Israel; New York: Da Capo, 1969.

> 1785–1792. Journal account (perhaps rewritten) of exploring in the north Pacific; stops at Unalaska, Kodiak and Fox Islands with descriptions of Aleuts and their customs.

VAN CLEVE, BENJAMIN, 1773–1821   **1419**

Bond, B.W., ed. "Memoirs of Benjamin Van Cleve." HISTORICAL AND PHILOSOPHICAL SOCIETY OF OHIO QUARTERLY PUBLICATIONS 17 (1922):11–14, 30–41, 45–58.

> Nov 1785–Apr 1786. Scattered extracts; migration from New Jersey to Pennsylvania; journey from Fort Washington to Philadelphia on official business; military career, including trial for making soldiers drunk; surveying and farming in Ohio; life in Cincinnati and Dayton; grocery work at Greenville; politics; a varied and interesting record.

"Journal of Benjamin Van Cleve." ILLINOIS STATE HISTORICAL SOCIETY TRANSACTIONS (1903):62–64.

> May–Jun 1794. Journey to Fort Massac and vicinity.

1786

DUNLAP, WILLIAM, 1766–1839   **1420**

DIARY OF WILLIAM DUNLAP (1766–1839): THE MEMOIRS OF A DRAMATIST, THEATRICAL MANAGER, PAINTER, CRITIC, NOVELIST, AND HISTORIAN. New York Historical Society Collections, vol. 62–64. New York: New York Historical Society, 1930. 3 vols. Reprint. New York: B. Blom, 1969. 3 vols. in 1.

> 1786–1834 (with gaps). Private activities of playwright and painter; personal and domestic entries; journeys to New England and Canada; a valuable diary for its picture of Dunlap and his circle.

HULL, HENRY, 1765–1834   **1421**

"Memoirs of the Life and Religious Labors of Henry Hull." FRIENDS' LIBRARY 4 (1840):236–325. Diary, pp. 242–304.

> 1786–1813. Conversion, travels and religious experiences of a ministering Quaker; southern states, Ireland, New York, Canada, Ohio; notes on slavery, social conditions, "Popery," education, child labor; interesting for reformist aspects of Quakerism.

JUDD, EBEN, 1761–1837   **1422**

VERMONT HISTORICAL GAZETEER 1 (1867):944–946.

> Sep 1786–Apr 1787. Scattered extracts of surveying in Essex County, Vermont; meetings, Thanksgiving celebrations.

MCCLEAN, ALEXANDER, 1744 or 1745?–1834   **1423**

Murphy, James L., ed. "Alexander McClean's Journal of the 1786 Survey of the Western Boundary of Pennsylvania." WESTERN PENNSYLVANIA HISTORICAL MAGAZINE 63 (1980):321–343.

> Aug–Oct 1786. Journal of survey led by Colonel Andrew Porter and Alexander McClean; rigors of wilderness surveying; camping, weather, contending with swamps and forests; equipment and tasks; contacts with Indians.

MATTHEWS (or MATHEWS), JOHN, b. 1765   **1424**

In PIONEER HISTORY, by Samuel P. Hildreth, pp. 170–192. Historical and Philosophical Society of Ohio Publications, vol. 1. Cincinnati: H.W. Derby; New York: A.S. Barnes, 1848.

In OHIO IN THE TIME OF THE CONFEDERATION, edited by Archer B. Hulbert, vol. 3, pp. 187–214. Marietta College Historical Collections, vol. 3; Ohio Company Series, vol. 3. Marietta, Ohio: Marietta Historical Commission, 1918.

> 1786–1788. Journey from Massachusetts to Ohio; incidents in survey of Seven Ranges, Ohio; topographical and surveying notes for proposed Ohio Company purchase; some social and Indian notes.

RUSSELL, GILBERT, 1760–1829   **1425**

In THE HISTORY OF NEW BEDFORD, BRISTOL COUNTY, MASSACHUSETTS, by Daniel Ricketson, pp. 169–175. New Bedford: The author, 1858.

> Oct–Dec 1786. Account of and extracts from Quaker travel journal; in Connecticut, New York and Massachusetts; notes on travel, taverns, food, meetings.

SEWALL, JOTHAM, 1760–1850   **1426**

A MEMOIR OF REV. JOTHAM SEWALL OF CHESTERVILLE, MAINE. By his son Jotham Sewall. Boston: Tappan & Whittemore; Bangor, Maine: E.F. Duren, 1853. 408 pp. passim.

> 1786–1850. Copious extracts of missionary journeys, religious meditations, social affairs, etc.

STEVENS, JAMES   **1427**

"Stevens' Diary." VIRGINIA MAGAZINE OF HISTORY AND BIOGRAPHY 29 (1921):385–401.

> May–Oct 1786, Jan 1787. Fragments of travel diary; voyage from Norfolk, Virginia, to Scotland; Glasgow; visits to friends, relatives, court of law in Scotland; amusing notes.

STRANGE, JAMES, 1753–1840   **1428**

JOURNAL AND NARRATIVE OF THE COMMERCIAL EXPEDITION FROM BOMBAY TO THE NORTHWEST COAST OF AMERICA. Introduction by A.V. Venkatarama. Madras: Printed by the Superintendent, Government Press, 1928. 63 pp.

> 1786. Commander's journal of an expedition with two ships, CAPTAIN COOK and EXPERIMENT, undertaken to establish fur trade between China and America; sailing conditions, port experiences, water supply for ships, scurvy and other health problems; observations, during one month in Nootka Sound and Prince William Sound, of Indian customs and ceremonies, love of music and dance; additions to Captain Cook's Nootka vocabulary; fur trading activities.

TRUMBULL, JOHN, 1756–1843   **1429**

AUTOBIOGRAPHY, REMINISCENCES, AND LETTERS OF JOHN TRUMBULL. New York and London: Wiley and Putnam; New Haven: B.L. Hamlen, 1841. 439 pp. Journal, pp. 101–146.

THE AUTOBIOGRAPHY OF COLONEL JOHN TRUMBULL. Edited by Theodore Sizer. New Haven: Yale University

Press, 1953. 404 pp.

Aug-Oct 1786. Artist's visit to France, Germany and Flanders; impressions of paintings, etc.

VIAL, PEDRO, d. 1814   1430

In PEDRO VIAL AND THE ROADS TO SANTA FE, by Noel Loomis and Abraham P. Nasatir, pp. 268-285.

Oct 1786-May 1787. Daily account of journey made by Vial and one companion to locate a route from San Antonio to Santa Fe; some details of dealings with Indians, including two month sojourn in a Tawakoni village while recovering from severe illness.

In PEDRO VIAL AND THE ROADS TO SANTA FE, pp. 372-405.

Extracts in THE SPANISH REGIME IN MISSOURI, by Louis Hauck, vol. 1, pp. 354-358. Chicago: R.R. Donnelly & Sons, 1909.

Extracts in "The First Santa Fe Expedition," edited by Alfred B. Thomas. CHRONICLES OF OKLAHOMA 9 (1931):195-208. Diary, pp. 200-208.

Extracts in SOUTHWEST ON THE TURQOISE TRAIL, edited by Archer B. Hulbert, pp. 48-54.

1792-1793. Diary of journey undertaken to open communication between Santa Fe and St. Louis; travel conditions, capture and detention by Kansas Indians; long stopover at St. Louis due to bad weather and fear of Indians; capture and liaison with Pawnees on return trip.

In PEDRO VIAL AND THE ROADS TO SANTA FE, pp. 433-438.

Oct-Nov 1805. Expedition to make peace with Pawnees; from Santa Fe to Arkansas River, where encounter with unidentified Indians and loss of supplies and arms necessitated return to Santa Fe.

WARDER, ANN, ca. 1758-1829   1431

"Extracts from the Diary of Mrs. Ann Warder." PENNSYLVANIA MAGAZINE OF HISTORY AND BIOGRAPHY 17 (1893):444-464; 18 (1894):51-63.

1786-1788. Life at Philadelphia; lively style and varied details of the social round of a young matron; visits, parties, dinners.

1787

ATTMORE, WILLIAM, d. 1800   1432

JOURNAL OF A TOUR TO NORTH CAROLINA. Edited by Lida T. Rodman. James Sprunt Historical Publications, vol. 17, no. 2. Chapel Hill: The University, 1922. 46 pp.

Nov-Dec 1787. Philadelphia merchant's voyage and tour in Virginia and North Carolina; entertainments, horse races, social affairs; lively and amusing picture of the Old South; long entries.

BARKLEY, FRANCES HORNBY TREVOR, 1769?-1845   1433

Lamb, W. Kaye. "The Mystery of Mrs. Barkley's Diary." BRITISH COLUMBIA HISTORICAL QUARTERLY 6 (1942):31-55. Diary, pp. 49-55.

1787-1792. Extracts, copied by John T. Walbran before diary was lost in a fire, from diary of wife of Captain Charles William Barkley of IMPERIAL EAGLE, or LOUDEN, the name used when under Portuguese flag; west coast of Vancouver Island; discovery of Strait of Juan de Fuca; coast of Alaska; descriptions of Indians, particularly of dress and lip ornaments.

BROWN, JAMES, 1761-1834   1434

Collins, Clarkson A., III, ed. "James Brown's Diary." RHODE ISLAND HISTORY 6 (1947):99-107; 7 (1948):9-11, 51-57.

1787-1789. Private diary of son of prominent merchant, John Brown; brief entries of weather, social activities, news.

Swann, Bradford F., ed. "James Brown's Diary." RHODE ISLAND HISTORY, 4 (1945):84-85.

Jan 1801. Brief notes of weather, business, current events; report of town fire, estimate of damages.

CLINTON, CORNELIA   1435

Gibson, James R., ed. "A Portion of a Journal of Cornelia, Daughter of Governor George Clinton." NEW YORK GENEALOGICAL AND BIOGRAPHICAL RECORD 20 (1889):40-41.

1787. Extract relating to her visit to the governor.

COGSWELL, MASON FITCH, 1761-1830   1436

Bartlett, Ellen Strong, ed. "Extracts from the Diary of Dr. Mason Fitch Cogswell." CONNECTICUT MAGAZINE 5 (1899):532-537, 562-569, 606-614.

Nov-Dec 1787. Horseback journeys through Connecticut; entertaining social observations combined with reminiscences.

DEWEES, MARY COBURN   1437

"Mrs. Mary Dewees's Journal from Philadelphia to Kentucky." PENNSYLVANIA MAGAZINE OF HISTORY AND BIOGRAPHY 28 (1904):182-198.

JOURNAL OF A TRIP FROM PHILADELPHIA TO LEXINGTON IN KENTUCKY. Crawfordsville, Ind.: R.E. Banta, 1936. 16 pp.

Blair, John L., ed. "Mrs. Mary Dewees's Journal from Philadelphia to Kentucky." KENTUCKY HISTORICAL SOCIETY REGISTER 63 (1965):195-217.

Extracts in PEN PICTURES OF EARLY WESTERN PENNSYLVANIA, edited by John W. Harpster, pp. 177-185. Pittsburgh: University of Pittsburgh Press, 1938.

Sep 1787-Jan 1788. Lively descriptions of trip from Philadelphia to Lexington, Kentucky, by wagon and flat boat.

DICKINSON, REBECCA, b. 1738   1438

In HISTORY OF HATFIELD, MASSACHUSETTS, by Daniel W. Wells and Reuben F. Wells, pp. 206-207. Springfield, Mass.: F.C.H. Gibbons, 1910.

1787-1802. A good diary of a spinster's personal life; visits, social affairs, deaths, illnesses, opinions.

HARDY, PHINEAS, 1763-1829   1439

"Capt. Hardy's Journal." NEW ENGLAND HISTORICAL AND GENEALOGICAL REGISTER 7 (1853):352.

Jan-Feb 1787. Brief military journal of march from Andover to suppress Shays' Rebellion.

HASWELL, ROBERT, 1768-1805   1440

"Log of the First Voyage of the COLUMBIA." In VOYAGES OF THE COLUMBIA TO THE NORTHWEST COAST,

1787-1790 AND 1790-1793, edited by Frederic W. Howay, pp. 3-107. Massachusetts Historical Society Collections, vol. 79. Boston: Massachusetts Historical Society, 1941. Reprint. Bibliotheca Australiana, extra series. Amsterdam: N. Israel; New York: Da Capo. 1969.

> 1787-1789. Third mate's record of sailing conditions along the Oregon and Washington coast to Nootka Sound; meetings and trading with Indians.

Elliott, T.C., ed. "Captain Robert Gray's First Visit to Oregon." OREGON HISTORICAL QUARTERLY 29 (1928): 162-188.

> Sep-Oct 1787, Aug-Sep 1788. Mate's description of Gray's 1788 voyage in the sloop WASHINGTON from California to Nootka Sound preceded by a few entries describing preparations and departure from Boston the previous autumn; account of Indian attack; British-American rivalry and encounter with John Meares.

In HISTORY OF THE NORTHWEST COAST, by Hubert H. Bancroft, vol. 1, pp. 187-207 passim. San Francisco: A.L. Bancroft & Co., 1884.

> Aug 1788-May 1789. Extracts of exploring the northwest coast.

"Log of the Second Voyage of the COLUMBIA." In VOYAGES OF THE COLUMBIA TO THE NORTHWEST COAST, pp. 293-359.

> 1791-1792. Log of first officer under Captain Gray; sailing conditions and coastal observations along the west coast from Alaska, Queen Charlotte Islands, Strait of Juan de Fuca to Grays Harbor; discovery of the Columbia River; trading relations with the Indians; language notes.

KINGSBURY, JONATHAN, 1751-1806   1441

In NEEDHAM EPITAPHS, p. 41.

> 1787-1788. Colonel's notes on Shays' Rebellion; some courts-martial.

LEDYARD, JOHN, 1751-1788   1442

JOHN LEDYARD'S JOURNEY THROUGH SIBERIA, 1787-1788; THE JOURNAL AND SELECTED LETTERS. Edited by Stephen D. Watrous. Madison: University of Wisconsin Press, 1966. 293 pp.

> Jun 1787-Apr 1788. Expedition intended to traverse whole of Siberia and eventually North America by former colleague of Captain James Cook; St. Petersburg to Irkutsk, where expedition was cut short by Ledyard's arrest and forced march back to Moscow; much written during winter delay in Yakutsk; notes on Siberians, terrain, wildlife, farming; entertaining accounts of best and worst of Siberian hospitality, rigorous overland and river travel.

LITTLE, DANIEL, d. 1801   1443

"Extract from the Journal of Rev. Daniel Little." BANGOR HISTORICAL MAGAZINE 5 (1889-1890):168-169.

> Sep 1787. Fight with drunken fur trader at Condeskeeg, Maine.

MARES, JOSE   1444

"Journal of José Mares, Santa Fe to Bexar." In PEDRO VIAL AND THE ROADS TO SANTA FE, by Noel M. Loomis and Abraham P. Nesatir, pp. 289-302.

> Jul-Oct 1787. Travel diary of unsuccessful expedition to determine a route for road from Santa Fe to San Antonio.

"Itinerary and Diary of José Mares, Bexar to Santa Fe." In PEDRO VIAL AND THE ROADS TO SANTA FE, pp. 306-314.

> Jan-Apr 1788. Return of the expedition seeking a shorter route between San Antonio and Santa Fe.

PRESTON, SAMUEL   1445

"Extracts from the Journal of Samuel Preston, Surveyor." PENNSYLVANIA MAGAZINE OF HISTORY AND BIOGRAPHY 22 (1898):350-365.

> Jun-Jul 1787. Journey to survey lands in Pike County, Pennsylvania; stories of Indian captures.

VAUGHAN, SAMUEL, 1720-1802   1446

Williams, Edward G., ed. "Samuel Vaughan's Journal or 'Minutes Made by S.V., from Stage to Stage, on a Tour to Fort Pitt.'" WESTERN PENNSYLVANIA HISTORICAL MAGAZINE 44 (1961):51-65, 159-173, 261-285.

> Jun-Jul 1787. British merchant's horseback trip from Philadelphia to Pittsburgh over new Pennsylvania State Road and over Braddock's Road to Maryland and Virginia; topography, settlements, inhabitants, crops, and Mount Vernon.

1788

BACKUS, JAMES, 1764-1816   1447

In A GENEALOGICAL MEMOIR OF THE BACKUS FAMILY, by William W. Backus, pp. 16-102. Norwich, Conn.: Press of The Bulletin, 1889.

> 1788-1791. Journey from Pennsylvania to Marietta, Ohio, and private life there; clearing for farm; good picture of pioneer life, settlers, Indians and their customs, hunting, weather, journeys, organization of community; work as agent for the Ohio Company.

BRISSOT DE WARVILLE, JACQUES PIERRE,   1448
1754-1793

NEW TRAVELS IN THE UNITED STATES OF AMERICA. New York: Printed by T.&J. Swords, for Berry & Rogers, 1792. 264 pp. Dublin: Printed by W. Corbet, for P. Byrne, A. Gueber, 1792. 483 pp. London: J.S Jordan, 1794. 2 vols. Boston: From the press of J. Bumstead, 1797. 276 pp. Bowling Green, Ohio: Historical Publications, 1919. 544 pp.

Extracts in "Boston in 1788." OLD SOUTH LEAFLETS, no. 126, 6 (1902):1-20.

Extracts in AMERICAN HISTORY TOLD BY CONTEMPORARIES, edited by Albert B. Hart, vol. 3, pp. 31-39, 53-56.

> May-Nov 1788. Letter-diary of journey through New England and some southern states. Translated from the French.

BULFINCH, HANNAH, 1768-1841   1449

In THE LIFE AND LETTERS OF CHARLES BULFINCH, by Charles Bulfinch, edited by Ellen Susan Bulfinch, pp. 91, 104-109, 141-143, 187-190. Boston and New York: Houghton, Mifflin, 1896.

> 1788-1815. Bostonian's private diary; brief, scattered quotations.

CONCHA, FERNANDO DE LA   1450

Feather, Adlai, ed. "Colonel Don Fernando de la Concha Diary, 1788." NEW MEXICO HISTORICAL REVIEW 34 (1959):285-304.

Aug-Oct 1788. New Mexico governor's military expedition against the Gila and Mimbres Apaches; route, terrain, search for elusive Indians; one small engagement. Translated from the Spanish.

COPLAND, CHARLES 1451

Graves, Anna M., ed. "Extracts from Diary of Charles Copland." WILLIAM AND MARY COLLEGE QUARTERLY, 1st ser. 14 (1905-1906):44-50, 217-230.

1788-1823. Virginia lawyer's unmethodical register of domestic events, expenses, journeys, etc.; theater fire at Richmond; canal trip to Ohio.

DAY, JEREMIAH, 1737-1806 1452

"A Missionary Tour to Vermont." VERMONT HISTORICAL SOCIETY PROCEEDINGS, n.s. 1 (1930):169-176.

Extracts in SOME CHRONICLES OF THE DAY FAMILY, compiled by Ellen Day Putnam, pp. 15-17. Cambridge, Mass.: Printed at the Riverside Press, 1893.

Sep-Oct 1788. Brief notes in clergyman's journal of preaching tour in Vermont; travel; visits.

DUFFIN, ROBERT 1453

In VOYAGES MADE IN THE YEARS 1788 AND 1789, FROM CHINA TO THE NORTH WEST COAST OF AMERICA, by John Meares, app. London: Printed at the Logographic Press, 1790. Reprint. Bibliotheca Australiana, no. 22. Amsterdam: N. Israel; New York: Da Capo, 1967.

Jul 1788. Account of a member of an expedition investigating the possibilities of fur trade; days spent off his ship, the FELICE, exploring the Strait of Juan de Fuca by long boat.

FERNANDEZ, SANTIAGO 1454

"Diary of Santiago Fernández from Santa Fe to the Taovayas and Return to Santa Fe." In PEDRO VIAL AND THE ROADS TO SANTA FE, by Noel M. Loomis and Abraham P. Nasatir, pp. 318-326.

Jun-Dec 1788. Diary of commander of three cavalrymen ordered to escort Pedro Vial as far as country of the Taovayas and return to Santa Fe; distances traveled, trail conditions, herds of game; meetings with Comanches; notes on the lodgings and guides they provided.

FRAGOSA, FRANCISCO XAVIER 1455

"Diary of Francisco Xavier Fragosa, Santa Fe to Natchitoches, to San Antonio to Santa Fe." In PEDRO VIAL AND THE ROADS TO SANTA FE, by Noel M. Loomis and Abraham P. Nasatir, pp. 327-366.

1788-1789. One of Pedro Vial's party to explore a direct road to connect New Mexico with outposts in Louisiana and Texas; distances traveled; country traversed, especially rivers; friendly treatment by Comanches; warm reception at Fort of Natchitoches; long stay at San Antonio recuperating from illness.

HAMTON, JAMES, 1764-1792 1456

"James Hamton's Diary." FRIENDS' MISCELLANY 1 (1831):223-252, 258-282.

1788-1790. Pennsylvania Quaker's diary; work as schoolmaster; meetings; introspection.

MCCLELLAN, JOHN, 1767-1858 1457

McClellan, Jessy T., ed. "A Long Journey on Horseback in 1788." CONNECTICUT MAGAZINE 9 (1905):185-

189.

May-Jun 1788. Horseback journey from Lebanon, Connecticut, to Albany and return; notes on scenery and taverns.

MAY, ABIGAIL, 1754-1821 1458

Edes, Samuel S. "A Few Words Additional Relative to Col. John May, of Boston, and His Journeys to the Ohio Country in 1788 and 1789." NEW ENGLAND GENEALOGICAL AND HISTORICAL REGISTER 30 (1876): 43-49.

Apr-Sep 1788. Brief extracts of daily life in Boston; from diary kept while her husband was traveling in the West.

MAY, JOHN, 1748-1812 1459

THE WESTERN JOURNALS OF JOHN MAY, OHIO COMPANY AGENT AND BUSINESS ADVENTURER. Edited by Dwight L. Smith. Cincinnati: Historical and Philosophical Society of Ohio, 1961. 176 pp.

1788-1789. Business trips of Boston merchant to the Ohio frontier; rather harrowing travel, mostly on horseback; comments on settlers, with whom he often boarded en route, and on Indians; establishment of community at Marietta and contested land claims; much bemoaning of his health and circumstances; lively descriptions; interesting spellings.

JOURNAL AND LETTERS OF COL. JOHN MAY. With a biographical sketch by Richard S. Edes and illustrative notes by William M. Darlington. Historical and Philosophical Society of Ohio Publications, n.s. vol. 1. Cincinnati: R. Clarke & Co., 1873. 160 pp.

Extracts in "Letters and Journal of Col. John May, of Boston." NEW ENGLAND HISTORICAL AND GENEALOGICAL REGISTER 27 (1873):14-24.

Apr-Aug 1788.

"Journal of Col. John May, of Boston, Relative to a Journey to the Ohio Country, 1789." PENNSYLVANIA MAGAZINE OF HISTORY AND BIOGRAPHY 45 (1927):101-179.

Apr-Dec 1789.

MERCK, CARL HEINRICH 1460

SIBERIA AND NORTHWESTERN AMERICA, 1788-1792; THE JOURNAL OF CARL HEINRICH MERCK, NATURALIST WITH THE RUSSIAN SCIENTIFIC EXPEDITION LED BY CAPTAINS JOSEPH BILLINGS AND GAVRIIL SARYCHEV. Translated by Fritz Jaensch and edited by Richard A. Pierce. Materials for the Study of Alaska History, no. 17. Kingston, Ontario: Limestone Press, 1980. 215 pp.

1788-1792. German naturalist's account of the Northeastern Secret Geographical and Astronomical Expedition, sponsored by Catharine the Great, to explore and strengthen Russian claims to coastal north Pacific area; dismal outposts of Yakutsk and Okhotsk; explorations from Kolyma River to Bering Strait; extensive notes on plants and animals; the appearance, customs, and diseases of Kamchatkans, Aleuts, Unalaska and Kodiak Islanders.

PENN, JOHN, 1760-1834 1461

"John Penn's Journal of a Visit to Reading, Harrisburg, Carlisle, and Lancaster." PENNSYLVANIA MAGAZINE OF HISTORY AND BIOGRAPHY 3 (1879):284-295.

In EARLY NARRATIVES OF BERKS COUNTY, by James B. Nolan, pp. 121-130.

Apr 1788. Englishman's travel diary; pleasant descriptions; visit to Muhlenberg and General Mifflin.

PRICE, JOSEPH, b. 1753   1462

Barker, Charles R. "Joseph Price and His Diary." HISTORICAL SOCIETY OF MONTGOMERY COUNTY PENNSYLVANIA BULLETIN 1 (1937):55-66.

1788-1810. Extracts containing notes on gossip, morals, services, local affairs, deaths and weddings in Merion, Pennsylvania; interesting spellings.

SAUGRAIN DE VIGNI, ANTOINE FRANCOIS, 1763-1821   1463

Bliss, Eugene F. "Dr. Saugrain's Note-Books." AMERICAN ANTIQUARIAN SOCIETY PROCEEDINGS, n.s. 19 (1908-1909):222-238. Diary, pp. 230-238. Reprint. Worcester, Mass.: Davis Press, 1909. 21 pp.

May-Jul 1788. Journey from Louisville to Philadelphia; descriptions of towns and route. Translated from the French.

SHREVE, ISRAEL, 1739-1799   1464

Shreve, S.H. "Journal of Colonel Israel Shreve from Jersey to the Monongahala." MAGAZINE OF AMERICAN HISTORY 2 (1878):741-748.

In THE GENEALOGY AND HISTORY OF THE SHREVE FAMILY FROM 1641, by Luther P. Allen, pp. 603-611. Greenfield, Illinois: Privately printed, 1901.

"Journal from Jersey to the Monongahala." PENNSYLVANIA MAGAZINE OF HISTORY AND BIOGRAPHY 52 (1928): 193-204.

Jul-Aug 1788. Journey from New Jersey to Rottroven on the Monongahela; difficulties of travel with family and cattle; some interesting spellings.

WILLIAMS, TIMOTHY, 1764-1849   1465

In PUTNAM PATRIOT.

Jul-Aug 1788. Personal and local affairs in West Woodstock, Connecticut; notes of important public matters.

Apr-Mar 1815. Sermons, texts, notes.

1789

ANON.   1466

"Journal of a Survey of the South Shore of Lake Erie Made in 1789." BUFFALO HISTORICAL SOCIETY PUBLICATIONS 7 (1904):365-376.

Jun-Aug 1789. Little except surveying measurements, topography, etc.

CLARKE, ALETTA   1467

In SOME RECORDS OF SUSSEX COUNTY, DELAWARE, compiled by Charles H.B. Turner, pp. 350-369. Philadelphia: Allen, Lane & Scott, 1909.

1789-1793. Brief notes of family affairs, visits, domestic details; quite interesting view of everyday life; some interesting words.

COLNETT, JAMES, ca. 1755-1806   1468

THE JOURNAL OF CAPTAIN JAMES COLNETT. Edited by Frederic W. Howay. Champlain Society Publications, 26. Toronto: Champlain Society, 1940. 328 pp. Reprint. COLNETT'S JOURNAL ABOARD THE ARGONAUT. Champlain

Society Publications, 26. New York: Greenwood Press, 1968.

1789-1791. Commander's journal of trading expedition of United Merchants to China aboard PRINCE OF WALES and PRINCESS ROYAL; greatest portion of document covering trading voyage in the ARGONAUT to the northwest coast of America; largely dealing with capture of his vessels by the Spanish in Nootka Sound; historically valuable for Spanish-American-British political and trading relations.

Elliott, T.C., ed. "Bodega to Clayoquot in 1790 in a Long Boat." OREGON HISTORICAL QUARTERLY 42 (1941): 125-132.

Sep-Oct 1790. Extract containing orders for and summary of trading voyage undertaken by the ARGONAUT's long boat; from Bodega Bay to Vancouver Island.

DAVIS, SAMUEL, 1765-1829   1469

"Journal of a Tour to Connecticut." MASSACHUSETTS HISTORICAL SOCIETY PROCEEDINGS, 1st ser. 11 (1869-1870):9-32.

Aug-Sep 1789. Horseback journey from Plymouth, Massachusetts, to Fairfield, Connecticut, and by water to New York; good observations of people and places.

DEFOE, JULES   1470

THE DIARY OF JULES DEFOE. Research by Bess Foster Smith. Mountain Home, Idaho: Mountain Home News, 1977. 16 pp.

Jun-Oct 1789. Unauthenticated diary allegedly of French trapper, employee of Hudson's Bay Company, who was in Idaho fourteen years before Lewis and Clark; search for beaver; hardships and dangers, including a glimpse of ghastly slave labor among Spanish gold miners, which reads suspiciously like an adventure yarn.

DOUGLAS, WILLIAM   1471

In THE MEMORIAL OF JOHN MEARS TO THE HOUSE OF COMMONS RESPECTING THE CAPTURE OF VESSELS IN NOOTKA SOUND, with an introduction and notes by Nellie B. Pipes, pp. 56-76. Portland, Oreg.: Metropolitan Press, 1933.

Apr-Jun 1789. Account of seizure of Captain Douglas and the IPHEGENIA by Esteban José Martinez in Nootka Sound.

HAY, HENRY, b. 1765   1472

Quaife, Milo M., ed. "A Narrative of Life on the Old Frontier: Henry Hay's Journal from Detroit to the Mississippi River." STATE HISTORICAL SOCIETY OF WISCONSIN PROCEEDINGS (1914):208-261.

Quaife, Milo M., ed. "Fort Wayne in 1790." INDIANA HISTORICAL SOCIETY PUBLICATIONS 7 (1921):295-361.

Dec 1789-Apr 1790. Journey from Detroit to the Miami and winter at Fort Wayne; excellent picture of pioneer life in the Old Northwest among French settlers; border forays and horrors; social life and customs, fur trade, dances and amusements, music, games, etc.; a vivid diary.

MACKENZIE, Sir ALEXANDER, 1763-1820   1473

VOYAGES FROM MONTREAL, ON THE RIVER ST. LAURENCE, THROUGH THE CONTINENT OF NORTH AMERICA, TO THE FROZEN AND PACIFIC OCEANS: IN THE YEARS

1789 AND 1793. London: T. Cadell & W. Davies, 1801. 412 pp. Frequently reprinted; recently, Ann Arbor: University Microfilms, 1966.

A NARRATIVE OR JOURNAL OF VOYAGES AND TRAVELS THROUGH THE NORTH-WEST CONTINENT OF AMERICA IN THE YEARS 1789 AND 1793, by Mr. Maclauries. London: J. Lee, 1802. 91 pp. Reprint. Fairfield, Wash.: Ye Galleon Press, 1979.

FIRST MAN WEST; ALEXANDER MACKENZIE'S JOURNAL OF HIS VOYAGE TO THE PACIFIC COAST OF CANADA IN 1793. Edited by Walter Sheppe. Berkeley: University of California Press, 1962. 366 pp.

EXPLORING THE NORTHWEST TERRITORY; SIR ALEXANDER MACKENZIE'S JOURNAL OF A VOYAGE BY BARK CANOE FROM LAKE ATHABASCA TO THE PACIFIC OCEAN IN THE SUMMER OF 1789. Edited by Ted H. McDonald. Norman: University of Oklahoma, 1966. 133 pp.

THE JOURNALS AND LETTERS OF SIR ALEXANDER MAC-KENZIE. Edited by W. Kaye Lamb. Hakluyt Society, extra series, no. 41. Cambridge: Published for the Hakluyt Society at University Press, 1970. 551 pp.

> Jun-Sep 1789, Oct 1792-Aug 1793. Expeditions on behalf of Northwest Fur Company; the first from Fort Chippewayan on Lake Athabasca, to the Arctic; the second, an expedition to the Pacific. The classic of pioneer exploration in this area, written in simple style with good details and descriptions.

MACLAY, WILLIAM, 1734-1804   1474

JOURNAL OF WILLIAM MACLAY, UNITED STATES SENATOR FROM PENNSYLVANIA, 1789-1791. Edited by Edgar S. Maclay. New York: D. Appleton, 1890. 438 pp.

THE JOURNAL OF WILLIAM MACLAY. Introduction by Charles A. Beard. New York: A.&C. Boni, 1927. 429 pp. Reprint. New York: F. Ungar, 1965.

Abridgment published as SKETCHES OF DEBATE IN THE FIRST SENATE OF THE UNITED STATES IN 1789-90-91. Edited by George W. Harris. Harrisburg, Pa.: L.S. Hart, Printer, 1880. 375 pp. Reprint. New York: B. Franklin, 1969.

Extracts in "The Cantankerous Mr. Maclay." by Robert C. Albert. AMERICAN HERITAGE 25 (1974):48-50, 84-89.

Extracts in AMERICAN HISTORY TOLD BY CONTEMPORAR-IES, edited by Albert B. Hart, vol. 3, pp. 257-262, 265-269; DIARY OF AMERICA, edited by Josef Berger, pp. 135-144.

> 1789-1791. A candid insider's view of the first three sessions of First Congress; an outspoken antifederalist's valuable and lively picture of debates, ceremonies, and accompanying social and personal activities; good pictures of contemporary politicians and of himself; foreign affairs, ambition in politics, cures for ills, family affairs, social customs, dress, religion, regional characteristics; historically important and highly interesting.

MARTINEZ, ESTEBAN JOSE, 1742-1798   1475

In THE JOURNAL OF CAPTAIN JAMES COLNETT, edited by Frederic W. Howay, app. 3, pp. 308-318. Champlain Society Publications, 26. Toronto: Champlain Society, 1940. Reprint. COLNETT'S JOURNAL ABOARD THE ARGO-NAUT. Champlain Society Publications, 26. New York: Greenwood Press, 1968.

> Jul 1789. Account of capture of the ARGONAUT in Nootka Sound by Martinez to prevent occupation or claim by the British of land he claimed for Spain.

MEACHAM, JAMES, 1763-1820   1476

"A Journal and Travel of James Meacham." DUKE UNI-VERSITY TRINITY COLLEGE HISTORICAL PAPERS, ser. 9 (1912):66-95; ser. 10 (1914):87-102.

> May-Aug 1789, Jul-Dec 1791, Feb-Nov 1792, Oct-Dec 1796, Jan-Jun 1797. Extracts describing travels in Virginia of itinerant Methodist minister; anti-slavery sentiments.

MORRIS, GOUVERNEUR, 1752-1816   1477

THE DIARY AND LETTERS OF GOUVERNEUR MORRIS, MINISTER OF THE UNITED STATES TO FRANCE. Edited by Anne Cary Morris. New York: C. Scribner's Sons, 1888. 2 vols. Reprint. New York: Da Capo, 1970.

In THE LIFE OF GOUVERNEUR MORRIS, by Jared Sparks, vol. 1. Boston: Gray & Bowen, 1832.

A DIARY OF THE FRENCH REVOLUTION. Edited by Beatrix C. Davenport. Boston: Houghton Mifflin, 1939. 2 vols. Reprint. Freeport, N.Y.: Books for Libraries, 1971; Westport, Conn.: Greenwood, 1972.

> 1789-1793. Political and social diary of American statesman during French Revolution; social life in the doomed court of Louis XVI; euphemistic allusions to diarist's affair with a French countess; the fall of the Bastille; terror and tumult of Paris. The great American diary of the French Revolution; a splendid work for both historian and general reader.

PERKINS, NATHAN, 1749-1838   1478

A NARRATIVE OF A TOUR THROUGH THE STATE OF VER-MONT. Woodstock, Vt.: Elm Tree Press, 1920. 31 pp.

Extracts in "From a Narrative of a Tour through the State of Vermont." VERMONT QUARTERLY 19 (1951): 43-52.

> Apr-Jun 1789. Connecticut minister's journey to preach the gospel to the inhabitants of Vermont; through Connecticut, Massachusetts and Vermont, to Burlington, and return; hardships of travel; candid commentary on people, places, frontier conditions; very interesting.

PERKINS, THOMAS HANDASYD, 1764-1854   1479

In MEMOIR OF THOMAS HANDASYD PERKINS; CONTAINING EXTRACTS FROM HIS DIARIES AND LETTERS, by Thomas Greaves Cary, 304 pp. passim. Boston: Little, Brown, 1856.

> 1789-1835 (with gaps). Bostonian's diaries of foreign travel; in Batavia, with lengthy description of places and customs; events in Paris in spring of 1795; travel through France, Holland, England; general travel in Europe in 1835; full descriptions of places, people and customs, largely in style of travel book.

POWELL, ANN, b. 1769   1480

"Journal of Miss Powell of a Tour from Montreal to Detroit." MAGAZINE OF AMERICAN HISTORY 5 (1880): 34-47.

In THE LIFE OF WILLIAM DUMMER POWELL, by William R. Riddell, pp. 60-73. Lansing: Michigan Historical Commission, 1924.

Extracts in ANTHOLOGY AND BIBLIOGRAPHY OF NIAGARA FALLS, by Charles M. Dow, vol. 1, pp. 89-91.

> May-Jun 1789. Canadian's tour from Montreal to Detroit; seminarrative with irregular dates; des-

cription of St. Lawrence, Lake Ontario, Niagara Falls; camping; tourist observations.

WHATCOAT, RICHARD, 1736-1806   1481

In THE METHODISTS, A COLLECTION OF SOURCE MATERIALS, edited by William Warren Sweet, pp. 74-122. Religion on the American Frontier, vol. 4. Chicago: University of Chicago Press, 1946.

> 1789-1790. Abbreviated entries indicating the traveling conditions of this itinerant Methodist preacher; where he preached, exhorted or held a prayer meeting; kind and size of congregations in Maryland, Delaware, Virginia, Georgia, Tennessee and Kentucky.

1790

ANON.   1482

"Notes of a Journey from Philadelphia to New Madrid, Tennessee." PENNSYLVANIA MAGAZINE OF HISTORY AND BIOGRAPHY 36 (1912):209-216.

> Oct 1790-Jan 1791. Travel diary kept by member of Philadelphia firm of Reed and Forde; difficulties of navigation on the Ohio and Mississippi.

ARMSTRONG, JOHN   1483

In A HISTORY OF INDIANA FROM ITS EARLIEST EXPLORATION BY EUROPEANS TO THE CLOSE OF THE TERRITORIAL GOVERNMENT, by John Brown Dillon, pp. 245-248. Indianapolis: Bingham & Doughty, 1859.

Meek, Basil, ed. "General Harmar's Expedition." OHIO ARCHAEOLOGICAL AND HISTORICAL QUARTERLY 20 (1911):74-108. Journal, pp. 79-83.

> Sep-Oct 1790. Captain's journal of Harmar's punitive expedition against Indians above the Wabash headquarters; troop movements from Fort Washington; defeat by Indians.

BLOUNT, WILLIAM, 1749-1800   1484

"Governor Blount's Journal." AMERICAN HISTORICAL MAGAZINE 2 (1897):213-277.

THE BLOUNT JOURNAL, 1790-1796. By Territory of the United States, South of the River Ohio, Governor. Nashville: Benson Printing Co., 1955. 157 pp.

> 1790-1796. Official journal of the territorial governor of Tennessee; administrative and military details.

BOIT, JOHN, 1774-1829   1485

Meany, Edmond S., ed. "New Log of the Columbia." WASHINGTON HISTORICAL QUARTERLY 12 (1921):2-50. Reprint. Seattle: University of Washington Press, 1921.

Howay, Frederic W. and Elliott, T.C. "The John Boit Log and Captain Gray's Log of the Ship COLUMBIA." OREGON HISTORICAL QUARTERLY 22 (1921):257-356. Reprint. Portland, Oreg.: The Ivy Press, 1921.

"Remarks on the Ship COLUMBIA'S Voyage from Boston." In VOYAGES OF THE COLUMBIA TO THE NORTHWEST COAST, edited by Frederic W. Howay, pp. 363-431. Massachusetts Historical Society Collections, vol. 79. Boston: Massachusetts Historical Society, 1941. Bibliotheca Australiana, extra series. Amsterdam: N. Israel; New York: Da Capo, 1969.

VOYAGE OF THE COLUMBIA: AROUND THE WORLD WITH JOHN BOIT. Edited by Dorothy O. Johansen. Portland, Oreg.: Beaver Books, 1960. 92 pp.

Extracts in DIARY OF AMERICA, edited by Josef Berger, pp. 253-260.

> 1790-1793. Fifth officer on Captain Robert Gray's COLUMBIA, first American ship to sail to the northwest coast from Boston around the Horn; brief account of Hawaiian Islands; Northwest coast; Indians; discovery of the Columbia River; repair of the ship at the Spanish settlement at Nootka; drama of an Indian plot against Captain Gray which failed.

LOG OF THE UNION: JOHN BOIT'S REMARKABLE VOYAGE TO THE NORTHWEST COAST AND AROUND THE WORLD, 1794-1796. Edited by Edmund Hayes. North Pacific Studies, no. 6. Portland, Oreg.: Oregon Historical Society, 1981. 136 pp.

> 1794-1796. Captain of UNION on profitable and safe trading voyage from Boston to Canton; stops at northwest coast for furs and at Hawaiian Islands for supplies.

BROWN, WILLIAM   1486

In THE WILDERNESS ROAD, by Thomas Speed, pp. 56-63. Filson Club Publication no. 2. Louisville, Ky.: J.P. Morton, 1886.

> Aug-Nov 1790. Diary of travel from Hanover County, Virginia, to Kentucky, along the Ohio route; notes of distances, etc.

CHAPLIN, EBENEZER, 1733-1822   1487

Shumway, H.L. "An Old-Time Minister." WORCESTER SOCIETY OF ANTIQUITY PROCEEDINGS 5 (1882):44-66.

> 1790-1794. Extracts from clergyman's diary; brief notes of parish and church work, personal affairs and weather at Sutton, Massachusetts.

FERRIS, ZACHARIAH, 1716-1803   1488

Valinger, Leon de, Jr., ed. "Journal of Zachariah Ferris's Visits to Southern Friends' Meetings." FRIENDS' HISTORICAL ASSOCIATION BULLETIN 22 (1933): 58-70.

> Oct 1790-Feb 1791. Quaker's diary of journeys from Wrightsborough, Georgia, to Wilmington; preceded by brief memoranda of meetings visited on journey southward from Gaines River, Virginia; interesting spellings.

FULLER, ELIZABETH, 1775-1856   1489

In HISTORY OF THE TOWN OF PRINCETON, IN THE COUNTY OF WORCESTER AND COMMONWEALTH OF MASSACHUSETTS, by Francis Everett Blake, pp. 302-322. Princeton, Mass.: Published by the town, 1915.

Extracts in DIARY OF AMERICA, by Josef Berger, pp. 144-147.

> 1790-1792. Diary kept by minister's daughter; charming record of the minutiae of a girl's domestic and social life in Princeton; cookery, housewifery, visits, education; some doggerel verses; interesting vocabulary.

HARMAR, JOSIAH, 1753-1813   1490

Meek, Basil. "General Harmar's Expedition." OHIO ARCHAEOLOGICAL AND HISTORICAL QUARTERLY 20 (1911): 74-108. Journal, pp. 89-96.

> Sep-Nov 1790. Unsuccessful punitive expedition against Indians above Wabash headquarters; troop movements around Little and Great Miami, etc.

HEWARD, HUGH, d. 1803   1491

In THE JOHN ASKIN PAPERS, edited by Milo M. Quaife, vol. 1, pp. 339-360. Detroit: Detroit Library Commission, 1928.

> Mar-May 1790. Fur trader's account of journey from Detroit to the Illinois by canoe; full details of travel; impersonal but interesting.

HILL, WILLIAM   1492

In THE PRESBYTERIANS, 1783-1840, A COLLECTION OF SOURCE MATERIALS, edited by William Warren Sweet, pp. 755-777. Religion on the American Frontier, vol. 2. New York and London: Harper and Brothers, 1936.

> 1790-1791. Experience as a Presbyterian itinerant preacher in Virginia before ordination and first pastorate; an attempt to preach at Williamsburg, Virginia.

INGRAHAM, JOSEPH, 1762-1800   1493

JOSEPH INGRAHAM'S JOURNAL OF THE BRIGANTINE HOPE ON A VOYAGE TO THE NORTHWEST COAST OF AMERICA, 1790-92. Edited by Mark D. Kaplanoff. Barre, Mass.: Imprint Society, 1971. 248 pp.

Extracts in "An Account of a Recent Discovery of Seven Islands in the South Pacific Ocean," edited by Jeremy Belknap. MASSACHUSETTS HISTORICAL SOCIETY COLLECTIONS 2 (1793):20-24.

> 1790-1792. Journal of captain of the HOPE, involved in sea otter trade between the northwest coast and China; voyage from Boston to what is now British Columbia via Cape Horn, the Marquesas, Hawaii, then to China and back to the Northwest; daily events, inhabitants and natural history of places visited; details of trading process; relations with Hawaiians, Spanish, Indians; some interesting reflections on such topics as slavery and origin of races.

L'HOMMEDIEU, ABIGAIL, 1774-1851   1494

In OLD HOUSES OF THE ANTIENT TOWN OF NORWICH, by Mary Elizabeth Perkins, pp. 26-30. Norwich, Conn.: Press of the Bulletin, 1895.

> 1790-1841. Undated extracts containing fragmentary but interesting notes; personal, social, love affairs, journeys.

MACLAY, SAMUEL, 1741-1811   1495

Meginness, John F., ed. "Journal of Samuel Maclay." HISTORICAL JOURNAL 1 (1887):137-151, 169-187, 201-216.

JOURNAL OF SAMUEL MACLAY, WHILE SURVEYING THE WEST BRANCH OF THE SUSQUEHANNA, THE SINNEMAHONING AND THE ALLEGHENY RIVERS. Williamsport, Pa.: Gazette and Bulletin Printing House, 1887. 63 pp.

> Apr-Sep 1790. Surveying journal kept by member of lower house of Pennsylvania legislature; examining headwaters of Susquehanna and streams of recently purchased northwestern Pennsylvania territory; weather, taverns, adventures, camp life, relations with settlers; rather impersonal but quite interesting.

MARSHALL and BENZIAN   1496

In RECORDS OF THE MORAVIANS IN NORTH CAROLINA, edited by Adelaide L. Fries, vol. 5, pp. 1989-1997.

> 1790-1791. Journey made by two Moravians from Salem, North Carolina, accompanied by Brother Johann Samuel, a Negro; inspecting lands given by Henry Laurens; observations of the land, seeking opportunities for the brethren.

POPE, JOHN, 1770-1845   1497

A TOUR THROUGH THE SOUTHERN AND WESTERN TERRITORIES OF THE UNITED STATES OF NORTH-AMERICA. Richmond, Va.: Printed by J. Dixon for the author, 1792. 104 pp. Reprint. New York: C.L. Woodward, 1888.

Extracts relating to Tennessee in EARLY TRAVELS IN THE TENNESSEE COUNTRY, edited by Samuel C. Williams, pp. 318-319.

Extracts in AMERICAN HISTORY TOLD BY CONTEMPORARIES, edited by Albert B. Hart, vol. 3, pp. 110-114.

> 1790-1791. Diary of travel through the southern and western states, the Mississippi and Ohio valleys; notes on Creek Indians, scenery, towns, social customs; literary style.

QUIMPER, MANUEL, fl. 1790   1498

In SPANISH EXPLORATIONS IN THE STRAIT OF JUAN DE FUCA, by Henry R. Wagner, pp. 80-132. Santa Ana, Calif.: Fine Arts Press, 1933.

> 1790. Diary of the commander of PRINCESA REAL on a Spanish exploration into the Strait of Juan de Fuca; meetings with and descriptions of Indians, gifts exchanged, entertainments; weather and soundings; naming of islands; claiming the area for Spain with prescribed ceremonies.

SEVIER, JOHN, 1745-1815   1499

DeWitt, John H., ed. "Journal of John Sevier." TENNESSEE HISTORICAL MAGAZINE 5 (1919):156-194, 232-264; 6 (1920):18-60.

In ANDREW JACKSON AND EARLY TENNESSEE HISTORY, by Samuel G. Heiskell, vol. 2, pp. 503-614. Nashville: Ambrose Printing Co., 1920.

> 1790-1815. Personal diary of member of United States House of Representatives and first governor of Tennessee; mostly line-a-day; details of ordinary daily routine and thought; weather; chief public and social affairs; some linguistic interest.

SMITH, WILLIAM LOUGHTON, 1762-1812   1500

NEW YORK EVENING POST, 14, 21, 28 April, 5 May, and 2 June 1888.

"Journal of William Loughton Smith." MASSACHUSETTS HISTORICAL SOCIETY PROCEEDINGS 51 (1917-1918):20-88. Journal, pp. 20-75.

> Aug-Sep 1790. Diary kept while member of United States House of Representatives from South Carolina; visit to Rhode Island when it came into Union; descriptions of people and places.

> Apr-May 1791. Trip from Philadelphia to Charleston; detailed description of historic sights, such as Mount Vernon, on the way. Corrects earlier text.

STANLEY, WILLIAM, d. 1814   1501

"Diary of Major William Stanley." HISTORICAL AND PHILOSOPHICAL SOCIETY OF OHIO QUARTERLY PUBLICATIONS 14 (1919):19-32.

> 1790-1809. Private diary mainly concerned with his business and journeys as one of principal merchants of Cincinnati; hurried brief entries, but giving good picture of frontier trade; some interesting spellings.

WALCUTT, THOMAS, 1758-1840   1502

"Journal of Thomas Walcutt." MASSACHUSETTS HISTORI-CAL SOCIETY PROCEEDINGS, 1st ser. 17 (1879-1880): 174-206.

In HISTORIC HIGHWAYS OF AMERICA, by Archer B. Hulbert, vol. 12, pp. 43-63.

> Jan-Apr 1790. Travel to Marietta, Ohio, via Virginia route, and return to Philadelphia; substantial entries containing interesting details of public and social affairs in the new settlements; pleasant travel notes; taverns, food, etc.

1791

AUPAMUT, HENDRICK   1503

Coates, B.H. "A Narrative of an Embassy to the Western Indians." PENNSYLVANIA HISTORICAL SOCIETY MEMOIRS 2 (1827-1830):61-131. Diary, pp. 76-131.

> May-Oct 1791. Journey of chief of the Mohicans to and conferences with western Indians; interesting as Indian's description of his people and his opinions on their treatment by white men; speaking for United States against Britain; written up from notes.

BRADLEY, DANIEL, d. 1825   1504

JOURNAL OF CAPT. DANIEL BRADLEY. With copious comment by Frazer E. Wilson. Greenville, Ohio: F.H. Jobes & Son, 1935. 75 pp.

> 1791-1795. Military journals of the Ohio frontier; expeditions of St. Clair and Wayne against Maumee Indians; marches, skirmishes; some notes on countryside and garrison life.

CAMPBELL, PATRICK, d. 1823   1505

TRAVELS IN THE INTERIOR INHABITED PARTS OF NORTH AMERICA. Edinburgh: Printed for the author and sold by J. Guthrie, 1793. 387 pp.; Edited, with an introduction, by Hugh H. Langton, and with notes by William F. Ganong. Champlain Society Publications, 23. Toronto: Champlain Society, 1937. 326 pp.

> 1791-1792. Travel journal kept by former member of the Forty-second Regiment; from Scotland to St. John's, Fredericton, Quebec, Montreal, Niagara, Genesee, Albany, New York, New Jersey, St. John's and return to Scotland; notes on farming, Indians, soil, climate, social affairs, politics; good observations in simple style.

Extract in ONTARIO HISTORICAL SOCIETY PAPERS AND RECORDS 21 (1924):91-98.

> Nov 1791.

CRESSON, CALEB, 1742-1816   1506

DIARY OF CALEB CRESSON. Philadelphia: Privately printed, 1877. 214 pp.

> 1791-1792. Notes on life in Philadelphia; journey to New England, with good descriptions and accounts of historic scenes.

ERNST, JOHN FREDERICK   1507

"Rev. John Frederick Ernst's Account of His Removal from Pennsylvania to New York." PENNSYLVANIA MAGA-ZINE OF HISTORY AND BIOGRAPHY 42 (1918):172-173.

> Nov 1791. Journey by horseback, wagon and boat; details of migration interspersed with notations of pastoral functions.

FIDLER, PETER   1508

In JOURNALS OF SAMUEL HEARNE AND PHILIP TURNOR, edited by J.B. Tyrell, pp. 493-555. Champlain Society Publications, 21. Toronto: Champlain Society, 1934.

> Sep 1791-Apr 1792. Journal of exploration kept by surveyor's assistant, employed by Hudson's Bay Company; journey with Chippewa Indians to Slave Lake and east and west of Slave River; many notes of travel, personal observations; Indian affairs, customs; stories; a very entertaining account of fur-trading life.

GREEN, ASHBEL, 1762-1848   1509

THE LIFE OF ASHBEL GREEN. Prepared by Joseph H. Jones. New York: R. Carter & Brothers, 1849. 628 pp. Diary, pp. 204-472 passim.

> Jun-Jul 1791. Extracts from clergyman's travel diary; preaching, work as pastor of Second Presbyterian Church in Philadelphia; journeys into New England, etc.; work as president of College of New Jersey.

KERSHAW, JAMES, b. 1764   1510

In HISTORIC CAMDEN, by Thomas J. Kirkland and Robert M. Kennedy, vol. 1, pp. 404-413. Columbia, S.C.: The State Co., 1905.

> 1791-1815. Diary extracts containing very brief notes of social affairs in Camden, South Carolina; lively details of amusements, fashions, people, plays, etc.

LINCKLAEN, JOHN, b. 1768   1511

TRAVELS IN THE YEARS 1791 AND 1792 IN PENNSYL-VANIA, NEW YORK AND VERMONT. Edited by Helen L. Fairchild. New York and London: G.P. Putnam's Sons, 1897.

> 1791-1792 (with gaps). Journeys as agent of the Holland Land Company; descriptions of places; professional interests.

Butterworth, Elise W. "John Lincklaen of the Holland Land Company: I." HALVE MAEN 43 (1968):11-12, 16.

> Aug 1791. Excerpts covering travel through western Pennsylvania and New York; commercial prospects, particularly in maple sugar production.

MAIR, JOHN, 1744-1830   1512

"Journal of John Mair, 1791." AMERICAN HISTORICAL REVIEW 12 (1906-1907):77-94.

> Jan-Jul 1791. Englishman's visit to United States and Canada; London to Charleston, Philadelphia, New York, Boston, Hartford, Albany, Fort George, Montreal, Quebec; good descriptions of a "civilised" man looking at strange people in a strange country.

MARTIN, ISAAC, 1757-1828   1513

A JOURNAL OF THE LIFE, TRAVEL, LABOURS, AND RELI-GIOUS EXPERIENCES OF ISAAC MARTIN. Philadelphia: Printed by W.P. Gibbons, 1834. 160 pp.

> 1791-1823. New Jersey Quaker's notes on church work, travels, religious reflections, reading.

NEWMAN, SAMUEL, d. 1791   1514

Quaife, Milo M., ed. "A Picture of the First United States Army: The Journal of Captain Samuel Newman." WISCONSIN MAGAZINE OF HISTORY 2 (1918-1919):40-73.

Jul-Oct 1791. St. Clair's campaign against north-western Indians; good picture of army life; journey with his company to Philadelphia, then to Cincinnati, and advance northward; highly personal, with excellent details of deplorable moral and disciplinary state of army.

O'BRIEN, JOSEPH   1515

"Extracts from Interleaved Almanacs Kept in Newbury-port, Probably by Joseph O'Brien." ESSEX INSTITUTE HISTORICAL COLLECTIONS 44 (1908):332-337.

1791-1815. Brief notes of outstanding personal, local, and public events around Newburyport, Massachusetts.

PROCTOR, THOMAS, 1739-1806   1516

In PENNSYLVANIA ARCHIVES, 2d ser., vol. 4, pp. 465-524.

In AN AUTHENTIC AND COMPREHENSIVE HISTORY OF BUFFALO, by William Ketchum, vol. 1, pp. 413-426, vol. 2, pp. 305-318. Buffalo: Rockwell, Baker & Hill, Printers, 1864-1865.

Mar-May 1791. Carefully written official report of colonel sent by United States government as a commissioner to Indians; journey from Philadelphia to Buffalo Creek and around Lake Erie; accounts of Indians and their customs; treaty with Six Nations.

RAMSAY, MARTHA LAURENS, 1759-1811   1517

MEMOIRS OF THE LIFE OF MARTHA LAURENS RAMSAY, 2d ed. By David Ramsay. Charlestown, Mass.: Printed and sold by Samuel Etheridge, Jun'r, 1812. 270 pp. Journal, app. 5, pp. 122-208. Reprint of 1st edition. Philadelphia: American Sunday-School Union, 1845. 262 pp.

1791-1808. Religious reflections and self-analysis, self-abasements; a few notes of illnesses, deaths, church services.

SAUNDERS, DANIEL   1518

A JOURNAL OF THE TRAVELS AND SUFFERINGS OF DANIEL SAUNDERS, JUN., A MARINER ON BOARD THE SHIP COMMERCE, OF BOSTON, SAMUEL JOHNSON, COMMANDER, WHICH WAS CAST AWAY NEAR CAPE MOREBET, ON THE COAST OF ARABIA, JULY 10, 1792. Salem, Mass.: Printed by Thomas C. Cushing, 1794. 128 pp. Frequently reprinted, with various pagings.

Extract in THE SHIPS AND SAILORS OF OLD SALEM, by Ralph D. Paine, pp. 252-287.

1791-1794. Narrative, partly in diary form; escapes and sufferings in the Arabian desert.

SURIA, TOMAS DE, b. ca. 1761   1519

Wagner, Henry R., trans. and ed. "Journal of Tomás de Suria of His Voyage with Malaspina to the Northwest Coast of America in 1791." PACIFIC HISTORICAL REVIEW 5 (1936):234-276. Reprint. Glendale, Calif.: Arthur H. Clark, 1936.

Feb-Aug 1791. Journal of painter who joined the Malaspina expedition at Acapulco aboard the DESCUBIERTA; description of Cape Suckling, Prince William Sound and Strait of Bucareli; drawings of animals and inhabitants; notes of sailing conditions, meetings with Indians, trading and customs.

VENABLE, RICHARD N., 1763-1838   1520

Morrison, A.J., ed. "Diary of Richard N. Venable." TYLER'S QUARTERLY HISTORICAL AND GENEALOGICAL MAGAZINE 2 (1920-1921):135-138.

1791-1792. View of Virginia lawyer's life; traveling from court to court, relaxing at home, etc.; comments on George Washington's popularity; character traits admired in others; western land speculation.

1792

ALCALA-GALIANO, DIONISIO, 1760-1805   1521

"Extract of the Diary Executed by the Schooners SUTIL and MEXICANA under the Command of Don Dionisio Galeano and Don Cayetano Valdes in the Estrecho or Canal de Juan de Fuca in the Year 1792." In SPANISH EXPLORATIONS IN THE STRAIT OF JUAN DE FUCA, by Henry R. Wagner, pp. 210-227. Santa Ana, Calif.: Fine Arts Press, 1933.

Jun-Oct 1792. Narrative style diary of Spanish commander who met the ships of the Vancouver expedition at Boundary Bay and warily exchanged information; continuation of their explorations of channels and inlets of the Strait of Juan de Fuca, chiefly separately but sometimes jointly; feeling that English had the advantage with more and larger ships and more men.

BELL, EDWARD   1522

Meany, Edmond S., ed. "A New Vancouver Journal." WASHINGTON HISTORICAL QUARTERLY 5 (1914):129-137, 215-224, 300-308; 6 (1915):50-68.

Mar-Oct 1792. Sea journal supposedly kept by the clerk of the CHATHAM during Vancouver's voyage to northwest coast; accounts of Nootkas, etc.; descriptions of country, movements of expedition.

A NEW VANCOUVER JOURNAL ON THE DISCOVERY OF PUGET SOUND. Edited by Edmond S. Meany. Seattle, Wash.: 1915. 43 pp.

Apr-Sep 1792. Extracts covering Puget Sound, Vancouver Island and Nootka Sound. Authorship ascribed to Bell and to William Walker, the surgeon.

Barry, J. Neilson, ed. "Columbia River Exploration." OREGON HISTORICAL QUARTERLY 33 (1932):31-42, 143-155.

Oct-Nov 1792. From Vancouver Island to the Columbia; exploration up the river, some 120 miles; encounters with Indians; on to San Francisco.

CAAMAÑO, JACINTO, b. ca. 1750   1523

Grenfell, Harold, trans.; Wagner, Henry R., and Newcombe, W.A., eds. "The Journal of Jacinto Caamaño." BRITISH COLUMBIA HISTORICAL QUARTERLY 2 (1938):189-222, 265-301.

Mar-Sep 1792. Record kept by a lieutenant in the Royal Spanish Navy, commanding the frigate ARANZAZU on the exploring expedition along the west coast of North America from San Blas to Nootka Sound; detailed descriptions of Indians, their appearance, dress, masks; the explorers' reception and entertainment in a village.

CARPENTER, BENJAMIN 1524

In THE SHIPS AND SAILORS OF OLD SALEM, by Ralph D. Paine, pp. 417-439 passim.

May 1792. Extracts from sea journal; voyage of the HERCULES from Boston to the East Indies; notes on ports and trade.

CUTTING, NATHANIEL, d. 1822 1525

"Extracts from a Journal of a Gentleman Visiting Boston in 1792." MASSACHUSETTS HISTORICAL SOCIETY PROCEEDINGS, 1st ser. 12 (1871-1873):60-67.

Sep 1792-Jan 1793. Extracts from well written and interesting travel journal; visit to Boston from Providence; extensive notes describing sights, places, social life in Boston.

Brooks, William G., ed. "Nathaniel Cutting's Journal of an Embassy to Algiers in 1793, under Col. David Humphreys." HISTORICAL MAGAZINE 4 (1860):262-265, 296-298, 359-363.

Aug 1793-Feb 1794 (with gap). Voyage from Lisbon to Algiers.

ESPINOSA Y TELLO, JOSE, 1763-1815 1526

A SPANISH VOYAGE TO VANCOUVER AND THE NORTH-WEST COAST OF AMERICA BEING THE NARRATIVE OF THE VOYAGE MADE IN 1792 BY THE SCHOONERS SUTIL AND MEXICANA TO EXPLORE THE STRAIT OF JUAN DE FUCA. Translated from the Spanish with an introduction by Cecil Jane. London: Argonaut Press, 1930. 142 pp.

Jan-Nov 1792. Narrative style diary; preparations and supplies for the two ships; sailing conditions from Acapulco to Nootka Sound; meeting with various ships, including Captain Vancouver's ship DISCOVERY; manners, customs and mode of life of Indian tribes along the Northwest coast.

FARIS, WILLIAM, 1728-1804 1527

"Extracts from Diary of William Faris of Annapolis, Maryland." MARYLAND HISTORICAL MAGAZINE 28 (1933): 197-244.

1792-1804. Extracts providing brief but interesting notes; gossipy record of life, death, etc. in Annapolis.

FRYE, JOSEPH 1528

In FRYEBURG, MAINE, AN HISTORICAL SKETCH, by John Stuart Barrows, pp. 46-48. Fryeburg: Pequawket Press, 1938.

1792-1797. Extracts from private diary of town clerk; brief notes of his activities; musters, church, journeys, weather, etc.

HALL, RUFUS, b. 1744 1529

A JOURNAL OF THE LIFE, RELIGIOUS EXERCISES, AND TRAVELS IN THE WORK OF THE MINISTRY OF RUFUS HALL. Byberry, Pa.: J. and I. Comly, 1840. 176 pp.

1792-1814. New York Quaker's journal, partly auto-biographical; meetings and travel in New York, New England, Upper Canada, etc.

JOHNSON, ROBERT C., b. 1766 1530

Snow, Vernon F., ed. "The Grand Tour Diary of Robert C. Johnson." AMERICAN PHILOSOPHICAL SOCIETY PROCEEDINGS 102 (1958):60-105.

Nov 1792-Mar 1793. Prominent young lawyer's travel diary; crossing from New York to Bristol; social and intellectual life among important people in England, including Edmund Burke; debates in the House of Commons; theatre of Mrs. Siddons; the trial of Thomas Paine; travels in revolutionary France, where diarist witnessed the execution of Louis XVI; notes on Gouverneur Morris; journey to Italy, with continued enjoyment of architecture, art, drama and society.

LEE, BENJAMIN, 1765-1828 1531

In AMERICAN BACKLOGS: THE STORY OF GERTRUDE TYLER AND HER FAMILY, compiled by Edith Kermit Carow Roosevelt and Kermit Roosevelt, pp. 52-64, 66-77 passim. New York and London: C. Scribner's Sons, 1928.

1792-1793. Captain's account of voyage of the FAIR AMERICAN.

Feb-May 1796. Extracts covering voyage from New York to China.

MANBY, THOMAS, 1766-1834 1532

Howay, F.W. and Elliott, T.C., eds. "Vancouver's Brig CHATHAM in the Columbia." OREGON HISTORICAL QUARTERLY 43 (1942):318-327.

Oct-Nov 1792. Private journal kept by CHATHAM's master; description of perils of navigating the mouth of the Columbia; Indian customs; report of captain's explorations extending more than one hundred miles up the river.

MENZIES, ARCHIBALD, 1754-1842 1533

MENZIES' JOURNAL OF VANCOUVER'S VOYAGE. Edited by Charles F. Newcombe. Archives of British Columbia Memoir, no. 5. Victoria, B.C.: Printed by W.H. Collin, 1923. 171 pp.

Apr-Oct 1792. Journal kept by botanist and Royal Navy surgeon with Vancouver's expedition off the Northwest coast; general diary of happenings; natural history notes; scientific appendix.

MICKLE, SAMUEL, 1746-1830 1534

In NOTES ON OLD GLOUCESTER COUNTY, NEW JERSEY, edited by Frank H. Stewart, vol. 1, pp. 157-253.

Extracts in NEW JERSEY SOCIETY OF PENNSYLVANIA YEAR-BOOK, 1921-1924.

1792-1829. Brief entries in merchant's diary; personal and local affairs in Woodbury, New Jersey; literary and genealogical interests.

"Diary of Samuel Mickle." FRIENDS' HISTORICAL SOCIETY JOURNAL 22 (1925):78-79.

1821-1829. Extracts.

MINOR, STEPHEN 1535

Ross, Edward H. and Phelps, Dawson A., trans. and eds. "A Journey Over the Natchez Trace in 1792: A Document from the Archives of Spain." JOURNAL OF MISSISSIPPI HISTORY 15 (1953):252-273.

Mar-Apr 1792. Detailed account by emissary of Spanish government; negotiations with the Choctaws about Spanish and Indian land claims and trading at Fort Nogales, at the site of Vicksburg; journey over Indian trail, Path to the Choctaw Nation, which later became part of Natchez Trace.

PUGET, PETER, ca. 1764-1822　　　　**1536**

Anderson, Bern, ed. "The Vancouver Expedition: Peter Puget's Journal of the Exploration of Puget Sound." PACIFIC NORTHWEST QUARTERLY 30 (1939):177-217.

> May-Jun 1792. Extracts from sea journal of lieutenant aboard Vancouver's flagship DISCOVERY during exploration of Puget Sound from Port Discovery to Birch Bay; full notes on topography, natural history.

REID, JOHN　　　　**1537**

In AMERICAN BACKLOGS: THE STORY OF GERTRUDE TYLER AND HER FAMILY, compiled by Edith Kermit Carow Roosevelt and Kermit Roosevelt, pp. 50-52. New York and London: C. Scribner's Sons, 1928.

> Jan 1792. Ship's log kept by second mate on the FAIR AMERICAN; cruise from Boston to East Indies; mutiny; ship life; interesting spellings.

UNDERWOOD, THOMAS TAYLOR　　　　**1538**

JOURNAL, THOMAS TAYLOR UNDERWOOD. Cincinnati: Society of Colonial Wars in the State of Ohio, 1945. 33 pp.

> 1792-1800. Sporadic entries in officer's journal covering Wayne's campaign against the Indians; reports on marches, courts martial, duels, engagements, assignments and duties; notes on Andrew Jackson; gathering of Indians for the Treaty of Greenville.

VANCOUVER, GEORGE, 1758?-1798　　　　**1539**

A VOYAGE OF DISCOVERY TO THE NORTH PACIFIC OCEAN, AND ROUND THE WORLD. Edited by John Vancouver. London: Printed for G.G. and J. Robinson, 1798. 3 vols. Reprint. Bibliotheca Australiana, nos. 30-33. Amsterdam: N. Israel; New York: Da Capo, 1968.

A VOYAGE OF DISCOVERY TO THE NORTH PACIFIC OCEAN, AND ROUND THE WORLD. A new ed., with corrections. Edited by John Vancouver. London: Printed for J. Stockdale, 1801. 6 vols.

> 1792-1795. British naval officer's official report of explorations in Pacific and along Northwest coast; command of fleet comprised of DISCOVERY, CHATHAM and DAEDALUS; visit to Hawaii; exploration of Puget Sound and circumnavigation of Vancouver Island, claiming Spanish territory at Nootka Sound assigned to Britain by the Nootka Convention; activities along coasts of Washington and Oregon, with notes on Indians; calls at California missions and settlements.

Extracts in VANCOUVER'S DISCOVERY OF PUGET SOUND, by Edmond S. Meany, pp. 61-334. New York and London: Macmillan, 1907.

Extracts in "Oregon Coast as Seen by Vancouver in 1792," edited by T.C. Elliott. OREGON HISTORICAL QUARTERLY 30 (1929):33-42.

> Apr-Oct 1792.

VANCOUVER IN CALIFORNIA, 1792-1794; THE ORIGINAL ACCOUNT. Edited and annotated by Marguerite E. Wilbur. Early California Travel Series, 9-10, 22. Los Angeles: G. Dawson, 1953-1954. 3 vols. in 1.

> 1792-1794.

1793

ANON.　　　　**1540**

Knopf, Richard C., ed. "Two Journals of the Kentucky Volunteers 1793 and 1794." FILSON CLUB HISTORY QUARTERLY 27 (1953):247-281.

> Oct-Nov 1793. Uneventful campaign under Major General Charles Scott against Indians in Whitewater area; sightings of Indians but no real engagements; description of terrain; mutiny and desertion among the Kentucky Volunteers.

BARNO Y FERRUSOLA, JUAN FRANCISCO JOSE　　　　**1541**

In SPANISH WAR VESSELS ON THE MISSISSIPPI, by Abraham P. Nasatir, pp. 189-231. New Haven: Yale University Press, 1968.

> Nov 1793-Feb 1794. Cruise of LA FLECHA from Natchez to Nogales and Arkansas River to inspect every vessel for "seditious materials and suspicious persons"; to New Madrid to give aid, having received word of planned French attack; capture of Frenchman and two Americans; delivery of prisoners to post at Nogales.

BLANCHARD, JEAN PIERRE, 1753-1809　　　　**1542**

JOURNAL OF MY FORTY-FIFTH ASCENSION. Philadelphia: Printed for C. Cist, 1793. Reprint. MAGAZINE OF HISTORY, extra no. 64, 16 (1918):260-282.

> Jan 1793. Record of balloon ascension at Philadelphia on January 9.

BUELL, JOHN HUTCHINSON　　　　**1543**

"A Fragment from the Diary of Major John Hutchinson Buell, U.S.A., Who Joined the American Army at the Beginning of the Revolutionary War and Remained in Service until 1803." MILITARY SERVICE INSTITUTION OF THE UNITED STATES JOURNAL 40 (1907):102-113, 260-268.

> 1793-1795. Brief description of journey from Connecticut to Fort Washington (Cincinnati); military activities in the Northwest Territory in army commanded by Anthony Wayne; treaty negotiations with Indians; dueling.

ELLIOT, JAMES, 1775-1839　　　　**1544**

THE POETICAL AND MISCELLANEOUS WORKS OF JAMES ELLIOT, CITIZEN OF GUILFORD, VERMONT, AND LATE A NONCOMMISSIONED OFFICER IN THE LEGION OF THE UNITED STATES. Greenfield, Mass.: Printed by Thomas Dickman, 1798. 271 pp. Journal, book 3.

In PEN PICTURES OF EARLY WESTERN PENNSYLVANIA, edited by John W. Harpster, pp. 168-175. Pittsburgh: University of Pittsburgh Press, 1938.

> 1793-1796. Military journal kept during Whiskey Rebellion and Indian warfare in the Old Northwest, Pennsylvania, and Ohio.

EVANS, JOSHUA, 1731-1798　　　　**1545**

FRIENDS' MISCELLANY 10 (1837):43-212.

Extracts in "The Journal of Joshua Evans," by Thomas H. Fawcett. FRIENDS' HISTORICAL ASSOCIATION BULLETIN 28 (1939):30-36.

> 1793-1798. Quaker's diary of New England journeys; meetings in New York, Carolina, Canada; notes on slaves, Indians, racial problems, schools.

FOSS, JOHN, 1744–1800   **1546**

A JOURNAL OF THE CAPTIVITY AND SUFFERINGS OF JOHN FOSS. 2d ed. Newburyport, Mass.: Printed by A. March, 1798. 189 pp.

1793–1797. Captivity and imprisonment at Algiers; mainly narrative, with vivid description of treatment of American captives.

HEMPHILL, JAMES, 1774–1833   **1547**

Ward, Christopher L. "Leaves from the Log-Books and Letters of James Hemphill, Mariner and Merchant of Wilmington." DELAWARE HISTORICAL SOCIETY PAPERS, no. 64 (1914), pp. 1–35.

1793–1797. Extracts from sea journals and letters in biographical article; voyages from Wilmington to Europe and Asia.

Munroe, John A., ed. "James Hemphill's Account of a Visit to Maryland in 1802." DELAWARE HISTORY 3 (1948):61–78.

Oct-Nov 1802. Trip by chaise and stage down the peninsula to Berlin, Maryland, and return to Wilmington; distances covered, accommodations, travel hazards; events at town fair.

HUTCHINSON, JEREMY, 1738–1805   **1548**

"Jeremy Hutchinson Diary." DANVERS HISTORICAL COLLECTIONS 28 (1940):64–69.

May-Jun 1793. Journey on foot from Danvers, Massachusetts, to Danville to visit daughter; notes on distances, crops, farming, weather; interesting vocabulary.

LINCOLN, BENJAMIN, 1733–1810   **1549**

"Journal of a Treaty Held in 1793, with the Indian Tribes North-west of the Ohio, by Commissioners of the United States." MASSACHUSETTS HISTORICAL SOCIETY COLLECTIONS, 3d ser. 5 (1836):109–176.

Extracts in ANTHOLOGY AND BIBLIOGRAPHY OF NIAGARA FALLS, by Charles M. Dow, vol. 1, pp. 94–97.

Apr-Sep 1793. Journey from Philadelphia to Detroit via Albany and Niagara; negotiations and speeches; return via Montreal; many pleasant notes on travel and social affairs.

LINDLEY, JACOB, 1774–1857   **1550**

"Jacob Lindley's Account of a Journey to Attend the Indian Treaty." FRIENDS' MISCELLANY 2 (1831–1832): 49–156. Reprint. "Expedition to Detroit, 1793." MICHIGAN PIONEER AND HISTORICAL COLLECTIONS 17 (1890): 565–632.

Apr-Sep 1793. Quaker peace commissioner's journey to Philadelphia, and thence to Sandusky, to attend peace negotiations with Indians; long notes of scenic and social observations, customs of Indians, and interviews with them; travels around Detroit; sympathy toward Indians; a well written and valuable journal.

"Jacob Lindley's Journal." BUFFALO HISTORICAL SOCIETY PUBLICATIONS 6 (1903):169–182.

Oct-Nov 1797. Mission to Friends in Canada and to the Seneca Indians around Buffalo Creek and Niagara; mostly notes of travel and scenery.

LITTLEHALES, Maj.   **1551**

"Governor Simcoe's Tour through Southern Ontario Including Major Littlehale's Journal." LONDON AND MIDDLESEX HISTORICAL SOCIETY TRANSACTIONS 8 (1917):5–18. Reprinted from CANADIAN LITERARY MESSENGER, 1833.

Feb-Mar 1793. Travel journal of Simcoe's secretary; journey between Niagara and Detroit; notes on Moravians, Indian villages, etc.

MACDONELL, ALEXANDER, 1762–1842   **1552**

"Diary of Gov. Simcoe's Journey from Humber Bay to Matchetache Bay." ROYAL CANADIAN INSTITUTE TRANSACTIONS 1 (1889–1890):128–139.

Sep-Oct 1793. Travel with Simcoe.

In THE PROVINCE OF ONTARIO, by Jesse E. Middleton and Fred Landon, vol. 2, app. A, pp. 1246–1250.

Jan 1799. Domestic and business life in York (Toronto); political and police interests.

MACDONELL, JOHN, 1768–1850   **1553**

In FIVE FUR TRADERS OF THE NORTHWEST, edited by Charles M. Gates, pp. 63–119.

May-Oct 1793. Good narrative by fur trader working for the Northwest Company; first trading journey from Lachine to a post on the Upper Assiniboine River; valuable for account of canoe journey from Grand Portage to Lake of the Woods and for notes on life and customs of the voyageurs.

MICHAUX, ANDRE, 1746–1802   **1554**

In EARLY WESTERN TRAVELS, edited by Reuben G. Thwaites, vol. 3, pp. 27–104.

1793–1796. Extracts from travel diary of French diplomat and botanist; some comments on diplomatic and public affairs, but mainly notes of travel and botanical observations. Translated from the French.

MOORE, JOSEPH, 1732–1793   **1555**

"Joseph Moore's Journal." MICHIGAN PIONEER AND HISTORICAL COLLECTIONS 17 (1890):632–666.

Apr-Sep 1793. Quaker peace commissioner's journey from Philadelphia to Sandusky and Detroit to attend peace negotiations with Indians; less complete, but supplements Jacob Lindley's journal.

**MOREAU DE ST. MERY, MEDERIC LOUIS ELIA,   1556
1750–1819**

MOREAU DE ST. MERY'S AMERICAN JOURNEY. Translated and edited by Kenneth Roberts and Anna M. Roberts. Garden City, N.J.: Doubleday, 1947. 394 pp.

1793–1798. Exciting and well written diary of lawyer, statesman, man of letters and prominent refugee from Reign of Terror following French Revolution; harrowing winter Atlantic crossing; settlement in Philadelphia and activities among French community; observations on American conditions and manners, slavery; return to France on plague-ridden ship.

Norfleet, Fillmore, trans. and ed. "Baltimore as Seen by Moreau de Saint-Méry." MARYLAND HISTORICAL MAGAZINE 35 (1940):221–240.

1794. Extracts covering voyage by packet boat from Norfolk to Baltimore and by packet boat and stagecoach from there to Philadelphia; detailed description of Baltimore; brief descriptions of Wilmington and Philadelphia; most interesting information on travel conditions.

Norfleet, Fillmore, trans. and ed. "Norfolk, Portsmouth

and Gosport as Seen by Moreau de Saint-Méry." VIRGINIA MAGAZINE OF HISTORY AND BIOGRAPHY 48 (1940):12–30.

Mar–May 1794. Extracts describing difficulties encountered in obtaining accommodations for his family upon arrival in America.

NORMAN, JEREMIAH, 1771–1843   1557

Stokes, Durward. "Jeremiah Norman, Pioneer Methodist Minister in Augusta, and His Diary." RICHMOND COUNTY HISTORY 10 (1978):20–35.

1793–1801. Extracts from fourteen volume diary, drawn mainly from March through October 1798 during which time Stokes established the Methodist Episcopal Circuit of Augusta; reports of successful and unsuccessful worship services.

PRINCE, HEZEKIAH, 1771–1840   1558

Prince, George, ed. "Twelve Hundred Miles on Horseback One Hundred Years Ago." NEW ENGLAND MAGAZINE, n.s. 9 (1893–1894):723–734.

Nov 1793–Jan 1794. Partly narrative travel journal; from Kingston, Massachusetts, to Virginia; notes on scenery, people, places, sights; some social comments; tourist notes.

ROUSSEAU, PEDRO ANDRES   1559

"Log of His Majesty's Galoit, LA FLECHE." In SPAIN IN THE MISSISSIPPI VALLEY, 1765–1794, edited by Lawrence Kinnaird, vol. 4, pp. 111–133. American Historical Association Annual Report, 1945. Washington, D.C.: Government Printing Office, 1949.

"Diary of Captain of the Army Don Pedro Rousseau, Commander of the Quadron of Galleys, upon the War Galiot LA FLECHA, from Natchez to New Madrid in the Year 1793 by Order of Colonel of the Royal Army Don Manuel Gayosa de Lemos, Military and Political Governor of the Plaza of Natchez, January 5–March 25, 1793, Natchez to Madrid and Return." In SPANISH WAR VESSELS ON THE MISSISSIPPI, 1792–1796, by Abraham P. Nasatir, pp. 149–188. New Haven: Yale University Press, 1969.

Jan–Mar 1793. Conditions of river travel on Mississippi from Natchez, main base from which galleys operated on upper Mississippi, to New Madrid, most important military post in upper Louisiana; weather, distances, landmarks, meeting with Arkansas Indians and delivery of war materials to fort at New Madrid.

SAVERY, WILLIAM, 1750–1804   1560

A JOURNAL OF THE LIFE, TRAVELS, AND RELIGIOUS LABOURS, OF WILLIAM SAVERY. Compiled by Jonathan Evans. London: C. Gilpin, 1844. 316 pp.

"The Journal of William Savery." FRIENDS' LIBRARY 1 (1837):327–459.

1793–1798. Travels of ministering Quaker from Philadelphia; work among Indians around Great Lakes and in Virginia; voyage to and work in England, Ireland, Germany, France; much description of European places and persons.

TOULMIN, HARRY, 1767–1823   1561

THE WESTERN COUNTRY IN 1793; REPORTS ON KENTUCKY AND VIRGINIA. Edited by Marian Tinley and Godfrey Davies. San Marino, Calif.: Henry E. Huntington Library, 1948. 141 pp.

May–Aug 1793. Travel journal of English Unitarian

minister visiting America to report to his parishioners the suitability of America for emigrants; letter-journal of the voyage; detailed descriptions of Virginia, especially Norfolk and Richmond; land, farms, people, prices of products, food, lodging, wages, political and religious affairs, family life, education, slavery and banking.

WARD, SUSANNA, 1779–1860   1562

In THE HOLYOKE DIARIES, edited by George F. Dow, pp. 175–188.

1793–1856. Brief notes on family, personal, social and local affairs in Salem, Massachusetts; journeys and visits.

WILLIAMS FAMILY   1563

In A HISTORY OF EAST BOSTON, by William H. Sumner, pp. 331–339. Boston: J.E. Tilton, 1858.

1793–1801. Extracts from diary apparently kept by the daughters of Henry Howell Williams, 1736–1802; social affairs in and around Boston.

YARNALL, PETER, 1754–1798   1564

In THOMAS RICHARDSON OF SOUTH SHIELDS, compiled by Mary Thomas Seaman, pp. 176–196. New York: T.A. Wright, 1929.

"Peter Yarnall's Journal." FRIENDS' MISCELLANY 2 (1831–1832):253–308.

May–Dec 1793. Travel journal of Quaker from Byberry, Pennsylvania; visit to New York and Massachusetts; journey, meetings, visits to Friends; long but impersonal notes.

1794

ANON.   1565

Knopf, Richard C., ed. "Two Journals of the Kentucky Volunteers 1793 and 1794." FILSON CLUB HISTORY QUARTERLY 27 (1953):247–281.

Jul–Oct 1794. Major General Anthony Wayne's campaign against the Confederated Indians of Kentucky, as recorded by a Kentucky volunteer under Major General Charles Scott; difficulties of terrain, disorderly behavior of troops, problems with supplies; battles against Indians and their French and English allies; General Wayne's continual attempts at negotiation.

ANON.   1566

Smith, Dwight L., ed. "From Greene Ville to Fallen Timbers: A Journal of the Wayne Campaign." INDIANA HISTORICAL SOCIETY PUBLICATIONS 16 (1952):249–326.

Jul–Sep 1794. Account by member of General Anthony Wayne's campaign against the Confederated Indians of the Old Northwest; diarist's support of Wayne's subordinate General James Wilkinson in his machinations against Wayne; supply problems, difficulties of terrain; route, distances marched, encampments; other personalities of the campaign.

ANON.   1567

In TRAVEL ACCOUNTS OF INDIANA, compiled by Shirley S. McCord, pp. 38–41.

Sep–Oct 1794. Soldier's description of life in Kentucky Volunteers, probably under General Charles Scott, in area near Fort Wayne after defeat of Indians at battle of Fallen Timbers.

BALDWIN, JOHN, b. 1722   1568

"John Baldwin's Diary; or Journal of Time." FRIENDS' MISCELLANY 5 (1833-1834):249-269.

    1794-1798. Journal of Pennsylvania Quaker; introspection, schooling, meetings, personalities.

BAYARD, MARTHA   1569

THE JOURNAL OF MARTHA PINTARD BAYARD. Edited by Samuel Bayard Dod. New York: Dodd, Mead, 1894. 141 pp.

    1794-1797. Journal describing fashionable social life in London.

BISHOP, CHARLES, b. ca. 1760   1570

THE JOURNAL AND LETTERS OF CAPTAIN CHARLES BISHOP ON THE NORTHWEST COAST OF AMERICA, IN THE PACIFIC AND IN NEW SOUTH WALES. Edited by Michael Roe. Hakluyt Society, 2d ser., no. 131. Cambridge: Published for the Hakluyt Society at the University Press, 1967. 342 pp.

    1794-1799. Journal of British merchant-sailor and captain of the RUBY on a fur-trading expedition from Bristol to Pacific Northwest coast and what is now British Columbia via South America, Easter Islands, Hawaiian Islands; ship life; provisions, disease, discipline; brief description of armed skirmishes among Hawaiians; fuller details of Indians of Pacific Northwest coast, including comments about evidence for and against cannibalism; planting first known garden in territory which is now Washington and Oregon.

Elliott, T.C., ed. "Journal of Captain Charles Bishop of the RUBY in 1795." OREGON HISTORICAL QUARTERLY 29 (1928):337-347.

    Sep-Nov 1794, May 1795. Extracts covering departure from England, search for harbor along Oregon coast and arrival at the mouth of the Columbia River.

Elliott, T.C., ed. "Journal of the Ship RUBY." OREGON HISTORICAL QUARTERLY 28 (1927):258-280.

    May-Jun 1795, Oct 1795-Jan 1796. Extracts concerning RUBY's sojourn on the Columbia River while trading with Indians; good descriptions of hazards of crossing the bar into the Columbia and of European-Indian interactions.

BOYER, JOHN   1571

JOURNAL OF WAYNE'S CAMPAIGN AGAINST THE INDIANS. Cincinnati: Wm. Dodge, 1866. 23 pp.

Extracts in "Daily Journal of Wayne's Campaign." MICHIGAN PIONEER AND HISTORICAL COLLECTIONS 34 (1904):539-564.

    Jul-Nov 1794. Military journal of lieutenant in the Second Infantry Regiment; Wayne's campaign against Indians; purely military details; mainly movements of American forces.

BROWN, JOHN   1572

Newsome, A.R., ed. "John Brown's Journal of Travel in Western North Carolina in 1795." NORTH CAROLINA HISTORICAL REVIEW 11 (1934):284-313.

    Dec 1794-Jul 1795. Travel diary; interesting spellings.

CAZENOVE, THEOPHILE, 1740-1811   1573

CAZENOVE JOURNAL. Edited by Rayner W. Kelsey. Haverford College Studies, no. 13. Haverford: Pennsylvania History Press, 1922. 103 pp.

Extracts relating to Berks County, Pennsylvania, in EARLY NARRATIVES OF BERKS COUNTY, by James B. Nolan, pp. 157-165.

    Oct-Nov 1794. Travel journal of Holland Land Company agent; through New Jersey and Pennsylvania; shrewd, valuable observations on the land and its people; good descriptions of Moravians. Translated from the French.

CHEW, JOHN   1574

MAGAZINE OF WESTERN HISTORY 11 (1889-1890):383-388.

"The Diary of an Officer in the Indian Country in 1794." AMERICAN HISTORICAL MAGAZINE 3 (1908):639-643.

    Jun 1794. Account of expedition of Indians against Fort Recovery in Upper Canada; diarist thought to be officer of British Indian Department for Upper Canada.

CLARK, WILLIAM, 1770-1838   1575

McGrane, R.C., ed. "William Clark's Journal of General Wayne's Campaign." MISSISSIPPI VALLEY HISTORICAL REVIEW 1 (1914-1915):418-444.

    Jul-Oct 1794. Military journal of campaign against the Shawnee Indians in Ohio; interesting spellings.

THE FIELD NOTES OF CAPT. WILLIAM CLARK. Edited by Ernest S. Osgood. Yale Western Americana Series, 5. New Haven: Yale University Press, 1964. 335 pp.

    1803-1805. Day-by-day account of events at Camp Dubois, the winter quarters of the Lewis and Clark expedition party, opposite the mouth of the Missouri; trip up the Missouri to Mandan villages; notes about river, country, Indians; course and distance traveled.

WESTWARD WITH DRAGOONS; THE JOURNAL OF WILLIAM CLARK ON HIS EXPEDITON TO ESTABLISH FORT OSAGE. Edited for schools by Kate L. Gregg. Fulton, Mo.: Printed by the Ovid Bell Press, 1937. 97 pp. Journal, pp. 21-48.

    Aug-Sep 1808. Journey from St. Louis; picture of the country; many interesting spellings.

Barry, Louise, ed. "William Clark's Diary." KANSAS HISTORICAL QUARTERLY 16 (1948):1-39, 136-174, 274-305, 384-410.

    1826-1831. Official record of Office of Superintendent of Indian Affairs at St. Louis; weather, Mississippi River data, steamboat arrivals and departures; record of Indians visiting Superintendent Clark; most entries by his subordinates.

COOKE, JOHN, 1766-1824   1576

"General Wayne's Campaign in 1794 and 1795." AMERICAN HISTORICAL RECORD 2 (1873):311-316, 339-345.

    Jul-Nov 1794. Captain's military journal; from Greenville, Ohio; valuable account of movements, marches, fort building; impersonal, plain notes.

DAVY, WILLIAM, 1757-1827   1577

Wilkinson, Norman B., ed. "Mr. Davy's Diary." PENNSYLVANIA HISTORY 20 (1953):123-141, 258-279.

Sep-Nov 1794. Record of trip made by newly arrived English merchant with Joseph Priestley, Jr.; from Philadelphia to Northumberland, on the upper Susquehanna in the northern interior of Pennsylvania, where Priestley's father had recently settled; details of travel by carriage and on foot; description of countryside, especially around Northumberland, focusing on possibilities for profitable settlement.

DICKINSON, TIMOTHY, 1761-1813   1578

WORCESTER SOCIETY OF ANTIQUITY PROCEEDINGS 6 (1883):67-89.

1794-1808 (with gaps). Clergyman's journal; religious work and reflections; local news in Holliston, Massachusetts; visits to Boston, etc.

DOW, LORENZO, 1777-1834   1579

QUINTESSENCE OF LORENZO'S WORKS. HISTORY OF COSMOPOLITE; OR, THE FOUR VOLUMES OF LORENZO'S JOURNAL, CONCENTRATED IN ONE. 2d ed., cor. and enl. Philadelphia: Printed and sold by Joseph Rakestraw, 1815. 554 pp. Frequently published under different titles among which are the following:

PERAMBULATIONS OF COSMOPOLITE. Edited by Orrin Scofield. Rochester, N.Y.: Printed for the publisher, 1842. 421 pp.

THE DEALINGS OF GOD, MAN, AND THE DEVIL. With an introductory essay by John Dowling. New York: Cornish, Lamport, 1851; New York: Sheldon, Lambert & Blakeman, 1856. 2 vols. in 1.

HISTORY OF COSMOPOLITE. Rev. and cor. with notes. Philadelphia: J.B. Smith, 1859. 720 pp. Journal, pp. 9-349.

Discussed in AMERICAN DIARY LITERATURE, by Steven E. Kagle, pp. 54-57.

1794-1816. Religious diary with earlier autobiographical entries; account of his life as Methodist circuit rider and revivalist in United States, Canada, England, Ireland; six trips to Mississippi Territory; preaching, camp meetings, spiritual visitations, etc.; long, loud and lively; a valuable picture of religious zeal and of a great eccentric.

EYERLY, JACOB   1580

Wallace, Paul A.W., trans. and ed. "Jacob Eyerly's Journal, 1794: The Survey of Moravian Lands in the Erie Triangle." WESTERN PENNSYLVANIA HISTORICAL MAGAZINE 45 (1962):5-23.

May-Jun 1794. Surveyor's narrative journal; from Pittsburgh to Presque Isle on Lake Erie, and back; surveying tracts given by the state of Pennsylvania to the Moravians on which to establish Indian missions; comments on unrest among Indians; encounters with Indians; notes on the land and its fertility, etc.

FORD, DAVID, d. 1835   1581

"Journal of an Expedition Made in the Autumn of 1794." NEW JERSEY HISTORICAL SOCIETY PROCEEDINGS 8 (1856-1859):75-88.

Sep-Oct 1794. Captain's military journal; the Whiskey Rebellion; expedition into Pennsylvania from New Jersey; descriptions of towns; good accounts of "rebels."

GALES, JOSEPH, 1761-1841   1582

Powell, William S., ed. "The Diary of Joseph Gales." NORTH CAROLINA HISTORICAL REVIEW 26 (1949):335-347.

Sep 1794-Jul 1795. Summary of events leading up to departure of British printer/publisher and family from Germany aboard the CHARLES & HENRY in June 1795; daily entries of voyage to Philadelphia; mostly weather reports; description of boarding and questioning by British privateer.

GOULD, WILLIAM   1583

"Journal by Major William Gould." NEW JERSEY HISTORICAL SOCIETY PROCEEDINGS 3 (1848-1849):173-191.

Sep-Nov 1794. Military journal kept by member of New Jersey Infantry; the Whiskey Rebellion; march into Pennsylvania from Trenton, New Jersey; orders and movements.

HAMBLY, JOHN, 1751-1798   1584

Murdoch, Richard K., ed. "Mission to the Creek Nation in 1794." FLORIDA HISTORICAL QUARTERLY 34 (1956): 266-284.

Jan-Apr 1794. Diary of English trader employed by Panton, Leslie and Company, who carried out diplomatic mission to Creek Indians ordered by Juan Nepomucena de Quesada, governor of East Florida; conversations with chiefs; attempts to counteract influence of James Seagrove, American superintendent of Indian affairs; routine notes of travel.

Ross, Daniel J.J. and Chappell, Bruce S., eds. "Visit to the Indian Nations." FLORIDA HISTORICAL QUARTERLY 55 (1976):60-73.

Jun-Aug 1794. Second of three missions undertaken for Juan Nepomucena de Quesada; delivery of governor's messages of friendship to Creek Indians and attempts to learn about suspected American attempts to woo their allegiance away from Spain.

LAKIN, BENJAMIN, 1767-1849   1585

In THE METHODISTS, A COLLECTION OF SOURCE MATERIALS, edited by William Warren Sweet, pp. 203-260. Religion on the American Frontier, vol. 4. Chicago: University of Chicago Press, 1946.

1794-1820. Introspective journal of a Methodist circuit preacher concerning his doubts and concerns over "duties of religion," resignation to the will of God, examination of his past life and view of the goodness of God; accounts of superstitions and omens; travels in Kentucky, Tennessee and Ohio.

LORIMIER, PIERRE LOUIS   1586

"Journal of Lorimier during the Threatened Genet Invasion of Louisiana." In THE SPANISH REGIME IN MISSOURI, by Louis Houck, vol. 2, pp. 59-99. Chicago: R.R. Donnelly & Sons, 1909.

1794-1795. Journal of the commandant, a naturalized Spanish citizen, at Cape Girardeau, established to guard upper Louisiana (now Missouri) from the French; rumors of war, spies, Indian councils, movements of men and arms; written by his secretary, Louis François Largeau.

M'GILLIVRAY, DUNCAN, d. 1808   1587

THE JOURNAL OF DUNCAN M'GILLIVRAY OF THE NORTH WEST COMPANY. Edited by Arthur S. Morton. Toronto: Macmillan, 1929. 79 pp.

Jul 1794–May 1795. Journal of the fur trade; mostly journey to and winter at Fort St. George, Saskatchewan; account of trade and conduct of Indians; a very interesting picture of character and life of the Indians and of their relation to the traders.

MICHAEL, WILLIAM, 1768–1823 1588

Nead, Benjamin M., ed. "A Journal of the 'Whiskey Insurrection.'" HISTORICAL REGISTER 1 (1883):64–74, 134–147.

"Autobiography of William Michael. Part II." LANCASTER COUNTY HISTORICAL SOCIETY PAPERS 25, no. 7 (1921):69–77.

Oct–Nov 1794. Military journal of federal officer; march to western Pennsylvania to suppress Whiskey Rebellion; marches, army life, personal adventures; interpolation of long narrative of an unfortunate lady; literary allusions.

PARKIN, THOMAS, 1774–1797 1589

"Diary of a Baltimorean of the Eighteenth Century." MARYLAND HISTORICAL MAGAZINE 7 (1912):356–374.

Nov 1794–Oct 1795. Extracts from travel diary; voyage from Baltimore to London; description of London and Paris; tour through England; return to United States; interesting picture of the "Grand Tour" of a young American.

PARRY, NEEDHAM 1590

Beckner, Lucien, ed. "John D. Shane's Copy of Needham Parry's Diary of a Trip Westward in 1794." FILSON CLUB HISTORY QUARTERLY 22 (1948):227–247.

May–Jul 1794. Pennsylvania Quaker's prospecting journey down the Ohio, with saddles to trade for expenses; Wheeling, Muskingum, Gallipolis, Lexington, Georgetown, Frankfort, Springfield, Cythiana, Danville, Abington, Shelbyville; return eastward by Wilderness Road; reports of Indian skirmishes and depredations; notes on persons, places, soil; colloquial style.

"The Journal of Needham Parry." KENTUCKY STATE HISTORICAL SOCIETY REGISTER 34 (1936):379–391.

May–Jun 1794.

PLUMER, WILLIAM, 1759–1850 1591

In LIFE OF WILLIAM PLUMER, by William Plumer, Jr., edited by Andrew P. Peabody, pp. 1–543 passim. Boston: Phillips, Sampson, 1857.

WILLIAM PLUMER'S MEMORANDUM OF PROCEEDINGS IN THE UNITED STATES SENATE, 1803–1807. Edited by Everett S. Brown. New York: Macmillan, 1923. 673 pp.

Brown, Everett S. "The Senate Debate on the Breckenridge Bill for the Government of Louisiana, 1804." AMERICAN HISTORICAL REVIEW 22 (1917):340–364.

"Lord Timothy Dexter: Account of His Life Taken from the Diary of Governor William Plumer of New Hampshire." JOURNAL OF AMERICAN HISTORY 18 (1924):51–53.

1794–1842. Extracts from private and political diary of New Hampshire senator (1802–1807) and governor (1812–1813, 1816–1819); personal and public affairs; business in Congress; journeys; notes on health, political views, reading, etc.

POPE, AMOS, 1772–1837 1592

Marsh, Jasper, ed. "Amos Pope and His Almanacs with Extracts from His Diary." DANVERS HISTORICAL SOCIETY

COLLECTIONS 10 (1922):93–114. Diary, pp. 103–114.

1794–1807. Brief almanac notes; weather, domestic affairs, deaths, sermons, local events in Danvers, Massachusetts.

PUTNAM, ISRAEL, 1766–1824 1593

"A Journey to Marietta in 1794." NEW ENGLAND MAGAZINE, n.s. 13 (1895–1896):642–651.

Mar 1794–Jan 1795. Extracts from travel diary; journey from Brooklyn, Connecticut, to visit brother at Belpré, Ohio, and later return to New Jersey; colloquial style.

RANDOLPH 1594

Knopf, Richard C., ed. "A Precise Journal of General Wayne's Last Campaign in the Year 1794 against the Western Indians Taken down in the Course of the Campaign with an Account of the Attack Made on Fort Recovery by the Indians on the 30th June Preceding." AMERICAN ANTIQUARIAN SOCIETY PROCEEDINGS 64 (1954):273–302.

Jul–Nov 1794. Soldier's diary of General Anthony Wayne's campaign against northwestern Indians; details of camp life and marches; an apparent attempt by James Wilkinson, second in command, to murder Wayne; searches for Indians and occasional skirmishes; the establishment of Fort Wayne; amusingly elevated style in places.

ROUTH, MARTHA, 1743–1817 1595

"Memoir of the Life, Travels, and Religious Experience of Martha Routh, a Minister in the Religious Society of Friends." FRIENDS' LIBRARY 12 (1848):413–477. American journal, pp. 424–477.

1794–1797. Extracts from English Quaker's journal; journey to America; work in New England, Pennsylvania, and southern states; return to England; second visit to America; notes on journeys, meetings, religion.

RUSSELL, MARTHA, 1766–1807 1596

In THE RUSSELLS OF BIRMINGHAM IN THE FRENCH REVOLUTION AND AMERICA, by Samuel H. Jeyes, pp. 53–193. London: G. Allen, 1911.

1794–1795. Extracts from Englishwoman's travel adventure; capture by French and Americans; imprisonment in France during French Revolution; visit to New England, with lively descriptions and social notes.

STRICKLAND, Sir WILLIAM, 1753–1834 1597

JOURNAL OF A TOUR IN THE UNITED STATES OF AMERICA. Edited by J.E. Strickland with a facsimile edition of William Strickland's OBSERVATIONS ON THE AGRICULTURE OF THE UNITED STATES OF AMERICA. New York Historical Society Collections for the Year 1950. New York: New York Historical Society, 1971. 335 pp.

1794–1795. Visit to America of naturalist/farmer with list of questions from the British Board of Agriculture about agriculture in America; comments on education, manners, structure of society, agriculture; price of land, size of farms, yield of soils, systems of cultivation, crop rotation, fertilization, price of produce, farm wages and rents.

TRUDEAU (or TRUTEAU), JEAN BAPTISTE, 1748–1827 1598

SOUTH DAKOTA HISTORICAL COLLECTIONS 7 (1914):403–474.

"Journal of Truteau on the Missouri River." In BEFORE LEWIS AND CLARK, edited by Abraham P. Nasatir, vol. 1, pp. 259-311. St. Louis: St. Louis Historical Documents Foundation, 1952.

Extracts in "Journal of Jean Baptiste Trudeau among the Arikara Indians in 1795," translated and edited by Mrs. H.T. Beauregard. MISSOURI HISTORICAL SOCIETY COLLECTIONS 4 (1912):9-48.

> 1794-1795. Account by agent of the Company of the Missouri sent to establish trade and peaceful relations with Indians on upper Missouri River.

WANSEY, HENRY, 1752?-1827   1599

THE JOURNAL OF AN EXCURSION OF THE UNITED STATES OF NORTH AMERICA, IN THE SUMMER OF 1794. Salisbury: Printed and sold by J. Easton, 1796. 290 pp. Reprint. With a new introduction by Peter A. Fritzell. New York: Johnson Reprint, 1969.

In HENRY WANSEY AND HIS AMERICAN JOURNAL, edited by David J. Jeremy, pp. 39-147. Philadelphia: American Philosophical Society, 1970.

Extract in AMERICAN SOCIAL HISTORY AS RECORDED BY BRITISH TRAVELLERS, compiled and edited by Allan Nevins, pp. 44-57. New York: H. Holt, 1923.

> Mar-Jul 1794. English clothier's journey, mostly in Pennsylvania, New York and New England; observations on people, places, manners, industry and commerce, especially related to textiles; interesting details of ship and stagecoach travel.

WELLFORD, ROBERT, 1753-1823   1600

"A Diary Kept by Dr. Robert Wellford, of Fredericksburg, Virginia, during the March of the Virginia Troops to Fort Pitt." WILLIAM AND MARY COLLEGE QUARTERLY, 1st ser. 11 (1902):1-19.

> Sep-Dec 1794. Military surgeon's journal kept during march from Fredericksburg to Fort Pitt to suppress the Whiskey Rebellion; medical work, scenery, weather, social life; strong opinions.

WIGHAM, JOHN, 1749-1839   1601

MEMOIRS OF THE LIFE, GOSPEL LABOURS, AND RELIGIOUS EXPERIENCE OF JOHN WIGHAM. London: Harvey and Darton, 1842. 133 pp.

> 1794-1797. Scottish Quaker's travels in the United States; his ministry; notes on American Quakers.

1795

ANDERSON, ALEXANDER, 1775-1870   1602

In OLD NEW YORK, vol. 1, pp. 46-55, 85-93, 197-204, 233-253, vol. 2, pp. 88-105, 184-192, 217-226, 289-301, 428-436. New York: W.W. Pasko, 1889-1891.

> Jan-Nov 1795. Extract from an intimate and interesting diary; early work as engraver, but mostly life as medical student at Columbia College; amusing details of study, social life, reading.

ANDREWS, JOSEPH GARDNER   1603

A SURGEON'S MATE AT FORT DEFIANCE: THE JOURNAL OF JOSEPH GARDNER ANDREWS FOR THE YEAR 1795. Edited by Richard C. Knopf. Columbus: Ohio Historical Society, 1953. 91 pp. Reprint. OHIO HISTORICAL QUARTERLY 66 (1957):57-86, 159-186, 238-268.

> Jan-Dec 1795. Activities at Fort Defiance after General Wayne's victory at Fallen Timbers; Indians en route to sign Treaty of Greenville; dealings with traders and settlers; much attention to food and conviviality of officers' mess; good medical details and picture of fort life in frontier Ohio.

BAYARD, SAMUEL, 1767-1840   1604

Wilson, James G. "Judge Bayard of New Jersey, and His London Diary." NEW JERSEY HISTORICAL SOCIETY PROCEEDINGS, 2d ser. 8 (1884-1885):203-216.

Extracts in "Judge Bayard's London Diary," edited by James G. Wilson. NEW YORK GENEALOGICAL AND BIOGRAPHICAL RECORD 23 (1892):1-14.

> 1795-1796. Travel diary kept in London; political and legal notes; observations of political figures; account of Irish forgeries.

BURGES, GEORGE   1605

A JOURNAL OF A SURVEYING TRIP INTO WESTERN PENNSYLVANIA UNDER ANDREW ELLICOTT IN THE YEAR 1795 WHEN THE TOWN OF ERIE, WARREN, AND WATERFORD WERE LAID OUT. Mt. Pleasant, Mich.: John Cumming, 1965. 48 pp.

> May-Nov 1795. Lively diary of young surveyor's horseback journey from Philadelphia to western Pennsylvania; inns along the way; extensive surveying details; contacts with Indians.

CHAPMAN, THOMAS   1606

"Journal of a Journey through the United States." HISTORICAL MAGAZINE, 2d ser. 5 (1869):357-368; 6 (1869):70-75; 7 (1870):16-19.

> 1795-1796. Travels through the eastern United States; descriptions of towns, taverns, etc.

CONDICT, LEWIS, 1772-1862   1607

"Journal of a Trip to Kentucky in 1795." NEW JERSEY HISTORICAL SOCIETY PROCEEDINGS, n.s. 4 (1919):108-127.

> Jun-Dec 1795. Physician's horseback journey from Morristown, New Jersey, to Kentucky, and part of return; scenery and towns; comments on manners and morals of citizens of Wheeling, Pittsburgh and Cincinnati.

GAYOSO DE LEMOS, MANUEL   1608

"Diary of Gayoso de Lemos' Expedition on LA VIGILANTE." In SPANISH WAR VESSELS ON THE MISSISSIPPI, by Abraham P. Nasatir, pp. 233-326. Yale Western Americana Series, 18. New Haven: Yale University Press, 1968.

> Apr 1795-Jan 1796. Expedition from Natchez to Barrancas (Chickasaw Bluffs) to establish a fort, taking possession of the site in the name of the King of Spain; trip into Illinois to increase loyalty to Spain of both the French and Indians and to inspect their defenses.

HINSDALE, THEODORE, 1738-1818   1609

In HISTORY OF BERKSHIRE COUNTY, MASSACHUSETTS, vol. 1, pp. 82-86. New York: J.B. Beers, 1885.

> 1795-1797. Account of and extracts from clergyman's journal; church affairs at Hinsdale, Massachusetts; courtship of congregation; account of parish.

KOROBITSYN, NIKOLAY IVANOV 1610

"Journal of N.I. Korobitsyn, Clerk of the Russian-American Company." In RUSSIAN DISCOVERIES IN THE PACIFIC AND IN NORTH AMERICA IN THE EIGHTEENTH AND NINETEENTH CENTURIES, translated from the Russian by Carl Ginsburg, edited by Aleksandr I. Andreev, pp. 118–200. American Council of Learned Societies Russian Translation Project Series, 13. Ann Arbor, Mich.: Published for American Council of Learned Societies by J.W. Edwards, 1952.

> 1795–1807. Russian-American Company clerk's journal including stop at Hawaii in 1804 with descriptions of the people, trade and natural features there; from Hawaii to Kodiak Island and Sitka; sailing conditions; ports, settlements and all of their buildings; the business of the Russian-American Company; notes on Aleuts, their customs and appearance.

MACKAY, JAMES, 1759?–1822 1611

In THE SPANISH REGIME IN MISSOURI, by Louis Houck, vol. 2, pp. 182–192. Chicago: R.R. Donnelly & Sons, 1909.

In BEFORE LEWIS AND CLARK, edited by Abraham P. Nasatir, vol. 1, pp. 354–374. St. Louis: St. Louis Historical Documents Foundation, 1952.

> Oct 1795–Jan 1796. Report of the general agent of the Company of the Missouri who was sent to drive British from Indian villages along Platte and Missouri rivers and ensure Spanish supremacy.

Quaife, Milo M., ed. "Extracts from Capt. McKay's Journal--and Others." WISCONSIN STATE HISTORICAL SOCIETY PROCEEDINGS (1915):186–210. Journal, pp. 190–195.

> Jun 1796–? Extracts from notes of travel and exploration in the upper Missouri region; partly diaristic, possibly drawn up for Lewis and Clark.

PIERCE, JOHN, 1773–1849 1612

"Dr. Pierce's Manuscript Journal." MASSACHUSETTS HISTORICAL SOCIETY PROCEEDINGS, 2d ser. 3 (1886): 40–52.

> Sep 1795. Journey of Brookline, Massachusetts, clergyman to Providence and New Haven; inauguration of Timothy Dwight as president of Yale; notes on taverns, accident, etc.

"Commencements at Harvard." MASSACHUSETTS HISTORICAL SOCIETY PROCEEDINGS, 2d ser. 5 (1889–1890):167–263.

> 1803–1848. Extracts from diary of alumnus (1793), describing and commenting on commencement exercises at Harvard.

Smith, Charles C., ed. "The Rev. Dr. John Pierce's Memoirs." MASSACHUSETTS HISTORICAL SOCIETY PROCEEDINGS, 2d ser. 19 (1905):356–389. Journal, pp. 366–383.

> Dec 1812–Jan 1813. Trip from Brookline to Washington, via New York, Philadelphia, Baltimore; meeting with Madison; return; mostly account of churches and sermons.

SANDS, DAVID, 1745–1818 1613

JOURNAL OF THE LIFE AND GOSPEL LABOURS OF DAVID SANDS. London: C. Gilpin, 1848. 240 pp.

> 1795–1800. American Quaker's travels and ministry in England, Ireland and Germany; social conditions; Quaker meetings; dated entries, but narrative style.

SILLIMAN, BENJAMIN, 1779–1864 1614

In LIFE OF BENJAMIN SILLIMAN, M.D., LL.D., LATE PROFESSOR OF CHEMISTRY, MINEROLOGY, AND GEOLOGY IN YALE COLLEGE, by George Park Fisher, vol. 1, pp. 29–44. New York: C. Scribner, 1866.

> Aug 1795–Jan 1796. College diary kept at Yale; good picture of studies and social life.

A JOURNAL OF TRAVELS. New York: Printed by D.&G. Bruce, for E. Sargeant, 1810; 2d ed. Boston: Printed by T.B. Wait and Co., 1812. 2 vols. Reprint. New York: Arno, 1980.

JOURNAL OF TRAVELS. 3d ed. New Haven: S. Converse, 1820. 3 vols.

> 1805–1806. Atlantic crossings; travel through England, Scotland, Holland.

SMITH, ELIHU HUBBARD, 1771–1798 1615

THE DIARY OF ELIHU HUBBARD SMITH. Edited by James E. Cronin. American Philosophical Society Memoirs, vol. 95. Philadelphia: American Philosophical Society, 1973. 481 pp.

> 1795–1798. Self-conscious literary effort by an unusually intelligent young man who combined careers in medicine and literature; observations on society, politics, medicine, literature and personalities of the time.

Cronin, James E., ed. "John Adams on the History of the Revolution." PENNSYLVANIA MAGAZINE OF HISTORY AND BIOGRAPHY 73 (1949):92–93.

> Nov 1796. Extract containing interesting account of Adams's concern about preservation of primary sources for the writing of an accurate history of the American Revolution and his personal opinions about William Penn and James Otis.

STUART, ROBERT, 1772–1856 1616

"Journals of Robert Stuart." PRESBYTERIAN HISTORICAL SOCIETY JOURNAL 23 (1945):150–164.

> Jul–Aug 1795. Work of Presbyterian minister in West Lexington Presbytery of Kentucky.

> Sep–Dec 1806, Feb 1808. Missionary tours through other parts of Kentucky.

> Sep–Nov 1816. Missionary tour west of the Mississippi; good descriptions of frontier life; terrain.

TWINING, THOMAS, 1776–1861 1617

TRAVELS IN AMERICA 100 YEARS AGO. New York: Harper & Brothers, 1894. 180 pp.

> Nov 1795–May 1796. Seminarrative travel diary; India to England via the United States; Wilmington, Philadelphia, Baltimore, Washington, New York; notes on people and manners, life in the United States; particularly interesting account of George Washington.

WHITTEKER, WILLIAM, 1775–1853 1618

Cometti, Elizabeth, ed. "The Memorandum of William Whitteker." WEST VIRGINIA HISTORY 1 (1939–1940):207–224, 283–292.

> 1795–1810. Business journal of saltmaker and carpenter at Charleston in what became West Virginia; memoranda of travels to Java and West Indies from Baltimore and Philadelphia; notes on East Indian trade; trading and travel on the frontier; salt drilling; an unusual, varied, interesting journal.

ZUÑIGA, JOSE DE 1619

Hammond, G.P., trans. "The Zuñiga Journal, Tucson to Santa Fe: The Opening of the Spanish Trade Route, 1788-1795." NEW MEXICO HISTORICAL REVIEW 6 (1931): 40-65.

Apr-May 1795. Part of an attempt to establish trade route between Sonora, Mexico, and Santa Fe; unsuccessful efforts to find and defeat Apaches.

1796

ALLEN, SAMUEL 1620

In HISTORIC HIGHWAYS OF AMERICA, by Archer B. Hulbert, vol. 12, pp. 65-77.

Nov 1796. Letter-journal describing New England-er's journey from Alexandria and Cumberland to the Ohio via Braddock's Road; interesting spellings.

ARRILLAGA, JOSE JOAQUIN, 1750-1814 1621

JOSE JOAQUIN ARRILLAGA: DIARY OF HIS SURVEYS OF THE FRONTIER. Baja California Travels Series, 17. Los Angeles: Dawson's Book Shop, 1969. 103 pp.

Jun-Nov 1796. Expedition of the lieutenant governor of the Californias to investigate mission sites and possibly establish a land route from the coast to the Colorado River; good descriptive entries about the land and its fertility, water, trails, un-friendly encounters with Indians and Spanish attitudes toward the Indians.

AUDRAIN, PETER 1622

"Journal of Peter Audrain, Esq." PIONEER SOCIETY OF THE STATE OF MICHIGAN PIONEER COLLECTIONS 8 (1885):444-447.

1796-1797. A few entries describing army movements around Pittsburgh, Greenville, Forts Defiance and Miami, Detroit.

AUSTIN, MOSES, 1761-1821 1623

Garrison, George P. "A Memorandum of Mr. Austin's Journey from the Lead Mines in the County of Wythe in the State of Virginia to the Lead Mines in the Province of Louisiana West of the Mississippi." AMERI-CAN HISTORICAL REVIEW 5 (1899-1900):518-542.

Dec 1796-Mar 1797. Merchant's journey to the lead fields of southeastern Missouri.

"Journal of a Voyage down the Mississippi." In THE AUSTIN PAPERS, edited by Eugene C. Barker, vol. 1, pp. 69-74. American Historical Association Annual Report, 1919. Washington, D.C.: Government Printing Office, 1924.

Apr-May 1801. Description of traffic on Mississippi and Ohio rivers.

BAILY, FRANCIS, 1774-1844 1624

JOURNAL OF A TOUR IN UNSETTLED PARTS OF NORTH AMERICA. London: Baily Brothers, 1856. 439 pp.; Edited by Jack D.L. Holmes. Carbondale: Southern Illinois University, 1969. 336 pp.

Extracts relating to Pennsylvania and Ohio in HIS-TORIC HIGHWAYS OF AMERICA, by Archer B. Hulbert, vol. 11, pp. 106-150.

Extracts relating to Tennessee in EARLY TRAVELS IN THE TENNESSEE COUNTRY, edited by Samuel C. Williams, pp. 387-430.

1796-1797. Englishman's tour from Washington to Pittsburgh via Pennsylvania Road; good obser-vations on a leisurely tour.

CHAMBERS, CHARLOTTE, d. 1821 1625

In MEMOIR OF CHARLOTTE CHAMBERS, by Lewis H. Garrard, pp. 1-135 passim. Philadelphia: Printed for the author, 1856.

1796-1821. Scattered extracts from diary of social life and religious work at Cincinnati and Ludlow Station, Ohio; work for Bible Society in Ohio.

CLEAVELAND, MOSES, ca. 1755-1806 1626

In EARLY HISTORY OF CLEVELAND, OHIO, by Charles Whittlesey, pp. 181-184. Cleveland: Fairbanks, Bene-dict & Co., Printer, 1867.

Jul 1796. Extracts containing brief notes of sur-veying around Cleveland.

DUFOUR, JEAN JACQUES, d. 1827 1627

"Daybook of Jean Jaques Dufour." INDIANA HISTORICAL COLLECTIONS 13 (1925):234-347.

1796-1816. Mainly financial records; French and English text.

ELLICOTT, ANDREW, 1754-1820 1628

THE JOURNAL OF ANDREW ELLICOTT, LATE COMMIS-SIONER ON BEHALF OF THE UNITED STATES. Philadel-phia: Printed by Budd & Bertram, for Thomas Dobson, 1803; Philadelphia: Printed by William Fry, 1814. 299 pp. Reprint. New York: Arno, 1980; Chicago: Quad-rangle Books, 1962, 300 pp.

1796-1800. Surveyor's official journal, written up from notes; determining boundary between United States and French possessions; mainly journey down Ohio and Mississippi and proceedings in lower Mississippi Valley; occasional topographical and sociological notes.

EVANS, JOHN 1629

Quaife, Milo M., ed. "Extracts from Capt. McKay's Journal--and Others." WISCONSIN STATE HISTORICAL SOCIETY PROCEEDINGS (1915):186-210. Diary, pp. 195-200.

1796. Notes of travel and exploration in the upper Missouri region.

HASWELL, ANTHONY, 1756-1816 1630

Wood, Virginia S., ed. "From Bennington to New York City in 1796." VERMONT HISTORY 42 (1974):287-295.

Jun-Jul 1796. Vermont newspaper publisher's ac-count of travel difficulties, business dealings and illness.

HAWKINS, BENJAMIN, 1754-1818 1631

Hemperley, Marion R., ed. "Benjamin Hawkins' Trip across Georgia in 1796." GEORGIA HISTORICAL QUAR-TERLY 55 (1971):114-137.

Nov-Dec 1796. Travels through South Carolina, Georgia and Alabama of newly-appointed general superintendent of all Indians south of Ohio; Indian trails, scenery, terrain; agriculture of Indians and new settlers; amicable encounters with Indians and plans for "bettering their condition."

LETTERS OF BENJAMIN HAWKINS, 1796-1806. Georgia Historical Society Collections, vol. 9. Savannah:

Georgia Historical Society, 1916. 500 pp. Reprint. Hemperley, Marion R. "Benjamin Hawkins' Trip through Alabama." ALABAMA HISTORICAL REVIEW 31 (1969):207-236.

Dec 1796. Traversing Creek territory, using Indian trails; minute topographical notes; lodgings with settlers; conversations with Indians; obvious concern for Indian welfare and apparent abuse of it by settlers; many place and personal names, of both Indians and settlers.

In EARLY TRAVELS IN THE TENNESSEE COUNTRY, edited by Samuel C. Williams, pp. 370-372.

Mar 1797. Brief extracts from journal of surveying in western South Carolina; largely technical notes.

Hemperley, Marion R. "Benjamin Hawkins' Trip from New York to Coweta Tallahassee." ALABAMA HISTORICAL QUARTERLY 33 (1971):218-226.

Nov 1798. Trip to the Creek town of New York (Tallaposa County) to Coweta Tallahassee (Russell County), Alabama, along Indian trails; mainly distances, topographical features, place names.

HOLLEY, JOHN MILTON   1632

In EARLY HISTORY OF CLEVELAND, OHIO, by Charles Whittlesey, pp. 192-202, 206-207, 215-223, 242-249. Cleveland: Fairbanks, Benedict & Co., Printer, 1867.

Apr-Oct 1796. Journal of surveying for Cleveland Land Company; from Dover to Canandaigua and Western Reserve; notes on topography, natural history, etc.

HUNTER, GEORGE, 1755-1824   1633

THE WESTERN JOURNALS OF DR. GEORGE HUNTER. Edited by John F. McDermott. American Philosophical Society Transactions, n.s., vol. 53, pt. 4. Philadelphia: American Philosophical Society, 1963. 133 pp.

Extracts in TRAVEL ACCOUNTS OF INDIANA, compiled by Shirley S. McCord, pp. 45-49.

Jul-Sep 1796, Aug-Oct 1802. Two journals of private business ventures into Kentucky and Illinois territories to explore prospects for mining and land investment.

May 1804-Apr 1805. Chemist, responsible for scientific observations, on expedition authorized by Thomas Jefferson; mainly exploration of Washita River portion of Louisiana Purchase; notes on minerals, soil conditions, geological features, climate, vegetation, prospects for development; difficult travel overland and by canoe and riverboat; dealings with Indians.

KRAUSS, JOHN, 1779-1819   1634

"The Diary of John Krauss: Entries Pertaining to Organs." In THE HISTORY OF THE ORGAN IN THE UNITED STATES, by Orpha Ochse, pp. 430-438. Bloomington: Indiana University Press, 1975.

1796-1810. Entries establishing dates for organs built, repaired and rebuilt by John and Andrew Krauss; charges and compensations.

LATROBE, BENJAMIN HENRY, 1764-1820   1635

THE JOURNAL OF LATROBE: BEING THE NOTES AND SKETCHES OF AN ARCHITECT, NATURALIST AND TRAVELER IN THE UNITED STATES FROM 1797 TO 1820. New York: D. Appleton, 1905. 269 pp. Reprint. New York: B. Franklin, 1971.

IMPRESSIONS RESPECTING NEW ORLEANS; DIARY AND SKETCHES, 1818-1820. Edited by Samuel Wilson, Jr. New York: Columbia University Press, 1951. 196 pp.

THE VIRGINIA JOURNALS OF BENJAMIN HENRY LATROBE, 1795-1798. Edited by Edward C. Carter II and others. The Papers of Benjamin Henry Latrobe, ser. I. Journals, vols. 1-2. New Haven: Published for the Maryland Historical Society by Yale University Press, 1977. 2 vols.

THE JOURNALS OF BENJAMIN HENRY LATROBE, 1799-1820: FROM PHILADELPHIA TO NEW ORLEANS. Edited by Edward C. Carter II and others. The Papers of Benjamin Henry Latrobe, ser. I. Journals, vol. 3. New Haven: Published for the Maryland Historical Society by Yale University Press, 1981, c1980. 351 pp.

1796-1820. Naturalist's travel journals; comments and sketches of Virginia and Virginians; education; notes on Louisiana; extensive descriptions.

LEE, WILLIAM, 1772-1840   1636

In JOHN LEIGH OF AGAWAM, compiled by William Lee, pp. 233-237. Albany: J. Munsell's Sons, 1888.

A YANKEE JEFFERSONIAN: SELECTIONS FROM THE DIARY AND LETTERS OF WILLIAM LEE OF MASSACHUSETTS. Edited by Mary Lee Mann. Cambridge: Belknap Press of Harvard University Press, 1958. 312 pp. Diary, pp. 1-52.

1796-1798. Business and travel diary kept in Europe by Lee, who later served as United States commercial agent at Bordeaux under Jefferson and Madison and as auditor of the Treasury under Monroe and John Quincy Adams; survival of shipwreck on French coast; visits to various cities; tourist attractions and social customs in France, Belgium, England and the Netherlands; interesting especially for atmosphere of France in early post-revolutionary years as perceived by a young American of republican principles.

PAYNE, WILLIAM OSBORN, 1783-1812   1637

AN UNCONSCIOUS AUTOBIOGRAPHY: WILLIAM OSBORN PAYNE'S DIARY AND LETTERS. Edited by Thatcher T.P. Luquer. New York: Privately printed, 1938. 103 pp.

1796-1804. Charming diary of a teen-aged employee in a Baltimore counting house; some few business details; much on play-going, theaters, actors, performances; lively social life, visits to Boston; religious and philosophical reflections.

PEASE, SETH, 1764-1819   1638

In EARLY HISTORY OF CLEVELAND, OHIO, by Charles Whittlesey, pp. 178-181, 277-287. Cleveland: Fairbanks, Benedict & Co., Printer, 1867.

"Journals of Seth Pease." WESTERN RESERVE HISTORICAL SOCIETY TRACT, no. 94 (1914), pp. 27-124.

1796-1798 (with gaps). Surveying journals; journey to Western Reserve and surveys on behalf of Connecticut Land Company; from Cleveland to Canandaigua, New York; from there to Suffield and New Connecticut; life on Western Reserve; return to Connecticut; notes of surveys; general comments on people and places.

PETERS, JOHN   1639

"Abstract of Peters' Journal of the Peters-Hedden Survey of the Lower Magaguadavic and Lake Utopia in 1796." In HISTORICAL-GEOGRAPHICAL DOCUMENTS, RE-

LATING TO NEW BRUNSWICK, edited by William F. Ganong, vol. 3, pp. 173-174.

Sep-Nov 1796. Surveying journal.

POWELL, CUTHBERT, b. 1779   1640

Evans, James D., ed. "Journal of Cuthbert Powell." WILLIAM AND MARY COLLEGE QUARTERLY, 1st ser. 12 (1903-1904):221-231; 13 (1904-1905):53-63.

1796-1801. Virginian's sea journal; mainly notes of voyages, storms, trade at Alexandria, Virginia.

ROBBINS, THOMAS, 1777-1856   1641

DIARY OF THOMAS ROBBINS. Edited by Increase N. Tarbox. Boston: T. Todd, Printer, 1886-1887. 2 vols.

1796-1854. An extremely long and detailed diary of great value; life as teacher and preacher in Massachusetts and Connecticut; begun when student at Williams College; weather, Federalist politics; local affairs, church work.

SHELDON, CHARLOTTE, 1780-ca. 1840   1642

In CHRONICLES OF A PIONEER SCHOOL, compiled by Emily N. Vanderpoel, pp. 10-17.

May-Sep 1796. Extracts from private diary; notes on school life, personal and local affairs.

WILLISTON, SETH, 1770-1851   1643

Adams, John Quincy, ed. "The Diaries of the Rev. Seth Williston, D.D." PRESBYTERIAN HISTORICAL SOCIETY JOURNAL 7 (1913-1914):175-208, 234-254; 8 (1915-1916): 40-48, 123-144, 184-192, 226-235, 316-330; 9 (1917-1918):25-40, 368-383; 10 (1919-1920):24-35, 130-141.

1796-1800. Presbyterian clergyman's journal; interesting and valuable account of Presbyterians in Connecticut and missionary work in New York; reading, sermons, parish work, travel; a good deal of private life; illnesses, politics, spiritual experiences; notes on weather, etc.

1797

CHABOILLEZ, CHARLES JEAN BAPTISTE   1644

Hickerson, Harold, ed. "Journal of Charles Jean Baptiste Chaboillez." ETHNOHISTORY 6 (1959):265-316; 363-427.

In THE NORTHWEST, by B.C. Payette, pp. 143-222. Montreal: Printed privately for Payette Radio, 1964.

1797-1798. Journal of Northwest Company fur trader; routine notes of trading, especially with Chippewas; enumeration of items such as food, tobacco and liquor involved in barter for furs; names of traders and Indians coming and going at bustling trading post located at junction of Red and Pembina rivers.

CLARK, JOSEPH   1645

"Joseph Clark's Account of a Journey to the Indian Country." FRIENDS' MISCELLANY 1 (1831):367-380.

Oct-Nov 1797. Journey to upper New York, sponsored by Friends Yearly Meeting, to bring four Indian girls back to Philadelphia to be instructed in "the useful arts of domestic economy"; conferences with Indian leaders; illness of companion; opinions of Indians; return trip by sloop down the Hudson.

"Minutes of a Tour." FRIENDS' MISCELLANY 5 (1833-1834):171-176.

Nov 1800. Quaker's journey to distribute religious books and to visit with black families in New Jersey.

COMLY, REBECCA, b. 1773   1646

In JOURNAL OF THE RELIGIOUS LABOURS OF JOHN COMLY, LATE OF BYBERRY, PENNSYLVANIA, Philadelphia: Published by his children, T.E. Chapman, 1853. 645 pp.

1797-1829. Extracts from Quaker's journal; brief notes of Quaker work and travels.

COWLES, JULIA, 1785-1803   1647

THE DIARIES OF JULIA COWLES. Edited by Laura H. Moseley. New Haven: Yale University Press; London: H. Milford, Oxford University Press, 1931. 94 pp.

Extracts in CHRONICLES OF A PIONEER SCHOOL, compiled by Emily N. Vanderpoel, pp. 17-19.

1797-1803. Social and school life at Litchfield, Connecticut; records of private and school readings; long entries; well written, entertaining.

CROWNINSHIELD, JOHN, b. 1771   1648

"Journal of Capt. John Crowninshield at Calcutta, 1797-1798, when Master of the Ship BELISARIUS." ESSEX INSTITUTE HISTORICAL COLLECTIONS 81 (1945):354-382; 82 (1946):26-41, 122-136.

Dec 1797-Feb 1798. Diary kept by captain of vessel out of Salem while in port at Calcutta, assembling a cargo for return voyage and carrying out necessary repairs; considerable detail about trading methods and ship maintenance; description of behavior of certain sailors; illness; press gangs; a valuable account of the uncertainties and hazards of the Far East trade.

Corning, Howard, ed. "John Crowninshield in the AMERICA III, at Sumatra, 1801." ESSEX INSTITUTE HISTORICAL COLLECTIONS 80 (1944):139-157.

Jul 1801. Extracts from ship's log, describing trading for pepper in Sumatra; interesting account, not only of trading methods but also of the coming together of different cultures.

FRENCH, SAMSON, 1742-1834   1649

In A GENEALOGICAL HISTORY OF THE FRENCH AND ALLIED FAMILIES, by Mary E.Q. Beyer, pp. 132-135. Cedar Rapids, Iowa: Privately printed by the Torch Press, 1912.

1797-1833. Few extracts from business journal; mostly notes of purchases, with some diary entries.

FROST, AMRIAH, 1750-1819   1650

AMERICAN ANTIQUARIAN SOCIETY PROCEEDINGS (1879): 71-79.

Jun 1797. Clergyman's journey from Milford, Massachusetts, to Virginia; visit to Mount Vernon and reception by Washington.

GILMOR, ROBERT, 1774-1848   1651

"Gilmor Memorandums." BOSTON PUBLIC LIBRARY BULLETIN (1892):73-92.

Jul-Aug 1797. Seminarrative memoranda of journey

through Middle Atlantic and New England states; entertaining.

"The Diary of Robert Gilmor." MARYLAND HISTORICAL MAGAZINE 17 (1922):231–268, 319–347.

Dec 1826–Jun 1827. Domestic and business life in Baltimore; voyage to New York, Philadelphia, and return to Baltimore; an intimate picture of the life and hypochondria of a prominent citizen.

GRIFFIN, EDWARD DOOR, 1770–1837   1652

In MEMOIR OF THE REV. EDWARD D. GRIFFIN, by William B. Sprague, pp. 12–88. New York: Taylor & Dodd, 1839.

1797–1805. Clergyman's journal containing resolutions, self-analysis, moral reflections, devotions, self-abasement; long entries.

HARRISON, AARON, 1726–1819   1653

In HISTORY OF THE TOWN OF WOLCOTT (CONNECTICUT), by Samuel Orcutt, pp. 327–328. Waterbury, Conn.: Press of the American Printing Co., 1874.

1797–1812. Extracts from deacon's diary; sudden deaths, religious introspection, church admissions.

HILL, FRANCES BAYLOR   1654

Bottorff, William K. and Flannagan, Roy C., eds. "The Diary of Frances Baylor Hill of 'Hillsborough,' King and Queen County, Virginia." EARLY AMERICAN LITERATURE 2 (1967):3–53.

Jan–Dec 1797. Quiet pursuits of a Virginia girl; reading, sewing, games, family and neighborhood social life; illnesses and deaths among relatives and friends.

JORDAN, RICHARD, 1756–1826   1655

A JOURNAL OF THE LIFE AND RELIGIOUS LABOURS OF RICHARD JORDAN, A MINISTER OF THE GOSPEL IN THE SOCIETY OF FRIENDS, LATE OF NEWTON, IN GLOUCESTER COUNTY, NEW JERSEY. London: Harvey and Darton, 1829. 188 pp. Reprint. FRIENDS' LIBRARY 13 (1849): 292–349.

A JOURNAL OF THE LIFE AND RELIGIOUS LABOURS OF RICHARD JORDAN, A MINISTER OF THE GOSPEL OF THE SOCIETY OF FRIENDS. Philadelphia: T. Kite, 1829. 172 pp.; Philadelphia: Friends' Book Store, 1877. 218 pp.

1797–1825. Travels and experience as a Quaker preacher; ministry in Maryland, Pennsylvania, Connecticut, New Jersey; antislavery sentiment; visits to Ireland, Holland, France.

LOUIS PHILIPPE, king of the French,   1656
1773–1850

DIARY OF MY TRAVELS IN AMERICA. Translated from the French by Stephen Becker. New York: Delacorte Press, 1977. 202 pp.

Mar–May 1797. Unpretentious travel diary of the young duc d'Orléans, later to be king of France, and his two brothers, all refugees from the French Revolution; time in Philadelphia and Washington; details of a visit with retired George Washington at Mount Vernon, where he observed slavery; travel among frontiersmen and Indians of Kentucky and Tennessee; comments on health, religious tolerance, seemingly classless society of settlers and customs and appearance of Cherokees; interesting diary illustrated by his brother's romantic landscapes.

STEARNS, SAMUEL, 1770–1834   1657

In HISTORY OF THE TOWN OF BEDFORD, MIDDLESEX COUNTY, MASSACHUSETTS, by Abram E. Brown, pp. 61–62. Bedford: Published by the author, 1891.

1797–1798. Fragmentary notes in religious journal; presents, mainly food, he received during his first year as a minister.

SWAN, CALEB, d. 1809   1658

"The Northwest Country in 1797." MAGAZINE OF AMERICAN HISTORY 19 (1888):74–77.

Aug 1797. Military travel journal of paymaster-general of United States Army; round trip from Detroit through northwestern country; brief notes on topography and Indians.

THOMPSON, DAVID, 1770–1857   1659

Wood, W. Raymond. "David Thompson at the Mandan-Hidatsa Villages, 1797–1798: The Original Journals." ETHNOHISTORY 24 (1977):329–342.

Dec 1797–Jan 1798. Ethnographic field notes on Mandan-Hidatsa villages; fur-trading.

DAVID THOMPSON'S JOURNALS RELATING TO MONTANA AND ADJACENT REGIONS. Edited by M. Catherine White. Missoula: Montana State University Press, 1950. 345 pp.

1808–1812. Explorer's journal of geography, natural history and trading posts in western Montana.

In NEW LIGHT ON THE EARLY HISTORY OF THE GREATER NORTHWEST, by Alexander Henry, edited by Elliott Coues, vol. 2. New York: F.P. Harper, 1897. Reprint. Minneapolis: Ross & Haines, 1965.

DAVID THOMPSON'S NARRATIVE OF HIS EXPLORATIONS IN WESTERN AMERICA. Edited by Joseph B. Tyrrell. Champlain Society Publications, no. 12. Toronto: Champlain Society, 1916. 582 pp.

NARRATIVE. New ed. Edited by Richard Glover. Champlain Society Publications, no. 40. Toronto: Champlain Society, 1962. 410 pp.

1808–1811. Digests of the journeys in Oregon, Washington and Idaho; valuable notes on topography, geography, navigation.

Elliott, T.C., ed. "David Thompson's Journeys." WASHINGTON HISTORICAL QUARTERLY 8 (1917):183–187; 9 (1918):11–16; 11(1920):97–103, 163–173; 23 (1932):18–24, 88–93, 173–176.

1809–1811. Journeys in Pend Oreille and Spokane areas of Idaho and Washington.

Elliott, T.C., ed. "Journal of David Thompson." OREGON HISTORICAL QUARTERLY 15 (1914):39–63, 104–125.

Jul–Aug 1811. Journey down the Columbia.

Elliott, T.C., ed. "David Thompson's Journeys." WASHINGTON HISTORICAL QUARTERLY 8 (1917):261–264; 9 (1918):103–106, 169–173; 10 (1919):17–20.

Aug 1811–Mar 1812. Journeys in Spokane country of Washington.

TOWNSEND, EBENEZER, JR.   1660

"The Diary of Mr. Ebenezer Townsend, Jr." NEW HAVEN COLONY HISTORICAL SOCIETY PAPERS 4 (1888):1–115.

1797–1799. Supercargo's journal in a letter to his brother; aboard sealing ship NEPTUNE; from New York to South Pacific, Hawaii, Canton, and on to circumnavigate the globe; hunting, trading; elaborate descriptions of people and places; a full and very interesting journal.

WALLEY, SAMUEL HALL, 1778-1850　　　1661

MEMORIAL OF SAMUEL HALL WALLEY. Boston: Marvin, 1866. 168 pp.

1797-1850. Diary, largely of religious work and reading over a period of years in Boston; many references to Old South Church, Park Street Church, Rev. Channing, etc.; work with Sabbath Schools; trip with his family to Europe; deaths of family members and friends.

1798

ADAMS, THOMAS BOYLSTON, 1772-1832　　　1662

Paltsits, Victor H., ed. "Berlin and the Prussian Court in 1798." NEW YORK PUBLIC LIBRARY BULLETIN 19 (1915):803-843.

Jan-Dec 1798. Diplomatic and social life in Berlin.

BATES, TARLETON, 1775-1806　　　1663

Seely, Frederick F., ed. "Tarleton Bates' Journal." WESTERN PENNSYLVANIA HISTORICAL MAGAZINE 34 (1951):199-207.

Sep-Oct 1798. Journey by skiff down the Ohio from Pittsburgh to Cincinnati; navigational notes; description of settlements along the river.

CORSER, DAVID, 1754-1828　　　1664

In GENEALOGY OF THE CORSER FAMILY IN AMERICA, by Samuel B.G. Corser. Concord, N.H.: Printed by I.C. Evans, 1902.

1798-1800. Brief notes on personal affairs of resident of Boscawen, New Hampshire; sufferings from Tory neighbors.

FULLER, TIMOTHY, 1778-1835　　　1665

Fuller, Edith D. "Excerpts from the Diary of Timothy Fuller, Jr." CAMBRIDGE HISTORICAL SOCIETY PUBLICATIONS 11 (1916):33-53.

1798-1801. Harvard undergraduate's diary; student and social life; reading, debates, etc.; interesting.

Rostenberg, Leona, ed. "Diary of Timothy Fuller in Congress." NEW ENGLAND QUARTERLY 12 (1939):521-529.

Jan-Mar 1818. Extracts from diary of Margaret Fuller's father, kept while member of Congress from Massachusetts; political and social life in Washington.

HUMPHRIES, CLEMENT　　　1666

"Diary of Clement Humphreys, of Philadelphia." PENNSYLVANIA MAGAZINE OF HISTORY AND BIOGRAPHY 32 (1908):34-53.

Mar-Oct 1798. Account of services as envoy to France.

LEVY, ISAAC H.　　　1667

"Log Book of the Ship SANSOM." AMERICAN JEWISH HISTORICAL SOCIETY PUBLICATIONS 27 (1920):239.

1798-1799. Fragment of travel diary; voyage from New York to Madras and Calcutta; mainly log entries, but some general descriptions.

MATTHEWS, INCREASE, 1772-1856　　　1668

"Diary of a Journey from Massachusetts to the Ohio Country." NEW ENGLAND HISTORICAL AND GENEALOGICAL REGISTER 86 (1932):32-46.

Jun-Sep 1798. Journey from Oakham, Massachusetts, to the Ohio country; mainly travel notes; some notes on sects and politics; character sketches.

MENDONCA, HIPOLITO JOSE DE COSTA PEREIRA FURTADO DE, 1774-1823　　　1669

Smith, Robert C., ed. "A Portuguese Naturalist in Philadelphia." PENNSYLVANIA MAGAZINE OF HISTORY AND BIOGRAPHY 78 (1954):71-106.

Dec 1798-Apr 1799. Travel diary extracts covering sojourn in Philadelphia; descriptions of arrangement and procedures of Congress and the Supreme Court, president's residence; observations on various religious practices.

NIEMCEWICZ, JULIAN URSYN, 1758-1841　　　1670

Budka, Metchie J.E., ed. "A Visit to Harvard College." NEW ENGLAND QUARTERLY 34 (1961):510-514.

Jul 1798. Brief but detailed description by Polish poet, playwright and politician of Harvard College and the city-wide celebration of its commencement exercises.

Budka, Metchie J.E., trans. and ed. "Journey to Niagara." NEW YORK HISTORICAL SOCIETY QUARTERLY 44 (1960):73-113.

Oct 1805. Journey by carriage and wagon from Elizabeth, New Jersey, to Niagara Falls; road conditions, accommodations, land fertility and values, American characteristics, Indians, Niagara Falls, etc.

O'CONWAY, MATHIAS JAMES　　　1671

"Extracts from a Diary Kept during the Yellow Fever Plague in Philadelphia." AMERICAN CATHOLIC HISTORICAL SOCIETY OF PHILADELPHIA RECORDS 13 (1902):486-493.

Aug-Sep 1798. Deaths, flights, statistics. Authorship assumed.

STANFORD, JOHN, 1754-1834　　　1672

In MEMOIR OF THE REV. JOHN STANFORD, by Charles G. Sommers, pp. 62-314 passim. New York: Swords, Stanford, 1835.

1798-1834. Extracts from clergyman's journal; religious reflections; work as chaplain in orphanages, humane and criminal institutions in New York City.

1799

　　　1673
ANON.

O'Neil, Marion, ed. "The Peace River Journal." WASHINGTON HISTORICAL QUARTERLY 19 (1928):250-270.

Oct 1799-Apr 1800. Brief but entertaining notes in fur trader's journal; life at Rocky Mountain Fort on the Peace River.

APPLETON, NATHANIEL, d. 1819　　　1674

Phillips, James Duncan, ed. "Nathaniel Appleton's Journal of the Voyage of the Ship CONCORD around the

World." ESSEX INSTITUTE HISTORICAL COLLECTIONS 83 (1947):146-161, 220-246.

1799-1802. Journal kept by part-owner and, on this voyage, supercargo of CONCORD, the second Salem ship to circumnavigate the globe; interesting account of life under sail and sealing off the South American coast; unfortunately, no entries covering trading at Canton or return home.

AVERY, JOSEPH, b. 1743   1675

"Joseph Avery's Journal." NEW YORK STATE HISTORICAL ASSOCIATION QUARTERLY JOURNAL 2 (1921):251-266.

Jun-Sep 1799. Journey of Presbyterian clergyman to the Genesee country to form churches; return to Greenbush, Massachusetts; preaching and religious work; details of sects.

"Visit of Rev. Joseph Avery." BUFFALO HISTORICAL SOCIETY PUBLICATIONS 6 (1903):223-230.

Aug-Sep 1805. Visit to Buffalo and vicinity; preaching; notes on families, Niagara, etc.

BATEMAN, EPHRAIM, 1770-1829   1676

"Journal of Ephraim Bateman of Fairfield Township, Cumberland County." VINELAND HISTORICAL MAGAZINE 13 (1928):55-64, 80-89; 14 (1929):106-114, 127-135, 154-162, 174-182; 15 (1930):210-217, 235-246.

1799-1806. Brief notes in physician's diary; family and schooling details; work as teacher; church activities and politics; introspection and health.

BROOKES, JOSHUA, 1773-1859   1677

Vail, R.W.G., ed. "A Dinner at Mount Vernon." NEW YORK HISTORICAL SOCIETY QUARTERLY 31 (1947):72-85. Diary, pp. 73-76.

1799. Extract from Englishman's travel journal; detailed description of dinner with George and Martha Washington and Nellie Custis; additional extracts, written later or of uncertain date, describing Mount Vernon, Washington's funeral, Jefferson's opinion of Washington.

BULLEN, JOSEPH, 1751-1825   1678

Phelps, Dawson A., ed. "Excerpts from the Journal of the Reverend Joseph Bullen." JOURNAL OF MISSISSIPPI HISTORY 17 (1955):254-281.

Mar-Jun 1799, Jul-Nov 1800. Journal of representative of New York Missionary Society of the Presbyterian Church; journey on horseback from New York to Chickasaw settlement near present-day Tupelo, Mississippi; detailed description of Chickasaw beliefs, customs, etc.; missionary efforts, hardships; return to Vermont.

DEVEREUX, JOHN WILLIAM   1679

Weeks, O. Douglas, ed. "My Journal of One of My Trips to New York." GEORGIA HISTORICAL QUARTERLY 15 (1931):46-80.

Jun-Nov 1799. Interesting account of travel overland and by coastal ship from Georgia to New York; expense account.

EMERSON, JOHN, 1745-1826   1680

In THE IPSWICH EMERSONS, by Benjamin K. Emerson, p. 133. Boston: D. Clapp & Son, 1900.

Dec 1799-Oct 1800. Extracts from clergyman's diary; very brief notes of local affairs in Conway, Massachusetts, and payments.

GOSHEN, INDIANA, MORAVIAN CONGREGATION   1681

In THE MORAVIAN INDIAN MISSION ON WHITE RIVER: DIARIES AND LETTERS, edited by Lawrence H. Gipson, pp. 23-37, 53-62. Indiana Historical Collections, vol. 23. Indianapolis: Indiana Historical Bureau, 1938.

1799-1801. Extracts from journals of congregation on the Muskingum River; founding of the White River Mission; life and work of the Goshen community. Translated from the German.

Mortimer, Benjamin. "The Ohio River in 1812. Diary 'of the Indian Congregation at Goshen on the River Muskingum' for the Year 1812." OHIO ARCHAEOLOGICAL AND HISTORICAL QUARTERLY 22 (1913):205-266.

Jan-Dec 1812. Congregational journal; details of Moravian life and work; kept in English by Reverend Benjamin Mortimer.

GRANGER, ERASTUS, 1765-1826   1682

Granger, James N. "Connecticut and Virginia a Century Ago." CONNECTICUT QUARTERLY 3 (1897):100-105, 190-198.

1799-1804. Judge's horseback journeys from Suffield, Connecticut, to Virginia and West Virginia, investigating land titles.

HILL, THOMAS, d. 1828   1683

"A Journey on Horseback from New Brunswick, New Jersey, to Lycoming County, Pennsylvania." PENNSYLVANIA MAGAZINE OF HISTORY AND BIOGRAPHY 14 (1890): 189-198.

Jun-Jul 1799. Extract from travel diary.

HUNT, BENJAMIN, 1766-1812   1684

Cope, Gilbert, ed. "Diary of Benjamin Hunt." CHESTER COUNTY HISTORICAL SOCIETY BULLETIN (1898):1-20.

1799-1812. Notes, mainly of where he went and what he did; personal and family affairs; varied and interesting for local affairs in Westtown, Pennsylvania; some interesting spellings and vocabulary.

LOW, RUFUS   1685

Preble, George H. "The First Cruise of the United States Frigate ESSEX." ESSEX INSTITUTE HISTORICAL COLLECTIONS 10 (1869):1-108. Diary, pp. 70-85.

Dec 1799-Nov 1800. Log notes of the sailing master of the ESSEX; cruise to Batavia.

LYON, JOHN, d. 1814   1686

JOHN LYON, NURSERYMAN AND PLANT HUNTER, AND HIS JOURNAL. By Joseph and Nesta Ewan. American Philosophical Society, n.s., vol. 53, pt. 2. Philadelphia: American Philosophical Society, 1963. 69 pp.

1799-1814. Nurseryman's record of plant collecting field trips into Alleghenies, southern Appalachians in Tennessee, Georgia Sea Islands, up the St. Johns River, Florida; names of settlers with whom he stayed, taverns and ferries; trip to London for private sales and public auction of plants.

MCKENZIE, JAMES   1687

In LES BOURGEOIS DE LA COMPAGNIE DU NORD-OUEST, by Louis F.R. Masson, vol. 2, pp. 371-399.

Oct 1799–Aug 1800. Extracts from fur trading journal kept by Northwest Company bourgeois at and about Fort Chippewan in the Athabasca district; valuable for notes of competition and business methods; social affairs, lives of employees; very interesting for its personality and ironical humor.

PREBLE, EDWARD, 1761–1807　　1688

Preble, George H. "The First Cruise of the United States Frigate ESSEX." ESSEX INSTITUTE HISTORICAL COLLECTIONS 10 (1869):1–108. Diary, pp. 60–70.

1799–1800. Convoying from Salem; voyage around Cape Horn to Batavia and return to New York; mainly log entries.

"Commodore Preble and Tripoli." AMERICAN HISTORICAL RECORD 1 (1872):53–58.

"Diary of Commodore Edward Preble." MAGAZINE OF AMERICAN HISTORY 3 (1879):182–193.

1803–1805. Brief notes in memorandum diary; expedition to Mediterranean; movements of CONSTITUTION and American navy about Tripoli; return to America.

SIMMONS, HENRY, JR.　　1689

Congdon, Charles E., ed. "The Good News of Handsome Lake." NEW YORK FOLKLORE QUARTERLY 23 (1967): 290–297.

Jul–Aug 1799. Extract from Quaker schoolteacher's diary describing the visions of Handsome Lake, Seneca prophet, and Seneca ceremonies.

STEINER, ABRAHAM, 1758–1833　　1690

Fries, Adelaide L., ed. "Report of the Brethren Abraham Steiner and Friedrich von Schweinitz of Their Journey." NORTH CAROLINA HISTORICAL REVIEW 21 (1944):330–375.

In EARLY TRAVELS IN THE TENNESSEE COUNTRY, edited by Samuel C. Williams, pp. 448–525.

Nov–Dec 1799. Formal but interesting Moravian travel journal; visit to the Cherokees and Cumberland settlements; social and general observations.

STROTHER, JOHN　　1691

Williams, Samuel C., ed. "The North Carolina–Tennessee Boundary Line Survey." TENNESSEE HISTORICAL MAGAZINE 6, no. 2 (1920):46–57.

Apr–May 1799. Surveying journal; interesting for language and details of discomforts of commissioners.

STURGIS, WILLIAM, 1782–1863　　1692

THE JOURNAL OF WILLIAM STURGIS, edited by S.W. Jackman. Victoria, B.C.: Sona Nis Press, 1978. 136 pp.

Feb–May 1799. Youthful adventurer's search for experience as a seaman and fur trader on trip from Boston to Northwest coast of America; brisk trade with and his regard for the Indians.

1800

BROWN, POLY GUION, 1783–1871　　1693

Barry, Ann. "Diary of a 19th-Century Lass." SEVENTEEN 36 (1977):118–122.

1800–1807. Extracts from diary of girl of Westchester County, New York; balls, serious and fickle suitors; marriage to Samuel Brown, the boy next door.

CLEVELAND, WILLIAM　　1694

A DIARY OF WILLIAM CLEVELAND, CAPTAIN'S CLERK ON BOARD THE MASSACHUSETTS. Edited by Madoka Kanai. University of the Philippines Institute of Asian Studies Monograph Series, no. 1. Quezon City: Institute of Asian Studies, University of the Philippines, 1965. 43 pp.

In THE SHIPS AND SAILORS OF OLD SALEM, by Ralph D. Paine, pp. 352–375.

Jul–Nov 1800. Extracts from sea journal; account of Japanese topography and customs.

COMLY, JOHN, 1773–1850　　1695

JOURNAL OF THE RELIGIOUS LABOURS OF JOHN COMLY, LATE OF BYBERRY, PENNSYLVANIA. Philadelphia: Published by his children, T.E. Chapman, 1853. 645 pp. Journal, pp. 69–488.

1800–1832. Quaker's journal with autobiography and memoirs; spiritual life; notes of travels and religious work.

COPE, THOMAS PYM, 1768–1854　　1696

PHILADELPHIA MERCHANT: THE DIARY OF THOMAS P. COPE. Edited by Eliza Cope Harrison. South Bend, Ind.: Gateway Editions, 1978. 628 pp.

1800–1851. Experiences and observations of a sensitive and thoughtful merchant and public servant; political and philanthropic activities; Quaker life; notable people of nineteenth century Philadelphia; a valuable record.

Maass, Eleanor A., ed. "A Public Watchdog: Thomas Pym Cope and the Philadelphia Waterworks." AMERICAN PHILOSOPHICAL SOCIETY PROCEEDINGS 125 (1981): 134–154.

Jul 1800. A fact-finding trip taken by member of Philadelphia "Watering Committee" to investigate delays in delivery of waterworks machinery; references to Benjamin Latrobe and Nicholas Roosevelt; description of Soho, New Jersey, steam engine works, Schuyler cooper mine; New Jersey countryside and terrain; events and sights of New York; much technical information on steam engines and all sorts of machinery of the period by an enlightened amateur.

DAVIS, JOHN RUSSELL, b. 1775　　1697

"Diary of a Journey through Massachusetts, Vermont and Eastern New York in the Summer of 1800." VERMONT HISTORICAL SOCIETY PROCEEDINGS (1919–1920): 159–183.

May–Jun 1800. Notes on sights, scenes, inns; religious qualms and comments.

HARMON, DANIEL WILLIAMS, 1778–1845　　1698

A JOURNAL OF VOYAGES AND TRAVELS IN THE INTERIOR OF NORTH AMERICA. Edited by Daniel Haskel. Andover, Mass.: Printed by Flagg and Gould, 1820. 432 pp. New York: A.S. Barnes, 1903; New York: Allerton Book Co., 1922. 382 pp.

SIXTEEN YEARS IN THE INDIAN COUNTRY; THE JOURNAL OF DANIEL WILLIAMS HARMON. Edited by W. Kaye Lamb. Toronto: Macmillan Co. of Canada, 1957. 277 pp.

1800-1819. A very interesting journal of the general life of a trader and partner in the Northwest Company; voyages from Montreal to the Pacific Northwest; half of journal kept west of the Rockies; Lake Winnepeg, the Assiniboine, Fort William, Athabasca, Fort Vermillion, New Caledonia, Stuart's Lake.

HAYWARD, JONATHAN, 1788-1813   **1699**

"Diary of Jonathan Hayward." DANVERS HISTORICAL SOCIETY COLLECTIONS 3 (1915):53-58.

1800-1808. Occasional brief notes on local events at Danvers, Massachusetts; deaths, etc.

HENRY, ALEXANDER, d. 1814   **1700**

NEW LIGHT ON THE EARLY HISTORY OF THE GREATER NORTHWEST. Edited by Elliott Coues. New York: F.P. Harper, 1897. 3 vols. Reprint. Minneapolis: Ross & Haines, 1965. 3 vols. in 2.

1800-1814. Fur trader's exploration journal; travel from Lake Superior to Lake of the Woods, Winnipeg River, Red River, mouth of Park River; building trading post and its establishment; realistic accounts of journeys, business, Indian life, personal affairs, while in charge of the Northwest Company's business in Minnesota, North Dakota, and Manitoba area; from 1808 in charge of posts in Saskatchewan; long overland and river journeys; journey to Astoria and minute account of life at mouth of Columbia River in 1813-1814, with occasional journeys up the Columbia and Willamette rivers. A most valuable and interesting journal, although somewhat formal in style.

HENRY'S JOURNAL, COVERING ADVENTURES AND EXPERIENCES IN THE FUR TRADE ON THE RED RIVER. By Charles N. Bell. Historical and Scientific Society of Manitoba Transactions, nos. 31, 35, 37. Winnipeg: Manitoba Free Press, 1888-1889. 2 vols.

Extracts in NORTH DAKOTA HISTORICAL SOCIETY COLLECTIONS 3 (1910):360-368.

1800-1801. Relating to the Red River Valley.

JOHNSON, WILLIAM, 1779-1828   **1701**

"A Young Man's Journal of 1800-1813." NEW JERSEY HISTORICAL SOCIETY PROCEEDINGS, n.s. 7 (1922):49-59, 122-134, 210-216, 305-314; 8 (1923):150-154, 219-225, 313-321.

Extracts concerning New Orleans and return voyage to New York in "William Johnson's Journal." LOUISIANA HISTORICAL QUARTERLY 5 (1922):34-50.

1800-1813. Extracts from merchant's travel diary, with editorial narrative; from New Jersey to New Orleans; overland to Natchez and then voyage to New Orleans; stormy return voyage to New York; valuable picture of life and tastes of successful businessman.

KING, REUBEN, 1779-1867   **1702**

Wood, Virginia S. and Wood, Ralph V., eds. "The Reuben King Journal." GEORGIA HISTORICAL QUARTERLY 50 (1966):177-206, 296-335, 421-458; 51 (1967):78-120.

1800-1806. Daily notes of a penniless young New England tanner seeking his fortune in Georgia; travel from Sharon, Connecticut, to Darien; a series of odd jobs; small business transactions and purchases, including prices; beginnings of prosperity as a tanner; taking an apprentice and terms of indenture; sicknesses and relentless record of hard work.

KLUGE, JOHN PETER, 1768-1849   **1703**

In THE MORAVIAN INDIAN MISSION ON WHITE RIVER: DIARIES AND LETTERS, edited by Lawrence H. Gipson, pp. 39-52, 67-101, 455-465. Indiana Historical Collections, vol. 23. Indianapolis: Indiana Historical Bureau, 1938.

Oct-Nov 1800, Mar-May 1801, Sep-Nov 1806. Missionary travels with Brother Abraham Luckenbach; from Bethlehem, Pennsylvania, to Goshen on the Muskingum; from Goshen to White River; from White River to Bethlehem; notes on travel and Moravian life and work.

MCLEOD, ARCHIBALD NORMAN   **1704**

In FIVE FUR TRADERS OF THE NORTHWEST, edited by Charles M. Gates, pp. 123-185.

Nov 1800-Jun 1801. Diary of bourgeois, partner in Northwest Company, in charge of Swan River Department; supervising fur trading between Lake Winnipeg and the Assiniboine River; weather and social details; most interesting account of life of fur traders.

MAUDE, JOHN   **1705**

VISIT TO THE FALLS OF NIAGRA IN 1800. London: Longman, Rees, Orme, Brown & Green, 1826. 313 pp. Diary, pp. 3-279.

Extracts in ANTHOLOGY AND BIBLIOGRAPHY OF NIAGARA FALLS, by Charles M. Dow, vol. 1, pp. 115-122.

Jun-Oct 1800. Englishman's trip from New York through Upper Canada to Niagara and return to New York; long entries in travel-book style; tourist's adventures and impressions of scenery, towns, people, etc. Authorship assumed.

POSTLETHWAITE, SAMUEL, 1772-1825   **1706**

"Journal of a Voyage from Louisville to Natchez." MISSOURI HISTORICAL SOCIETY BULLETIN 7 (1951):312-329.

Sep 1800-Feb 1801. Merchant's account of journey by flatboat down the Ohio and Mississippi; navigational landmarks with occasional notes on settlements, Indians, business, etc., reflecting the multicultural nature of the region.

TENNENT, WILLIAM MACKAY   **1707**

"Journal of the Rev. William Mackay Tennent." PRESBYTERIAN HISTORICAL SOCIETY JOURNAL 22 (1944):124-135.

Oct-Dec 1800. Presbyterian clergyman and moderator of the General Assembly on fund-raising trip through Maryland; itinerary; names of people encountered; preaching.

THORNTON, ANNA MARIA, b. 1774?   **1708**

"Diary of Mrs. William Thornton." COLUMBIA HISTORICAL SOCIETY RECORDS 10 (1907):88-226; 19 (1916):172-182.

Jan-Dec 1800. Detailed and factual personal diary; social and domestic life in Washington, D.C.; account of friendship with George and Martha Washington, visits to Mount Vernon, etc.

Aug-Sep 1814. Good description of capture of Washington, D.C., by the British.

1801

ASSHETON, SUSANNAH, b. 1767   1709

Beatty, Joseph M. Jr., "Susan Assheton's Book." PENN-SYLVANIA MAGAZINE OF HISTORY AND BIOGRAPHY 55 (1931):174-186.

> 1801-1832. Philadelphian's brief, occasional memoranda of national, international and family affairs; comments on dead friends.

BADGER, JOSEPH, 1757-1846   1710

A MEMOIR OF REV. JOSEPH BADGER: CONTAINING AN AUTOBIOGRAPHY AND SELECTIONS FROM HIS PRIVATE JOURNAL AND CORRESPONDENCE. Hudson, Ohio: Sawyer, Ingersoll, 1851. 185 pp. Journal, pp. 27-167.

> 1801-1807. Presbyterian missionary work, mainly in Western Reserve settlement at Austinburg, Ohio; missionary tours in Ohio, Virginia, Pennsylvania; meetings, preaching; among Wyandots and in Sandusky Mission.

BASCOM, RUTH HENSHAW MILES, 1772-1848   1711

Roeber, A.G., ed. "A New England Woman's Perspective on Norfolk, Virginia, 1801-1802: Excerpts from the Diary of Ruth Henshaw Bascom." AMERICAN ANTI-QUARIAN SOCIETY PROCEEDINGS 88 (1979):277-325.

> Nov 1801-Jun 1802. Yankee visitor's observations of Norfolk; social life, commerce, slavery, church services and sermons; the "Easter Rebellion."

BUCKNER, PHILIP, 1747-1820   1712

McGroarty, William B., ed. "Diary of Captain Philip Buckner." WILLIAM AND MARY COLLEGE QUARTERLY, 2d ser. 6 (1926):173-207.

> Feb-Jun 1801. Diary extracts of journey from Bracken County, Kentucky, to Natchez by water; return by land; bare details of places and incidents.

CHURCH, D.W.   1713

"Stillman Foote: A Middlebury Man Migrates to York State." VERMONT QUARTERLY 21 (1953):52-56.

> Mar-May 1801. Millwright's account of transporting mill irons from Vermont, via Lake Champlain and the St. Lawrence River, to the new settlement which would become Canton, New York; travel difficulties; hardships of weather and illness.

DU PONT DE NEMOURS, VICTOR MARIE, 1767-1827   1714

JOURNEY TO FRANCE AND SPAIN. Edited by Charles W. David. Ithaca, N.Y.: Cornell University Press, 1961. 144 pp. Reprint. Port Washington, N.Y.: Kennikat, 1972.

> 1801-1802. Negotiations of a former French diplomat to enlist French investors in his father's proposed speculative ventures in America; engaging accounts of social life and entertainments, especially opera and theatre, in Rouen and Paris; Spanish journal chiefly noting mode of travel, where and with whom he dined to carry on business.

ELLICOTT, JOSEPH, 1760-1826   1715

In AN AUTHENTIC AND COMPREHENSIVE HISTORY OF BUFFALO, by William Ketchum, vol. 2, pp. 146-150. Buffalo: Rockwell, Baker & Hill, Printers, 1865.

> 1801-1802. Extracts from business journal kept by agent of the Holland Land Company; early real estate operations at Buffalo Creek, New York.

HASWELL, WILLIAM   1716

Jenkins, Lawrence W., ed. "Remarks on a Voyage in 1801 to the Island of Guam." ESSEX INSTITUTE HISTORICAL COLLECTIONS 53 (1917):193-214.

Extracts in THE SHIPS AND SAILORS OF OLD SALEM, by Ralph D. Paine, pp. 380-393.

> Oct 1801-Jan 1802. Boston ship officer's journal of voyage on barque LYDIA, from Manila to Guam; full and good descriptions of Zamboanga and Guam; resources, government, religion, customs, etc.

HOLYOKE, MARGARET, 1763-1825   1717

In THE HOLYOKE DIARIES, edited by George F. Dow, pp. 139-174.

> 1801-1823. Brief notes of social, personal and local affairs of Salem, Massachusetts.

LE RAYE, CHARLES   1718

In A TOPOGRAPHICAL DESCRIPTION OF THE STATE OF OHIO, INDIANA TERRITORY, AND LOUISIANA, by Jervis Cutler, pp. 158-204. Boston: Charles William, 1812.

> 1801-1805. French Canadian's trade journey along the Missouri River; capture by Indians; details of their mode of travel, encampment, food, villages, agriculture, celebrations and games; travel as far as Yellowstone River and Rocky Mountains; descriptions of Mandan, Gros Ventre, Flathead, Snake and Paunch Indians.

PICKERING, JOHN, 1777-1846   1719

In LIFE OF JOHN PICKERING, by Mary Orne Pickering, pp. 189-196. Boston: Printed for private distribution, 1887.

> Apr-May 1801. Travel diary of visit to Holland; Leyden, Amsterdam; notes on theaters, buildings, museums; return to England.

QUINCY, JOSIAH, 1772-1864   1720

"Journey of Josiah Quincy in 1801." MASSACHUSETTS HISTORICAL SOCIETY PROCEEDINGS, 2d ser. 4 (1887-1889):123-135.

> Jun 1801. Pleasant diary of tour from Boston through southeastern New England; descriptions of Providence, Tiverton, Martha's Vineyard; notes on persons.

SHELDON, LUCY, 1788-1889   1721

In CHRONICLES OF A PIONEER SCHOOL, by Emily N. Vanderpoel, pp. 43-53.

> Dec 1801-Feb 1802, Jan-Mar 1803. Extracts from school diary; studies and social life at Litchfield School.

SIEBENTHAL, FRANCOIS   1722

"The Crossing of Vevay's Founders." INDIANA MAGA-ZINE OF HISTORY 35 (1939):187-194.

> Mar-Apr 1801. Atlantic voyage of Swiss colonists from Vevey, France, to Norfolk, Virginia. Authorship assumed.

SMET, PIERRE JEAN DE, 1801-1873   1723

LIFE, LETTERS, AND TRAVELS OF FATHER PIERRE JEAN DE SMET, S.J. By Hiram M. Chittenden and Alfred T. Richardson. New York: Harper, 1905. 4 vols. Reprint. New York: Arno; Kraus, 1969.

> 1801-1873. Narrative and journal of Jesuit's missionary journeys and work; labors and adventures among the North American Indians; minute descriptions of manners, customs, games, warfare, legends, traditions; sketches of country from St. Louis to Puget Sound and the Athabasca.

VAN METER, ISAAC   1724

"Isaac Van Meter's Journal." TRANS-ALLEGHENY HISTORICAL MAGAZINE 1 (1901-1902):96-105.

> Apr-May 1801. Travel diary of tour through western Virginia; notes on scenery, towns, settlements, farming; sale and purchase of lands.

WHITE RIVER, INDIANA, MORAVIAN CONGREGATION   1725

"Diary of the Little Indian Congregation on the White River for the Year 1801." In THE MORAVIAN INDIAN MISSION ON WHITE RIVER: DIARIES AND LETTERS, edited by Lawrence H. Gipson, pp. 102-465. Indiana Historical Collections, vol. 23. Indianapolis: Indiana Historical Bureau, 1938.

> 1801-1808 (with gap). Life and work of a Moravian congregation; interesting details of Moravian missionary work and life; Indian life; weather, social affairs, etc. Translated from the German.

1802

BACON, MARY ANN, 1787-1815   1726

In CHRONICLES OF A PIONEER SCHOOL, by Emily N. Vanderpoel, pp. 66-71.

> Jun-Sep 1802. Charming diary extracts of school life at Litchfield, Connecticut.

BARTON, BENJAMIN SMITH, 1766-1815   1727

McAtee, W.L., ed. "Journal of Benjamin Smith Barton on a Visit to Virginia, 1802." CASTANEA 3 (1938):85-117.

> Jul-Sep 1802. Trip of physician and naturalist from Frederick, Maryland, to Virginia; lists of all plants and minerals observed; notes on medicinal use of several plants.

CRAFTS, SAMUEL, 1768-1853   1728

Bassett, T.D. Seymour, ed. "Samuel Crafts and His Dugout Canoe." VERMONT HISTORY 41 (1973):198-204. Diary, pp. 199-200.

> 1802. Summary and a few brief extracts of lost travel diary; journey from Vermont to Mississippi to investigate land prospects; part of trip spent in company with French botanist, François André Michaux.

DAVYDOV, GAVRIIL IVANOVICH, 1784-1809   1729

TWO VOYAGES TO RUSSIAN AMERICA, 1802-1807. Translated by Colin Bearne, edited by Richard A. Pierce. Materials for the Study of Alaska History, no. 10. Kingston, Ontario: The Limestone Press, 1977. 257 pp.

> 1802-1804. Young Russian naval officer's two treks across Siberia and visits to Kodiak Island in service of the Russian-American Company; incredi-ble rigors of Siberian travel; notes on people, customs and terrain; detailed descriptions of Kodiak life, including festivals.

DIEFENBACH, HEINRICH, 1771-1837?   1730

Yoder, Don, trans. and ed. "From the Yadkin to the Delaware--Pastor Diefenbach Rides to Synod in 1802." PENNSYLVANIA DUTCHMAN 3, no. 12 (November 15, 1951):1, 5-6.

> Apr-Jun 1802. Minister's journey to the Reformed Synod in Philadelphia; examination and ordination; return trip; visiting relatives; preaching in various locales; report of foiled slave revolt.

Yoder, Don, trans. and ed. "Over the Alleghenies in 1825--Pastor Diefenbach's Journal of His Removal Westward." PENNSYLVANIA DUTCHMAN 3, no. 14 (December 15, 1951):1, 5-6.

> Jun-Jul 1825. Journey of Reformed pastor and family in covered wagon from Berks County, Pennsylvania, over route through Lancaster, Gettysburg, Hagerstown, Wheeling and into Highland County, Ohio; pleasant description of travel sights and events.

EATON, WILLIAM, 1764-1811   1731

In THE LIFE OF THE LATE GEN. WILLIAM EATON, compiled by Charles Prentiss, pp. 237-238, 268-277, 301-335. Brookfield: Printed by E. Merriam, 1813.

> 1802-1805. General's military diary; notes on Tunisian pickpockets, cruise to Malta, social life at Cairo, march from Alexandria to Barca Desert; notes on difficulties of journey.

GILPIN, JOSHUA, 1765-1841   1732

"Journey to Bethlehem." PENNSYLVANIA MAGAZINE OF HISTORY AND BIOGRAPHY 46 (1922):15-38, 122-153.

> May 1802. Journey from Wakefield to Bethlehem via Germantown, Easton, Stroudsburg; full descriptions of sights; expenses; farming conditions; long account of the Moravian settlement at Bethlehem.

"Journal of a Tour from Philadelphia Thro the Western Counties of Pennsylvania in the Months of September and October, 1809." PENNSYLVANIA MAGAZINE OF HISTORY AND BIOGRAPHY 50 (1926):64-78, 163-178, 380-382; 51 (1927):172-190, 351-375; 52 (1928):29-58.

PLEASURE AND BUSINESS IN WESTERN PENNSYLVANIA: THE JOURNAL OF JOSHUA GILPIN. Edited by Joseph E. Walker. Harrisburg: Pennsylvania Historical and Museum Commission, 1975. 156 pp.

> Sep-Oct 1809. Travel diary of a combination business trip and family vacation undertaken by Gilpin, his wife, eight-year-old son and servants; round-trip between Philadelphia and Pittsburgh by private carriage; great descriptive detail of countryside; soil, crops, topography, towns, manufactures; notes on expenses and accommodations of trip; business prospects, economic conditions and potential.

LITTLE, NATHANIEL W.   1733

"Journal of Nathaniel W. Little." OLD NORTHWEST GENEALOGICAL QUARTERLY 10 (1907):237-245.

> Jul-Oct 1802. Travel diary from Blandford to northwestern Ohio, via New York, Princeton, Philadelphia, Lancaster, Pittsburgh, Chillicothe, Muskingum, Greensburg, etc.; usual travel observations.

MICHAUX, FRANCOIS ANDRE, b. 1770?   **1734**

Bassett, T.D. Seymour, ed. "Samuel Crafts and His Dugout Canoe." VERMONT HISTORY 41 (1973):198–204. Journal, pp. 201–204.

> Jul–Oct 1802. Extracts from travel journal of French botanist; journey down Ohio River with Samuel Crafts of Vermont.

OLIVER, WILLIAM WAIT, 1778–1869   **1735**

"Journal of William Wait Oliver of Salem." ESSEX INSTITUTE HISTORICAL COLLECTIONS 81 (1945):124–137, 227–256, 348–353.

> Jun 1802–Mar 1803. Daily activities of employee at Salem Custom House; books read, sermons heard, ship arrivals and departures; illnesses and deaths; appointment as deputy collector; criticism of Jefferson for treating the position of collector as political appointment.

SIBLEY, JOHN, 1757–1837   **1736**

"The Journal of Dr. John Sibley." LOUISIANA HISTORICAL QUARTERLY 10 (1927):474–497.

> Jul–Oct 1802. Voyage from Charleston, South Carolina, to New Orleans; descriptions of city and surrounding country; up Mississippi to Washington in Mississippi Territory.

TAYLOR, JOHN, 1762–1840   **1737**

In THE DOCUMENTARY HISTORY OF THE STATE OF NEW YORK, by E.B. O'Callaghan, vol. 3, pp. 673–696.

Extracts in THE ANNALS OF ALBANY, by Joel Munsell, vol. 6, pp. 219–222. Albany: J. Munsell, 1855.

> Jul–Oct 1802. Missionary journey from Deerfield, Massachusetts, to the Mohawk and Black River country of New York; lengthy descriptive notes.

TUCKER, MARY ORNE, 1775–1806   **1738**

"Diary of Mary Orne Tucker." ESSEX INSTITUTE HISTORICAL COLLECTIONS 77 (1941):306–338.

> Apr–May 1802. Full and well-written entries of domestic and social life in Essex County, Massachusetts; notes on reading.

TURNER, CHARLES, 1760–1839   **1739**

"Journal of Charles Turner, Jr." MASSACHUSETTS HISTORICAL SOCIETY PROCEEDINGS, 1st ser. 17 (1879–1880):206–216.

> Aug–Oct 1802. Extracts from surveying journal; surveying grants and sales of land in Nova Scotia; Campobello, Grand Manan, etc.; some general and social notes.

WILLIAMS, WILLIAM, 1763–1824   **1740**

JOURNAL OF THE LIFE, TRAVELS AND GOSPEL LABOURS OF WILLIAM WILLIAMS. Cincinnati: Lodge, L'Hommedieu, and Hammond, Printers, 1828. 272 pp. Cincinnati, 1839. 195 pp.

> 1802–1822. Quaker journal of journeys and visits to Friends' meetings in southern states; tours in Atlantic and trans-Allegheny states; move to Indiana and work there; various tours in the East.

WINCH, JOEL   **1741**

Peach, Arthur W., ed. "The Rev. Joel Winch--Pioneer Minister: Selections from His Diaries." VERMONT HISTORICAL SOCIETY PROCEEDINGS 9 (1941):235–270; 10 (1942):21–35, 83–103.

> 1802–1806. Methodist circuit rider's diary with summary of his life prior to 1802; circuits in Vermont, Maine and New Hampshire; manners and mores of frontier folk; rigors of itineration; controversy with Congregationalists; sickness and drastic treatment with mercury; a lively picture of New England Methodism of the time; unusual spellings.

1803

BUCKMINSTER, JOSEPH STEVENS, 1784–1812   **1742**

In MEMOIRS OF REV. JOSEPH BUCKMINSTER, by Eliza Buckminster Lee, pp. 237–278. Boston: W. Crosby and H.P. Nichols, 1849.

> 1803–1806. A record of studies modeled on Gibbon's journal; notes on religious and philosophical reading; journey to Europe; notes on literary acquaintances in London and at Strasbourg.

COVELL, LEMUEL   **1743**

"Visit of Rev. Lemuel Covell to Western New York and Canada." BUFFALO HISTORICAL SOCIETY PUBLICATIONS 6 (1903):207–216.

> Sep–Nov 1803. Baptist minister's travel journal; attendance at meetings; comments on Indians.

COWDERY, JONATHAN, 1767–1852   **1744**

AMERICAN CAPTIVES IN TRIPOLI. 2d ed. Boston: Printed and sold by Belcher & Armstrong, 1806. 35 pp.

> 1803–1805. Journal of the surgeon's mate on the PHILADELPHIA; capture and captivity in Tripoli; medical work in bashaw's family; daily life of the American prisoners.

CUROT, MICHEL   **1745**

"A Wisconsin Fur-Trader's Journal." WISCONSIN HISTORICAL SOCIETY COLLECTIONS 20 (1911):396–471.

> Jul 1803–Jun 1804. Fur trader in charge of Yellow River Post in northern Wisconsin; travels, trade, daily life, notes on Indians. Translated from the French.

FORBES, JOHN   **1746**

"A Journal of John Forbes, May, 1803; the Seizure of William Augustus Bowles." FLORIDA HISTORICAL SOCIETY QUARTERLY 9 (1931):279–289.

> May 1803. Indian affairs in Florida; seizure of leader of Indians, William Augustus Bowles.

HARRIS, THADDEUS MASON, 1768–1842   **1747**

THE JOURNAL OF A TOUR INTO THE TERRITORY NORTHWEST OF THE ALLEGHANY MOUNTAINS. Boston: Printed by Manning & Loring, 1805. 271 pp. Journal, pp. 11–85.

In EARLY WESTERN TRAVELS, edited by Reuben G. Thwaites, vol. 3, pp. 309–382.

> Mar–Jun 1803. Minister's journal of travel from Lancaster, Pennsylvania, to Ohio, via Strasbourg,

Shippensburg, Marietta, and return via Wheeling, Somerset, Bedford, Yorktown; notes on geography, topography; historical account of Ohio.

IRVING, WASHINGTON, 1783–1859   1748

JOURNALS AND NOTEBOOKS. Edited by Nathalia Wright et al. Complete Works of Washington Irving, vols. 1–5. Madison: University of Wisconsin Press; Boston: Twayne, 1969–(in progress).

1803–1842. Travel diaries of the peripatetic author; detailed descriptions of persons and places; notes for tales.

JOURNAL, 1803. Edited by Stanley T. Williams. London and New York: Oxford University Press, 1934. 43 pp.

Irving, Pierre M., ed. "Washington Irving Visits Ogdenburg." YORK STATE TRADITION 25 (1971):22–28.

Jul–Aug 1803. Journey to Ogdensburg (Oswegatchie) with Josiah Moffman, Thomas Ogden and others, and into the Black River country; juvenile, romantic observations on the frontier.

NOTES AND JOURNAL OF TRAVEL IN EUROPE. Edited by William P. Trent. New York: Grolier Club, 1921. 3 vols. Reprint. Scholarly Press, 1972.

1804–1805. Young Irving on his European travels; France, Italy, Switzerland, Greece, Germany, Belgium.

THE JOURNALS OF WASHINGTON IRVING (HITHERTO UNPUBLISHED). Edited by William P. Trent and George S. Hellman. Boston: Bibliophile Society, 1919. 3 vols. Reprint. New York: Haskell House, 1970.

1815–1842. Travels in Wales, France, Germany, Austria, Bohemia, Spain; horseback trip onto the Great Plains with Indian Commissioner Henry Leavitt Ellsworth and others to investigate land set aside for removal of Indians from settled areas; travel on Ohio, Mississippi and Arkansas rivers; meetings with the prisoner Black Hawk and other chiefs; much on ways of Indians and settlers; trading posts, missions to Indians, buffalo hunts; trip from New York to Spain.

TOUR IN SCOTLAND, 1817, AND OTHER MANUSCRIPT NOTES. Edited by Stanley T. Williams. New Haven: Yale University Press, 1927. 146 pp. Journal, pp. 21–72, 75–79.

Jun–Sep 1817. Journey from Liverpool to Runcorn with William C. Preston; then from London to Edinburgh and tour through Scotland; interesting notes on people, places and tales.

JOURNAL OF WASHINGTON IRVING. Edited by Stanley T. Williams. Cambridge: Harvard University Press, 1931. 244 pp.

Jul–Aug 1824. Kaleidoscopic notes in England, France, Germany, Holland.

Myers, Andrew B., ed. "Washington Irving's Madrid Journal 1827–1828 and Related Letters." NEW YORK PUBLIC LIBRARY BULLETIN 62 (1958):217–227, 300–311, 407–419.

May 1827–Feb 1828. Literary and social activities in Madrid; trips to the Escorial, Aranjuez and Toledo.

JOURNAL OF WASHINGTON IRVING 1828 AND MISCELLANEOUS NOTES ON MOORISH LEGEND AND HISTORY. Edited by Stanley T. Williams. New York: American Book Co., 1937. 80 pp. Journal, pp. 1–65.

Mar–Apr 1828. Irving's first stay in Granada; part of journey from Madrid into southern Spain.

WASHINGTON IRVING DIARY, SPAIN 1828–1829. Edited by Clara Louise Penny. New York: Hispanic Society of America, 1926. 142 pp.

Apr 1828–Feb 1829. Journey from Madrid into southern Spain; generally brief notes.

THE WESTERN JOURNALS OF WASHINGTON IRVING. Edited by John F. McDermott. Norman: University of Oklahoma Press, 1944. 201 pp. 2d ed. 1966. 206 pp.

Sep–Nov 1832.

JEWITT, JOHN RODGERS, 1783–1821   1749

A JOURNAL KEPT AT NOOTKA SOUND. Boston: Printed for the author, 1807. 48 pp. Reprint. New York: Garland, 1976; With an introduction by Norman L. Dodge. Boston: C.E. Goodspeed, 1931. 91 pp.

1803–1805. Journal of survivor of ship BOSTON; captivity by Nootka Indians; brief notes of daily life in Indian fashion; in Defoe-like style; apparently written by Richard Alsop from interviews.

LEWIS, MERIWETHER, 1774–1809   1750

THE JOURNALS OF CAPTAIN MERIWETHER LEWIS AND SERGEANT JOHN ORDWAY, KEPT ON THE EXPEDITION OF WESTERN EXPLORATION 1803–1806. Edited by Milo M. Quaife. Wisconsin State Historical Society Collections, vol. 22. Madison: Wisconsin State Historical Society, 1916. 444 pp. Journal, pp. 31–76.

Aug–Dec 1803. Exploration down Ohio River and up the Mississippi; mainly topographical notes.

HISTORY OF THE EXPEDITION UNDER THE COMMAND OF CAPTAINS LEWIS AND CLARK, TO THE SOURCES OF THE MISSOURI, THENCE ACROSS THE ROCKY MOUNTAINS AND DOWN THE RIVER COLUMBIA TO THE PACIFIC OCEAN. Edited by Nicholas Biddle and Paul Allen. Philadelphia: Bradford and Inskeep; New York: Abm. M. Inskeep, J. Maxwell, Printer, 1814. 2 vols. Frequently reprinted.

HISTORY OF THE EXPEDITION. Edited by Elliott Coues. New York: Harper, 1893. 4 vols. Reprint. New York: Dover, 1965. 3 vols.

ORIGINAL JOURNALS OF THE LEWIS AND CLARK EXPEDITION, 1804–1806. Edited by Reuben G. Thwaites. New York: Dodd, Mead, 1904–1905. 8 vols. Reprint. New York: Antiquarian Press, 1959.

THE JOURNALS OF LEWIS AND CLARK. Edited by Bernard De Voto. Boston: Houghton Mifflin, 1953. 504 pp. Abridgment.

THE JOURNALS OF LEWIS AND CLARK. A new selection by John Bakeless. New York: New American Library, 1964. 384 pp. Abridgment.

Extracts in THOSE TREMENDOUS MOUNTAINS: THE STORY OF THE LEWIS AND CLARK EXPEDITION, by David Freeman Hawke. New York: Norton, 1980. 273 pp.

Extracts in AMERICAN HISTORY TOLD BY CONTEMPORARIES, edited by Albert B. Hart, vol. 3, pp. 381–384.

1804–1806. Extensive account of the exploration to the Northwest with William Clark; distances, topography, etc.

"Lewis and Clark in North Dakota." NORTH DAKOTA HISTORY 14 (1947):5–45, 73–145, 173–241, 287–391; 15 (1948):15–74.

1804–1806. Extracts relating to North Dakota.

Peebles, John J., ed. "On the Lolo Trail: Route and Campsites of Lewis and Clark." IDAHO YESTERDAYS 9, no. 4 (1965):2–15; 10, no. 2 (1966):16–27.

Sep 1805–Jun 1806. Extracts relating to northern Idaho.

Peebles, John J., ed. "Rugged Waters: Trails and Campsites of Lewis and Clark in the Salmon River Country." IDAHO YESTERDAYS 8, no. 2 (1964):2–17.

Aug–Sep 1805. Extracts relating to Salmon River area of Idaho.

For a publishing history of the journals, see A HISTORY OF THE LEWIS AND CLARK JOURNALS, by Paul Russell Cutright. Norman: University of Oklahoma Press, 1976.

MILLS, ROBERT, 1781–1855   1751

Cohen, Hennig, ed. "An Unpublished Diary by Robert Mills." SOUTH CAROLINA HISTORICAL AND GENEALOGICAL MAGAZINE 51 (1950):187–194.

Jul 1803. Personal diary of Baltimore architect employed by Benjamin Latrobe; thoughts on religion and man's depravity; reports on his social life; some notes on his work, reading and current events.

Evans, Richard Xavier, ed. "The Daily Journal of Robert Mills." MARYLAND HISTORICAL MAGAZINE 30 (1935):257–271.

Jan–Dec 1816. Brief personal and business notes.

Cohen, Hennig, ed. "The Journal of Robert Mills." SOUTH CAROLINA HISTORICAL AND GENEALOGICAL MAGAZINE 52 (1951):133–139, 218–224; 53 (1952):31–36, 90–100.

1828–1830. Correspondence and financial accounts; occasional prayers; some references to work on Washington Monument.

SALTONSTALL, LEVERETT, 1783–1845   1752

In THE SALTONSTALL PAPERS, 1607–1815 vol. 2, pp. 125–295, 326–343, 366–440, 549–555. Massachusetts Historical Society Collections, vol. 81. Boston: Massachusetts Historical Society, 1974.

1803–1814. Personal and social life of young lawyer of prominent family in Haverhill and Salem, Massachusetts; professional studies; journey through Maine with descriptions of towns; first Bowdoin College Commencement at which he took an A.M. degree; local, national and international events; political opinions, religious services; trip from Salem to New York State with details of Shaker worship service.

Moody, Robert, ed. "Leverett Saltonstall: A Diary Beginning Jany. A.D. 1806." MASSACHUSETTS HISTORICAL SOCIETY PROCEEDINGS 89 (1977):127–177.

1806–1807. Diary located after those published in THE SALTONSTALL PAPERS.

SELKIRK, THOMAS DOUGLAS, 5th earl of, 1771–1820   1753

LORD SELKIRK'S DIARY. Edited by Patrick C.T. White. Reprint. Champlain Society Publications, vol. 35. New York: Greenwood Press, 1969. 359 pp.

Bryce, George, ed. "Extracts from Lord Selkirk's Diaries in Upper and Lower Canada in the Years 1803 and 1804." ROYAL SOCIETY OF CANADA PROCEEDINGS AND TRANSACTIONS, 3d ser. 6 (1912):3–9.

1803–1804. Scottish philanthropist's account of travels in Canada, where he was overseeing the settlement of impoverished Irish and Scottish immigrants, New York and New England; great interest in the arts, commerce, manufacture, education, and especially agriculture; very detailed picture of northeastern United States and its people; city dwellers, Indians, frontiersmen.

SETON, ELIZABETH ANN BAYLEY, 1774–1821   1754

In MEMOIR, LETTERS AND JOURNAL OF ELIZABETH SETON, CONVERT TO THE CATHOLIC FAITH AND SISTER OF CHARITY, by Robert Seton, 2 vols. passim. New York: P. O'Shea, 1869.

1803–1816. Extract from journal of trip to Italy for her husband's health; conversion; devotion; deaths of her daughters.

SHARPLES, ELLEN WALLACE, 1769–1849   1755

In THE SHARPLES; THEIR PORTRAITS OF GEORGE WASHINGTON AND HIS CONTEMPORARIES, by Katharine McCook Knox, pp. 127–133, app., pp. 117–122. New Haven: Yale University Press, 1930, 1972.

1803–1814. Extracts from English artist's diary kept during two trips to America; notes on numerous portraits of eminent Americans, including George Washington, painted by herself, her husband, James, her daughter, Rolinda, and her two sons, James and Felix; other paintings and handiwork, including embroidery.

SWEARINGEN, JAMES STRODE   1756

In CHICAGO AND THE OLD NORTHWEST, by Milo M. Quaife, pp. 373–377. Chicago: University of Chicago Press, 1913.

Jul–Aug 1803. Brief notes on journey from Detroit to Chicago; topography, weather, etc.

WEIR, JAMES, 1777–1845   1757

In A HISTORY OF MUHLENBERG COUNTY, by Otto A. Rothert, pp. 443–448. Louisville, Ky.: J.P. Morton, 1913.

Mar–Jul 1803. Travel diary; Natchez, Baton Rouge, New Orleans, Philadelphia, Pittsburgh; imprisonment by Spaniards at Baton Rouge; notes on towns, waterspout, etc.

WERTMUELLER, ADOLF ULRIC, 1751–1811   1758

Scott, Franklin D., trans. and ed., "Wertmüller's Diary: The Transformation of Artist into Farmer." SWEDISH PIONEER HISTORICAL QUARTERLY 6 (1955):34–54.

Apr–Jul 1803. Noted Swedish artist's record of establishing small farm in southeastern Pennsylvania; acquisition of stock, tools; problems of finding laborers to assist him.

WHITE, MARY WILDER, 1780–1811   1759

In MEMORIALS OF MARY WILDER WHITE, by Elizabeth A.W. Dwight, edited by Mary W. Tileston, pp. 1–409 passim. Boston: Everett Press, 1903.

1803–1805. Scattered extracts of religious and social life in Concord, Massachusetts.

YARNALL, HANNAH HAINES, 1765–1822   1760

In THOMAS RICHARDSON OF SOUTH SHIELDS, DURHAM COUNTY, ENGLAND, by Mary Thomas Seaman, pp. 197–222. New York: T.A. Wright, 1929.

Sep–Nov 1803. Quaker travel journal; visit to Friends in Canada; meetings, work, weather, religious reflections; notes on Indians and Methodist rivalries.

1804

CAMERON, DUNCAN 1761

In LES BOURGEOIS DE LA COMPAGNIE DU NORD-OUEST, by Louis F.R. Masson, vol. 2, pp. 267-300.

Aug-Dec 1804. Extracts of fur-trading journal by employee of Northwest Company; kept at Nipigon Department, between Lake Superior and Hudson's Bay; travel about the territory, establishment of fort, criticism of Indians; rivalry with Hudson's Bay Company.

CLARK, WILLIAM JOSEPH, 1776-1813 1762

"Diary of William Joseph Clark." KENTUCKY HISTORICAL SOCIETY REGISTER 25 (1927):193-206.

Nov 1804-Jun 1805. Lawyer's business trip from Kentucky to St. Louis and return; description of weather impeding travel; various "entertainments" he enjoyed; return of Lewis and Clark Expedition and visit to their barge; Indian ceremony; record of expenses; some confusion in entry dates.

DUNBAR, WILLIAM, 1749-1810 1763

In DOCUMENTS RELATING TO THE PURCHASE & EXPLORATION OF LOUISIANA, by William Dunbar, pp. 7-189. Boston and New York: Houghton Mifflin, 1904.

LIFE, LETTERS AND PAPERS OF WILLIAM DUNBAR. Compiled by Eron O.M. Rowland. Jackson: Mississippi Historical Society, 1930. 410 pp. Journal, pp. 216-320.

Oct 1804-Jan 1805. Mississippi surveying and exploration journal; from St. Catherine's Landing to Hot Springs; Red, Black and Washita rivers.

FARIES, HUGH 1764

In FIVE FUR TRADERS OF THE NORTHWEST, edited by Charles M. Gates, pp. 189-241.

Jul 1804-May 1805. Fur-trading journal of employee of Northwest Company in charge of fur trading around Rainy Lake post during absence of supervisor; work and life at the post; valuable notes on social life of the voyageurs.

FLOYD, CHARLES, ca. 1781-1804 1765

AMERICAN ANTIQUARIAN SOCIETY PROCEEDINGS, n.s. 9 (1893-1894):238-252.

In ORIGINAL JOURNALS OF THE LEWIS AND CLARK EXPEDITION, edited by Reuben G. Thwaites, vol. 7, pp. 3-26. New York: Dodd, Mead, 1905. Reprint. New York: Antiquarian Press, 1959.

Mar-Aug 1804. Entertaining record of sergeant on the Lewis and Clark Expedition; bare details of the exploration; interesting spellings.

FOORD, JAMES, 1761-1821 1766

Still, Bayrd. "To the West on Business in 1804." PENNSYLVANIA MAGAZINE OF HISTORY AND BIOGRAPHY 64 (1940):1-21.

Jan-May 1804. Brief entries of business trip from Massachusetts to Kentucky to investigate titles; Boston, New York, Philadelphia, Frankfort, Ohio Valley; travel by stage and horseback; notes on stages, inns, social affairs.

GASS, PATRICK, 1771-1870 1767

A JOURNAL OF THE VOYAGES AND TRAVELS OF A CORPS OF DISCOVERY, UNDER THE COMMAND OF CAPT. LEWIS AND CAPT. CLARKE. Pittsburgh: David M'Keehan, 1807. 262 pp. Frequently reprinted; recently, Minneapolis: Ross & Haines, 1958. 317 pp.

GASS'S JOURNAL OF THE LEWIS AND CLARK EXPEDITION. Introduction by James K. Hosmer. Chicago: A.D. McClurg, 1904. 208 pp.

1804-1806. Exploration journal of member of Lewis and Clark Expedition; first published account of the expedition; very good reading, although journal was polished for publication.

HOPKINS, GERARD T. 1768

Extracts in TRAVEL ACCOUNTS OF INDIANA, compiled by Shirley McCord, pp. 49-52.

Mar-Apr 1804. Extracts from Quaker missionary's account of attempt to help Chief Little Turtle, at his request, and Miami Indians with an agricultural experiment.

"Visit of Gerard T. Hopkins: A Quaker Ambassador to the Indians Who Visited Buffalo in 1804." BUFFALO HISTORICAL SOCIETY PUBLICATIONS 6 (1903):217-222.

May 1804. Quaker travel journal; visit to Buffalo; account of the country and notes on farming.

JOHNSTON, JOHN, 1781-1851 1769

In JOHN JOHNSTON OF NEW YORK, MERCHANT, by Emily Johnston De Forest, 196 pp. passim. New York: Privately printed, 1909.

1804-1847. Scattered extracts of business journals; business life in New York; travel abroad.

LOOMIS, HEZEKIAH, 1779-1862 1770

Middlebrook, Louis F., ed. "Journal of Hezekiah Loomis, Steward of U.S. Brig VIXEN, Captain John Smith, U.S.N., in War with Tripoli." ESSEX INSTITUTE HISTORICAL COLLECTIONS 63 (1927):285-308; 64 (1928): 33-48, 129-144, 225-235.

1804-1805. Sea journal of cruise in Mediterranean during war with Tripoli; ship movements and work as steward; some social details.

MALHIOT, FRANCOIS VICTOR, 1776-1840 1771

"A Wisconsin Fur-Trader's Journal." WISCONSIN STATE HISTORICAL SOCIETY COLLECTIONS 19 (1910):163-233.

Jul 1804-Jun 1805. Journal by clerk of Northwest Company while in charge of Fond du Lac Department, south of Lake Superior; repairing and rebuilding post; interesting notes on life of fur trader; good source for economics of fur trade. Translated from the French-Canadian patois.

MASON, JONATHAN, 1756-1831 1772

"Diary of the Hon. Jonathan Mason." MASSACHUSETTS HISTORICAL SOCIETY PROCEEDINGS, 2d ser. 2 (1885-1886):5-34.

Nov 1804-Apr 1805. Horseback journey from Boston to Savannah; comments on and descriptions of people, places, social life, theaters; expense list; pleasant journal.

ORDWAY, JOHN, ca. 1775-ca. 1817   1773

In THE JOURNALS OF CAPTAIN MERIWETHER LEWIS AND SERGEANT JOHN ORDWAY, KEPT ON THE EXPEDITION OF WESTERN EXPLORATION 1803-1806, by Meriwether Lewis, edited by Milo M. Quaife, pp. 79-402. Wisconsin State Historical Society Collections, vol. 22. Madison: Wisconsin State Historical Society, 1916. Reprint. 1965.

    1804-1806. Exploration journal kept on Lewis and Clark Expedition; River Dubois, Floyd's Creek, Teton River, Fort Mandan, Marias River, Great Falls, Great Divide, down Columbia River to Pacific Ocean; at Fort Clatsop, Walla Walla River, headwaters of Missouri River.

SAYER, JOHN   1774

In FIVE FUR-TRADERS OF THE NORTHWEST, by Charles M. Gates, pp. 245-278.

    Sep 1804-Apr 1805. Fur-trading journal of employee of Northwest Company; winter in region of Cross Lake and Snake River; building of trading post; trading activities and varied work around the post; notes on Indian customs and habits; a most interesting narrative, with some linguistic interest. Attributed by Gates to Thomas Connor; for discussion of authorship, see Birk, Douglas A. and White, Bruce M. "Who Wrote the Diary of Thomas Connor?" MINNESOTA HISTORY 46 (1979):170-188, and "Guilty as Charged." MINNESOTA HISTORY 47 (1980):162.

SHALER, WILLIAM, 1778?-1833   1775

"Journal of a Voyage between China and the North-Western Coast of America Made in 1804." AMERICAN REGISTER 3, pt. 1 (1808):137-175. Reprint. Introduction by Lindly Bynum. Claremont, Calif.: Saunders Studio Press, 1935. 108 pp.

Extracts in A HISTORY OF CALIFORNIA, by Robert G. Cleland, pp. 470-482. New York: Macmillan, 1922.

    1804-1805. Voyage from Canton to California; Gulf of California, Fonseca Bay, Santa Catalina Island, Cape San Lucas, Hawaiian Islands, Canton; personal observations and material derived from travel books.

SUTCLIFF, ROBERT, d. 1811   1776

TRAVELS IN SOME PARTS OF NORTH AMERICA. Philadelphia: B.&T. Kite, 1812. 289 pp.

    1804-1806. English visitor's pleasant, journalistic style travel diary; from England to New York; extensive travels in Pennsylvania, New Jersey, New York, Virginia; tourist's notes of scenery, occupations, people, customs.

TILLINGHAST, WILLIAM E.   1777

"The Journal of Capt. Tillinghast." RHODE ISLAND HISTORICAL COLLECTIONS 32 (1939):8-16, 80-84.

    Aug-Oct 1804. Journey from Providence through New York State to Saratoga and Lake George; notes on towns, scenery, taverns, farming; interesting spellings.

WHITE, EBENEZER, 1727-1817   1778

In HISTORY OF MIDDLESEX COUNTY, CONNECTICUT, pp. 501-502. New York: J.B. Beers, 1884.

    Jul-Sep 1804. Brief scattered notes of personal and local affairs; farming, sermons, weather.

WHITEHOUSE, JOSEPH   1779

In ORIGINAL JOURNALS OF THE LEWIS AND CLARK EXPEDITION, ed. by Reuben G. Thwaites, vol. 7, pp. 29-190. New York: Dodd, Mead, 1905.

    1804-1805. Private with Lewis and Clark Expedition; useful supplement to better-known journals of the expedition; some linguistic interest.

Cutright, Paul Russell. "The Journal of Private Joseph Whitehouse, a Soldier with Lewis and Clark." MISSOURI HISTORICAL SOCIETY BULLETIN 28 (1971-1972):143-161.

    Nov 1805-Apr 1806. Paraphrased version, discovered in 1966, of Whitehouse's journal, which extends coverage and fills in gaps in other edition.

1805

ANON.   1780

"From Bardstown to Washington in 1805." AMERICAN HISTORICAL MAGAZINE AND TENNESSEE HISTORICAL SOCIETY QUARTERLY 8 (1903):91-100.

    Apr 1805. Notes and general comments on scenery, towns and taverns, from Bardstown, Kentucky, to Washington, D.C.

AYER, SARAH CONNELL, 1791-1835   1781

DIARY OF SARAH CONNELL AYER. Portland, Maine: Lefavor-Tower, 1910. 404 pp.

    1805-1935. Extensive notes on religious and social life in Andover and Newburyport, Massachusetts, Concord and Bow, New Hampshire, Portland and Eastport, Maine; beginning with the visits, reading and chitchat of a child and developing into a dominantly religious record in later years.

BARTLETT, HENRY   1782

"Henry Bartlett's Diary to Ohio and Kentucky." VIRGINIA MAGAZINE OF HISTORY AND BIOGRAPHY 19 (1911): 68-86.

    Apr-Jun 1805. Expenses and brief descriptive notes of journey from Frederick County, Virginia, to Ohio and Kentucky; good narrative of a backwoods preacher appended.

BIGELOW, TIMOTHY, 1767-1821   1783

JOURNAL OF A TOUR TO NIAGARA FALLS. Boston: Press of J. Wilson and Son, 1876. 121 pp.

Extract in HISTORIC HIGHWAYS OF AMERICA, by Archer B. Hulbert, vol. 12, pp. 116-142.

    Jul-Aug 1805. Trip from Massachusetts to Niagara; return via Montreal, Lake Champlain, Vermont and New Hampshire; good, full notes on topography, towns, taverns, agriculture, etc.

DIARY OF A VISIT TO NEWPORT, NEW YORK AND PHILADELPHIA. Boston: Printed for private distribution, 1880. 29 pp.

    Jul 1815. General travel details and descriptions.

BLAKE, NOAH, b. 1790 or 1791   1784

DIARY OF AN EARLY AMERICAN BOY. Edited by Eric Sloane. New York: W. Funk, 1962. 108 pp.; New York: Ballantine Books, 1974.

    1805. Diary of farm life of a fifteen year old boy; chores, social life, sugaring, bridge-building and mill construction.

BREATHITT, JOHN, 1786-1834   **1785**

"Commencement of a Journal from Kentucky to the State of Pennsylvania." KENTUCKY HISTORICAL SOCIETY REGISTER 52 (1954):5-24.

Mar-Aug 1805. Youth's travel journal; details of route through Kentucky, Ohio, Virginia and Pennsylvania; visit to wax figure display; magic lantern show; sojourn with relatives in and around Bedford County, Pennsylvania; social life, flirtations; trips to Hagerstown, Maryland; visit to the warm springs in Berkeley County, West Virginia; July Fourth in Winchester, Virginia; trip home.

BURR, ISAAC   **1786**

Burr, Daniel Swift. "Diary of a Journey a Century Ago." JOURNAL OF AMERICAN HISTORY 3 (1909):447-452.

Sep-Nov 1805. Journey through New York and Atlantic states to Virginia; notes on travel difficulties, taverns, expenses.

CATLIN, GUY, b. 1782?   **1787**

Muller, H.N., ed. "Floating a Lumber Raft to Quebec City, 1805: The Journal of Guy Catlin of Burlington." VERMONT HISTORY 39 (1971):116-124. Journal, pp. 119-122.

May-Jul 1805. Brief notes describing the voyage of a lumber raft from St. John on the Richelieu River to Quebec; hazards of the transport; intricacies of the timber trade.

ESPY, JOSIAH MURDOCH, 1771-1847   **1788**

MEMORANDUMS OF A TOUR MADE BY JOSIAH ESPY IN THE STATES OF OHIO AND KENTUCKY AND INDIANA TERRITORY. Ohio Valley Historical Series, no. 7: Miscellanies, pt. 1. Cincinnati: R. Clarke, 1870. 28 pp.

Jun-Nov 1805. Tour from Bedford, Pennsylvania, into Ohio and Kentucky; visits to relatives; description of springs, scenery, Cincinnati, Louisville, New Lancaster.

HOOKER, EDWARD, 1785-1846   **1789**

"Diary of Edward Hooker." AMERICAN HISTORICAL ASSOCIATION ANNUAL REPORT 1896, pp. 842-929.

1805-1808. Diary extracts; graduation at Yale, journey to Charleston, South Carolina; tutorship at Caroline College, Columbia; experiences in South; mainly political history of South with a few social and general items.

ISELIN, ISAAC   **1790**

Cromwell, James, ed. "Journal of a Trading Voyage around the World." NEW YORK HISTORICAL SOCIETY QUARTERLY 62 (1978):86-137.

1805-1808. Swiss immigrant's account of voyage of the brig MARYLAND on which he served as supercargo; information on commercial dealings and life at sea; views of many port cities visited in Chile, California, Mexico, Hawaii and Canton.

KENNY, PATRICK, 1763-1840   **1791**

Griffin, Martin I.J. and Willcox, Joseph, eds. "Extracts from the Diary of Rev. Patrick Kenny." AMERICAN CATHOLIC HISTORICAL SOCIETY OF PHILADELPHIA 7 (1896):94-137; 9 (1898):64-76, 77-128, 223-256, 305-342, 422-458.

1805-1833 (with gaps). Priest's diaries; details of

Catholic missions at Coffee Run, West Chester, Wilmington; churches of St. Mary and Holy Trinity, Philadelphia; many private notes of expenses, opinions of people, social affairs, parish and farm work; daily life and infirmities; weather; touched with sarcastic and whimsical humor.

LAROCQUE, FRANCOIS ANTOINE   **1792**

Hazlitt, Ruth, trans. and ed. "The Journal of François Antoine Larocque from Assiniboine River to the Yellowstone." THE FRONTIER AND MIDLAND 14 (1933-1934):241-247, 332-339; 15 (1934-1935):67-75, 88. Reprint. FRONTIER OMNIBUS, edited by John W. Hakola, pp. 2-28; MONTANA STATE UNIVERSITY, MISSOULA. HISTORICAL REPRINTS, SOURCES OF NORTHWEST HISTORY, no. 20.

Extracts in LES BOURGEOIS DE LA COMPAGNIE DU NORD-OUEST, by Louis F.R. Masson, vol. 1, pp. 299-313.

Jun-Oct 1805. Diary of fur-trader and clerk of Northwest Company; journey from Fort de la Bosse trading post on Assiniboine to the Yellowstone; notes on daily life, fur trade and trapping; early account of the Crow Indians; many lively incidents.

LEVY, AARON   **1793**

"Items Relating to the Moses and Levy Families, New York." AMERICAN-JEWISH HISTORICAL SOCIETY PUBLICATIONS 27 (1920):331-345.

1805-1834. Extracts relating to Jews in New York; business, service as paymaster in army, necrology.

NUTT, RUSH   **1794**

Jennings, Jesse D., ed. "Nutt's Trip to the Chickasaw Country." JOURNAL OF MISSISSIPPI HISTORY 9 (1947): 34-61.

Jul-Sep 1805. Diary selections relating to the study of the Natchez Trace; smattering of information about the Choctaws; copious description of Chickasaw culture; notes on natural resources; journey to Nashville.

PAYSON, EDWARD, 1783-1827   **1795**

In A MEMOIR OF THE REV. EDWARD PAYSON, by Asa Cummings, pp. 35-436 passim. New York: J. Leavitt, 1830.

1805-1825. Extracts from Portland, Maine, clergyman's journal; religious reflections, self-analysis and exercises, resolves, prayers, religious reading, health, hopes and despairs.

PIKE, ZEBULON MONTGOMERY, 1779-1813   **1796**

AN ACCOUNT OF EXPEDITIONS TO THE SOURCES OF THE MISSISSIPPI AND THROUGH THE WESTERN PARTS OF LOUISIANA, TO THE SOURCES OF THE ARKANSAW, KANS, LA PLATTE AND PIERRE JAUN RIVERS. Philadelphia: C.&A. Conrad, 1810. 1 vol., various paging.

THE EXPEDITIONS OF ZEBULON MONTGOMERY PIKE, TO HEADWATERS OF THE MISSISSIPPI RIVER. Edited by Elliott Coues. New York: F.P. Harper, 1895. 3 vols.

JOURNALS. Edited by Donald Jackson. Norman: University of Oklahoma Press, 1966. 2 vols.

1805-1807. Official United States exploring expedition to sources of the Mississippi River and its western tributaries; tour through New Mexico and Colorado.

AN ACCOUNT OF A VOYAGE UP THE MISSISSIPPI RIVER FROM ST. LOUIS TO ITS SOURCE. Washington, D.C., 1807? 68 pp. Reprint. MINNESOTA HISTORICAL SOCIETY COLLECTIONS 1 (1902):302-342.

1805-1806. Paraphrase in third person of voyage up Mississippi; probably compiled by Nicholas King.

THE SOUTHWESTERN EXPEDITION OF ZEBULON M. PIKE. Edited by Milo M. Quaife. Chicago: R.R. Donnelley & Sons, 1925. 239 pp.

1806-1807.

In OVERLAND TO THE PACIFIC, edited by Archer B. Hulbert, vol. 1, pp. 1-200; vol. 2, pp. 203-280. Colorado Springs: The Stewart Commission of Colorado College; Denver: Denver Public Library, 1932. Vol. 1 reprinted as ZEBULON PIKE'S ARKANSAW JOURNAL. Westport, Conn.: Greenwood Press, 1972.

1806-1807. Journal relating to southern Louisiana Purchase boundary line; tour of New Mexico and Colorado.

PUTNAM, ARCHELAUS, 1787-1818   1797

"Diary of Archelaus Putnam of New Mills." DANVERS HISTORICAL SOCIETY COLLECTIONS 4 (1916):51-72; 5 (1917):49-69; 6 (1918):11-29.

1805-1817. Interesting and varied details of local affairs, personal matters, work as apothecary, religious introspection, literary ambitions; a poem.

RATCLIFF, MILDRED, 1773-1847   1798

MEMORANDA AND CORRESPONDENCE OF MILDRED RATCLIFF. Philadelphia: Friends' Book Store, 1890. 210 pp. Journal, pp. 38-172 passim.

1805-1833. Extracts from Quaker journal; travels and work in Virginia, Carolinas, Ohio; visits to Baltimore, Philadelphia; meetings west of Alleghenies and in South; religious exercises, travel notes, introspection.

SMITH, LYDIA   1799

"Lydia Smith's Journal." MASSACHUSETTS HISTORICAL SOCIETY PROCEEDINGS 48 (1914-1915):508-534.

Dec 1805-Jan 1806. Journal of Boston traveler, notes kept irregularly and sent to America in letters; social life in London; very literary and stylish; revealing picture of well-bred young American.

WHITE, TRYPHENA ELY, b. 1784   1800

TRYPHENA ELY WHITE'S JOURNAL. New York: Grafton Press, 1904. 40 pp.

Jun-Sep 1805. Private diary kept during first months of family's settlement at Genesee Street, New York; housework, gardening, meals, layout of farms, roads, etc.; religious services, housebuilding, neighbors; very interesting diary of woman's side of pioneer life.

1806

ASHE, THOMAS, 1770-1835   1801

TRAVELS IN AMERICA. London: R. Phillips, 1808. 3 vols. Reprint. Newburyport, Mass.: E.M. Blunt, 1808. 366 pp.

Oct-Nov 1806. Englishman's travel book and general gazetteer arranged as a diary; impersonal descriptions; from Pittsburgh to New Orleans; sociological and economic observations.

ATKINS, QUINTIUS F., 1782-1859   1802

Baldwin, C.C. "Wyandot Missions in 1806-7." WESTERN RESERVE AND NORTHERN OHIO HISTORICAL SOCIETY TRACT, no. 50 (1879), pp. 110-113.

1806-1807. Journal of missionary to Wyandot Indians on Sandusky River; mostly summary; useful as historical record.

BRIGHT, JACOB   1803

Ryan, Harold W., ed. "Jacob Bright's Journal of a Trip to the Osage Indians." JOURNAL OF SOUTHERN HISTORY 15 (1949):509-523.

Aug 1806. Trader's account of negotiating trading arrangements with leaders of the Osage Indians residing along the Arkansas River; subsequent attack by unidentified Indians, possibly Choctaws.

HENKEL, PAUL, 1754-1825   1804

Martzolff, Clement L. and Cooper, F.E., ed. and trans. "Rev. Paul Henkel's Journal: His Missionary Journey to the State of Ohio." OHIO ARCHAEOLOGICAL AND HISTORICAL QUARTERLY 23 (1914):162-218.

Jul-Sep 1806. Lutheran missionary's journal of journey from New Market, Virginia, to Point Pleasant, Ohio; visits to German community; preaching and accounts of country and German settlers; a solid and pleasant diary.

INGERSOLL, HENRY   1805

"Diary and Letters of Henry Ingersoll, Prisoner at Carthagena." AMERICAN HISTORICAL REVIEW 3 (1897-1898):674-702. Diary, pp. 681-684.

1806-1808. Scattered entries in travel diary with post facto narrative; Miranda's expedition to South America; travel; imprisonment at Cartagena.

JACKSON, HALLIDAY   1806

Snyderman, George S., ed. "Halliday Jackson's Journal of a Visit Paid to the Indians of New York." AMERICAN PHILOSOPHICAL SOCIETY PROCEEDINGS 101 (1957):565-588.

Sep 1806. Journal of Quaker mission to Seneca Indians; attempts, with mixed success, to persuade Indians to adopt fixed agriculture, build cabins, spin, weave, etc.; problems of hunger, idleness, drunkenness resulting from disruption of traditional Indian culture and hunting economy; assistance to Quaker efforts by Seneca prophet Handsome Lake and Chief Cornplanter; narrative style.

KHVOSTOV, NIKOLAI ALEKSANDROVICH, 1776-1809   1807

In REZANOV RECONNOITERS CALIFORNIA, 1806: A NEW TRANSLATION OF RESANOV'S LETTER, PARTS OF LIEUTENANT KHVOSTOV'S LOG OF THE SHIP JUNO, AND DR. GEORG VON LANGSDORFF OBSERVATIONS, by Richard A. Pierce, pp. 44-54. Book Club of California Publications 140. San Francisco: Book Club of California, 1972.

Jan-Jun 1806. Account of exploring trip along west coast of America from Sitka to San Francisco; determining strength of Spanish presidio; entertaining and charming Spanish Governor Arillaga in San Francisco.

LENOIR, THOMAS, 1780-1861   1808

Patton, James W., ed. "Thomas Lenoir's Journey to Tennessee in 1806." TENNESSEE HISTORICAL QUARTERLY 17 (1958):156-166.

Jun–Jul 1806. Journey from North Carolina to Tennessee to collect debts and survey family land holdings; primarily details of business and survey activities with some notes on land quality, settlements.

PHILIPS, JOHN   1809

Deardorff, Merle H. and Snyderman, George S., eds. "A Nineteenth-Century Journal of a Visit to the Indians of New York." AMERICAN PHILOSOPHICAL SOCIETY PROCEEDINGS 100 (1956):582–612.

Sep 1806. Quaker mission to Seneca Indian reservation in New York to promote peace between new settlers and Indians and to help Indians with transition from hunting life to fixed agriculture; mainly undated entries; interesting spellings.

ROE, DANIEL, 1740–1820   1810

THE DIARY OF CAPTAIN DANIEL ROE. Introduction by Alfred S. Roe. Worcester: Blanchard Press, 1904. 64 pp.

1806–1808. Notes on weather, farming, crops, household and family affairs in Brookhaven, Long Island; interesting spellings.

STUART, JOHN C., 1783–1853   1811

"A Journal Remarks or Observations in a Voyage down the Kentucky, Ohio, Mississippi Rivers, etc." KENTUCKY HISTORICAL SOCIETY REGISTER 50 (1952):5–25.

Feb–Jul 1806. Activities and impatience during several weeks of waiting for necessary river level; flatboat navigation to New Orleans, impressions of that city; exhausting return trip on foot to Natchez, Nashville and on to Kentucky; a fresh, interesting description.

1807

ANON.   1812

Beeman, Richard R., ed. "Trade and Travel in Post-Revolutionary Virginia: A Diary of an Itinerant Peddler." VIRGINIA MAGAZINE OF HISTORY AND BIOGRAPHY 84 (1976):174–188.

Oct 1807–Jan 1808. Vivid and often humorous account of Irish peddler's activities; trade and travel hardships; entertainments enjoyed.

BALDWIN, BENJAMIN   1813

"Extracts from the Rev. Benjamin Baldwin's Journal of a Missionary Tour." MASSACHUSETTS BAPTIST MISSIONARY MAGAZINE 2 (1808–1810):37–43.

Oct–Dec 1807. Baptist missionary tour on Susquehannah River and vicinity.

BEDFORD, JOHN R., 1782–1827   1814

"A Tour in 1807 down the Cumberland, Ohio and Mississippi Rivers from Nashville to New Orleans." TENNESSEE HISTORICAL MAGAZINE 5 (1919):40–63, 107–122.

Jan–Mar 1807. Travel notes of scenery, character sketches; personal and social items.

BLENNERHASSETT, HARMAN, 1765–1831   1815

In THE BLENNERHASSETT PAPERS, by William H. Safford, pp. 303–507. Cincinnati: Moore, Wilstach, Keys, 1861; R. Clarke, 1891.

Aug–Nov 1807. Incidents surrounding Aaron Burr from the time of his arrest in Kentucky until his discharge in Richmond, Virginia.

BURCKARD, JOHANN CHRISTIAN   1816

PARTNERS IN THE LORD'S WORK: THE DIARY OF TWO MORAVIAN MISSIONARIES IN THE CREEK INDIAN COUNTRY, 1807–1813. Translated and edited by Carl Mauelshagen and Gerald H. Davis. Georgia State College School of Arts and Sciences Research Papers, no. 21. Atlanta: Georgia State College, 1969. 77 pp.

1807–1812. Official diary, kept collectively by immigrant Moravian missionaries, Johann Burckhard and Karsten Petersen, of a largely unsuccessful attempt to Christianize the Creek Indians of Georgia; difficulties of tribal warfare, lack of response of Indians, ill health of missionaries; self-sacrificing dedication to preach to and counsel with all, Indian, white, slave or free.

CASE, ISAAC, 1762–1852   1817

"Extract from the Rev. Isaac Case's Journal." MASSACHUSETTS BAPTIST MISSIONARY MAGAZINE 2 (1808–1810): 14–18, 161–166.

Extracts in HISTORY OF THE BAPTISTS IN MAINE, by Henry S. Burrage, 497 pp. passim. Portland: Marks Printing House, 1904.

1807–1809. Baptist preaching tours, meetings, visits, etc., in Monmouth, Canaan, Islesboro, Fairfield and Harmony, Maine.

CLUBB, STEPHEN, b. 1762   1818

A JOURNAL; CONTAINING AN ACCOUNT OF THE WRONGS, SUFFERINGS AND NEGLECT EXPERIENCED BY AMERICANS IN FRANCE. Boston, 1809. 60 pp. Reprint. MAGAZINE OF HISTORY, extra no. 51, 13 (1916):1–59.

1807–1809. Prison diary after capture by French while sailing as second mate of the HYADES from Charleston; imprisonment with his wife at Arras; long notes on travels and prison experiences; comments on French people and customs; teaching English.

COLLETTE, ELIZABETH VAN HORNE, 1776–1846   1819

JOURNEY TO THE PROMISED LAND: JOURNAL OF ELIZABETH VAN HORNE. Pittsburgh: Historical Society of Western Pennsylvania, 1939. 23 pp.

Oct–Nov 1807. Diary kept by daughter of Baptist minister who, with family of six daughters and one son, made arduous overland trip from Plains, New Jersey, to Lebanon, Ohio; daily descriptions of travelers, boats, roads and accommodations; death of the father at Pittsburgh and sympathetic, generous care of strangers there.

EARLY, JOHN, 1786–1873   1820

Denny, Collins, ed. "Diary of John Early, Bishop of the Methodist Episcopal Church, South." VIRGINIA MAGAZINE OF HISTORY AND BIOGRAPHY 33 (1925):166–174, 283–287; 34 (1926):130–137, 237–251, 299–312; 35 (1927):7–12, 280–286; 36 (1928):175–179, 239–248, 328–332; 37 (1929):130–138, 256–260; 38 (1930):251–258; 39 (1931):41–45, 146–151; 40 (1932):70–74, 147–154 (incomplete).

Extracts in DIARY OF AMERICA, edited by Josef Berger, pp. 165–169.

1807–1812. Extracts of experiences and travels, mainly in Virginia; preaching on various circuits; notes on religion and politics.

GAINES, EDMUND PENDLETON   1821

Stone, James H. "Surveying the Gaines Trace." ALABAMA HISTORICAL QUARTERLY 33 (1971):135–152.

Stone, James H. "Edmund Pendleton Gaines' Description of the Upper Tombigbee River." ALABAMA HISTORICAL QUARTERLY 33 (1971):227–239.

Dec 1807–Jan 1808. Military survey for road between Tennessee River and Tombigbee River of southern Alabama; to enable Alabama settlers to circumvent severe tax on goods coming through Spanish territory; topographical features, surveying details.

IRVING, PETER, 1771–1838   1822

Beach, Leonard B., Hornberger, Theodore and Wright, Wyllis E., eds. "Peter Irving's Journals." NEW YORK PUBLIC LIBRARY BULLETIN 44 (1940):591–608, 649–670, 745–772, 814–842, 888–914. Reprint. New York: New York Public Library, 1943. 128 pp.

Apr–Sep 1807 (with gaps). Travel diaries of elder brother of Washington Irving; travel in France, Italy, Switzerland, England and Scotland; long and matter-of-fact notes of a "Grand Tour"; mostly formal and Baedeker-like in style; notes on paintings, buildings, scenery, towns, etc.; varied by occasional personal items and literariness.

JACKSON, JOHN RICHARD, 1787–1847   1823

"Converson of Mr. John Richard, Related by Himself." UNITED STATES CATHOLIC HISTORICAL MAGAZINE 1 (1887):92–100.

1807–1808. Extracts from religious journal; journey to Montreal; conversion to Catholicism; scenic description with mystical aspects.

MORSE, ASAHEL   1824

"Extract from the Rev. Asahel Morse's Journal of a Mission." MASSACHUSETTS BAPTIST MISSIONARY MAGAZINE 2 (1808–1810):149–155.

Aug–Oct 1807. Baptist preaching tour in northwestern New York and upper Canada.

PURSH, FREDERICK, 1774–1820   1825

JOURNAL OF A BOTANICAL EXCURSION IN THE NORTHEASTERN PARTS OF THE STATES OF PENNSYLVANIA AND NEW YORK. Philadelphia: Brinckloe & Marot, Printers, 1869. 87 pp. Reprint. Edited by William M. Beauchamp. Syracuse, N.Y.: Dehler Press, 1923. 113 pp.; Port Washington, N.Y.: I.J. Friedman, 1969.

May–Oct 1807. Botanical journal; travel and scientific notes; followed by report.

STONE, JOHN, 1781–1849   1826

"Notes from Memorandum Book of John Stone, Deacon of the First Church, Salem." ESSEX INSTITUTE HISTORICAL COLLECTIONS 61 (1925):97–112, 259–264.

1807–1847. Religious and some social affairs of the church at Salem, Massachusetts.

SWIFT, JOSEPH GARDNER, 1783–1865   1827

THE MEMOIRS OF GEN. JOSEPH GARDNER SWIFT. Worcester, Mass.: Press of F.S. Blanchard, 1890. 292 pp.

Journal, pp. 9–289.

1807–1865. Partly written up as memoirs; military life, engineering, politics, agriculture, history, antisecessionist politics; private and family affairs; extensive and varied observations and reflections.

1808

ANON.   1828

O'Brien, Dennis, ed. "A Lost Diary of the West Virginia Frontier." WEST VIRGINIA HISTORY 40 (1978): 55–68.

Jul 1808. Diary of horseback journey through what is now West Virginia; notes on road conditions, land quality and value, crops, etc.

AMANGUAL, FRANCISCO, ca. 1739–1812   1829

"Diary of Francisco Amangual from San Antonio to Santa Fe; Santa Fe to San Elzeario; and San Elzeario to San Antonio." In PEDRO VIAL AND THE ROADS TO SANTA FE, by Noel M. Loomis and Abraham P. Nasatir, pp. 462–533.

Mar–Dec 1808. Military expedition assessing United States pressure from north and east; searching for a northern route from San Antonio to Santa Fe, locating watering places and making friends with Indians; notes on the country, weather and Indians, some of whom are identified as Comanche, Yamparica or Caddo.

BURR, AARON, 1756–1836   1830

THE PRIVATE JOURNAL OF AARON BURR. Edited by Matthew L. Davis. New York: Harper & Brothers, 1838. 2 vols. Reprint. Upper Saddle River, N.J.: Literature House, 1970.

THE PRIVATE JOURNAL OF AARON BURR. Edited by William H. Samson. Rochester, N.Y.: Post Express Printing, 1903. 2 vols.

1808–1812 (with gaps). Kept during author's residence in Europe, especially London and Paris; opening as diaristic jottings, diary develops as daily narrative; private and social affairs, visits, comments on people and places.

CLAUS, WILLIAM   1831

"Diary of Col. Wm. Claus." MICHIGAN PIONEER AND HISTORICAL SOCIETY COLLECTIONS 23 (1893):47–60.

May–Aug 1808. Treaty journal; negotiations and other dealings with Ottawas, Hurons, etc., at and about Amherstburg.

CONNEAU, THEOPHILUS   1832

A SLAVER'S LOG BOOK, OR 20 YEARS' RESIDENCE IN AFRICA. Englewood Cliffs, N.J.: Prentice-Hall, 1976. 370 pp.

1808–1854. Overwritten and self-aggrandizing record of a French-born American ship captain and slave trader; slave revolts, capture by pirates, mutinies, sea battles, imprisonment by both French and British, negotiations with African slave dealers, and witnessing of tribal rites; youthful revulsion at grosser cruelties of slave trade giving way to acceptance and rationalization.

CRAM, JACOB, 1762–1833   1833

JOURNAL OF A MISSIONARY TOUR. Rochester, N.Y.:

Genesee Press, 1909. 37 pp.

Jun 1808-Feb 1809. Congregational minister's missionary tour through settlements of northern New Hampshire and Vermont; horseback travel, meetings, notes on religious provision of towns.

CURTIS, HOLBROOK, 1787-1858   1834

In LETTERS AND JOURNALS, compiled by Elizabeth Curtis, pp. 49-53, 64-77. Hartford, Conn.: Case, Lockwood & Brainard, 1926.

1808-1813, 1821-1822. Journeys in Connecticut; weather, news, reading; visit to Philadelphia; philosophical and religious reflections; interesting self-portrait.

FEW, FRANCES, 1789-1885   1835

Cunningham, Noble E., ed. "The Diary of Frances Few." JOURNAL OF SOUTHERN HISTORY 29 (1963):345-361.

Oct 1808-Mar 1809. Niece's account of her visit with the Gallatins in Washington, D.C.; descriptive evaluations of Thomas Jefferson, James and Dolly Madison, various legislators and notables; New York to Washington, D.C., trip and return; record of her reading.

FRASER, SIMON, 1776-1862   1836

In LES BOURGEOIS DE LA COMPAGNIE DU NORD-OUEST, by Louis F.R. Masson, vol. 1, pp. 157-221.
LETTERS AND JOURNALS. Edited by W. Kaye Lamb. Toronto: Macmillan, 1960. 292 pp.

May-Aug 1808. Exploration journey mainly by canoe from Fraser River in the Rocky Mountains to the Pacific coast; well-written narrative, with interesting details of Atmah and Chilkotin Indians and adventures.

HARTWELL, JESSE   1837

"Extract from Elder Hartwell's Missionary Journal." MASSACHUSETTS BAPTIST MISSIONARY MAGAZINE 2 (1808-1810):304-307.

Sep-Nov 1808. Baptist's missionary preaching tour in Connecticut, New York and Delaware.

IRISH, DAVID   1838

"Extract from Mr. Irish's Missionary Journal." MASSACHUSETTS BAPTIST MISSIONARY MAGAZINE 2 (1808-1810): 238-243.

Nov-Dec 1808. Preaching tour in Massachusetts by Baptist minister from Aurelius, New York.

MARTHA FURNACE   1839

In IRON IN THE PINES: THE STORY OF NEW JERSEY'S GHOST TOWNS AND BOG IRON, by Arthur D. Pierce, pp. 1-244 passim. New Brunswick, N.J.: Rutgers University Press, 1957.

1808-1815. Diary kept by clerks, Caleb Earle and others, at the Martha Furnace on Wading River, two miles from Harrisville, Pennsylvania; activities of the workers and community; producing stoves, firebacks, sash weights, sugar kettles, shot, cannon wheels and cooking utensils from molds.

MASSIE, HENRY, b. 1784   1840

"Journal of Capt. Henry Massie." TYLER'S QUARTERLY HISTORICAL AND GENEALOGICAL MAGAZINE 4 (1922-

1923):77-86.

Apr-Jun 1808. Touristic notes of journey with friend; from Fredericksburg, Virginia, to Boston.

MORAGA, GABRIEL, b. 1767   1841

THE DIARY OF ENSIGN GABRIEL MORAGA'S EXPEDITION OF DISCOVERY IN THE SACRAMENTO VALLEY. Translated and edited by Donald C. Cutter. Early California Travels Series, no. 41. Los Angeles: Glen Dawson, 1857. 36 pp.

Sep-Oct 1808. Diary of the leader of a small group of soldiers from the San Francisco Company exploring inland, especially up and down rivers and streams, from San Jose into the Sacramento Valley; efforts to find adaptable sites for new mission locations and Indian villages.

OSBORN, CHARLES, 1775-1850   1842

JOURNAL OF THAT FAITHFUL SERVANT OF CHRIST, CHARLES OSBORN. Cincinnati: Printed by Achilles Pugh, 1854.

1808-1840, 1850. Private diary of Quaker minister, editor and publisher of THE PHILANTHROPIST, reputedly the first anti-slavery newspaper in the United States; religious visits to Friends throughout the eastern and midwestern states; Great Britain, Ireland and Europe; evaluation of meetings for worship, his testimony, preaching; spiritual and social concerns; illnesses; Hicksite controversy; division over testimony against slavery.

PILLSBURY, PHINEHAS, b. 1767   1843

"Extracts from the Journal of Elder Phinehas Pillsbury of Nobleboro, Me." NEW ENGLAND HISTORICAL AND GENEALOGICAL REGISTER 63 (1909):373-379; 64 (1910): 75-76, 154-157, 374-375; 66 (1912):274-281, 359-366.

Jul-Dec 1808. Journal mainly of genealogical interest; deaths, births, etc.

ROWLEY, SAMUEL   1844

"Extracts from the Rev. Samuel Rowley's Missionary Journal." MASSACHUSETTS BAPTIST MISSIONARY MAGAZINE 2 (1808-1810):169-172.

Aug-Oct 1808. Baptist minister's journal; preaching on west side of Lake Champlain, in Essex, Franklin and St. Lawrence counties.

SUMMERS, LEWIS, 1778-1843   1845

"Lewis Summer's Journal of a Tour from Alexandria, Virginia, to Gallipolis, Ohio." SOUTHERN HISTORICAL MAGAZINE 1 (1892):49-81.

Jun-Aug 1808. Travel journal; through Valley of Virginia, down New and Kanawha rivers, to Gallipolis, Ohio; seeking location for his father; notes on character of the land, descriptions of towns, some political notes, visits, farming notes; a useful journal, with some interesting southern locutions.

TULLY, WILLIAM   1846

THE JOURNAL OF WILLIAM TULLY, MEDICAL STUDENT AT DARTMOUTH. Edited by Oliver S. Hayward and Elizabeth H. Thomson. New York: Science History Publications, 1977. 88 pp.

Sep 1808-Jan 1809. Lively diary of observant and opinionated medical student; departure from Saybrook, Connecticut, and stagecoach journey to Hanover, New Hampshire; Dartmouth students and faculty, especially professor Dr. Nathan Smith; people, sights, taverns and mores of Hanover.

WILLISTON, JOSIAH 1847

"Extracts from the Diary of Josiah Williston of Boston." NEW ENGLAND HISTORICAL AND GENEALOGICAL REGISTER 65 (1911):366-371.

> 1808-1814. Selections of genealogical interest; births, deaths, etc.

1809

ARNOLD, SETH SHALER, 1788-1871 1848

Peach, Arthur W., ed. "As the Years Pass--the Diaries of Seth Shaler Arnold (1788-1871), Vermonter." VERMONT HISTORICAL SOCIETY PROCEEDINGS, n.s. 8 (1940):107-193.

> 1809-1850. Extracts from private diary; facts and views of social, economic, industrial and religious life of Westminster, Vermont; account of silkworm industry; great local interest.

BRADBURY, JOHN, fl. 1809 1849

TRAVELS IN THE INTERIOR OF AMERICA. Liverpool: Printed for the author by Smith and Galway; London: Sherwood, Neely and Jones, 1817. 364 pp. Reprint. Ann Arbor, Mich.: University Microfilms, 1966. 2d ed. London: Sherwood, Neely and Jones, 1819. 346 pp.

In EARLY WESTERN TRAVELS, edited by Reuben G. Thwaites, vol. 5.

> 1809-1811. Narrative with day-to-day entries by London botanist; travel in Louisiana, Ohio, Kentucky, Indiana, Tennessee, Illinois and western territories; notes on places, Indians, botany; Osage word list.

COLBY, JOHN, 1787-1817 1850

THE LIFE, EXPERIENCE AND TRAVELS OF JOHN COLBY, PREACHER OF THE GOSPEL. 3d ed. Cornish, Maine: S.W. and C.C. Cole, 1829. 2 vols. in 1. Reprint. Lowell, Mass.: N. Thurston & A. Watson, 1838.

> 1809-1817. Baptist minister's travel and preaching journal; Vermont, New Hampshire, Maine, Rhode Island and Ohio; partly narrative and autobiography; left unfinished.

CUTLER, EPHRAIM, 1767-1853 1851

In LIFE AND TIMES OF EPHRAIM CUTLER, by Julia P. Cutler, pp. 90-103, 229-238. Cincinnati: R. Clarke, 1890.

> Jul-Sep 1809, May-Dec 1837. Travel notes while delegate to Presbyterian General Assembly at Philadelphia; visits, taverns, towns and farms while driving cattle from Ohio River to Baltimore; good picture of country life.

FOSS, DANIEL 1852

A JOURNAL OF THE SHIPWRECK AND SUFFERINGS OF DANIEL FOSS. Boston: Printed for N. Coverly, Jr., 1812, 1816. 24 pp. Reprint. MAGAZINE OF HISTORY, extra no. 28, 7 (1914):29-51.

> 1809-1814. Castaway's diary kept by sole survivor of wreck of brig NEGOCIATOR; five years alone on Pacific island; occasional notes of a Robinson Crusoe-like life. Appears to be narrative written afterwards.

GALE, WILLIAM A. 1853

In HISTORY OF THE NORTHWEST COAST, by Hubert H. Bancroft, vol. 2, pp. 133-134. Works, vol. 28. San Francisco: A.L. Bancroft, 1886.

> Jun 1809. Sea journal of captain's assistant on the ALBATROSS; day-by-day efforts to find a trading post on the Columbia River.

HARVEY, MARGARET BOYLE, 1786-1832 1854

JOURNAL OF A VOYAGE FROM PHILADELPHIA TO CORK. Philadelphia: West Park Publishing Co., 1915. 78 pp. Reprint. FRIENDS' HISTORICAL SOCIETY JOURNAL 24 (1927):3-20.

> 1809. Philadelphia Quaker's diary of travels in Cork, Dublin and Clonmel; life among the Quakers in Ireland; notes on Irish life.

JONES, PETER 1855

JOURNAL OF THE PROCEEDINGS, INDIAN TREATY, FORT WAYNE, SEPTEMBER 30th, 1809. Connerville, Ind.: 1910. 24 pp.

> Sep 1809. Journal of secretary to commissioners of proceedings for Indian treaty of Fort Wayne.

MARIN, FRANCISCO DE PAULA, 1774-1837 1856

DON FRANCISCO DE PAULA MARIN: A BIOGRAPHY, by Ross H. Gast: THE LETTERS AND JOURNAL OF FRANCISCO DE PAULA MARIN. Edited by Agnes C. Conrad. Honolulu: University Press of Hawaii for the Hawaiian Historical Society, 1973. 344 pp. Journal, pp. 199-331.

> 1809-1826. Brief entries by influential Spaniard who became major landowner, vintner and physician to the Hawaiian royal household; news of shipping, trade, sickness, quarrels; encounters with missionaries; horticultural interests.

MARTIN, WILLIAM DICKINSON, 1789-1833 1857

JOURNAL: A JOURNEY FROM SOUTH CAROLINA TO CONNECTICUT IN THE YEAR 1809. Prepared by Anna D. Elmore. Charlotte, N.C.: Heritage House, 1959. 53 pp.

> Apr-May 1809. Law student's trip north to attend law lectures; description of towns, sights, events, accommodations; visit with Moravians at Salem, North Carolina; social life and opinions of Irish, bachelors, etc; travel by stagecoach and coastal packet.

ROBBINS, CAIRA, 1794-1881 1858

Stone, Ellen A., ed. "Diary and Letters of Caira Robbins." LEXINGTON HISTORICAL SOCIETY PROCEEDINGS 4 (1905-1910):61-81.

> 1809-1823. Extracts and brief notes on schooling, domestic and social affairs of East Lexington, Massachusetts; literature, theaters, journeys.

SHORT, PEYTON, 1761-1825 1859

"Tour of Mobile, Pensacola, etc." HISTORICAL AND PHILOSOPHICAL SOCIETY OF OHIO QUARTERLY PUBLICATIONS 5 (1910):3-15.

> Nov-Dec 1809. Travel diary of tour through part of Mississippi Territory; notes on soil, climate, scenery, social and commercial conditions; people encountered.

WILLIAMSON, WILLIAM 1860

Klett, Guy S., ed. "A Missionary Journey in Ohio in 1809." JOURNAL OF THE PRESBYTERIAN HISTORICAL SOCIETY 27 (1949):229-234.

Nov-Dec 1809. Missionary journey with James Gilliland to scattered frontier folk of Ohio; brief daily notes of itinerary, names of hosts, reactions of congregations to sermons, numbers present for preaching.

1810

ANON. 1861

In THE DISCOVERY OF THE OREGON TRAIL, by Robert Stuart, edited by Philip A. Rollins, app. A, pp. 267-280. New York and London: C. Scribner's Sons, 1935.

1810-1812. An account based on diaries now lost of sea journey from New York to mouth of Columbia River. Translated from the French.

BELL, MARGARET VAN HORN DWIGHT, 1790-1834 1862

A JOURNEY TO OHIO IN 1810 AS RECORDED IN THE JOURNAL OF MARGARET VAN HORN DWIGHT. Edited by Max Farrand. New Haven: Yale University Press, 1912. 64 pp.

Extract in EARLY NARRATIVES OF BERKS COUNTY, by James B. Nolan, pp. 57-67.

Oct-Nov 1810. Travel journal addressed to her cousin Elizabeth; a journey by wagon from Milford, Connecticut, to Warren, Ohio; long, lively entries in rattling style, describing adventures, inns, characters; a good diary.

BISHOP, RICHARD 1863

"Journal of a Passage, London to New York." NAUTICAL RESEARCH JOURNAL 19 (1972):182-184, 222-233.

Jul-Nov 1810. Journal of steerage passenger aboard the ISABELLA; weather, provisions, hardships, limited space, vermin, theft, etc.; severity of punishments.

BUDD, JOHN 1864

"Copied from John Budd's Diary." VINELAND HISTORICAL MAGAZINE 38 (1954):163-166.

1810-1821. Marriages, births and deaths in and around Cumberland County, New Jersey; sermons and religious activities of Methodists; genealogical interest.

COLBERT, WILLIAM 1865

Yoder, Don, ed. "A Methodist Circuit Rider among the Berks County Dutch." PENNSYLVANIA DUTCHMAN 2, no. 13 (December 1, 1950):1, 5-6.

May-Aug 1810. Events while riding circuit; preaching; illness, losing his way, losing his horse; camp meeting; opinions of Pennsylvania Dutch; reading account of the Lewis and Clark Expedition.

FRANCHERE, GABRIEL, 1786-1863 1866

NARRATIVE OF A VOYAGE TO THE NORTHWEST COAST OF AMERICA IN THE YEARS 1811, 1812, 1813, AND 1814; OR, THE FIRST AMERICAN SETTLEMENT ON THE PACIFIC. Translated and edited by J.V. Huntington. New York: Redfield, 1854. 376 pp.

ADVENTURE AT ASTORIA, 1810-1814. Translated and edited by Hoyt C. Franchére. Norman: University of Oklahoma Press, 1967. 190 pp.

1810-1814. Journal written up from his own diary notes by French-Canadian (later American) in the Astoria fur trade; exploration, trading, personages of the Northwest fur trade; Indians, account of TONQUIN ship massacre, adventures in Hawaii; exciting and historically useful journal.

McBRIDE, JAMES, 1788-1859 1867

"Journey to Lexington, Kentucky." HISTORICAL AND PHILOSOPHICAL SOCIETY OF OHIO QUARTERLY PUBLICATIONS 5 (1910):21-27.

Jun-Jul 1810. Brief notes in letter-journal of journey to Lexington.

NUTTALL, THOMAS, 1786-1859 1868

Graustein, Jeannette E., ed. "Nuttall's Travels into the Old Northwest; an Unpublished 1810 Diary." CHRONICA BOTANICA 14 (1951):1-88.

Apr-Sep 1810. English naturalist's first expedition in the United States made for Benjamin Smith Barton; plagued by malaria during trip from Philadelphia to Pittsburgh, Lake Erie, Ohio Territory, down Ohio River by boat to Detroit; botanical descriptions, diseases and treatment, minerals, small animals, insects; notes on Huron Indians; joining the Astoria land party for part of trip and accompanying Aaron Greely, surveyor of Michigan Territory, for another.

A JOURNAL OF TRAVELS INTO THE ARKANSA TERRITORY. Philadelphia: T.H. Palmer, 1821. 296 pp. Reprint. Cleveland: A.H. Clark, 1905; Ann Arbor, Mich.: University Microfilms, 1966.

A JOURNAL OF TRAVELS INTO THE ARKANSAS TERRITORY. Edited by Savoie Lottinville. American Exploration and Travel Series, vol. 66. Norman: University of Oklahoma Press, 1980. 361 pp.

1818-1820. Valuable botanical and ethnological notes of naturalist's travels down the Ohio and in the Arkansas country; Fort Smith to the Red River, Cave-in-Rock, Shawneetown, etc.

STEBBINS, WILLIAM, 1786-1858 1869

THE JOURNAL OF WILLIAM STEBBINS; STRATFORD TO WASHINGTON IN 1810. With an introduction by Leonard W. Labaree and notes by Pierce W. Gaines. Connecticut: The Acorn Club, 1968. 57 pp.

Jan-Feb. 1810. Yale graduate's trip to Washington in search of employment; fascinating details of stagecoach travel; route, discomforts and hardships, the mixed lot of fellow travelers, accommodations and meals; meeting, in Washington, with Secretary of Treasury Albert Gallatin, attending both houses of Congress, intimations of impending war with Britain; religious reflections, lively reactions to people and events.

1811

BACON, LYDIA B. STETSON, 1786-1853 1870

In THE BIOGRAPHY OF MRS. LYDIA B. BACON. pp. 6-85. Boston: Massachusetts Sabbath School Society, 1856.

Crawford, Mary M., ed. "Mrs. Lydia B. Bacon's Journal." INDIANA MAGAZINE OF HISTORY 40 (1944): 367-386; 41 (1945):59-79.

1811–1812. Chronological arrangement of letters and journal entries of officer's wife in the Old Northwest; report of battle of Tippecanoe; eyewitness account of attack on Detroit, capture and parole after its fall; interesting descriptions of travel by horseback, wagon and boat; the region and army life. Crawford contends journal in biography is "heavily edited."

BAKER, DANIEL, 1791–1857   1871

In THE LIFE AND LABOURS OF THE REV. DANIEL BAKER, by William Mumford Baker, pp. 35–343 passim. Philadelphia: W.S.&A. Martien, 1858.

1811–1848. Extracts from religious journals; notes while student at Hampden Sidney College; work at Winchester, Virginia; efforts for formation of religious college at Austin, Texas; work at Holly Springs; mission to Texas.

BRACKENRIDGE, HENRY MARIE, 1786–1871   1872

VIEWS OF LOUISIANA. Pittsburgh: Cramer, Spear and Eichbaum, 1814. 304 pp. Reprint. Chicago: Quadrangle Books, 1962; Ann Arbor, Mich.: University Microfilms, 1966.

JOURNAL OF A VOYAGE UP THE RIVER MISSOURI. Baltimore: Coale and Maxwell, 1815. 247 pp. Reprint. In EARLY WESTERN TRAVELS, edited by Reuben G. Thwaites, vol. 6, pp. 21–166.

Apr–Aug 1811. Travel up the Missouri River; travels in Louisiana Purchase from St. Charles to Manuel Lisa's fort near Mandan village; residence and return; with Lisa in pursuit of the Astorians.

ELY, EZRA STILES, 1786–1861   1873

THE JOURNAL OF THE STATED PREACHER TO THE HOSPITAL AND ALMSHOUSE IN THE CITY OF NEW YORK FOR THE YEAR OF OUR LORD 1811. New York: Whiting and Watson, 1812. 300 pp.

THE SECOND JOURNAL OF THE STATED PREACHER TO THE HOSPITAL AND ALMSHOUSE IN THE CITY OF NEW YORK, FOR A PART OF THE YEAR OF OUR LORD 1813. Philadelphia: M. Carey, 1815. 255 pp.

VISITS OF MERCY, OR THE JOURNALS OF THE REV. EZRA STILES ELY, D.D., WRITTEN WHILE HE WAS STATED PREACHER TO THE HOSPITAL AND ALMSHOUSES, IN THE CITY OF NEW YORK. Philadelphia: Samuel F. Bradford, 1829. 2 vols.

1811–1813. Ministry to the destitute, blind, sick, disabled and insane in hospitals, almshouses and prisons of early nineteenth century New York; sermons, conversations with individual patients and inmates including aged revolutionary war veterans; deplorable conditions of such institutions and tireless work of a minister who suffered with his unfortunate flock.

GUBBINS, JOSEPH   1874

NEW BRUNSWICK JOURNALS OF 1811 AND 1813. Edited by Howard Temperley. Fredericton, N.B.: Kings Landing Corporation, 1980. 92 pp.

Jul–Aug 1811, Jul 1813. Diary of British colonel sent to New Brunswick to oversee local militia during War of 1812; life among New Brunswick settlers, mostly Loyalist refugees from American colonies, French Acadians, British aristocracy; rugged journeys through wilderness to inspect regiments; awareness of socially leveling effect of frontier life and availability of land; religious

climate, manners and mores of settlers and soldiers.

GUTIERREZ DE LARA, JOSE BERNARDO, 1774–1841   1875

West, Elizabeth Howard, trans. and ed. "Diary of José Bernardo Gutiérrez de Lara." AMERICAN HISTORICAL REVIEW 34 (1928):55–77, 281–294.

Nov 1811–May 1812. Fragmentary diary of Mexican revolutionary's journey through Tennessee to Washington, D.C.; efforts to secure United States aid for his cause; sea voyage from Philadelphia to New Orleans and up Mississippi River to Natchitoches; interesting account of sights seen as well as the many factors at work in international relations on the eve of the War of 1812.

HEMPSTEAD, STEPHENS S., 1754–1831   1876

Jensen, Dana O., ed. "I at Home." MISSOURI HISTORICAL SOCIETY BULLETIN 13 (1956–1957):30–56, 283–317; 14 (1957–1958):59–96, 272–288; 15 (1958–1959):38–48, 224–247; 22 (1965–1966):61–94, 180–206, 410–445.

1811–1831. Extracts from farmer's diary; daily life of farm family from Connecticut who settled near St. Louis; weather, farm tasks, work of slaves, illnesses, births, deaths, marriages, social, civil and religious activities.

HUNT, WILSON PRICE, 1783?–1842   1877

THE OVERLAND DIARY OF WILSON PRICE HUNT. Translated from the French and edited by Hoyt C. Franchère. Ashland: Oregon Book Society, 1973. 67 pp.

In THE DISCOVERY OF THE OREGON TRAIL, by Robert Stuart, edited by Philip A. Rollins, app. A, pp. 281–308. New York and London: C. Scribner's Sons, 1935.

Jul 1811–Feb 1812. Exploration journal on overland trip with companions from St. Louis to mouth of Columbia River by a new route across the Rockies; notes on adventures, topography, natural history; good reading.

HYDE, NANCY MARIA, 1792–1816   1878

THE WRITINGS OF NANCY MARIA HYDE. Norwich, Conn.: Printed by Russell Hubbard, 1816. 252 pp. Diary, pp. 27–210.

1811–1812. Private diary of work as teacher in a girls' school at Norwich; full entries in literary style; Christian reading, literary reading (Scott, Rogers, Burns, etc.); sermons, gardening, social life, reflections; many original verses; genteel diary.

KENDALL, AMOS, 1789–1869   1879

AUTOBIOGRAPHY OF AMOS KENDALL. Edited by William Stickney. Boston: Lee and Shepard, 1872. 700 pp. Reprint. New York: Peter Smith, 1949. Four pages in reduced print on each page.

1811–1872. Journal entries interspersed with letters and memoirs; studying law in Groton with Mr. Richardson; observations on political situation, War of 1812, churches and religion; dangerous illness of Mr. Richardson and diarist during epidemic of "lung-fever"; trip by public coach to Washington, D.C., and Pittsburgh; by boat, horse and foot to Lexington, Kentucky; tutoring undisciplined children of Henry Clay and enjoying his library; various ill-fated professional and business ventures in Georgetown, Kentucky, where he remained as editor of GEORGETOWN PATRIOT and practiced law.

MACLEAN, WILLIAM, 1756-1825   1880

Keith, Alice B., ed. "William Maclean's Travel Journal." NORTH CAROLINA HISTORICAL REVIEW 15 (1938): 378-388.

May-Jun 1811. Physician's diary of trip from Lincolnton, North Carolina, to Nashville, Tennessee; notes of inns, people, towns, expenses.

MACLEOD, JOHN, b. 1788?   1881

Gunn, H.G. "Diary, Etc., of Chief Trader John MacLeod, Senior, of Hudson's Bay Company, Red River Settlement, 1811." NORTH DAKOTA STATE HISTORICAL SOCIETY COLLECTIONS 2 (1908):115-134.

1811-1848. Diary and narrative of fur trader sent to establish new trading post at Red River, later at Thieves River and other places; difficulties with Northwest Company, including a battle in 1815; loss of his horse and seventy mile walk carrying trade goods; building what later became Fort Douglas.

MILLER, ROBERT JOHNSTONE, 1758-1834   1882

In PRINCIPAL TRANSACTIONS OF THE SYNOD OF THE LUTHERAN MINISTRY IN NORTH CAROLINA FROM 1811-1812, pp. 12-23. New Market, Va., 1812.

In REPORT OF THE TRANSACTIONS DURING THE SYNOD OF THE LUTHERAN MINISTRY, BEGUN AND HELD IN THE STATE OF NORTH CAROLINA, IN THE YEAR OF OUR LORD 1813, pp. 28-45. Raleigh, N.C., 1814.

Wight, Willard E., ed. "The Journals of the Reverend Robert J. Miller, Lutheran Missionary in Virginia." VIRGINIA MAGAZINE OF HISTORY AND BIOGRAPHY 61 (1953):141-166.

Jun-Sep 1811, May-Jul 1813. Missionary journeys in Virginia, Tennessee and North Carolina; preaching and other pastoral services; observations on religious situation in places visited.

Wight, Willard E., ed. "Two Lutheran Missionary Journals." SOUTH CAROLINA HISTORICAL MAGAZINE 55 (1954):6-14.

Nov-Dec 1811. Activities during missionary tour in South Carolina.

MORSE, SAMUEL FINLEY BREESE, 1791-1872   1883

SAMUEL F.B. MORSE, HIS LETTERS AND JOURNALS. Edited by Edward Lind Morse. Boston: Houghton Mifflin, 1914. 2 vols. passim.

1811-1831. Scattered extracts from his diary covering visits to Europe and a difficult crossing of the Atlantic aboard the CERES.

TAYLOR, ROWSE   1884

"A Journey by Carriage from Newport, Rhode Island, to Smithfield, Ohio." FRIENDS' HISTORICAL SOCIETY BULLETIN 8 (1918):90-100; 9 (1919):1826.

Jul-Dec 1811. Quaker family's journey by carriage from Rhode Island to Ohio; notes on scenery, towns, local customs, horrors of taverns; settlement and farming at Smithfield.

TIPTON, JOHN, 1786-1839   1885

INDIANAPOLIS NEWS, 5 May 1879. Reprint. "John Tipton's Tippecanoe Journal." INDIANA QUARTERLY MAGA-

ZINE OF HISTORY 2 (1906):170-184.

Sep-Nov 1811. Military journal of Tippecanoe campaign; interesting spellings.

In REMOVAL OF THE POTTAWATTOMIE INDIANS FROM NORTHERN INDIANA, by Daniel McDonald. Plymouth, Ind.: D. McDonald & Co., Printers, 1899.

Nov 1811. Extracts describing battle of Tippecanoe.

INDIANAPOLIS NEWS, 17 April, 1879. Reprint. "The Journal of John Tipton." INDIANA QUARTERLY MAGAZINE OF HISTORY 1 (1905):9-15, 74-79.

Extracts in TRAVEL ACCOUNTS OF INDIANA, compiled by Shirley McCord, pp. 102-110.

May-Jul 1820. Surveyor's expedition to locate the state capital of Indiana and determine the boundary between Indiana and Illinois.

In REMOVAL OF THE POTTAWATTOMIE INDIANS FROM NORTHERN INDIANA, by Daniel McDonald.

Sep 1838. Military commander's account of Potawatomies' journey to Sandusky Point, Illinois; reports of long marches, difficulty in obtaining water and provisions; illness, deaths.

WALKER, ADAM   1886

A JOURNAL OF TWO CAMPAIGNS OF THE FOURTH REGIMENT OF U.S. INFANTRY. Keene, N.H.: Printed at the Sentinel Press, 1816. 143 pp.

In MESSAGES AND LETTERS OF WILLIAM HENRY HARRISON, edited by Logan Esarey, vol. 1, pp. 693-710. Indiana Historical Collections, vol. 7. Indianapolis: Indiana Historical Commission, 1922.

In AMERICAN STATE PAPERS: MILITARY AFFAIRS V: vol. 1, pp. 268-295.

1811-1812. Two campaigns in Michigan and Indiana; good narrative but written up from notes.

WARDEN, DAVID BAILIE, 1774-1845   1887

"Journal of a Voyage from Annapolis to Cherbourg." MARYLAND HISTORICAL MAGAZINE 11 (1916):127-141, 204-217.

Aug-Sep 1811. Sea journal aboard frigate CONSTITUTION.

WATSON, JOHN, 1774-1864   1888

Smith, Dwight L. and Smith, S. Winifred, eds. "The Journey of a Pennsylvania Quaker to Pioneer Ohio." CINCINNATI HISTORICAL SOCIETY BULLETIN 26 (1968): 3-40, 174-210.

Apr-Aug 1811. Journey on horseback from Philadelphia to Pittsburgh, by flatboat down the Ohio to Cincinnati and by horse to the Quaker settlement near West Milton; return to Bucks County home via Chillicothe, Zane's Trace and Wheeling; notes on crops, settlements, Ohio River travel, Quaker meeting; sickness and treatment; Indian mounds, fossil hunting.

1812

ANON.   1889

THE VOYAGE OF THE RACOON; A "SECRET" JOURNAL OF A VISIT TO OREGON, CALIFORNIA AND HAWAII, 1813-1814. Edited by John A. Hussey. San Francisco: The Book Club of California, 1958. 36 pp.

1812-1814. Journal kept aboard H.M.S. RACOON, the ship sent by Great Britain to take possession of the American fur-trading post at Astoria during the War of 1812; life aboard a British man-of-war; information on capture of United States frigate ESSEX; descriptions of San Francisco, Monterey and the Hawaiian Islands.

ANON.   1890

Quaife, Milo M., ed. "A Diary of the War of 1812." MISSISSIPPI VALLEY HISTORICAL REVIEW 1 (1914-1915): 272-278.

    Aug-Sep 1812. Notes on border warfare by scout of Seventeenth United States Infantry Regiment; relief of Detroit and Fort Wayne.

ASKIN, CHARLES, b. 1780   1891

In CANADA ARCHIVES PUBLICATIONS 7 (1912):235-248.

Quaife, Milo M., ed. "The Fort Dearborn Massacre." MISSISSIPPI VALLEY HISTORICAL REVIEW 1 (1914-1915): 561-573. Diary, pp. 563-565.

    Jul-Sep 1812. Extracts from military and personal diary of Canadian militiaman; service during war; surrender of Detroit; account of Fort Dearborn Massacre.

ASKIN, JOHN   1892

"Extracts from the Diary of John Askin." PIONEER AND HISTORICAL SOCIETY OF THE STATE OF MICHIGAN HISTORICAL COLLECTIONS 32 (1902):468-474.

    1812-1815. Scattered, brief and miscellaneous entries of news and events of the war.

AUSTIN, STEPHEN FULLER, 1793-1836   1893

"Stephen F. Austin's Diary." In THE AUSTIN PAPERS, by Moses Austin, edited by Eugene C. Barker, vol. 2, pt. 1, pp. 205-209. American Historical Association Annual Report, 1919. Washington, D.C.: Government Printing Office, 1924.

    May 1812-Feb 1813. Observations on Mississippi River navigation; effects of earthquake at New Madrid, Missouri; travel in Mississippi.

"Journal of Stephen F. Austin on His First Trip to Texas." TEXAS HISTORICAL ASSOCIATION QUARTERLY 7 (1903-1904):286-307.

    Jun-Sep 1821. Exploration for site for colony; from New Orleans to Natchitoches by boat and then inland; mainly impersonal descriptions.

"Stephen F. Austin's Diary." In THE AUSTIN PAPERS, vol. 2, pt. 1, pp. 885-887.

    Aug-Sep 1824. Military campaign against the Karankaways.

Garrison, George P., ed. "The Prison Journal of Stephen F. Austin." TEXAS STATE HISTORICAL ASSOCIATION QUARTERLY 21 (1898-1899):183-210.

    Dec 1833-Apr 1834. Trip to Mexico City to present grievances of Texas settlers to Mexican government; comments on towns, people and countryside; strong disapproval of Catholic practices, especially power of clergy; arrest in Mexico City for treason; imprisonment there; reflections on his life, aspirations for Texas and religion.

BEALL, WILLIAM K   1894

"Journal of William K. Beall." AMERICAN HISTORICAL REVIEW 17 (1911-1912):783-808.

    Jul-Aug 1812. Military diary of assistant quarter-

master general of United States Army; in the Ohio country under Hull; capture by British; comic-opera plot.

BLACKMAN, LEARNER, 1781-1815   1895

Phelps, Dawson A., ed. "The Diary of a Chaplain in Andrew Jackson's Army: The Journal of the Reverend Mr. Learner Blackman." TENNESSEE HISTORICAL QUARTERLY 12 (1953):264-281.

    Dec 1812-Apr 1813. Methodist chaplain's account of Tennessee Volunteers; river journey from Nashville to Natchez; encampment at Camp Jackson, near Washington, Mississippi, and return to Nashville via the Natchez Trace; mostly record of preaching and ministering to soldiers and civilians, concern about effectiveness of his labors.

CARR, FRANCIS   1896

"Diary of Hon. Francis Carr of Bangor, Member of Congress 1812-13." BANGOR HISTORICAL MAGAZINE 2 (1886-1887):214-216.

    May-Jul 1812. Political diary kept during author's service as congressman; brief, mainly political, notes.

CUSHING, DANIEL LEWIS, 1764-1815   1897

CAPTAIN CUSHING IN THE WAR OF 1812. Edited by Harlow Lindley. Ohio Historical Collections, vol. 11. Columbus: Ohio State Archaeological and Historical Society, 1944. 133 pp. Diary, pp. 74-124.

    Oct 1812-Jul 1813. Artillery captain's account of military activities under William Henry Harrison in Ohio; marches, duties, routines of army life; reports of engagements; two sieges of Fort Meigs; detailed, readable and interesting.

DARNELL, ELIAS   1898

A JOURNAL, CONTAINING AN ACCURATE AND INTERESTING ACCOUNT OF THE HARDSHIPS, SUFFERINGS, BATTLES, DEFEAT AND CAPTIVITY OF THOSE HEROIC KENTUCKY VOLUNTEERS. Philadelphia: Grigg & Elliott, 1834. 87 pp.; Philadelphia: Lippincott, Grambo, 1854. 98 pp. Reprint. New York: W. Abbatt, 1914; MAGAZINE OF HISTORY, extra no. 31, 8 (1914):183-235.

    Aug 1812-Feb 1813. Winchester's expedition against Canada with Kentucky volunteers and regulars; hardships, battles, captivity.

EVANS, AMOS ALEXANDER, 1785-1848   1899

"Journal Kept on Board the United States Frigate CONSTITUTION, 1812, by Amos A. Evans, Surgeon United States Navy." PENNSYLVANIA MAGAZINE OF HISTORY AND BIOGRAPHY 19 (1895):152-169, 374-386, 468-480.

Ash, M. Howard, ed. "Extracts from the Diary of Dr. Amos Alexander Evans." PATRIOTIC MARYLANDER 3 (1916-1917):177-186.

    Jun 1812-Feb 1813. Surgeon's account of cruise on the CONSTITUTION.

FLAGET, BENEDICT JOSEPH, 1763-1850   1900

Howlett, W.J., ed. "Bishop Flaget's Diary." AMERICAN CATHOLIC HISTORICAL SOCIETY OF PHILADELPHIA RECORDS 29 (1918):37-59, 153-169, 231-249.

    Jan-Nov 1812. Diary of the bishop of Kentucky; diocesan work; journey to Baltimore; mostly brief, formal notes of his work, but more expansive at Baltimore. Translated from the French.

GODDARD, BENJAMIN, 1766–1861   1901

Baker, Edward W., ed. "Extracts from the Diary of Benjamin Goddard." BROOKLINE HISTORICAL SOCIETY PROCEEDINGS 18 (1911):16–48.

> 1812–1821. Extracts, mostly from 1812–1815 and arranged topically, from a diary kept by a Brookline, Massachusetts, merchant and farmer; family and social life of a prominent Brookline family; opinions on local and national politics, War of 1812.

HEALD, NATHAN, b. 1775   1902

In CHICAGO AND THE OLD NORTHWEST, by Milo M. Quaife, pp. 402–405. Chicago: University of Chicago Press, 1913.

> 1812–1822. Officer's account of march from Chicago to Detroit; attack by Indians; miscellaneous biographical items thereafter; brief scattered notes.

HORRY, PETER, 1747–1815   1903

Salley, A.S., ed. "Journal of General Peter Horry." SOUTH CAROLINA HISTORICAL AND GENEALOGICAL MAGAZINE 38 (1937):49–53, 81–86, 116–119; 39 (1938):46–49, 96–99, 125–128, 157–159; 40 (1939):11–14, 48–51, 91–96, 142–144; 41 (1940):15–18; 42 (1941):8–11, 72–75, 118–121, 189–193; 43 (1942):57–60, 125–128, 181–184, 251–255; 44(1943):55–58, 124–129, 196–199, 255–257; 45 (1944):51–55, 116–119, 177–181, 222–225; 46 (1945):54–56, 110–114, 176–179, 218–222; 47 (1946):58–60, 121–123, 181–183, 243–244; 48 (1947):53–54, 115–116.

> 1812–1814. Personal diary of plantation and domestic details; work, relaxation, musings; good picture of an elderly, well-to-do, active Southerner in Winyah Bay, South Carolina.

HUNTINGTON, SUSAN MANSFIELD, 1791–1823   1904

In MEMOIRS OF THE LATE MRS. SUSAN HUNTINGTON, OF BOSTON, MASS., by Benjamin B. Wisner, pp. 62–353 passim. Boston: Crocker & Brewster, 1826. 3rd ed. New York: J. Leavitt, 1829.

> 1812–1822. Extracts from a diary recording the Lord's dealings with her; reflections on religion and her own life; self-analysis; family notes in this light.

JONES, NOAH   1905

JOURNALS OF TWO CRUISES ABOARD THE AMERICAN PRIVATEER YANKEE. Introduction by E.M. Eller. New York: Macmillan, 1967. 156 pp.

In TALES OF AN OLD SEA PORT, by Wilfred H. Monro, pp. 225–288. Princeton: Princeton University Press, 1917.

> Jul 1812–Mar 1813. Journals kept by the captain's clerk of first two cruises in the War of 1812 of the YANKEE, a privateer with the record of greatest profits of any American vessel; trip to Cape Verdes to Cape Lopez with stops at ports and off coast of Brazil; weather conditions and changes in sails; duties and health of crew; ships sighted and boarded, capture of over $200,000 in prizes from eight ships; Old Neptune's ceremonies upon crossing equator.

LUCAS, ROBERT, 1781–1853   1906

Parish, John C., ed. "The Robert Lucas Journal." IOWA JOURNAL OF HISTORY AND POLITICS 4 (1906):343–437.

> Apr–Sep 1812. Captain's journal of disastrous Hull campaign of the volunteers in Ohio until surrender of Detroit; return across Lake Erie and down Ohio to Portsmouth; valuable account of military affairs; interesting spellings.

Smith, Dwight L., ed. "An Unsuccessful Negotiation for Removal of the Wyandot Indians from Ohio." OHIO STATE ARCHAEOLOGICAL AND HISTORICAL QUARTERLY 58 (1949):305–331. Journal, pp. 319–322.

> Sep 1834. Official record of attempt by Ohio governor to negotiate removal of Wyandots to trans-Mississippi area; arguments of both sides; terms and compensations.

LUTTIG, JOHN C., d. 1815   1907

JOURNAL OF A FUR-TRADING EXPEDITION ON THE UPPER MISSOURI. Edited by Stella M. Drumm. St. Louis: Missouri Historical Society, 1920. 192 pp.; New York: Argosy Antiquarian, 1964. 213 pp.

> May 1812–Mar 1813. Fur trading journal kept by clerk of Missouri Fur Company; expedition on the upper Missouri; extremely interesting for social life of traders and Indians; some German-English features in spelling and syntax.

PORTER, DAVID, 1780–1843   1908

JOURNAL OF A CRUISE MADE TO THE PACIFIC OCEAN, BY CAPTAIN DAVID PORTER, IN THE UNITED STATES FRIGATE ESSEX. Philadelphia: Bradford and Inskeep, 1815. 2 vols. in I. 2d ed. New York: Wiley & Halsted, 1822. 2 vols. Reprint. Upper Saddle River, N.J.: Gregg, 1970.

> 1812–1814. Captain's account of cruise aboard the ESSEX; descriptions of the Cape Verde Islands, coast of Brazil, Patagonia, Chile, Peru; the Galapagos and Marquesas Islands.

REYNOLDS, JAMES   1909

JOURNAL OF AN AMERICAN PRISONER AT FORT MALDEN AND QUEBEC IN THE WAR OF 1812. Edited by George M. Fairchild, Jr. Quebec: Privately printed by F. Carrel, 1909. 32 pp.

> Jul–Oct 1812. Prison journal of surgeon's mate with Hull's expedition against Canada; capture with his patients near Fort Malden; journey to Quebec and life on prison ship there; patriotic and antimonarchistic notes; some interesting spellings.

ROACH, ISAAC, d. 1848   1910

"Journal of Major Isaac Roach." PENNSYLVANIA MAGAZINE OF HISTORY AND BIOGRAPHY 17 (1893):129–158, 281–315.

> 1812–1824. War services around Buffalo; battle of Lake Erie; notes on later army life; possibly inaccurate.

STUART, ROBERT, 1785–1848   1911

THE DISCOVERY OF THE OREGON TRAIL: ROBERT STUART'S NARRATIVES OF HIS OVERLAND TRIP EASTWARD FROM ASTORIA. Edited by Philip A. Rollins. New York and London: C. Scribner's Sons, 1935. 391 pp.

ON THE OREGON TRAIL: ROBERT STUART'S JOURNEY OF DISCOVERY. Edited by Kenneth A. Spaulding. Norman: University of Oklahoma Press, 1953. 192 pp.

> Jun 1812–May 1813. Journal of Scottish fur trader with the Northwest Company; journey, mainly by canoe, up Columbia River from Astoria, via Tongue-Point, Klickitat River, Walla Walla River, Vinson Wash, American Falls, McCoy Creek, Moody Creek, Sweetwater River, North Platte, Nebraska, to St. Louis; horseback journey from St. Louis to Green River, Kentucky; extensive entries on scenery, natural history, Indians, etc.; a good journal of exploration.

WALL, GARRETT   1912

In NOTES AND QUERIES, edited by William H. Egle, 1900, pp. 165–166.

> Oct 1812–Apr 1813. Brief notes of marches and encampment at Sandusky.

WATERHOUSE, BENJAMIN, 1754–1846   1913

A JOURNAL OF A YOUNG MAN OF MASSACHUSETTS, LATE A SURGEON ON BOARD AN AMERICAN PRIVATEER. Boston: Printed by Rowe and Hooper, 1816. 272 pp. Reprint. New York: W. Abbatt, 1911; MAGAZINE OF HISTORY, extra no. 18, 5 (1911):200–272.

> 1812–1815. Prison journal kept by physician recently of Harvard medical faculty; capture at sea by the British and imprisonment at Melville Island, Halifax, and later at Chatham and Dartmoor, England; an extensive, literary diary recounting daily life and news; much general comment and reflection.

1813

ANON.   1914

LEAVES FROM THE WAR LOG OF THE NANCY. Comments by H.J. Snider. Toronto: Rous & Mann, 1936. xliv pp.

> Jul–Dec 1813. Scottish seaman's record of life on board the British troop ship NANCY OF MOY on maneuvers through the Great Lakes during War of 1812.

BAYARD, JAMES ASHETON, 1767–1815   1915

PAPERS OF JAMES A. BAYARD. Edited by Elizabeth Donnan. Annual Report of the American Historical Association for the year 1913, vol. 11. Washington, D.C., 1913. 539 pp. Diary, pp. 385–516.

> 1813–1814. European diary of commissioner in negotiations with Great Britain; activities at Gothenburg, St. Petersburg, Riga, Berlin, Holland, London, Brussels, etc; greater part in Russia at time Alexander I was attempting mediation; very interesting details and impressions of diplomatic and aristocratic life and characters.

BEAUMONT, WILLIAM, 1785–1853   1916

In LIFE AND LETTERS OF DR. WILLIAM BEAUMONT, by Jesse S. Myer, pp. 38–47. St. Louis: C.V. Mosby, 1912. 317 pp. Reprint. 1939.

> Mar–May 1813. Medical notes of a surgeon's mate in the War of 1812; battle of Little York; storming of Fort George.

In LIFE AND LETTERS OF DR. WILLIAM BEAUMONT, pp. 74–85.

> May–Sep 1820. Travel diary extracts; trip from Plattsburg to Mackinac; descriptions; long quotations from Benjamin Franklin.

BONNER, JAMES   1917

"Diary of Capt. James Bonner." WESTERN RESERVE AND NORTHERN OHIO HISTORICAL SOCIETY TRACT, no. 49 (1879), pp. 103–104.

> Oct 1813–Apr 1814. Extracts covering military events at Upper Sandusky and Fort Meigs, Ohio; notes about Indians.

CHEVER, JAMES, 1791–1857   1918

In THE SHIPS AND SAILORS OF OLD SALEM, by Ralph D. Paine, pp. 489–495.

> Dec 1813–Apr 1814. Extracts from privateersman's journal; cruise of the AMERICA.

CRAWFORD, WILLIAM HARRIS, 1772–1834   1919

THE JOURNAL OF WILLIAM H. CRAWFORD. Edited by Daniel C. Knowlton. Smith College Studies in History, vol. 11, no. 1. Northampton, Mass.: Department of History of Smith College, 1925. 64 pp. Journal, pp. 9–52.

Extracts in GIANT DAYS, OR THE LIFE OF WILLIAM H. CRAWFORD, by John E.D. Shipp, pp. 101–115. Americus, Ga.: Southern Printers, 1909.

> Jun–Nov 1813. Diplomat's journey from Washington to Pennsylvania; service as minister at French Court; meetings with famous politicians and statesmen; notes on places, social affairs, reading, plays, etc.; interesting.

DOW, PEGGY, 1780–1820   1920

In THE DEALINGS OF GOD, MAN, AND THE DEVIL: AS EXEMPLIFIED IN THE LIFE, EXPERIENCE, AND TRAVELS OF LORENZO DOW, by Lorenzo Dow, pt. 2. New York: Cornish, Lamport, 1851; Sheldon, Lampert & Blakeman, 1856.

In HISTORY OF COSMOPOLITE, by Lorenzo Dow, pp. 663–708. Philadelphia: J.B. Smith, 1859.

> 1813–1816. Religious journal of the wife of an evangelist; notes on camp meeting religion.

FOGG, WILLIAM, 1790–1859   1921

"A Journal from This Time Forward." OLD ELIOT 3 (1899):7–9, 15–19, 33–36, 41–43, 76–80, 108–112, 124–127, 137–139, 164–168, 178–184, 195–198.

> 1813–1821. Clergyman's journal; brief notes on weather, local affairs at Kittery, Maine; marriages, deaths, war news, church affairs, farming, parish meetings, fashions, journeys; description of President Monroe; verses.

FRANKLOW, JOHN PHILIP, d. 1829   1922

Wight, Willard E., ed. "Two Lutheran Missionary Journals." SOUTH CAROLINA HISTORICAL MAGAZINE 55 (1954):6–14. Journal, pp. 11–14.

> Mar–Apr 1813. Description of activities during missionary journey in South Carolina; mainly efforts to ameliorate discord between a Lutheran pastor and his congregation.

GALLATIN, JAMES, 1796–1876   1923

A GREAT PEACEMAKER: THE DIARY OF JAMES GALLATIN, SECRETARY TO ALBERT GALLATIN. New York: C. Scribner's Sons, 1914. 314 pp. New ed. THE DIARY OF

JAMES GALLATIN. New York: C. Scribner's Sons, 1916. Reprint. Westport, Conn.: Greenwood, 1979.

1813-1827. Political and diplomatic diary; Russian offer of mediation, Treaty of Ghent, treaty of commerce; ministry in France; restoration of Bourbons, assassination of Duc de Berry; return to America; special mission to England; intimate picture of family; valuable politically and personally.

GERRY, ELBRIDGE, 1791-1883   1924

THE DIARY OF ELBRIDGE GERRY, JR. With a preface and footnotes by Claude G. Bowers. New York: Brentano's, 1927. 222 pp.

"Extracts from the Diary of Elbridge Gerry, Jr." MASSACHUSETTS HISTORICAL SOCIETY PROCEEDINGS 47 (1914):523-528.

May-Jul 1813. Horseback journey through Ohio, Virginia, Washington, Pennsylvania; notes on social life of Washington; descriptions of Moravians; detailed and interesting notes.

HAMTON, AARON   1925

Jacobsen, Edna L., ed. "Aaron Hamton's Diary." NEW YORK HISTORY 21 (1940):324-334, 341-442.

May-Jun 1813. Travel journal of New Jersey Quaker; New Jersey to Holland Purchase in New York State; notes on taverns, towns, people, Indians; original verses.

HARTSELL, JACOB, 1786-1843   1926

McCown, Mary H., ed. "'The J. Hartsell Memora': The Journal of a Tennessee Captain in the War of 1812." EAST TENNESSEE HISTORICAL SOCIETY PUBLICATIONS 11 (1939):93-115; 12 (1940):118-146.

Oct 1813-Jan 1814. Military journal covering movements and camp life; comments on Indians; farming; interesting incidents and good picture of diarist.

HICKS, ELIAS, 1748-1830   1927

JOURNAL OF THE LIFE AND RELIGIOUS LABOURS OF ELIAS HICKS. New York: I.T. Hopper, 1832. 451 pp. Reprint. New York: Arno, 1969. Journal, pp. 132-387.

1813-1820. Quaker's private life and religious work at Jericho, New York; journeys and preaching in middle and southern states, New York, New England, Pennsylvania, Ohio, etc.; social life, reading, domestic work, etc.; journal introduced and followed by autobiography and memoirs; a good Quaker journal.

HOWE, JOSEPH P.   1928

Pears, Thomas C., Jr., ed. "A Journal of Two Missionary Tours Made in Kentucky and Tennessee." PRESBYTERIAN HISTORICAL SOCIETY JOURNAL 16 (1934-1935): 373-388.

In THE PRESBYTERIANS, 1783-1840: A COLLECTION OF SOURCE MATERIALS, edited by William Warren Sweet, pp. 778-796. Religion on the American Frontier, vol. 2. New York and London: Harper and Brothers, 1936.

Oct-Dec 1813, Sep-Oct 1814. Travels on horseback of a Presbyterian minister; preaching at various meetings, manner of securing appointments, and the reception of listeners.

INDERWICK, JAMES, d. 1815   1929

Paltsits, Victor H., ed. "Cruise of the U.S. Brig ARGUS in 1813: Journal of Surgeon James Inderwick." NEW YORK PUBLIC LIBRARY BULLETIN 21 (1917):383-405. Journal, pp. 395-405.

Jul-Aug 1813. Extracts from naval surgeon's journal; naval warfare; raiding English shipping off English and Irish coasts; defeat and capture of H.M.S. PELICAN.

LEE, MARY JACKSON, 1783-1860   1930

In HENRY AND MARY LEE, LETTERS AND JOURNALS, prepared by Frances R. Morse, pp. 167-226. Boston: T. Todd, Printers, 1926.

1813-1816. Journal kept at home in Boston for her merchant husband in India; mostly domestic matters, illnesses of children, social visits; merchant ships in and out of Boston harbor; incidents in War of 1812; views on war and Napoleon; religious reading; reflections of an obviously well educated woman.

MORRELL, JAMES   1931

"James Morrell's Account of a Trip to Ballston and Saratoga Springs." PENNSYLVANIA MAGAZINE OF HISTORY AND BIOGRAPHY 39 (1915):425-433.

Aug 1813. Travel diary.

PALMER, BENJAMIN FRANKLIN, 1793-1824   1932

THE DIARY OF BENJAMIN F. PALMER, PRIVATEERSMAN. Acorn Club Publications, no. 11. New Haven, Conn.: Tuttle, Morehouse & Taylor, 1914. 274 pp.

1813-1815. Prison diary kept while diarist was aboard British warships, in prison at Melville Island and at Dartmoor, England; detailed accounts of prison life; philosophizing; an excellent prison diary with poem, letters, prison regulations appended.

PECK, JOHN MASON, 1789-1858   1933

FORTY YEARS OF PIONEER LIFE. By Rufus Babcock. Philadelphia: American Baptist Publication Society, 1864. 360 pp. Reprint. Carbondale: Southern Illinois University Press, 1965.

1813-1857. Baptist missionary journals covering extensive missionary journeys in trans-Allegheny region, mostly Illinois and Missouri; everyday affairs, weather, adventures, social conditions; wide interests and good observations.

"The Boon's Lick Country." MISSOURI HISTORICAL SOCIETY BULLETIN 6 (1950):442-490.

1818-1819. Extracts describing Boon's Lick area of Missouri.

RODNEY, DANIEL, 1764-1846   1934

In RODNEY'S DIARY AND OTHER DELAWARE RECORDS, compiled by Charles H.B. Turner, pp. 3-14. Philadelphia: Allen, Lane & Scott, 1911.

1813-1829. Record of naval engagements in the Delaware; destruction of British cruisers; later entries covering ship movements; business.

SCHILLINGER, WILLIAM   1935

Green, James A., ed. "Journal of Ensign William Schillinger, a Soldier of the War of 1812." OHIO AR-

CHAEOLOGICAL AND HISTORICAL QUARTERLY 41 (1932): 51-85.

Feb-Aug 1813. Account of service with Hosbrook's company of Ohio militia, mainly at Fort Amanda building boats; garrisoning and provisioning of stockade and general work; news of siege of Fort Meigs; dislike of Kentucky troops.

SEARCY, ROBERT   1936

"The Departure from Nashville: A Journal of the Trip down the Mississippi." In CORRESPONDENCE OF ANDREW JACKSON, ed. by John Spencer Bassett, vol. 1, pp. 256-271. Carnegie Institution of Washington, Publication no. 371. Washington, D.C.: Carnegie Institution of Washington, 1926.

Jan-Mar 1813. Journal probably kept by aide to Andrew Jackson; difficulties of Army of Tennessee volunteers trying to move on ice choked Ohio in bitter winter weather; down Mississippi River; miserable state of inhabitants, courageous rescue of men on sinking boat, colorful arrival at Natchez and encampment there.

TAIT, JAMES A., 1791-1855   1937

Brannon, Peter A., ed. "Journal of James A. Tait." GEORGIA HISTORICAL QUARTERLY 8 (1924):229-239.

1813-1814. Account of military expedition under Captain Smith against Creek Indians; portraits of officers; battle of Auttose; notes on Indians.

VALPEY, JOSEPH, 1792-1816   1938

JOURNAL OF JOSEPH VALPEY, JR., OF SALEM. Detroit: Michigan Society of Colonial Wars, 1922. 71 pp.

1813-1815. Seaman's prison diary; capture on the MONKEY of Boston; imprisonment at Halifax and subsequently at Dartmoor, England; notes on prison conditions, daily activities; interesting linguistically and for poems by diarist and his comrades.

WINSLOW, HARRIET WADSWORTH LATHROP,   1939
1796-1833

A MEMOIR OF MRS. HARRIET WADSWORTH WINSLOW, COMBINING A SKETCH OF THE CEYLON MISSION. By Miron Winslow. New York: Leavitt, Lord; Boston: Crocker & Brewster, 1835. 408 pp. passim.

MEMOIR OF MRS. HARRIET L. WINSLOW, THIRTEEN YEARS A MEMBER OF THE AMERICAN MISSION IN CEYLON. New York: American Tract Society, 1840. 479 pp. passim.

1813-1832. Extracts of missionary journal; religious self-analysis; social items; mission work in Ceylon; teaching in school for the poor; journey to New England; marriage; voyage to Calcutta and Jaffna.

YOST, ROBERT   1940

"Robert Yost His Book." OHIO ARCHAEOLOGICAL AND HISTORICAL QUARTERLY 23 (1914):150-161.

Dec 1813-Jan 1814. Military journal of march from St. Clairsville, Ohio, to Fort Detroit; general comments on proceedings, places and people; some interesting spellings.

1814

ANDERSON, RICHARD CLOUGH, 1788-1826   1941

THE DIARY AND JOURNAL OF RICHARD CLOUGH ANDERSON, JR. Edited by Alfred Tischendorf and E. Taylor Parks.

Durham, N.C.: Duke University Press, 1964. 342 pp.

1814-1826. Political and private diary of Kentucky state legislator, United States congressman, and finally Minister to Simón Bolivar's ill-fated Gran Columbia; the working of state and federal government; candid comments on fellow politicians, family and social life in Kentucky and Washington; diplomatic work in Colombia, including arduous travels reported in geographic detail; deaths of several children in the United States and of his wife in Colombia, his own declining health, sense of loss and tragedy.

ANDERSON, THOMAS GUMMERSALL, 1779-1875   1942

"Anderson's Journal at Fort McKay." WISCONSIN STATE HISTORICAL SOCIETY COLLECTIONS 9 (1882):207-261. Reprint. 1909.

Aug-Nov 1814. Officer's journal kept at Fort McKay, Prairie du Chien, Wisconsin; military affairs and dealings with Fox, Sauk, Paun and Sioux Indians; interesting and valuable record.

BAKER, ISAAC L.   1943

"Journal of Capt. Isaac L. Baker." SOUTHWESTERN HISTORICAL QUARTERLY 30 (1926-1927):272-282.

Jul-Aug 1814. March from Nashville, Tennessee, to Huntsville, Alabama; signing of treaty with Creek Indians; many references to General Andrew Jackson.

BAXLEY, JOHN, d. 1849   1944

In LIFE OF JOHN H.W. HAWKINS, compiled by William H. Hawkins, pp. 11-14. Boston: J.P. Jewett; New York: Sheldon, Blakeman, 1859; Boston: E.P. Dutton, 1863.

Sep 1814. Baltimore clergyman's diary; account of British fleet off Baltimore and bombardment of Fort McHenry.

BRACE, JOHN PIERCE   1945

Extracts in MORE CHRONICLES OF A PIONEER SCHOOL FROM 1792 TO 1833, compiled by Emily N. Vanderpoel, pp. 81-163. New York: Cadmus, 1927.

1814-1815. Charming and ingenuous journal of a beleaguered young schoolmaster at Litchfield Female Academy; his teaching, poetic musings, romances or lack of them; frequent embarrassments, both academic and social.

BRECK, SAMUEL, 1771-1862   1946

Wainwright, Nicholas B., ed. "The Diary of Samuel Breck." PENNSYLVANIA MAGAZINE OF HISTORY AND BIOGRAPHY 102 (1978):469-508; 103 (1979):85-113, 222-251, 356-382, 497-527.

1814-1840. Extracts from diary of Philadelphia gentleman, builder of Fairmount Park's Sweetbriar, and an active and highly regarded public servant; cultural, economic and political affairs of the day; life among upper class.

CALLAWAY, JAMES, 1783-1815   1947

Wesley, Edgar B. "James Callaway in the War of 1812." MISSOURI HISTORICAL SOCIETY COLLECTIONS 5 (1927-1928):38-81. Diary, pp. 74-77.

Aug-Sep 1814. Taylor's expedition against Sac and Fox Indians; march from Cap au Gris; battle of Credit Rock; good diary with interesting spellings.

CAROW, ISAAC   1948

In AMERICAN BACKLOGS: THE STORY OF GERTRUDE TYLER AND HER FAMILY, compiled by Edith Kermit Carow Roosevelt and Kermit Roosevelt, pp. 202–230. New York and London: C. Scribner's Sons, 1928.

     Dec 1814–Jun 1815. Travel diary; voyage from New York to England and touring there.

     1827–1828. Travel in England, France, Switzerland and Germany; interesting picture of a "Grand Tour"; lively touristic details, with some literary interests; notes on customs, meals, inns, etc.

DARLINGTON, WILLIAM, 1782–1863   1949

Harpster, John W., ed. "Major William Darlington's Diary of Service in the War of 1812." WESTERN PENNSYLVANIA HISTORICAL MAGAZINE 20 (1937):197–214.

     Sep–Dec 1814. Marches with Pennsylvania Volunteer Light Infantry; Darlington's court-martial for objecting to regular army discipline; peaceful life of amateur soldiers.

DICKSON, Sir ALEXANDER   1950

Ritchie, Carson I.A., ed. "Journal of Operations in Louisiana." LOUISIANA HISTORICAL QUARTERLY 44 (July–October 1961):1–110.

     Dec 1814–Feb 1815. Journal of the commander of the British artillery in Louisiana campaign; detailed account of British effort to take New Orleans; evidence regarding the importance of Jackson's frontier riflemen.

DULLES, JOSEPH HEATLY, 1795–1876   1951

"Extracts from the Diary of Joseph Heatly Dulles." PENNSYLVANIA MAGAZINE OF HISTORY AND BIOGRAPHY 35 (1911):276–289.

     Aug 1814. A young Yale man's jaunt to Plattsburg, New York, and Burlington, Vermont.

ELLIS, WILLIAM   1952

AURORA (Philadelphia), 4 January 1815.

     Aug–Sep 1814. Captive's diary; capture by British and Creek Indians; removal to Pensacola.

EVANS, WILLIAM, 1787–1867   1953

JOURNAL OF THE LIFE AND RELIGIOUS SERVICES OF WILLIAM EVANS. Philadelphia: For sale at Friends' Book Store, 1870. 710 pp. passim.

     1814–1862. Quaker journal, set in autobiography; very detailed and extensive notes of travels and religious work.

GRAY, FRANCIS CALLEY   1954

THOMAS JEFFERSON IN 1814, BEING AN ACCOUNT OF A VISIT TO MONTICELLO, VIRGINIA. Notes and introduction by Henry S. Rowe and T. Jefferson Coolidge, Jr. Boston: The Club of Odd Volumes, 1924. 79 pp.

     Dec 1814–Jan 1815. A young Boston intellectual's trip by stagecoach to visit Thomas Jefferson; fellow travelers, including George Ticknor; difficulties of winter journey; wretchedness of inns; the patient hospitality of the much visited and elderly Jefferson; diarist's delight with his host's renowned library.

MERRITT, WILLIAM HAMILTON, 1793–1862   1955

In SELECT BRITISH DOCUMENTS OF THE CANADIAN WAR OF 1812, edited by William C.H. Wood, vol. 3, pp. 623–648. Champlain Society Publications, vol. 15. Toronto: Champlain Society, 1928.

     Jul–Dec 1814. Prison diary; march as captive from Buffalo to Cheshire, New York, and imprisonment there; social life and general war news; an entertaining diary.

MICHELL, JOHN   1956

Ritchie, Carson I.A., ed. "Diary of Major J. Michell." LOUISIANA HISTORICAL QUARTERLY 44 (July–October 1961):127–130.

     Dec 1814–Feb 1815. British artillery officer's diary outlining events during the struggle for New Orleans; observations from his strategic position on the battlefield.

MURPHY, PLEASANTS, 1786–1863   1957

"Pleasants Murphy's 'Journal and Day Book'." WILLIAM AND MARY COLLEGE QUARTERLY, 2d ser. 3 (1923): 231–238.

     Dec 1814–Jan 1815. Private and military diary; mostly notes of parades and marches.

NAPIER, HENRY EDWARD, 1789–1853   1958

NEW ENGLAND BLOCKADED IN 1814: THE JOURNAL OF HENRY EDWARD NAPIER. Edited by Walter M. Whitehill. Salem: Peabody Museum, 1939. 88 pp. Journal, pp. 3–58.

     Mar–Sep 1814. Journal of British naval officer aboard H.M.S. NYMPHE during blockade of New England; service off Halifax and off Massachusetts coast; notes on attitudes of New Englanders and relations of Quakers with British; weather, ship movements, amusements and horseplay; good, full entries; a spirited journal.

PIERCE, NATHANIEL, 1795–1823   1959

"Journal of Nathaniel Pierce of Newburyport, Kept at Dartmoor Prison." ESSEX INSTITUTE HISTORICAL COLLECTIONS 73 (1937):24–59.

     Nov 1814–Jul 1815. Prison diary; capture at sea by British and imprisonment at Dartmoor, England; notes on daily activities, weather, food, escapes, release; interesting spellings.

PLEASANTS, THOMAS FRANKLIN, 1790–1817   1960

"Extracts from the Diary of Thomas Franklin Pleasants." PENNSYLVANIA MAGAZINE OF HISTORY AND BIOGRAPHY 39 (1915):322–336, 410–424.

     Apr–Dec 1814. Lawyer's activities as member of Philadelphia militia; camp life, detailed account of an affair of honor; unintentionally comic.

QUINCY, ELIZA SUSAN, b. 1798   1961

In THE ARTICULATE SISTERS, by M.A. DeWolfe Howe, pp. 9–46.

     1814–1821. Diary of eldest daughter of Josiah Quincy; careful account of peace celebration of 1815; visits from John Adams and John Quincy Adams; an excursion on the Middlesex Canal; Harvard Commencement of 1821; parties described in detail; social interactions with many prominent people.

CAMBRIDGE HISTORICAL SOCIETY PUBLICATIONS 4 (1909):90–92.

Jun 1825, 1828–1829. Brief extracts relating to Harvard.

STEVENS, JOSEPH LOWE, 1790–1879   1962

Munro, Wilfred H., ed. "The Fifth Cruise of the Privateer YANKEE." RHODE ISLAND HISTORICAL SOCIETY COLLECTIONS 12 (1919):76–83.

Mar–Jul 1814. Naval surgeon's journal of cruise aboard privateer YANKEE off Madeira, etc.; mainly general memoranda.

TATUM, HOWELL, fl. 1775–1815   1963

MAJOR HOWELL TATUM'S JOURNAL WHILE ACTING TOPOGRAPHICAL ENGINEER (1814) TO GENERAL JACKSON, COMMANDING THE SEVENTH MILITARY DISTRICT. Edited by John S. Bassett. Smith College Studies in History, vol. 7, nos. 1–3. Northampton, Mass.: Department of History of Smith College, 1922. 138 pp.

Aug 1814–Jan 1815. Topographical engineer's military exploration journal; survey of Alabama River, with good topographical details; New Orleans campaign until just before capture of Fort Bowyer by the British; latter part in narrative style with full descriptions; of some general and historical interest.

Hamilton, Peter J. and Owen, Thomas M., eds. "Topographical Notes and Observations on the Alabama River." ALABAMA HISTORICAL SOCIETY PUBLICATIONS 2 (1898):130–177.

Aug 1814.

THACKARA, WILLIAM WOOD, 1791–1839   1964

Golovin, Anne C., ed. "William Wood Thackara, Volunteer in the War of 1812." PENNSYLVANIA MAGAZINE OF HISTORY AND BIOGRAPHY 91 (1967):299–325.

Sep 1814–Jan 1815. Diary of Philadelphia engraver who answered call for volunteers after British burned Washington, D.C.; an interesting and readable account of life in army camps near Kennett Square, Pennsylvania, and Wilmington, Delaware; camp conditions and soldier's misadventures.

WITHEROW, JOHN   1965

Walker, Joseph E., ed. "A Soldier's Diary for 1814." PENNSYLVANIA HISTORY 12 (1945):292–303.

Mar–Sep 1814. Record kept by corporal with Pennsylvania troops on the Niagara frontier; movements, engagements, camp activities; daily, generally brief entries.

1815

BALLARD, JOSEPH, 1789–1877   1966

ENGLAND IN 1815 AS SEEN BY A YOUNG BOSTON MERCHANT. Boston and New York: Houghton Mifflin, 1913. 180 pp.

Mar–Nov 1815. Travels in England; notes on London, towns and scenery in the north of England; interest in antiquities.

BINGHAM, HIRAM, 1789–1869   1967

Miller, Char, ed. "'Teach Me O My God': The Journal of Hiram Bingham." VERMONT HISTORY 48 (1980):225–235.

1815–1816. Extracts from student diary of the future Congregational missionary to the Hawaiian Islands; his studies at Middlebury College and Andover Theological School; evidence of his religious background and development towards missionary vocation.

CHESTER, CAROLINE, 1801–1870   1968

In CHRONICLES OF A PIONEER SCHOOL, compiled by Emily N. Vanderpoel, pp. 150–154.

Nov 1815–Jan 1816. Extract giving a detailed account of a fourteen-year-old's life at Litchfield Female Academy; studies, reading, friends, religious thoughts and activities; a pleasant diary.

In MORE CHRONICLES OF A PIONEER SCHOOL, compiled by Emily N. Vanderpoel, pp. 164–196. New York: Cadmus, 1927.

Jun–Sep 1816.

COTTON, JOHN, b. 1792   1969

"From Rhode Island to Ohio in 1815." JOURNAL OF AMERICAN HISTORY 16 (1922):36–49, 249–260.

Extracts in "Journal of John Cotton, M.D." OLD NORTHWEST GENEALOGICAL QUARTERLY 13 (1910):59–67.

Sep–Nov 1815. Plymouth, Massachusetts, physician's travel diary; to New York by boat, then through New York, Pennsylvania and Ohio; general, social and touring notes in narrative style.

CRABBE (or CRABB), THOMAS, 1788?–1872   1970

Aimone, Alan C. "The Cruise of the U.S. Sloop HORNET in 1815." MARINER'S MIRROR 61 (1975):377–384.

Jan–Jun 1815. Officer's account of action at sea; engagements, misdeeds and punishments of crew; observation of slave market in Bahia, Brazil.

DE MUN, JULES   1971

Beauregard, Nettie H., trans., and Marshall, Thomas M., ed., "The Journals of Jules De Mun." MISSOURI HISTORICAL SOCIETY COLLECTIONS 5 (1927–1928):167–208, 311–326.

Sep–Nov 1815. Journals of French trading expeditions; from St. Louis to upper Arkansas River.

Feb–Apr 1816. From Huerfano Creek to Gasconade River.

Jun–Aug 1816. From St. Louis to lower Kansas River.

GREEN, NATHAN, 1787?–1825   1972

In THE SHIPS AND SAILORS OF OLD SALEM, by Ralph D. Paine, pp. 500–503.

Mar–Apr 1815. Extracts from journal of captain aboard the privateer GRAND TURK.

HILL, SAMUEL, b. 1777   1973

Snyder, James W., Jr., ed. "Voyage of the OPHELIA from Boston to Canton: Excerpts from the Journal of Captain Samuel Hill." NEW ENGLAND QUARTERLY 10 (1937):355–380.

1815–1817. Captain's sea journal; fitting out ship; sailing details; life and work aboard ship; notes on Valparaiso, Hawaiian Islands, South Seas, etc.; detailed descriptions.

IZARD, GEORGE, 1776–1828   1974

Ryan, Harold W., ed. "Diary of a Journey by George Izard." SOUTH CAROLINA HISTORICAL MAGAZINE 53 (1952):67–76, 155–160, 223–229.

> Nov 1815–Apr 1816. Journal of a trip from Philadelphia to Charleston and back; visits with friends and family; land business deals; description of roads and accommodations; characteristics of Virginians.

KEMPER, JAMES, 1753–1834   1975

Fishwick, Marshall W., ed. "Journey through the Wilderness." VIRGINIA MAGAZINE OF HISTORY AND BIOGRAPHY 57 (1949):134–139.

> Oct–Dec 1815. Extracts from journal of Presbyterian minister's horseback journey through Virginia; missionary activities; comments on the state of religion in various areas and activities of other denominations; a visit with parson Mason L. Weems and his family.

KENNEDY, ALBERT, 1792–1864   1976

In HISTORY OF THE HUME, KENNEDY AND BROCKMAN FAMILIES, by William E. Brockman, pp. 128–130. Washington, D.C.: Press of Chas. H. Potter, 1916.

> 1815–1829. Summary and extracts from diary of Madison County, Virginia, teacher; trips to Kentucky, visits; brief notes of genealogical interest.

KOTZEBUE, OTTO VON, 1787–1846   1977

VOYAGE OF DISCOVERY IN THE SOUTH SEA, AND TO BEHRING'S STRAITS IN SEARCH OF A NORTH–EAST PASSAGE. London: Printed for Sir Richard Phillips, 1821. 220 pp.

> 1815–1818. Exploration journal of voyage on board the RURICK; descriptions of coastal areas from Alaska to California with some detail of San Francisco; the land, people, ceremonies and natural history of the Hawaiian Islands.

MCKENZIE, M.   1978

DeWitt, John H., ed. "Lieutenant McKenzie's Reconnoissance on Mobile Bay." TENNESSEE HISTORICAL MAGAZINE 1 (1915):66–69.

> Jan 1815. Sea journal of a British naval officer.

MILLS, SAMUEL JOHN, 1783–1818   1979

In MEMOIRS OF THE REV. SAMUEL J. MILLS, LATE MISSIONARY TO THE SOUTH WESTERN SECTION OF THE UNITED STATES, by Gardiner Spring, pp. 74–217 passim. New York: New York Evangelical Missionary Society, J. Seymour Printer, 1820.

> 1815–1818. Missionary work in New Orleans, distributing Bibles among American soldiers and British prisoners; voyage to Africa and missionary work and travel in West Africa around Sierra Leone; notes on scenery, sites, dealings with African people; schools in Freetown.

MONTLEZUN, BARTHELEMI SERNIN DU MOULIN DE LA BARTHELLE, baron de, b. 1762?   1980

Yeager, Henry J., ed. "By Steamboat across New Jersey and Back." NEW JERSEY HISTORY 87 (1969):105–118.

> 1815–1816. Anti-Bonaparte aristocrat's account of journey across New Jersey from New York to Philadelphia and return; descriptions of New Jersey and its towns, steamboat accommodations and women encountered while traveling.

Moffatt, L.G. and Carriere, J.M., eds. "A Frenchman Visits Norfolk, Fredericksburg and Orange County." VIRGINIA MAGAZINE OF HISTORY AND BIOGRAPHY 53 (1945):101–123, 197–214.

> Aug–Sep 1816. Extracts of account of journey through Virginia; highly critical of Americans and their society but charmed by President Madison and his family whom he visited at Montpelier.

Carriere, J.M. and Moffatt, L.G., trans. and ed. "A Frenchman Visits Albemarle." ALBEMARLE COUNTY HISTORICAL SOCIETY PAPERS 4 (1943–1944):39–55.

> Sep 1816. Extracts regarding horseback journey from Madison's Montpelier to Monticello; description of Jefferson's Indian artifacts, natural history collections, paintings and other art objects, his house and estate; visit with Monroe at Ash Lawn; return to Montpelier.

Moffatt, Lucius G. and Carriere, Joseph M., eds. "A Frenchman Visits Charleston." SOUTH CAROLINA HISTORICAL AND GENEALOGICAL MAGAZINE 49 (1948):131–154.

> Apr 1817. Travel journal with critical remarks concerning Charleston, its inhabitants and culture; Protestantism; plight of French refugees from Santo Domingo.

NIXON, THOMAS, 1793–1872   1981

In A COMPLETE HISTORY OF METHODISM AS CONNECTED WITH THE MISSISSIPPI CONFERENCE OF THE METHODIST EPISCOPAL CHURCH, SOUTH, by John G. Jones, vol. 1, pp. 396–397. Nashville, Tenn.: Southern Methodist Publishing House, 1887. Rev. ed., by E. Russ Williams, Jr. Baton Rouge: Claitor's Book Store, 1966.

> Nov 1815. Extract from circuit rider's diary kept on return journey with colleagues from Tennessee Conference; from Maury County, Tennessee, to the Pearl River below the Indian Territory; accommodations and mishaps of journey.

PLESSIS, JOSEPH OCTAVE, 1763–1825   1982

Lindsay, Lionel, trans. "Pastoral Visitation of Bishop Plessis of Quebec." AMERICAN CATHOLIC HISTORICAL SOCIETY OF PHILADELPHIA RECORDS 15 (1904):377–402.

> Aug–Sep 1815. Bishop's pastoral visitation along St. Lawrence; visit to Indian mission at Point Pleasant, Maine, and return via Portland, Boston, Worcester, Hartford, New Haven, Albany, Lake Champlain; extracts relating to Catholicism in New England.

REICHEL, GOTTHOLD BENJAMIN, 1785–1833   1983

Bell, Helen, trans. "A Journey to Bethlehem and Nazareth." MORAVIAN HISTORICAL SOCIETY TRANSACTIONS 4 (1892):125–161.

> Sep–Oct 1815. Moravian pastor's journey from Friedensstadt, North Carolina, to Bethlehem and Nazareth, Pennsylvania; pleasant, full descriptions of Moravian communities and people.

RICHARDSON, WILLIAM, 1791–1863   1984

TRAVEL DIARY OF WILLIAM RICHARDSON FROM BOSTON TO NEW ORLEANS BY LAND. New York: Privately printed for Valve Pilot Corporation, 1938. 32 pp.

JOURNAL FROM BOSTON TO THE WESTERN COUNTRY AND DOWN THE OHIO AND MISSISSIPPI RIVERS TO NEW ORLEANS. New York: Privately printed for Valve Pilot Corporation, 1940. 40 pp.

1815-1816. Journal of arduous trip by stagecoach, horseback, steamer and river boat; route, distances covered, road conditions, accommodations; sights along the way; hazards of travel; especially detailed notes on river boat experiences.

ROBERTSON, THOMAS BOLLING, 1779?-1828   1985

JOURNAL OF EVENTS IN PARIS. Philadelphia: Printed and published by M. Carey, 1815. 80 pp.

LETTERS FROM PARIS, WRITTEN DURING THE PERIOD OF THE LATE ACCESSION AND ABDICATION OF NAPOLEON. Washington City: Published by R.C. Weightman, 1816. 201 pp.

    Jun-Jul 1815. Observations of an American congressman in Paris during the accession and abdication of Napoleon.

SCHAFFER, GEORG ANTON, b. 1779   1986

In RUSSIA'S HAWAIIAN ADVENTURE, 1815-1817, by Richard A. Pierce, pp. 157-215. Berkeley: University of California Press, 1965.

    1815-1818. Journal of German doctor's trip to Hawaiian Islands on Russian ship; making trade agreements and negotiating for Russian settlement and return of cargo of Russian American Company's ship BERING; gaining favor with King Kamehameha in spite of interference of Americans; concluding an Act of Subordination; notes on productivity of islands and numerous intrigues.

TICKNOR, GEORGE, 1791-1871   1987

LIFE, LETTERS, AND JOURNALS OF GEORGE TICKNOR. Edited by George S. Hillard. Boston: J.R. Osgood, 1876. 2 vols. Reprint. New York: Houghton Mifflin, 1900; Johnson Reprint, 1968.

    1815-1857. Personal and travel diaries of Harvard professor and author; travel to England and France, study in Göttingen, Italy, Spain, England; residence in England, with travels and visits; professorship at Harvard; efforts for reform there; studies in English and Italian; further extensive travels in Europe; notes on literary and scholarly affairs and on public and literary figures such as Coleridge, Scott, Edgeworth and Macaulay.

1816

ANON.   1988

"Pedestrian Tour." NORTH AMERICAN REVIEW 4 (1817): 175-186.

    May 1816. Journey on foot through Vermont and New England.

BRECKENRIDGE, RICHARD, 1781-1840   1989

Halbert, H.S., ed. "Diary of Richard Breckenridge." ALABAMA HISTORICAL SOCIETY TRANSACTIONS 3 (1898-1899):142-153.

    Aug-Sep 1816. Travel diary fragment; hardships of journey in Tennessee River country; good narrative.

BROWN, URIA, b. 1769   1990

"Uria Brown's Journal." MARYLAND HISTORICAL MAGAZINE 10 (1915):262-283, 344-369; 11 (1916):42-49, 142-157, 218-237, 348-375.

    Jun 1816-Mar 1817. Travel and business journal of journey from Baltimore to Pennsylvania, Virginia, Ohio and Maryland to settle land claims; amusing adventures along the Cumberland Road.

CHAMBERLAIN, ELI, 1795-1817   1991

Chamberlain, Walter, ed. "The Voyage of the GENTOO." ESSEX INSTITUTE HISTORICAL COLLECTIONS 66 (1930): 479-493.

    1816-1817 (with gap). Voyage of the GENTOO from Salem to Calcutta via Cape of Good Hope and return.

CHAMISSO, ADELBERT VON, 1781-1838   1992

In THE VISIT OF THE RURIK TO SAN FRANCISCO IN 1816, by August C. Mahr, pp. 31-51. Stanford University Publications, University Series, History, Economics and Political Science, vol. 2, no. 2. Stanford, Calif.: Stanford University Press, 1932.

    Oct-Nov 1816. Account of poet and naturalist aboard RURIK commanded by Otto von Kotzebue; exchanges between Don Pablo Vicente de Sola, governor of New California, and Kotzebue regarding Russian settlement and trading at Fort Ross (at Port Bodega); criticism of missionaries.

CLERC, LAURENT, 1785-1869   1993

THE DIARY OF LAURENT CLERC'S VOYAGE FROM FRANCE TO AMERICA IN 1816. West Hartford, Conn.: American School for the Deaf, 1952. 22 pp.

    Jun-Aug 1816. Atlantic crossing on board the MARY-AUGUSTA of young Frenchman coming to teach in first American school for the deaf; his time employed in studying English and teaching sign language to Thomas Gallaudet; development of their friendship; religious thoughts and reading; Gallaudet's preaching.

COFFIN, EBENEZER, d. ca. 1816   1994

Easterby, J.H., ed. "Shipbuilding on St. Helena Island in 1816: A Diary of Ebenezer Coffin." SOUTH CAROLINA HISTORICAL AND GENEALOGICAL MAGAZINE 47 (1946): 117-120.

    Feb-Apr 1816. Terse description of goods and services supplied to repair the brig PILGRIM at Coffin's Point Plantation.

FLOWER, GEORGE, ca. 1780-1862   1995

Schmidt, Otto L., ed. "The Mississippi Valley in 1816 through an Englishman's Diary." MISSISSIPPI VALLEY HISTORICAL REVIEW 14 (1927-1928):137-155.

"George Flower: Diarist." CHICAGO HISTORY 1 (1948): 364-368.

    Aug-Nov 1816. Extracts of a young Englishman's journey through New York, Pennsylvania, Ohio, Kentucky, Virginia; observations of slavery, frontier life, taverns, towns; a visit with Thomas Jefferson at Monticello.

GILLAM, JAMES SKELTON   1996

"A Trip to the North." TYLER'S QUARTERLY HISTORICAL AND GENEALOGICAL MAGAZINE 2, no. 1 (July 1920): 294-309.

    Jul-Sep 1816. Trip from Petersburg, Virginia, to Saratoga via Philadelphia and New York; travel and social notes; account with running extracts.

HIGBEE, WILLIAM F. 1997

"Diary of Wm. F. Higbee of a Trip Made to Western Pennsylvania." PENNSYLVANIA MAGAZINE OF HISTORY AND BIOGRAPHY 47 (1923):80-84.

Dec 1816-Aug 1817. Brief notes of journey from Cumberland County, New Jersey, to Kittanning, Pennsylvania, to survey his father's property; return to Somerset via Indiana; expense list; some interesting spellings.

HONEYWELL, ENOCH 1998

In TRAVEL ACCOUNTS OF INDIANA, by Shirley McCord, pp. 73-78.

May-Jun 1816. Extracts from visiting farmer's description of travels on Indiana frontier; notes on soil, water, timber; a meeting of Shaking Quakers and an Indian dance.

LARCOM, JONATHAN, 1768-1834 1999

"Diary of Jonathan Larcom of Beverly, Massachusetts." ESSEX INSTITUTE HISTORICAL COLLECTIONS 87 (1951): 65-95.

1816-1818. Diary of toll keeper at the Essex Bridge connecting Salem and Beverly; mainly weather reports; ship arrivals and departures; some community news; deaths, fires, etc.; grief for the loss of his son; regular entries through early January, 1818; very few thereafter.

MERCER, WILLIAM NEWTON, 1792-1869 2000

Davis, Edwin A. and Andreassen, John C.L., eds. "A Journey from Baltimore to Louisville in 1816." OHIO ARCHAEOLOGICAL AND HISTORICAL QUARTERLY 45 (1936):351-364.

Jul-Sep 1816. Travel diary of planter and surgeon; Baltimore to Louisville by stagecoach, flatboat and horseback; notes on strange sights and characters, scenery, medicinal springs and Indian mounds; interesting.

Davis, Edwin A. and Andreassen, John C.L., eds. "From Louisville to New Orleans in 1816." JOURNAL OF SOUTHERN HISTORY 2 (1936):390-402.

Sep-Oct 1816. Continuation of the same journey; from Louisville to New Orleans by steamboat.

MILLER, JOHN E., 1792-1847 2001

Cross, Jasper W., ed. "John Miller's Missionary Journal." JOURNAL OF PRESBYTERIAN HISTORY 47 (1969): 226-261.

Oct 1816-May 1817. Record of missionary journey through the South and Midwest covering 2,500 miles by horseback; size and reactions of congregations; agricultural and economic conditions; diarist's concern for many communities without ministers; revulsion toward slavery, especially auctions, and desire to educate and evangelize slaves.

NORTH, ASAHEL, 1782-1846 2002

North, Marcus, ed. "Asahel North--Biographical Sketch and Diary." ILLINOIS HISTORICAL SOCIETY JOURNAL 15 (1922-1923):679-687.

Jun-Jul 1816. Journey from Windsor, Vermont, to the Illinois Territory; names of towns; distances.

OGDEN, ELIZA 2003

In CHRONICLES OF A PIONEER SCHOOL, by Emily N. Vanderpoel, pp. 160-176.

1816-1818. Extracts from school diary; lengthy accounts of classes and sermons at Litchfield Female Academy.

PODUSHKIN, IAKOV ANIKIEVICH 2004

Extract in RUSSIA'S HAWAIIAN ADVENTURE, 1815-1817, by Richard A. Pierce, pp. 65-71. Berkeley: University of California Press, 1965.

Mar-Jun 1816. Account by commander of the OTKRY-TIE ordered to Hawaii to reclaim property seized from Russian American Company's ship BERING the previous year by Kaumualii, ruler of Kauai; negotiations with Kamehameha and Kaumualii, exchange of goods, entertainments, return of seized cargo.

ROBERTSON, POWHATAN 2005

"Diary of Powhatan Robertson during His Student Days at William and Mary." WILLIAM AND MARY COLLEGE QUARTERLY, 2d ser. 11 (1931):61-68.

May-Jul 1816, Sep 1818. College diary of student at William and Mary; social life, cutting classes, studies.

SEELY, CATHARINE, 1799-1838 2006

MEMOIRS OF CATHARINE SEELY AND DEBORAH S. ROBERTS. New York: D. Goodwin, 1844. 252 pp. Diary, pp. 16-208 passim.

1816-1838. Religious diary; self-analysis, prayers, self-abasement, illnesses; occasional family notes.

TAYLOR, OLIVER ALDEN, 1801-1851 2007

MEMOIR OF THE REV. OLIVER ALDEN TAYLOR, A.M., LATE OF MANCHESTER, MASSACHUSETTS. By Timothy A. Taylor. Boston: Tappan and Whittemore, 1853. 396 pp. passim.

1816-1851. Extracts from clergyman's journal; undergraduate studies at Union College and theology at Andover; pastoral life at Manchester, Massachusetts; reflections on backslidings; notes on public and local affairs, gold rush, parish trials; a good clerical journal.

THOMAS, DAVID, 1776-1859 2008

TRAVELS THROUGH THE WESTERN COUNTRY IN THE SUMMER OF 1816. Auburn, N.Y.: Printed by David Rumsey, 1819. 320 pp.

Extract in INDIANA AS SEEN BY EARLY TRAVELERS, by Indiana Historical Commission, pp. 42-135.

May-Jul 1816. Journey through western New York, Pennsylvania, West Virginia, southern Ohio, Kentucky, Indiana, Wabash region; pleasant touristic notes, social life, taverns, customs, topography, Indians of Ohio Valley.

WALKER, JAMES 2009

Watts, Emma P., ed. "Diary of the Wilderness Road." KENTUCKY STATE HISTORICAL SOCIETY REGISTER 34 (1941):224-229.

Mar-Jun 1816. Work as manager of Wilderness Road; travel in Kentucky; inns, prices, camping, riding.

1817

ANON.   2010

"A Journey to the West in 1817: Notes of Travel by a Salem Mechanic on His Way to the Ohio." ESSEX INSTITUTE HISTORICAL COLLECTIONS 8 (1866):226-250.

Sep 1817-Feb 1818. Notes of a journey to Ohio, via Bedford and Pittsburgh, and return to New England; an excellent, lively account of trip and criticism of what he saw.

BANGS, HEMEN, 1790-1869   2011

THE AUTOBIOGRAPHY AND JOURNAL OF THE REV. HEMEN BANGS. New York: N. Tibbals and Son, 1872. 385 pp.

1817-1869. Journal of a New England Methodist circuit rider; exhausting travels in all kinds of weather; camp meetings, love feasts, class meetings and conversions; outlines of sermons; religious introspections; many references to teachings of John Wesley; temperance work; controversy over slavery and rented pews; travels in the South and distress over Civil War; a good picture of Methodist work over many years.

BIRKBECK, MORRIS, 1764-1825   2012

NOTES ON A JOURNEY IN AMERICA FROM THE COAST OF VIRGINIA TO THE TERRITORY OF ILLINOIS. Philadelphia: Caleb Richardson, 1817. 139 pp. Frequently reprinted.

Extracts in AMERICAN HISTORY TOLD BY CONTEMPORARIES, edited by Albert B. Hart, vol. 3, pp. 463-467; INDIANA AS SEEN BY EARLY TRAVELERS, by Indiana Historical Commission, pp. 171-190.

Apr-Aug 1817. Englishman's land-hunting journey with George Flower; from Richmond, Virginia, through Pennsylvania, Ohio, Indiana and Illinois; day-by-day narrative of adventures; notes on taverns, characters, towns; a critical commentary by a keen observer and valuable for its picture of frontier life.

BROADDUS, ANDREW, 1770-1848   2013

Blair, John L., ed. "A Baptist Minister Visits Kentucky: The Journal of Andrew Broaddus I." KENTUCKY HISTORICAL SOCIETY REGISTER 71 (1973):393-425.

Oct-Nov 1817. Noted minister's journey from Caroline County, Virginia, to Hopkinsville, Kentucky, to consider appointment as president of the Hopkinsville Academy, which he declined; difficult horseback travel through Cumberland Gap and west on the Wilderness Road; homesickness; visit to Shakers at South Union in Logan County; an interesting, well-written account.

CHESEBROUGH, SILAS, 1796-1845   2014

McGuire, Peter S., ed. "Journal of a Journey to the Westward." AMERICAN HISTORICAL REVIEW 37 (1931-1932):65-88.

Sep-Nov 1817. Extracts from journal of trip from Stonington, Connecticut, to the Ohio Territory, via New Jersey and Pennsylvania; descriptions of route.

COBBETT, WILLIAM, 1763-1835   2015

A YEAR'S RESIDENCE IN THE UNITED STATES OF AMERICA. New York: Printed for the author by Clayton and Kingsland, 1818. 3 pts. in 2 vols.; 2d ed. London:

Sherwood, Neely and Jones, 1819. 3 pts. in 1 vol.; 3d ed. London: The author, 1828. 370 pp.; London: Chapman & Dodd, 1922. 275 pp.; Carbondale: Southern Illinois University Press; Fontwell, Sussex: Centaur, 1964. 338 pp.

Extracts relating to the Birkbeck settlement in INDIANA AS SEEN BY EARLY TRAVELERS, by Indiana Historical Commission, pp. 508-521.

May 1817-Apr 1818. American diary of the noted British reformer, politician and agriculturalist; a year's farming on Long Island; notes on soil, farming, economics, expenses, manners and customs, political and religious institutions.

DEAN, THOMAS, 1783-1844   2016

Dean, John C. and Dean, Randle C., eds. "Journal of Thomas Dean: A Voyage to Indiana in 1817." INDIANA HISTORICAL SOCIETY PUBLICATIONS 6 (1918):273-345.

May-Oct 1817. Journey to Indiana with representative Brothertown Indians to help acquire lands for them; travel by boat to Lake Ontario and through Lakes; portage to mouth of Wabash, by canoe and foot in southern Indiana; return from Fort Wayne to Detroit; good practical details of country and matter-of-fact description of difficulties.

DELAFIELD, JOSEPH, 1790-1875   2017

THE UNFORTIFIED BOUNDARY: A DIARY OF THE FIRST SURVEY OF THE CANADIAN BOUNDARY LINE FROM ST. REGIS TO THE LAKE OF THE WOODS. Edited by Robert McElroy and Thomas Riggs. New York: Privately printed, 1943. 490 pp.

1817-1823. Diary of United States agent directed to survey and determine the boundary as defined by the Treaty of Ghent; careful descriptions of work, route, weather and natural features of country; special personal and scientific interest in mineralogy.

DOUGLASS, DAVID BATES, 1790-1849   2018

Jackman, Sydney W., ed. "David Bates Douglass' Journal: An Account of the Survey of the Eastern Entrance to Long Island Sound." AMERICAN NEPTUNE 24 (1964):280-293.

May-Aug 1817. West Point topographer's journal of a coastal survey conducted for the Army Corps of Engineers; technical details revealing navigational and map-making skills of the time; a few social notes, including dinner with President Monroe.

AMERICAN VOYAGEUR: THE JOURNAL OF DAVID BATES DOUGLASS. Edited by Sydney W. Jackman and John F. Freeman. Marquette: Northern Michigan University Press, 1969. 128 pp.

Apr-Sep 1820. Journal of the 5000 mile Cass Expedition to explore and map upper Great Lakes and northern Mississippi River area; route from Detroit to Fort Gratiot, Mackinac, Sault Sainte Marie, west with excursions to see natural phenomena, up St. Louis River, Sandy Lake, to St. Anthony's Falls; assessment of potential of vast area for commerce and development of resources; negotiations with Indians for land and acute observations of Indian life; notes on geology, botany and canoe travel; activities of Cass and Schoolcraft.

DURAN, NARCISO, 1776-1846   2019

EXPEDITION ON THE SACRAMENTO AND SAN JOAQUIN RIVERS. Edited by Charles E. Chapman. Academy of Pacific Coast History Publication, vol. 2, no. 5.

Berkeley: University of California Press, 1911. 21 pp.

May 1817. Record of priest who accompanied short exploring expedition from San Francisco Presidio up the Sacramento and San Joaquin Rivers; description of rivers, villages and meeting with Indians. Translated from the Spanish.

FLETCHER, CALVIN, 1798-1866   2020

THE DIARY OF CALVIN FLETCHER. Edited by Gayle Thornbrough. Indianapolis: Indiana Historical Society, 1972-(in progress). 6 vols.

1817-1860. Daily life and family vicissitudes of an Indiana lawyer, prosperous farmer, land owner and banker; personal introspection and thoughts on religion of a staunch Methodist; costs and cares of raising a family of eleven children.

FLUEGEL, J.G., d. 1855   2021

Flugel, Felix, ed. "Pages from a Journal of a Voyage down the Mississippi to New Orleans." LOUISIANA HISTORICAL QUARTERLY 7 (1924):414-440.

Jan-Jun 1817. German trader's journal of a trip down the Mississippi to New Orleans.

FORDHAM, ELIAS PYM, b. 1763   2022

PERSONAL NARRATIVE OF TRAVELS IN VIRGINIA, MARYLAND, PENNSYLVANIA, OHIO, INDIANA, KENTUCKY; AND OF A RESIDENCE IN THE ILLINOIS TERRITORY. Edited by Frederic A. Ogg. Cleveland: Arthur H. Clark, 1906. 248 pp. Diary, pp. 136-169.

Dec 1817-Feb 1818. English immigrant diary; daily happenings at English Prairie, Illinois; trip down the Patoka; winter work; journey to Kentucky; trip across the Wabash in search of lands; interesting account of Birkbeck settlement.

GATES, GUERDON   2023

Guthrie, Blaine A., ed. "A Visit by That Confidential Character--President Monroe." FILSON CLUB HISTORY QUARTERLY 51 (1977):44-48.

Sep 1817. Washington College student's reaction to visit of President Monroe to Washington, Pennsylvania.

Guthrie, Blaine A., and Guthrie, Mitchell R., eds. "Catfish, Cornmeal and the Broad Canopy of Heaven: The Journal of the Reverend Guerdon Gates." KENTUCKY HISTORICAL SOCIETY REGISTER 66 (1968):3-34.

Dec 1841-Mar 1842. Baptist minister's account of arduous journey up the Red River by keelboat with party formed in Louisville and bound for free land offered near present Dallas-Fort Worth area; return by skiff to Shreveport; a fascinating account reflecting many human elements of the westward movement and settlement of Texas.

GREENE, WELCOME ARNOLD, 1795-1870   2024

THE JOURNALS OF WELCOME ARNOLD GREENE. Edited by Howard Greene and Alice E. Smith. Madison: State Historical Society of Wisconsin, 1956-1957. 2 vols.

1817-1820. Sea diary of young Quaker on merchant ship PERSEVERANCE; ports of call in Norway, Spain, South America, Cuba; cargo, trade, scenes and mores of places visited.

1822-1824. Business trip to the South, partly to try to find long missing relative; horseback, stagecoach and river steamer travel throughout southern states; visits with Quakers and business contacts; notes on agriculture, scenery, prospects for development of frontier areas; anecdotes of people along the way; interesting and detailed.

KEEN, JAMES   2025

"James Keen's Journal of a Passage from Philadelphia to Blackbeard Island, Georgia, for Live Oak Timber." AMERICAN NEPTUNE 35 (1975):227-247.

Nov 1817-Apr 1818. New England shipwright's account of life and work at a live oak logging camp where he was cutting timber for building United States Navy ships; work of New England loggers and Georgia slaves; problems with sickness and drunkenness among workers.

KELLOGG, EBENEZER, 1789-1846   2026

Martin, Sidney W., ed. "Ebenezer Kellogg's Visit to Charleston." SOUTH CAROLINA HISTORICAL AND GENEALOGICAL MAGAZINE 49 (1948):1-14.

Nov-Dec 1817. Extracts from journal Williams College professor kept for one of his colleagues during a trip south for his health; descriptions of Charleston streets, architecture, religious life, the condition of house slaves.

Martin, Sidney W., ed. "A New Englander's Impressions of Georgia." JOURNAL OF SOUTHERN HISTORY 12 (1946):247-262.

Dec 1817-Jan 1818. Extracts covering impressions of Georgia; travel by stagecoach; descriptions of physical and social environment, notes on Savannah, comments on slavery and comparisons between North and South.

KEYS, WILLARD   2027

"A Journal of Life in Wisconsin One Hundred Years Ago." WISCONSIN MAGAZINE OF HISTORY 3 (1919-1920): 339-363, 443-465.

1817-1819. Canoe journey to Wisconsin with Peters colony and two years at Prairie du Chien; school-teaching, milling, logging; brief notes of his own activities; a valuable diary of early Wisconsin life.

LAFITTE, JEAN, 1782-1854?   2028

Warren, Harris G., trans. and ed. "Documents Relating to the Establishment of Privateers at Galveston." LOUISIANA HISTORICAL QUARTERLY 21 (1938):1086-1109. Journal, pp. 1102-1107.

Mar-May 1817. Pirate's journal of voyage from New Orleans to Galveston, kept while he was in the service of Spain; privateers at Galveston.

LANGSLOW, RICHARD   2029

"A Niagara Falls Tourist of the Year 1817." BUFFALO HISTORICAL SOCIETY PUBLICATIONS 5 (1902):111-133.

Sep-Oct 1817. Travel journal of a captain in the East India service; from New London to New York by steamboat, by coach to Albany, Utica, Buffalo, Niagara, Batavia, Utica, and return; tourist's notes on inns, food, scenery, etc.; expense list.

LIPPINCOTT, THOMAS, 1791-1869   2030

Rammelkamp, Charles H., ed. "Thomas Lippincott, a Pioneer of 1818 and His Diary." ILLINOIS HISTORICAL SOCIETY JOURNAL 10 (1917-1918):237-255.

In A FAMILY HISTORY IN LETTERS AND DOCUMENTS,

1667–1837, edited by Emily H.G. Noyes, pp. 331–342. St. Paul, Minn.: Privately printed, 1919.

Nov 1817–Feb 1818. Journey with wife and baby through Easton, Steubenville, Marietta, Maysville, Augusta, St. Louis; notes on companions, conditions of travel, places, etc.; a good narrative.

LONG, STEPHEN HARRIMAN, 1784–1864   2031

THE NORTHERN EXPEDITIONS OF STEPHEN H. LONG: THE JOURNALS OF 1817 AND 1823 AND RELATED DOCUMENTS. Edited by Lucile M. Kane, June D. Holmquist and Caroline Gilman. Minneapolis: Minnesota Historical Society, 1978. 407 pp.

Jul–Aug 1817, Apr–Oct 1823. Journals from two Corps of Topographical Engineers exploring expeditions; from Belle Fontaine to the Falls of St. Anthony, from Philadelphia to Minnesota, and return via old Canadian fur trade route; Indian relations; long descriptions of places and antiquities.

VOYAGE IN A SIX-OARED SKIFF TO THE FALLS OF SAINT ANTHONY IN 1817. With an introductory note by Edward D. Neill. Minnesota Historical Society Collections pt. 1. Philadelphia: H.B. Ashmead, Printer, 1860. 2d ed. Minnesota Historical Society Collections, vol. 2. St. Paul, Minn., 1889.

Jul–Aug 1817.

In THE BAPTISTS, 1783–1830: A COLLECTION OF SOURCE MATERIAL, edited by William Warren Sweet, pp. 625–628. Religion on the American Frontier, vol. 1. New York: H. Holt, 1931.

Jun 1823.

LYE, JOSEPH, 1792–1834   2032

Tapley, Henry F., ed. "An Old New England Town as Seen by Joseph Lye, Cordwainer." LYNN HISTORICAL SOCIETY REGISTER 19 (1915):36–54.

1817–1832. Extracts from private diary of Lynn, Massachusetts, shoemaker; notes on weather, church and local affairs, reading, fishing, camp meetings.

PALMER, JOHN   2033

JOURNAL OF TRAVELS IN THE UNITED STATES OF NORTH AMERICA. London: Sherwood, Neely and Jones, 1818. 456 pp.

Mar–Oct 1817. Englishman's travel journal of voyage to New York; by stage to Pittsburgh, via Bedford, Stoyestown and Greensburg; by boat down the Ohio; information on land prices, economics and towns in Ohio, Indiana, Illinois and Missouri.

PERKINS, SAMUEL HUNTINGTON, 1797–1874   2034

McLean, Robert C., ed. "A Yankee Tutor in the Old South." NORTH CAROLINA HISTORICAL REVIEW 47 (1970): 51–85.

Oct 1817–Mar 1818. Journey from Connecticut, by boat and gig, to teaching post in North Carolina; thoughts during first months of residence; remarks on dissipation, health and hospitality of inhabitants of Virginia and North Carolina; observations of and opinions on slavery.

SCHULZ, THOMAS   2035

"School Diary of Thomas Schulz." In RECORDS OF THE MORAVIANS IN NORTH CAROLINA, edited by Adelaide L. Fries, vol. 7, pp. 3332–3343.

Aug–Dec 1817. Diary of teacher in the Moravian boys' school in Salem, North Carolina; school life, classes in morning, activities in afternoon; weather; severe attack of fever.

SEWALL, WILLIAM, 1797–1846   2036

DIARY OF WILLIAM SEWALL. Edited by John Goodell. Lincoln, Ill.: Printed by Gordon and Feldman, 1930. 283 pp.

1817–1846. Extracts from private diary; extensive daily record; travels in Maine, Maryland, Virginia and Illinois; schooling, farming, weather, visits, church and local matters, courtship; an interesting record of country life in Augusta, Maine.

SMITH, RICHARD, 1784–1824   2037

Crosfield, John Dymond, ed. "Richard Smith and His Journal." FRIENDS' HISTORICAL SOCIETY JOURNAL 13 (1916):49–58, 89–98, 129–141; 14 (1917):15–25, 59–71, 108–121.

1817–1824. Quaker journal; joining Friends in Ohio; journey to New York through Pennsylvania; Kentucky; trade, religion and journeys.

1818

ANON.   2038

"Mission among the Cherokees." MISSIONARY HERALD 14 (1818):200–204, 213–216, 242–245; 15 (1819):17–22, 154–159, 176–182; 16 (1820):34–39, 49–53, 87–92, 145–149; 17 (1821):21–23, 43–49, 71–74, 283–287, 305–307, 337–342; 18 (1822):13–16, 105–107, 284–287, 305–309; 19 (1823):44–46, 169–172, 341–343.

1818–1823. Missionary's official journal, kept at Brainerd mission in Cherokee Nation; at Hoyt, Butrick, Chamberlain; interesting details of Indians and missionary work, social life and visits.

ABBOT, ABIEL, 1770–1828   2039

Moore, John Hammond, ed. "The Abiel Abbot Journals: A Yankee Preacher in Charleston Society." SOUTH CAROLINA HISTORICAL MAGAZINE 68 (1967):51–73, 115–139, 232–254.

Nov–Dec 1818, Nov 1827. Interesting view of life in Charleston provided by Unitarian minister sojourning there to restore his health; detailed descriptions of social and cultural institutions; library, hospital, churches, etc.; socializing with prominent residents, including Samuel F.B. Morse; commentary on slavery; brief critiques of sermons; visit to Henry Izard's plantation, The Elms.

BACON, SAMUEL, 1781–1820   2040

In MEMOIR OF THE LIFE AND CHARACTER OF THE REV. SAMUEL BACON, A.M., LATE AN OFFICER OF MARINES IN THE UNITED STATES' SERVICE; AFTERWARDS, ATTORNEY AT LAW IN THE STATE OF PENNSYLVANIA; AND SUBSEQUENTLY, A MINISTER OF THE EPISCOPAL CHURCH, AND PRINCIPAL AGENT OF THE AMERICAN GOVERNMENT FOR PERSONS LIBERATED FROM SLAVE-SHIPS, ON THE COAST OF AFRICA, by Jehudi Ashmun, pp. 138–274 passim. Washington, D.C.: J. Gideon, Junior, Printer, 1822.

1818–1820. Extracts describing work in Sunday school movement in New York, and later as minister; work for African agency of Bible Society; journey to Africa on behalf of African slaves; work and death in Sierra Leone.

BINGHAM, HENRY VEST, 1785?-1823   2041

Windell, Marie G., ed. "The Road West in 1818: The Diary of Henry Vest Bingham." MISSOURI HISTORICAL REVIEW 40 (1945-1946):21-54, 174-204.

Extracts in TRAVEL ACCOUNTS OF INDIANA, compiled by Shirley S. McCord, pp. 88-92.

> May-Jul 1818. Diary kept by father of artist George Caleb Bingham during trip from Virginia to Missouri and back; through Kentucky, Tennessee, Indiana and Illinois, scouting possibilities for family's move west; detailed description of countryside and settlements; land quality and prices.

BRIDGHAM, ELIZA WILLIAMS, 1799-1882   2042

"A Journey through New England and New York in 1818." MAGAZINE OF HISTORY 2 (1905):14-27, 90-95.

> Jul-Aug 1818. Newport, Rhode Island, resident's diary, written for her sister; travel in New England and New York; descriptions of places and social details.

BUTLER, ROBERT S.   2043

In BEGINNINGS OF WEST TENNESSEE, by Samuel C. Williams, app. A, pp. 283-300. Johnson City, Tenn.: Watauga Press, 1930.

> Sep-Oct 1818. Journal kept by secretary to Indian treaty commission; treaty with Chickasaw Indians at Old Town (near Tuscumbia, Alabama); conferences, etc.

CAMPBELL, GEORGE WASHINGTON, 1769-1848   2044

Jordan, Weymouth T., ed. "Diary of George Washington Campbell, American Minister to Russia." TENNESSEE HISTORICAL QUARTERLY 7 (1948):152-170, 259-280.

Extracts concerning official duties in "Excerpts from the Diary of a Tennessean at the Court of the Tsar," edited by Weymouth T. Jordan. EAST TENNESSEE HISTORICAL SOCIETY PUBLICATIONS 15 (1943):104-109.

> 1818-1820. Personal diary of Minister to Russia, focusing on family and social rather than official activities; sea voyage to Russia with stops at Isle of Wight and Copenhagen; sights of St. Petersburg and nearby area; death of three of his children in one week; sea voyage to London, sightseeing and social activities there.

CAMPBELL, HUGH, 1797-1879   2045

Brooks, George R., ed. "The Journal of Hugh Campbell." MISSOURI HISTORICAL SOCIETY BULLETIN 23 (1867):241-268.

> Jun-Oct 1818. Written for family and friends in 1819 from notes of previous year's journey from Ireland to America; misfortunes, kindness and generosity of strangers; being "smuggled" into United States; search for job in New York City and Philadelphia; travel through New Jersey.

CARY, ANNE M.   2046

In THE CARY LETTERS, edited by Caroline G.C. Curtis, pp. 247-269. Cambridge, Mass.: Printed at the Riverside Press, 1891.

> Jul 1818. Letter-diary containing touristic notes of a journey from Chelsea, Massachusetts, to Canada; Albany, Schenectady, Lake Ontario.

CLARK, LAURA DOWNS, 1798-1863   2047

"The Original Diary of Mrs. Laura (Downs) Clark, Wakeman, Ohio." FIRELANDS PIONEER, n.s. 21 (1920): 2309-2326.

> Jun-Oct 1818. Excellent and detailed diary of doctor's wife; domestic matters; loneliness and nostalgia; valuable and intimate record of pioneer life in Firelands, Ohio, area.

COX, CALEB   2048

Jensen, Mrs. Dana O., ed. "New Orleans to St. Louis and Return, 1819." MISSOURI HISTORICAL SOCIETY BULLETIN 8 (1952):151-174.

> Aug 1818-Feb 1819. Diary kept on board a Mississippi River steamboat for his fiance; grounding of boat, illness and deaths of several crewmen; diarist's attempts to aid the sick who were refused treatment on shore; his own eventual illness; effusive and lovelorn in places.

CUTLER, BENJAMIN CLARKE, 1798-1863   2049

In MEMOIRS OF REV. BENJAMIN C. CUTLER, D.D., LATE RECTOR OF ST. ANN'S CHURCH, BROOKLYN, N.Y., by Horatio Gray, pp. 16-334 passim. New York: A.D.F. Randolph, 1865.

> 1818-1860. Extracts from private and religious diary; college life; work and reflections.

ENDICOTT, MARY, 1800-1871?   2050

SALEM PRESS HISTORICAL AND GENEALOGICAL RECORD 2 (1892):112-122, 171-176. Continued in "Mary Endicott's Diary." PUTNAM'S MONTHLY HISTORICAL MAGAZINE 1 (1892-1893):28-31, 61-63, 125-127, 250-253.

> 1818-1863. Extracts from private diary, selected mainly for genealogical interest; births, deaths, marriages; some general notes and local affairs in Danvers, Massachusetts.

ENGELBRECHT, JACOB, 1797-1878   2051

THE DIARY OF JACOB ENGELBRECHT. Edited by William R. Quynn. Frederick, Md.: Historical Society of Frederick County, 1976. 3 vols.

> 1818-1878. Uncorrected diary of tailor in Frederick, Maryland, kept until one month before his death; reads like a newspaper; deaths and marriages of town folk and notable people in other parts of the country; political affairs, elections (all elected named); religious life; participation in musical events; business affairs, prices of goods; natural disasters and unusual occurrences; quotations, rhymes and riddles; views on Civil War and its effects on Frederick; occasional entries in German.

FAUX, WILLIAM   2052

MEMORABLE DAYS IN AMERICA. London: W. Simpkin and R. Marshall, 1823. 488 pp. Reprint. In EARLY WESTERN TRAVELS, edited by Reuben G. Thwaites, vol. 11, pp. 16-305, vol. 12, pp. 11-138; New York: AMS Press, 1969.

Extracts relating to Indiana in INDIANA AS SEEN BY EARLY TRAVELERS, by Indiana Historical Commission, pp. 290-326.

> 1818-1820. English farmer's journey to America to ascertain prospects for British emigrants, especially in Birkbeck settlement; Boston, Charleston, Washington, Philadelphia, New York, Illinois,

English Prairie; return to England; satirical, abusive picture of American life and domestic manners.

GALE, JOHN, 1795?-1830   **2053**

THE MISSOURI EXPEDITION, 1818-1820: THE JOURNAL OF SURGEON JOHN GALE. Edited by Roger L. Nichols. American Exploration and Travel Series, no. 56. Norman: University of Oklahoma Press, 1969. 145 pp.

1818-1820. Army surgeon's account of movement of men and supplies up the Missouri River under grueling conditions; encounters and dealings with Indians, including quotation of eloquent self-defense of Indian chief on trial. Journal originally attributed to Lieutenant Thomas W. Kavanaugh.

GILMAN, REBECCA, 1746-1823   **2054**

In A FAMILY HISTORY IN LETTERS AND DOCUMENTS, by Emily H.G. Noyes, vol. 1, pp. 351-352. St. Paul, Minn.: Privately printed, 1919.

1818-1819. Fragments from private diary; visit to Providence; reading, domestic affairs.

GUILD, JAMES, 1797-1841   **2055**

"From Tunbridge, Vermont, to London, England." VERMONT HISTORICAL SOCIETY PROCEEDINGS, n.s. 5 (1937):249-314.

1818-1824. Travels of Vermont peddler and jack-of-all-trades in various states; Vermont, New York, Pennsylvania, etc.; journey to England; occasional work as tinker, schoolmaster, portrait painter; experiences and impressions from time to time; occasional verses; a most unusual and entertaining diary with some linguistic interest.

HITCHCOCK, ETHAN ALLEN, 1798-1870   **2056**

FIFTY YEARS IN CAMP AND FIELD, DIARY OF MAJOR-GENERAL ETHAN ALLEN HITCHCOCK. Edited by W.A. Croffut. New York and London: G.P. Putnam's Sons, 1909. 514 pp. Reprint. Freeport, N.Y.: Books for Libraries, 1971.

1818-1868. Extracts with running editorial narrative; life at West Point; Florida wars, Mexican War, Civil War; abundant non-military notes, travel abroad, comments on literature, philosophy, etc.

A TRAVELER IN INDIAN TERRITORY; THE JOURNAL OF ETHAN ALLEN HITCHCOCK. Edited by Grant Foreman. Cedar Rapids, Iowa: Torch Press, 1930. 270 pp.

Nov 1841-Apr 1842. Journal kept during investigation in Indian Territory of the charges of fraud and profiteering against contractors who removed Indians west of the Mississippi River; private notes of what he saw and heard and his impressions; a valuable account of the seamier side of frontier life and the misfortunes of the Indians.

HOBSON, SAMUEL   **2057**

"1818: A Tour in the United States." In TRAVEL IN THE TWO LAST CENTURIES OF THREE GENERATIONS, edited by Samuel R. Roget, pp. 136-157. London: T.F. Unwin, 1921; New York: D. Appleton, 1922.

May-Jul 1818. Extracts from Englishman's travel diary; from Philadelphia to Lancaster, noting prosperous farms; bad roads over the Allegheny Mountains; Pittsburgh, with its gloomy appearance from manufacturing; seven and a half days down

the Ohio on a "clumsy contrivance . . . like an orange box," seeing self-sufficient farms and congenial people along the banks; Cincinnati; to Louisville in a skiff, noting steamboat traffic between Louisville and New Orleans; to Birkbeck's settlement and New Harmony, Indiana, with brief description of community there.

HODGE, CHARLES, 1797-1878   **2058**

Cashdollar, Charles D., ed. "The Pursuit of Piety: Charles Hodge's Diary." JOURNAL OF PRESBYTERIAN HISTORY 55 (1977):267-283.

1818-1820. Spiritual diary kept during time between graduation from Princeton Theological Seminary and appointment to the faculty; preaching in small churches in Philadelphia area; doubts of his own piety and worthiness to be a minister.

HULME, THOMAS   **2059**

"Mr. Hulme's Journal Made during a Tour in the Western Countries of America." In A YEAR'S RESIDENCE IN THE UNITED STATES OF AMERICA, by William Cobbett, pp. 253-283. New York: Printed for the author by Clayton and Kingsland, 1818. 3 pts. in 2 vols.; 2d ed. London: Sherwood, Neely and Jones, 1819. 3 pts. in 1 vol.; 3d ed. London: The author, 1828. 370 pp.; London: Chapman & Dodd, 1922. 275 pp.; Carbondale: Southern Illinois University Press; Fontwell, Sussex: Centaur, 1964. 338 pp. Reprint. In EARLY WESTERN TRAVELS, edited by Reuben G. Thwaites, vol. 10, pp. 17-84.

Sep 1818-Aug 1819. English farmer's tour in Ohio, Indiana, Illinois; by stage and Ohio riverboat; return overland; description of Birkbeck's settlement.

LEIGHTON, SAMUEL, 1771-1848   **2060**

Jewell, Margaret H. "Country Life in Maine, a Century Ago: Gleanings from the Diary of General Samuel Leighton of Alfred, Maine." OLD-TIME NEW ENGLAND 23 (1932):28-38, 71-82.

1818-1848. Summary, sprinkled with quotations, of diary kept by farmer/innkeeper, who at various times also served as jailor, justice of the peace and judge; work activities, family news, local events, etc.

NEWTON, EBENEZER, 1790-1859   **2061**

Newton, Charlotte, ed. "Ebenezer Newton's 1818 Diary." GEORGIA HISTORICAL QUARTERLY 53 (1969):205-219.

Oct-Nov 1818. Presbyterian's diary of carriage trip from Athens, Georgia, to Tennessee; lodgings along the way, often with settled, Christian Cherokee Indians, and at mission stations; visits with relatives; reactions to church services and camp meetings.

OWEN, JOHN, 1786-1848   **2062**

"John Owen's Journal of His Removal from Virginia to Alabama in 1818." SOUTHERN HISTORICAL ASSOCIATION PUBLICATIONS 1 (1897):89-97.

Oct-Dec 1818. Move of diarist and family from Norfolk County to Tuscaloosa; brief notes of stages and minor hardships.

PINCKNEY, CHARLES COTESWORTH, 1746-1825   **2063**

In PLANTATION AND FRONTIER DOCUMENTS, edited by Ulrich B. Phillips, vol. 1, pp. 203-208.

Easterly, J.H., ed. "Charles Cotesworth Pinckney's Plantation Diary." SOUTH CAROLINA HISTORICAL AND GENEALOGICAL MAGAZINE 41 (1940):135-150.

Apr-Dec 1818. Work on plantation on Pinckney Island, near Charleston, South Carolina; plantation management, planting and tending crops; supplies for slaves.

RUSSELL, JONATHAN, 1771-1832   2064

"Journal of Jonathan Russell." MASSACHUSETTS HISTORICAL SOCIETY PROCEEDINGS 51 (1917-1918):369-498.

Oct 1818-May 1819. Lengthy notes in diplomat's travel diary; journey from Stockholm to Berlin, Vienna, and through Italy; meetings with Metternich and other important Europeans; opinions on objets d'art, ruins, towns, customs, religion, etc.; intelligent American appraisals.

SCHOOLCRAFT, HENRY ROWE, 1793-1864   2065

A VIEW OF THE LEAD MINES OF MISSOURI. New York: Charles Wiley, 1819. 299 pp.

SCENES AND ADVENTURES IN THE SEMI-ALPINE REGION OF THE OZARK MOUNTAINS OF MISSOURI AND ARKANSAS. Philadelphia: Lippincott, Grambo, 1853. 256 pp.

1818. Daily notes of journey up the Mississippi, from the mouth of the Ohio to St. Louis; notes on mineralogy, geography, sociology, etc.

JOURNAL OF A TOUR INTO THE INTERIOR OF MISSOURI AND ARKANSAS. Collection of Modern and Contemporary Voyages and Travels, 3d ser., vol. 4, no. 5. London: Printed for Sir R. Phillips, 1821. 102 pp.

Nov 1818-Feb 1819. From Potosi in Missouri Territory through Arkansas to the Rockies; long descriptions of geography, topography, people and personal adventures.

NARRATIVE JOURNAL OF TRAVELS THROUGH THE NORTH-WESTERN REGIONS OF THE UNITED STATES. Albany: E.&E. Hosford, 1821. 419 pp. Reprint. TRAVELS THROUGH THE NORTHWESTERN REGIONS OF THE UNITED STATES. Ann Arbor: University Microfilms, 1966.

NARRATIVE JOURNAL OF TRAVELS THROUGH THE NORTH-WESTERN REGIONS OF THE UNITED STATES. Edited by Mentor L. Williams. East Lansing: Michigan State College Press, 1953. 520 pp.

SUMMARY NARRATIVE OF AN EXPLORATORY EXPEDITION TO THE SOURCES OF THE MISSISSIPPI RIVER. Philadelphia: Lippincott, Grambo, 1855. 596 pp.

Extracts in "Dubuque in 1820, August 7th," edited by William Salter. IOWA HISTORICAL RECORD 16 (1900): 100-106.

Mar-Sep 1820. Journal kept while member of Governor Cass's expedition; description and travel in the Old Northwest from Detroit through the Great Lakes to the sources of the Mississippi.

TRAVELS IN THE CENTRAL PORTIONS OF THE MISSISSIPPI VALLEY. New York: Collins and Hannay, 1825. 459 pp.

1821. With General Cass on expedition down Wabash and Ohio rivers to Shawneetown; by wagon across southern Illinois to St. Louis; up the Mississippi and Illinois rivers to Peoria; by horseback to Chicago; Indian treaty; notes on geography, Indians.

1819

ANON.   2066

"Mission among the Choctaws." MISSIONARY HERALD 15 (1819):220-225; 16 (1820):1-5, 149-155, 169-176; 17 (1821):48-52, 74-76, 287-292, 307-313, 342-344; 18 (1822):76-80, 179-182, 378-379; 19 (1823):114-116.

1819-1822. Very interesting official journal kept by American Board missionary at Elliott Mission among the Choctaw Nation; farming and mission work; journey to found a new mission.

BAGLEY, LOWELL, 1784-1860   2067

In THE HISTORY OF A HOUSE, by Mary H.B. Longyear, pp. 12-32. Brookline, Mass.: Zion Research Foundation, 1925; 2d ed., rev., pp. 8-33. Brookline, Mass.: Longyear Foundation, 1947.

1819-1850. Pleasant diary of a man of consequence in Amesbury, Massachusetts; merchant, farmer, justice of the peace; family life, church, business; the delights of nature; visits to Boston.

BROWN, JACOB, 1775-1828   2068

BUFFALO HISTORICAL SOCIETY PUBLICATIONS 24 (1920): 296-323.

May-Jul 1819. Army general's military journal, covering inspection tour around garrisons of Great Lakes via Brownville, Oswego, Genesee, Niagara, Fort George, Buffalo, Detroit, Mackinac, Green Bay, etc.; mostly descriptions of scenery and social notes.

CHAMBERLAIN, DANIEL, 1782-1860   2069

THREE CHAMBERLAIN JOURNALS (1819-1823) FROM BOSTON TO THE SANDWICH ISLANDS AND BACK. Prepared by Calvin S. Hathaway. Philadelphia, 1965. 4, 50, 28, 60 leaves.

Nov 1819-Jul 1820; Mar-May 1823. Diaries of New England lay missionary, member of first Hawaiian venture of the American Board of Commissioners for Foreign Missions; voyages on ships THADDEUS and PEARLE described in detail; life in Hawaii with his wife and children, religious practices and other customs of Hawaiians, acceptance of Christianity by some; persecution of missionaries by Captain of PEARLE.

ELLIS, IRA J.   2070

"A Trip to Kentucky: Diary of Ira J. Ellis." VIRGINIA MAGAZINE OF HISTORY AND BIOGRAPHY 41 (1933):33-40.

May-Jun 1819. Travel diary; horseback from Pittsylvania County, Virginia, to Kentucky, and return.

EMERSON, RALPH WALDO, 1803-1882   2071

THE JOURNALS AND MISCELLANEOUS NOTEBOOKS. Edited by William H. Gilman et al. Cambridge: Belknap Press of Harvard University, 1960-1982. 16 vols.

JOURNALS OF RALPH WALDO EMERSON. Edited by Edward Waldo Emerson and Waldo Emerson Forbes. Boston and New York: Houghton, Mifflin, 1909-1914. 10 vols.

THE HEART OF EMERSON'S JOURNALS. Edited by Bliss Perry. Boston and New York: Houghton, Mifflin, 1926. 357 pp. Reprint. New York: Dover, 1958.

JOURNALS. Abridged and edited by Robert N. Linscott. New York: Modern Library, 1960. 463 pp.

1819-1882. Copious journals, notebooks and common-place books; Emerson's reading, reflections, ideas for poems and essays; his doubts and soul-search-ings; glimpses of friends, intellectual companions and adversaries, such as Channing, Thoreau, Web-ster and Alcott; work as a Unitarian minister, decision to leave the ministry; lecture tours, the processes of philosophical thinking and essay-writing; a vast, important and unclassifiable work.

EMERSON IN HIS JOURNALS. Edited by Joel Porte. Cambridge: Belknap Press of Harvard University, 1982. 588 pp.

1820-1874. Extracts.

ESTUDILLO, JOSE MARIA   2072

Gayton, A.H. "Estudillo among the Yokuts." In ESSAYS IN ANTHROPOLOGY PRESENTED TO A.L. KROEBER IN CELEBRATION OF HIS SIXTIETH BIRTHDAY, pp. 67-85. Berkeley: University of California Press, 1936.

Oct-Nov 1819. Diary kept by the commandant of Presidio of Monterey on a campaign ordered by Governor Don Pablo Vizente de Sola for reconnais-sance of rancherios on plains of Sierra Nevada; observations on Indians and their customs, nature and fertility of the land; advice to proselytize Yokut Indians in their homeland to prevent leaving coastal missions and recommendation of Kings River as good location for a new mission and garrison.

In DIARIES AND ACCOUNTS OF THE ROMERO EXPEDITIONS IN ARIZONA AND CALIFORNIA, 1823-1826, pp. 30-51. Palm Springs, Calif.: Palm Springs Desert Museum, 1962.

Nov 1823-Jan 1824. Expedition to open a road to Colorado River; from San Diego to rendezvous point with Romero at San Gabriel; description of each day's march across the desert; distances, terrain, supplies, availability of water and pasture, difficulties with pack mules and horses; return without reaching river due to lack of provisions and loss of horses.

FIELD, GABRIEL, d. 1823   2073

Nichols, Roger L., ed. "The Camp Missouri-Chariton Road, 1819: The Journal of Lt. Gabriel Field." MIS-SOURI HISTORICAL SOCIETY BULLETIN 24 (1967-1968): 139-152.

Oct-Nov 1819. Journal kept by young army officer in charge of surveying the route for a road which would link the newly established Camp Missouri, near Council Bluffs, with settlements farther down the Missouri River; straightforward descriptions of countryside.

FORSYTH, THOMAS, 1771-1833   2074

"Journal of a Voyage from St. Louis to the Falls of St. Anthony." WISCONSIN STATE HISTORICAL SOCIETY COLLECTIONS 6 (1872, reprint 1908):188-219. Reprint. MINNESOTA HISTORICAL SOCIETY COLLECTIONS 3 (1870-1880):139-167.

Jun-Sep 1819. Travel diary of Peoria, Illinois, fur trader with Leavenworth's expedition to establish Fort Snelling; by water from St. Louis to Falls of St. Anthony and return; interesting details, especially about the lead mines and Indians of the upper Mississippi.

FRANCIS, CONVERS, 1795-1863   2075

Woodall, Guy R., ed. "The Journals of Convers Francis (Part One)." In STUDIES IN THE AMERICAN RENAIS-SANCE, 1981, edited by Joel Myerson, pp. 265-343. Boston: Twayne, 1981.

1819-1824. Preaching and pastoral work of a humble and conscientious Congregationalist minis-ter, later Unitarian and transcendentalist in Watertown, Massachusetts; pulpit exchanges, notes on other ministers, Unitarian controversy.

Myerson, Joel, ed. "Convers Francis and Emerson." AMERICAN LITERATURE 50 (1978):17-36.

1835-1863. Extracts relating to Unitarian minister's contacts with and reactions to Emerson; lectures, conversations, meetings of a "society for the dis-cussion of great subjects"; encounters with Bronson Alcott, George Ripley and other Boston area transcendentalists.

GOLDIE, JOHN, 1793-1886   2076

DIARY OF A JOURNEY THROUGH UPPER CANADA AND SOME OF THE NEW ENGLAND STATES, 1819. Toronto: W. Tyrrell, 1897. 56 pp.

1819. Scottish botanist's travel diary of journey, mostly afoot, through eastern Canada and New England; mainly botanical and travel notes with a few political entries and echoes of the War of 1812.

GREENLEAF, MARY COOMBS, 1800-1857   2077

LIFE AND LETTERS OF MISS MARY C. GREENLEAF. Boston: Massachusetts Sabbath School Society, 1858. 446 pp. Diary, pp. 20-340 passim.

1819-1857. Extracts containing notes on religious life and reflections, health, family; missionary work among Chickasaw Indians.

HALLOCK, WILLIAM ALLEN, 1794-1880   2078

MEMORIAL OF REV. WM. A. HALLOCK, D.D., FIRST SECRETARY OF THE AMERICAN TRACT SOCIETY. By Helen C. Knight. New York: American Tract Society, 1882. 110 pp. Journal, pp. 13-75 passim.

1819-1851. Life in seminary at Andover; preaching tours; founding of American Tract Society and his work for it; family notes.

HAMBLETON, JOHN NEEDLES, b. 1798   2079

Vivian, James F., ed. "The Orinoco River and Angos-tura, Venezuela, in the Summer of 1819: The Narrative of a Maryland Naval Chaplain." THE AMERICAS: A QUARTERLY REVIEW OF INTER-AMERICAN CULTURAL HISTORY 24 (1967):160-183.

Jul-Aug 1819. Record of Commodore Oliver Hazard Perry's mission to suppress Latin American piracy and privateering against United States ships; patrolling of Orinoco River in ships JOHN ADAMS and NONSUCH; notes on Indians, Spaniards; the town of Angostura, its inhabitants and officials; government policies of Venezuela; yellow fever epidemic on board ships.

HAWKINS, JOHN HENRY WILLIS, 1797-1858   2080

In LIFE OF JOHN H.W. HAWKINS, compiled by William G. Hawkins, pp. 23-191 passim. Boston: E.P. Dutton, 1863. 433 pp.

1819–1842. Clergyman's journal; tour from Baltimore through western states, Ohio, Pennsylvania; work in Massachusetts, Boston, etc.

HOW, MOSES, 1798–1882   2081

DIARY OF REV. MOSES HOW, PASTOR OF THE MIDDLE STREET CHRISTIAN CHURCH, NEW BEDFORD. New Bedford, Mass.: Reynolds Printing, 1932. 29 pp.

   1819–1826, Dec 1836. Work as pastor; local and social affairs; political notes; poems.

HUNNEWELL, JAMES, 1794–1869   2082

JOURNAL OF THE VOYAGE OF THE "MISSIONARY PACKET," BOSTON TO HONOLULU. Cambridge, Mass.: University Press, 1880. 77 pp.

   Nov 1819–Apr 1820. Extracts from journal kept by officer on the brig THADDEUS, bringing the first American missionaries to Hawaii; weather, navigational position, passengers' health, arrival in Honolulu.

   Jan–Oct 1826. Captain's journal of voyage of small, inadequately built vessel, owned by the American Board; mainly weather and navigation reports; some notes on ship's condition, repairs, crew troubles; in port at Rio de Janeiro, Falkland Islands, Valparaiso; arduous passage through the Straits of Magellan.

JUDSON, ADONIRAM, 1788–1850   2083

In A MEMOIR OF THE LIFE AND LABORS OF THE REV, ADONIRAM JUDSON, by Francis Wayland. 2 vols. passim. Boston: Phillips, Sampson, 1853.

   1819, 1832 (and other scattered dates). Memoir containing many letters and diary extracts of Baptist missionary to Burma; successes and failures in spreading the gospel among Burmese, including plea for honesty in publishing of missionary efforts; good primary document in nineteenth century American missions.

MASON, RICHARD LEE, d. 1824   2084

NARRATIVE OF RICHARD LEE MASON IN THE PIONEER WEST. New York: Printed for C.F. Heartman, 1915. 74 pp.

Extracts relating to Indiana in INDIANA AS SEEN BY EARLY TRAVELERS, by Indiana Historical Commission, pp. 235–238.

   Oct–Dec 1819. Physician's journey from Pennsylvania to Illinois, through Ohio, Kentucky and Indiana, to locate bounty land near Alton, Illinois; acute observations on people and customs; impersonal but interesting.

OTIS, HARRIET   2085

In THE CARY LETTERS, edited by Caroline G.C. Curtis, pp. 269–281. Cambridge, Mass.: Printed at the Riverside Press, 1891.

   Jul–Aug 1819. Letter-diary containing tourist's notes of a journey to Saratoga Springs; social and literary details.

PEALE, TITIAN RAMSAY, 1799–1885   2086

Weese, A.O., ed. "The Journal of Titian Ramsay Peale, Pioneer Naturalist." MISSOURI HISTORICAL REVIEW 41 (1947):147–163, 266–284.

   1819–1820. Journal kept by Peale while serving as assistant naturalist on Major Stephen H. Long's expedition to the Rocky Mountains; journey from Pittsburgh to Fort Osage, Missouri; fauna, settlements, grave sites of the Mound Builders; steamboat navigation.

"The Six Journals of Mr. Peale, Naturalist." BIOLOGICAL LEAFLET, no. 55 (1951), pp. 1–3.

   1819–1820, 1841. Extracts from artist/naturalist's journals of Long and Wilkes expeditions.

In TITIAN RAMSAY PEALE, 1799–1885, AND HIS JOURNALS OF THE WILKES EXPEDITION, by Jessie Poesch, pp. 124–203. Philadelphia: American Philosophical Society, 1961.

   1838–1842. Naturalist with Wilkes Exploring Expedition to the South Pacific; Virginia to Madeira, South America, the Antarctic, Tahiti, Samoa, Australia, New Zealand, Fiji, Hawaii, Oregon, California, Manila and Singapore; sketches and paintings of ship life, birds and animals.

DIARY OF TITIAN RAMSEY PEALE: OREGON TO CALIFORNIA, OVERLAND JOURNEY, SEPTEMBER AND OCTOBER, 1841, edited by Clifford M. Drury. Los Angeles: G. Dawson, 1957. 85 pp.

   Sep–Oct 1841. Overland party of the Wilkes Expedition; trip from Oregon Territory to San Francisco; terrain; plants, gathering seeds, animals; visit to Catholic missions; notes on Indians.

RICHARDSON, JACOB, JR.   2087

Richardson, George L. "Going West in 1820." HYDE PARK HISTORICAL RECORD 4 (1904):49–67.

   1819–1921. Account of diary, with extracts; journey from New Hampshire to Arkansas, via Cincinnati; life as schoolmaster in Arkansas and Natchez; notes on Indians.

RUGGLES, SAMUEL   2088

"From a Missionary Journal." ATLANTIC MONTHLY 134 (1924):648–657.

   Oct 1819–Aug 1820. Diary kept jointly by young missionary couple, Samuel and Nancy Ruggles, for family and friends in New England; voyage to Hawaii on board THADDEUS; impressions of Hawaii and its people; negotiations with Hawaiian royalty about establishment of schools and churches; great concern to spread Christianity and literacy.

SLADE, JEREMIAH   2089

Bassett, John S., ed. "General Slade's Journal of a Trip to Tennessee." TRINITY COLLEGE HISTORICAL PAPERS, ser. 6 (1906):37–56.

   Jun 1819. Journal of trip from Martin County, North Carolina, to Nashville, Tennessee; hospitality on the way; flowery descriptions.

SMITH, THOMAS, b. ca. 1797   2090

Appleton, Thomas H., Jr., ed. "An Englishman's Perception of Antebellum Kentucky: The Journal of Thomas Smith, Jr., of Lincolnshire." KENTUCKY HISTORICAL SOCIETY REGISTER 79 (1981):57–62.

   May–Oct 1819. Summary of contents of journal kept during trip to investigate American agriculture with an eye to future immigration prospects for his family; extracts describing American customs, comparison of farm life in Ohio and Kentucky.

SPARKS, JARED, 1789-1866   2091

Moore, John H., ed. "Jared Sparks Visits Harper's Ferry." WEST VIRGINIA HISTORY 25 (1963-1964):81-91.

Aug-Sep 1819. Travel diary of Unitarian minister, later editor of NORTH AMERICAN REVIEW and noted historian; trip by stage from Baltimore, via western Maryland and mineral springs of southern Pennsylvania, to Philadelphia; return to Baltimore by way of York and Gettysburg; his observations of Harper's Ferry compared to Jefferson's in NOTES ON VIRGINIA; commentary on countryside, settlements, sermons, reading, traveling companions, acquaintances, etc.

Moore, John H., ed. "Jared Sparks Visits South Carolina." SOUTH CAROLINA HISTORICAL MAGAZINE 72 (1971):150-160.

Nov-Dec 1819. Extracts from travel diary; brief description of Fayetteville, North Carolina; route to Charleston, South Carolina, and notes on ordination of Unitarian minister there.

Apr-May 1826. Extracts from travel diary; search for papers and correspondence dealing with American Revolution; Augusta, Columbia, and Camden, South Carolina; observations of slavery.

In THE LIFE AND WRITINGS OF JARED SPARKS, by Herbert B. Adams, vol. 1, pp. 415-545. Boston and New York: Houghton, Mifflin, 1893.

Mar-Oct 1826. Notes of a tour from Boston to South Carolina, Virginia, Pennsylvania, Delaware, and return; visits with friends; research in New York and New England.

Moore, John H., ed. "Jared Sparks in Georgia." GEORGIA HISTORICAL QUARTERLY 47 (1963):425-435.

Apr 1826. Research in historical records at Milledgeville; comments on agriculture, slavery, social mores, lottery for distribution of Creek Indian lands; notes on Governor George Michael Troup; attendance at Unitarian, Presbyterian and Baptist services.

Moore, John H. "Jared Sparks in North Carolina." NORTH CAROLINA HISTORICAL REVIEW 40 (1963):285-294.

May 1826. Burrowing through primary sources in government archives at Raleigh; notes on travel in North Carolina; meeting with John Marshall; comments on southern cooking.

Proctor, "CC," ed. "After-Dinner Anecdotes of James Madison: Excerpt from Jared Sparks' Journal for 1829-31." VIRGINIA MAGAZINE OF HISTORY AND BIOGRAPHY 60 (1952):255-265.

Apr 1830. Visit to Montpelier to examine Madison's letters from Washington; record of some of Madison's observations and anecdotes relating to early history of the United States government.

TROWBRIDGE, CHARLES CHRISTOPHER   2092

Brown, Ralph H., ed. "With Cass in the Northwest in 1820: The Journal of Charles C. Trowbridge." MINNESOTA HISTORY 23 (1942):126-148, 233-252, 328-348.

Nov 1819-Sep 1820. Journal of enthusiastic twenty-year-old member of Cass Expedition to explore the Great Lakes and sources of the Mississippi; canoe travel, terrain, portages; negotiations with Sioux and Chippewa Indians; activities of Lewis Cass, David Douglass and Henry Schoolcraft.

"Journal and Letters of Charles Christopher Trowbridge, Expedition of 1820." In NARRATIVE JOURNAL OF TRAVELS THROUGH THE NORTHWESTERN REGIONS OF THE UNITED STATES, by Henry R. Schoolcraft, edited by Mentor L. Williams, pp. 461-499. East Lansing: Michigan State College Press, 1953.

May-Aug 1820.

WATSON, WILLIAM, 1773-1836   2093

"Extracts from the Diary of William Watson of Hartford, Conn." NEW ENGLAND HISTORICAL AND GENEALOGICAL REGISTER 79 (1925):298-310, 401-409; 80 (1926): 54-72.

1819-1836. Extracts mainly of genealogical interest; births, deaths, etc., in Hartford, Connecticut.

YARNALL, ELIAS, 1757-1847   2094

"A Visit to Friends in Charleston, South Carolina." FRIENDS' HISTORICAL SOCIETY OF PHILADELPHIA BULLETIN 9 (1920):118-127.

Nov-Dec 1819. Fragment of Quaker's travel journal; trip from Philadelphia to Charleston as member of committee to investigate condition of Friends there; mainly details of voyage.

1820

ADAMS, CHARLES FRANCIS, 1807-1886   2095

DIARY. Edited by Aïda DiPace Donald and David H. Donald. Cambridge: Belknap Press of Harvard University, 1964-(in progress).

1820-. A sixty-year record of people and events; early diaries covering Harvard years and legal studies in Daniel Webster's office; subsequent volumes to include Massachusetts and national politics, Free Soil Party, service in Congress, crucial events of 1860-1861, diplomacy and politics while serving as minister to Great Britain; a very important view of nineteenth century America.

DIARY. 1st Atheneum ed. Edited by Aïda DiPace Donald and David H. Donald. New York: Atheneum, 1967. 2 vols.

1820-1829.

Adams, Henry, ed. "Charles Francis Adams Visits the Mormons in 1844." MASSACHUSETTS HISTORICAL SOCIETY PROCEEDINGS 68 (1944-1947):266-300.

Apr-Jun 1844. Journey, primarily by stagecoach and steamboat, from New England to Illinois; lively and interesting descriptions of modes of travel, "western" manners, places; Washington, D.C., Cincinnati, Louisville, St. Louis, Detroit, Niagara Falls, etc.; meeting with Joseph Smith and life at Nauvoo.

AUDUBON, JOHN JAMES, 1785-1851   2096

JOURNAL OF JOHN JAMES AUDUBON MADE DURING HIS TRIP TO NEW ORLEANS IN 1820-1821. Edited by Howard Corning. Foreward by Ruthven Deane. Boston: The Club of Odd Volumes, 1929. 234 pp.

1820-1821. Botanical journal; bird life, hunting.

THE 1826 JOURNAL OF JOHN JAMES AUDUBON. Transcribed with introduction by Alice Ford. Norman: University of Oklahoma Press, 1967. 409 pp.

Apr-Dec 1826. Detailed journal, kept for his wife, of journey to England and Scotland in search of publisher for BIRDS OF AMERICA; ocean crossing on the DELOS; travel by stagecoach; English countryside and Liverpool, Manchester, Edinburgh; meetings with artists, publishers and scientists; lively, with considerable introspection and humor.

JOURNAL OF JOHN JAMES AUDUBON MADE WHILE OBTAINING SUBSCRIPTIONS TO HIS BIRDS OF AMERICA 1840-1843. Edited by Howard Corning. Foreword by Francis H. Herrick. Boston: The Club of Odd Volumes, 1929. 179 pp.

Extracts in AUDUBON AND HIS JOURNALS, by Maria R. Audubon, with zoological and other notes by Elliott Coues. New York: C. Scribner's Sons, 1897. 2 vols. Reprint. New York: Dover, 1960.

> 1840-1843. Travel and description in United States and Canada.

Mott, David C., ed. "John J. Audubon and His Visit to Iowa." ANNALS OF IOWA, 3d ser. 16 (1928):403-419.

> 1843. Extracts relating to Iowa.

Peterson, William J., ed. "Birds Along the Missouri." PALIMPSEST 52 (1971):550-570.

> May 1843. Portion of trip up the Missouri on board the OMEGA; birds and animals along the way; notes on fur traders, United States dragoons; description of Indians in squalid conditions; full and interesting account.

Peterson, William J., ed. Barging Down from Fort Union." PALIMPSEST 52 (1971):571-583.

> Aug-Oct 1843. Return down the Missouri on the barge UNION; notes on wildlife, bears, buffalo and a variety of birds.

BELL, JOHN R., 1784 or 1785-1825   2097

THE JOURNAL OF CAPTAIN JOHN R. BELL; OFFICIAL JOURNALIST FOR THE STEPHEN H. LONG EXPEDITION TO THE ROCKY MOUNTAINS, 1820. Edited by Harlin M. Fuller and LeRoy R. Hafen. Far West and the Rockies, vol. 6. Glendale, Calif.: Arthur H. Clark, 1957. 349 pp.

> Mar-Nov 1820. Explorer's diary; by riverboat from West Point to New York City; by stagecoach to join Major Long at Pittsburgh; by riverboat to St. Louis; expedition on horseback to Council Bluffs, exploring the Platte, Arkansas and Mississippi rivers; careful report of route, natural features of the land, settlements and their prospects, supplies, people and Indians.

BENTON, HENRY P.   2098

Riker, Dorothy, ed. "Two Accounts of the Upper Wabash Country." INDIANA MAGAZINE OF HISTORY 37 (1941):384-395.

> Feb-Apr 1820. Journal of deputy surveyor of public lands in Indiana; surveying boundaries of Big Miami Reserve, south of Wabash River; details of work, weather, camps, etc.

CUTLER, GEORGE YOUNGLOVE   2099

In CHRONICLES OF A PIONEER SCHOOL, compiled by Emily N. Vanderpoel, pp. 193-207.

> May-Dec 1820. Extracts from law student's diary; amusing account of social life in Litchfield, Connecticut, especially in relation to the young ladies of Litchfield School.

DOTY, JAMES DUANE, 1779-1865   2100

"Papers of James Duane Doty." WISCONSIN HISTORICAL COLLECTIONS 13 (1895):163-219.

> May-Aug 1820. Official travel journal of the expedition of Cass and Schoolcraft to Lake Superior and sources of the Mississippi; investigation of northern Indians, topography and resources.

ENGLAND, JOHN, 1786-1842   2101

"Diurnal of the Right Rev. John England, First Bishop of Charleston, S.C." AMERICAN CATHOLIC HISTORICAL SOCIETY OF PHILADELPHIA RECORDS 6 (1895):29-55, 184-224.

> 1820-1823. Account of church and diocesan work during his first three years as bishop in America.

FITCH, JEREMIAH   2102

"An Account and Memoranda of My Journey to Saratoga Springs." MASSACHUSETTS HISTORICAL SOCIETY PROCEEDINGS 50 (1916-1917):189-196.

> Jul-Aug 1820. Pleasure jaunt from Boston to Saratoga Springs, New York, and return; notes on inns and sights along the way.

FORSTER, WILLIAM, 1784-1854   2103

MEMOIRS OF WILLIAM FORSTER. Edited by Benjamin Seebohm. London: A.W. Bennett, 1865. 2 vols.

Extracts relating to Indiana in INDIANA AS SEEN BY EARLY TRAVELERS, by Indiana Historical Commission, pp. 256-268.

> 1820-1825. Travel journal of English ministering Quaker; New England, Canada, New York, New Jersey, Pennsylvania, Delaware, Maryland, Ohio, Indiana, Illinois; travel, work, meetings.

HAWLEY, ZERAH   2104

A JOURNAL OF A TOUR THROUGH CONNECTICUT, MASSACHUSETTS, NEW YORK, THE NORTH PART OF PENNSYLVANIA AND OHIO, INCLUDING A YEAR'S RESIDENCE IN THAT PART OF THE STATE OF OHIO, STYLED NEW CONNECTICUT, OR WESTERN RESERVE. New Haven, Conn.: Printed by S. Converse, 1822. 158 pp.

> 1820-1821. Interesting notes on many towns, scenery, crops, trade, etc.

HOLMAN, LUCIA RUGGLES, 1793-1886   2105

JOURNAL OF LUCIA RUGGLES HOLMAN. Bernice Pauhi Bishop Museum Special Publications, no. 17. Honolulu: The Museum, 1931. 40 pp.

> 1820. Optimistic journal of missionary sent with her husband, Dr. Thomas Holman, to Hawaii by American Board of Commissioners for Foreign Missions; voyage from Boston aboard the THADDEUS; descriptions of storms, fish and birds; arrival in Hawaii, manners of the people, reception by the king and their residence in his town as objects of curiosity.

KEARNY, STEPHEN WATTS, 1794-1848   2106

Porter, Valentine M., ed. "Journal of Stephen Watts Kearny." MISSOURI HISTORICAL SOCIETY COLLECTIONS 3 (1908-1911):8-29, 99-131. Reprint. THE 1820 JOURNAL OF STEPHEN WATTS KEARNY. St. Louis: Missouri Historical Society, 1908; "An Expedition Across Iowa in 1820." ANNALS OF IOWA, 3d ser. 10 (1912):343-371.

> Jul-Aug 1820. Frontier soldier's account of Council Bluffs-St. Peters military exploration expedition, between the upper Missouri and Mississippi rivers, to open up route between Camp Missouri near Omaha and Camp Cold Water near Minneapolis; descriptions of forts, town, Indian villages, geography; some personal items.

LEWIS, JANE R.   2107

In CHRONICLES OF A PIONEER SCHOOL, compiled by Emily N. Vanderpoel, pp. 221–225.

> Summer 1820. Brief notes on daily studies at Litchfield School, by Jane R. and Mary Ann Lewis.

NETTLETON, ASAHEL, 1783–1844   2108

In MEMOIR OF THE LIFE AND CHARACTER OF REV. ASAHEL NETTLETON, D.D., by Bennet Tyler, pp. 108–123. Hartford, Conn.: Robins & Smith, 1844; 2d ed., 1845.

> Apr–Jun 1820. Religious work in Nassau, near Albany; meetings in schools, taverns, etc.; revivals.

SCHWEIZER, JOHANNES, 1785–1831   2109

"Account of a Journey to North America and through the Most Significant Parts Thereof." In THE OLD LAND AND THE NEW: THE JOURNALS OF TWO SWISS FAMILIES IN AMERICA IN THE 1820'S. Edited and translated by Robert H. Billigmeier and Fred A. Picard, pp. 3–147. Minneapolis: University of Minnesota Press, 1965.

> May–Dec(?) 1820. Part diary and part undated journal of intelligent and observant Swiss immigrant, kept for interest of friends and relatives and usefulness to future immigrants; ocean crossing, homesickness and seasickness, sense of God's providence; social life, customs and character of new land, especially in Pennsylvania; disappointment with moral condition of Swiss and German immigrants; work as a traveling Bible salesman; advantages and disadvantages of immigration.

SIMPSON, GEORGE, 1792–1860   2110

JOURNAL OF OCCURRENCES IN THE ATHABASCA DEPARTMENT. Edited by E.E. Rich. Champlain Society Publications, Hudson's Bay Company Series, 1. Toronto: The Champlain Society, 1938. 498 pp. Reprint. Hudson's Bay Record Society Publications, 1. Nendeln, Liechtenstein: Kraus Reprint, 1968.

> Jul 1820–Jun 1821. Highly personal and revealing journal of governor of Hudson's Bay Company, beginning at Rock Depot on Hayes River; mostly in Athabasca Department; business details, his own activities in the early days of his service; an important journal.

FUR TRADE AND EMPIRE: GEORGE SIMPSON'S JOURNAL. Edited by Frederick Merk. Harvard Historical Studies, 31. Cambridge: Harvard University Press; London: H. Milford, Oxford University Press, 1931. 370 pp. Journal, pp. 3–174. Rev. ed. Cambridge: Belknap Press of Harvard University Press, 1968.

> Aug 1824–Jun 1825. Voyage from York Factory to Fort George and return; very important in Northwest history.

NARRATIVE OF A JOURNEY ROUND THE WORLD, DURING THE YEARS 1841 AND 1842. London: H. Colburn, 1847. 2 vols.

> 1841–1842. Tour of inspection of properties of Hudson's Bay Company; four chapters on California; notes on a world tour.

WEST, JOHN, 1775?–1845   2111

THE SUBSTANCE OF A JOURNAL DURING A RESIDENCE AT THE RED RIVER COLONY, BRITISH NORTH AMERICA. London: Printed for L.B. Seeley and Son, 1824. 210 pp.; 2d ed., enl. London: L.B. Seeley and Son, 1827. 326 pp.

"Extracts from the Substance of a Journal during a Residence at the Red River Colony, British North-America." NORTH DAKOTA HISTORICAL SOCIETY COLLECTIONS 3 (1910):441–490.

> 1820–1823. Religious and missionary journal of chaplain to Hudson's Bay Company; journey from England to Winnipeg; residence as chaplain at Red River colony; daily events; accounts of the country, Indians, missionaries and state of religion; return to London; an interesting journal.

WOODS, JOHN, d. 1829   2112

TWO YEARS' RESIDENCE IN THE SETTLEMENT ON THE ENGLISH PRAIRIE, IN THE ILLINOIS COUNTRY, UNITED STATES. London: Longman, Hurst, Rees, Orme, and Brown, 1822. 310 pp.

TWO YEARS' RESIDENCE ON THE ENGLISH PRAIRIE OF ILLINOIS. Edited by Paul M. Angle. Chicago: Lakeside Press, 1968. 242 pp.

In EARLY WESTERN TRAVELS, edited by Reuben G. Thwaites, vol. 10, pp. 177–357.

> 1820–1821. English farmer's very full account of his life and prospects and the progress of Birkbeck's settlement; travel notes and comments on agriculture, towns and villages, American customs, etc.; a valuable and interesting diary.

1821

ANON.   2113

PROMINENT FEATURES OF A NORTHERN TOUR. Charleston, S.C.: Printed for the author by C.C. Sebring, 1822. 48 pp.

> Jun–Nov 1821. Travel diary; from Charleston, South Carolina, to Rhode Island, Massachusetts, New Hampshire, Vermont, Canada, New York, Maine, and return to Charleston.

BECKNELL, THOMAS (or WILLIAM?)   2114

MISSOURI INTELLIGENCER, 22 April 1823. Reprint. "The Missouri–Santa Fe Trade." MISSOURI HISTORICAL SOCIETY COLLECTIONS 2, no. 6 (1906):55–67.

"The Journals of Capt. Thomas Becknell from Boone's Lick to Santa Fe and from Santa Cruz to Green River." MISSOURI HISTORICAL REVIEW 4 (1909–1910): 65–84. Journal, pp. 65–81.

In SOUTHWEST ON THE TURQUOISE TRAIL, edited by Archer B. Hulbert, pp. 56–68.

> 1821–1822. Journey from Boone's Lick, Missouri, to Santa Fe; description of Santa Fe; return trip; account of second expedition over similar route; post facto and dated irregularly.

MISSOURI INTELLIGENCER, 25 June 1825. Reprint. "The Journals of Capt. Thomas Becknell from Boone's Lick to Santa Fe and from Santa Cruz to Green River." MISSOURI HISTORICAL REVIEW 4 (1909–1910):65–84. Journal, pp. 81–84.

> Nov–Dec 1824? Journey from Santa Cruz to the Green River, "several hundred miles from Santa Fe"; descriptions of country and Indians. Undated account written for newspaper article.

COGGESHALL, GEORGE   2115

"Voyage in the Pilot-Boat Schooner SEA-SERPENT." In FIVE SEA CAPTAINS, edited by Walter M. Teller, pp. 309–351. New York: Atheneum, 1960.

> 1821–1822. Sea captain's trading venture to Lima,

Peru; cargoes, prices, incidents at sea and in port; full entries. Later memoirs, of which this journal is a part, were popular sea narratives in their day.

CROSWELL, HARRY, 1778-1858 2116

Dexter, Franklin B. "The Rev. Harry Croswell, D.D., and His Diary." NEW HAVEN COLONY HISTORICAL SOCIETY PAPERS 9 (1918):46-69. Reprint. In A SELECTION FROM THE MISCELLANEOUS HISTORICAL PAPERS OF FIFTY YEARS, by Franklin B. Dexter, pp. 349-365. New Haven, Conn.: Tuttle, Morehouse & Taylor, 1918.

> 1821-1848. Extracts arranged to illustrate his parish work, character, congregational thought, politics, interest in New Haven, etc.

DRAKE, SYLVIA, 1784-1868 2117

Murray, Donald M. and Rodney, Robert M. "Sylvia Drake 1784-1868: The Self-Portrait of a Seamstress of Weybridge." VERMONT HISTORY 34 (1966):123-135.

> 1821-1824. Summary of manuscript diary with lengthy extracts describing household activities, social life and travel; commencement exercises at nearby Middlebury College; Vermont village life; numerous brief quotations concerning religion and her friendship with Charity Bryant, aunt of William Cullen Bryant.

FINNEY, ALFRED 2118

"Mission among the Cherokees of the Arkansaw." MISSIONARY HERALD 17 (1821):147-152, 211-214.

> 1821. Alfred Finney's and Cephas Washburn's journal of trip from Elliot mission to Walnut Hills on Arkansas River to seek site for new mission; hardships of travel, lack of food and severe illnesses.

FLETCHER, SARAH HILL, 1801-1854 2119

In THE DIARY OF CALVIN FLETCHER, edited by Gayle Thronbrough, vol. 1, pp. 39-79, 170-172, 474-478. Indianapolis: Indiana Historical Society, 1972.

> 1821-1838. Chiefly her daily life during the first two years of her marriage to Calvin Fletcher; keeping house, planting garden, visiting, studies supervised by her husband, record of weather.

FOWLER, JACOB, 1765-1850 2120

THE JOURNAL OF JACOB FOWLER. Edited by Elliott Coues. New York: F.P. Harper, 1898. 183 pp. Reprint. Minneapolis: Ross & Haines, 1965; With a preface and additional notes by Ramond W. Settle, Mary L. Settle and Harry R. Stevens. Lincoln: University of Nebraska Press, 1970. 152 pp.

> Sep 1821-Jul 1822. Diary of travel from Arkansas through the Indian Territory; Oklahoma, Kansas, Colorado, New Mexico; to the sources of the Rio Grande; valuable geographically; impersonal, but very interesting for spellings and language.

CHRONICLES OF OKLAHOMA 8 (1930):181-188.

> Sep-Oct 1821. Section relating to Oklahoma.

GARRY, NICHOLAS 2121

Garry, Francis N.A., ed. "Diary of Nicholas Garry." ROYAL SOCIETY OF CANADA PROCEEDINGS AND TRANSACTIONS, 2d ser. 6 (1900):sec. 2, 73-204.

> Mar-Nov 1821. Travel diary of deputy governor of Hudson's Bay Company; from England to New York; meeting with Astor; Montreal; visiting company's posts in Northwest Territories; descriptions, often social and scenic; return voyage to England; well written and entertaining.

HALL, WILLIAM, 1773-1837 2122

Monaghan, Jay, ed. "From England to Illinois in 1821: The Journal of William Hall." ILLINOIS STATE HISTORICAL SOCIETY JOURNAL 39 (1946):21-67, 208-253.

> 1821-1826. Sailing from England, walking by family's wagon from Philadelphia to Pittsburgh, floating in an ark down the Ohio to Illinois; overland by foot and wagon to the English settlement established by Birkbeck and Flower; emphasis on beauty of land and abundance of food; account of family's life in new home, providing many details of getting started; buying property, planting orchard, raising cabin, etc.; daily routines of farm; a camp meeting; Robert Owen's new settlement; death of Birkbeck; an interesting diary.

HARRIS, THOMPSON S. 2123

"Journals of Rev. Thompson S. Harris." BUFFALO HISTORICAL SOCIETY PUBLICATIONS 6 (1903):281-380.

> 1821-1828. Missionary work among the Senecas at Buffalo Creek and Cattaraugus reservations; rather impersonal account of religious and school work, with some religious reflections and moralizing.

PARSONS, ANNA QUINCY THAXTER 2124

"A Newburyport Wedding One Hundred and Thirty Years Ago." ESSEX INSTITUTE HISTORICAL COLLECTIONS 87 (1951):309-332.

> Mar-Apr 1821. "Journal of events" kept by the half-sister of the bride, at the request of her mother and sister, to be sent to the bride's brother; details of preparations for a fashionable wedding; selection of home furnishings, dressmaking, food preparation, etc.; sprightly, humorous account of a joyous time, with a poignant note as diarist reveals the unhappiness of her own marriage.

PEARSON, JOHN 2125

NOTES MADE DURING A JOURNEY IN 1821, IN THE UNITED STATES OF AMERICA. London: Printed by W. and S. Couchmann, 1822. 72 pp.

Extracts in PEN PICTURES OF EARLY WESTERN PENNSYLVANIA, edited by John W. Harpster, pp. 277-285. Pittsburgh: University of Pittsburgh Press, 1938.

Extracts in SIX WHO RETURNED: AMERICA VIEWED BY BRITISH REPATRIATES, by Wilbur S. Shepperson, pp. 46-53. Nevada Studies in History and Political Science, no. 3. Carson City: University of Nevada Press, 1961.

> 1821. Travel diary of Englishman, lured by writing of Morris Birkbeck to join English settlement in America; arrival at Philadelphia; examination of Pennsylvania farms; disillusioned return to Philadelphia and home to England; vigorous and lively abuse of Americans, Scotsmen, innkeepers, dogs, towns, etc.

ROBERTS, PHOEBE MCCARTY, b. 1766? 2126

Gray, Leslie R., ed. "Phoebe Roberts' Diary of a Quaker Missionary Journey to Upper Canada." ONTARIO HISTORICAL SOCIETY PAPERS AND RECORDS 42 (1950): 7-46.

Sep 1821–Feb 1822. Pennsylvania Quaker's religious visit to upstate New York and Ontario; travel, meetings attended, individuals encountered.

RODMAN, SAMUEL, 1792–1876   2127

THE DIARY OF SAMUEL RODMAN. Edited by Zephaniah W. Pease. New Bedford, Mass.: Reynolds Printing, 1927. 349 pp. Reprinted from THE MORNING MERCURY.

1821–1829. Long and detailed record of life in New Bedford; regular notes of work, social affairs and church life; reading and reflections; valuable and interesting.

NEW BEDFORD IN 1827 AS TOLD IN SAMUEL RODMAN'S DIARY. Edited by Bradford Swan. New Bedford, Mass.: Reynolds Printing, 1935.

1827. Section missing from the Pease edition.

STEELE, J.D.   2128

Remini, Robert V., ed. "A New York 'Yankee' in Tennessee." TENNESSEE HISTORICAL QUARTERLY 37 (1978):278–292.

Jan–Mar 1821. Travel on horseback through middle Tennessee; commentary, generally critical, on terrain, weather, accommodations, lifestyles and politics in Tennessee; encounters with and evaluation of Andrew Jackson.

TEAS, THOMAS SCATTERGOOD, 1794–1850   2129

In INDIANA AS SEEN BY EARLY TRAVELERS, by Indiana Historical Commission, pp. 246–255.

Jul 1821. Extracts from Quaker carpenter's travel diary; journey afoot from Philadelphia to Indiana by way of Pittsburgh; long descriptive entries; details of Indians, scenery, towns, etc.

Ideson, Julia and Higginbotham, Sanford W., eds. "A Trading Trip to Natchez and New Orleans." JOURNAL OF SOUTHERN HISTORY 7 (1941):380–399.

Apr–Oct 1822. Down the Ohio and Mississippi to New Orleans, sea voyage to Philadelphia and overland back to Ohio; travel by flatboat, sailing vessel, stage, skiff, canoe and on foot; interesting descriptions of the commerce of the rivers, Natchez, New Orleans, conditions of slavery, etc.

VAN LIEW, ELIZABETH, 1790–1873   2130

"Jottings from an Old Journal." SOMERSET COUNTY HISTORICAL QUARTERLY 7 (1918):55–61, 123–127.

1821–1856. Arranged by editor as jottings on Six Mile Run, weather, necrology, family visits to West and lake country.

WHITALL, JOHN M., 1800–1877   2131

In JOHN M. WHITALL. THE STORY OF HIS LIFE, by Hannah Whitall Smith, pp. 112–287 passim. Philadelphia: Printed for the family, 1879.

1821–1867. Scattered extracts on religion, reflections, life as sailor; becoming a Quaker; captain of an East Indiaman; mainly notes on his shortcomings and on business life in Philadelphia and mission work there.

WILLIAMSON, WILLIAM D., 1779–1846   2132

"Extracts from the Diary of the Late Hon. William D. Williamson, of Bangor, Maine." NEW ENGLAND HISTORICAL AND GENEALOGICAL REGISTER 30 (1876):189–191, 429–431.

"Extracts from the Diary of the Late Hon. William D. Williamson, of Bangor, Maine." BANGOR HISTORICAL MAGAZINE 8 (1893):50–54.

Nov 1821–May 1822. Maine congressman's journey from Bangor to Washington to attend Seventeenth Congress; brief travel and political notes.

ZAHM, MATTIAS, 1789–1874   2133

Goodell, Robert H., ed. "Mattias Zahm's Diary." LANCASTER COUNTY HISTORICAL SOCIETY PAPERS 47 (1943):61–92.

1821–1822, 1836–1849. Extracts from brushmaker's diary; local events in Lancaster, Pennsylvania; weather, deaths, fires, visits of General Harrison and President Taylor; inauguration of city water and street lighting; court cases, celebrations, etc., as well as events of personal life; reactions to national political and economic issues and popular enthusiasms of the period; an engaging record.

"An Old Diary." LANCASTER COUNTY HISTORICAL SOCIETY PAPERS 12 (1901):184–194.

1839–1849. Extracts; scattered notes of local events; work as tipstaff and crier in Lancaster courts.

1822

ANON.   2134

A JOURNAL OF AN EXCURSION MADE BY THE CORPS OF CADETS, OF THE AMERICAN LITERARY, SCIENTIFIC AND MILITARY ACADEMY, UNDER CAPT. ALDEN PARTRIDGE. Concord, N.H.: Printed by Hill and Moore, 1822. 38 pp.

Jun 1822. School travel journal; from Vermont to Concord, New Hampshire, via Enfield and Salisbury; return through Hopkinton, Hillsborough and Newport; notes on countryside, drills, etc. Authored by committee.

JOURNAL OF AN EXCURSION, PERFORMED BY A DETACHMENT OF CADETS, BELONGING TO THE A.L.S.&M. ACADEMY UNDER THE COMMAND OF CAPTAIN ALDEN PARTRIDGE. Middletown, Conn.: Printed by E.&H. Clark, 1826. 22 pp.

Nov 1826. School travel journal; from Middletown, Connecticut, to Poughkeepsie, West Point and New York City. Authored by committee.

JOURNAL OF A TOUR OF A DETACHMENT OF CADETS, FROM A.L.S.&M. ACADEMY. Middletown, Conn.: W.D. Starr, 1827. 100 pp.

Dec 1826. School travel journal; from Middletown to Washington, D.C. Authored by committee.

ANON.   2135

"A Diary of 1822." PENNSYLVANIA MAGAZINE OF HISTORY AND BIOGRAPHY 49 (1925):61–74.

Oct–Dec 1822. Journey from Horsham, Pennsylvania, to New Lisbon, Ohio, mainly over the Erie Pike; return by southern route to Pittsburgh and Pennsylvania way; notes on taverns, food, towns and minor adventures; some interesting spellings.

ANON.   2136

Kleet, Guy S., ed. "A Diary of a Journey from Cincinnati to Natchez in a Flatboat." PRESBYTERIAN HISTORICAL SOCIETY JOURNAL 21 (1943):167–185.

Nov 1822–Apr 1823. Down the Ohio and Mississippi rivers with a cargo of furniture; weather, navigation, river traffic, stops and sales along the way; settling in Natchez; work in newspaper office; establishment of Natchez Harmonical Society, a singing society; attendance at various churches; journey on horseback to Jackson; search for teaching position.

BIERCE, LUCIUS VERUS   2137

TRAVELS IN THE SOUTHLAND, 1822–1823; THE JOURNAL OF LUCIUS VERUS BIERCE. Edited by George W. Knepper. Columbus: Ohio State University Press, 1966. 139 pp.

1822–1823. Walking tour throughout the South of young graduate of Ohio University; descriptions of countryside, towns and villages; vignettes of people, manners and mores of southerners; slavery, condition of Indians; a lively and informative diary.

BOMPART, LOUIS   2138

Myer, Mrs. Max W., trans. "To Fort Lisa by Keelboat." MISSOURI HISTORICAL SOCIETY BULLETIN 16 (1959–1960):14–19.
In THE WEST OF WILLIAM H. ASHLEY; THE INTERNATIONAL STRUGGLE FOR THE FUR TRADE OF THE MISSOURI, ROCKY MOUNTAINS AND THE COLUMBIA, edited by Dale L. Morgan, pp. 9–11. Denver: Old West Publishing Co., 1964.

May–Jun 1822. Journal fragment; daily record of travel of group of French fur traders up the Missouri River; brief entries focusing on distances covered and camp locations but also communicating the tumult of the travel and trade.

BRINCKLE, SAMUEL C., 1796–1863   2139

In THE HISTORY OF OLD ST. DAVID'S CHURCH, RADNOR, IN DELAWARE COUNTY, PENNSYLVANIA, app., pp. 198–206. Philadelphia: J.C. Winston, 1907.

1822–1832. Extracts from diary kept while diarist was rector of Old St. David's and St. Peter's Church, Chester Valley; churches, sermons, vestry meetings, parish work.

CANBY, EDMUND, 1804–1848   2140

Hoffecker, Carol E., ed. "The Diaries of Edmund Canby, a Quaker Miller." DELAWARE HISTORY 16 (1974):79–131, 184–243.

1822–1848. Selections from seventeen volumes of diaries kept by Whig businessman, a member of one of the prominent Quaker families owning mills on the Brandywine; business, political and religious concerns; business reverses, loss of mill, employment as bank teller; conversion from Quaker to Episcopalian; trips through Middle Atlantic and New England states, Virginia, Maryland, Ohio, with vacations at Cape May, New Jersey; cholera epidemic of 1832; family life; local events in Wilmington; reports on railways and steam navigation; an interesting reflection of economic, political and social environment of the period.

COLLINS, STEPHEN, 1797–1871   2141

THE AUTOBIOGRAPHY OF STEPHEN COLLINS, M.D. Philadelphia: Published for the author by J.B. Lippincott, 1872. 235 pp.

1822–1860. Philadelphia physician's private diary, focusing on religious life after his conversion; notes on religion, reflection, prayer, self-abasement, etc.

HADLOCK, SAMUEL, 1792–1833   2142

GOD'S POCKET: THE STORY OF CAPTAIN SAMUEL HADLOCK, JUNIOR, OF CRANBERRY ISLES, MAINE. By Rachel L. Field. New York: Macmillan, 1934. 163 pp.

1822–1826. Extensive and highly entertaining diary extracts within biography of American showman; travels through England, Ireland, Germany and France with a small circus and troupe of Indians; performances at inns, fairs, even the courts of Europe; verses; interesting spellings.

KHROMCHENKO, VASILIY STEPANOVICH, d. 1849   2143

V.S. KHROMCHENKO'S COASTAL EXPLORATIONS IN SOUTHWESTERN ALASKA. Edited by James W. Vanstone, translated by David H. Kraus. Fieldiana: Anthropology, vol. 64. Chicago: Field Museum of Natural History, 1973. 95 pp.

Apr 1822. Diary of naval officer of Russian American Company on expedition to obtain information about Eskimo inhabitants of southwestern Alaska with intention of expanding fur trade; command of GOLOVNIN; explorations in small boats, baydarkas; implements, weapons and language.

LAY, JOHN   2144

Severance, Frank H., ed. "The Journeys and Journals of an Early Buffalo Merchant." BUFFALO HISTORICAL SOCIETY PUBLICATIONS 4 (1896):125–145.

1822–1824. Extracts relating to travel in Scotland and England; meetings with some famous literary men; return to Boston; comments on theater, etc.

LIEBER, FRANCIS, 1800–1872   2145

THE LIFE AND LETTERS OF FRANCIS LIEBER. Edited by Thomas S. Perry. Boston: J.R. Osgood, 1882. 439 pp. Diary, pp. 44–296 passim.

1822–1857. Scholar's diary; journal kept in Greece; early life in Germany and London; immigration to America; notes on study, reading, journeys; tours in Europe, where diarist had many eminent acquaintances in the literary world; teaching and research at Columbia University; social and artistic life in New York.

MORGAN, YOUNGS L., 1797?–1888   2146

Headline, Clarissa and Gallup, Milton N., eds. "The Diary of an Early Fur Trader." INLAND SEAS 18 (1962):300–305; 19 (1963):30–38, 113–122, 227–232, 277–283.

1822–1823. Young man's diary of time spent trading furs in the northern Great Lakes region; good picture of the loneliness, hardships and danger of the venture.

PRINCE, HEZEKIAH, 1800–1843   2147

JOURNALS OF HEZEKIAH PRINCE, JR. Introduction by Walter M. Whitehill, foreword by Robert G. Albon. New York: Published for the Maine Historical Society by Crown, 1965. 448 pp.

1822–1828. A pleasant account of daily life; work as customs inspector in Thomaston, Maine, noting arrival and departure of ships and their cargos; local governmental affairs, political events, debates at his clubs; an active social life of outings, parties and balls; important events affecting his family and friends; weather and crops; some introspection each year on his birthday.

RAVENEL, HENRY, b. 1790   2148

In RAVENEL RECORDS, A HISTORY AND GENEALOGY OF THE HUGUENOT FAMILY OF RAVENEL, OF SOUTH CAROLINA, by Henry E. Ravenel, pp. 251-253. Atlanta: Franklin Printing and Publishing Co., 1898.

1822-1853. Private diary of physician in Pooshee, South Carolina; brief notes of family affairs, work, journeys, weather; continues his father's diary.

ROBERTS, DEBORAH S., b. 1802   2149

In MEMOIRS OF CATHARINE SEELY AND DEBORAH S. ROBERTS, pp. 216-250. New York: D. Goodwin, 1844.

1822-1838. Reflections of a recluse-like woman on God and herself, Negroes, morals, Christian consolation; self-abasement and afflictions, illness.

ROSATI, JOSEPH, 1789-1843   2150

"Documents from Our Archives: Diary of Bishop Rosati." ST. LOUIS CATHOLIC HISTORICAL REVIEW 3 (1921):311-369; 4 (1922):76-108, 165-184, 245-271; 5 (1923):60-88.

1822-1826. Catholic diocesan journal; travel and daily work of archbishop; detailed but impersonal.

SHERMAN, ALPHEUS, 1780-1866?   2151

Schroeder, Peter B., ed. "By Horse and Waggon: The Diary of Alpheus Sherman." NEW YORK HISTORY 37 (1956):432-451.

Sep-Oct 1822. Travel diary of attorney, political leader; from New York City through upstate New York; Montgomery, Monticello, Ithaca, Lake Oneida, Schenectady, Albany, Poughkeepsie, etc.; details of travel; descriptions of towns and countryside, especially noting land values.

STEWART, CHARLES SAMUEL, 1795-1870   2152

CHRISTIAN ADVOCATE 2 (1824):277-283, 320-324; 3 (1825):216-222, 266-270, 314-319, 359-363, 407-408, 452-455, 552.

JOURNAL OF A RESIDENCE IN THE SANDWICH ISLANDS. With an introduction and occasional notes by William Ellis. London: H. Fisher, Son, and Jackson, 1828. 407 pp.; 2d ed., corrected and enl. New York: J.P. Haven, 1828. 320 pp.; 3d ed. London: H. Fisher and P. Jackson, 1830. 407 pp. Reprint. Honolulu: University of Hawaii Press for Friends of the Library of Hawaii, 1970, 430 pp.; 5th ed., enl. Boston: Weeks, Jordan, 1839. 348 pp.

Extracts in "Private Journal of a Voyage to the Pacific Ocean, and Residence at the Sandwich Islands." AMERICAN QUARTERLY REVIEW 3 (1828):342-369.

1822-1825. American missionary's journal; voyage from Philadelphia around Cape Horn to Hawaiian Islands; missionary work in the islands; notes on manners and customs of the inhabitants; account of Lord Byron's visit; description of interment of king and queen on Oahu; linguistic, anthropological and social notes; literary style.

STOCKTON, BETSEY   2153

CHRISTIAN ADVOCATE 2 (1824):232-235, 564-566; 3 (1825):36-41.

Nov 1822-Jul 1823. Negro missionary's journal; voyage from Philadelphia around Cape Horn to Hawaiian Islands; good descriptions of cruise, fishing, ceremonies, social life, arrival at Hawaii; an interesting journal.

SUMNER, WILLIAM H., 1780-1861   2154

"Incidents in the Life of John Hancock." MAGAZINE OF AMERICAN HISTORY 19 (1888):504-510.

Nov 1822. Extract from army general's private diary; incidents in the life of John Hancock as related by his widow to the diarist.

TOKETA   2155

Barrére, Dorothy and Sahlins, Marshall. "Tahitians in the Early History of Hawaiian Christianity: The Journal of Toketa." HAWAIIAN JOURNAL OF HISTORY 13 (1979):19-35.

May-Jun 1822. Tahitian missionary to Hawaii and teacher in the schools of the Hawaiian chiefs; tour of island of Hawaii with Governor John Adams Kuakini while teaching him to read; Hawaiian customs, modes of work, recreation; considerable drunkenness and fighting among governor's family and retinue. Translated from the Hawaiian.

TYERMAN, DANIEL, 1773-1828   2156

JOURNAL OF VOYAGES AND TRAVELS BY THE REV. DANIEL TYERMAN AND GEORGE BENNET, DEPUTED FROM THE LONDON MISSIONARY SOCIETY TO VISIT THEIR VARIOUS STATIONS IN THE SOUTH SEA ISLANDS, CHINA, INDIA, ETC., BETWEEN THE YEARS 1821 AND 1829. Compiled from original documents by James Montgomery. London: Frederick Westley and A.H. Davis, 1831. 2 vols. Journal, vol. 1, pp. 374-480.

Apr-Aug 1822. Missionary activities by London Missionary Society and American Board of Foreign Missions in Hawaii reported by London visitors; descriptions of the islands, people and customs; cordial reception by Kamehameha II.

WILBOR, MARY L., b. 1806   2157

In CHRONICLES OF A PIONEER SCHOOL, compiled by Emily N. Vanderpoel, pp. 234-241.

May-Aug 1822. School diary; studies and social life at Litchfield School.

1823

ALTIMERA, JOSE   2158

"Journal of a Mission-Founding Expedition North of San Francisco." HUTCHINGS' ILLUSTRATED CALIFORNIA MAGAZINE 5 (1860):58-62, 115-119.

Jun-Jul 1823. Priest's account of founding of Mission of Sonoma; journey by barge to the locality of Sonoma; evaluation of natural resources; killing of many bears as "animals offensive to humanity"; exploration of surrounding area of Napa and Petaluma; introductory meeting with Indians; formal founding ceremony.

ANTHONY, JOSEPH, b. 1797   2159

LIFE IN NEW BEDFORD A HUNDRED YEARS AGO. Edited by Zephaniah W. Pease. New Bedford, Mass.: Published under the auspices of the Old Dartmouth Historical Society by G.H. Reynolds, 1922. 91 pp.

1823-1824. Full and varied diary; social and local affairs, reading, trips to New York, business, ship affairs; an intimate and very interesting record of a small New England town.

BETZ, JOHANN LORENZ, 1792-1840   2160

In FINDING THE GRAIN, edited by Norbert Krapf, pp. 20-46. Jasper, Ind.: Dubois County Historical Society and Herald Printing, 1977.

1823-1839. Extracts from journal of German immigrant, who settled first in Wheeling, Virginia, and then near Jasper, Indiana; chiefly, significant dates for his family, voyage on the GANGES to America, working and acquiring land.

BROOKS, WILLIAM G.   2161

"Journal of an Excursion to Manchester, Vermont by a Party of Norwich Cadets." VERMONT HISTORICAL SOCIETY PROCEEDINGS (1915-1916):93-107.

Sep-Oct 1823. School travel journals kept by cadet at the American Literary, Scientific and Military Academy, Vermont; excursion to Manchester and Windsor, Vermont; formal style, but interesting picture of military school life.

BUTRICK, DANIEL S., 1789-1851   2162

"Mission among the Cherokees: Tour of Rev. Mr. Butrick." MISSIONARY HERALD 20 (1824):8-14.

Feb-Aug 1823. Windsor, Massachusetts, clergyman's missionary journal.

CHAMBERLAIN, NATHAN B., b. ca. 1809   2163

In THREE CHAMBERLAIN JOURNALS (1819-1823) FROM BOSTON TO THE SANDWICH ISLANDS AND BACK, prepared by Calvin S. Hathaway, Philadelphia: 1965. 60 leaves.

Mar-Aug 1823. Journal of fourteen-year-old son of missionary, Daniel Chamberlain, aboard PEARLE on return from Hawaii to New England; family life and children's escapades; meals, weather, rages of the captain, many nautical details; good sea diary of an observant boy who enjoyed the voyage.

COLHOUN, JAMES E.   2164

In THE NORTHERN EXPEDITIONS OF STEPHEN H. LONG: THE JOURNALS OF 1817 AND 1823 AND RELATED DOCUMENTS, by Stephen H. Long, edited by Lucile M. Kane, June D. Holmquist and Caroline Gilman, pp. 269-327. Minneapolis: Minnesota Historical Society, 1978.

July 1823. Only other surviving journal of the Stephen H. Long Expedition; from encampment at Lake Pepin up Minnesota River valley into watershed of Red River; many literary allusions, descriptions of Indians, countryside, food and plants.

DARRELL, JOHN HARVEY   2165

"Diary of John Harvey Darrell: Voyage to America." BERMUDA HISTORICAL QUARTERLY 5 (1948):142-149.

Jul 1823. Voyage from Bermuda to Richmond, Fredericksburg and Washington, D.C.; good description of stagecoach journeys. American section of longer diary serialized in BERMUDA HISTORICAL QUARTERLY.

GLENN, JOSHUA NICHOLS   2166

"A Diary of Joshua Nichols Glenn: St. Augustine in 1823." FLORIDA HISTORICAL QUARTERLY 24 (1945):121-161.

Feb-Dec 1823. Missionary diary of young Georgia Methodist, a humble, hardworking parson of charitable disposition; travel by small coastal boats and horseback to St. Augustine; zealous ministry to black and white alike; discouragements and illnesses; distress over rivalry with Presbyterian minister Eleazar Lathrop; comments on Spanish Catholics; interesting spellings.

JOHNS, JAMES, 1797-1874   2167

"James Johns, Vermont Pen Printer." VERMONT HISTORICAL SOCIETY PROCEEDINGS, n.s. 4 (1936):69-88.

1823-1826 (with later entries). Private and business diaries of writer in Huntington, Vermont; entertaining, sympathetic and observant notes on happenings in a small town; births, deaths, marriages, accidents; a seizure by the Devil, rape, court battles, jail break; celebrations; later notes on beginning of Civil War.

KENNERLY, JAMES, 1792-1840   2168

Wesley, Edgar B., ed. "Diary of James Kennerly." MISSOURI HISTORICAL SOCIETY COLLECTIONS 6 (1928-1931):41-97.

1823-1826. Business diary of sutler at Council Bluffs; early entries retrospective; business records, life at post, weather; good picture of life and work.

LONG, ZADOC, 1800-1873   2169

In A HISTORY OF BUCKFIELD, OXFORD COUNTY, MAINE, by Alfred Cole and Charles F. Whitman, pp. 469-508. Buckfield: 1915.

FROM THE JOURNAL OF ZADOC LONG. Edited by Peirce Long. Caldwell, Idaho: Caxton Printers, 1943. 316 pp.

1823-1860. Mostly impersonal but interesting extracts, revealing local life in Buckfield; trade, weather, family, religion, journeys, prices, accidents and providences.

MINOR, LUCIAN, 1802-1858   2170

"The Shenandoah Regime." In PLANTATION AND FRONTIER DOCUMENTS, edited by Ulrich B. Phillips, vol. 1, pp. 254-256.

Nov 1823. Observations of William and Mary College graduate; description of Shenandoah Valley farms belonging to Dutch settlers from Pennsylvania, and of his landlord's improved loom, corn-shelling machine and apple-parer.

"A Virginian in New England Thirty-five Years Ago." ATLANTIC MONTHLY 26 (1870):333-341.

Jun 1834. Louisa County, Virginia, lawyer's journey, mainly by stagecoach, to Baltimore, Philadelphia, Washington and Boston.

"A Journey to the West in 1836." MASSACHUSETTS HISTORICAL SOCIETY PROCEEDINGS, 2d ser. 7 (1891-1892): 263-294.

Nov-Dec 1836. A very pleasant travel diary with

substantial and well-written entries; from Charlottesville, Virginia, to junction of Ohio and Wabash rivers; scenery, social and personal comments; a good deal of literary interest (Dickens, Johnson, Congreve, etc.).

NEAD, PETER, 1796-1877   2171

Durnbaugh, Donald F. "Vindicator of Primitive Christianity: The Life and Diary of Peter Nead." BRETHREN LIFE AND THOUGHT 14 (1969):196-223.

> 1823-1824. Evangelistic tour of Shenandoah Valley by self-appointed Methodist preacher, inclined toward German Baptist Brethren (or Dunkers) whom he eventually joined; contacts with Brethren, Baptists, Methodists and Christians (Disciples); preaching in homes and meeting houses; his own depressions and constant search for evidence of God's calling; illumination of the religious diversity of the area and time; many personal names, interesting spellings.

PRESCOTT, WILLIAM HICKLING, 1796-1859   2172

LITERARY MEMORANDA. Edited by C. Harvey Gardiner. Norman: University of Oklahoma Press, 1961. 2 vols.

> 1823-1858. Notebooks of his literary activity forming documentary record of the historian's work; books read and plan of writing; little social or domestic information.

RAVENSCROFT, JOHN STARK, 1772-1830   2173

"Manuscript Journal of John Stark Ravenscroft, First Bishop of North Carolina." PROTESTANT EPISCOPAL CHURCH HISTORICAL MAGAZINE 5 (1936):42-46.

> Jun-Jul 1823. Journal of first visitation of North Carolina; sharp, entertaining comments.

ROMERO, JOSE   2174

In DIARIES AND ACCOUNTS OF THE ROMERO EXPEDITIONS IN ARIZONA AND CALIFORNIA, by Lowell J. Bean, pp. 14-24. Palm Springs, Calif.: Palm Springs Desert Museum, 1962.

> Jun-Jul 1823. Expedition charged to open a land route from Colorado River to California; return trip from Tucson to Mission San Miguel, accompanied by Father Felix Caballero, who was much respected by Indians; brief travel notes on distances, conditions, aid of Indians and their desire for missions.

SIMMONS, W.H.   2175

"Journal of Dr. W.H. Simmons." FLORIDA HISTORICAL SOCIETY QUARTERLY 1 (April 1908):28-36.

> Sep-Oct 1823. Commissioner's journey from St. Augustine to Tallahassee to choose site for capital.

STOW, BARON, 1801-1869   2176

THE MODEL PASTOR: A MEMOIR OF THE LIFE AND CORRESPONDENCE OF REV. BARON STOW. By John C. Stockbridge. Boston: Lee and Shepard, 1871. 376 pp. New ed., 1894. 392 pp. passim.

> 1823-1866. Copious extracts from clergyman's journal; student life at Columbia College, preaching tour in Virginia, ministry at Portsmouth and Boston; parish work and religious reflections; secretary of triennial convention; revival meetings; trip to Europe; Italy, Switzerland, Germany, England.

TAYLOR, JAMES BRAINERD, 1801-1829   2177

In MEMOIR OF JAMES BRAINERD TAYLOR, 2d ed., rev., by John H. Rice and Benjamin H. Rice, pp. 131-405 passim. New York: American Tract Society, 1833.

> 1823-1828. Extracts from clergyman's journal; religious exercises, self-analysis and prayers, illness; study at Nassau Hall (Princeton) and in seminary; preaching in South Carolina.

TODD, JOHN, 1800-1873   2178

JOHN TODD, THE STORY OF HIS LIFE. Compiled and edited by John Edwards Todd. New York: Harper & Brothers, 1876. 529 pp. passim.

> 1823-1871. Extracts from clergyman's journal; life at Andover, Groton, Northampton and Pittsfield, Massachusetts; personal and family affairs; full and well-written notes.

VIZCARRA, JOSE ANTONIO   2179

Brugge, David M. "Vizcarra's Navajo Campaign of 1823." ARIZONA AND THE WEST 6 (1964):223-244.

> Jun-Aug 1823. New Mexico governor's record of his campaign against elusive Navajos to settle land and livestock disputes; route, marching conditions, skirmishes, casualties. Translated from the Spanish.

WHEATON, NATHANIEL SHELDON, 1792-1862   2180

JOURNAL OF A RESIDENCE DURING SEVERAL MONTHS IN LONDON. Hartford, Conn.: H.&F.J. Huntington; New York: G.C. and H. Carvill, 1830. 520 pp.

> 1823-1824. American clergyman's travels in England and France; notes on Liverpool, London, Ely, Cambridge, Bath, Bristol, Edinburgh; considerable detail on churches, sermons, historic sites.

WILLIAMS, JOHN LEE   2181

FLORIDA HISTORICAL SOCIETY QUARTERLY 1 (April 1908):37-44; 1 (July 1908):18-27.

> Oct-Nov 1823. Commissioner's sea voyage from Pensacola to St. Marks, Florida; selection of Tallahassee as site for capital.

WORK, JOHN, 1791?-1861   2182

> Journals of trader for Hudson's Bay Company; richly descriptive accounts of fur trading and exploration; business details; important as records of the fur trade of the Northwest at the time of its greatest prosperity.

Sage, Walter N. "John Work's First Journal." CANADIAN HISTORICAL ASSOCIATION ANNUAL REPORT (1929):21-29.

> 1823-1824. Account of and extracts from journal of first journey, with Peter Skene Ogden, from York Factory to Columbia River; journeys to and from Spokane House and Fort Astoria.

Elliott, T.C., ed. "Journal of John Work." WASHINGTON HISTORICAL QUARTERLY 3 (1912):198-228; 5 (1914):83-115, 163-191, 258-287; 6 (1915):26-49.

> Nov-Dec 1824. Fort George to the Fraser River, and return.

> 1825-1826. Trading on the Columbia River.

Pipes, Nellie B., ed. "The Journal of John Work." OREGON HISTORICAL QUARTERLY 45 (1944):138-146.

Mar–May 1825. Journal kept while Work was responsible for transfer of Hudson's Bay Company goods up the Columbia from Fort George (now Astoria, Oregon) to Fort Vancouver.

Lewis, William S. and Meyers, Jacob A., eds. "Journal of a Trip from Fort Colville to Fort Vancouver and Return in 1828." WASHINGTON HISTORICAL QUARTERLY 11 (1920):104–114.

May–Aug 1828. River travel to Fort Vancouver and back to mouth of Spokane River; notes on cargo, boat repairs, relations with Indians, salmon catch, etc.

Elliott, T.C., ed. "Journal of John Work." OREGON HISTORICAL QUARTERLY 10 (1909):296–313.

Apr–May 1830. Snake River fur brigade; Fort Colville to Fort Vancouver.

Elliott, T.C., ed. "Journal of John Work." OREGON HISTORICAL QUARTERLY 13 (1912):363–371; 14 (1913):280–314.

THE SNAKE COUNTRY EXPEDITION OF 1830–1831. Edited by Francis D. Haines, Jr. American Exploration and Travel Series, vol. 59. Norman: University of Oklahoma Press, 1971. 172 pp.

Aug 1830–Jul 1831. Hudson's Bay Company fur trapping expedition, commanded by Work, under orders to deplete the Snake River drainage area of furs, thus discouraging further American settlement; descriptions of terrain, wildlife; encounters with Snake, Nez Perce and Blackfoot Indians; sufferings of trappers and their families from cold and hunger.

THE JOURNAL OF JOHN WORK, A CHIEF-TRADER OF THE HUDSON'S BAY CO. Edited by William S. Lewis and Paul C. Phillips. Cleveland: Arthur H. Clark, 1923. 209 pp.

Aug 1831–Jul 1832. Expedition from Fort Vancouver to the Flathead and Blackfoot Indians of the Pacific Northwest.

Maloney, Alice B., ed. "Fur Brigade to the Bonaventura; John Work's California Expedition of 1832–33 for the Hudson's Bay Company." CALIFORNIA HISTORICAL SOCIETY QUARTERLY 22 (1943):193–222, 323–346; 23 (1944): 19–40, 123–146.

1832–1833. Expedition of 100 men, women and children from Fort Vancouver through Oregon and into California to the Sacramento River and return; much sickness and hunger among trappers and their families; difficulties of terrain and weather; dealings with Indians; Spanish missions; results of hunting and trapping.

Scott, Leslie M., ed. "John Work's Journey." OREGON HISTORICAL QUARTERLY 24 (1923):238–268.

May–Jul 1834. Fort Vancouver to the Umpqua River and return.

Dee, Henry D., ed. "The Journal of John Work, 1835. Being an Account of His Voyage Northward from the Columbia River to Fort Simpson." BRITISH COLUMBIA HISTORICAL QUARTERLY 8 (1944):127–146, 227–244, 307–308; 9 (1945):49–69, 129–146.

THE JOURNAL OF JOHN WORK. With an introduction and notes by Henry D. Dee. Archives of British Columbia Memoir, no. 10. Victoria, British Columbia: Printed by C.F. Banfield, 1945. 96 pp.

Extracts in THE NORTHWEST, compiled by B.C. Payette, pp. 646–666. Montreal: Printed privately for Payette Radio, 1964.

Jan–Oct 1835. Maritime fur trade aboard LAMA; sea

otter, beaver; fishing; dangers faced from Haida Indians; Columbia River area.

1824

ANON.   2183

"Cherokees of the Arkansas: Journal of the Mission at Dwight." MISSIONARY HERALD 21 (1825):48–51, 175–176, 244–248.

Jul 1824–Mar 1825. Journal of American Board missionary.

ADAMS, RILEY M., 1808–1894   2184

Andrews, Frank D. "A Journal of Riley M. Adams." VINELAND HISTORICAL MAGAZINE 4 (1919):10–15, 33–36, 56–60, 74–78, 85–87, 107–110, 127–130, 153–159.

Aug–Dec 1824. Diary of cadet at Norwich Military Academy; substantial entries describing excursion of cadets to the White Mountains and camping there.

ASHLEY, WILLIAM HENRY, 1778–1838   2185

In THE ASHLEY-SMITH EXPLORATIONS AND THE DISCOVERY OF A CENTRAL ROUTE TO THE PACIFIC, edited by Harrison C. Dale, pp. 117–161. Cleveland: Arthur H. Clark, 1918; rev. ed. Glendale, Calif.: Arthur H. Clark, 1941.

Nov 1824–Aug 1825. Narrative, partly in journal form, of fur trader, exploring the Rocky Mountains from Fort Atkinson; notes on topography, etc.

Morgan, Dale L., ed. "The Diary of William H. Ashley, March 25–June 27, 1825: A Record of Exploration West across the Continental Divide, down the Green River and into the Great Basin." MISSOURI HISTORICAL SOCIETY BULLETIN 11 (1954–1955):9–40, 158–186, 279–302.

In THE WEST OF WILLIAM H. ASHLEY; THE INTERNATIONAL STRUGGLE FOR THE FUR TRADE OF THE MISSOURI, THE ROCKY MOUNTAINS AND THE COLUMBIA, edited by Dale L. Morgan, pp. 104–129. Denver: Old West Publishing, 1964.

Mar–Jun 1825. Trail-breaking expedition across the Medicine Bow mountain range and down the Green River. Text of the original manuscript diary, heretofore attributed to William Sublette but correctly identified in 1951; evidence now indicates that the narrative described above was written from memory rather than with the diary at hand.

BETHUNE, JOANNA GRAHAM, b. 1770   2186

In MEMOIRS OF MRS. JOANNA BETHUNE, by George W. Bethune, pp. 125–250. New York: Harper & Brothers, 1863.

1824–1847. Religious reflections and prayers; some domestic and family notes; work for infant schools in New York City.

BLOXAM, ANDREW   2187

DIARY OF ANDREW BLOXAM; NATURALIST ON THE BLONDE ON HER TRIP FROM ENGLAND TO THE HAWAIIAN ISLANDS. Bernice P. Bishop Museum Special Publications, 10. Honolulu: Bernice P. Bishop Museum, 1925. 95 pp.

Sep 1824–Aug 1825. Voyage of the BLONDE, sent by the British government to return the bodies of King Kamehameha II and Queen Kamamalu, who died on a trip to England; reception by Hawaiians and the funeral; gathering information on the natural history of Hawaii; reports on vegetation, cultivation, food, trips into the interior, volcanoes, waterfalls. This edition includes all of diary concerning Hawaii, with abstacts of the voyage to and from England.

CLARK, JOHN, 1745–1833 2188

Peach, Arthur W., ed. "John Clark's Journal." VERMONT HISTORICAL SOCIETY PROCEEDINGS 10 (1942):187–213.

1824–1832. Journal of elderly shoemaker/farmer; spiritual state, physical ailments, financial concerns.

DOBBIN, WILLIAM, 1771–1858 2189

In JOHN DOBBIN OF CONNAGER, DESCENDANTS, by William J. Foster, pp. 75–82. Schenectady, N.Y. and Lancaster, Pa.: Science Press Printing, 1936.

Jul–Aug 1824. Lengthy entries describing voyage from Ireland to Montreal; notes on seasickness, religious and social life on board.

DOUGLAS, DAVID, 1798–1834 2190

Hooker, W.J., ed. "A Brief Memoir of the Life of Mr. David Douglas, with Extracts from His Letters." COMPANION TO THE BOTANICAL MAGAZINE 2 (1836):79–182.

"Sketch of a Journey to the Northwestern Parts of the Continent of North America." OREGON HISTORICAL QUARTERLY 5 (1904):325–369; 6 (1905):76–97, 206–227.

"Second Journey to the Northwestern Parts of the Continent of North America." OREGON HISTORICAL QUARTERLY 6 (1905):288–309.

"Sketch of a Second Journey to the Northwestern Parts of the Continent of North America and to Sandwich Islands." OREGON HISTORICAL QUARTERLY 6 (1905):417–449.

JOURNAL KEPT BY DAVID DOUGLAS DURING HIS TRAVELS IN NORTH AMERICA, 1823–1827. London: W. Wesley & Son, 1914. 364 pp. Reprint. New York: Antiquarian Press, 1959.

DOUGLAS OF THE FORESTS: THE NORTH AMERICAN JOURNALS OF DAVID DOUGLAS. Edited by John Davies. Seattle: University of Washington Press, 1980. 188 pp. Abridgment, selections mainly from 1824–1827.

1824–1834. Two journeys to the Pacific Northwest on behalf of the Royal Horticultural Society of London; first journey to mouth of Columbia River, with various explorations in Oregon, etc.; overland with McLoughlin via Red River settlement and York Factory; return to England in October 1829; second trip to Northwest, January–December 1830, including journey to California; trip from Columbia River to Hawaiian Islands, October 1833–January 1834.

DUNCAN, ELIZABETH CALDWELL, 1808–1876 2191

Putnam, Elizabeth D., ed. "Diary of Mrs. Joseph Duncan (Elizabeth Caldwell Smith)." ILLINOIS HISTORICAL SOCIETY JOURNAL 21 (1928–1929):1–91. Supplements in "The Life and Services of Joseph Duncan, Governor of Illinois, 1834–1838," by Elizabeth D. Putnam. ILLINOIS STATE HISTORICAL SOCIETY TRANSACTIONS, no. 26 (1919), pp. 126–127, 164–167, 177–178.

Nov 1824–Feb 1825, 1828–1848. Early school life in Newark; domestic and social life in Jacksonville, Illinois.

KITTSON, WILLIAM 2192

In SNAKE COUNTRY JOURNALS, 1824–25 AND 1825–26, by Peter Skene Ogden, edited by E.E. Rich, pp. 209–250. Hudson's Bay Record Society Publications, 13. London: Hudson's Bay Record Society, 1950.

Dec 1824–Aug 1825. Journal of member of the Ogden fur trapping expedition in Oregon Territory; horse racing with Indians; some discrepancies with Ogden journal in locations and distances traveled.

Miller, David E., ed. "William Kittson's Journal Covering Peter Skene Ogden's 1824–1825 Snake Country Expedition." UTAH HISTORICAL QUARTERLY 22 (1954):125–142.

Apr–May 1825. Extract covering penetration into Utah.

LORD, DANIEL WALKER, 1800–1880 2193

Padgett, James A., ed. "Journal of Daniel Walker Lord, Kept while on a Southern Trip." GEORGIA HISTORICAL QUARTERLY 26 (1942):166–195.

Feb–May 1824. Trip of business and pleasure from Baltimore to Savannah and return to Virginia; sporadic entries describing travel by carriage, stagecoach, packet and steamship, lodgings and road conditions; major towns, including Charleston, Wilmington, Raleigh, Savannah, Baltimore, Washington, D.C., Alexandria, Williamsburg, and Richmond; trade, slavery.

MACDONALD, DONALD, 1791–1872 2194

THE DIARIES OF DONALD MACDONALD. Introduction by Caroline D. Snedeker. Indiana Historical Society Publications, vol. 14, no. 2, pp. 147–379. Indianapolis: Indiana Historical Society, 1942. Diary, pp. 159–379. Reprint. Clifton, N.J.: A.M. Kelley, 1973.

1824–1826. Travels and labors of young Scottish officer, companion and assistant to British socialist Robert Owen in effort to establish utopian community at New Harmony, Indiana; weather, conditions of travel over land and sea, agriculture, industry; notes on slavery kept during visit to New Orleans; steamboat travel on the Mississippi, with detailed observations of passengers, conditions of travel, towns, especially New Orleans; valuable as a record of travel and of the less than harmonious experiment at New Harmony.

In BEFORE MARK TWAIN: A SAMPLER OF OLD, OLD TIMES ON THE MISSISSIPPI, ed. by John F. McDermott, pp. 40–47, 278–286. Carbondale: Southern Illinois University Press, 1968.

Mar 1826. Extracts covering Mississippi River trip to New Orleans.

MARMADUKE, MEREDITH MILES, 1791–1864 2195

MISSOURI INTELLIGENCER, 2 September 1825.

Sampson, F.A., ed. "Santa Fe Trail: M.M. Marmaduke Journal." MISSOURI HISTORICAL REVIEW 6 (1911–1912):1–10.

In SOUTHWEST ON THE TURQUOISE TRAIL, edited by Archer B. Holbert, pp. 69–77.

May–Aug 1824, and May 1825. Trip from Franklin, Missouri, to Santa Fe and return next year; brief notes, mainly of stages of journey and on people and customs of New Mexico.

MARSHALL, ADAM, d. 1825 2196

Durkin, Joseph T., ed. "Journal of the Revd. Adam Marshall, Schoolmaster, U.S.S. NORTH CAROLINA." AMERICAN CATHOLIC HISTORICAL SOCIETY OF PHILADELPHIA RECORDS 53 (1942):152-168; 54 (1943):44-65.

> Dec 1824-Aug 1825. Extracts from diary of Jesuit teacher and chaplain to midshipmen on Atlantic and Mediterranean cruise under Commodore John Rodgers; teaching duties, escapades of midshipmen and corporal punishment, dangers and rigors of naval life; extensive comments about his visits to Gibraltar and Spain; a cheerful diary despite the tuberculosis to which he succumbed on return voyage.

OGDEN, PETER SKENE, 1790-1854 2197

SNAKE COUNTRY JOURNALS, 1824-25 AND 1825-26. Edited by E.E. Rich. Hudson's Bay Record Society Publications, 13. London: Hudson's Bay Record Society, 1950. 283 pp.

> 1824-1826. Fur trapping and trading expedition from Flathead Post to Snake Country, the unknown eastern and southern area of Oregon; difficulties with freemen and American trappers; privations, rugged life; opinions on Hudson's Bay Company policy; venture as far south as Taos and first brigade into Ogden Valley.

Elliott, T.C., ed. "The Peter Skene Ogden Journals." OREGON HISTORICAL QUARTERLY 10 (1909):331-365; 11 (1910):201-222, 355-396.

> 1825-1829. Reports of Snake River expeditions; notes on fur trapping, Indian affairs, statistics; important geographically.

Miller, David E., ed. "Peter Skene Ogden's Journal of His Expedition to Utah." UTAH HISTORICAL QUARTERLY 20 (1952):160-186.

> 1825. Extract covering Utah portion of expedition.

SNAKE COUNTRY JOURNAL, 1826-27. Edited by K.G. Davies. Hudson's Bay Record Society Publications, 23. London: Hudson's Bay Record Society, 1961. 255 pp.

> Sep 1826-Jul 1827. From Fort Vancouver into southern Oregon Territory; long entries giving details of Indian customs, personal opinions on fur trapping.

PETER SKENE OGDEN'S SNAKE COUNTRY JOURNALS, 1827-28 and 1828-29. Edited by Glyndwr Williams. Hudson's Bay Record Society Publications, 28. London: Hudson's Bay Record Society, 1971. 201 pp.

> 1827-1829. Journals kept in Oregon Territory and northern Nevada; discovery of Humboldt River; comments on British-American relations and competition; concern over destruction of beaver population.

OWEN, WILLIAM, 1802-1842 2198

DIARY OF WILLIAM OWEN. Edited by Joel W. Hiatt. Indiana Historical Society Publications, vol. 4, no. 1. Indianapolis: Bobbs-Merrill, 1906. 134 pp. Reprint. Clifton, N.J.: A.M. Kelley, 1973.

> Nov 1824-Apr 1825. Scottish immigrant's diary of travels and life at New Harmony, Indiana; social life, work, visits, friends, church activities, amusements; trips to New York, Philadelphia, Washington, Cincinnati, Pittsburgh; a pleasant and intelligent diary.

PAINE, ABIEL WARE, 1787-1852 2199

Extracts in THE DISCOVERY OF A GRANDMOTHER: GLIMPSES INTO THE HOMES AND LIVES OF EIGHT GENERATIONS OF A IPSWICH-PAINE FAMILY, by Lydia Augusta Paine Carter, pp. 76-131. Newtonville, Mass.: H.H. Carter, 1920.

> 1824-1851. Family and domestic affairs, religious life, visits; an intimate record of diarist's life, mainly at Winslow, Massachusetts.

PORTER, MOSES, 1794-1858 2200

"Diary for the Year 1824." DANVERS HISTORICAL SOCIETY COLLECTIONS 1 (1913):31-51; 2 (1914):54-63. Diary, pp. 54-63.

> Jan-Dec 1824. Daily work and social life of a farmer; markets and prices; notes on Danvers and Salem; a pleasant diary.

QUINCY, MARGARET MORTON, b. 1806 2201

In THE ARTICULATE SISTERS, by M.A. DeWolfe Howe, pp. 49-145.

> 1824-1828. Journal of daughter of Josiah Quincy; the pleasures and gaiety of the summer resort, Nahant; General Lafayette's visit to Boston; a party at Quincy; after her marriage to Benjamin Daniel Greene, travel by ship to Havana with a stopover at Charleston, South Carolina; return via New Orleans, where she attended the opera, LA DAME BLANCHE; on to New York and home to Boston.

RIDOUT, HORATIO, 1769-1834 2202

"Journal of a Voyage down the Chesapeake Bay on a Fishing Expedition." MARYLAND MAGAZINE OF HISTORY 51 (1956):140-153.

> Sep-Oct 1824. Lively account of a fishing trip, which included visits to Norfolk, Hampton and Fortress Monroe.

ROSS, ALEXANDER, 1783-1856 2203

Elliott, T.C., ed. "Journal of Alexander Ross--Snake Country Expedition." OREGON HISTORICAL QUARTERLY 14 (1913):366-388.

> 1824-1825. Scotsman's journal of a Hudson's Bay Company expedition; notes on hunting, Indians and interesting account of trouble with Piegans.

SCOULER, JOHN, 1804-1871 2204

"Account of a Voyage to Madeira, Brazil, Juan Fernandez, and the Gallapagos Islands." EDINBURGH JOURNAL OF SCIENCE 5 (1826):195-214; 6 (1827):51-73, 228-236.

"Dr. John Scouler's Journal of a Voyage to Northwest America." OREGON HISTORICAL QUARTERLY 6 (1905):54-75, 159-205, 276-287.

> 1824-1826. Travel journal of Hudson's Bay Company surgeon aboard the Hudson's Bay ship WILLIAM AND ANNE; voyage from England to the Columbia River; Vancouver, Nootka Sound; zoological notes.

WHITCOMB, SAMUEL, b. 1792? 2205

Peden, William, ed. "A Book Peddler Invades Monticello." WILLIAM AND MARY QUARTERLY, 3d ser. 6 (1949):631-636.

May–Jun 1824. Book peddler's summaries of separate conversations with Thomas Jefferson and James Madison; discussions with Jefferson covering political and theological topics and old age; with Madison, mainly political matters; description of both men and comparisons of their personalities.

1825

ANON. 2206

Reid, Russell and Gannon, Clell G., eds. "Journal of the Atkinson-O'Fallon Expedition." NORTH DAKOTA HISTORICAL QUARTERLY 4 (1929):5-56.

May–Oct 1825. Official journal of the expedition; up the Missouri from St. Louis to the mouth of the Yellowstone; careful details of movements, mileage, topography; useful geographically.

ATKINSON, HENRY, 1782–1842 2207

In THE WEST OF WILLIAM H. ASHLEY; THE INTERNATIONAL STRUGGLE FOR THE FUR TRADE OF THE MISSOURI, THE ROCKY MOUNTAINS AND THE COLUMBIA, edited by Dale L. Morgan, pp. 130-136. Denver: The Old West, 1964.

Aug–Sep 1825. Exploration journal of the Atkinson-O'Fallon Expedition; the return trip from Yellowstone to Fort Atkinson; chiefly travel conditions and securing of provisions.

BROBSON, WILLIAM P., 1786–1850 2208

Gibson, George H., ed. "William P. Brobson Diary." DELAWARE HISTORY 15 (1972-1973):55-84, 124-155, 195-217, 295-311.

1825–1828. Diary of Wilmington Quaker and Whig member of Delaware legislature; local events, obituaries and discourses on political, social and literary topics; opinions on slavery, Elias Hicks, etc.; observations of Congress, particularly noting John Randolph's behavior.

DAVIS, JOSEPH 2209

In THE ROAD TO SANTA FE: THE JOURNAL AND DIARIES OF GEORGE CHAMPLIN SIBLEY AND OTHERS, edited by Kate L. Gregg, pp. 162-168. Albuquerque: University of New Mexico Press, 1952.

Sep–Oct 1825. Diary of member of Sibley survey party on return from Mexican boundary; route, travel conditions, weather.

DEADERICK, DAVID ANDERSON, 1797–1873 2210

Williams, Samuel C., ed. "Journal of Events of David Anderson Deaderick." EAST TENNESSEE HISTORICAL SOCIETY PUBLICATIONS 8 (1936):121-137; 9 (1937):93-110.

1825–1872. Notes on chief public events, especially those relating to east Tennessee; journalistic and impersonal, arranged as annals.

DERBY, EDWARD GEORGE GEOFFREY SMITH STANLEY, 14th earl of, 1799–1869 2211

JOURNAL OF A TOUR IN AMERICA. London: Privately printed, 1930. 342 pp.

Jan 1825. English nobleman's journal of travel through Canada and United States; trip by steamboat up the Alabama River from Mobile to Montgomery and on horseback to Augusta; description of land and lifestyle, accommodations and road conditions; remarks added later on Creek Indians, controversy over Indian lands, slavery.

FINAN, P. 2212

JOURNAL OF A VOYAGE TO QUEBEC. Newry, Mass.: Printed by A. Peacock, 1828. 400 pp.

Apr–Aug 1825. Voyage to Quebec, combined with recollections of Canada during the War of 1812.

FOLSOM, GEORGE WILLIAM, 1803–1827 2213

In EARLY YEARS OF THE MCLEAN HOSPITAL, RECORDED IN THE JOURNAL OF GEORGE WILLIAM FOLSOM, by Nina Fletcher Little, pp. 27-148. Boston: Francis A. Countway Library of Medicine, 1972.

Feb–Dec 1825. Harvard medical student's record of his apprenticeship at the Asylum for the Insane at Charlestown, Massachusetts; daily rounds among patients, preparation of medicines; reading, both medical and religious; comments on prominent doctors of Boston area, especially Dr. Rufus Wyman, with whom he lived; a quiet social life and his increasingly bad health; an interesting picture of early nineteenth century medical education and institutional care of the insane.

HOWE, SAMUEL GRIDLEY, 1801–1876 2214

LETTERS AND JOURNALS OF SAMUEL GRIDLEY HOWE. Edited by Laura E. Richards. Boston: D. Estes, 1906-1909. 2 vols. passim.

1825–1829. Extracts covering Byronic adventures in Greece during the Revolution; account of Missolonghi, siege of Athens; philanthropic work at Corinth; literary and romantic interests.

JONES, PETER, 1802–1856 2215

LIFE AND JOURNALS OF KAH-KE-WA-QUO-NA-BY: (REV. PETER JONES,) WESLEYAN MISSIONARY. Published under the direction of the Missionary Committee, Canada Conference. Toronto: A. Green, 1860. 424 pp.

1825–1856. Methodist missionary journals of Chippewa chief; extensive and detailed notes of work and life, mainly among Chippewas, also Moravian and Munceytown Indians.

LAURENS, CAROLINE OLIVIA 2216

King, Louise C., ed. "Journal of a Visit to Greenville from Charleston." SOUTH CAROLINA HISTORICAL MAGAZINE 72 (1971):164-173, 220-233.

May–Nov 1825. Trip by carriage from Charleston to Greenville; sojourn there and in nearby Pendleton, and return to Charleston; social life, views on slavery, description of a Masonic lodge.

LONGACRE, JAMES B., 1794–1869 2217

"Extracts from the Diary of James B. Longacre." PENNSYLVANIA MAGAZINE OF HISTORY AND BIOGRAPHY 29 (1905):134-142.

Jul–Aug 1825. Extracts from engraver's diary of travel from Philadelphia to New York, Albany, Boston, Rhode Island, and Connecticut; particular attention to art in New York and Boston.

OWEN, ROBERT DALE, 1801–1877 2218

TO HOLLAND AND TO NEW HARMONY: ROBERT DALE OWEN'S TRAVEL JOURNAL. Edited by Josephine M.

Elliott. Indiana Historical Society Publications, vol. 23, no. 4. Indianapolis: Indiana Historical Society, 1969. 296 pp. Journal, pp. 175-296.

May 1825-Jan 1826. Travel journal of son of Robert Owen, leader of New Harmony community; care of his father's cotton mills at New Lanark, Scotland; voyage to America; visits to New York and Philadelphia; trip by keelboat, icebound for a month during which time he hunted and explored the countryside; continuation of trip to Mount Vernon, Indiana, and thence by horseback to New Harmony.

ROBERT DALE OWEN'S TRAVEL JOURNAL, 1827. Edited by Josephine M. Elliott. Indiana Historical Society Publications, vol. 25, no. 4. Indianapolis: Indiana Historical Society, 1978. 71 pp.

May-Aug 1827. Trip down Ohio and Mississippi rivers, accompanying Frances Wright to her utopian community at Nashoba, Tennessee; Atlantic crossing and travels as tourist in England and France.

PAINE, ALBERT BULKELEY, 1807-1885   2219

In HISTORY OF SAMUEL PAINE, JR., edited by Albert P. Paine, pp. 92-100. Randolph Center, Vt., 1923.

1825-1828. Farmer's diary kept at Randolph, Vermont; work, weather, visits, illness, family affairs; interesting.

PEARD, GEORGE, 1783-1837   2220

TO THE PACIFIC AND ARCTIC WITH BEECHEY: THE JOURNAL OF LT. GEORGE PEARD OF H.M.S. BLOSSOM. Edited by Harry M. Gough. Hakluyt Society Works, 2d ser., no. 143. Cambridge: Published for the Hakluyt Society at the University Press, 1973. 272 pp.

1825-1828. Journal of Frederick William Beechey's scientific mission from England to the North Pacific, attempting to meet Sir John Franklin's party in its search for Northwest Passage; two stops in Hawaii for provisions, with observations on beauty and richness of land; food, towns, customs and organization of Hawaiians; call at San Francisco; description of its mission, including conversion of Indians by coercive means; Indian customs; prices; botanical and geological observations; call at Monterey; explorations along coast of Alaska, with notes on Indians and bartering; some entries long and in narrative style.

Gough, Barry M., ed. "The Views of Lt. George Peard, R.N., on Alta California." SOUTHERN CALIFORNIA QUARTERLY 56 (1974):213-229.

1826-1827. Extract relating to California.

REED, ISAAC, 1787-1858   2221

THE CHRISTIAN TRAVELLER. New York: Printed by J.J. Harper, 1828. 242 pp.

Extract in "Early Presbyterianism in East Central Illinois," by Ira W. Allen. ILLINOIS STATE HISTORICAL SOCIETY TRANSACTIONS, no. 22 (1916), pp. 71-78. Diary, pp. 74-76.

1825. Presbyterian clergyman's travels in Indiana and eastern Illinois to organize Presbyterian church; trip to Paris, Illinois.

REEVES, BENJAMIN H.   2222

In THE ROAD TO SANTA FE: THE JOURNAL AND DIARIES OF GEORGE CHAMPLIN SIBLEY AND OTHERS, edited by

Kate L. Gregg, pp. 169-174. Albuquerque: University of New Mexico Press, 1952.

Oct 1825. Brief notes of member of Santa Fe Trail Commission on a surveying expedition with George Sibley.

SIBLEY, GEORGE CHAMPLAIN, 1782-1863   2223

In THE ROAD TO SANTA FE: THE JOURNAL AND DIARIES OF GEORGE CHAMPLIN SIBLEY AND OTHERS, edited by Kate L. Gregg, pp. 49-161. Albuquerque: University of New Mexico Press, 1952.

1825-1827. Private journal of government trader at Fort Osage and commissioner to survey and mark road from Missouri frontier to Mexican settlements; St. Louis to Santa Fe and Taos; official activities of marking the route, conditions of travel, game; notes on people and events; meeting with Indians.

WESTERN JOURNAL 5 (1852):178 ff. Reprint. In SOUTHWEST ON THE TURQUOISE TRAIL, edited by Archer B. Hulbert, pp. 133-174.

Oct 1825-Mar 1826. Survey of the Santa Fe Trail; some personal, business and social items.

TAYLOE, EDWARD THORNTON, 1803-1876   2224

MEXICO, 1825-1828: THE JOURNAL AND CORRESPONDENCE OF EDWARD THORNTON TAYLOE. Edited by C. Harvey Gardiner. Chapel Hill: University of North Carolina Press, 1959. 212 pp.

1825-1828. Travels throughout Mexico of secretary to Joel Roberts Pionsett, who was later to be first United States minister to Mexico; meetings with President Guadalupe Victoria and other dignitaries; interest in Indians, ruins, religion, festivals, hospitals, politics, natural history; many aspects of Mexican life.

UNDERWOOD, JOSEPH ROGERS, 1791-1876   2225

Stickles, Arndt M., ed. "Joseph R. Underwood's Fragmentary Journal of the New and Old Court Contest in Kentucky." FILSON CLUB HISTORY QUARTERLY 13 (1939):202-210.

1825-1826. Fragments relating to the Old and New Court contest.

Stickles, Arndt M., ed. "Joseph R. Underwood's Fragmentary Journal: Closing Entries Giving His Views on Political Campaigns and President Jackson in Kentucky." FILSON CLUB HISTORY QUARTERLY 15 (1941): 41-44.

Sep 1832. Interviews with President Jackson.

1826

ALCOTT, AMOS BRONSON, 1799-1888   2226

THE JOURNALS OF BRONSON ALCOTT. Edited by Odell Shepard. Boston: Little, Brown, 1938. 559 pp. Reprint. Port Washington, N.Y.: Kennikat, 1966. 2 vols.

1826-1882. Selections from the extensive and far-ranging journals of the Boston area transcendentalist, self-styled Socratic teacher and utopian reformer; teaching experiences; resolves and aspirations; family life; views on religion, philosophy, science, art and reading; interactions with and comments on numerous people; important for a glimpse of a mind preoccupied with speculative thought and of Alcott's influential circle.

Myerson, Joel, ed. "Bronson Alcott's 'Journal for 1836'." In STUDIES IN THE AMERICAN RENAISSANCE,

1978, edited by Joel Myerson, pp. 17–104. Boston: Twayne, 1978.

Jan–Dec 1836. Record of teaching, reading, writing, thoughts, beliefs, etc; impressions of Emerson; mention of many persons prominent in the New England intellectual world of that time; much material excluded by Shepard.

Carlson, Larry A., ed. "Journal for 1837 (Part One)." In STUDIES IN THE AMERICAN RENAISSANCE, 1981, edited by Joel Myerson, pp. 27–132. Boston: Twayne, 1981.

Jan–Dec 1837. A difficult year, which saw failure of Bronson's Temple School; views on the nature of children and how to educate them; public reaction to his CONVERSATIONS WITH CHILDREN ON THE GOSPELS; notes on lectures of others; break in friendship with William Ellery Channing; visits with Emerson, Fuller, Ripley and others; as in all his journals, much philosophical reflection.

ALEXANDER, JOSEPH ADDISON, 1809–1860   2227

In THE LIFE OF JOSEPH ADDISON ALEXANDER, by Henry Carrington Alexander, 2 vols. passim. New York: Scribners, 1870.

1826?–1860? Biography interspersed with journal extracts of brilliant Biblical scholar, linguist and professor at Princeton Theological Seminary.

ARNETT, THOMAS, 1791–1877   2228

JOURNAL OF THE LIFE, TRAVELS AND GOSPEL LABORS OF THOMAS ARNETT. Chicago: Publishing Association of Friends, 1884. 422 pp. passim.

1826–1861. Journal of religion life, work and travels of an itinerant Quaker minister; entries set in autobiography.

BRYSON, HENRY, 1799–1874   2229

Williams, John R., ed. "Frontier Evangelist: The Journal of Henry Bryson." ALABAMA HISTORICAL QUARTERLY 42 (1980):5–39.

Dec 1826–Jun 1827. Evangelistic trip through Georgia, Tennessee, Alabama and Florida of young man licensed to preach by the Associate Reformed Presbyterian Church; services, lodgings, with names and places of hosts, expenses; religious condition of people along the way.

CLINTON, GEORGE W.   2230

"Journal of a Tour from Albany to Lake Erie by the Erie Canal." BUFFALO HISTORICAL SOCIETY PUBLICATIONS 14 (1910):273–305.

Apr–Jun 1826. Excursion of the Rensselaer School from Albany to Lake Erie, by the Erie Canal; mainly natural history notes and botanical nomenclature.

ELSON, THOMAS   2231

In TO THE PACIFIC AND ARCTIC WITH BEECHEY: THE JOURNAL OF LT. GEORGE PEARD OF H.M.S. BLOSSOM, by George Peard, edited by Harry M. Gough, pp. 159–167. Hakluyt Society Works, 2d ser., no. 143. Cambridge: Published for the Hakluyt Society at the University Press, 1973.

Aug–Oct 1826. Account by master's mate of the BLOSSOM, sent in barge to explore coast of Alaska as far as Point Barrow and to search for Sir John Franklin; difficulties with inhabitants, weather and crushing ice.

GLOVER, JOHN, 1778–1857   2232

Windell, Marie G., ed. "Westward along the Boone's Lick Trail in 1826, the Diary of Colonel John Glover." MISSOURI HISTORICAL REVIEW 39 (1945):184–199.

Oct–Nov 1826. Journey on horseback from Kentucky through Indiana and Illinois to Missouri and back, to investigate prospects for settlement in Missouri; mostly record of fees charged for accommodations and ferrying.

HUTCHISON, SUSAN NYE, b. 1790   2233

De Treville, Virginia E. "Extracts from the Journal of Susan Nye Hutchison while She Was Living at Augusta, Ga." RICHMOND COUNTY HISTORY 11 (1979):26–33.

1826–1833. Private diary reflecting everyday life in Augusta; reports of arson and fears of slave insurrection; river and sea voyage back to New York after husband's death.

MCLEOD, ALEXANDER RODERICK   2234

In SNAKE COUNTRY JOURNAL, by Peter Skene Ogden, edited by K.G. Davies, pp. 141–219. Hudson's Bay Record Society Publications, 23. London: Hudson's Bay Record Society, 1961.

May 1826–Mar 1827. Journal of Hudson's Bay Company fur trader leading expedition from Fort Vancouver through western Oregon Territory; trapping, trading, negotiations with Indians, hunting for food.

In THE TRAVELS OF JEDEDIAH SMITH, edited by Maurice S. Sullivan, pp. 112–135. Santa Ana, Calif.: Fine Arts Press, 1934.

Sep–Dec 1831. Travel journal from Fort Vancouver southward; recovering property of Jedediah Smith taken by Indians after the massacre on Umpqua River.

READ, ALMIRA HATHAWAY, 1797–1831   2235

Darden, Genevieve, M., ed. "A Visit to Saratoga." NEW YORK HISTORY 50 (1969):283–301.

Aug–Sep 1826. Travel journal reflecting a pious young woman's search for health and spiritual salvation; journey to Saratoga Springs by sloop, steamer and stagecoach.

ROGERS, HARRISON G., d. 1828   2236

In THE ASHLEY-SMITH EXPLORATIONS AND THE DISCOVERY OF A CENTRAL ROUTE TO THE PACIFIC, edited by Harrison C. Dale, pp. 197–228. Cleveland: Arthur H. Clark, 1918; rev. ed. Glendale, Calif.: Arthur H. Clark, 1941.

Extracts in THE SPLENDID WAYFARING; THE STORY OF THE EXPLOITS AND ADVENTURES OF JEDEDIAH SMITH AND HIS COMRADES, THE ASHLEY-HENRY MEN, DISCOVERERS AND EXPLORERS OF THE GREAT CENTRAL ROUTE FROM THE MISSOURI RIVER TO THE PACIFIC OCEAN, by John G. Neihardt, pp. 262–268. New York: Macmillan, 1920.

Nov 1826–Jan 1827. Journal of fur traders' clerk on J.S. Smith's southwestern expedition; San Gabriel and San Bernardino; interesting details of Spanish life and religion; some linguistic interest.

May–Jul 1828. March through northern California and southern Oregon; detailed account of Indians and the country; personal items; an interesting journal.

SCHIRMER, JACOB FREDERICK, 1803–1880　　2237

"The Schirmer Diary." SOUTH CAROLINA HISTORICAL MAGAZINE 67 (1966):167–171, 229–233; 68 (1967):37–41, 97–100; 69 (1968):59–65, 139–144, 204–208, 262–266; 70 (1969):59–63, 122–125, 196–199; 72 (1971):115–118; 73 (1972):97–98, 156–158, 220–221; 74 (1973):39–40, 103–104, 170–172, 311–315; 75 (1974):50–52, 121–122, 187–188, 249–251; 76 (1975):35–37, 87–88, 171–173, 250–252; 77 (1976):49–51, 127–129, 194–195; 78 (1977):71–73, 168–169, 264; 79 (1978):72–74, 166, 250–252; 80 (1979): 88–90, 192, 265–266; 81 (1980):92–93; 82 (1981):85–86, 194–196, 288; (in progress).

    1826–. Extracts from prominent Charlestonian's personal diary; mainly record of births, marriages and deaths; brief notes on local building, business; elections, entertainment, national politics and Mexican War.

"Extracts from the Schirmer Diary, 1860." SOUTH CAROLINA HISTORICAL MAGAZINE 61 (1960):163, 232.

    Jan–Mar 1860. Local events in Charleston.

"Extracts from the Schirmer Diary, 1861." SOUTH CAROLINA HISTORICAL MAGAZINE 62 (1961):54, 113–114, 182, 237.

    Jan–Dec 1861. The capture of Fort Sumter and effects of the Union blockade; reports of war news.

SHILLITOE, THOMAS, 1754–1836　　2238

"Journal of the Life, Labours and Travels of Thomas Shillitoe." FRIENDS' LIBRARY 3 (1839):74–486. Journal, pp. 341–478.

    1826–1829. English ministering Quaker's tour of the United States; voyage from Liverpool; travels and religious work in New York, Canada, Buffalo, New England, Baltimore, Philadelphia, New Jersey, Ohio, Indiana, Kentucky; visits to Indians, President Adams, prisons and Moravians; account of Hicksites; comments on slavery; considerable interest.

JOURNAL OF THE LIFE, LABORS AND TRAVELS OF THOMAS SHILLITOE. London: Harvey and Darton, 1839. 2 vols.

    1828–1829.

SMITH, JOHN, 1796–1886　　2239

"Journal of John Smith." ESSEX INSTITUTE HISTORICAL COLLECTIONS 106 (1970):88–107.

    Nov 1826–Mar 1827. Journal of Andover, Massachusetts, manufacturer's trip back to Scotland; reunion with family and friends at Brechin; factory tours in Glasgow, etc.

VAN VLECK, CHARLES A., 1794–1845　　2240

Fries, Adelaide L., ed. "Travel Journal of Charles A. Van Vleck." NORTH CAROLINA HISTORICAL REVIEW 8 (1931):187–206.

    Oct 1826. Moravian minister's journey from Salem, North Carolina, to Bethlehem, Pennsylvania; difficulties of travel with a family.

WHITALL, HANNAH, d. 1848　　2241

Extracts in JOHN M. WHITALL: THE STORY OF HIS LIFE, by Hannah Whitall Smith, pp. 42–58. Philadelphia: Printed for the family, 1879.

    1826–1844. Notes on family and personal affairs, deaths, religious reflections, work as a schoolmistress.

1827

ANON.　　2242

Albree, John. "An Old Diary of a Young Man." LYNN HISTORICAL SOCIETY REGISTER, no. 25, pt. 2 (1923–1928), pp. 121–123.

    Sep 1827–Mar 1828. Account, with quotations, of army officer's diary; politics, social life, plays in Washington, D.C.

AIME, VALCOUR, 1798–1867　　2243

PLANTATION DIARY OF THE LATE MR. VALCOUR AIME. New Orleans: Clark & Hofeline, 1878. 192 pp.

Extracts in PLANTATION AND FRONTIER DOCUMENTS, edited by Ulrich B. Phillips, vol. 1, pp. 214–230.

    1827–1853. Notes on the pioneer operation of the St. James sugar plantation and refinery near New Orleans; cutting and hauling wood, with the amounts required to produce sugar; other crops produced.

BILL, JOHN　　2244

THE ENGLISH PARTY'S EXCURSION TO PARIS, IN EASTER WEEK 1849, TO WHICH IS ADDED, A TRIP TO AMERICA. London: Longman, 1850. 557 pp. Journal, pp. 152–440.

    1827–1828. Englishman's travel journal to America and return; New York, down the Ohio and Mississippi to New Orleans; revised for publication.

BOLLING, WILLIAM, b. 1777　　2245

"Diary of Col. William Bolling of Bolling Hall." VIRGINIA MAGAZINE OF HISTORY AND BIOGRAPHY 43 (1935): 237–250, 330–342; 44 (1936):15–24, 120–128, 238–245, 323–334; 45 (1937):29–39; 46 (1938):44–51, 146–152, 234–239, 321–328; 47 (1939):27–31.

    1827–1828. Details of running three plantations in Goochland County, Virginia; trips to Fredericksburg for church convention and to Richmond for anti-Jackson convention; primarily a farming diary, with valuable details of large-scale agriculture.

CLOPPER, EDWARD NICHOLAS, 1803–1828　　2246

In AN AMERICAN FAMILY: ITS UPS AND DOWNS THROUGH EIGHT GENERATIONS, by Edward N. Clopper, pp. 156–169. Huntington, W. Va.: Printed by Standard Printing & Publishing, 1950.

    Nov 1827–Mar 1828. Journal of river travel, scenery and shipping activities on the Ohio and Mississippi rivers from Cincinnati to New Orleans; sea travel to Galveston, Texas; up Buffalo River to settle in Harrisburg; establishing mercantile business in Austin Colony, building warehouse and house, gardening.

CLOPPER, JOSEPH CHAMBERS, 1802–1861　　2247

In AN AMERICAN FAMILY: ITS UPS AND DOWNS THROUGH EIGHT GENERATIONS, by Edward N. Clopper, pp. 170–197. Huntington, W. Va.: Printed by Standard Printing & Publishing, 1950.

    1827–1828. Irregularly dated entries of trip with his brother, Edward Nicholas Clopper; details of ocean voyage from New Orleans to Galveston; seafood treats after sea sickness; settling in Harrisburg; following lumber raft down river; trading trips to San Felipe; descriptions of Colonel Austin, other personalities and social life of

Austin Colony; death of his brother during trip to San Antonio.

"J.C. Clopper's Journal and Book of Memoranda." TEXAS STATE HISTORICAL ASSOCIATION QUARTERLY 13 (1909-1910):44-80.

Nov 1827-Oct 1828.

CORCORAN, JOHN　　　　　　　　　　　　2248

Ravenswaay, Charles Van, ed. "The Diary of John Corcoran." MISSOURI HISTORICAL SOCIETY BULLETIN 13 (1956-1957):264-274.

Jun-Sep 1827. Straightforward account of family's journey from the Red River in Hudson's Bay Territory to St. Louis by cart and canoe; hardships of travel; unfortunately, geographical locations not clarified.

ERMATINGER, EDWARD, 1797-1876　　　　2249

Ermatinger, C.O. and White, James, eds. "Edward Ermatinger's York Factory Express Journal." ROYAL SOCIETY OF CANADA PROCEEDINGS AND TRANSACTIONS, 3d ser. 6 (1912):sec. 2, 67-127.

1827-1828. Hudson's Bay Company journal; journeys between Fort Vancouver and Hudson's Bay; mainly brief, undeveloped notes of stages, weather, hunting, etc.

HIGGINSON, LOUISA S.　　　　　　　　　2250

"Cambridge Eighty Years Since." CAMBRIDGE HISTORICAL SOCIETY PUBLICATIONS 2 (1906-1907):20-32.

Oct 1827-Mar 1828. Extracts from diary-letters of Thomas Wentworth Higginson's mother; social life and gossip in Cambridge, Massachusetts, while her husband was steward and patron at Harvard; entertaining.

HOBBIE, HANNAH, 1806-1831　　　　　　2251

Extracts in MEMOIR OF HANNAH HOBBIE: OR, CHRISTIAN ACTIVITY, AND TRIUMPH IN SUFFERING, by Robert G. Armstrong, pp. 32-225 passim. New York: American Tract Society, 1837?

1827-1831. Young woman's religious journal; reflections, self-abasement, consolations; family notes and religious visits.

IDE, SIMEON, 1794-1889　　　　　　　　2252

Extracts in SIMEON IDE, YEOMAN, FREEMAN, PIONEER PRINTER, by Louis W. Flanders, pp. 9-347 passim. Rutland, Vt.: Tuttle, 1931.

1827-1878. Biographical and social notes of a Windsor, Vermont, printer.

JUDAH, SAMUEL, b. 1777　　　　　　　　2253

Judah, John M., ed. "A Journal of Travel from New York to Indiana." INDIANA MAGAZINE OF HISTORY 17 (1921):338-352.

Oct-Dec 1827. Travel from New York to Vincennes, Indiana, to visit his lawyer son.

KEENEY, SALMON, 1794-1847　　　　　　2254

Everett, Helen, ed. "Salmon Keeney's Visit to Michigan." MICHIGAN HISTORY 40 (1956):433-446.

Jun-Aug 1827. Trip from Pennsylvania to Michigan to acquire land; distances, route, including names of towns and people with whom he lodged; travel by coach, lake and canal boats and canoe; potential for farming in Michigan.

KELLY, THOMAS, d. 1870　　　　　　　　2255

THOMAS KELLY AND FAMALY'S (SIC) JOURNAL: BEING THE DIARY OF ONE THOMAS KELLY, A MANXMAN FROM JURBY. Edited by Margery West. n.p.: Isle of Man Examiner, 1935; Douglas, Isle of Man: Times Press, 1965. 51 pp.

Apr 1827-Jan 1828. Scattered entries for 1830, 1845, 1870; tender journal of private thoughts about Isle of Man, his native land, its legends, myths and ruins; trip to New York aboard sailing ship ANACREON, thence to Plainsville, Ohio, where he settled with his family.

LAPHAM, INCREASE ALLEN, 1811-1875　2256

Thomas, Samuel W. and Conner, Eugene H., eds. "The Falls of the Ohio River and Its Environs: The Journals of Increase Allen Lapham." FILSON CLUB HISTORY QUARTERLY 45 (1971):5-34, 199-226, 315-341, 381-403. Reprint. THE JOURNALS OF INCREASE ALLEN LAPHAM FOR 1827-1830. Edited by Samuel Thomas and Eugene H. Conner. Louisville, Ky.: Clark, 1973. 127 pp.

1827-1830. Teen-aged engineer's extensive record of work on the Ohio Canal built to circumvent the falls of the Ohio River; technical and practical details of canal excavation, building, design of locks, etc; cultural life of Louisville; the diarist's scientific reading, geological and zoological observations, chemical experiments, and sporadic formal education; sickness and remedies; interesting diary of a hard-working and precocious young man.

MITCHELL, ELISHA, 1793-1857　　　　　2257

DIARY OF A GEOLOGICAL TOUR. Introduction and notes by Kemp P. Battle. University of North Carolina. James Sprunt Historical Monograph, no. 6. Chapel Hill: University of North Carolina, 1905. 73 pp.

Dec 1827-Aug 1828. Professor's diary-letters to his wife, kept during vacation while he was doing field work in North Carolina, etc; partly personal, but mostly geological.

POTTS, WILLIAM S., 1802-1852　　　　2258

Smoot, Joseph G., ed. "A Presbyterian Minister Calls on President John Quincy Adams." NEW ENGLAND QUARTERLY 34 (1961):379-382.

Nov 1827. Brief but detailed account of diarist's interview with Adams to request a donation, which he declined to give, for the education of ministers; description of Washington, D.C., the White House and Capitol.

Smoot, Joseph G., ed. "An Account of Alabama Indian Missions and Presbyterian Churches in 1828." ALABAMA REVIEW 18 (1965):134-152.

Mar-Apr 1828. Presbyterian minister's horseback journey from Macon, Georgia, through Alabama, visiting missions to Creek and Cherokee Indians; notes on Presbyterian congregations and the annual session of the South Alabama Presbytery; interesting, detailed descriptions.

Smoot, Joseph G., ed. "A Presbyterian Minister Calls on Presidential Candidate Andrew Jackson." TENNESSEE HISTORICAL QUARTERLY 21 (1962):287-290.

Apr 1828. Account of visit to the Hermitage; evaluative description of Andrew Jackson, his wife, home and hospitality.

SANCHEZ, JOSE MARIA 2259

Castaneda, Carlos E., trans. "A Trip to Texas." SOUTHWESTERN HISTORICAL QUARTERLY 29 (1925-1926): 249-288.

Nov 1827-Jun 1828. Journal of a draftsman with a commission to arrange boundary between Mexico and the United States; travels through Laredo, Bexar, Austin, Nacogdoches; details of Indians; historical notes.

SMITH, JEDEDIAH, 1798-1831 2260

THE TRAVELS OF JEDEDIAH SMITH. Edited by Maurice S. Sullivan. Santa Ana, Calif.: Fine Arts Press. 195 pp. Journal, pp. 1-105.

1827-1828. Travel journal of trader and explorer in and west of the Rockies; fur trade; walk across Utah desert; second journey into California; escapes from Mojaves and adventures in California and Oregon; details of life of a trader and of Indian life; an important journal.

SNELLING, JOSIAH, 1782-1828 2261

Dick, Helen D. "A Newly Discovered Diary of Colonel Josiah Snelling." MINNESOTA HISTORY 18 (1937):399-406.

1827-1828. Quotations from diarist's activities at Fort Snelling.

TOWNSEND, PETER SOLOMON, 1796-1849 2262

Rosen, George, ed. "An American Doctor in Paris in 1828: Selections from the Diary of Peter Solomon Townsend." JOURNAL OF THE HISTORY OF MEDICINE 6 (1951):64-115, 209-252.

Dec 1827-Aug 1828. Physician's trip to Paris; sightseeing, visiting museums and theaters, attending a masked ball which he called "the most stupid amusement I ever witnessed"; visits to medical schools and hospitals, meeting many prominent medical men, and involvement in controversy over contagious or non-contagious nature of yellow fever.

VINTON, JOHN R., 1801-1847 2263

Bonner, James C., ed. "Journal of a Mission to Georgia in 1827." GEORGIA HISGORICAL QUARTERLY 44 (1960):74-84.

Feb-Mar 1827. Diary of envoy sent by President John Quincy Adams to Governor George M. Troup of Georgia to mediate controversy between state and federal governments over lands taken from Creek Indians; dealings with the governor; stage coach travel over wretched roads; interesting conversation of fellow traveler, Professor William Montgomery Greene; distaste for manners and mores of Milledgeville, the frontier capital.

WOODRUFF, SAMUEL 2264

Extract in LIFE OF JOSEPH BRANT-THAYENDANEGEA, by William Leete Stone, vol. 1, app. I-lvii. New York: A.V. Blake, 1838. Reprint. Albany: J. Munsell, 1865.

Oct 1827. Travel to Saratoga; reflections on Burgoyne's campaign.

1828

BAILLIE, JOHN, 1772-1833 2265

"An Englishman's Pocket Note Book." MAGAZINE OF AMERICAN HISTORY 19 (1888):331-338, 424-428, 511-512; 20 (1888):61-64.

Nov 1828-Mar 1829. Travel diary of British Orientalist and member of Parliament; tour of America from Washington to Veracruz; highly critical notes of Americans and their inns, travel facilities, manners and food; route down the Mississippi to New Orleans and voyage to Veracruz.

COLE, THOMAS, 1801-1848 2266

Campbell, Catherine H. "Two's Company: The Diaries of Thomas Cole and Henry Cheever Pratt on Their Walk through Crawford Notch." HISTORICAL NEW HAMPSHIRE 33 (1978):308-333.

Oct 1828. Article comparing diary entries of artists during their journey by coach and on foot from Concord, New Hampshire, to Crawford Notch; description of route, scenery, views sketched.

THE COURSE OF EMPIRE, VOYAGE OF LIFE, AND OTHER PICTURES OF THOMAS COLE. By Louis L. Noble. New York: Cornish, Lamport, 1853. 415 pp. Journal, pp. 132-380 passim. THE LIFE AND WORKS OF THOMAS COLE, 3d ed. New York: Sheldon, Blakeman, 1856.

1831-1848. Extracts of painter's travels in Italy, New York State and Catskills; notes on painting and painters, scenery, poetry, etc.

COOPER, JAMES FENIMORE, 1789-1851 2267

LETTERS AND JOURNALS. Edited by James F. Beard. Cambridge: Belnap Press of Harvard University Press, 1960-1968. 6 vols.

1828-1848. Novelist's journal; travel in Holland, Belgium, Switzerland and Italy; notes on towns and scenery; visit with Lafayette in Paris; vacationing with his family in France, Belgium, Germany and Switzerland; visit to Paris and London before return to America; intimate picture of home life at Cooperstown, New York; work, reading, weather, etc.

PUTNAM'S MAGAZINE (1868):730-737, 167-172.

1828-1830.

CORRESPONDENCE OF JAMES FENIMORE COOPER. Edited by his grandson, James Fenimore Cooper. New Haven: Yale University Press, 1922. 2 vols. Journal, vol. 2, app., pp. 727-752.

Jan-May 1848.

COZINE, JOHN C. 2268

THE DAY-BOOK ACCOUNT OF JOHN C. COZINE: A JOURNEY FROM HARRODSBURG, KENTUCKY, TO NEW YORK, AND RETURN. Lexington, Ky.: King Library Press, University of Kentucky Libraries, 1976. 56 pp.

Sep-Nov 1828. Trip by stage and boat to settle estate claim; sightseeing in Baltimore, Philadelphia, New York City; up the Hudson to Albany and through the Erie Canal; visits with family and friends in upper New York State; view of Niagara Falls; good description of stage travel; religious and political interests; record of expenses.

DUFFIELD, GEORGE, 1794–1868　　2269

VanderVelde, L.G., ed. "Notes on the Diary of George Duffield." MISSISSIPPI VALLEY HISTORICAL REVIEW 24 (1937–1938):53–67.

　1828–1868. Extracts from diary of Presbyterian minister; conduct of ministry; religious, business and political notes; mostly summaries.

ERMATINGER, FRANK, 1798–1857　　2270

"Earliest Expedition against Puget Sound Indians." WASHINGTON HISTORICAL QUARTERLY 1 (January 1907): 16–29.

　Jun–Jul 1828. Hudson's Bay Company clerk's record of McLeod expedition against the Clallam Indians of Puget Sound; Fort Vancouver; good narrative.

GRIMKE, ANGELINA, 1805–1879　　2271

Extracts in THE GRIMKE SISTERS: SARAH AND ANGELINA GRIMKE, THE FIRST AMERICAN WOMEN ADVOCATES OF ABOLITION AND WOMAN'S RIGHTS, by Catherine H. Birney, pp. 55–123 passim. Boston: Lee and Shepard; New York: C.T. Dillingham, 1885.

　1828–1835. Reflections on slavery and account of work against it.

HEAD, Sir GEORGE, 1782–1855　　2272

FOREST SCENES AND INCIDENTS IN THE WILDS OF NORTH AMERICA. London: J. Murray, 1829. 362 pp. 2d ed. 1838.

　Dec 1828–Jul 1829. Englishman's travel diary; Halifax, Nova Scotia, to Presque Isle, thence to Riviére de Cape and York, Upper Canada; four months' residence in the woods on border of Lakes Huron and Simcoe; journey from Lake Simcoe to Quebec via Niagara; touristic notes.

HENSHAW, LEVI, 1769–1843　　2273

In CHRONICLES OF OLD BERKELEY, A NARRATIVE HISTORY OF A VIRGINIA COUNTY, by Mabel Henshaw Gardiner and Ann Henshaw Gardiner, pp. 259–281. Durham, N.C.: Seeman, 1938.

　Nov 1828–Mar 1829. Miller's journey from Mill Creek to Kentucky; notes on towns, crops, countryside, visits, local people and characters; expenses.

HONE, PHILIP, 1780–1851　　2274

THE DIARY OF PHILIP HONE. Edited by Bayard Tuckerman. New York: Dodd, Mead, 1889. 2 vols.

THE DIARY OF PHILIP HONE. Edited by Allan Nevins. New York: Dodd, Mead, 1927. 2 vols. Reprint. New York: Kraus, 1969; Arno, 1970; Library Editions, 1970.

Extracts in OLD NEW YORK, vol. 1, pp. 316–331. New York: W.W. Pasko, 1890.

Extracts in DIARY OF AMERICA, edited by Josef Berger, pp. 197–212.

　1828–1851. Important and extensive diary of a wealthy and influential citizen; observations on politics, literature, art, industry, social life in New York; literary but intimate.

JUDSON, EMILY CHUBBUCK, 1817–1854　　2275

In THE LIFE AND LETTERS OF MRS. EMILY C. JUDSON, by Asahel C. Kendrick, pp. 16–30, 246–249, 319–328. New York: Sheldon; Boston: Gould & Lincoln, 1860.

　1828–1833. Apparently autobiography of childhood, arranged as diary, followed by extracts from a missionary journal, 1847–1850, kept at Maulmain, Burma.

LUNDY, BENJAMIN, 1789–1839　　2276

THE LIFE, TRAVELS AND OPINIONS OF BENJAMIN LUNDY. Philadelphia: W.D. Parrish, 1847. 316 pp. Diary, pp. 26–28.

　May–Oct 1828. Travel diary of Virginia abolitionist; journey to antislavery societies in New England and New York.

In GENIUS OF UNIVERSAL EMANCIPATION, 1832. Reprint. Landon, Fred, ed. "The Diary of Benjamin Lundy Written during His Journey through Upper Canada." ONTARIO HISTORICAL SOCIETY PAPERS AND RECORDS 19 (1922):110–133; THE DIARY OF BENJAMIN LUNDY. Edited by Fred Landon. Toronto, 1922. 24 pp.

　Jan 1832. Tour in Upper Canada, from Queenston to Detroit; description of Wilberforce settlement of Negroes; propagandist journey; historically interesting.

THE LIFE, TRAVELS AND OPINIONS OF BENJAMIN LUNDY. Diary, pp. 32–186.

　1833–1835. Journey from New Orleans to Texas and New Mexico; San Felipe de Austin, San Antonio de Bexar, Monclova, Laredo, Aransas Bay; return to New Orleans and Cincinnati; second journey to Texas and Mexico; notes on scenery, natural history, adventures, weather, people and customs.

MCCOY, ISAAC, 1784–1846　　2277

Barnes, Lela, ed. "Journal of Isaac McCoy for the Exploring Expedition of 1828." KANSAS HISTORICAL QUARTERLY 5 (1936):227–277, 339–377.

　Jul–Oct 1828, Aug–Nov 1830. Baptist missionary's exploration journals; first, an expedition west of Mississippi with Indian tribes to be relocated; Michigan to St. Louis and first tour with northern Indians; highly interesting details of Indians and some personal notes; second, an expedition to survey lands assigned to relocated Delawares near Topeka.

McDermott, John F., ed. "Isaac McCoy's Second Exploring Trip in 1828." KANSAS HISTORICAL QUARTERLY 13 (1945):400–462.

　Oct–Nov 1828. Continued exploration west from St. Louis to help resettle Chickasaw, Choctaw and Creek Indians; service as treasurer for expedition under Captain G.H. Kennerly; concern about exploitation of Indians.

MCDONALD, ARCHIBALD　　2278

PEACE RIVER: A CANOE VOYAGE FROM HUDSON'S BAY TO PACIFIC. Edited by Malcolm McLeod. Ottawa: J. Durie & Son, 1872. 112 pp. Journal, pp. 1–39.

　Jul–Oct 1828. Journal kept by chief factor of Hudson's Bay Company of a canoe voyage with Sir George Simpson.

MAYO, ABIGAIL DE HART, 1761–1843　　2279

AN AMERICAN LADY IN PARIS. Edited by Mary Mayo Crenshaw. Boston and New York: Houghton Mifflin, 1927. 144 pp.

　1828–1829. Diary of aristocratic social life in Paris; visits, meetings with Lafayette and diplomats; notes on monuments, museums, galleries, plays, operas, balls.

NETSVETOV, IAKOV EGOROVICH, 1804-1864   2280

THE JOURNALS OF IAKOV NETSVETOV: THE ATKHA YEARS. Translated and with an introduction by Lydia Black. Materials for the Study of Alaska History, no. 16. Kingston, Ontario: Limestone Press, 1980. 340 pp.

1828-1842. Official record of day-to-day activities of a parish priest, as required by Orthodox Church; work of the first indigenous priest for the new church at Atkha, Alaska; organization of the Russian American Company school, which became Atkha parish school; remarks on hunting, life of the Aleuts, geography, trading, the Russian American Company; vital statistics for each year.

PARKER, PETER, 1804-1888   2281

In THE LIFE, LETTERS AND JOURNALS OF THE REV. AND HON. PETER PARKER, M.D., by George B. Stevens, pp. 357-362. Boston: Congregational Sunday School and Publishing Society, 1896.

1828-1880. Presbyterian medical missionary's journal interspersed with letters and biographical narrative; undergraduate studies at Amherst and Yale, followed by medical and theological studies; appointment to China under American Board of Commissioners for Foreign Missions; work as medical missionary in Singapore; founding of Ophthalmic Hospital in Canton; trip to Japan, interruption of work during Opium War, 1839; return to United States, marriage, trip to England and France to raise funds for Chinese missions; presentation to Louis Phillipe; appointment as United States commissioner to China.

PUGH, SARAH, 1800-1884   2282

THE MEMORIAL OF SARAH PUGH: A TRIBUTE OF RESPECT FROM HER COUSINS. Philadelphia: J.B. Lippincott, 1888. 136 pp.

1828-1882. Journal and letters of abolitionist and women's suffrage activist raised as a Quaker but later separated from Society of Friends; participation in Women's Anti-Slavery Convention of 1837, but denied admission as delegate to British and Foreign Anti-Slavery Society Convention, London, 1840, because she was a woman; later work with suffrage movement in company with Lucretia Mott.

SEDGWICK, CATHARINE MARIA, 1789-1867   2283

LIFE AND LETTERS OF CATHARINE M. SEDGWICK. Edited by Mary E. Dewey. New York: Harper, 1871. 466 pp.

1828-1867. Long journal extracts, interspersed with letters, of a popular and genteel author of moral domestic literature; reading and writing, travel, social life, religious thoughts and charitable activities, especially on behalf of the Women's Prison Association of New York; comments on Harriet Martineau and Fanny Kemble.

Stearns, Bertha M. "Miss Sedgwick Observes Harriet Martineau." NEW ENGLAND QUARTERLY 7 (1934):533-541.

1837-1849. Previously unpublished extracts revealing her changing attitude toward Harriet Martineau during the latter's sojourn in America and after publication of SOCIETY IN AMERICA.

STARK, FREDERICK G.   2284

Stark, George, ed. "A Journey from New Hampshire to Philadelphia." GRANITE MONTHLY 5 (1882):42-46.

Oct 1828. Merchant's business trip from Manchester to Philadelphia; by stage to Providence, steamer to New York, stage to Trenton, steamer to Philadelphia; substantial entries describing towns, scenery, etc.

VAN DER LYN, HENRY, 1784-1865   2285

Curran, Thomas J., ed. "The Diary of Henry Van Der Lyn." NEW YORK HISTORICAL SOCIETY QUARTERLY 55 (1971):119-152.

1828-1856. Diary of prominent upstate New York lawyer; comments on the turbulent politics of the period from perspective of concern for stability of the Union; diarist's change of political support from antislavery to anti-abolitionist, Jackson to Whigs, Whigs to Democrats, Democrats to Know-Nothing and back to the Democrats.

WETMORE, ALPHONSO, 1793-1849   2286

UNITED STATES CONGRESS. SENATE EXECUTIVE DOCUMENT 90, 22d Congress, 1st Session.

Stephens, F.F., ed. "Major Alphonso Wetmore's Diary of a Journey to Santa Fe." MISSOURI HISTORICAL REVIEW 8 (1913-1914):177-197. Diary, pp. 184-195.

In SOUTHWEST ON THE TURQUOISE TRAIL, edited by Archer B. Hulbert, pp. 182-195.

May-Aug 1828. Extract of travel journal; from Franklin, Missouri, to Santa Fe; a lively and flippant narrative in a letter to the secretary of war.

1829

ABEEL, DAVID, 1804-1846   2287

"Journal of Mr. Abeel." MISSIONARY HERALD 27 (1831): 374-378; 28 (1832):68-71, 97-100, 139-142, 173-177, 252-255; 39 (1843):251-255, 449-452; 40 (1844):193-198, 397-401; 41 (1845):87-89, 183-187.

1829-1833. Journal of Dutch Reformed missionary to China, Singapore and Thailand; moral, social and religious discussion; irregular day-by-day entries.

ALEXANDER, WILLIAM PATTERSON, 1805-1884   2288

In WILLIAM PATTERSON ALEXANDER IN KENTUCKY, THE MARQUESAS, HAWAII, compiled by Mary C. Alexander, 516 pp. passim. Honolulu: Privately printed under the direction of Yale University Press, 1934.

1829-1872. Extracts, within a biography, of journal of Presbyterian missionary to the South Pacific; studies at Princeton; religious reflections; marriage; voyage on whaling ship around Cape Horn to the Marquesas and work as missionary there and on Waioli, Lahainaluna and Wailuku.

MISSION LIFE IN HAWAII: MEMOIR OF REV. WILLIAM P. ALEXANDER. By James M. Alexander. Oakland, Calif.: Pacific Press, 1888. 196 pp.

1831-1872. Memoir containing extracts of work in Hawaii.

ARMIJO, ANTONIO   2289

In OLD SPANISH TRAIL, SANTA FE TO LOS ANGELES, by LeRoy R. Hafen and Ann W. Hafen, pp. 159-165. Far West and the Rockies, vol. 1. Glendale, Calif.: Arthur H. Clark, 1954.

Nov 1829-Mar 1830. Commander's very brief official diary of a New Mexico to California expedition important in the development of the Old Spanish Trail and subsequent trade; mostly just route, names of rivers, creeks, mountains.

In SOUTHWEST ON THE TURQUOISE TRAIL, edited by Archer B. Hulbert, pp. 284-289.

Hafen, LeRoy R., ed. "Armijo's Journal." HUNTINGTON LIBRARY QUARTERLY 11 (1947):87-101.

Hafen, LeRoy R., ed. "Armijo's Journal of 1829-30; the Beginning of Trade between New Mexico and California." COLORADO MAGAZINE 27 (1950):120-131.

Nov 1829-Jan 1830.

BALDWIN, CHRISTOPHER COLUMBUS, 1800-1835   2290

DIARY OF CHRISTOPHER COLUMBUS BALDWIN, LIBRARIAN OF THE AMERICAN ANTIQUARIAN SOCIETY. Edited by Nathaniel Paine. American Antiquarian Society Transactions and Collections, vol. 8. Worcester, Mass.: American Antiquarian Society, 1901. 380 pp.

Extracts in AMERICAN ANTIQUARIAN SOCIETY PROCEEDINGS (1812-1849):308-324. Diary, pp. 314-320.

Extracts in "Christopher Columbus Baldwin's Diary," edited by John Nelson. AMERICANA 28 (1934):319-341.

1829-1835 (lacking year 1832-1833). Librarian's diary; notes of antiquarian and bibliographical interests, general reading, life and work of his friends and acquaintances, weather, natural history, visits, his work on the catalogue of the society; an interesting scholar's record.

BAYFIELD, HENRY WOLSEY, 1795-1885   2291

Boulton, Captain. "Paper on Admiral Bayfield." LITERARY AND HISTORICAL SOCIETY OF QUEBEC TRANSACTIONS, no. 28 (1910), pp. 27-95.

1829-1853. Surveying journals; coasts and harbors, mainly around St. Lawrence River.

BLAKE, GEORGE SMITH, d. 1871   2292

McInnis, Katherine. "When Smallpox Struck." UNITED STATES NAVAL INSTITUTE PROCEEDINGS 97 (1971):78-82.

May 1829. Naval lieutenant's account of smallpox epidemic aboard the GRAMPUS; his own illness, treatment and recovery from the disease; return of ship from Caribbean to Pensacola to be fumigated because of epidemic; reassignment north to restore health.

BROWNELL, THOMAS CHURCH, 1779-1865   2293

Beardsley, William A., ed. "Bishop Thomas C. Brownell's Journal of His Missionary Tours." HISTORICAL MAGAZINE OF THE PROTESTANT EPISCOPAL CHURCH 7 (1938):303-322.

Nov 1829-Mar 1830. Missionary journal of Episcopal bishop of Connecticut; journey via Philadelphia, Pittsburgh, Cincinnati, Louisville, Lexington, New Orleans, Mobile and return; notes on preaching, people and places.

Nov 1834-Apr 1835. Missionary journey to New Orleans; mostly comments on church there.

COVINGTON, LEVEN   2294

Extracts in PLANTATION AND FRONTIER DOCUMENTS, edited by Ulrich B. Phillips, vol. 1, pp. 231-244.

1829-1830. Extracts from diary of cotton and corn plantation owner in Adams County, Mississippi; plowing, planting, hoeing, clearing new field; the work of women slaves, consisting of piling brush, "cleaning up before ploughs," cutting briars and spinning.

DUNCAN, JOSEPH, 1794-1844   2295

Putnam, Elizabeth D. "The Life and Services of Joseph Duncan, Governor of Illinois." ILLINOIS STATE HISTORICAL SOCIETY TRANSACTIONS, no. 26 (1919), pp. 106-187.

Putnam, Elizabeth D. "Governor Joseph Duncan of Illinois." TENNESSEE HISTORICAL MAGAZINE 7 (1922): 243-251.

1829-1830. Political diary; notes on politics in Washington while he was a member of Congress; personal affairs in Kentucky and Illinois.

FOSTER, ABSALOM   2296

Riegler, Gordon A., ed. "Journal and Report of the Rev. A. Foster, of Willington, South Carolina." PRESBYTERIAN HISTORICAL SOCIETY JOURNAL 13 (1928-1929): 289-296.

Dec 1829-May 1830. Letter-journal to American Home Mission Society; report on missionary activities at Pendleton, South Carolina.

GREEN, JONATHAN S.   2297

"North-West Coast: Extracts from the Report of an Exploring Tour on the North-West Coast of North America." MISSIONARY HERALD 26 (1830):343-345, 369-373; 27 (1831):33-39, 75-79, 105-107.

JOURNAL OF A TOUR ON THE NORTH WEST COAST OF AMERICA. New York: Reprinted for C.F. Heartman, 1915. 104 pp.

Extracts in THE OREGON CRUSADE: ACROSS LAND AND SEA TO OREGON, edited by Archer B. Hulbert and Dorothy P. Hulbert, pp. 45-78. Overland to the Pacific, vol. 5. Colorado Springs: The Stewart Commission of Colorado College; Denver: Denver Public Library, 1935.

Mar-Oct 1829. Exploring and missionary journal; tour on barque VOLUNTEER, work on Pacific Northwest coast; New Archangel, Kiganee, Norfolk Sound; and in California; descriptions of country, government, Russian settlements, northern Indians, California missions, his own adventures; religious commentary; an important and interesting journal.

GREEN, THOMAS, 1798-1883   2298

Gatewood, Joanne L., ed. "Richmond during the Virginia Constitutional Convention." VIRGINIA MAGAZINE OF HISTORY AND BIOGRAPHY 84 (1976):287-332.

Oct 1829-Jan 1830. Extracts from diary of Richmond attorney; observations as spectator at Virginia Constitutional Convention; family, social and business activities.

HILLARD, HARRIET LOW, 1809-1877   2299

MY MOTHER'S JOURNAL; A YOUNG LADY'S DIARY OF FIVE YEARS SPENT IN MANILA. Edited by Katharine Hillard. Boston: G.H. Ellis, 1900. 320 pp.

"Harriet Low's Journal," abridged by Katharine Hillard. In THE CHINA TRADE POSTBAG OF THE SETH LOW FAMILY OF SALEM AND NEW YORK, edited by Elma Loines, pp. 100-233. Manchester, Maine: Falmouth Publishing House, 1953.

1829-1834. Young Massachusetts girl's lively journal of life in Macao among the American and

British merchant elite; church, dinners, balls, operas; voyages to and from Macao aboard SUMATRA and LORCHA; a good picture of tedium of formal social life.

JONES, ALEXANDER, 1764-1840 2300

"Two Journals of Alexander Jones, Esq., of Providence, Rhode Island." HISTORICAL MAGAZINE OF THE PROTESTANT EPISCOPAL CHURCH 10 (1941):6-30.

May, Aug 1829. Travels of Episcopal layman; from Providence to New York via Hartford and New Haven; interesting notes on churchmen; comments on social life and travel; from Providence to New York and Philadelphia to attend convocation of Protestant Episcopal Church as delegate from Rhode Island.

Chorley, E. Clowers, ed. "Journal of a Tour to New York to Attend the Triennial Convention of the Episcopal Church." HISTORICAL MAGAZINE OF THE PROTESTANT EPISCOPAL CHURCH 1 (1932):6-18.

Oct-Nov 1832. From Providence to New York to attend triennial convention of his church as a lay deputy; account of debates; unusual and interesting diary.

LONGFELLOW, HENRY WADSWORTH, 1807-1882 2301

LIFE OF HENRY WADSWORTH LONGFELLOW, WITH EXTRACTS FROM HIS JOURNALS AND CORRESPONDENCE. Edited by Samuel Longfellow. Boston: Ticknor, 1886. 2 vols. passim.

WORKS OF HENRY WADSWORTH LONGFELLOW. Edited by Samuel Longfellow. Boston and New York: Houghton, Mifflin, 1886-91. 14 vols. Journal, vols. 12-14.

LIFE OF HENRY WADSWORTH LONGFELLOW. Edited by Samuel Longfellow. Boston and New York: Houghton Mifflin, 1891. 3 vols. Reprint. New York: Greenwood, 1969.

May 1829, Jul 1835, 1838-1840, 1845-1881. Poet's journals; travel in Germany; in Stockholm; reading, translations, lectures, visits with literary people; Emerson's lectures; reflections, writing and college work, social affairs, some verses, literary plans, friendships; a valuable and interesting record.

PAINE, HORACE HALL, 1810-1864 2302

In HISTORY OF SAMUEL PAINE, JR., edited by Albert P. Paine, pp. 85-88. Randolph Center, Vt., 1923.

Dec 1829-Jan 1830. Merchant's diary first kept while author was clerk in a dry goods store in New York City; fire; impressions of New York; brief but interesting.

QUINCY, MARIA SOPHIA, b. 1805 2303

In THE ARTICULATE SISTERS, by M.A. DeWolfe Howe, pp. 149-189.

1829. A tour from Cambridge, Massachusetts, to Malta, New York, by carriage; delay at Brattleborough due to sister Anne's illness; stay at Ballston Spa and Sans Souci resort; return to Cambridge and Harvard Commencement of 1829, the first year her father, Josiah Quincy, was president; Phi Beta Kappa exercises the following day.

RILEY, BENNET, 1787-1853 2304

Perrine, Fred S., ed. "Military Escorts on the Santa Fe Trail." NEW MEXICO HISTORICAL REVIEW 3 (1928): 265-300.

May-Nov 1829. Official military journal, evidently written by Lieutenant James F. Izard on behalf of Major Riley; expedition from Jefferson Barracks, Missouri, to the crossing of the Arkansas River by the Sante Fe Trail, via Leavenworth; interesting account of encounter with raiding Indians.

STONE, WILLIAM LEETE, 1792-1844 2305

"From New York to Niagra: Journal of a Tour, in Part by the Erie Canal." BUFFALO HISTORICAL SOCIETY PUBLICATIONS 14 (1910):207-264.

Extracts in MAGAZINE OF AMERICAN HISTORY 20 (1888): 316-324, 395-399, 489-494; 21 (1889):46-49.

Sep-Oct 1829. Editor's trip from New York City to Niagara; careful observations and humorous reflections; literary style.

VOGLER, JOHN 2306

"Diary of the Journey of John Vogler and Van N. Zevely to the Cherokee Indian Mission." In RECORDS OF THE MORAVIANS IN NORTH CAROLINA, edited by Adelaide L. Fries, vol. 8, pp. 3902-3909.

Mar-May 1829. Trip from Salem, North Carolina, to Cherokee Mission; horseback travel through poor country, staying with a variety of people, distributing missionary tracts; joyful reception at the mission.

WAILES, BENJAMIN LEONARD COVINGTON, 1797-1862 2307

Moore, J.H., ed. "A View of Philadelphia in 1829: Selections from the Journal of B.L.C. Wailes of Natchez." PENNSYLVANIA MAGAZINE OF HISTORY AND BIOGRAPHY 78 (1954):353-360.

Dec 1829. Notes of sightseeing in Philadelphia, including Philadelphia Museum Company, Academy of Fine Arts, United States Mint, the Fairmont Waterworks.

Sydnor, Charles S., ed. "Diary of a Journey in Arkansas in 1856." MISSISSIPPI VALLEY HISTORICAL REVIEW 22 (1935-1936):419-433.

Oct-Nov 1856. Journey from Vicksburg to Arkansas; life on river packet; inspection of property in Arkansas; Pine Bluff, Little Rock; expenditures.

WILLIAMS, L.S. 2308

"Choctaws: Continued Attention to Religion." MISSIONARY HERALD 25 (1829):251-253.

Feb 1829. Extracts from clergyman's missionary journal; life and work among the Choctaw Indians.

1830

BACKHOUSE, HANNAH CHAPMAN GURNEY, 1787-1850 2309

EXTRACTS FROM THE JOURNAL AND LETTERS OF HANNAH CHAPMAN BACKHOUSE. London: R. Barrett, Printer, 1858. 291 pp. Journal, pp. 78-185.

1830–1835. Extracts relating to English Quaker's voyage to the United States; visits to Philadelphia, Baltimore, New York, Ohio, Indiana, New England, South Carolina, Tennessee, Kentucky; travels and visits to Friends and their meetings; pleasant description and comment on scenery, people and institutions.

BALLANCE, CHARLES, 1800–1872   2310

East, Ernest, E., ed. "The Journal of Charles Ballance of Peoria." ILLINOIS HISTORICAL SOCIETY JOURNAL 30 (1937–1938):70–84.

1830–1843. Lawyer's journal of travel in Kentucky and Illinois; description of Peoria; business records; irregular entries.

CAMPBELL, WILLIAM M., 1805–1849   2311

"Diary of William C. Campbell." MISSOURI HISTORICAL SOCIETY GLIMPSES OF THE PAST 3 (1936):138–150.

Apr–May, Dec 1830. Lawyer's business and prospecting trip in Missouri; St. Charles County to Jefferson City, Boonville, Chariton, Howard, Callaway counties, etc.; notes on places, soil, etc.

CARR, JOHN B.   2312

"The Diary of a Naturalist." HAZARD'S REGISTER OF PENNSYLVANIA 8 (1831–1832):13–15.

Mar–Jun 1830. Nature diary kept at the Bartram Botanical Garden on the Schuylkill River near Philadelphia; weather, arrival of birds, flowering of plants, etc.

COLLINS, DANIEL LAKE, 1808–1887   2313

In A GENEALOGY OF THE LAKE FAMILY OF GREAT EGG HARBOUR, IN OLD GLOUCESTER COUNTY IN NEW JERSEY, by Arthur Adams and Sarah A. Risley, app. 6, pp. 280–293. Hartford: Privately printed, 1915.

Aug 1830–Feb 1831. Travel diary of farmer and surveyor; journey to the west and return; New York State, Buffalo, Pennsylvania, Ohio, Ohio Canal, Cincinnati, Kentucky, Indianapolis, Wabash, down Mississippi to New Orleans, by sea to New York; notes on scenery, social life, economic conditions; mostly narrative written up from diary.

DAVIS, HANNAH   2314

"Journal of 1830." VINELAND HISTORICAL MAGAZINE 17 (1932):164–165.

Aug 1830. Journey from Shiloh, New Jersey, to Alford and Friendship, New York, with five companions; brief daily notes.

EARLE, PLINY, 1809–1892   2315

In MEMOIRS OF PLINY EARLE, M.D., WITH EXTRACTS FROM HIS DIARY AND LETTERS, edited by Franklin B. Sanborn, 409 pp. passim. Boston: Damrell & Upham, 1898.

1830–1864. Alienist's diary of travels, work and social observations in New England and Philadelphia; travel and residence in England, France, Switzerland, Italy; work with the insane; work in South Carolina; visit to Cuba; residence in New York and Washington; comments on the Civil War; a very detailed and interesting diary of social life and work in Europe and America.

EGGLESTON, DICK HARDAWAY   2316

In THE PLANTATION SOUTH, by Katharine M. Jones, pp. 245–255. Indianapolis: Bobbs-Merrill, 1957.

Jan–Sep 1830. Brief extracts from the diary of Woodville, Mississippi, cotton planter; agricultural work of slaves, some social notes.

EVERETT, ANNE GORHAM, 1823–1843   2317

In MEMOIR OF ANNE GORHAM EVERETT, WITH EXTRACTS FROM HER CORRESPONDENCE AND JOURNAL, by Philippa C. Bush, 320 pp. passim. Boston: Privately printed, 1857.

1830–1843? Girlhood diary and letters of Edward Everett's daughter; family life and school in Boston, extensive travels in Europe with her mother while continuing her studies; two years' residence in England; great interest in the fine arts; onset of tuberculosis from which she died in London.

FERRIS, WARREN ANGUS, 1810–1873   2318

WESTERN LITERARY MESSENGER 2 (Jan 1843); 3 (May 1844).

LIFE IN THE ROCKY MOUNTAINS. Arranged by Herbert S. Auerback, annotated by J. Cecil Alter. Salt Lake City, Utah: Rocky Mountain Book Shop, 1940. 272 pp.

1830–1835. Fur trading journal kept while diarist was employee of American Fur Company; trapping, trading, clerking; notes on life in the Rockies, Indian affairs.

FOWLER, JOHN   2319

JOURNAL OF A TOUR IN THE STATE OF NEW YORK. London: Whittaker, Treacher, and Arnot, 1831. 333 pp.

Extracts in "Central New York in 1830." YORK STATE TRADITION 27 (1973):44–48.

Jun–Dec 1830. Englishman's tour in New York State; Flushing, Albany, Buffalo, Niagara, Rochester, New Hartford, Poughkeepsie, New York City; shipwreck; return by western islands; notes for settlers on scenery and travel facilities.

GREENE, ROLAND, 1770–1859   2320

"A Visit to East Farnham, Canada." FRIENDS' HISTORICAL SOCIETY OF PHILADELPHIA BULLETIN 2 (1908): 119–121.

Jul 1830. Quaker's journey from Barton, Vermont, to East Farnham, Quebec; notes on scenery and farms.

HALSEY, JACOB, d. 1842   2321

Robinson, Doane, ed. "Fort Tecumseh and Fort Pierre Journal and Letter Books." SOUTH DAKOTA HISTORICAL COLLECTIONS 9 (1918):69–167. Journal, pp. 93–167.

1830–1833. Abstract, with gaps, of journal of partner in American Fur Company; records of forts on upper Missouri, near mouth of Teton River; brief notes on life at forts, arrivals and departures of traders and trappers; mention of famous persons.

HENSHAW, HIRAM   2322

In CHRONICLES OF OLD BERKELEY, A NARRATIVE HISTORY OF A VIRGINIA COUNTY, by Mabel Henshaw Gardiner and Ann Henshaw Gardiner, pp. 282–314. Durham, N.C.: Seeman Press, 1938.

Jan–May 1830. Journey from Berkeley County, West Virginia, to Kentucky via Ohio; notes on scenery, farming, mills, towns, visits, expenses.

HERR, BENJAMIN 2323

"Benjamin Herr's Journal." GERMAN–AMERICAN ANNALS 5 (1903):8–31.

Sep–Oct 1830. Touristic notes of journey from Strasburg, Pennsylvania, to Philadelphia, New York City, Saratoga, Schenectady, Buffalo, Sandusky; Ohio, Illinois, Kentucky, Virginia, Pennsylvania, and return to Strasburg.

HEWINS, AMASA, 1795–1855 2324

HEWIN'S JOURNAL: A BOSTON PORTRAIT PAINTER VISITS ITALY. Edited by Francis H. Allen. Boston: The Boston Athenaeum, 1931. 145 pp.

1830–1833. Travel and study of painting in Europe, mostly in Italy; notes on travel conditions, galleries, paintings, sculpture; also travel in Spain, France and England.

KEATING, Sir HENRY SINGER, 1804–1888 2325

Posner, Russell M., ed. "Philadelphia in 1830: An English View." PENNSYLVANIA MAGAZINE OF HISTORY AND BIOGRAPHY 95 (1971):239–243.

1830–1831. Extract from British law student's journal of travel to America; three week sojourn in Philadelphia; evaluation of such customary sights as waterworks, Bank of the United States, Academy of Arts and prison; observations on "mere monied" aristocracy.

KENRICK, FRANCIS PATRICK, 1797–1863 2326

DIARY AND VISITATION RECORD OF THE RT. REV. FRANCIS KENRICK. Edited by Francis E. Tourscher. Lancaster, Pa.: Wickersham, 1916. 298 pp. Diary, pp. 29–267.

1830–1852. Diary of Catholic bishop of Philadelphia; diocesan work, religious reflections, administration; some travel notes and reflections on Mexican War.

LYMAN, SARAH JOINER, 1805–1885 2327

SARAH JOINER LYMAN OF HAWAII; HER OWN STORY. Compiled from the journal and letters by Margaret Greer Martin. Hilo, Hawaii: Lyman House Memorial Museum, 1970. 201 pp.

1830–1841. Missionary diary; courtship, call to mission service under American Board, life aboard whaler AVERICK en route to Hawaii with her husband and other missionaries; description of teaching and church activities; death of Queen Kaahumanu; births and raising of her children; a full and ingenuous diary.

MCCALL, JAMES, 1774–1856 2328

"M'Call's Journal." WISCONSIN HISTORICAL COLLECTIONS 12 (1892):177–205.

Jun–Sep 1830. Official journal of visit to Wisconsin to settle differences between Winnebagos and Menominees; first part at Detroit; voyage to Green Bay; interviews with Indians; return; some good description.

NORTHRUP, ENOS 2329

"First Trip to Michigan." MICHIGAN PIONEER COLLECTIONS 5 (1882):69–70.

May–Jun 1830. Travel from Hinckley, Ohio, to Gull Prairie, Michigan; brief notes of stages.

PHELPS, CAROLINE 2330

"Mrs. Caroline Phelps' Diary." ILLINOIS HISTORICAL SOCIETY JOURNAL 23 (1930–1931):209–239.

1830–1840. Interesting account of woman pioneering on the Illinois frontier; narrative with few dates.

POOR, MARY, 1747–1834 2331

Mariotti, Eva. "The Diary of Mary Poor of Indian Hill Farm." NEW ENGLAND MAGAZINE, n.s. 13 (1895–1896):316–322.

1830–1834. Extracts from the diary of an old woman at Indian Hill Farm, Massachusetts; brief notes of weather, social and family life.

TOLMIE, WILLIAM FRASER, 1812–1886 2332

THE JOURNALS OF WILLIAM FRASER TOLMIE, PHYSICIAN AND FUR TRADER. Vancouver, B.C.: Mitchell Press, 1963. 413 pp.

1830–1843. Journal of medical school studies in Glasgow followed by trip to Fort Vancouver on GANYMEDE to serve as Hudson's Bay Company physician and trader; details of studies on board ship, dissecting birds and fish; stopover at Honolulu where he collected plants and observed activities of Hawaiians and missionaries; life and medical work at Fort Vancouver, fur trade and farm administration at Fort Nisqually.

"Journal of William Fraser Tolmie." WASHINGTON HISTORICAL QUARTERLY 3 (1912):229–241.

Apr–May 1833. Excellent descriptions of Fort Vancouver and Indians of the area; botanical notes.

WHARTON, THOMAS KELAH, 1814–1862 2333

Rodabaugh, James H., ed. "From England to Ohio, 1830–1832." OHIO HISTORICAL QUARTERLY 65 (1956):1–27, 111–151.

1830–1832. Journal of English teen-ager who immigrated with his family to Ohio; a month in New York City; travel by canal and lake boat; across Lake Erie aboard the ENTERPRISE, thence to Piqua, Ohio; excellent descriptions enhanced with many drawings by the diarist.

WILLARD, EMMA HART, 1787–1870 2334

JOURNAL AND LETTERS FROM FRANCE AND GREAT BRITAIN. Troy, N.Y.: N. Tuttle, Printer, 1833. 391 pp.

1830–1831. Educator's journal with letters interspersed; trip to France, England and Scotland to visit girls' or women's schools to compare with her own methods used at Troy Female Academy; school of Madame Morin, Paris, and schools in New Lanark, Scotland, and St. Denis; detailed descriptions of traditional tourist attractions; porcelain manufacture at Sevres, calico printing at Glasgow and cotton thread factory at New Lanark; soirees in Paris including several with her old friend General Lafayette.

WYATT, RICHARD WARE, 1806–1881   2335

King, George H.S., ed. "Diary of Colonel Richard Ware Wyatt on Horseback Trip to the Western Country." KENTUCKY STATE HISTORICAL SOCIETY REGISTER 39 (1941):106–115.

> 1830. Horseback journey into the Blue Ridge, Ohio River area, and Kentucky, etc.; notes on scenery, towns, people.

1831

BURGESS, GEORGE, 1809–1866   2336

In MEMOIR OF THE LIFE OF THE RIGHT REVEREND GEORGE BURGESS, D.D., FIRST BISHOP OF MAINE, edited by Alexander Burgess, pp. 33–47. Philadelphia: Claxton, Remsen, and Haffelfinger, 1869.

> 1831–1834. Extracts from European travel diary of Episcopal bishop; university life in Göttingen, Bonn and Berlin; travel in other parts of Germany; notes on universities, lectures, literary figures, scenery; religious reflections.

CLEVELAND, MOSES C., 1795–1883   2337

Howell, N.R., ed. "Journal of a Tour from Riverhead, Long Island, to the Falls of Niagara." NEW YORK HISTORY 27 (1946):352–364.

> Jun 1831. Cordwainer's journey to Niagara Falls by sloop, steamer, canal boat and stagecoach; descriptions of countryside, towns and the Falls.

EMERSON, JOHN SMITH, 1800–1867   2338

Extracts in PIONEER DAYS IN HAWAII, by Oliver P. Emerson, 257 pp. passim. Garden City, N.Y.: Doubleday, 1928.

> 1831–1857. Diary of missionary to Hawaii, among the fifth band sent by American Board of Commissioners for Foreign Missions; voyage on whaler AVERICK: work as a pastor, teacher, doctor, farmer and mechanic.

EMERSON, URSULA SOPHIA NEWELL, d. 1888   2339

Extracts in PIONEER DAYS IN HAWAII, by Oliver P. Emerson, 257 pp. passim. Garden City, N.Y.: Doubleday, 1928.

> 1831–1837. Missionary diary; voyage to Hawaii on the AVERICK; warm and loving notes of her work as a new missionary wife, learning language and customs, making a home, teaching women and children.

FLOYD, JOHN, 1783–1837   2340

In THE JOHN P. BRANCH HISTORICAL PAPERS OF RANDOLPH-MACON COLLEGE, vol. 5, pp. 119–233. Richmond, Va.: Department of History, Randolph-Macon College, 1918.

In THE LIFE AND DIARY OF JOHN FLOYD, by Charles H. Ambler, pp. 123–237. Richmond, Va.: Richmond Press, 1918.

> 1831–1834. Social and political diary of governor of Virginia; public, political and social life; national and international news activities in Washington during the Jacksonian period; mainly political interest, with notes on many eminent national figures.

FOWLER, THOMAS, fl. 1832   2341

THE JOURNAL OF A TOUR THROUGH BRITISH AMERICA TO THE FALLS OF NIAGARA. Aberdeen: L. Smith, 1832. 288 pp.

> 1831. Englishman's journal of a tour through Canada to Niagara Falls; descriptions of country, towns, manners, customs, scenery.

GOULD, DENISON, 1788–1866   2342

"RAINS FINELY TODAY": THE DIARY AND ACCOUNT BOOK OF DENISON GOULD. Edited by Harrison C. Baldwin. n.p., 1974. 128 pp.

> 1831–? New Hampshire farmer's diary; weather, crops, prices; local news in Antrim area.

HALL, SHERMAN, 1800–1879   2343

"Extracts from the Journal of Mr. Hall." MISSIONARY HERALD 29 (1833):410–414, 472–473; 30 (1834):24–27.

> 1831–1833. Journal of missionary sent by American Board to work among the Ojibwas; journey from Mackinaw to St. Mary's River, to south shore of Lake Superior; visit to Lac du Flambeau.

HARLAN, RICHARD, 1796–1843   2344

MONTHLY JOURNAL OF GEOLOGY AND NATURAL SCIENCE 1, no. 2 (August 1831):58–67.

Rachal, William M.E., ed. "Richard Harlan's 'Tour to the Caves in Virginia' in 1831." ALBEMARLE COUNTY HISTORICAL SOCIETY PAPERS 7 (1946–1947):37–46.

> May 1831. Account of trip from Fairfax through Charlottesville to the Blue Ridge; visits to Montpelier, Monticello and the University of Virginia; fossil-hunting at Wyer's Cave; north through Harper's Ferry to Washington, D.C.; comments on slavery, geology of the region, road conditions.

HUNTINGTON, CHARLES P.   2345

"Diary and Letters of Charles P. Huntington." MASSACHUSETTS HISTORICAL SOCIETY PROCEEDINGS 57 (1923–1924):244–277. Diary, pp. 244–269.

> 1831–1834. Diary extracts containing political, literary and social opinions; domestic affairs, gossip, political maneuverings in Massachusetts state legislature.

KUHN, GEORGE HORATIO, 1795–1879   2346

Clarke, George K., ed. "Extracts from a Journal of Hon. George H. Kuhn." DEDHAM HISTORICAL REGISTER 8 (1897):91–94.

> Jan-Nov 1831. Business journal; extracts relating to early manufacturing in Dedham, Massachusetts, and vicinity; projects for factories.

MCLELLAN, HENRY BLAKE, 1810–1833   2347

JOURNAL OF A RESIDENCE IN SCOTLAND, AND A TOUR THROUGH ENGLAND, FRANCE, GERMANY, SWITZERLAND AND ITALY. Complied by I. McLellan, Jr. Boston: Allan and Ticknor, 1834. 377 pp.

> 1831–1833. Atlantic crossing; travels through Britain and Europe, with special interest in churches, sermons and monuments.

MOTTE, JACOB RHETT, 1811–1868   2348

CHARLESTON GOES TO HARVARD: THE DIARY OF A HARVARD STUDENT OF 1831. Edited by Arthur H. Cole. Cambridge: Harvard University Press, 1940. 108 pp.

> May–Sep 1831. College diary kept by junior at Harvard; full and highly entertaining notes on college life and work; sprightly and intimate; interesting for Harvard personalities and curriculum; some notes on the town of Cambridge.

O'BRYAN, WILLIAM, 1778–1868   2349

A NARRATIVE OF TRAVELS IN THE UNITED STATES OF AMERICA. London: Published for the author, 1836. 419 pp.

> 1831–1834. Englishman's voyage from Liverpool to New York and extensive travels in New York, New Jersey, Pennsylvania, Ohio, etc.; personal adventures and general description; manners, institutions, advice to settlers.

PHILBRICK, JOHN, 1791–1874   2350

Philbrick, Charles. "Nobody Laughs, Nobody Cries: The Journal of John Philbrick." THE NEW-ENGLAND GALAXY 8 (1966):27–38.

> 1831–1874. Scattered extracts from journal kept by New Hampshire farmer, businessman, legislator, etc.; his activities; reports of local and national events; evaluations of fellow citizens upon their demise.

PORTER, JEREMIAH   2351

Beeson, Lewis, ed. "A Missionary in Early Sault Sainte Marie." MICHIGAN HISTORY 38 (1954):321–370.

> Nov 1831–Feb 1832. Thoughts, labors and prayers of a young Presbyterian missionary to upper Michigan frontier; ministry to settlers, Indians, and soldiers of garrison at Fort Brady; temperance work; many references to local people, including Indian agent Schoolcraft and his wife, and to Baptist minister Abel Bingham; a detailed and interesting diary.

Anderson, Charles A., ed. "Mackinac to Sault Sainte Marie by Canoe in 1831." MICHIGAN HISTORY 30 (1946): 466–475.

> Nov 1831. Extract covering missionary's hazardous winter trip across part of Lake Huron in canoe dispatched by Schoolcraft.

ROEBLING, JOHANN AUGUST, 1806–1869   2352

DIARY OF MY JOURNEY FROM MUEHLAUSEN IN THURINGIA VIA BREMEN TO THE UNITED STATES. Translated from the original German by Edward Underhill. Trenton, N.J.: Privately printed, The Roebling Press, 1931. 124 pp.

> May–Aug 1831. Immigrant diary; life at sea and in Philadelphia; detailed descriptions and accounts.

SHANE, CHARLES G.   2353

"Journal of C.G. Shane." PRESBYTERIAN HISTORICAL SOCIETY JOURNAL 22 (1944):52–77.

> Dec 1831–Feb 1832. Voyage of young Presbyterian doctor to Liberia aboard CRAWFORD taking former slaves to settle there; most graphic description of storms, seasickness and life on board ship; interesting details of work in helping to settle the colonists; dealings with local people; trade.

SHELBY, THOMAS HART   2354

A JOURNAL AND OTHER PAPERS CONCERNING THE TRAVELS OF MAJOR THOMAS H. SHELBY, SR. Edited by William C. Scott. New York: Privately printed, 1962. 32 pp.

Scott, William C., ed. "Journal of Travels East in 1831." KENTUCKY HISTORICAL SOCIETY REGISTER 65 (1967):163–186.

> Apr–Aug 1831. An apparently well connected gentleman's interesting account of tour through Middle Atlantic and New England states by stagecoach, steamboat and canal boat; good tourist descriptions of Washington, D.C., Baltimore, Philadelphia; New York City, Hudson River valley, Boston, Niagara Falls; dinner and tour of White House with President Jackson; ride on horse-drawn railroad.

SILSBEE, FRANCIS, 1811–1848   2355

Booth, Alan R., ed. "Francis Silsbee's August Odyssey." ESSEX INSTITUTE HISTORICAL COLLECTIONS 100 (1964):59–69.

> Aug 1831. Young Harvard graduate's journal of trip with friends through New England; travel by stagecoach and wagon through Maine, New Hampshire, Massachusetts, Connecticut River valley; description of climbing Mount Washington in the White Mountains; notes on New England towns.

SIMPSON, MATTHEW, 1811–1884   2356

In THE LIFE OF BISHOP MATTHEW SIMPSON, OF THE METHODIST EPISCOPAL CHURCH, by George R. Crooks, 512 pp. passim. New York: Harper & Brothers, 1890.

> 1831–1854. Biography containing extracts of an intermittently kept diary of a zealous churchman; early theological and medical studies; itinerant work and bishopric; trips to California and Panama; religious reflections.

STRANG, JAMES JESSE, 1813–1856   2357

THE DIARY OF JAMES J. STRANG. Deciphered, translated, introduced and annotated by Mark A. Strang. East Lansing: Michigan State University Press, 1961. 78 pp.

In THE KINGDOM OF SAINT JAMES; A NARRATIVE OF THE MORMONS, by Milo M. Quaife, pp. 195–234. New Haven: Yale University Press; London: H. Milford, Oxford University Press, 1930.

> 1831–1836. Early diary of man later to become a rival to Brigham Young's leadership of Mormons; life at Chautauqua County, New York, prior to his conversion to Mormonism; reading, debating, teaching school; philosophical and religious speculations; a dramatic sense of his own destiny.

SUPPIGER, JOSEPH   2358

Titus, Leo G., ed. "Swiss Emigrants Seek Home in America." HISTORICAL AND PHILOSOPHICAL SOCIETY OF OHIO BULLETIN 14 (1956):167–185.

> Aug 1831. Diary covering part of the journey of two Swiss families who settled in western Illinois; thirteen-day trip from Buffalo to Cleveland and Marietta by canal boat and then by river steamer on the Muskingum and Ohio; reports on land values, expenses, wages, American customs, etc.; long daily entries apparently directed towards those contemplating emigration.

TOCQUEVILLE, ALEXIS DE, 1805–1859   2359

JOURNEY TO AMERICA. Translated by George Lawrence, edited by J.P. Mayer. New Haven: Yale University Press, 1959. 424 pp. Reprint. Garden City, N.Y.: Doubleday, 1971.

> 1831–1832. The diaries which became source for his celebrated DEMOCRACY IN AMERICA, containing material which never appeared in the later work; hasty but detailed notes, freshness of first impressions of scenes, people, institutions and character of young country that fascinated and sometimes puzzled the observant Frenchman; travel by horseback, stagecoach and steamboat from East Coast to frontier; conversations with Americans of all kinds, from government leaders and urban elite to frontiersmen.

WASHBURN, AMASA CORNWALL   2360

"Canoeing on the Kankakee in 1831." SOCIETY OF INDIANA PIONEERS YEARBOOK (1944):5–13.

> Jun 1831. Journey of emigrant from Putney, Vermont; on the St. Joseph and Kankakee rivers; hazardous trip through marshes; difficulties obtaining supplies and fresh water.

1832

ANON.   2361

"The Fort Tecumseh and Pierre Journal." In THE AMERICAN FUR TRADE OF THE FAR WEST, by Hiram M. Chittenden, vol. 2, pp. 975–983. New York: F.P. Harper, 1902; Press of the Pioneers, 1935; R.R. Wilson, 1936; Stanford, Calif.: Academic Reprints, 1954.

> Mar–Sep 1832. Extracts from diary kept at fur trading posts; comings and goings of Indians, trappers, fur traders and hunters, by land and Missouri River boats; day-to-day work and routine of fur trade.

ANON.   2362

"A Diary of the Black Hawk War." IOWA JOURNAL OF HISTORY AND POLITICS 8 (1910):265–269.

> Apr–May 1832. Details of the Black Hawk War; brief notes of Indian activities.

ALLEN, JAMES   2363

"Journal and Letters of Lieutenant James Allen." In NARRATIVE OF AN EXPEDITION THROUGH THE UPPER MISSISSIPPI TO ITASCA LAKE, by Henry R. Schoolcraft. New York: Harper & Brothers, 1834; EXPEDITION TO LAKE ITASCA, by Henry R. Schoolcraft, edited by Philip P. Mason, pp. 163–241. East Lansing: Michigan State University Press, 1958.

> May–Aug 1832. Exploration diary of commander of military escort accompanying Henry Rowe Schoolcraft on his second expedition to Lake Itasca and the source of the Mississippi; canoe and overland travel; notes on Indians; especially Chippewas, lakes, rivers, land features; some dissension with Schoolcraft.

BALL, JOHN, b. 1794   2364

Powers, Kate N.B., ed. "Across the Continent Seventy Years Ago." OREGON HISTORICAL QUARTERLY 3 (1902): 82–106.

> 1832–1833. Extracts from exploration journal of Nathaniel Wyeth's expedition; Baltimore to Oregon and life in Oregon; adventures and incidents of journey; notes on Indians, scenery, natural history, climate.

BETTLE, JANE, 1773–1840   2365

EXTRACTS FROM THE MEMORANDUMS OF JANE BETTLE, WITH A SHORT MEMOIR RESPECTING HER. 2d ed. Philadelphia: J. & Kite, 1843. 116 pp.; London, 1845. 94 pp. Journal, pp. 13–66.

> 1832–1840. Journal of Pennsylvania Quaker; wholly concerned with her bodily and spiritual conditions; implorings and thanks to the Lord.

BIGGS, ASA, 1811–1878   2366

AUTOBIOGRAPHY OF ASA BIGGS, INCLUDING A JOURNAL OF A TRIP FROM NORTH CAROLINA TO NEW YORK IN 1832. Edited by Robert D.W. Connor. North Carolina Historical Commission Publications, Bulletin no. 19. Raleigh: Edwards & Broughton Printing Co., 1915. 51 pp. Journal, pp. 41–51.

> Apr–May 1832. A trip from Williamston, North Carolina, to New York and return; Mount Vernon, Washington, Baltimore, Philadelphia, New York; some lively descriptions of places and of the proceedings in the Senate.

BOUTWELL, WILLIAM THURSTON   2367

"Extracts from the Journal of Mr. Boutwell, on a Tour to the Source of the Mississippi." MISSIONARY HERALD 30 (1834):132–136, 177–180, 222–223, 259–262.

MINNESOTA HISTORICAL SOCIETY COLLECTIONS 1 (1902): 121–140. Reprint of 1850–1856 vols.

In EXPEDITION TO LAKE ITASCA, by Henry R. Schoolcraft, edited by Philip P. Mason, pp. 306–351. East Lansing: Michigan State University Press, 1958.

> Jun–Aug 1832. Exploration diary of missionary accompanying Henry Rowe Schoolcraft's second expedition to Lake Itasca and source of the Mississippi; missionary work with Chippewas and comments on their ways.

BRADFORD, PHOEBE GEORGE, 1794–1840   2368

Wilson, W. Emerson, ed. "Phoebe George Bradford Diaries." DELAWARE HISTORY 16 (1974):1–21, 132–151, 244–267, 337–357.

> 1832–1839. Extracts from twenty-three volumes of diaries kept by woman of prominent family in Wilmington, Delaware; family and social life; church activities and controversies; gardening; pro-Whig political comments; trip through northern New Jersey; building and occupancy of home which became a Wilmington landmark; commencement at Delaware College.

BROWN, SALLY EXPERIENCE   2369

THE DIARIES OF SALLY AND PAMELA BROWN, 1832–1838, AND HYDE LESLIE, 1887, OF PLYMOUTH NOTCH, VT. Springfield, Vt.: William L. Bryant Foundation, 1970. 176 pp.

> 1832–1838. Diary begun by Sally and continued by Pamela; brief notes of household chores, reading, visits, church services, school teaching, illnesses and deaths of friends and neighbors.

BROWNING, ORVILLE HICKMAN, 1806–1881   2370

In THE BLACK HAWK WAR, by Frank E. Stevens, pp. 117–118. Chicago: F.E. Stevens, 1903.

Apr–May 1832. March to Yellow Banks during Black Hawk War; brief notes of movements.

THE DIARY OF ORVILLE HICKMAN BROWNING. Edited by Theodore C. Pease and James G. Randall. Springfield: The Trustees of the Illinois State Historical Library, 1925–1933. 2 vols.

1850–1881. Senator's private diary, a huge and regularly kept work; law practice in Quincy, Illinois; rather bucolic life of family, church, small town society; attention to the beauties and changes of nature; much legal interest in railroads; opinions on slavery and on Civil War and its leading participants; views on Abraham Lincoln and reaction to his assassination; political life of Washington, D.C.; work as secretary of the interior; an important diary.

BUNTING, HANNAH SYNG, 1801–1832   2371

MEMOIR, DIARY, AND LETTERS, OF MISS HANNAH SYNG BUNTING, OF PHILADELPHIA. Compiled by T. Merritt. New York: T. Mason and G. Lane, 1837. 2 vols. in 1.

1818–1832. Methodist woman's scattered entries bearing spiritual "angst"; death notices and deathbed scenes; brief descriptions of activities with longer religious reflection on same.

CAMPBELL, ROBERT, 1808–1894   2372

NORTH DAKOTA HISTORICAL QUARTERLY 1 (1926):35–45.

Nov 1832–Sep 1833. Journey to Kentucky to buy sheep for Red River Colony.

CARR, GEORGE KIRWAN   2373

"A Short Tour through the United States and Canadas, 1832: The Journal of Lieutenant George Kirwan Carr." NEW YORK PUBLIC LIBRARY BULLETIN 41 (1937):743–774.

Oct–Dec 1832. Journey along the St. Lawrence and Hudson rivers; visits to Baltimore, Philadelphia and return to Halifax, Nova Scotia; notes on scenery, taverns, customs, fashions, persons; full, pleasant entries, apparently written up after return.

CHAMBERLAIN, EBENEZER MATTOON, b. 1805   2374

Fogle, Louise, ed. "Journal of Ebenezer Mattoon Chamberlain." INDIANA MAGAZINE OF HISTORY 15 (1919): 233–259.

1832–1835. Journey from Maine to Indiana; description of natural history, manners, customs; two poems; flowery style.

CLAYBROOKE, THOMAS W., b. 1800?   2375

Harris, M.H., ed. "Diary of Travels from Virginia to Tennessee." WILLIAM AND MARY COLLEGE QUARTERLY, 2d ser. 13 (1933):163–169.

Oct–Nov 1832. Mostly brief details of trip; some personal notes, descriptions and expenses.

COLEMAN, ANN RANEY THOMAS, 1810–1897   2376

VICTORIAN LADY ON THE TEXAS FRONTIER: THE JOURNAL OF ANN RANEY COLEMAN. Edited by C. Richard King. Norman: University of Oklahoma Press, 1971. 206 pp.

1832–1890. Journey from England to Texas; frontier life, Texas Revolution, Civil War; rewritten from her journals for her niece.

ELLSWORTH, HENRY LEAVITT   2377

WASHINGTON IRVING ON THE PRAIRIE; OR A NARRATIVE OF A TOUR IN THE SOUTHWEST IN THE YEAR 1832. Edited by Stanley T. Williams and Barbara D. Simison. New York: American Book Co., 1937. 152 pp.

Oct–Nov 1832. Letter-journal, kept for his wife, of Indian commissioner's expedition to resettle in Oklahoma Territory the Indians expelled by Indian Removal Bill; interesting more for content on Washington Irving, who accompanied him, than for information on Indians and Indian problems, which is scant.

FOLTZ, JONATHAN MESSERSMITH, 1810–1877   2378

In SURGEON OF THE SEAS: THE ADVENTUROUS LIFE OF SURGEON GENERAL JONATHAN M. FOLTZ IN THE DAYS OF WOODEN SHIPS. Told from his notes by Charles S. Foltz, pp. 35–300 passim. Indianapolis: Bobbs-Merrill, 1931.

1832–1867. Extensive quotations within biography of navy surgeon; cruises and expeditions; his personal affairs, reading, jottings on history and scenery, Civil War, Indies, South America, etc.; lively and entertaining.

GRATIOT, HENRY   2379

Quaife, Milo M., ed. "Journals and Reports of the Black Hawk War." MISSISSIPPI VALLEY HISTORICAL REVIEW 12 (1925–1926):392–409. Journal, pp. 396–401.

Jan–Jun 1832. Journal of "sub-Indian agent"; events and proceedings with the Winnebago Indians at Rock River; Black Hawk War; vaccination of Indians; speeches.

GRAY, MILLIE, 1800–1851   2380

THE DIARY OF MILLIE GRAY, 1832–1840 (NEE MILDRED RICHARDS STONE, WIFE OF COL. WM. FAIRFAX GRAY) RECORDING HER FAMILY LIFE BEFORE, DURING AND AFTER COL. WM. F. GRAY'S JOURNEY TO TEXAS IN 1835; AND THE SMALL JOURNAL, GIVING PARTICULARS OF ALL THAT OCCURED DURING THE FAMILY'S VOYAGE TO TEXAS IN 1838. Houston: Printed by F. Young, 1967. 158 pp.

1832–1840. Diary of home and family life, health, visiting and being visited, religious life, writing and giving music lessons in Fredericksburg, Virginia; notes of Colonel Gray's business affairs and reverses; sad farewell, moving, settling and making new friends in Houston.

GRIFFITH, BARTON, d. 1834   2381

THE DIARY OF BARTON GRIFFITH, COVINGTON, INDIANA. Crawfordsville, Ind.: R.E. Banta, 1932. 17 pp.

Oct 1832–May 1833. Account of an Indiana merchant's failed romance.

May 1834. Horseback trip from Covington to Cincinnati via Indianapolis and return; description of cities and accommodations; anti-Jacksonian political opinions.

Jun–Aug 1834. Journey to New Orleans by flatboat and steamboat down Ohio and Mississippi to get his goods to market; hazards of river transportation as Griffith anxiously tries to get to New Orleans before pork spoils.

HOUGHTON, DOUGLASS   2382

In EXPEDITION TO LAKE ITASCA, by Henry R. Schoolcraft, edited by Philip P. Mason, pp. 242–305.

East Lansing: Michigan State University Press, 1958.

Jun–Aug 1832. Exploration diary of physician and botanist with Henry Rowe Schoolcraft's second expedition to Lake Itasca and the source of the Mississippi; medical work with Chippewas, including vaccination for smallpox, formulas for medicines; collection of botanical and geological specimens.

KEMBLE, FRANCES ANNE, 1809–1893　　　　2383

JOURNAL. London: J. Murray; Philadelphia: Carey, Lea & Blanchard, 1835. 2 vols. Reprint. THE JOURNAL OF FRANCES ANNE BUTLER, BETTER KNOWN AS FANNY KEMBLE. New York: Blom, 1970.

Extracts in AMERICAN HISTORY TOLD BY CONTEMPORARIES, by Albert B. Hart, vol. 3, pp. 564–567; DIARY OF AMERICA, edited by Josef Berger, pp. 179–185.

Aug 1832–Jul 1833. Travels of the celebrated English actress in Middle Atlantic and New England cities; largely social and theatrical notes.

JOURNAL OF A RESIDENCE ON A GEORGIAN PLANTATION. London: Longman, Green, Longman, Roberts & Green, 1863. 434 pp. New York: Harper & Brothers, 1863. 337 pp. Reprint. Chicago: Afro-American Press, 1969.

JOURNAL OF A RESIDENCE ON A GEORGIAN PLANTATION. Edited by John A. Scott. London: Jonathan Cape; New York: Knopf, 1961. 415 pp.

1838–1839. An agonized record of Fanny Kemble Butler's five months on her husband's plantation and the everyday lives and mutual bondage of slaves and masters; her untenable position as slaves' advocate to her husband, particularly on behalf of the women; notes on social mores of plantation owners and their families; her sense of degradation of slavery; not published until the Civil War and credited by some with swinging British sympathies from Confederate to Union cause.

KING, WILLIAM C.　　　　2384

Landon, Fred. "Extracts from the Diary of William C. King, a Detroit Carpenter." MICHIGAN HISTORY MAGAZINE 19 (1935):65–70.

Jan–Sep 1832. Brief notes of work during a cholera epidemic; social and public affairs.

LONGFELLOW, FANNY APPLETON, 1817–1861　　　　2385

MRS. LONGFELLOW: SELECTED LETTERS AND JOURNALS. Edited by Edward Wagenknecht. New York: Longmans, Green, 1956. 255 pp.

1832–1853. Mainly letters, with some journal entries, of Longfellow's second wife; girlhood in Boston; travels in Europe where she met Longfellow; lengthy courtship, marriage; experience as first woman in America to have anesthetic for childbirth; literary interests, social life of Boston, care of children, much about her husband and other distinguished people: Emerson, Hawthorne, Whittier, Fanny Kemble, Carlisle, Lowell.

LYONS, LORENZO, 1807–1886　　　　2386

MAKUA LAIANA: THE STORY OF LORENZO LYONS. Compiled by Emma L. Doyle. Honolulu: Privately printed, Honolulu Star-Bulletin, 1945. 259 pp. Rev. and en. ed. Honolulu: Advertiser Publishing Co., 1953. 278 pp.

1832–1886. Significant missionary diary of beloved "Father" Lyons who worked for fifty-four years in the Waimea Highlands of Hawaii; voyage aboard whaler AVERICK with his bride and other missionaries; preaching, medical work, hymn writing in Hawaiian language, arduous tours to various islands, dealings with government during reigns of four Kamehamehas; throughout diary, keen observation, love for Hawaiian people; revelation of diarist's character and attitudes.

MARSH, CUTTING, 1800–1873　　　　2387

"Extracts from Marsh's Journal, during the Black Hawk War." WISCONSIN HISTORICAL SOCIETY COLLECTIONS 15 (1900):60–65.

Jun–Jul 1832. Extracts from journal of Congregational missionary to Stockbridge Indians; incidents in the Black Hawk War in Wisconsin; his emotions; descriptions of Indians.

MEEKER, JOTHAM, 1804–1855　　　　2388

In JOTHAM MEEKER, PIONEER PRINTER OF KANSAS, by Douglas C. McMurtrie and Albert H. Allen, pp. 45–126. Chicago: Eyncourt Press, 1930.

1832–1855. Missionary journal; brief notes of his work as missionary to the Indians and printer for Baptist mission in Kansas; notes on farming, printing, binding, translations into Ottawa, etc.

MILLER, AARON　　　　2389

"Diary of Aaron Miller, Written while in Quest of Ohio Wheat Lands." OHIO ARCHAEOLOGICAL AND HISTORICAL QUARTERLY 33 (1924):69–79.

Apr–Jun 1832. Travels through Ohio in search of farm land; route through Williamsport, Brownsville, Zanesville, Columbus, Urbana, Cincinnati, Chillicothe, Wheeling, Winchester; general comments on soil and developments.

MUNCK, CHRISTOPH JACOB　　　　2390

Mahr, August C., ed. "Down the Rhine to the Ohio: The Travel Diary of Christoph Jacob Munck." OHIO STATE ARCHAEOLOGICAL AND HISTORICAL QUARTERLY 57 (1948):266–310.

Apr–Aug 1832. German immigrant's diary covering travels within Germany, Atlantic crossing on the GEORGE NOLGEN, and journey to Ohio; prayers and religious thoughts of a Pietist; concerns for his wife, who opposed leaving Germany, and his small children traveling with him. In German and English.

POURTALES, ALBERT, 1812–1861　　　　2391

ON THE WESTERN TOUR WITH WASHINGTON IRVING: THE JOURNAL AND LETTERS OF COUNT DE POURTALES. Edited by George F. Spaulding, translated by Seymour Feiler. American Exploration and Travel Series, 54. Norman: University of Oklahoma Press, 1968. 96 pp.

Sep–Dec 1832. Diary of a romantic nineteen-year-old Swiss nobleman who, mounted on a race horse, traveled in Oklahoma Indian Territory with Washington Irving and new Indian Commissioner Henry Leavitt Ellsworth; camping, buffalo hunting; an abortive attempt to join an Osage hunting expedition; sympathetic description of life and plight of Indians; a lively, humorous and totally youthful diary.

PRATT, ORSON, 1811–1881　　　　2392

"History of Orson Pratt." UTAH GENEALOGICAL AND HISTORICAL MAGAZINE 27 (1936):117–124, 163–169; 28

(1937):42–48, 92–96, 118–125; 29 (1938):34–36.

> 1832–1844. Extracts from diary of Mormon apostle; notes on religious, business, social, domestic activities; valuable as a collection of dates, facts, etc.

"Extracts from the Private Journal of Orson Pratt." UTAH GENEALOGICAL AND HISTORICAL MAGAZINE 15 (1924):55–59, 104–109, 166–171; 16 (1925):19–24, 71–76, 118–123, 160–167; 17 (1927):118–126, 209–214.

> Mar–Jul 1846. Journey of Mormons from Nauvoo to Great Salt Lake; founding of city; long detailed entries giving an excellent record of the migration.

SCOTT, JACOB RICHARDSON, 1815–1861   2393

TO THEE THIS TEMPLE: THE LIFE, DIARY AND FRIENDS OF JACOB RICHARDSON SCOTT. Edited by Elizabeth Hayward and Roscoe Ellis Scott. Chester, Pa.: American Baptist Historical Society, 1955. 405 pp.

> 1832–1860. Personal diary of Baptist minister, author of hymns, including "To Thee This Temple"; student years at Brown University and Newton Theological Seminary; pastorates in white and black churches in Richmond and Hampton, Virginia; chaplaincy of University of Virginia; pastorates in Portland, Maine, Fall River, Massachusetts, Rochester and Yonkers, New York; local trips and European tour; generally longer entries during school years becoming brief notes of religious activities and personal life thereafter.

SMITH, ABIGAIL TENNEY, 1809–1885   2394

Extracts in LOWELL AND ABIGAIL, A REALISTIC IDYLL, by Mary D. Frear, pp. 39–279 passim. New Haven, Conn.: Yale University Press, 1934.

> 1832–1885. Missionary journal; educational work in connection with her husband's mission at Kaumakapili, Hawaii.

SMITH, LOWELL, 1802–1891   2395

In LOWELL AND ABIGAIL, A REALISTIC IDYLL, by Mary D. Frear, pp. 39–283 passim. New Haven, Conn.: Yale University Press, 1934.

> 1832–ca. 1885. Missionary work as pastor of Kaumakapili Church, Hawaii.

STOCK, JOSEPH WHITING, 1815–1855   2396

THE PAINTINGS AND THE JOURNAL OF JOSEPH WHITING STOCK. Edited by Juliette Tomlinson. Middletown, Conn.: Wesleyan University Press, 1976. 180 pp. Journal, pp. 169–180.

> 1832–1846. New England artist's combination autobiography, diary and account book; details of the accident which left him unable to walk, the doctor who devised a wheel chair for him, and his travels from town to town to paint portraits; each painting recorded with patron, size and price.

WYETH, NATHANIEL JARVIS, 1802–1856   2397

"The Correspondence and Journals of Captain Nathaniel J. Wyeth." SOURCES OF THE HISTORY OF OREGON 1, pts. 3–6 (1899):155–219, 221–256. Reprint. New York: Arno, 1973.

THE JOURNALS OF CAPTAIN NATHANIEL J. WYETH. Fairfield, Wash.: Ye Galleon, 1969. 131 pp.

Extract in THE CALL OF THE COLUMBIA, edited by

Archer B. Hulbert, pp. 112–153. Denver: Denver Public Library, 1934.

> 1832–1833, May 1834–Apr 1835. Journals of two exploring expeditions in Oregon Territory; the first across Nebraska, Wyoming, Idaho and Oregon to the mouth of the Columbia; the second around the Columbia; detailed notes of movements, topography, etc.; fine descriptions of Indians.

1833

ANON.   2398

Bagley, Clarence B., ed. "Journal of Occurrences at Nisqually House." WASHINGTON HISTORICAL QUARTERLY 6 (1915):179–197, 264–278; 7 (1916):59–75, 144–167.

Farrar, Victor J., ed. "The Nisqually Journal." WASHINGTON HISTORICAL QUARTERLY 10 (1919):205–230; 11(1920):59–65, 136–149, 218–229, 294–302; 12 (1921): 68–70, 137–148, 219–228, 300–303; 13 (1922):57–66, 131–141, 225–232, 293–299; 14 (1923):145–148, 223–234, 299–306; 15 (1924):63–66, 126–143, 215–226, 289–298.

Extracts in TOLD BY THE PIONEERS, by United States Work Projects Administration. Olympia, Wash., 1837–1838.

> 1833–1835, 1849–1852. Fur-trading journals recording activities and events at Fort Nisqually; trading, Indians, farming; work at the fort.

ABDY, EDWARD STRUTT, 1791–1846   2399

JOURNAL OF A RESIDENCE AND TOUR IN THE UNITED STATES. London: J. Murray, 1835. 3 vols. Reprint. New York: Negro Universities Press, 1969.

> 1833–1834. Travel journal of a fellow of Jesus College, Cambridge; visits to New England, Canada, Washington, D.C., the southern and midwestern states; caustic anti-slavery and anti-American comments.

ALLIBONE, SUSAN, 1813–1854   2400

A LIFE HID WITH CHRIST IN GOD, BEING A MEMOIR OF SUSAN ALLIBONE, CHIEFLY COMPILED FROM HER DIARY AND LETTERS. By Alfred Lee. Philadelphia: J.B. Lippincott, 1856. 295 pp.

> 1833–1854. Religious diary; devotion to St. Andrews Church, Philadelphia, and to her spiritual advisors, especially the Rev. Dr. Bedell; reflections on her spiritual life, unworthiness and acceptance of suffering.

BARNARD, HENRY, b. ca. 1811   2401

Steiner, Bernard C., ed. "The South Atlantic States in 1833, as Seen by a New Englander." MARYLAND HISTORICAL MAGAZINE 13 (1918):267–386.

> 1833. Combination of diary and letters describing events in Washington, D.C., during the peak of the nullification controversy; notes on people and places visited during a three month tour through Virginia, North Carolina and South Carolina.

BENTON, COLBEE CHAMBERLAIN, 1805–1880   2402

A VISITOR TO CHICAGO IN INDIAN DAYS: "JOURNAL TO THE FAR-OFF WEST." Edited by Paul M. Angle and James R. Getz. Chicago: The Caxton Club, 1957. 121 pp.

> Jul–Aug 1833. Adventurous New Englander's trip to see frontier Chicago and especially Indians and their ways; travel by stagecoach, lake steamer

and horseback; all the tourist attractions en route, including Niagara Falls; great delight and interest in almost everything and good natured tolerance of rigors of travel; excellent descriptions of Chicago and of Indians of northern Illinois and southern Wisconsin.

BOTSFORD, JABEZ KENT   2403

Extracts in ADVENTURES IN ANCESTORS; ACTIVITIES OF AND ANECDOTES CONCERNING SOME OF THE BOTSFORD PIONEERS IN AMERICA, by Eli H. Botsford, vol. 1, pp. 61-75. Williamstown: McClelland, 1936.

Apr-Aug 1833. Social and travel diary; social life in Newton, Massachusetts; visit to New York, theaters; journey to Chicago by Erie Canal, Great Lake steamers; travel notes; a pleasant diary.

CAMPBELL, ROBERT, 1804-1879   2404

Brooks, George R., ed. "The Private Journal of Robert Campbell." MISSOURI HISTORICAL SOCIETY BULLETIN 20 (1963-1964):3-24, 107-118.

Sep-Dec 1833. Fur trading journal; challenge of Campbell and his partner, William Sublette, to the power of the American Fur Company; account of life at Fort William, their trading post near confluence of Yellowstone and Missouri rivers; competition with nearby American Fur Company post; notes on trading with Indians.

DAVID, GEORGE   2405

"Diary of George David, a Trip from London to Chicago." MICHIGAN HISTORY MAGAZINE 18 (.1934):53-66.

Sep-Oct 1833. Extracts from travel diary; trip from Sandusky through Michigan, Indiana and Illinois to Chicago; comments on farms, forests, taverns, American institutions; lively, varied, critical and entertaining.

DAVIDSON, MARGARET MILLER, 1823-1838   2406

Harding, Walter, ed. "Sentimental Journal: The Diary of Margaret Miller Davidson." RUTGERS UNIVERSITY LIBRARY JOURNAL 13 (1949):19-24.

May-Jul 1833. Travel journal of precocious child who gained posthumous fame for her poetry; visits to Ticonderoga, Saratoga Springs, Hoboken, Coney Island; much sentiment.

DOMETT, ALFRED, 1811-1887   2407

THE CANADIAN JOURNAL OF ALFRED DOMETT: BEING AN EXTRACT FROM A JOURNAL OF A TOUR IN CANADA, THE UNITED STATES AND JAMAICA. Edited by E.A. Horsman and Lillian R. Benson. London, Canada: University of Western Ontario, 1955. 66 pp.

1833-1834. Englishman's visit to Niagara Falls, with vivid, detailed and effusive descriptions of the falls; candid and disparaging remarks about accommodations, conditions of travel and manners of the "Yankees."

ELDRIDGE, CHARLES WILLIAM, 1811-1883   2408

"Journal of a Tour through Vermont to Montreal and Quebec." VERMONT HISTORICAL SOCIETY PROCEEDINGS 2 (1931):53-82.

Jun-Aug 1833. Amateur painter's tour through Connecticut, Vermont, Montreal, Quebec; observations of country and people; literary allusions; narrative style.

EVANS, HUGH, 1811-1836   2409

Perrine, Fred S., ed. "Journal of Hugh Evans, Covering the First and Second Campaigns of the United States Dragoon Regiment." CHRONICLES OF OKLAHOMA 3 (1925):175-215.

Oct 1833-Sep 1834. Ordinary soldier's account of the first summer campaign with Henry Dodge to the Rocky Mountains.

Perrine, Fred S., ed. "Hugh Evans' Journal of Colonel Henry Dodge's Expedition to the Rocky Mountains in 1835." MISSISSIPPI VALLEY HISTORICAL REVIEW 14 (1927-1928):192-214.

May-Aug 1835. Long notes on march, military life with the dragoons; Indians; some interesting spellings.

FLOY, MICHAEL, 1808-1837   2410

THE DIARY OF MICHAEL FLOY, JR., BOWERY VILLAGE. Edited by Richard A.E. Brooks. New Haven: Yale University Press, 1941. 269 pp.

1833-1837. Diary of nurseryman with avocational interests in mathematics, music, book collecting and reading; detailed account of his conversion to Methodism, class meetings, services, etc.; trips to Harlem to tend the nursery stock; lists and prices of books purchased; notes, some humorous, on family, friends and events.

HARRIS, DILUE, b. 1825   2411

"The Reminiscences of Mrs. Dilue Harris." TEXAS HISTORICAL ASSOCIATION QUARTERLY 4 (1900-1901):85-127, 155-189.

1833-1837. Monthly entries, largely reminiscence; begun by her father, Dr. Pleasant W. Rose; life in Harrisburg, Texas; interesting.

LEE, JASON, 1803-1845   2412

"Diary of Rev. Jason Lee." OREGON HISTORICAL SOCIETY QUARTERLY 17 (1916):116-146, 240-266, 397-430.

Extracts in CHRISTIAN ADVOCATE, 3 and 30 October 1834.

Extracts in THE OREGON CRUSADE; ACROSS LAND AND SEA TO OREGON, edited by Archer B. Hulbert and Dorothy P. Hulbert, pp. 147-160, 167-184. Overland to the Pacific, vol. 5. Colorado Springs: The Stewart Commission of Colorado College; Denver: Denver Public Library, 1935.

1833-1838. Missionary diary; travel from Canada to Liberty, Missouri, thence overland to Fort Vancouver; life on the trail as seen by a troubled missionary.

LYONS, JOSEPH, 1813-1837   2413

In MEMOIRS OF AMERICAN JEWS, 1775-1865, by Jacob R. Marcus, vol. 1, pp. 239-260. New York: Ktav Publishing House, 1974.

1833-1835. Diary of a nineteen-year-old Jewish man during years studying law in Savannah, Georgia; frequent trips to Charleston, South Carolina; often in despair, perhaps because of illness.

MERRILL, MOSES, 1803-1840   2414

"Extracts from the Diary of Rev. Moses Merrill, a Missionary to the Otoe Indians." NEBRASKA HISTORICAL SOCIETY TRANSACTIONS 4 (1892):157-191.

1833–1839. Account of work among Oto Indians in the Platte River country; interesting details of Oto life and customs; religious and educational work, personal activities and adventures of missionary.

NICHOLS, SARAH PEIRCE, b. 1804   2415

"Journal of Sarah Peirce Nichols of Salem." ESSEX INSTITUTE HISTORICAL COLLECTIONS 82 (1946):211-227.

Apr-Dec 1833. Woman's diary recording daily habits, such as a twelve mile walk, and activities; brief allusions to visits of Andrew Jackson and Henry Clay to Salem.

OTEY, JAMES HERVEY, 1800-1863   2416

Extracts in MEMOIR OF RT. REV. JAMES HERVEY OTEY, THE FIRST BISHOP OF TENNESSEE, by William Mercer Green, pp. 151-169. New York: J. Pott, 1885.

1833–1863. Clergyman's diary; activities of the first Episcopal bishop of Tennessee; diocesan work, visitations, journeys in the South, religious reflections, affairs of his family, illnesses, weather, gossip.

PORTER, CHARLES HENRY, 1811-1841   2417

Extracts in MEMOIR OF CHARLES HENRY PORTER, A STUDENT IN THEOLOGY, by Elizur G. Smith, pp. 13-151 passim. New York: American Tract Society, 1849.

1833–1841. Religious journal; preparation for college, study at Westfield Academy, Massachusetts; reflections and resolves; visits to sick, meetings, preaching.

PURCELL, JOHN BAPTIST, 1800-1883   2418

"Bishop Purcell's Journal." CATHOLIC HISTORICAL REVIEW 5 (1919-1920):239-255.

1833–1836. Journal of Catholic bishop of Ohio; journey to his diocese; lively commentary on local conditions, drunkenness, bigotry; gossip about nuns; notes on his work; personal and highly amusing.

QUINCY, ANNA CABOT LOWELL, b. 1812   2419

In THE ARTICULATE SISTERS, by M.A. DeWolfe Howe, pp. 193-244.

1833–1834. Diary of daughter of President Josiah Quincy of Harvard; parties in Boston; attending the theater to see Fanny Kemble in FAZIO and other performances; President Jackson's visit to Cambridge; domestic affairs recorded for her sisters who were on a trip.

SHAFTER, OSCAR LOVELL, 1812-1873   2420

Extracts in LIFE, DIARY AND LETTERS OF OSCAR LOVELL SHAFTER, ASSOCIATE JUSTICE SUPREME COURT OF CALIFORNIA. Edited by Flora H. Loughead, 323 pp. passim. San Francisco: Blair-Murdock, 1915.

1833–1863. Judge's diary; migration and early life in California.

STEELE, MILLICENT POLLOCK   2421

"Diary of a Voyage from London to Upper Canada in 1833 by Millicent Pollock Steele and Ellen Frances Steele." ONTARIO HISTORICAL SOCIETY PAPERS AND RECORDS 23 (1926):483-510.

Apr-Aug 1833. Letter-diaries describing journey from London to Simcoe County, Upper Canada, via

New York; lively details of social life aboard ship, American and overland journey, clearing site, home-making and social activities.

STEINES, HERMANN   2422

"The Followers of Duden." MISSOURI HISTORICAL REVIEW 14 (1919-1920):56-59, 436-446.

1833–1837 (with gaps). Journey from Baltimore to Pittsburgh; searching in Missouri for land on which to settle; life there with other German political refugees, followers of Gottfried Duden.

TRAVIS, WILLIAM BARRET, 1809-1836   2423

THE DIARY OF WILLIAM BARRET TRAVIS. Edited by Robert E. Davis, Spanish translation by Thomas W. Walker. Waco: Texian Press, 1966. 206 pp.

Aug 1833–Jun 1834. Diary of lawyer later to be a hero in the Texas Revolution; legal and financial matters; sales and prices of goods, horses, land and slaves; names of many Anglo-American Texans; little personal information.

VAILL, WILLIAM F.   2424

"Journal of Mr. Vaill during a Preaching Tour." MISSIONARY HERALD 29 (1833):366-371.

May 1833. Journal of a missionary under the American Board of Commissioners for Foreign Missions; travel to and preaching in the principal Osage villages; interesting details of Osage customs; notes on Santa Fe traders.

WALKER, MARY RICHARDSON, 1814-1897   2425

Extracts in ELKANAH AND MARY WALKER, PIONEERS AMONG THE SPOKANES, by Clifford M. Drury, 250 pp. passim. Caldwell, Idaho: The Caxton Printers, 1940.

Extracts in MARY RICHARDSON WALKER: HER BOOK, by Ruth K. McKee, 357 pp. passim. Caldwell, Idaho: The Caxton Printers, 1945.

1833–1850. Missionary diary; sense of vocation, courtship and marriage to Elkanah Walker; exhausting horseback journey to Oregon Territory; frank assessments of people in the party; difficult stay with the Whitmans at Walla Walla under crowded conditions; notes on people who frequented the mission; work among Indians at Tshimakain near Spokane; childbearing and rearing; endless domestic chores; guilt over allowing family duties to take precedence over mission work; avowals of love for her husband but frequent sense of his disapproval; news of the Whitman massacre; a fine diary which obviously served a cathartic purpose.

Extracts in WOMEN OF THE WEST, by Cathy Luchetti, pp. 61-75. St. George, Utah: Antelope Island Press, 1982.

1833–1847.

Extracts in FIRST WHITE WOMEN OVER THE ROCKIES, by Clifford M. Drury, vol. 2, pp. 21-44, 63-356.

1838–1848.

Extracts in "The Diary of Mary Richardson Walker," edited by Rufus A. Coleman. THE FRONTIER: A MAGAZINE OF THE NORTHWEST 11 (1931):284-300; FRONTIER OMNIBUS, pp. 79-99.

Extracts in THE DIARY OF MARY RICHARDSON WALKER, edited by Rufus A. Coleman. Sources of Northwest History, Historical Reprints, no. 15. Missoula: State University of Montana, 1931. 19 pp.

Jun–Dec 1838. Last weeks of journey; stay at Whitman mission.

1834

ANON. 2426

Carey, Charles H., ed. "The Mission Record Book of the Methodist Episcopal Church, Willamette Station." OREGON HISTORICAL SOCIETY QUARTERLY 23 (1922):230–266.

1834–1838. Journal of Methodist missionary in the Willamette Valley, Oregon; hardships, work and worship; notes on Indians; intimate portrait of the mission; marriage records, etc., appended.

ANON. 2427

JOURNAL OF AN EXCURSION TO THE UNITED STATES AND CANADA. By A Citizen of Edinburgh. Edinburgh: J. Anderson, 1835. 168 pp.

Mar–Jun 1834. Travel mainly in New York State; conventional descriptions and advice for emigrants.

ANON. 2428

Pelzer, Louis, ed. "Journal of Marches by the First United States Dragoons." IOWA JOURNAL OF HISTORY AND POLITICS 7 (1909):331–378.

May–Sep 1834, May–Aug 1835. Officer's account of marches of the dragoons in the Mississippi Valley; to Pawnee, Pict and Comanche villages on the Red River; from Fort Gibson to Des Moines; from Des Moines to near mouth of the Boone River and to Minnesota; brief notes of first journey, developed narrative of second.

ALLIS, SAMUEL 2429

"Communications from Mssrs. Dunbar and Allis." MISSIONARY HERALD 32 (1836):68–70.

Oct 1834. Journal of a missionary under the American Board of Commissioners for Foreign Missions; travel with the Rev. John Dunbar to the Pawnee Indians; details of his work and comments on the Pawnees.

ANDERSON, WILLIAM MARSHALL, 1807–1881 2430

THE ROCKY MOUNTAIN JOURNALS OF WILLIAM MARSHALL ANDERSON. Edited by Dale L. Morgan and Eleanor T. Harris. San Marino, Calif.: Huntington Library, 1967. 430 pp.

Mar–Sep 1834. Account of a trip to and from the Rockies with the Sublette party; size and personnel of the group; landmarks along route from Chimney Rock, Nebraska, to the Green River rendezvous, Wyoming; Rocky Mountain fur trade; founding of Fort Laramie, with daily record of fur trade rendezvous; merger of Fitzpatrick, Sublette and Bridger with Fontenelle, Drips and Company and return to St. Louis by pirogue with Fitzpatrick.

CIRCLEVILLE DEMOCRAT AND WATCHMAN, 29 September, 13 October 1871.

Partoll, Albert J., ed. "Anderson's Narrative of a Ride to the Rocky Mountains in 1834." FRONTIER AND MIDLAND 19 (1938):54–63. Reprint. FRONTIER OMNIBUS, pp. 67–78; Sources of Northwest History, Historical Reprints, no. 27. Missoula: State University of Montana, 1938. 11 pp.

May–Jun 1834. Chimney Rock to the Green River rendezvous.

AN AMERICAN IN MAXIMILIAN'S MEXICO, 1865–1866; THE DIARIES OF WILLIAM MARSHALL ANDERSON. Edited by Ramon E. Ruiz. San Marino, Calif.: Huntington Library, 1959. 132 pp.

1865–1866. Diary of surveyor commissioned by Maximilian to survey lands of Coahuila for colonization by Confederates; detailed description of Coahuila; social, economic and political notes; comments on the Southerners who settled in Mexico after the Civil War.

BOSWORTH, JOANNA SHIPMAN 2431

A TRIP TO WASHINGTON. n.p.: Privately published by Henry M. Dawes, 1914. 44 pp.

Oct–Nov 1834. Young girl's travel diary; a carriage trip from Athens, Ohio, to Philadelphia, Baltimore and Washington, D.C., with her father, Charles Shipman, and her sister, Betsy; accommodations; pleasures and problems of carriage travel; visits to churches and tourist attractions of Washington and surrounding area.

BOWEN, GEORGE, 1816–1888 2432

Extracts in GEORGE BOWEN OF BOMBAY: MISSIONARY, SCHOLAR, MYSTIC, SAINT; A MEMOIR, by Robert E. Speer, 366 pp. passim. New York: Privately printed, 1938.

1834–1880? Diary extracts and letters of missionary to India under American Board of Commissioners for Foreign Missions; boyhood, early travels in Europe, conversion, education at Union Theological Seminary; work in India, relinquishing salary to support himself as an independent missionary; later affiliation with Methodists; extensive writing, including editorship of the BOMBAY GUARDIAN; much religious reflection.

BROKE, FREDERICA SOPHIA 2433

"Diary of an American Tour." UNIVERSITY OF ROCHESTER LIBRARY BULLETIN 4 (1949):26–43.

Aug–Sep 1834. Englishwoman's account of railroad trip from near Albany to Niagara Falls; notes on accommodations, travel conditions, American accents, visit to Tuscarora Indian village and church; lengthy description of Niagara Falls.

CHARDON, FRANCIS AUGUSTE, d. 1848 2434

CHARDON'S JOURNAL AT FORT CLARK. Edited by Annie H. Abel. Pierre, S. Dak., 1932. 458 pp.

1834–1839. Fur trader's journal; experiences at and around Fort Clark in the upper Missouri country among the Mandans, Gros Ventres and their neighbors; very detailed account of work and private life; Indian affairs; vivid picture of the smallpox epidemic of 1837; a good journal.

Quaife, Milo M., ed. "The Smallpox Epidemic on the Upper Missouri." MISSISSIPPI VALLEY HISTORICAL REVIEW 17 (1930–1931):278–299.

Extract in DIARY OF AMERICA, edited by Josef Berger, pp. 278–288.

1837. Extract relating to smallpox epidemic.

CLARKE, C.H. 2435

In DIARIES FROM THE DAYS OF SAIL, edited by R.C. Bell, pp. 11–69. London: Barrie & Jenkins; New York: Holt, Rinehart and Winston, 1974.

1834. A young Englishman's diary of travel in America; comments on his modes of travel; sailing and steamships, canal boat, stagecoach and train; notes on Niagara Falls, St. Lawrence River, Erie Canal and eastern American countryside and cities.

CLARKE, JAMES FREEMAN, 1810-1888　　　　2436

JAMES FREEMAN CLARKE: AUTOBIOGRAPHY, DIARY AND CORRESPONDENCE. Edited by Edward Everett Hale. Boston and New York: Houghton, Mifflin, 1891. Reprint. New York: Negro Universities Press, 1968. Diary, pp. 107-275.

1834-1861. Diary of Unitarian clergyman and abolitionist; scattered notes on church affairs and theology; Civil War news.

CLELAND, JOHN　　　　2437

Martin, Kenneth R. "Wilmington's First Whaling Voyage." DELAWARE HISTORY 16 (1974):152-170.

1834-1837. Scattered extracts from diary kept by the son of the founder of the Wilmington Whaling Company; life aboard the CERES; work as a whaleman; tensions of an unsuccessful voyage.

DANA, RICHARD HENRY, 1815-1882　　　　2438

Allison, James, ed. "Journal of a Voyage from Boston to the Coast of California." AMERICAN NEPTUNE 12 (1952):177-185.

1834-1836. The diary upon which Dana based his TWO YEARS BEFORE THE MAST; brief notes of voyage on board the PILGRIM and ALERT; names of crew and of other ships; weather, navigational details, rounding of Cape Horn, ports of call in South America and California.

THE JOURNAL OF RICHARD HENRY DANA, JR. Edited by Robert F. Lucid. Cambridge: Belknap Press of Harvard University Press, 1968. 3 vols.

1841-1860. Long, articulate daily entries of Boston lawyer already famous as author; busy legal career, especially in maritime law, with cases described in detail; involvement in Free-Soil Party and abolitionist cause; family matters and life among the social, intellectual and literary elite of Boston and Cambridge; Episcopal church work and religious reading and thoughts; well described travels in the United States, to England and eventually a sea voyage around the world to recover health; occasional escapes from Boston and domesticity to the mountains, sea or less savory areas of New York; a monumental diary revealing much of the ideas, society, mores and politics of mid-nineteenth century New England and of the mind and character of the diarist.

Extract in DIARY OF AMERICA, edited by Josef Berger, pp. 395-402.

1854. Account of legal defense of runaway slave apprehended in Boston.

Extract in "Attack on a United States Court-House." AMERICAN HISTORY TOLD BY CONTEMPORARIES, edited by Albert B. Hart, vol. 4, pp. 87-91.

1854.

DODGE, HENRY, 1782-1867　　　　2439

Harlan, E.R., ed. "Colonel Henry Dodge and His Regiment of Dragoons on the Plains in 1834." ANNALS OF IOWA 17 (1930):173-197.

AMERICAN STATE PAPERS: MILITARY AFFAIRS, V:373-382.

In UNITED STATES CONGRESS. HOUSE EXECUTIVE DOCUMENT no. 2, 23d CONGRESS, 2d SESSION, 1834, pp. 70-91.

Jun-Aug 1834. Military journal of colonel with United States Dragoons; exploration on the southwestern plains; mainly councils with Indians at the Toyash village.

UNITED STATES CONGRESS. HOUSE EXECUTIVE DOCUMENT no. 181, 24th CONGRESS, 1st SESSION, 1836. 38 pp.

May-Aug 1835. With detachment of dragoons in the Rockies; journey from Fort Leavenworth; among Pawnees.

DUNBAR, JOHN　　　　2440

"Extracts from the Journal of Mr. Dunbar." MISSIONARY HERALD 31 (1835):343-349, 376-381, 417-421.

Jun 1834-Apr 1835. Journal of missionary under the American Board of Commissioners for Foreign Missions; journey from Fort Leavenworth to Indian villages between the Platte and Missouri rivers; work at Grand Pawnee village; interesting details of Pawnee customs.

FISHER, SIDNEY (or SYDNEY) GEORGE, 1809-1871　　　　2441

Wainwright, Nicholas B., ed. "The Diaries of Sydney George Fisher." PENNSYLVANIA MAGAZINE OF HISTORY AND BIOGRAPHY 76 (1952):177-220, 330-352, 440-467; 77 (1953):76-100, 198-211; 86 (1962):49-90, 181-203, 319-349, 454-478; 87 (1963):63-88, 189-225, 324-347, 431-453; 88 (1964):70-93, 199-226, 328-367, 456-484; 89 (1965):79-110, 207-227, 331-366, 459-485.

A PHILADELPHIA PERSPECTIVE; THE DIARY OF SIDNEY GEORGE FISHER. Edited by Nicholas B. Wainwright. Philadelphia: Historical Society of Pennsylvania, 1967. 626 pp.

1834-1871 (with gaps). Extracts from the seventy-nine volumes of diaries of a Philadelphia gentleman, who evidently had little use for the democracy of Jacksonian America; reports of social life and politics of the day; evaluations of political figures such as Jackson, Clay, Calhoun, Webster and Nicholas Biddle.

GILRUTH, JAMES, 1793-1873　　　　2442

In THE METHODISTS: A COLLECTION OF SOURCE MATERIALS, by William Warren Sweet, pp. 370-467. Religion on the American Frontier, vol. 4. Chicago: University of Chicago Press, 1946.

1834-1835. Lively day by day record of a Methodist circuit rider during the rapid settlement of the Detroit area; sermon texts and topics, conference affairs, books read and difficulties of travel; domestic matters including plans for a log house, remedies for ague, plans for instruction in spelling and a description of a threshing machine in operation.

GRANT, HUGH FRASER, d. 1873　　　　2443

PLANTER MANAGEMENT AND CAPITALISM IN ANTE-BELLUM GEORGIA: THE JOURNAL OF HUGH FRASER GRANT. Edited by Albert V. House. Columbia University Studies in the History of American Agriculture. New York: Columbia University Press, 1954. 329 pp.

1834-1861. Journal and account book of owner of Elizafield Plantation, Georgia; production, financial and marketing problems of rice-grower; some notes on health and activities of family; lists of slaves.

HEYWOOD, ROBERT, 1786-1868   2444

A JOURNEY TO AMERICA IN 1834. Edited by Mary Heywood Haslam. Cambridge: Privately printed, 1919. 112 pp.

Main May-Oct 1834. Englishman's travel diary; voyage from Liverpool to New York; tour by stage and steamer; comments on New York, Philadelphia, Washington, Maysville, Lexington, Louisville, Cincinnati, Columbus, Pittsburgh, Erie, Buffalo, Niagara Falls, Montreal, Quebec, Albany and Boston; sightseeing, descriptions of eminent persons, scenery, taverns, costs, customs, etc.; a full and interesting diary.

INGALLS, CHARLES FRANCIS   2445

Dixon, Mary F.C., ed. "The Coming of the Ingalls Family to Illinois." ILLINOIS HISTORICAL SOCIETY JOURNAL 18 (1925):416-421.

Apr-May 1834. Journey from Abington, Connecticut, to Buffalo, Erie, Detroit and Chicago; statistical notes.

JARRETT, DAVID   2446

Reed, W.H., ed. "An Overland Trip to the Great West in 1834." HISTORICAL SOCIETY OF MONTGOMERY COUNTY HISTORICAL SKETCHES 6 (1929):121-136.

May-Jun 1834. Account of overland trip to the West with a party from Montgomery County, Pennsylvania; travel through Virginia and Ohio; notes on distances, towns, roads, country, inns, and on towns of Richmond, Somerset, Wheeling, Shippensburg, Carlisle, etc.

KEMPER, JACKSON, 1789-1870   2447

"Journal of an Episcopalian Missionary's Tour to Green Bay." WISCONSIN HISTORICAL COLLECTIONS 14 (1898): 394-449.

1834. Trip of inspection to the Green Bay Mission, Wisconsin; notes on society, education, Indians, scenery, religious and personal matters; detailed, extensive and interesting.

"A Trip through Wisconsin in 1838." WISCONSIN MAGAZINE OF HISTORY 8 (1924-1925):423-445.

Jul-Aug 1838. Episcopal bishop's travel from Dubuque to Fond du Lac.

"Extracts from Bishop Kemper's Diary in Regards to Beginnings of Nashotah." NASHOTAH SCOLIAST 1, nos. 1-8 (1883-1884).

1841-1859 (with gaps). Bishop's diary of diocesan work.

"Bishop Jackson Kemper's Visit to Minnesota in 1843." MINNESOTA HISTORY 7 (1926):264-273.

1843. Visit to Minnesota, with extracts from his letters.

"Kemper's Journal and Letters." HISTORICAL MAGAZINE OF THE PROTESTANT EPISCOPAL CHURCH 4 (1935): 225-242. Journal, pp. 231-234.

1856. Diocesan journal; visitation of Nebraska and Kansas; notes of visits.

KENNEDY, ALEXANDER   2448

In CHARDON'S JOURNAL AT FORT CLARK, edited by Annie H. Abel, app. A, pp. 323-330. Pierre, S. Dak., 1932.

May-Jun 1834. Fragment from fur trader's journal kept at Fort Clark among Mandan Indians; mostly weather notes.

KERR, J.   2449

"Mission to the Western Indians: Journal of Rev. J. Kerr." CHRISTIAN ADVOCATE 12 (1834):517-519.

May-Aug 1834. Missionary journal; brief notes of work among the Shawnee Indians.

MAVERICK, SAMUEL AUGUSTUS, 1803-1870   2450

In SAMUEL MAVERICK, TEXAN: A COLLECTION OF LETTERS, JOURNALS AND MEMOIRS, edited by Mary Rowena Maverick Green, pp. 1-430 passim. San Antonio: Privately printed, 1952.

1834-1836, Sep 1842-Apr 1843, Aug-Dec 1848. Brief journals of an important Texas pioneer; the siege of San Antonio de Bexar, capture of Bexar, forced march of American prisoners to Perote, Mexico; Colonel Jack Hays' expedition to Chihuahua; comments on Santa Anna.

NOTES ON THE STORMING OF BEXAR IN THE CLOSE OF 1835. Edited and privately printed by Frederick C. Chabot. San Antonio: Artes Graficas, 1942. 31 pp.

1835.

MELVILLE, GANSEVOORT   2451

Leyda, Jay, ed. "An Albany Journal by Gansevoort Melville." BOSTON PUBLIC LIBRARY QUARTERLY 2 (1950):327-347.

Jan-Mar 1834. Interesting fragment of a journal kept, as a young man, by Herman Melville's older brother; work in fur and hat business left in failing condition by his late father; social life and interest in the belles of Albany; passion for books, with comments on his reading; debates at the Young Men's Association; legal problems over father's debts; only occasional mention of Herman Melville.

PRESTON, Mrs. WILLIAM   2452

"Personal Recollections of Eminent Men." THE LAND WE LOVE 3 (1867):334-336, 419-422, 512-514; 4 (1867-1868): 402-404; 5 (1868):119-122.

1834-1838. Diary extracts on Calhoun, Webster, etc.

RUSSELL, OSBORNE, 1814-ca. 1865   2453

JOURNAL OF A TRAPPER; OR, NINE YEARS IN THE ROCKY MOUNTAINS. Edited by Lem A. York. Boise, Idaho: Syms-York, 1914. 105 pp. 2d ed., 1921. 149 pp.

JOURNAL OF A TRAPPER. Edited by Aubrey L. Haines. Portland: Oregon Historical Society, 1955. 179 pp. Reprint. Gloucester, Mass.: P. Smith, 1965; Lincoln: University of Nebraska Press, 1965.

Extracts in WHERE ROLLS THE OREGON, edited by Archer B. Hulbert, pp. 177-219. Overland to the Pacific, vol. 3. Colorado Springs: The Stewart Commission of Colorado College; Denver: Denver Public Library, 1933.

1834-1843. Journal of fur trader employed by the Northwest Company; activities in the Rocky Mountains, mainly in Yellowstone country, Snake valley, Great Salt Lake, Green River; trading among Crow and Blackfoot Indians; meeting with Oregon missionaries; good account of his experiences, details of trapping and Indian life.

SHIPLEY, JOHN 2454

"She Blows! She Breeches! An Odyssey of an Industry of Other Days." THE NATION'S BUSINESS 11, no. 10 (September 1923):21-23.

1834-1837. Extracts from journal kept by a passenger during unsuccessful voyage of whaler CERES of Wilmington, Delaware; notes on weather, whaling, burials at sea, Penrhyn Island, Tahiti and Society Islands and their inhabitants.

SMITH, JOSEPH, 1805-1844 2455

THE JOURNAL OF JOSEPH SMITH; A PERSONAL HISTORY OF A MODERN PROPHET. Compiled by Leland R. Nelson. Provo, Utah: Council Press, 1979. 255 pp.

1834-1844. Activities of founder of Mormonism in Kirtland, Ohio, and Nauvoo, Illinois; persecution, interaction with "gentiles," preaching, religious services, baptisms; dealings with other Mormon leaders, including Brigham Young and Heber C. Kimball; prayers, reflections. Early life summarized for 1805-1833; dated entries beginning 1834, largely dictated to scribes.

STEPHENS, ALEXANDER HAMILTON, 1812-1883 2456

Rabun, James A., ed. "Alexander H. Stephen's Diary." GEORGIA HISTORICAL QUARTERLY 36 (1952):71-96, 163-188.

1834-1837. Youthful diary of man who became vice-president of the Confederacy; introspections, reading, rather meager social life of Crawfordville, Georgia; desultory law studies and occasional court work; diary possibly cathartic, exhibiting ambitions and dissatisfactions, contempt for most of the human race, but a marvelous flair for description and anecdote.

RECOLLECTIONS OF ALEXANDER H. STEPHENS: HIS DIARY KEPT WHEN A PRISONER AT FORT WARREN, BOSTON HARBOUR, 1865. Edited by Myrta L. Avary. New York: Doubleday, Page, 1910. 572 pp.

May-Oct 1865. Confederate political prisoner's journal; letters to his brother and various officials copied into journal; daily life and treatment; long discourses on political philosophy, reading, news.

TOWNSEND, JOHN KIRK, 1809-1851 2457

Extracts in WALDIE'S SELECT CIRCULATING LIBRARY, vol. 2, pp. 427-432. Philadelphia: A. Waldie, 1835. Reprint. In EARLY WESTERN TRAVELS, edited by Reuben G. Thwaites, vol. 21, pp. 107-369.

Jul-Sep 1834. Travel journal of a Philadelphia physician and naturalist; trip across the Rockies to the headwaters of the Columbia River with a party led by Thomas Nuttall.

UNDERWOOD, AMMON, 1810-1887 2458

Greer, James K., ed. "Journal of Ammon Underwood." SOUTHWESTERN HISTORICAL QUARTERLY 32 (1928-1929): 124-151.

1834-1848. Voyage from Boston to Texas; social, political and business life in Texas; activities as a merchant and legislator; notes on Texas Revolution; Texas Republic; interesting spellings.

WHEELER, DANIEL, 1771-1840 2459

EXTRACTS FROM THE LETTERS AND JOURNAL OF DANIEL WHEELER. London: Harvey & Darton, 1839; Philadelphia: Printed by J. Rakestraw, 1840. 324 pp.

1834-1837. Journal of British Quaker who visited Hawaii, November 1835-May 1836, preached at religious meetings, and visited schools; notes on Hudson's Bay Company ships BEACON and COLUMBIA.

"Memoirs of the Life and Gospel Labours of the Late Daniel Wheeler." FRIENDS' LIBRARY 7 (1843):290-305.

Dec 1838-Oct 1839. American travels of British Quaker; visits to Quaker meetings in Philadelphia, Baltimore, New York, New England, Nova Scotia and Ohio.

WHEELOCK, THOMPSON B., 1801-1836 2460

In UNITED STATES CONGRESS. SENATE EXECUTIVE DOCUMENT no. 1, 23d CONGRESS, 2d SESSION, 1834, pp. 73-93.

In AMERICAN STATE PAPERS: MILITARY AFFAIRS V: 373-382.

Shirk, George H., ed. "Peace on the Plains; Journal of Colonel Dodge's Expedition from Ft. Gibson to the Pawnee Pict Village." CHRONICLES OF OKLAHOMA 28 (1950):2-41.

Jun-Aug 1834. Military diary of Leavenworth Expedition of United States Dragoons to Wichita village for purpose of negotiating treaties with Kiowa and Wichita Indians; much sickness of men and horses, severe heat; extensive negotiations with Indians, speeches of chiefs and officers, particularly Colonel Henry Dodge; participation of artist George Catlin in the expedition.

1835

ALLING, PRUDDEN, 1809-1879 2461

"An Adventurous Journey to Chicago in 1835." THE FIRELANDS PIONEER, n.s. 20 (1918):2016-2024.

May-Jun 1835. Incomplete diary of a trip from Norwalk, Ohio, to Chicago; adventures traveling by coach in Indiana and Michigan to Chicago and Ottawa, Illinois; comments on trade, prospects, unusual events, land values in Chicago.

BARNARD, JOSEPH HENRY, 1804-1860 or 1861 2462

DR. J.H. BARNARD'S JOURNAL: A COMPOSITE OF KNOWN VERSIONS OF THE JOURNAL OF DR. JOSEPH H. BARNARD, ONE OF THE SURGEONS OF FANNIN'S REGIMENT. Edited by Hobart Huson. Goliad Bicentennial ed. Refugio?, Tex., 1949. 67 pp.

Dec 1835-Jun 1836. Journal of Canadian physician who immigrated to Texas to join fight for independence; service as surgeon to Fannin's troops; surrender of Fannin and subsequent execution of most of the prisoners; experiences and treatment as a prisoner of war; succinct and readable account giving notion of the patriotic fervor of the period. Diary destroyed by Mexicans and later reconstructed from memory and fragmentary notes.

BASSETT, HANNAH, 1815-1855   2463

MEMOIR OF HANNAH BASSETT WITH EXTRACTS FROM HER DIARY. Lynn, Mass.: W.W. Kellogg, Printer, 1860. 72 pp. passim.

> 1835-1853. Quaker diary; religious reflections and rather agonized introspections; attendance at Quaker meetings; deaths of friends and relatives; her own frequent ill health.

BOYNTON, LUCIEN C., 1811-1886   2464

Buck, Solon J., ed. "Selections from the Journal of Lucien C. Boynton." AMERICAN ANTIQUARIAN SOCIETY PROCEEDINGS, n.s. 43 (1933):329-380.

> 1835-1853. Extracts from the diary of Boston teacher and lawyer; lively notes on his education, reading, love affairs; honest and observant appraisal of American life.

BRADLEY, CYRUS PARKER, 1818-1838   2465

OHIO ARCHAEOLOGICAL AND HISTORICAL SOCIETY QUARTERLY 15 (1906):207-270.

> Jun 1835. College student's holiday tour in Ohio and Michigan; long entries at Marietta, Cincinnati, Portsmouth, Chillicothe, Circleville, Columbus, Sandusky City, Lake Erie, Pontiac, Cleveland; a lively picture of social and political conditions and descriptions of scenery, people, towns, inns; humorous style.

BRUNSON, ALFRED, 1793-1886   2466

"A Methodist Circuit Rider's Horseback Tour from Pennsylvania to Wisconsin." WISCONSIN HISTORICAL COLLECTIONS 15 (1900):264-291.

> Sep-Dec 1835. Methodist minister's journey from Meadville, Pennsylvania, to Wisconsin; religious comments; general descriptions of country, etc.

CHAMPION, GEORGE   2467

JOURNAL OF THE REV. GEORGE CHAMPION, AMERICAN MISSIONARY IN ZULULAND. Edited by Alan R. Booth. Cape Town: C. Struik, 1967. 135 pp.

> 1835-1839. Record of first ill-fated attempt of American Board of Commissioners for Foreign Missions to establish a mission to Zulus in South Africa; trek inland by wagon, establishment of school, preaching; dealings with unpredictable King Dingane, warfare between Boers and Zulus, customs of Zulus; diarist's sorrow at apparent failure of the enterprise; eventual expulsion.

COBDEN, RICHARD, 1804-1865   2468

AMERICAN DIARIES. Edited by Elizabeth H. Cawley. Princeton, N.J.: Princeton University Press, 1952. 233 pp. Reprint. New York: Greenwood, 1969.

> 1835, 1859. Diaries of two trips by British businessman, later statesman; in 1835, a series of one-night stops across eastern United States, forming optimistic assessments of the country and its almost utopian potential; in 1859, longer stays in homes of illustrious Americans, including President Buchanan; notes on Philadelphia, Chicago, New York, Washington, D.C.; in both diaries, hurried but detailed notes on homes, businesses, factories, farms, churches, politics, modes of travel; engaging sketches of people.

CROWNINSHIELD, CLARA, 1811-1907   2469

DIARY; A EUROPEAN TOUR WITH LONGFELLOW. Edited by Andrew Hilen. Seattle: University of Washington Press, 1956. 304 pp.

> 1835-1836. Travel diary of companion of Mary and Henry Wadsworth Longfellow on a trip through Europe; hardships of steamship travel; notes on parties, literary talk; Mary's death.

DEAS, EDWARD, b. ca. 1812   2470

Litton, Gaston, ed. "The Journal of a Party of Emigrating Creek Indians." JOURNAL OF SOUTHERN HISTORY 7 (1941):225-242.

> Dec 1835-Feb 1836. Official journal of emigration of Creek Indians from Alabama to Arkansas; hardships and mishaps.

DE LA SAGRA, RAMON   2471

Stewart, Watt, ed. "A Pilgrimage through New York State in 1835." NEW YORK HISTORY 19 (1938):407-418.

Stewart, Watt, ed. "A Spanish Traveler Visits Rochester." ROCHESTER HISTORICAL SOCIETY PUBLICATIONS 18 (1940):106-117.

> Jul-Aug 1835. Extracts from the travel diary of a Cuban botanist; careful notes on New York, West Point, Schenectady, Utica, Erie Canal, Rochester, Albany, Genesee. Translated from the Spanish.

FORD, LEMUEL, 1788-1850   2472

Pelzer, Louis, ed. "Captain Ford's Journal of an Expedition to the Rocky Mountains." MISSISSIPPI VALLEY HISTORICAL REVIEW 12 (1925-1926):550-579.

MARCH OF THE FIRST DRAGOONS TO THE ROCKY MOUNTAINS IN 1835: THE DIARIES AND MAPS OF LEMUEL FORD. Edited by Nolie Mumey. Denver: Eames Brothers Press, 1957. 116 pp.

> May-Sep 1835, Feb 1836-Sep 1837. Officer's account of peaceful expedition of mounted dragoons under Colonel Henry Dodge across Nebraska, Kansas and Colorado to secure treaties with Indians; daily details of march; distances, terrain, camps, weather; councils with Indians, encounters with traders, names of soldiers; in 1836, return home to Indiana and recruiting work there; resignation from army.

GAGE, JOHN, 1802-1890   2473

"Selections from the Autobiography of John Gage, Who Settled in Vineland in 1864." VINELAND HISTORICAL MAGAZINE 9 (1924):177-183, 188-191, 216-220; 10 (1925):29-31, 47-51, 66-68, 229-232.

> 1835-1836. Tour in New York, Pennsylvania, Maryland and Michigan; visits to principal towns, smelting works, the new industrial scene; social descriptions in Washington, Baltimore and Chicago; building flour mill at Chicago; an interesting diary.

GORDON, JOHN MONTGOMERY, 1810-1884   2474

Gordon, Douglas, ed. "A Virginian and His Baltimore Diary." MARYLAND HISTORICAL MAGAZINE 49 (1954):196-216; 50 (1955):109-119; 51 (1956):224-236; 56 (1961):198-203.

> 1835. Diary of a prominent Baltimore lawyer and banker; daily life, weather, reading, visits, local

events, business matters, etc.; short visit to Philadelphia.

Gordon, Douglas H. and May, George S., eds. "Michigan Journal." MICHIGAN HISTORY 43 (1959):1–42, 129–149, 257–293, 433–478.

Jul–Oct 1836. Record of an expedition to Michigan to buy land for speculation; full and erudite notes on scenes and experiences; many modes of travel, including stagecoach, train, river boat, canal packet, lake steamer and horseback; great interest in people and their foibles; notes on New York and Detroit; difficult trip from Buffalo to Detroit on steamer MICHIGAN; horseback journey across Michigan via Territorial Road; prices of land and timber; prospects for agriculture and commerce; notes on Indians, including Treaty of Washington; reading, introspections.

GRAY, WILLIAM F., d. 1841　　　2475

FROM VIRGINIA TO TEXAS, 1835. DIARY OF COL. WILLIAM F. GRAY GIVING DETAILS OF HIS JOURNEY TO TEXAS AND RETURN IN 1835–1836, AND A SECOND JOURNEY TO TEXAS IN 1837. Preface by A.C. Gray. Houston: Gray Dillaye, Printers, 1909. 230 pp. Reprint. Fletcher Young Publishing, 1965.

1835–1837. Lawyer's journey from Virginia to Texas via the Ohio and Mississippi rivers and exploration through Mississippi; stay in New Orleans; up the Red River to Natchitoches and overland to Texas; notes on route, expenses, accommodations, fellow travelers, land values; news concerning Texas and affairs there, including fall of the Alamo.

GUSTORF, FREDERICK JULIUS, 1800–1845　　　2476

THE UNCORRUPTED HEART: JOURNAL AND LETTERS OF FREDERICK JULIUS GUSTORF. Edited by Fred Gustorf, translated from German by Fred Gustorf and Gisela Gustorf. Columbia: University of Missouri Press, 1969. 182 pp.

1835–1836. Travel diary of a cultivated German immigrant impressed with scenery of America but not with its people or prospects, especially other immigrants whom he saw as struggling, disillusioned and often degraded; travel by train and canal; notes on hotels, farming, business, people met en route from Philadelphia to St. Louis; courtship of English immigrant Harriet Benson.

Gustorf, Fred, ed. "Frontier Perils Told by an Early Illinois Visitor." ILLINOIS HISTORICAL SOCIETY JOURNAL 55 (1962):136–156, 255–270.

1835–1836. Extracts pertaining mainly to Indiana and Illinois; notes on New Harmony, Albion, Vandalia and Peoria; hardships of farming and frontier life experienced by German settlers.

HAWTHORNE, NATHANIEL, 1804–1864　　　2477

HAWTHORNE'S FIRST DIARY, WITH AN ACCOUNT OF ITS DISCOVERY AND LOSS. By Samuel R. Pickard. Boston and New York: Houghton, Mifflin, 1897. 115 pp. Reprint. New York: Haskell House, 1972.

An early undated diary referring to boyhood in Maine, adventures, games, reading, etc. Authenticity questioned by some scholars.

HAWTHORNE'S LOST NOTEBOOKS. Transcript and preface by Barbara S. Mouffe, introduction by Hyatt H. Waggoner, foreword by Charles Ryskamp. University Park: Pennsylvania State University Press, 1978. 30 pp.

1835–1841. Notebooks and diaries covering Hawthorne's "solitary years" before his marriage to Sophia Peabody; his life in Salem; sights and reflections during long walks about Salem and Boston; extensive notes for stories; odd snippets of information about people; considerable gloom and irony.

THE COMPLETE WORKS OF NATHANIEL HAWTHORNE. With introductory notes by George P. Lathrop. Riverside ed. Boston and New York: Houghton Mifflin, 1914. Diary, vols. 7–10.

THE CENTENARY EDITION OF THE WORKS OF NATHANIEL HAWTHORNE. Edited by William Charvat et al. Columbus: Ohio State University Press, 1963–1982. Diary, vols. 8, 14.

THE HEART OF HAWTHORNE'S JOURNALS. Edited by Newton Arvin. Boston and New York: Houghton Mifflin, 1929. 345 pp.

1837–1860. Notebooks and travel journals; observations of New England life; ideas for stories, descriptions of places, persons and events; careful descriptive notes of England, France and Italy.

THE AMERICAN NOTEBOOKS. Edited by Randall Stewart. New Haven: Yale University Press; London: H. Milford, Oxford University Press, 1932. 350 pp.

1837–1853.

THE ENGLISH NOTEBOOKS. Edited by Randall Stewart. Modern Language Association of America General Series, 13. New York: Modern Language Association of America; London: Oxford University Press, 1941. 667 pp. Reprint. New York: Russell & Russell, 1969.

1853–1860.

HOLLEY, MARY AUSTIN, 1784–1846　　　2478

THE TEXAS DIARY. Edited by J.P. Bryan. Austin: University of Texas Press, 1965. 120 pp.

1835–1838. Diary of member of famous Texas colonial family and first historian of Texas; description of life on coastal plains near the mouth of the Brazos River during her second and third trips to the area; notes on transportation, living conditions, political and social activities, principal towns and plantations, with mention of many early Texas leaders.

HOPKINS, LOUISA, 1812–1862　　　2479

Extracts in THE LIFE AND LETTERS OF ELIZABETH PRENTISS, by Elizabeth Payson Prentiss, pp. 203–206. New York: A.D.F. Randolph, 1882.

1835–1840. Literary notes, reading, meeting with Richard Henry Dana.

JAMES, JOSHUA　　　2480

A JOURNAL OF A TOUR IN TEXAS: WITH OBSERVATIONS, ETC., BY THE AGENTS OF THE WILMINGTON EMIGRATING SOCIETY. Wilmington, N.C.: T. Loring, 1835. 16 pp.

Apr–Jul 1835. Journal of mission to explore western lands; by boat from Wilmington to Natchitoches and on horseback into Texas; description and evaluation of area; crop yields, prices of land, goods, slaves, etc.; commercial prospects and general advantages and disadvantages of life in Texas; remarks on cotton economy, slavery in Texas; return trip by steamboat to Mobile and up the Alabama River to Montgomery.

JOHNSON, WILLIAM, 1809–1851   2481

WILLIAM JOHNSON'S NATCHEZ: THE ANTE-BELLUM DIARY OF A FREE NEGRO. Edited by William R. Hogan and Edwin A. Davis. Baton Rouge: Louisiana State University Press, 1951. 812 pp. Reprint. Port Washington, N.Y.: Kennikat, 1968.

Extracts in DIARY OF AMERICA, edited by Josef Berger, pp. 185–190.

> 1835–1851. Personal and business diary of an ante-bellum free Negro, a prosperous barber and land-owner who was himself a slave holder; the colorful, violent life of old Natchez reported from an unusual perspective by a keen observer; births, deaths, marriages, business transactions, family quarrels, gambling, horse races, epidemics of yellow fever and cholera, Mississippi politics, prices of goods and slaves, and the economic impact of the Panic of 1837; a fresh, ingenuous diary of an active entrepreneur and man of consequence.

KINGSBURY, GAINES PEASE   2482

In UNITED STATES CONGRESS. SENATE EXECUTIVE DOCUMENT no. 209, 24th CONGRESS, 1st SESSION, 1836.

> May–Sep 1835. Military journal of lieutenant of United States Dragoons; exploration from Fort Leavenworth up the South Platte, Fountain Creek, Manitou, Bent's Fort, down Arkansas River, Santa Fe Trail, Fort Leavenworth; topographical details.

KITE, JAMES, 1808–1856   2483

"Notes on a Tour Made in 1835." FRIENDS' HISTORICAL ASSOCIATION BULLETIN 32 (1943):80–86; 33 (1944):5–16.

> Jun 1835. Quaker's journey from Philadelphia north to Schenectady, then to western New York and Pennsylvania; interesting descriptions of New York City and packet boat travel on the Erie Canal, also travel by steamboat and stagecoach; comments on fellow travelers, scenery; opinions on Jacksonian politics.

KLINE, JOHN, 1797–1864   2484

LIFE AND LABORS OF ELDER JOHN KLINE: THE MARTYR MISSIONARY. Collated from his diary by Benjamin Funk. Elgin, III.: Brethren Publishing House, 1900. 480 pp.

> 1835–1864. Diary extracts, many of them paraphrased, interspersed among sermon texts and editor's commentary; work of a Brethren minister in Rockingham County, Virginia, with missionary journeys to western Virginia, Ohio, Maryland, Pennsylvania and Indiana; horseback travel; some mention of Civil War events.

LINCECUM, GIDEON, 1793–1874   2485

Bradford, A.L. and Campbell, T.N., eds. "Journal of Lincecum's Travels in Texas." SOUTHWESTERN HISTORICAL QUARTERLY 53 (1949):180–201.

> Jan–Mar 1835. Mississippian's reconnaissance of southeast Texas to determine prospects for settlement, agriculture and commerce; data on soil, range land, navigability of rivers; flora and fauna; problems between settlers and Indians; difficult travel on horseback.

LINCOLN, WILLIAM, 1802–1843   2486

Chase, Charles A. "William Lincoln." AMERICAN ANTIQUARIAN SOCIETY PROCEEDINGS, n.s. 7 (1890–1891):

424–436. Diary, pp. 434–435.

> Nov 1835, Jan 1841. Extracts, selected as illustrative of his character, from diary of Worcester, Massachusetts, lawyer; introspective observations; notes on politics.

MCPHAIL, LEONARD, d. 1867   2487

Jones, Harold W., ed. "Diary of Assistant Surgeon Leonard McPhail on His Journey to the Southwest." CHRONICLES OF OKLAHOMA 18 (1940):281–292.

> Jun–Aug 1835. Surgeon's military journal; journey from Fort Gibson into the Indian country with the dragoons; completion of treaty with Comanches and return.

PAINE, ALBERT WARE, 1812–1907   2488

In THE DISCOVERY OF A GRANDMOTHER; GLIMPSES INTO THE HOMES AND LIVES OF EIGHT GENERATIONS OF AN IPSWICH-PAINE FAMILY, by Lydia Augusta Paine Carter, pp. 202–244. Newtonville, Mass.: H.H. Carter, 1920.

> Aug 1835–Jun 1836. Lawyer's diary; comments on slavery, French war, political news, Texas Revolution, Indian warfare in the Southwest, Deposit Bill; public, personal and social life in Bangor, Maine; theaters, clubs, temperance and church work; notes on Daniel Webster; an interesting diary with long, well written entries.

PARKER, SAMUEL, 1779–1866   2489

JOURNAL OF AN EXPLORING TOUR BEYOND THE ROCKY MOUNTAINS. Ithaca, N.Y.: The author, 1838. 371 pp. 2d ed. Mack, Andrus & Woodruff, Printers, 1840. 400 pp. New York: M.H. Newman, 1846. 422 pp. Minneapolis: Ross & Haines, 1967. 380 pp.

Report of tour in MARCUS WHITMAN, CRUSADER, edited by Archer B. Hulbert and Dorothy P. Hulbert, vol. 1, pp. 89–135. Overland to the Pacific, vols. 6–8. Colorado Springs: The Stewart Commission of Colorado College; Denver: Denver Public Library, 1936.

> 1835–1837. Journal of Congregational missionary under the American Board of Commissioners for Foreign Missions; overland journey via St. Louis, Independence, Colorado, Columbia River, Fort Vancouver; notes on scenery, Nez Perce Indians, Indian vocabularies; return via Hawaii.

PATTERSON, ROBERT, 1792–1881   2490

"Observations of an Early American Capitalist." JOURNAL OF AMERICAN HISTORY 1 (1907):653–668.

> May–Jun 1835. Extracts from Philadelphia merchant's travel diary; journey from Philadelphia to the upper Mississippi; travel over Wilderness Road and on the Mississippi; notes on people, customs, inns, farming; visit to Washington's birthplace and to Monticello.

POOLE, CAROLINE B., 1802–1844   2491

Padgett, James A., ed. "A Yankee School Teacher in Louisiana." LOUISIANA HISTORICAL QUARTERLY 20 (1937):651–679.

> 1835–1837. New England teacher's diary; voyage from Boston to New Orleans; then up the Mississippi, Red and Black rivers; school work at Monroe, Louisiana; trip to Louisville in summer of 1836; school again; an effective picture of Yankee loneliness in the midst of Southern hospitality.

PROUDFOOT, WILLIAM, 1787-1851   2492

Garland, M.A., ed. "From Upper Canada to New York in 1835: Extracts from the Diary of the Rev. William Proudfoot." MISSISSIPPI VALLEY HISTORICAL REVIEW 18 (1931-1932):378-396.

    1835. Journey of Canadian Presbyterian clergyman to New York to raise funds.

SPENCER, CAROLINE   2493

"A Trip to Niagara in 1835." MAGAZINE OF AMERICAN HISTORY 22 (1889):331-342.

    Jul 1835. Trip to Niagara Falls; a lively and interesting record.

STRONG, GEORGE TEMPLETON, 1820-1875   2494

DIARY. Edited by Allan Nevins and Milton H. Thomas. New York: Macmillan, 1952. 4 vols. Reprint. New York: Octagon Books, 1974.

    1835-1875. A monumental diary, in the tradition of Pepys, Evelyn or Sewall, begun by precocious fifteen-year-old son of a prominent New York family and continued throughout a distinguished law career and life of public service.

    Vol. 1, 1835-1849. Studies at Columbia; apprenticeship in law under his father and Marshall S. Bidwell; reading, music, social life; courtship and marriage; beginnings of lifelong service to Trinity Church; death of his father and his first child.

    Vol. 2, 1850-1859. Family life; law practice; New York society; public service, including active part on Columbia Board of Trustees; lay work for Trinity Church; strong opinion on events, politics, the arts, religion; growing unease over slavery.

    Vol. 3, 1860-1865. His great Civil War diary; tireless work as treasurer of Sanitary Commission; committee meetings, visits to encampments and battlefields, recruitment of volunteers and raising of funds, raging frustration with callous ineptitude of United States Medical Department, the secretary of state and the surgeon general.

    Vol. 4, 1865-1875. Financial problems, some important legal cases, depression over corruption and stupidity in civic life; continued service as trustee of Columbia and vestryman of Trinity Church; musical soirees at home, founding of Church Music Association and presidency of Philharmonic Society; final illness.

Thomas, Milton H. "Mid-Nineteenth Century Life in New York: More Revelations from the Diary of George Templeton Strong." NEW YORK HISTORICAL SOCIETY QUARTERLY 37 (1953):5-39.

    1835-1871. Biographical sketch containing diary extracts; Strong's view of life in New York City, mainly in the 1850's; evaluation of General Winfield Scott.

Miller, Harry L., ed. "Footnotes on the Astor Library's History from George Templeton Strong's Diary." NEW YORK PUBLIC LIBRARY BULLETIN 58 (1954):167-173.

    1840-1873. Scattered extracts relevant to the history of the Lenox Library and the Astor Library.

DIARY OF THE CIVIL WAR. Edited by Allan Nevins. New York: Macmillan, 1962. 664 pp.

    1860-1865. Reprint of vol. 3 of DIARY.

Extracts in DIARY OF AMERICA, edited by Josef Berger, pp. 499-510.

    1865-1875.

WHITMAN, MARCUS, 1802-1847   2495

Young, F.G., ed. "Journal and Report by Dr. Marcus Whitman of His Tour of Exploration with Rev. Samuel Parker in 1835 beyond the Rocky Mountains." OREGON HISTORICAL QUARTERLY 28 (1927):239-257.

MARCUS WHITMAN, CRUSADER. Edited by Archer B. Hulbert and Dorothy P. Hulbert. Overland to the Pacific, vols. 6-8. Colorado Springs: The Stewart Commission of Colorado College; Denver: Denver Public Library, 1936-1941. 3 vols. Journal, vol. 1.

    May-Oct 1835. Exploration journal of notable missionary doctor; travel from Liberty, Missouri, via Bellevue, Nebraska and Fort Laramie on the Oregon Trail; mostly religious and Indian notes.

1836

ALMONTE, JUAN NEPOMUCENO, 1804-1869   2496

Asbury, Samuel E., ed. "The Private Journal of Juan Nepomuceno Almonte." SOUTHWESTERN HISTORICAL QUARTERLY 48 (July 1944):10-32.

    Feb-Apr 1836. War diary of Texas Revolution kept by Santa Anna's aide de camp; marches, condition of troops, battle of the Alamo, the Bexar campaign. Diary translated and published serially in the NEW YORK HERALD in June and July 1836; some question of its authenticity.

ATHERTON, FAXON DEAN, 1815-1877   2497

THE CALIFORNIA DIARY. Edited by Doyce B. Nunis, Jr. California Historical Society Special Publications, no. 39. San Francisco: California Historical Society, 1964. 246 pp.

    1836-1839. Youthful diary of early California settler employed as clerk by merchant Alpheus B. Thompson; social life of Spanish California; journeys by ship and overland to various parts of California on business; sea voyage to Hawaii en route to Boston; names of people, places and ships; much local color.

BARROW, BENNET HILLIARD, 1811-1854   2498

PLANTATION LIFE IN THE FLORIDA PARISHES OF LOUISIANA. By Edwin A. Davis. Columbia University Studies in the History of American Agriculture, no. 9. New York: Columbia University Press, 1943. 457 pp. Diary, pp. 71-385. Reprint. New York: AMS Press, 1967.

    1836-1846. Concise daily entries showing the management of a Louisiana cotton plantation; buying and selling of land, planting, cultivating, picking and selling cotton, maintaining machinery and tools, overseeing slaves; family and social life, visiting, hunting and racing; comments on national political affairs.

BRADLEY, CALEB, 1772-1861   2499

"The Day We Celebrate: From the Journal of a Country Parson." ATLANTIC MONTHLY 94 (1904):108-113.

    1836-1860. A few interesting extracts relating to Fourth of July celebrations, as well as local, social and personal notes of Westbrook, Maine.

"Milestones: Being a Brief Record Which Concerns the Coming and Going of Years, and the Rise and Fall of Administrations." ATLANTIC MONTHLY 95 (1905):83-90.

    1836-1861. Minister's reactions to national events; presidential elections, Mexican War, etc.; local and parish notes.

BROCKWAY, GEORGE W., d. 1837 2500

Cornet, Florence D., ed. "The Experience of a Midwest Salesman in 1836." MISSOURI HISTORICAL SOCIETY BULLETIN 29 (1972–1973):227–235.

Jan–Apr 1836. Record of a business trip from St. Louis to towns along the Mississippi and in the Illinois River valley; description of steamboat travel in winter conditions; lively notes on country through which diarist passed and people he met; account of lynching of a Negro in St. Louis.

BURCHARD, GEORGE, 1810–1880 2501

"Excerpts from a Whaler's Diary." WISCONSIN MAGAZINE OF HISTORY 18 (1934–1935):422–441; 19 (1935–1936): 103–107, 227–241, 342–355.

Sep 1836–? Extracts from whaling journal kept aboard the COLUMBIA of Newark, New Jersey; voyage around Cape Horn and in the Pacific; return to New York; some interesting whaling and social details.

CATHER, THOMAS 2502

VOYAGE TO AMERICA: THE JOURNALS OF THOMAS CATHER. Edited by Thomas Yoseloff. New York and London: T. Yoseloff, 1961. 176 pp. Reprint. New York: Greenwood, 1973.

Feb 1836–Jan 1837. Daring and extensive American travels of a young Irish gentleman; detailed description of trans-Atlantic crossings; social life, balls, etc., in New York and Baltimore; travels to the Great Lakes, the South and to Indian Territory, where he sojourned among the Potawatomi; opinions on American character, slavery, Texas Revolution, Indians, etc.; a side-trip to Cuba.

COHEN, MYER M. 2503

NOTICES OF FLORIDA AND THE CAMPAIGNS. Charleston, S.C.: Burges and Honor, 1836. Reprint. Reproduction with introduction by O.Z. Tyler, Jr. Gainesville: University of Florida Press, 1964. 240 pp. Journal, pp. 106–184.

Jan–Apr 1836. Volunteer's journal, probably kept for publication, of his four month tour of duty in Florida during the Seminole Wars; difficulties of movement in trackless wilderness, battles and privations described in flamboyant style.

CONANT, AUGUSTUS HAMMOND, 1811–1863 2504

Extracts in A MAN IN EARNEST: LIFE OF A.H. CONANT, by Robert Collyer, pp. 43–110. Boston: H.B. Fuller; Chicago: J.R. Walsh, 1868.

Abridgment in AUGUSTUS CONANT, ILLINOIS PIONEER AND PREACHER, by Robert Collyer, pp. 31–55 passim. Boston: American Unitarian Association, 1905.

1836–1857. Diary of preacher and farmer at Desplaines River, Illinois; notes of farming, reading, Methodist preaching, studies and writing sermons, missionary work.

CROCKETT, DAVID, 1786–1836 2505

DAVY CROCKETT'S OWN STORY AS WRITTEN BY HIMSELF: THE AUTOBIOGRAPHY OF AMERICA'S GREAT FOLK HERO. New York: Citadel Press, 1955. 377 pp. Diary, pp. 363–373.

Extract in DIARY OF AMERICA, edited by Josef Berger, pp. 190–194; THE WORLD'S GREAT DIARIES, edited by Philip Dunaway, pp. 60–64.

Feb–Mar 1836. Account in diary form of the defense of the Alamo. Presumedly found and added posthumously to his autobiography; some question of authenticity.

DAVIDSON, JAMES D., ca. 1810–1882 2506

Kellar, Herbert A., ed. "A Journey through the South in 1836." JOURNAL OF SOUTHERN HISTORY 1 (1935):345–377.

Oct–Dec 1836. Lexington, Virginia, lawyer's tour in Ohio, Indiana, Kentucky, Louisiana, Alabama, Georgia, South Carolina; down Ohio and Mississippi rivers and up Atlantic coast; frank views on slavery, morals, northern and southern cities.

"Diaries of James D. Davidson (1836) and Greenlee Davidson (1857) during Visits to Indiana." INDIANA MAGAZINE OF HISTORY 24 (1928):130–134.

Oct 1836. Extracts relating to Indiana.

DAVIS, MARY ELIZABETH MORAYNE, 1815–1903 2507

THE NEGLECTED THREAD, A JOURNAL FROM THE CALHOUN COMMUNITY. Edited by Delle M. Craven. Columbia: University of South Carolina Press, 1951. 256 pp.

1836–1842. Journal of a literary southern woman; views on literary figures, music, education and slavery; domestic life in her parents' home, social life of Abbeville, South Carolina; religious conversion, church work, personal conflicts as she considered marriage; abandoning of fiction writing to marry minister William Hervey Davis; interesting picture of an intelligent young woman's activities and problems amidst extended circle of family and friends.

DAWSON, JAMES WILLIAM, 1808–1880 2508

Extracts in THE GENEALOGY OF THE LAMBORN FAMILY, compiled by Samuel Lamborn, pp. 118–119. Philadelphia: Press of M.L. Marion, 1894.

1836–1839. Notes kept during whaling voyages from Wilmington, Delaware, to the Pacific.

DELASSUS, CARLOS DEHAULT, 1767–1842? 2509

McDermott, John F., ed. "Diary of Charles Dehault Delassus from New Orleans to St. Louis." LOUISIANA HISTORICAL QUARTERLY 30 (1947):359–438.

Jun–Dec 1836. Travel up the Mississippi aboard the steamboat GEORGE COLLIER; six-month sojourn in St. Louis trying to sell his Missouri lands; social life among the prominent French families of the city; a frank, unpretentious diary.

FONTAINE, EDWARD 2510

Halsell, Willie D., ed. "A Stranger Indeed in a Strange Land." ALABAMA HISTORICAL QUARTERLY 30 (1968):61–75.

Nov 1836. Educated young Virginian's horseback trip from Cumberland County, Kentucky, through Alabama to Chickasaw cession lands in northern Mississippi; interesting notes on land, timber, soil, towns, inns and traveling companions.

GOMEZ, RAFAEL 2511

Beggs, Beatrice, trans. "The Diary of Rafael Gomez: Monterey in 1836." SOUTHERN CALIFORNIA QUARTERLY 45 (1963):265–270.

Jan–Apr 1836. Mexican lawyer's brief diary kept at Monterey, California; ships at anchor, ranching problems, frequent small earthquakes, a few legal and political matters.

GRAY, WILLIAM HENRY, 1809–1889   2512

"From Rendezvous to the Columbia." OREGON HISTORICAL QUARTERLY 38 (1937):355–369.

Jul–Sep 1836. Missionary's journey from Rendezvous to Fort Walla Walla; extract in a letter based on memoranda set down during the journey.

"The Unpublished Journal of William Henry Gray." WHITMAN COLLEGE QUARTERLY 16 (June 1913):1–79.

JOURNAL OF HIS JOURNEY EAST. Edited by Donald R. Johnson. Fairfield, Wash., 1980. 87 pp.

Dec 1836–Oct 1837. Travel from Vancouver to Walla Walla and Spokane to explore opportunities for establishing his own mission among the Flathead Indians.

Drury, Clifford M., ed. "Gray's Journal of 1838." PACIFIC NORTHWEST QUARTERLY 29 (1938):277–282.

In FIRST WHITE WOMEN OVER THE ROCKIES, edited by Clifford M. Drury, vol. 3, pp. 240–245.

Apr–May 1838. Journey from Independence, Missouri, to Oregon Mission at Walla Walla; chiefly distances and locations of camps.

HARRIS, LEWIS BIRDSALL, 1816–1893   2513

"Journal of Lewis Birdsall Harris." SOUTHWESTERN HISTORICAL QUARTERLY 25 (1921–1922):63–71, 131–146, 185–197.

Mar–May 1836. Journey from Pennsylvania to Texas, via Pittsburgh, St. Louis, New Orleans; arrival in Galveston at period of Alamo, etc.; notes on Sam Houston after defeat of Santa Anna; interesting descriptions; narrative summary of events from 1836–1842.

HENTZ, CAROLINE LEE, 1800–1856   2514

Ellison, Rhoda C., ed. "Caroline Lee Hentz's Alabama Diary." ALABAMA REVIEW 4 (1951):254–269.

Feb–Jul 1836. Diary extracts within article about a popular novelist; hardships of the diarist's life as contrasted with the luxurious settings she created in her sentimental romances; trials and tribulations of managing a school and teaching in Florence, Alabama.

HOLLINGSWORTH, HENRY, 1808–1855   2515

Horn, Stanley F., ed. "Tennessee Volunteers in the Seminole Campaign of 1836." TENNESSEE HISTORICAL QUARTERLY 1 (1942):269–274, 344–366; 2 (1943):61–73, 163–178, 236–256.

Sep 1836–Jan 1837. Officer's account of march from Alabama to Florida; movements of army and encounters with Indians; fulmination against hardships of army life, mismanagement by commanders and lack of adequate provisions; descriptions of natural surroundings, soldiers' diversions, voyage from Tampa Bay to New Orleans.

HOLMAN, RICHARD HENRY, 1817–1841   2516

Hamilton, Holman, ed. "An Indiana College Boy in 1836." INDIANA MAGAZINE OF HISTORY 49 (1953):281–306.

May–Sep 1836, Aug 1837. Student's diary kept at Indiana College in Bloomington; notes on fellow students, attractive young ladies, rivalry of literary societies.

LAING, CAROLINE HYDE BUTLER, 1804–1892   2517

A FAMILY HERITAGE: LETTERS AND JOURNALS OF CAROLINE HYDE BUTLER LAING. Edited by Edith N.S. Ward. East Orange, N.J.: Abbey Printers, 1957. 161 pp. Journal, pp. 32–60, 88–137.

1836, 1839. First journal covering voyage aboard the clipper ship ROMAN from New York to Macao and return; life aboard ship, reading, music-making, seasickness, descriptions of sailors, Chinese, limited social life at Macao; later journal of a trip from Paris to Rome by rail and extended visit there; colorful descriptions of places and events, including a Papal procession, St. Peter's, Pompeii.

MCLEOD, MARTIN, 1813–1860   2518

Nute, Grace L., ed. "The Diary of Martin McLeod." MINNESOTA HISTORY BULLETIN 4 (1922):351–357.

Extracts in PERSONAL RECOLLECTIONS OF MINNESOTA AND ITS PEOPLE, by John H. Stevens, pp. 345–357. Minneapolis: Tribune Job Printing Co., 1890.

1836–1841. Mainly record of a trip across Minnesota in fall of 1836; adventures, original poems, quotations from Shakespeare and romantic poets; interesting.

MEEK, ALEXANDER BEAUFORT, 1814–1865   2519

Mahon, John K., ed. "The Journal of A.B. Meek and the Second Seminole War." FLORIDA HISTORICAL QUARTERLY 38 (1960):302–318.

Feb–Apr 1836. Young Alabama lawyer's account of war against the Seminoles; departure for Florida with romantic notions of heroism and the glories of war; tedious marches and encampments of volunteers; disorder and lack of discipline, which diarist abetted; skirmishes with Indians.

NICOLLET, JOSEPH NICOLAS, 1786–1843   2520

THE JOURNALS OF JOSEPH N. NICOLLET: A SCIENTIST ON THE MISSISSIPPI HEADWATERS. Translated from the French by André Fertey, edited by Martha C. Bray. St. Paul: Minnesota Historical Society, 1970. 288 pp.

1836–1837. French geographer and astronomer's exploration and mapping expedition to the source of the Mississippi and up the St. Croix River, resulting in accurate maps which became basic to subsequent settlement and development of area; geographical features, Indian names of lakes and streams, plants and animals; beauty of forests and rivers; copious notes on Chippewa and Sioux Indians; canoe travel, diarist's life in Indian villages.

JOSEPH N. NICOLLET ON THE PLAINS AND PRAIRIES. Translated from the French and edited by Edmund C. Bray and Martha C. Bray. St. Paul: Minnesota Historical Society, 1976. 294 pp.

1838–1839. Leader's journal of mapping expedition under the Corps of Topographical Engineers to chart the region between the Mississippi and Missouri rivers; careful observations on geography, botany, customs and ceremonies of the Dakota Indians; assistance of John C. Fremont and botanist Charles A. Geyer.

Powers, William H., ed. "Journal of J.N. Nicollet in 1838 as It Relates to the Present South Dakota." SOUTH DAKOTA ACADEMY OF SCIENCES PROCEEDINGS 13 (1929–1930):115–139.

1838.

PEÑA, JOSE ENRIQUE DE LA, b. 1807   2521

WITH SANTA ANNA IN TEXAS: A PERSONAL NARRATIVE OF THE REVOLUTION. Translated and edited by Carmen Perry. College Station: Texas A. and M. University Press, 1975. 202 pp.

Feb–Aug 1836. Highly descriptive and polemical account of the Texas Revolution by officer under Santa Anna; condition and management of the Mexican army; battle of the Alamo and massacre of survivors; diarist's criticism of such atrocities by Santa Anna and fellow officers; General Vicente Filisola's inept leadership. Although the work was elaborated for publication, some diary entries remain unaltered.

PERRY, OLIVER HAZARD, 1817–1864   2522

HUNTING EXPEDITIONS OF OLIVER HAZARD PERRY, VERBATIM FROM HIS DIARIES. Cleveland: For private distribution, 1899. 246 pp.

1836–1853. Deer and elk hunting expeditions in Ohio and Michigan; terrain, hunting and camping methods, travel on foot and by canoe; encounters with Indians, lodging with frontier families; good picture of a wilderness shortly to disappear.

Burroughs, Raymond D., ed. "Perry's Deer Hunting in Michigan." MICHIGAN HISTORY 42 (1958):35–58.

1838–1855. Extracts and summary of Michigan portions of Perry's hunting diaries.

PICKELL, JOHN   2523

White, Frank, Jr., ed. "The Journals of Lt. John Pickell." FLORIDA HISTORICAL QUARTERLY 38 (1959): 142–171.

Jul–Aug 1836, Nov–Dec 1837. Seminole War journals covering scouting expedition near Jacksonville; exploration of St. Johns River area with notes on flora and fauna and survey of Lake Pickell; failure of the Cherokee mission to persuade Seminoles to emigrate west; resumption of fighting under General Thomas S. Jesup.

PRENTISS, ELIZABETH PAYSON, 1818–1878   2524

THE LIFE AND LETTERS OF ELIZABETH PRENTISS. New York: A.D.F. Randolph, 1882. 573 pp. Diary, pp. 50–154 passim.

THE LIFE OF ELIZABETH PRENTISS, AUTHOR OF STEPPING HEAVENWARD. Rev. ed. New York: A.D.F. Randolph, 1898. 2 vols.

1836–1878. Diary in letters and journal entries interspersed with narrative by editor; wide reading and criticism, especially of German classics; teaching in Mr. Persico's School, Richmond, Virginia; descriptions of teachers and pupils; religious aspirations; return home to Portland, Maine; personal discipline and spiritual growth; exasperation with women's social groups; another term at Richmond and return home for surgery; marriage to the Reverend George Lewis Prentiss, pastor of South Trinitarian Church, New Bedford, Massachusetts; births and deaths of several children; life as professor's wife when husband taught at Union Theological Seminary; writing of children's books, moral stories and hymns.

RIEGER, JOSEPH, 1811–1867   2525

Beck, William G. "The Followers of Duden." MISSOURI HISTORICAL REVIEW 28 (1923–1924):212–249. Diary, pp. 216–225.

Nov 1836–Aug 1837. Extract covering the life of a Bavarian missionary in Illinois, Iowa and Missouri.

THOMPSON, PHILO E., b. 1811   2526

Farr, Joel A., ed. "Philo E. Thompson's Diary of a Journey on the Main Line Canal." PENNSYLVANIA HISTORY 32 (1965):295–304.

Mar–Apr 1836. Journey by steamboat, railroad and canal boat from Connecticut across Pennsylvania, down the Ohio River and up the Mississippi to Payson, Illinois, to settle; description of settlements along the way; terse but detailed account of travel on the Pennsylvania Main Line Canal.

TOUMEY, WILLIAM S., ca. 1819–1848   2527

Hardin, J. Fair and Breazeale, Phanor, eds. "A Young Lawyer of Natchitoches of 1836." LOUISIANA HISTORICAL QUARTERLY 17 (1934):64–79, 315–326.

1836–1842. Diary of young Irish immigrant lawyer; studies and law practice; business, social life and local events at Natchitoches, Louisiana; brief description of Sam Houston.

VENIAMINOV, IOANN, 1797–1879   2528

Gibson, James R., ed. "A Russian Orthodox Priest in a Mexican Catholic Parish." PACIFIC HISTORIAN 15 (1971):57–66.

Jun–Oct 1836. Account by a Russian Orthodox priest of his trip from Sitka, Alaska, to Fort Ross, California, and missions near San Francisco, including Mission San José; record of ecclesiastical activities.

WHITMAN, NARCISSA PRENTISS, 1808–1847   2529

In FIRST WHITE WOMEN OVER THE ROCKIES, by Clifford M. Drury, vol. 1, pp. 71–114, 119–127.

Jul 1836–Mar 1837. Missionary's letter-diary; travel from Liberty, Missouri, to Fort Hall, Vancouver, and up the Columbia to Walla Walla in Oregon Territory; life at Waiilatpu Mission, getting settled in new home, domestic activities; description of Cayuse Indians, plans for their worship and education; homesickness; joy of motherhood.

"A Journey across the Plains in 1836." OREGON PIONEER ASSOCIATION TRANSACTIONS OF THE 19TH ANNUAL REUNION (1891):40–68.

Elliott, T.C. "The Coming of the White Women." OREGON HISTORICAL QUARTERLY 38 (1937):44–62. Reprint. In THE COMING OF THE WHITE WOMEN, by Narcissa P. Whitman, pp. 1–113 passim. Portland, Oreg.: Oregon Historical Society, 1937.

Jul–Dec 1836.

"Mrs. Whitman's Letters." OREGON PIONEER ASSOCIATION TRANSACTIONS OF THE 21ST ANNUAL REUNION (1893):53–219. Letter-diary, pp. 143–153.

Extracts in THE SOUVENIR OF WESTERN WOMEN, edited by Mary O. Douthit, pp. 19–21. Portland, Oreg.: Presses of Anderson & Duniway, 1905.

Mar 1842. Account of the difficult life of the missionaries at Waiilatpu.

WILEY, OREN, 1806–1889   2530

Graf, LeRoy P., ed. "The Journal of a Vermont Man in Ohio." OHIO STATE ARCHAEOLOGICAL AND HISTORICAL QUARTERLY 60 (1951): 175–199.

  1836–1842. Travel to Ohio with many others migrating west; employment at Ohio City and later in Dayton; religious reflections of an ardent Universalist; a great fight between the men of Ohio City and Cleveland over placement of the Columbus Street bridge.

WILLSON, ELIZABETH LUNDY, d. 1838   2531

A JOURNEY IN 1836 FROM NEW JERSEY TO OHIO. Edited by William C. Armstrong. Morrison, Ill.: Shawver Publishing Co., 1929. 47 pp.

  May–Jul 1836. Wagon trip of a Quaker family of eight from New Jersey to Ohio and back; accommodations, condition of land and crops along the way, bad roads, crossing flooded streams; a simple, charming diary.

WOODCOCK, THOMAS SWANN, 1805–1863   2532

Fulton, Deoch, ed. "New York to Niagara." NEW YORK PUBLIC LIBRARY BULLETIN 42 (1938):675–694. Reprint. New York: New York Public Library, 1938. 22 pp.

  May 1836. Engraver's trip from New York to Niagara and back; description of Falls, but mainly notes on trade, manufactures and land values.

WOODRUFF, WILFORD, 1807–1898   2533

Jessee, Dean C., ed. "The Kirtland Diary of Wilford Woodruff." BRIGHAM YOUNG UNIVERSITY STUDIES 12 (1971–1972):365–399.

  Nov 1836–May 1837. Extract, dealing with Kirtland period, of a longer Mormon diary; insight into early Mormon leadership and institutions; the struggle for community at Kirtland, Ohio; description of Joseph Smith.

1837

ANON.   2534

Parkinson, Mary W. "Travels in Western America in 1837." JOURNAL OF AMERICAN HISTORY 3 (1909):511–516.

  Jun–Jul 1837. A young girl's travel diary in a letter describing wagon trip from Keene, Ohio, across Illinois, via Paris, Springfield and Beardstown; interesting feminine and domestic details.

ANON.   2535

JOURNAL OF AN EXCURSION TO THE FRANCONIA MOUNTAINS: BY A CORPS OF CADETS OF THE NORWICH UNIVERSITY. Northfield, Vt., 1837. 14 pp.

  Jul 1837. Students' composite journal of a school excursion conducted by Captain Alden Partridge.

BACKUS, ELECTUS, 1804–1862   2536

"Diary of a Campaign in Florida." HISTORICAL MAGAZINE 10 (1866):279–285.

  Nov 1837–Apr 1838. Officer's bare notes of a campaign against Indians in Florida.

BIGGS, JOSEPH, 1809–1895   2537

TO AMERICA IN THIRTY–NINE DAYS, BEFORE STEAMSHIPS CROSSED THE ATLANTIC. 2d ed. Oxford: Village Press, 1927. 26 pp.

  May–Jul 1837. Englishman's voyage across Atlantic and remarks on American society during visit to New York, Philadelphia, Baltimore, Virginia, etc.; good description of Fourth of July celebration; observations on Iroquois Indians and on slavery; begun as diary but continued as narrative.

BONNEY, HENRY M.   2538

Martin, Kenneth R. "The Successful Whaling Voyage of the LUCY ANN of Wilmington." DELAWARE HISTORY 15 (1972):85–103.

  1837–1839. Scattered extracts from third mate's diary; account of one of the most successful whaling ventures of the Wilmington Whaling Company.

BROWN, PETER, 1784–1863   2539

Careless, J.M.S., ed. "Diary of Peter Brown." ONTARIO HISTORY 42 (1950):113–151.

  Apr–Jun 1837. Scottish merchant's immigration to America with his son, George; hazards and discomforts of voyage from Liverpool to New York aboard the ELIZA WARWICK; overcrowded quarters, inept captain; notes on fellow passengers; efforts to establish business in New York City; steamboat trip up the Hudson to Kingston; long, descriptive entries revealing a staunch Presbyterian and loyal British subject.

BUCHANAN, ROBERT CHRISTIE, 1811–1878   2540

White, Frank F., ed. "A Journal of Lt. Robert C. Buchanan during the Seminole War." FLORIDA HISTORICAL QUARTERLY 29 (1940):132–151.

  Nov 1837–Jan 1838. Officer's account of march from Tampa to Okeechobee; death of friend from typhus; detailed description of battle of Okeechobee with statistics of casualties.

BUCKNER, PHILIP JOHNSON, 1800–1853   2541

McGroarty, William Buckner, ed. "Diary of Philip Johnson Buckner, M.D." WILLIAM AND MARY COLLEGE QUARTERLY, 2d ser. 23 (1943):69–84.

  Nov 1837–Jan 1838. Account of flatboat trip from Kentucky to New Orleans on Ohio and Mississippi rivers with a cargo of farm products; brief entries on navigational information, mileage, towns, islands.

CHAMBERS, THOMAS JEFFERSON, 1802–1865   2542

Day, James M., ed. "Major General Thomas Chambers, Texas Army of the Reserves." TEXAS MILITARY HISTORY 4 (1964):223–263.

  Jan–Dec 1837. Diary of controversial Texas lawyer, adventurer and landowner, covering his return to Texas after recruiting the abortive Army of the Reserves; visits with relatives; steamboat trip from New Orleans to Galveston; business transactions, prices; comments on the new Republic of Texas.

CLARK, JOHN ALONZO, 1801–1843   2543

GLEANINGS BY THE WAY. Philadelphia: W.J. & J.K. Simon, 1842. 352 pp. Diary, pp. 25–180.

  Jun–Aug 1837. Episcopal clergyman's record of trip to restore health; long entries on journey through Pennsylvania, down the Ohio, up the Mississippi and over Great Lakes to New York; travel by canal boat, Allegheny Portage Railroad and steamboat; notes on scenery, towns, slavery, character of

Kentuckians, Dunkards, religious quality of life and Christian testimony.

COBB, EUNICE PARSONS, 1793-1877   2544

In MOTHER COBB OR SIXTY YEARS' WALK WITH GOD, by Mary Weems Chapman, 237 pp. passim. Chicago: T.B. Arnold, 1896.

1837-1874. Methodist diary kept chiefly in and around Marengo and Warren, Illinois; prayers, camp meetings, classes, love-feasts, good works and strenuous efforts to secure the conversion of others; temptations and victories, sense of God's presence and direction; a few family details.

DALLAS, GEORGE MIFFLIN, 1792-1864   2545

DIARY OF GEORGE MIFFLIN DALLAS, WHILE UNITED STATES MINISTER TO RUSSIA. Edited by Susan Dallas. Philadelphia: J.B. Lippincott, 1892. 443 pp. Reprint. New York: Arno, 1970.

1837-1839, 1856-1861. Diplomat's diary; first part kept while author was minister to Russia and second while minister to England; discreet, modest general entries in political setting; court and national news and comments, social life, some gossip and notes on famous people; many items of literary interest and some original verse; pleasant, readable diaries.

Nichols, Roy F., ed. "The Mystery of the Dallas Papers." PENNSYLVANIA MAGAZINE OF HISTORY AND BIOGRAPHY 73 (1949):349-392, 475-517. Diaries, pp. 475-517.

1844-1849. Diaries and letters relating mainly to author's service as vice president of the United States; observations as presiding officer of Senate; insight into the Polk administration.

Nichols, Roy F., ed. "The Missing Diaries of George Mifflin Dallas." PENNSYLVANIA MAGAZINE OF HISTORY AND BIOGRAPHY 75 (1951):295-338.

Jan-Oct 1856. Arrival in London to settle Central America question; Clayton-Bulwer Treaty. This portion of diary omitted from published book.

DAUBENY, CHARLES GILES BRIDLE, 1795-1867   2546

JOURNAL OF A TOUR THROUGH THE UNITED STATES AND IN CANADA. Oxford: Printed by T. Combe, 1843. 231 pp.

1837-1838. English naturalist's diary of travel in United States and Canada; journey along east side of Mississippi River to St. Louis, later up Mississippi and Ohio rivers; visits to American scientists and scholars; notes on scientific matters in a literary style.

DAYTON, MARIA ANNIS TOMLINSON, b. 1815   2547

Extracts in GENEALOGICAL STORY (DAYTON AND TOMLINSON), by Laura P. Fessenden, pp. 90-103. Cooperstown, N.Y.: Crist, Scott & Parshall, 1902.

1837-1882. Pleasant notes on social and domestic life, family, children, etc.; verses.

DWINNELL, JOSEPH PORTER, 1820-1839   2548

"Extracts from Diary of Joseph Porter Dwinnell." DANVERS HISTORICAL SOCIETY COLLECTIONS 26 (1938): 23-41.

1837-1838. Brief notes of local affairs at Danvers, Massachusetts; work, carpentry, reading and education; an interesting record of country life.

EDWARDS, PHILIP LEGET, 1812-1869   2549

"California in 1837." THEMIS 2 (September 13-27, 1890). Reprint. Sacramento: A.J. Johnston, 1890. 47 pp. THE DIARY OF PHILIP LEGET EDWARDS; THE GREAT CATTLE DRIVE FROM CALIFORNIA TO OREGON IN 1837. Rare Americana Series, no. 4. San Francisco: Grabhorn Press, 1932.

Jan-Sep 1837. Account of cattle drive along the Pacific coast with Willamette Cattle Company; from Des Sables, Willamette, Fort George, Port Bodega; voyage to San Francisco; early account of San Francisco and Monterey; an interesting diary of California before the gold rush days; vigorous and personal.

FARNHAM, JERUSHA LOOMIS, b. 1804   2550

In LOG CITY DAYS: TWO NARRATIVES ON THE SETTLEMENT OF GALESBURG, ILLINOIS, introduction by Ernest Calkins, pp. 11-57. Galesburg, Ill.: Knox College Centenary Publications, 1937.

May-Jul 1837. Schoolteacher's diary; trip from Tully, New York, to the Gale colony at Log City, Illinois; events during journey and pious reflections; weather, farming, domestic life; activities of her children; good diary of a pioneer woman.

FEATHERSTONHAUGH, GEORGE WILLIAM, 1780-1866   2551

A CANOE VOYAGE UP THE MINNAY SOTOR: WITH AN ACCOUNT OF THE LEAD AND COPPER DEPOSITS IN WISCONSIN: OF THE GOLD REGION IN THE CHEROKEE COUNTRY. London: R. Bentley, 1847. 2 vols. Reprint. St. Paul: Minnesota Historical Society, 1970.

Patton, James W., ed. "The Tennessee Valley as Seen by a British Traveler in 1837." TENNESSEE HISTORICAL MAGAZINE, 2d ser. 3 (1932):45-58.

1837. British geologist's canoe trip in Wisconsin Territory; very full entries describing topography and scenery, mineralogy, customs, adventures, Indians and Indian life; trip through Tennessee Valley.

FOULKE, JOSEPH, 1786-1863   2552

Cox, John, Jr., ed. "Visit of Joseph Foulke among the Friends of Long Island." FRIENDS' HISTORICAL ASSOCIATION BULLETIN 20 (1931):27-31.

May-Jun 1837. Schoolmaster's visit with family to Quakers on Long Island; social life and meetings; in seminarrative style.

FOWLER, LITTLETON, 1802-1846   2553

Arthus, Dora Fowler. "Jottings from the Old Journal of Littleton Fowler." TEXAS HISTORICAL ASSOCIATION QUARTERLY 2 (1898-1899):73-84.

Aug 1837-Apr 1838. Journal extracts within narrative kept by Methodist missionary in Texas; notes on religion and politics.

FRANCIS, JAMES-HANMER, 1796-1863   2554

Holman, Winifred L., ed. "Diary of the Rev. James-Hanmer Francis." OHIO STATE ARCHEOLOGICAL AND HISTORICAL QUARTERLY 51 (1942):41-61.

Jun 1837-May 1838. Massachusetts minister's preaching trip to New York, Ohio, Michigan, Indiana, Illinois and Iowa; travel by stagecoach, horseback and foot; names of people encountered; itinerary and expenses.

GARRIOCH, PETER, b. 1811   2555

"Peter Garrioch at St. Peter." MINNESOTA HISTORY 20 (1939):119-128.

Jul-Nov 1837. Extracts describing a trip from Red River Colony to St. Peter, Minnesota, by cart and canoe; negotiations with Chippewas; account of Kaposia Mission and Falls of St. Anthony.

GEORGE'S CREEK COAL AND IRON COMPANY   2556

THE LONACONING JOURNALS: THE FOUNDING OF A COAL AND IRON COMMUNITY. Edited by Katherine A. Harvey. American Philosophical Society Transactions, vol. 67, pt. 2. Philadelphia: American Philosophical Society, 1977. 78 pp.

1837-1840. Journals kept by the superintendents, chiefly John Henry Alexander, Philip T. Tyson, Charles B. Shaw, and chief clerk, Frederick Pauer, of the George's Creek Coal and Iron Company at Lonaconing, Maryland; building an experimental iron furnace, developing a company town; problems of supply, transportation, construction, labor, discipline and health.

HACKER, JEREMIAH, 1801-1895   2557

"Journal of Jeremiah Hacker." VINELAND HISTORICAL MAGAZINE 17 (1932):204-211; 18 (1933):232-237, 268-275, 305-312, 340-343; 19 (1934):22-27.

1837-1844. Journal of a pamphleteer and peppery crusader for various causes and against all manner of evil; lively account of religious life, meetings and revivals in Portland, Maine; temperance work; editorship of PORTLAND PLEASURE BOAT.

HENRY, JOSEPH, 1797-1878   2558

THE PAPERS OF JOSEPH HENRY. Edited by Nathan Reingold. Washington, D.C.: Smithsonian Institution Press, 1972-(in progress). Diary, vol. 3, pp. 171-464 passim.

Mar-Aug 1837. European tour of scientist and professor at Princeton; travels in England, Scotland and France; visits with eminent scientists, including Michael Faraday; observation of and participation in experiments, particularly in the field of electro-magnetism; notes on lectures and demonstrations; purchase of scientific equipment for Princeton; interesting tourist notes; lengthy quotations from the diary of physics colleague, Alexander Dallas Bache; a good picture of cooperation, as well as competition, between American and European scientists.

HIGBEE, LUCY ANN   2559

THE DIARY OF LUCY ANN HIGBEE. Cleveland: Privately printed, 1924. 57 pp.

May-Jul 1837. Diary of a trip from Trenton, New Jersey, to Ohio and return via Niagara Falls and Saratoga; travel by stagecoach and steamer; notes on scenery, social affairs.

HINDS, RICHARD BRINSLEY   2560

Kay, E. Alison, trans. and ed. "The Sandwich Islands: From Richard Brinsley Hinds' Journal of the Voyage of the SULPHUR." HAWAIIAN JOURNAL OF HISTORY 2 (1968):102-135.

Jul 1837, May-Jun 1839. Hawaiian portions of diary kept by surgeon aboard British ship on a round the world expedition; events in Honolulu; comments on Hawaiian royalty and common people, missionaries, and officers of his own and other ships; detailed botanical and anthropological notes.

JARVIS, NATHAN S.   2561

Jarvis, Nathan S., ed. "An Army Surgeon's Notes of Frontier Service." MILITARY SERVICE INSTITUTION OF THE UNITED STATES JOURNAL 39 (1906):131-135, 255-286, 451-460; 40 (1907):269-277.

1837-1839. Surgeon's record of service in Florida during Seminole War; activities at St. Augustine, Jupiter Inlet, Tampa, etc.; notes on army life, capture of Osceola, engagements and marches, negotiations with Seminoles; Seminole customs; report of a massacre. Includes letters beginning in 1833.

JOHNSON, JOSEPH A.   2562

Hoole, W. Stanley, ed. "Echoes from the 'Trail of Tears'." ALABAMA REVIEW 6 (1953):135-152. Diary, pp. 147-149.

Sep-Oct 1837. Extremely brief entries of wagon trip with companion, Johnson Jones Hooper, from Alabama to Texas; expenses, mileage, places along route, weather.

JUDD, SYLVESTER, 1813-1853   2563

Extracts in LIFE AND CHARACTER OF THE REV. SYLVESTER JUDD, by Arethusa Hall, pp. 113-185 passim. Boston: Crosby, Nichols; New York: C.S. Francis, 1854.

1837-1841. Clergyman's diary; life in divinity school at Harvard; appointment to pastorate at Augusta, Maine, and notes of work there.

LILLYBRIDGE, C.   2564

"Foreman, Grant, ed. "Journal of a Party of Cherokee Emigrants." MISSISSIPPI VALLEY HISTORICAL REVIEW 18 (1931-1932):232-245.

Mar 1837. Journal of a physician accompanying emigrating Cherokees; travel on Tennessee, Ohio, Mississippi and Arkansas rivers; data on health of Indians; official and impersonal but interesting.

LINDSAY, ELIZABETH DICK, 1792-1845   2565

DIARY OF ELIZABETH DICK LINDSAY. Introduction by Jo White Linn. Salisbury, N.C.: Salisbury Publishing Co., 1975. 1 vol. unpaged.

1837-1861. Plantation diary kept in Guilford County, North Carolina; way of life on a prosperous plantation; crops planted, instructions for grafting fruit trees, remedies for sickness; neighborhood events and family records. Facsimile of manuscript.

MANN, HORACE, 1796-1859   2566

In LIFE OF HORACE MANN, by Mary Tyler Peabody Mann, 609 pp. passim. Boston: Walker, Fuller and Co., 1865. Reprint. Centennial ed., in facsimile. Washington, D.C.: National Education Association of the United States, 1937.

1837-1853. Educator's journal entries interspersed with letters and comment; notes on ideals of organized system of common education, the Massachusetts Temperance Society, books read, legal matters, view on slavery; work as secretary to the Massachusetts Board of Education, political activities, teaching and presidency at Antioch College;

visit to Washington, D.C., and trip to Europe to observe schools.

MICKLE, ISAAC, 1822-1855   2567

A GENTLEMAN OF MUCH PROMISE: THE DIARY OF ISAAC MICKLE. Edited by Philip E. Mackey. Philadelphia: University of Pennsylvania Press, 1977. 2 vols.

     1837-1845. Extensive diary, kept from age fourteen to twenty-two, of son of a cultivated Quaker family in Camden, New Jersey; education, interest in books, music, debating, politics, local history; eventual work as attorney and newspaper editor; the loosening of Quaker ties; flirtations and carousing; some youthful pomposities and prejudices, but much charm; a self-revealing diary.

NYE, THOMAS, 1801-1877   2568

JOURNAL OF THOMAS NYE WRITTEN DURING A JOURNEY BETWEEN MONTREAL & CHICAGO. Edited by Hugh McLellan. Champlain, N.Y.: Privately printed at the Moorsfield Press, 1932. 30 pp.

     Oct-Dec 1837. Canadian lawyer's journey by stagecoach to Ontario, by steamer through the Great Lakes; return with his bride overland to Detroit, by steamer to Cleveland and then overland to Montreal; brief notes of activities, scenes, conversations and accommodations; good description of a prairie fire.

PEAKE, JOHN, 1756-1841   2569

Crookes, Harold F., ed. "Diary of John Peake." ILLINOIS HISTORICAL SOCIETY JOURNAL 8 (1915-1916):114-131.

     Jan-Dec 1837. Brief notes of daily occupations, devotions, etc., of resident of Sangamon County, Illinois.

PETIT, BENJAMIN MARIE   2570

THE TRAIL OF DEATH: LETTERS OF BENJAMIN MARIE PETIT. By Irving McKee. Indiana Historical Society Publications, 14, no. 1. Indianapolis: Indiana Historical Society, 1941. 141 pp. Journal, pp. 119-134.

     1837-1838. Young Indiana priest's attempt to defend the Potawatomi; daily missionary work recorded in notes added to his account book.

PORTER, DEBORAH H. CUSHING, 1809-1847   2571

Extracts in MEMOIR OF MRS. DEBORAH H. PORTER, by Anne T. Drinkwater, pp. 34-226 passim. Portland, Maine: Sanborn & Carter, 1848.

     1837-1845. Religious journal of parson's wife at Bangor, Maine; self-analysis, lamentations, trials, prayers, omens, consolations and despairs; church meetings and interactions with various preachers.

SIMPKINSON, FRANCIS GUILLEMARD, 1819-1906   2572

In H.M.S. SULPHUR AT CALIFORNIA, 1837 AND 1839: BEING THE ACCOUNTS OF MIDSHIPMAN FRANCIS GUILLEMARD SIMPKINSON AND CAPTAIN EDWARD BELCHER, edited by Richard A. Pierce and John H. Winslow, pp. 1-70. San Francisco: Book Club of California, 1969.

     Oct-Dec 1837. Midshipman's description of entry into San Francisco's Golden Gate and the three or four houses then comprising waterfront settlement; shipmate's tales of grievances against Captain Belcher on first charting of Sacramento River for navigation; glimpses of California and a naturalist's interest in the terrain and wildlife.

SMITH, JOSHUA TOULMIN, 1816-1869   2573

JOURNAL IN AMERICA. Edited by Floyd B. Streeter. Heartman's Historical Series, no. 41. Metuchen, N.J.: Printed for C.F. Heartman, 1925. 54 pp.

     Aug 1837-Jul 1838. English lawyer's diary of travel in America; voyage from England to New York; visits to Albany, Utica, Buffalo, Detroit, with notes on Detroit and Michigan; disappointment at not finding utopia; return to Utica; comments on American "barbarisms," prisons, elections, women, cookery, linguistics; a lively and provocative analysis, with the first part written by his wife.

SMITH, WILLIAM RUDOLPH, 1787-1868   2574

INCIDENTS OF A JOURNEY FROM PENNSYLVANIA TO WISCONSIN TERRITORY IN 1837, BEING THE JOURNAL OF GEN. WILLIAM RUDOLPH SMITH, U.S. COMMISSIONER FOR TREATY WITH THE CHIPPEWA INDIANS OF THE UPPER MISSISSIPPI. Chicago: W. Howes, 1927. 82 pp. Journal, pp. 27-72.

"Journal of William Rudolph Smith." WISCONSIN MAGAZINE OF HISTORY 12 (1928-1929):192-220, 300-321.

     Jul-Oct 1837. By canal and river from Pennsylvania to Wisconsin, via Pittsburgh, Steubenville, Wheeling, Marietta, Cincinnati, Louisville, Evansville, St. Louis, Alton, Dubuque, Prairie du Chien; part of return journey; notes on towns and incidents of journey, social and general observations; quite interesting.

STEBBINS, SALMON, 1795-1882   2575

"Journal of Salmon Stebbins." WISCONSIN MAGAZINE OF HISTORY 9 (1925-1926):188-212.

     1837-1838. Methodist preacher's journal; trip to Wisconsin; travel and preaching there; simple, direct notes of work, etc.

SUMNER, CHARLES, 1811-1874   2576

In MEMOIR AND LETTERS OF CHARLES SUMNER, by Edward L. Pierce, vol. 1, pp. 213-286. Boston: Roberts Brothers, 1877.

     Dec 1837-Apr 1838. Foreign travel diary of Boston lawyer and politician; voyage across Atlantic, tour in France, with notes on Rouen, Paris and study at Ecole de Droit; theaters and museums, contacts with American and English colony; observation of trials; detailed and interesting notes of life of Americans in Paris.

THOREAU, HENRY DAVID, 1817-1862   2577

THE WRITINGS OF HENRY DAVID THOREAU. Edited by Bradford Torrey and Franklin B. Sanborn. Boston and New York: Houghton, Mifflin, 1906. 20 vols. Journal, vols. 7-20. Reprint. New York: AMS Press, 1968.

JOURNAL. Edited by Bradford Torrey and Francis H. Allen. Walden ed. His Writings. Boston: Houghton Mifflin, 1949. 14 vols.

JOURNAL. John C. Broderick, general editor, edited by Elizabeth H. Witherell. Princeton, N.J.: Princeton University Press, 1981-(in progress).

     1837-1861. Thoreau's life work and masterpiece, which exhibits his best writing and the varied facets of his character; both poetic and scientific observations of nature; notes on his philosophical Concord neighbors, Alcott, Channing, Emerson, etc., as well as unnamed and interesting local characters; musings on religion, morality, philosophy, civil disobedience, work, human foibles, nature of the interior life; on each page, unfailing beauty, wisdom, common sense or ironic humor.

EARLY SPRING IN MASSACHUSETTS: FROM THE JOURNAL OF HENRY D. THOREAU. Edited by Harrison G. Blake. Boston: Houghton, Mifflin, 1881. 318 pp. Continued as SUMMER. 1884. 382 pp. WINTER. 1888. 439 pp. Reprint in two parts. Cambridge: Riverside Press, 1963, 1967. AUTUMN. 1892. 470 pp.

THE HEART OF THOREAU'S JOURNALS. Edited by Odell Shepard. Boston and New York: Houghton Mifflin, 1927. 348 pp. Revision. New York: Dover, 1961. 228 pp.

MEN OF CONCORD AND SOME OTHERS AS PORTRAYED IN THE JOURNAL OF HENRY DAVID THOREAU. Edited by Francis H. Allen, with illustrations by N.C. Wyeth. Boston: Houghton Mifflin, 1936. 255 pp. Reprint. New York: Bonanza Books, 197-?

SELECTED JOURNALS. Edited by Carl Bode. New York: New American Library, 1967. 327 pp. Reprint. THE BEST OF THOREAU'S JOURNALS. Carbondale: Southern Illinois University Press, 1971.

TWO FRAGMENTS FROM THE JOURNALS. Edited by Alexander C. Kern. Iowa City: Windhover Press, University of Iowa, 1968. 16 pp.

ESSAYS, JOURNALS AND POEMS. Edited by Dean Flower. Greenwich, Conn.: Fawcett Publications, 1975. 637 pp.

Extracts in WORLD'S GREAT DIARIES, edited by Philip Dunaway, pp. 293-299.

> 1837-1861. Extracts covering various aspects and periods of his life.

CONSCIOUSNESS IN CONCORD: THE TEXT OF THOREAU'S HITHERTO "LOST JOURNAL." Notes and a commentary by Perry Miller. Boston: Houghton Mifflin, 1958. 243 pp.

> 1840-1841.

WARREN, JOHN COLLINS, 1778-1856   2578

In THE LIFE OF JOHN COLLINS WARREN, compiled by Edward Warren, 2 vols. passim. Boston: Ticknor and Fields, 1860.

> 1837-1856. Journals of Boston surgeon; voyage to Europe, England, Ireland, France, Italy; touristic travels and notes, visits to medical schools and doctors; journal of professional life and work in Boston; some domestic and social items; further travel in Europe.

WILLS, WILLIAM HENRY, 1809-1889   2579

Wills, George S., ed. "A Southern Sulky Ride in 1837." SOUTHERN HISTORICAL ASSOCIATION PUBLICATIONS 6 (1902):471-483; 7 (1903):7-16, 79-84, 186-192.

> Apr-May 1837. Clergyman's travel diary; by sulky from Tarboro, North Carolina, through Florida, Georgia and Alabama, looking for site for home; comments on taverns, food, sectarians, farming, towns; detailed list of expenses; long entries, personal and amusing.

Wills, George S., ed. "A Southern Traveler's Diary in 1840." SOUTHERN HISTORICAL ASSOCIATION PUBLICATIONS 7 (1903):349-352, 427-432; 8 (1904):23-29, 129-138.

> Apr-May 1840. Journey by hack from Tarboro to Washington, by train to Baltimore; over mountains to Cumberland and Wheeling; Ohio, Kentucky, Illinois, Tennessee, Mississippi, Alabama and return; vigorous and amusing comments on social habits, institutions and places.

1838

ANON.   2580

LYCOMING HISTORICAL SOCIETY OCCASIONAL PAPER, no. 6 (1928).

NOW AND THEN 5 (1936):151-169.

> Apr-Nov 1838. English farmer's travel diary; trip from England to New York, New Jersey and Pennsylvania; farming in Murray Valley, Pennsylvania; beginning of voyage home.

ANON.   2581

Smith, Dwight L., ed. "A Continuation of the Journal of an Emigrating Party of Potawatomi Indians." INDIANA MAGAZINE OF HISTORY 44 (1948):393-408.

> Nov-Dec 1838. An account of the Potawatomi Indians' removal, led by William Polke; first stages of the resettlement of the Indians; establishment of winter quarters in Missouri and issuing of provisions.

ALLEN, WILLIAM Y., 1805-1855   2582

TEXAS PRESBYTERIAN, 19 March, 16, 30 April, 7 May, 6, 20 August, 8, 29 October, 31 December 1880; 4 March, 23 December 1881; 31 March 1882; 26 January, 29 June, 14 December 1883. Reprint. "Extracts from the Diary of W.Y. Allen," edited by William S. Red. SOUTHWESTERN HISTORICAL QUARTERLY 17 (1913-1914): 43-60.

> 1838-1939. Diary of the chaplain of the Congress of the Texas Republic; notes on his experiences in Texas, religious affairs, Indians.

BAKER, CHARLES MINTON, d. 1872   2583

"On the Road to Wisconsin." WISCONSIN MAGAZINE OF HISTORY 5 (1921-1922):389-401.

> Sep-Oct 1838. Journey from Hortonville, Vermont, to Wisconsin; notes on towns, inns, canals.

BAKER, JOHN R., b. ca. 1811   2584

Stevens, Harry R., ed. "Western Travels." HISTORICAL AND PHILOSOPHICAL SOCIETY OF OHIO BULLETIN 6 (1948):127-155. Diary, pp. 135-155.

> Jun-Aug 1838. Merchant's journey from Philadelphia to Cincinnati, Louisville, St. Louis, Chicago, Detroit, Cleveland, Buffalo and return; details of travel by rail, canal packet boat, stagecoach and steamboat; visits to Niagara Falls and Shaker village near Albany; notes on Ottawa and Seneca Indians.

BARRETT, SELAH HIBBARD, 1822-1883   2585

AUTOBIOGRAPHY OF SELAH HIBBARD BARRETT, THE SELF-EDUCATED CLERGYMAN. Rutland, Ohio.: The author, 1872. 396 pp.

> 1838-1872. Methodist journal; ministerial labors and travels in Ohio and occasional missions in other parts of the United States and Canada; revival meetings, work for religious press.

BLACKFORD, JOHN, ca. 1780-1839   2586

FERRY HILL PLANTATION JOURNAL. Edited by Fletcher M. Green. James Sprunt Studies In History and Political Science, vol. 43. Chapel Hill: University of North Carolina Press, 1961. 139 pp.

1838-1839. Plantation journal; management and social life at Ferry Hill Plantation on Maryland side of the Potomac River; accounts, production of various grains, hay, fruits, potatoes, livestock and timber, for sale and home consumption; daily life, visitors; operation of ferry to Shepherdstown.

COLVOCORESSES, GEORGE MUSALAS, 1816-1872 2587

FOUR YEARS IN A GOVERNMENT EXPLORING EXPEDITION. New York: Cornish, Lamport & Co., 1852. 371 pp. 2d ed. New York: R.T. Young, 1853.

1838-1842. Exploration journal by a member of Charles Wilkes' expedition; life aboard the VINCENNES; scenery, customs, government, religion, commerce of such diverse and far-flung places as Madeira, Cape Verde Islands, Brazil, Patagonia, Chile, Peru, Paumato Group, Society Islands, Navigator Group, Fiji Islands, Hawaii, New Zealand, Friendly Islands, Northwest coast of America, Oregon, California, East Indies, St. Helena, etc.; Captain Wilkes' climb of Mauna Loa in Hawaii, surveying of Northwest coast, Fourth of July celebration at Fort Nisqually in Washington, overland expedition to San Francisco. Journal entries interspersed with short essays and quotations from other diarists of the VINCENNES.

COOMBE, GEORGE, 1788-1858 2588

NOTES ON THE UNITED STATES OF NORTH AMERICA, DURING A PHRENOLOGICAL VISIT. Philadelphia: Carey & Hart, 1841. 2 vols.

In COLLECTIONS ON THE HISTORY OF ALBANY, FROM ITS DISCOVERY TO THE PRESENT TIME, edited by Joel Munsell, vol. 2, pp. 343-353. Albany: J. Munsell, 1867.

1838-1840. Extracts from American travel diary of Scottish phrenologist; visit to Albany, New York, and environs; description of Shakers, Albany politics, manners, etc.

DEARBORN, HENRY ALEXANDER, 1783-1851 2589

"Journals of Henry A.S. Dearborn." BUFFALO HISTORICAL SOCIETY PUBLICATIONS 7 (1904):39-225.

Aug-Dec 1838, Aug 1839. Journals of treaty negotiations with Indians; journey to Niagara frontier to negotiate with Seneca and Tuscarora Indians; travel from Roxbury, Massachusetts, to Albany, Buffalo, Genesee, Nunda Falls, Niagara, Buffalo Creek, Lewiston, Rochester, Oswego, Kingston, Ogdensburg, Rossie lead mines, Montreal and Burlington; very extensive entries describing scenery, Indians and their customs, myths and sports; notes on farming, fortifications, etc.; mission to Buffalo to negotiate treaty of emigration with Senecas; mainly personal items, weather, reading, comments on politics, Red Jacket, etc.; in August 1839, journey from Boston to Cattaraugus, New York, by railroad to attend council of Six Nations.

DOUGHERTY, PETER, b. 1805 2590

Anderson, Charles A., ed. "Diaries of Peter Dougherty." PRESBYTERIAN HISTORICAL SOCIETY JOURNAL 30 (1952):95-114, 175-192, 236-253.

1838-1842 (with gaps). Diary of Presbyterian missionary to Chippewas of northern Michigan; trip from New York to Michigan; search for site for mission; canoe travel; Indian language, customs, individuals; religious and educational work among Indians and settlers; an intelligent diary and excellent picture of area and time.

DUYCKINCK, GEORGE LONG, 1823-1863 2591

Schubert, Leland, ed. "A Boy's Journal of a Trip into New England in 1838." ESSEX INSTITUTE HISTORICAL COLLECTIONS 86 (1950):97-105.

Jun-Jul 1838. Brief account by the future editor of THE LITERARY WORLD and CYCLOPAEDIA OF AMERICAN LITERATURE of a trip through New England with his brother, Evert, and a friend; visit with Longfellow and a tour of Salem with Hawthorne; notes on Shaker village, factories, etc.

EELLS, MYRA FAIRBANKS, 1805-1878 2592

"Journal of Myra F. Eells." OREGON PIONEER ASSOCIATION TRANSACTIONS OF THE 17TH ANNUAL REUNION (1889):54-88a.

In FIRST WHITE WOMEN OVER THE ROCKIES, by Clifford M. Drury, vol. 2, pp. 47-118.

1838. Missionary's travel diary, intended for her family; factual account of events on the overland journey to the Oregon Mission at Walla Walla.

ELLICE, JANE 2593

THE DIARY OF JANE ELLICE. Edited by Patricia Godsell. Toronto: Oberon Press, 1975. 211 pp. Diary, pp. 16-104.

1838. Englishwoman's trip from Montreal to New York, Philadelphia, Washington and Niagara Falls; travel by train and river boat; colorful descriptions of people, places, manners and customs.

EVANS, MARY PEACOCK, 1821-1912 2594

THE JOURNAL OF MARY PEACOCK: LIFE A CENTURY AGO AS SEEN IN BUFFALO AND CHAUTAUQUA COUNTY BY A SEVENTEEN YEAR OLD GIRL. Buffalo, N.Y.: Privately printed, 1938. 1 vol., unpaged.

1838. Schoolgirl's journal; lessons, social life and family matters in Buffalo; description of soldiers passing through to war in Canada; visiting lecturers, including one on animal magnetism; uneventful but pleasant.

GALE, ANNA D. 2595

Hoyt, Edward A. and Brigham, Loriman S. "Glimpses of Margaret Fuller: The Green Street School and Florence." NEW ENGLAND QUARTERLY 29 (1956):87-98.

1838. Extracts from journal kept by a pupil of Margaret Fuller's at the Green Street School in Providence, Rhode Island; her teacher's opinions on several topics; the concept of evil, the millennium, charity, status of women, etc.; evidences of Fuller's teaching style.

GEYER, CHARLES A., 1809-1853 2596

Extracts in JOSEPH N. NICOLLET ON THE PLAINS AND PRAIRIES, by Joseph N. Nicollet, translated from the French and edited by Edmund C. Bray and Martha C. Bray, pp. 111-130. St. Paul: Minnesota Historical Society, 1957.

Jul-Oct 1838. Naturalist's notes on the expedition led by Joseph Nicolas Nicollet to chart region between Mississippi and Missouri rivers.

GREY, CHARLES, 1804–1870 2597

CRISIS IN THE CANADAS: 1838–1839; THE GREY JOURNALS AND LETTERS. Edited by William Ormsby. Toronto: Macmillan, 1964. 244 pp.

1838–1839. Journal of British officer, commander of Seventy-first Light Infantry who, as a result of rebellions in Upper and Lower Canada, undertook special diplomatic mission to Washington, D.C., to improve Anglo-American relations; travel from Quebec to Albany by coach, by steamer to New York and coach to Washington; meeting with President Van Buren, visit to House of Representatives, where he heard Daniel Webster speak on Maine–New Brunswick boundary question.

HAPPOLDT, CHRISTOPHER, 1823–1878 2598

THE CHRISTOPHER HAPPOLDT JOURNAL: HIS EUROPEAN TOUR WITH THE REV. JOHN BACHMAN. Edited by Claude H. Neuffer. Charleston, S.C.: Charleston Museum, 1960. 214 pp. Journal, pp. 119–214.

Jun–Dec 1838. Journal of a fourteen-year-old Charleston boy on a European tour with Audubon's collaborator, Lutheran clergyman and naturalist, John Bachman; ocean crossing on the CHICORA; sightseeing and meeting with distinguished people, including Audubon, with whom they traveled in England; visits to museums, zoological gardens in England and Europe.

HERNDON, JOHN HUNTER, b. 1813 2599

Muir, Andrew F., ed. "Diary of a Young Man in Houston." SOUTHWESTERN HISTORICAL QUARTERLY 53 (1950):276–307.

Jan–May 1838. Record of young Kentucky lawyer's first few months in Texas; social life and hunting expeditions; a few legal matters; election as engrossing clerk of Texas House of Representatives.

HULL, JACOB 2600

Smith, Dwight L., ed. "Jacob Hull's Detachment of the Potawatomie Emigration of 1838." INDIANA MAGAZINE OF HISTORY 45 (1949):285–288.

Sep–Oct 1838. Brief account of the journey of a small detachment of Potawatomi who were left behind the main removal because of illness; notes of events of march, but mainly record of miles covered and camp locations; overtaking of the original group under William Polke.

JENKS, M.H. 2601

Extracts in TRAVEL ACCOUNTS OF INDIANA, compiled by Shirley S. McCord, pp. 169–173.

May 1838. Philadelphian's trip to Indiana; notes on agriculture, prospects for development; lodging and difficulties of travel.

KASHEVAROV, ALEKSANDR FILIPPOVICH, 1809–1870 2602

A.F. KASHEVOROV'S COASTAL EXPLORATIONS IN NORTHWEST ALASKA. Edited by James W. Vanstone, translated by David H. Kraus. Fieldiana: Anthropology, vol. 69. Field Museum of Natural History Publication 1268. Chicago: Field Museum of Natural History, 1977. 104 pp.

Jul–Sep 1838. Russian explorer's detailed description of northern Alaska coast; information on Eskimos; villages and camps, names of settlements, tribal groupings; descriptions of houses and tents, clothing and personal adornment, activities; notes on plant and animal life of area.

MILLER, HENRY B. 1814–1847 2603

Marshall, Thomas M., ed. "The Journal of Henry B. Miller." MISSOURI HISTORICAL SOCIETY COLLECTIONS 6 (1928–1931):213–287.

1838–1839. Notes on political and social life of St. Louis; a trip to Iowa and Illinois; comments on Natchez; an interesting diary, but "trivial or merely personal" matter has been omitted by the editor.

NICHOLS, WILLIAM HENRY 2604

A JOURNAL OF A WHALING VOYAGE TO THE SOUTH ATLANTIC, INDIAN AND PACIFIC OCEANS ON BOARD BARQUE EMERALD OF SALEM. Edited by Henry C. Nichols. Salem, Mass.: Naumkeag Publications, 1973. 183 pp.

1838–1840. Whaling diary of cooper, ship's clerk and oarsman aboard the EMERALD under Captain Joseph Dexter; routine notes of weather, sightings of whales; more detail on harrowing chases and sailing conditions; a useful source on both whaling and seamanship.

OLIN, STEPHEN, 1797–1851 2605

THE LIFE AND LETTERS OF STEPHEN OLIN, LATE PRESIDENT OF THE WESLEYAN UNIVERSITY. New York: Harper & Brothers, 1853. 2 vols. Diary, vol. 1, pp. 223–345, vol. 2, pp. 10–28.

1838–1840. Diary of travel in France, Italy, Ireland and Germany, inspecting antiquities, scenery, crops, business; journey down the Danube to Turkey; general social and touring observations.

PETERS, JOHN, 1812–1871 2606

Brown, Margaret L., ed. "John Peters' Diary." MISSISSIPPI VALLEY HISTORICAL REVIEW 21 (1934–1935): 529–542.

1838–1841. Merchant's diary of business life in Vicksburg, Mississippi; attempt to recover his fortunes after the panic of 1837; a few personal details.

POLKE, WILLIAM 2607

"Journal of an Emigrating Party of Pottawattomie Indians." INDIANA MAGAZINE OF HISTORY 21 (1925): 315–336.

Aug–Nov 1838. Journal of the leader of Potawatomi removal from Twin Lakes, Marshall County, Indiana, to the Osage River in Western Territory; events during the march, deaths and sickness; details of Indian life and travel; an interesting journal. Generally attributed to Polke, but authorship uncertain.

SANDERS, CYRUS, 1817–1887 2608

"Journal of Cyrus Sanders." IOWA JOURNAL OF HISTORY AND POLITICS 37 (1939):52–88.

1838–1845. Journey from Ohio to Johnson County, Iowa, to settle; interesting details on such diverse items as taverns, cooking, gambling, dentists, etc.; work as a surveyor; some literary allusions.

SARGENT, JOHN GRANT, 1813–1883   2609

SELECTIONS FROM THE DIARY AND CORRESPONDENCE OF JOHN GRANT SARGENT, A MINISTER OF THE SOCIETY OF FRIENDS. Newport: J.E. Southall, 1885. 320 pp.

> 1838–1882. English Quaker's travels and ministry in England, France, Norway, Ireland and America; Quaker life and meetings; religious introspections.

SMITH, SARAH GILBERT WHITE,   2610
1813 or 1814–1855

In FIRST WHITE WOMEN OVER THE ROCKIES, by Clifford M. Drury, vol. 3, pp. 61–125.

> 1838. Missionary diary intended for her family at home; high religious idealism which induced her to undertake the arduous overland journey to the Oregon Mission at Walla Walla; description of difficulties; list of recommended clothing for men and women for overland trip; school teaching at Waiilatpu.

SPALDING, HENRY HARMON, 1803–1874   2611

THE DIARIES AND LETTERS OF HENRY H. SPALDING AND ASA BOWEN SMITH, RELATING TO THE NEZ PERCE MISSION. Edited by Clifford M. Drury. Glendale, Calif.: Arthur H. Clark, 1958. 379 pp. Diary, pp. 245–333.

> 1838–1843. Mission activities at Lapwai, dissension among missionaries, relations with Nez Percé; building a home, mill, school, print shop and cultivating the land; his philosophy of missions; attempt to settle Indians for instruction because they could not rely indefinitely on nomadic food-gathering.

STEELE, JOHN HARDY, 1789–1865   2612

Lindenbusch, John, ed. "Journal Kept on a Journey from Peterborough, N.H. to Salisbury, North Carolina in the Months of November & December, 1838." HISTORICAL NEW HAMPSHIRE 18 (December 1963):3–41.

> Nov–Dec 1838. Journal of Peterborough cotton manufacturer's trip to his birthplace after an absence of thirty years; descriptions of travel by stage, steamboat, train and foot, countryside, New York, Philadelphia, Washington, D.C., Congress in session; political views of a Jacksonian Democrat; emotions on meeting boyhood friends; expense account.

STERNE, ADOLPHUS, 1801–1852   2613

Smither, Harriet, ed. "Diary of Adolphus Sterne." SOUTHWESTERN HISTORICAL QUARTERLY 30 (1926–1927): 139–155, 219–232, 305–324; 31 (1927–1928):63–83, 181–187, 285–291, 374–383; 32 (1928–1929):87–94, 165–179, 252–257, 344–351; 33 (1929–1930):75–79, 160–168, 231–242, 315–325; 34 (1930–1931):69–76, 159–166, 257–265, 340–347; 35 (1931–1932):77–82, 151–168, 238–242, 317–324; 36 (1932–1933):67–72, 163–166, 215–229, 312–316; 37 (1933–1934):45–60, 136–148, 215–222, 320–323; 38 (1934–1935):53–70, 149–152, 213–228.

HURRAH FOR TEXAS! THE DIARY OF ADOLPHUS STERNE. Edited by Archie P. McDonald. Waco, Tex.: Texian Press, 1969. 269 pp.

> 1838–1851. Private and business diary of German immigrant to Texas; records of deaths; notes on taxes, politics, early life in Texas; an interesting and valuable source.

STEVENS, HENRY, 1791–1867   2614

"The Diary of Henry Stevens." VERMONT HISTORICAL SOCIETY PROCEEDINGS 2 (1931):115–128.

> 1838–1842. Brief entries covering farming, everyday life and politics in Burlington, Vermont.

SWARTZELL, WILLIAM   2615

MORMONISM EXPOSED, BEING A JOURNAL OF A RESIDENCE IN MISSOURI FROM THE 28TH OF MAY TO THE 20TH OF AUGUST, 1838. Pekin, Ohio: By the author, 1840. 48 pp.

> May–Aug 1838. Journal of a residence in Missouri, written by a former Mormon deacon.

WALKER, ELKANAH, 1805–1877   2616

In FIRST WHITE WOMEN OVER THE ROCKIES, by Clifford M. Drury, vol. 3, pp. 254–265.

> 1838. Missionary's travel diary of conditions of the overland journey to the Oregon Mission at Walla Walla; distances traveled, weather, health and concern for his mission.

NINE YEARS WITH THE SPOKANE INDIANS. Edited by Clifford Drury. Glendale, Calif.: Arthur H. Clarke, 1976.

> 1838–1848. Continuation of his diary from volume three of FIRST WHITE WOMEN OVER THE ROCKIES; years at Tshimakain among the Spokane Indians; struggle to learn the language; criticism of his colleague Cushing Eells; regular religious services; discouragement at trying to teach biblical truths to Indians and the demands of pioneer life.

WARNER, ABRAHAM JOSEPH, b. 1821   2617

THE PRIVATE JOURNAL OF ABRAHAM JOSEPH WARNER. Extracted by Herbert B. Enderton. San Diego? Calif., 1973. 319 pp.

> 1838–1864. Episcopal clergyman's diary; studies at Trinity College, Hartford, Connecticut; ordination; tutoring at Jubilee College; marriage; missionary work in Sterling, Illinois; pastorate at Grand Detour, Illinois; Civil War chaplaincy with Twelfth Illinois Cavalry Regiment.

WEBSTER, DANIEL, 1782–1852   2618

"Daniel Webster's Diary." OLD ELIOT 8 (1908):29–32.

> Jul 1838–Jan 1839. Fragments of statesman's diary; personal and autobiographical notes; visits to Eliot, Maine.

YOUNG, JOHN A., 1812–1873   2619

"Traveling to the Middle West in 1838." ANNALS OF IOWA 19 (1933):139–145.

> Dec 1838–Apr 1839. Physician's journey to Cincinnati on Ohio steamer; flirtations, Junius Brutus Booth's performance of JULIUS CEASAR and RICHARD III; journey to Monmouth to begin practice, trip to St. Louis, general social entries; a frank and rather amusing diary.

1839

BACHE, SOREN, 1814–1890   2620

A CHRONICLE OF OLD MUSKEGO, THE DIARY OF SOREN BACHE. Translated and edited by Clarence A. Clausen and Andreas Elviken. Northfield, Minn.: Norwegian-American Historical Association, 1951. 237 pp.

1839-1847. Diary of well-to-do Norwegian immigrant, who later returned to Norway; accounts of settlements in Illinois, which were devastated by malaria, and in Muskego, Wisconsin; business dealings, assistance to fellow Norwegians; comments on frontier Lutheran Church and pastors, whom Bache accused of Papist leanings; travels throughout eastern and middle United States; reactions to American politics and institutions.

BELKNAP, KITTURAH PENTON, 1820-1913   2621

Riley, Glenda, ed. "Family Life on the Frontier: The Diary of Kitturah Penton Belknap." ANNALS OF IOWA, 3d ser. 44 (1977-1979):31-51.

> 1839-1848. Covered wagon journey from Allen County, Ohio, to Des Moines River in Iowa; rigors of pioneer life; births and deaths of babies; church services and social life in log cabins; preparations for migration to Oregon; long narrative entries kept sporadically.

In WOMEN OF THE WEST, by Cathy Luchetti, pp. 127-150. St. George, Utah: Antelope Island Press, 1982.

> 1842-1848.

BENEDICT, J.W.   2622

"Diary of a Campaign against the Comanches." SOUTHWESTERN HISTORICAL QUARTERLY 32 (1928-1929):300-310.

> Sep-Nov 1839. Military campaign in Texas; little contact with Indians; description of country.

BREWER, HENRY BRIDGEMAN, 1813-1886   2623

Canse, John M., ed. "The Diary of Henry Bridgeman Brewer Being a Log of the LAUSANNE." OREGON HISTORICAL QUARTERLY 29 (1928):189-208, 288-309, 347-362; 30 (1929):53-62, 111-119.

> 1839-1843. Methodist missionary diary; voyage on the LAUSANNE with his family, from New York around Cape Horn to Fort Vancouver to reinforce Oregon Mission at The Dalles; notes on weather, cruise, religious life on board, reading; comments on the Hawaii missionary community during stop there; briefer entries covering events at the Oregon Mission; description of travel on the Columbia River.

BROWNELL, GEORGE, 1793-1872   2624

"The Journal of George Brownell on a Voyage to England in 1839." LOWELL HISTORICAL SOCIETY CONTRIBUTIONS 2 (1921-1926):325-371.

> Feb-May 1839. New England manufacturer's visit to England to study industrial methods and conditions; voyage out by sailing ship and home by steamship; interesting details of travel and of industrial and social life in England.

COOKE, AMOS STARR, 1810-1871   2625

THE CHIEFS' CHILDREN'S SCHOOL, A RECORD COMPILED FROM THE DIARY AND LETTERS OF AMOS STARR COOKE AND JULIETTE MONTAGUE COOKE. Compiled by Mary Atherton Richards. Honolulu: Printed by Honolulu Star-Bulletin, 1937. 372 pp. Rev. ed. THE HAWAIIAN CHIEFS' SCHOOL. Rutland, Vt.: C.E. Tuttle, 1970.

> 1839-1850. Interesting diaries of missionary teachers, husband and wife, requested by King Kamehameha to educate his chiefs and all the royal children in Hawaii; boarding school life, affectionate and detailed vignettes of various children; differences in culture and religion; prominent pupils, Lot Kamehameha and Bernice (Pauahi) Bishop, dealings with Dr. G.P. Judd, visit of Commodore Charles Wilkes of the United States Exploring Expedition.

CROSBY, JESSE W., 1820-1893   2626

"The History and Journal of the Life and Travels of Jesse W. Crosby." ANNALS OF WYOMING 11 (1939):145-218.

> 1839-1858 (with many gaps and added biographical matter). Mormon diary; joining Mormons in Missouri during "Mormon War"; missionary journey in England; the migration to Utah and building of Salt Lake City; governmental troubles; an excellent picture of western America and some interesting details of Victoria's England.

FIELD, MATTHEW C., 1812-1844   2627

Carson, William G.B., ed. "The Diary of Mat Field: St. Louis, April 2-May 16, 1839." MISSOURI HISTORICAL SOCIETY BULLETIN 5 (1949):91-108, 157-184.

> Apr-May 1839. Very personal journal of a young man's work as an actor, struggles with illness, probably a gastric ulcer; religious beliefs and doubts, longings for love and marriage.

PRAIRIE AND MOUNTAIN SKETCHES. Edited by Kate L. Gregg and John F. McDermott. American Exploration and Travel Series, 23. Norman: University of Oklahoma Press, 1957. 239 pp.

> Jun-Oct 1843. Diary of actor turned journalist accompanying Scottish sportsman, Sir William Stewart, and a heterogeneous group of gentlemen and amateur hunters on an excursion to the Rocky Mountains; notes on scenery, geography and hardships; anecdotes about Indians and mountain men. Diaries interspersed with sketches he was writing for various publications.

FULLER, MARGARET, 1810-1850   2628

Hudspeth, Robert N., ed. "Margaret Fuller's 1839 Journal: Trip to Bristol." HARVARD LIBRARY BULLETIN 27 (1979):445-470.

> 1839. Private journal, once in the possession of Emerson, of Fuller's visit with the wealthy De Wolfe family and others of Bristol, Rhode Island; conversations; lively observations of people and scenes; reading; introspections; admiration for her hostess, Mary Soley DeWolfe.

Myerson, Joel, ed. "Margaret Fuller's 1842 Journal: At Concord with the Emersons." HARVARD LIBRARY BULLETIN 21 (1973):320-340.

> Aug-Sep 1842. A rare picture of the Emersons at home; conversations with Emerson and William Ellery Channing; Fuller's own thoughts and much on Emerson's philosophy; rambles to Walden Pond.

Extracts in LADIES ON THE LOOSE: WOMEN TRAVELLERS OF THE 18TH AND 19TH CENTURIES, edited by Leo Hamalian, pp. 27-47. New York: Dodd, Mead, 1981.

> 1847-1848. Letter-diary from Italy.

Rostenberg, Leona, ed. "Margaret Fuller's Roman Diary." JOURNAL OF MODERN HISTORY 12 (1940):209-220.

> Jan-May 1849. Travel diary kept in Rome; notes on Mazzini, clericalism, political disturbances.

HAMILTON, JOHN, b. ca. 1800   2629

"John Hamilton's Journal." HISTORICAL JOURNAL 1 (1887):110-118.

Nov-Dec 1839. Travel diary; journey from Pine Creek, Clinton County, to Philadelphia by Union Canal, and return.

HASKEW, PETER, b. 1803   2630

"A St. Joseph Diary of 1839." FLORIDA HISTORICAL SOCIETY QUARTERLY 17 (1938-1939):132-151.

Apr-Dec 1839. Methodist missionary diary kept while author was serving with St. Joseph Mission and Apalachicola Mission in Florida; religious work; personal and domestic details; comments on Negroes.

KNOWLES, DAVID E., 1801-1848   2631

"Some Account of a Journey to the Cherokees." FRIENDS' HISTORICAL SOCIETY OF PHILADELPHIA BULLETIN 6 (1915):70-78; 7 (1916):15-21, 42-50.

Nov 1839-Sep 1840. Quaker travel journal; trip from East Farnham, Quebec, to Cincinnati, Arkansas, Indiana; horseback and stagecoach travel; visits to Friends and their meetings and to Cherokee missions.

LAMSON, MARY SWIFT, 1822-1909   2632

In THE FIRST STATE NORMAL SCHOOL IN AMERICA; THE JOURNALS OF CYRUS PEIRCE AND MARY SWIFT, with an introduction by Arthur O. Norton, pp. 79-224. Harvard Documents in the History of Education, vol. 1. Cambridge: Harvard University Press; London: H. Milford, Oxford University Press, 1926.

Extracts in WOMAN'S "TRUE" PROFESSION: VOICES FROM THE HISTORY OF TEACHING, by Nancy Hoffman, pp. 64-73. Old Westbury, N.Y.: Feminist Press; New York: McGraw-Hill, 1981.

Aug 1839-Apr 1840. Journal of an early student at the normal school in Lexington, Massachusetts; assignments, recitations, experiments, discussion; notes on methods of teaching; abstracts of lessons and sermons.

MUNGER, ASAHEL   2633

"Diary of Asahel Munger and Wife." OREGON HISTORICAL QUARTERLY 8 (1907):387-405.

May-Sep 1839. Letter-diary of Asahel and Eliza Munger; journey from Ohio to Oregon; notes on travel and religion; criticism of fur companies.

NICHOLS, THOMAS LOW, 1815-1901   2634

JOURNAL IN JAIL, KEPT DURING A FOUR MONTH'S IMPRISONMENT FOR LIBEL, IN THE JAIL OF ERIE COUNTY. Buffalo, N.Y.: Dinsmore, 1840. 248 pp. Reprint. New York: Arno, 1970.

Jun-Oct 1839. Prison diary of Buffalo newspaper editor; details of life in jail interspersed with rhymes and letters to female admirers; notes on contemporary events; constant and high-minded praise of the "fair sex"; breezy style, with many literary allusions.

OAKLEY, OBADIAH, 1815-1850   2635

In TO THE ROCKIES AND OREGON, edited by LeRoy R. Hafen and Ann W. Hafen, pp. 25-66.

May-Nov 1839. Partially written-up journal based on daily notes of member of Peoria Party; by horse from Independence, Missouri, to Brown's Hole, Colorado; suffering in miserable weather, fording rivers and streams, hunting and fishing for food; meeting other companies and trappers, sharing food and shelter; encounters with Indians; descriptions of country traversed; return to Peoria after a number of splits and desertions of the party.

OLMSTED, FRANCIS ALLYN   2636

INCIDENTS OF A WHALING VOYAGE. New York: D. Appleton, 1841. 360 pp. Reprint. With preface to the new edition by W. Storrs Lee. Rutland, Vt.: C.E. Tuttle, 1969.

1839-1841. Whaling diary of young Yale graduate who went to sea to recover his health; life, work and mishaps aboard the NORTH AMERICA; ports in Azores, South America; journey around the Horn to Hawaii, Society Islands, Tahiti and back; notes on islanders and missionaries; every possible facet of whaling life covered in a diary which became a best-seller of its day.

PAIGE, HARIETTE STORY WHITE, 1809-1863   2637

DANIEL WEBSTER IN ENGLAND. Edited by Edward Gray. Boston and New York: Houghton Mifflin, 1917. 370 pp.

May-Sep 1839. Travel diary of Boston companion to Daniel Webster's wife on trip to England; mainly notes of social life among important political figures.

PEIRCE, CYRUS, 1790-1860   2638

THE FIRST STATE NORMAL SCHOOL IN AMERICA; THE JOURNALS OF CYRUS PEIRCE AND MARY SWIFT. With an introduction by Arthur O. Norton. Harvard Documents in the History of Education, vol. 1. Cambridge: Harvard University Press; London: H. Milford, Oxford University Press, 1926. 299 pp. Journal, pp. 1-78.

1839-1841. Journal of the first principal of the normal school at Lexington, Massachusetts; an account of daily routines and studies; his philosophy of education, goals, frustrations and achievements.

SHERIDAN, FRANCIS CYNRIC, ca. 1812-1843   2639

GALVESTON ISLAND; OR A FEW MONTHS OFF THE COAST OF TEXAS. Edited by Willis W. Pratt. Austin: University of Texas Press, 1954. 172 pp.

1839-1840. Travel diary of a British diplomat sent to gather information about Texas and the desirability of Britain's recognizing it as a republic; travel from Barbados on board the PILOT; comments on settlers and their mores; colorful description of Galveston, Austin and Houston; business and trade, agriculture, slavery, social life, important personages; the diarist's own sophisticated reading. Dated entries through February 3, 1840, continued as narrative.

SMITH, ASA BOWEN, 1809-1886   2640

In THE DIARIES AND LETTERS OF HENRY H. SPALDING AND ASA BOWEN SMITH, RELATING TO THE NEZ PERCE MISSION. Edited by Clifford M. Drury, pp. 121-124, 195-198. Glendale, Calif.: Arthur H. Clark, 1958.

Nov 1839-Jan 1840, Oct-Dec 1840. Missionary's diary of difficulties in the mission at Waiilatpu; removal and beginning of mission to Nez Percé Indians at Kamiah.

SMITH, ELIAS WILLARD, b. 1816   **2641**

"Journal of E. Willard Smith while with the Fur Traders, Vasquez and Sublette, in the Rocky Mountain Region." OREGON HISTORICAL QUARTERLY 14 (1913):250–279.

Extracts in ANNALS OF WYOMING 11 (1939):31–41; 15 (1943):287–297.

Hafen, LeRoy R., ed. "With Fur Traders in Colorado." COLORADO MAGAZINE 27 (1950):161–188.

In TO THE ROCKIES AND OREGON, edited by LeRoy R. Hafen and Ann W. Hafen, pp. 151–195.

> Aug 1839–Jul 1840. Young engineer's journey with Louis Vasquez and Andrew Sublette by wagon from Independence, Missouri, along the Santa Fe Trail to Bent's Fort on the Arkansas River; north across the Continental Divide and down the South Platte to Fort Vasquez; by horseback to Brown's Hole on the Green River; by mackinaw boat from Fort Vasquez with cargo of buffalo robes and tongues down the Platte and Missouri to St. Louis; descriptions of Indians and mountain men, trading posts, buffalo hunts, winter on the Continental Divide.

SMITH, SIDNEY, 1809–1880   **2642**

In TO THE ROCKIES AND OREGON, edited by LeRoy R. Hafen and Ann W. Hafen, pp. 67–93.

> Jun–Oct 1839. Day-by-day notes of Peoria Party's journey to Oregon; weather, scenery, hunting, camps, hardships of travel, encounters with Indians.

SPRAGUE, JOHN T., 1810–1878   **2643**

White, Frank, Jr., ed. "Macomb's Mission to the Seminoles: John T. Sprague's Journal Kept during April and May, 1839." FLORIDA HISTORICAL QUARTERLY 35 (1956):130–193.

> Apr–May 1839. Aide de camp's well developed account of Major General Alexander Macomb's unsuccessful attempt to negotiate an ending to the Seminole Wars and a peaceful removal of Seminoles from lands settled by pioneers; travel from Washington by train, steamboat and coach; Savannah social life; encampments in Indian territory; diarist's sympathy for Indian position as well as respect for Macomb's diplomatic efforts.

WEBSTER, CAROLINE LE ROY, 1797–1882   **2644**

"MR. W. & I," BEING THE AUTHENTIC DIARY OF CAROLINE LE ROY WEBSTER, DURING A FAMOUS JOURNEY WITH THE HONORABLE DANIEL WEBSTER TO GREAT BRITAIN AND THE CONTINENT. Introduction by Claude M. Fuess. New York: I. Washburn, 1942. 264 pp.

> May–Dec 1839. Diary of travel in England and France with her husband, Daniel Webster; Atlantic crossing on the LIVERPOOL and train travel in England; balls and receptions of the London season; house parties throughout England and Scotland; meetings with Queen Victoria, Dickens, Carlyle, Macaulay, Southey and Wordsworth; English manners and customs; in Paris, social life at the court of Louis-Philippe; important as a social document, but reveals little of importance of this trip to future British-American relations.

WOOLSON, HANNA COOPER POMEROY   **2645**

In FIVE GENERATIONS (1785–1923) BEING SCATTERED CHAPTERS FROM THE HISTORY OF THE COOPER, POM-

EROY, WOOLSON AND BENEDICT FAMILIES, WITH EXTRACTS FROM THEIR LETTERS AND JOURNALS, edited by Clare Benedict, vol. 1, pp. 167–214. London: Ellis, 1930?

> 1839. Travel diary by niece of James Fenimore Cooper; summer trip from New Hampshire to Chicago and Great Lakes; travel by stagecoach and steamship; notes on conditions, fellow travelers, scenery.

YOUNG, BRIGHAM, 1801–1877   **2646**

MILLENNIAL STAR, published serially beginning in 1867.

THE JOURNAL OF BRIGHAM YOUNG: BRIGHAM YOUNG'S OWN STORY IN HIS OWN WORDS. Compiled by Leland R. Nelson. Provo, Utah: Council Press, 1980. 223 pp.

> 1839–1847. Diary of Mormon leader; life and persecution in Nauvoo, Illinois; migration to Salt Lake; administrative and religious matters on the trail and in early years of settlement and development of Mormon community in Utah; consultations with elders, advice and admonition to the people, spiritual insights, prayers and healings. Later years dictated to scribes.

DIARY OF BRIGHAM YOUNG, 1857. Edited by Everett L. Cooley. Salt Lake City: University of Utah Library, 1980. 105 pp.

> May–Sep 1857. Complete diary for part of one year, showing brief period of Young's life as spiritual and temporal leader of Mormons in Utah; routine administrative matters; work as territorial governor, superintendent of Indian affairs, church leader and business entrepreneur; the narrowly averted "Utah War" with federal troops dispatched by President Buchanan; an amazing mosaic of leadership activities but little that is personally revealing. Diary originally dictated to scribes.

1840

ANON.   **2647**

Extracts in GLEANINGS FROM OLD SHAKER JOURNALS, by Clara E. Sears, pp. 225–256. Boston and New York: Houghton Mifflin, 1916. 298 pp. Reprint. Westport, Conn.: Hyperion Press, 1975.

> 1840–1853. Extracts selected to illustrate time, duration and events of Shaker public meetings; the work of the "family"; farming, blacksmithing, furniture making, logging, saw mill work, bookbinding, gathering herbs; the work of apprentices; customs relating to death and funerals; activities in Boston and Fitchburg.

ANON.   **2648**

In TEXAS IN 1840, OR THE EMIGRANT'S GUIDE TO THE NEW REPUBLIC, introduction by A.B. Lawrence, pp. 29–80. New York: William W. Allen, 1840. Reprint. New York: Arno, 1973.

> Jan 1840. Travel diary; reports on land and crops made by settlers who were part of the original Austin colony; notes on stock, poultry, wildlife; incidents with Indians; education, religion and towns, particularly Austin.

ADAMS, GIBBINS, 1787–1862   **2649**

"Extracts from the Journal of Gibbins Adams." ESSEX INSTITUTE HISTORICAL COLLECTIONS 82 (1946):74–90.

> Jan 1840–Apr 1841. A lively personal journal recounting everyday affairs at Newburyport, Mas-

sachusetts, as well as political issues of the day; 1840 Presidential campaign; tensions arising from antislavery movement.

BALLARD, ADDISON MONTAGUE, 1799–1879　　　**2650**

"Addison Montague Ballard Diary." KENTUCKY HISTORICAL SOCIETY REGISTER 52 (1954):125–133.

> Aug 1840–Jan 1841. Account of carriage trip from Henry County, Kentucky, to Spotsylvania County, Virginia, and return; notes on sights along the way, places where he stopped, some expenses, road conditions.

BREWSTER, EDWARD, 1793–1886　　　**2651**

Beeson, Lewis, ed. "From New York to Illinois by Water in 1840." MICHIGAN HISTORY 32 (1948):270–289.

> Feb–May 1840. Preparations for leaving and journey by canal boat and Great Lakes steamer to settle on farm in Kane County, Illinois; much introspection about the significance of his westward migration; good descriptions of scenes along the way, experiences of travel, people, all in somewhat elevated style.

"From Illinois to Lake Superior and the Upper Peninsula by Steamer in 1852." MICHIGAN HISTORY 33 (1949):328–336.

> 1852. Undated entries of steamer travel on Lake Superior; comments on vegetation and mining of the area; much information and lore picked up from fellow travelers.

CLAYTON, WILLIAM, 1814–1879　　　**2652**

MANCHESTER MORMONS, THE JOURNAL OF WILLIAM CLAYTON. Edited by James B. Allene and Thomas G. Alexander. Classic Mormon Diaries Series, vol. 1. Santa Barbara, Calif.: Peregrine Smith, 1974. 248 pp.

> 1840–1842. Journal of a young English convert to Mormonism, who ministered to a working class congregation in Manchester before immigrating to the United States; poverty, dissension within the flock, arbitration of disputes; importance of dreams, speaking in tongues, millennial expectation; diarist's personal struggles and temptations; ocean crossing to United States with other Mormons; storms, sickness, problems with food, water and sanitation; interactions with important Mormon leaders, Willard Richards, Theodore Turley, Heber Kimball and Brigham Young, some in England and others in Nauvoo, Illinois.

WILLIAM CLAYTON'S JOURNAL; A DAILY RECORD OF THE JOURNEY OF THE ORIGINAL COMPANY OF "MORMON" PIONEERS FROM NAUVOO, ILLINOIS, TO THE VALLEY OF THE GREAT SALT LAKE. Published by the Clayton Family Association. Salt Lake City: Deseret News, 1921. 376 pp. Reprint. New York: Arno, 1973.

Extracts, combined with Orson Pratt's journal, in "The Pioneers of 1847." HISTORICAL RECORD (Salt Lake City) 9 (1890).

Extracts in THE OLD OREGON TRAIL: HEARINGS BEFORE THE COMMITTEE ON ROADS, HOUSE OF REPRESENTATIVES, SIXTY-EIGHTH CONGRESS, SECOND SESSION ON H.J. RES. 232, H.J. RES. 328, and S. 2053, by United States Congress, House, Committee on Roads, pp. 90–156. Washington, D.C.: Government Printing Office, 1925.

Extracts in EYE-WITNESSES TO WAGON TRAINS, by James Hewitt, pp. 124–133. New York: Scribner, 1974.

1846–1847. Official journal of Mormon historian and high priest; journey of Mormons overland from Nauvoo, Illinois, to settle in the Salt Lake valley; a good narrative with many intimate details; scenery, natural history, daily activities of the company, mob violence, factionalism and personalities; an account of the return to Winter Quarters after Brigham Young established the settlement at Salt Lake.

COMFORT, ELWOOD, b. 1822　　　**2653**

Mason, Philip P., ed. "Philadelphia to Michigan." MICHIGAN HISTORY 38 (1954):395–409.

> Apr–May 1840. Eighteen-year-old Quaker's account of journey with his father to settle on farm in Raisin, Michigan; distances, towns, inns, weather, conditions of travel, by wagon and Lake Erie steamer LEXINGTON; much interest in agriculture; happy, intelligent diary.

CURTIS, WILLIAM EDMUND, 1823–1880　　　**2654**

In LETTERS AND JOURNALS, compiled by Elizabeth Curtis, pp. 93–347. Hartford, Conn.: Case, Lockwood & Brainard, 1926.

> 1840–1880. Diary interspersed with letters, begun at Washington (Trinity) College, Hartford, Connecticut; college studies, reading, criticism, some verses; social life; travels with usual touristic notes; work as lawyer and judge; an interesting diary of a man of wide interests.

DOUGLAS, Sir JAMES, 1803–1877　　　**2655**

Leader, Herman, ed. "A Voyage from the Columbia to California in 1840." CALIFORNIA HISTORICAL SOCIETY QUARTERLY 8 (1929):97–115.

JAMES DOUGLAS IN CALIFORNIA, 1841; BEING THE JOURNAL OF A VOYAGE FROM THE COLUMBIA TO CALIFORNIA. Edited by Dorothy Blakey Smith. Vancouver, B.C.: The Library's Press, 1965. 56 pp.

> Dec 1840–Jan 1841. Official journal of Hudson's Bay Company factor on a mission to California to buy sheep and cattle for the stocking of ranches in the Columbia River valley, part of Britain's plan for increasing settlement and strengthening its claims to the area; coastal trip in the ship COLUMBIA; negotiations with Governor Alvarado about Hudson's Bay fur trapping; glimpse of trade and politics during turbulent period in California; notes on Monterey, inland journey to Santa Clara valley.

FAWCETT, JOSEPH W.　　　**2656**

JOURNAL OF JOS. W. FAWCETT (DIARY OF HIS TRIP DOWN THE OHIO AND MISSISSIPPI RIVERS TO THE GULF OF MEXICO AND UP THE ATLANTIC COAST TO BOSTON). Introduction by Eugene D. Rigney. Chillicothe, Ohio: David K. Webb, Private Press, 1944. 59 pp.

> Feb–Apr 1840. Travel diary of young man going to see the sights before he died of tuberculosis; vivid description of New Orleans, river steamer and sailing ship travel.

FROST, JOHN H., d. ca. 1863　　　**2657**

Pipes, Nellie B., ed. "Journal of John H. Frost." OREGON HISTORICAL QUARTERLY 35 (1934):50–73, 139–167, 235–262, 348–375.

> 1840–1843. Extracts from journal of Methodist missionary; notes on Fort Vancouver, life in a mission on the Clatsop plains; return to Boston via San Francisco and Oahu; partly narrative.

GARDINER, MARGARET, 1822–1857   2658

LEAVES FROM A YOUNG GIRL'S DIARY; THE JOURNAL OF MARGARET GARDINER. New Haven, Conn.: Tuttle, Morehouse and Taylor, 1925. 69 pp. 1927. 178 pp.

   May–Oct 1840. Nineteen-year-old girl's European travel diary, beginning in Venice and concluding in England; sightseeing, social life and weather in Italy, Switzerland, Germany, Netherlands, Belgium and England; notes on tourist attractions, accommodations, scraps of history; detailed, evaluative descriptions.

GREGG, JOSIAH, 1806–1850   2659

DIARY & LETTERS OF JOSIAH GREGG. Edited by Maurice G. Fulton. American Exploration and Travel, no. 7. Norman: University of Oklahoma Press, 1941–1944. 2 vols.

   1840–1850. Diary of trader on the Santa Fe Trail; trips into Texas; medical studies; service with Arkansas Volunteers and with Wool's column in Mexico; visits to Monterrey and Saltillo; a fine diary.

HALE, MARY A., 1824–1910   2660

"A Trip to the White Mountains in 1840." ESSEX INSTITUTE HISTORICAL COLLECTIONS 83 (1947):23–29.

   Aug 1840. Young woman's trip with her parents by carriage; description of various New Hampshire towns, a Shaker community; climbing Mount Lafayette.

HOBBS, THOMAS HUBBARD, 1826–1862   2661

THE JOURNAL OF THOMAS HUBBARD HOBBS: A CONTEMPORARY RECORD OF AN ARISTOCRAT FROM ATHENS, ALABAMA, WRITTEN BETWEEN 1840, WHEN THE DIARIST WAS FOURTEEN YEARS OLD, AND 1862, WHEN HE DIED SERVING THE CONFEDERATE STATES OF AMERICA. Edited by Faye A. Axford. University, Ala.: University of Alabama Press, 1976. 272 pp.

   1840–1862. Teen-age accounts of school, reading and church activities; La Grange College student pranks, studies, debates and patriotic celebrations; studies at Hoffman's Law Institution, Philadelphia, with expense accounts, books bought at auction; domestic life, religious reflections, public service as a legislator with special interests in education, agriculture and transportation; organization of and service with Company F of the Ninth Alabama Infantry until he died of injuries received at Gaines' Mill.

LAUGHLIN, SAMUEL H., b. 1796   2662

Sioussat, St. George L., ed. "Diaries of S.H. Laughlin, of Tennessee." TENNESSEE HISTORICAL MAGAZINE 2 (1916):43–55.

   Apr–May 1840. Diary of editor of NASHVILLE UNION; journey from McMinnville, Tennessee, to Washington and Baltimore as delegate to Democratic National Convention; interesting for travel details and politics of Andrew Jackson and James Knox Polk.

   Sep–Nov 1843. Political diary kept while author was member of Tennessee Senate and of "the immortal thirteen"; valuable, detailed account of procedure of legislators.

LORD, LOUISA   2663

MISS LOUISA LORD'S DIARY OF A VOYAGE ON THE SHIP ST. PETERSBURG. New York: Ivy Press, 1975. 49 pp.

   May–Sep 1840. A charming picture of life aboard ship for the captain's family in a fine new square rigger, as recorded by the long-time "female companion" of the captain's wife; ocean crossings to and from England; clothes, food, pastimes, storms; the work and deportment of the sailors observed from a genteel distance.

LOVELL, LUCY BUFFUM   2664

In TWO QUAKER SISTERS: FROM THE ORIGINAL DIARIES OF ELIZABETH BUFFUM CHACE AND LUCY BUFFUM LOVELL, with introduction by Malcolm R. Lovell, pp. 49–109. New York: Liveright, 1937.

   1840–1843. Domestic notes of the Quaker wife of a Baptist minister; births of children and their upbringing; pleasant reading.

LOWE, CHARLES, 1828–1874   2665

Extracts in MEMOIR OF CHARLES LOWE, by Martha Perry Lowe, pp. 5–514 passim. Boston: Cupples, Upham, 1884.

   1840–1872. Clergyman's diary; early studies at Harvard, general and religious reading in the divinity school; parish work in New Bedford, Massachusetts; Sunday School work; journey to Europe, Egypt and Near East; parish work in Boston; further travels in England and Europe; a journal of wide interests.

MARSTON, DAVID   2666

In HISTORY OF THE TOWN OF HAMPTON, NEW HAMPSHIRE, by Joseph Dow, pp. 579–580. Salem, Mass.: Printed by the Salem Press, 1893.

   1840–1879. Outstanding events, providences, weather, etc.

MORRISON, ANNA R., b. 1820   2667

Worthington, Miriam M., ed. "Diary of Anna R. Morrison, Wife of Isaac L. Morrison." ILLINOIS HISTORICAL JOURNAL 7 (1914):34–50.

   Nov 1840–Mar 1841. Journey from New York to Jacksonville, Illinois.

MOTT, LUCRETIA, 1793–1880   2668

SLAVERY AND "THE WOMAN QUESTION": LUCRETIA MOTT'S DIARY OF HER VISIT TO GREAT BRITAIN TO ATTEND THE WORLD'S ANTI-SLAVERY CONVENTION OF 1840. Edited by Frederick B. Tolles. Friends' Historical Society Journal, suppl. 23. Haverford, Pa.: Friends' Historical Association, 1952. 86 pp.

In JAMES AND LUCRETIA MOTT, edited by Anna Davis Hallowell, pp. 146–175. Boston and New York: Houghton, Mifflin, 1884.

   May–Sep 1840. Journey to England to attend the World's Anti-Slavery Convention at which Mott, Elizabeth Cady Stanton and other female delegates were denied seating; description of the convention; travel in England, Ireland and Scotland with impressions of typical tourist attractions; encounters with many people prominent in antislavery or woman suffrage organizations, as well as other religious, philanthropic and social causes; a lively, straightforward account.

PENNY, CHARLES W., 1812–1892   2669

NORTH TO LAKE SUPERIOR: THE JOURNAL OF CHARLES W. PENNY. Edited by James L. Carter and Ernest H.

Rankin. Marquette, Mich.: John M. Longyear Research Library, 1970. 84 pp.

May–Jul 1840. Exploration diary of merchant traveling with geologist Douglass Houghton in search of mineral resources along south shore of Lake Superior; people, terrain, prospects for copper mining along the old voyageur route from Madinac to LaPointe; pleasures and trials of life in the wilderness.

PHILIPS, MARTIN W., 1806–1889   **2670**

Riley, Franklin L., ed. "Diary of a Mississippi Planter." MISSISSIPPI HISTORICAL SOCIETY PUBLICATIONS 10 (1909):305–481.

1840–1863. Plantation diary; largely records of Log Hall cotton plantation; crops, planting, etc., with a few personal entries; interesting as a clear, factual record of a "progressive" Southern planter; little about the Civil War.

REATH, B.B.   **2671**

Bedford, George R., ed. "A Visit to Wilkes-Barre by a Young Philadelphian in the Year 1840." WYOMING HISTORICAL GEOLOGICAL SOCIETY PROCEEDINGS AND COLLECTIONS 15 (1917):157–172.

Aug 1840. Travel to Wilkes-Barre, Pennsylvania; conventional literary descriptions; notes on gallantries; a good picture of diarist.

STARIN, FREDERICK J.   **2672**

"Diary of a Journey to Wisconsin in 1840." WISCONSIN MAGAZINE OF HISTORY 6 (1922–1923):73–94, 207–232, 334–345.

1840–1841 (with a few entries in 1847). Journey from Montgomery County, New York, to Milwaukee, thence to East Troy, Whitewater, Madison, Fort Madison, etc.; valuable picture of early settlements in south and southeast Wisconsin.

STEELE, ELIZA R. STANSBURY   **2673**

A SUMMER JOURNEY IN THE WEST. New York: John S. Taylor, 1841. 278 pp.

Jun–Jul 1840. A diary, partly in letters, of a four thousand mile trip by stagecoach and steamboat from New York to the Great Lakes, Illinois, Mississippi, Ohio and Illinois rivers and over the Allegheny Mountains; extensive details of scenery, towns and tourist attractions, including Niagara Falls.

"A Lady Writer Reports Some Incidents of Steamboat Travel." In BEFORE MARK TWAIN: A SAMPLER OF OLD, OLD TIMES ON THE MISSISSIPPI, pp. 70–82. Carbondale: Southern Illinois University Press, 1968.

STICKNEY, ELIZABETH, 1781–1868   **2674**

Extracts in RECORDS OF A CALIFORNIA FAMILY; JOURNALS AND LETTERS OF LEWIS C. GUNN AND ELIZABETH LE BRETON GUNN, edited by Anna Lee Marston, pp. 10–11. San Diego, Calif., 1928.

1840–1842. Extracts from diary kept at Philadelphia; social life, reading, antislavery interests.

SUTHERLAND, JOHN, 1819–1886   **2675**

Lonn, Ella, ed. "Life and Journal of John Sutherland." MISSISSIPPI VALLEY HISTORICAL REVIEW 4 (1917–1918):362–370.

May 1840. Detailed extract from journal covering Whig gathering at Tippecanoe, Indiana; interesting spellings and word formations.

1841

ALLAN, GEORGE T.   **2676**

"Journal of a Voyage from Fort Vancouver, Columbia River, to York Factory, Hudson's Bay." OREGON PIONEER ASSOCIATION TRANSACTIONS OF THE 9TH ANNUAL REUNION (1881):38–55.

Mar–Jul 1841. Travel of Hudson's Bay Company employee from Fort Vancouver to York Factory, accompanying Ermatinger; narrative style.

"A Gallop through the Willamette." OREGON PIONEER ASSOCIATION TRANSACTIONS OF THE 9TH ANNUAL REUNION (1881):56–59.

Nov 1841. Brief account of horseback trip through the Willamette Valley.

BIDWELL, JOHN, 1819–1900   **2677**

A JOURNEY TO CALIFORNIA. Missouri, 1842. 32 pp. Reprint. A JOURNEY TO CALIFORNIA, WITH OBSERVATIONS ABOUT THE COUNTRY, CLIMATE AND THE ROUTE TO THIS COUNTRY. San Francisco: J.H. Nash, Printer, 1937. 43 pp.

In JOHN BIDWELL, PIONEER, STATESMAN, PHILANTHROPIST, by Charles C. Royce, pp. 8–37. Chico, Calif., 1906.

May–Nov 1841. Travel with Captain Bartleson's party from Independence, Missouri, to California; first emigrant train to California; descriptions of country, natural history, crops, weather, social conditions, incidents.

BRACKENRIDGE, WILLIAM DUNLOP, 1810–1893   **2678**

Sperlin, O.B., ed. "Our First Official Horticulturalist." WASHINGTON HISTORICAL QUARTERLY 21 (1930): 218–229, 298–305; 22 (1931):42–58, 129–145, 216–227.

Apr–Oct 1841. Scottish botanist's diary kept while assistant naturalist with Oregon-California portion of Wilkes Expedition; plants identified; descriptions of Mount Shasta and Sacramento Valley; visit at Sutter's settlement.

Maloney, Alice Bay. "A Botanist on the Road to Yerba Buena." CALIFORNIA HISTORICAL SOCIETY QUARTERLY 24 (1945):321–342. Diary, pp. 326–336.

Oct 1841.

BURRITT, ELIHU, 1810–1879   **2679**

ELIHU BURRITT: A MEMORIAL VOLUME CONTAINING A SKETCH OF HIS LIFE AND LABORS, WITH SELECTIONS FROM HIS WRITINGS AND LECTURES, AND EXTRACTS FROM HIS PRIVATE JOURNALS IN EUROPE AND AMERICA. Edited by Charles Northend. New York: D. Appleton, 1879. 479 pp. passim.

THE LEARNED BLACKSMITH; THE LETTERS AND JOURNALS OF ELIHU BURRITT. By Merle Curti. New York: Wilson-Erickson, 1937. Journal, pp. 11–138.

1841–1858. Extracts from the diaries of an educated blacksmith and reformer; reading and languages; crusades for world peace and penny postage in America and Europe; work in antislavery movement.

DALL, CAROLINE WELLS HEALY, d. 1912   **2680**

Myerson, Joel, ed. "Caroline Dall's Reminiscences of Margaret Fuller." HARVARD LIBRARY BULLETIN 22

(1974):414-428.

Mar-May 1841. A memoir written in 1895 which contains quotations from her own diary of 1841 when she was nineteen and first knew Margaret Fuller; notes on Fuller's lectures, conversation and appearance; reactions of other people to Fuller and her ideas; hints of diarist's own emancipated views. Isolated notes from 1851 (Bronson Alcott's lecture about Margaret Fuller), 1865 and 1877.

EMMONS, GEORGE FOSTER, 1811-1884　　　　**2681**

THE EMMONS JOURNAL. Eugene, Ore.: Koke-Tiffany Co., n.d. 11 pp.

"Extracts from the Emmons Journal." OREGON HISTORICAL QUARTERLY 26 (1925):263-273.

Jul-Aug 1841. Naval exploration journal of a lieutenant with the Wilkes Expedition; overland trip to San Francisco after wreck of the PEACOCK at the mouth of the Columbia; stay at Fort Vancouver with Dr. McLoughlin to provision for the trip.

EWING, THOMAS, 1789-1871　　　　**2682**

"Diary of Thomas Ewing." AMERICAN HISTORICAL REVIEW 18 (1912-1913):97-112.

Aug-Sep 1841. Extract from diary of President Tyler's secretary of the treasury; account of breach between Tyler and his cabinet.

FALCONER, THOMAS, 1805-1882　　　　**2683**

LETTERS AND NOTES ON THE TEXAN SANTA FE EXPEDITION. Introduction and notes by Frederick W. Hodge. New York: Dauber & Pine Bookshops, 1930. Diary, app., pp. 105-118.

Aug-Oct 1841. Travel diary of English judge; account of what befell the main party of Texans left behind when Cooke set out in search of the New Mexico settlements; long, interesting entries. The diary supplements his "narrative" of the expedition.

GLEASON, JAMES HENRY　　　　**2684**

Gleason, Duncan. "James Henry Gleason: Pioneer Journal and Letters." HISTORICAL SOCIETY OF SOUTHERN CALIFORNIA QUARTERLY 31 (1949):9-52. Journal, pp. 11-16.

Aug-Dec 1841. Young Bostonian's voyage to Hawaii via Cape Horn aboard the CALIFORNIA. From 1841-1856, letters to his sister, written from Hawaii.

HAYES, RUTHERFORD BIRCHARD, 1822-1893　　　　**2685**

DIARY AND LETTERS OF RUTHERFORD BIRCHARD HAYES, NINETEENTH PRESIDENT OF THE UNITED STATES. Edited by Charles R. Williams. Ohio State Archaeological and Historical Society. Hayes Series, vols. 3-7. Columbus: Ohio State Archaeological and Historical Society, 1922-1926. 5 vols. Reprint. New York: Kraus, 1972.

1841-1893. Private and political diary, begun at Kenyon College and continued until his death; study at Kenyon, Columbus and Harvard Law School; law practice at Sandusky; work in Cincinnati; service in Civil War; governorship of Ohio; presidency; an extensive and valuable record of public life with a good deal of private and general matter.

HAYES: THE DIARY OF A PRESIDENT 1875-1881, COVERING THE DISPUTED ELECTION, THE END OF RECONSTRUCTION, AND THE BEGINNING OF CIVIL SERVICE. Edited by Thomas Harry Williams. New York: D. McKay, 1964. 329 pp.

1875-1881.

JOHNSON, DANIEL NOBLE, 1822-1863　　　　**2686**

THE JOURNALS OF DANIEL NOBLE JOHNSON, UNITED STATES NAVY. Edited by Mendel L. Peterson. Smithsonian Miscellaneous Collections, vol. 136, no. 2. Washington, D.C.: Smithsonian Institution, 1959. 268 pp.

1841-1844. Young Navy clerk's highly descriptive diary of life on board sailing ships DELAWARE and ENTERPRISE and experiences in South American ports; deaths and burials at sea, flogging of sailors, calms and storms, routines of naval seamanship; humorous vignettes of officers and sailors; notes on ports of Buenos Aires and Rio de Janeiro; customs, homes, food, prominent people, appalling condition of slaves.

KEENE, JOHN FITHIAN, 1816-1895　　　　**2687**

"Diary of John Fithian Keene." VINELAND HISTORICAL MAGAZINE 34 (1949):46-51.

Jun-Dec 1841. Diary kept in and near Greenwich, New Jersey, dealing mainly with weather, local and family matters.

LYELL, Sir CHARLES, 1797-1875　　　　**2688**

TRAVELS IN NORTH AMERICA: WITH GEOLOGICAL OBSERVATIONS ON THE UNITED STATES, CANADA, AND NOVA SCOTIA. London: J. Murray, 1845. 2 vols. 2d ed. London: J. Murray, 1855.

TRAVELS IN NORTH AMERICA IN THE YEARS 1841-2. New York: Wiley and Putnam, 1845. 2 vols. in 1. Reprint. J. Wiley, 1852; Wiley & Halsted, 1856.

LYELL'S TRAVELS IN NORTH AMERICA IN THE YEARS 1841-2. Abridged and edited by John P. Cushing. New York: C.E. Merrill, 1909. 172 pp.

1841-1842. Englishman's diary of travel in New England and Canada; geological and topographical observations; notes on society and customs, meetings with prominent Americans, etc.

A SECOND VISIT TO THE UNITED STATES OF NORTH AMERICA. New York: Harper & Brothers; London: J. Murray, 1849. 2 vols. 3d ed. London: J. Murray, 1855.

Sep 1845-Jun 1846. Atlantic crossing from Liverpool to Halifax; travel in New England, down Atlantic coast to Louisiana, up the Mississippi; geological and social notes.

MARTIN, JOHN F., b. ca. 1819　　　　**2689**

"There She Blows!" CHICAGO HISTORY 3 (1951):21-27.

1841-1844. Extracts from harpooner's diary kept on board the LUCY ANN of Wilmington, Delaware; excellent description of taking a whale; work and amusements of whalers, including outrageous yarns; a gift of cockroaches to whaleship FLORENCE to control bedbugs.

Martin, Kenneth R. and Sinclair, Bruce. "A Pennsylvanian in the Wilmington Whaling Trade." PENNSYLVANIA HISTORY 41 (1974):27-52.

1841-1844. Substantial extracts within an article summarizing a whaling voyage around the world; details of life on ship; food, pranks, death; the hazards of whaling.

MEYERS, WILLIAM H., b. 1815   2690

JOURNAL OF A CRUISE TO CALIFORNIA AND THE SAND-WICH ISLANDS IN THE UNITED STATES SLOOP-OF-WAR CYANE. Edited by John H. Kemble. San Francisco: Book Club of California, 1955. 68 pp.

> 1841-1844. Journal of gunner on CYANE while cruis-ing with the Pacific Squadron; daily routine, special events on board or during port visits, mainly in Hawaii and California; reported with humor.

PARKMAN, FRANCIS, 1823-1893   2691

THE JOURNALS OF FRANCIS PARKMAN. Edited by Mason Wade. New York: Harper, 1947. 2 vols. Reprint. New York: Kraus, 1969.

> 1841-1885. Travel journals, part personal and part working notes of the renowned New England historian; youthful camping trips to trace invasion route of French and Indian wars and to do research on Ottawa chief Pontiac; "Grand Tour" of Europe; harrowing ocean crossing on the NAUTILUS; interest in Catholic countries and institutions; his most famous adventure, the trip across Oregon Trail, which became basis of his best-known book, but cost him his health; detailed notes on Indians, landscape, fellow travelers, conditions of travel; later journals covering Acadian areas of Canada, Lake George, Ticonderoga, Quebec, the Carolinas and Florida; excellent descriptions and dialogues throughout, as well as revelation of the diarist.

PRICHARD, JOHN LAMB, 1811-1862   2692

Extracts in MEMOIR OF REV. JOHN L. PRICHARD, LATE PASTOR OF THE FIRST BAPTIST CHURCH, WILMINGTON, N.C., by James D. Hufham, pp. 32-133 passim. Ra-leigh, N.C.: Hufman & Hughes, 1867.

> 1841-1861. Journal of Baptist minister; meetings, preaching, visits, travels, sermons, weather, reading, some political notes.

SWAN, LANSING B., 1809-1861   2693

JOURNAL OF A TRIP TO MICHIGAN IN 1841. Rochester, N.Y., 1904. 53 pp.

> Jun 1841. Trip from Rochester, New York, to Michi-gan by stagecoach, steamer and railroad; lively, full descriptions of towns, countryside, hardships of travel, etc.

TOMLINSON, RUFFIN WIRT, 1817-1844   2694

Sanders, John L., ed. "The Journal of Ruffin Wirt Tomlinson: The University of North Carolina." NORTH CAROLINA HISTORICAL REVIEW 30 (1953):86-114, 233-260.

> 1841-1842. University senior's detailed account of student life; curriculum, romances, activities of literary society, pranks, opinions of teachers and fellow students, etc.; interesting and engaging document.

VAN LENNEP, MARY ELIZABETH HAWES, 1821-1844   2695

Extracts in MEMOIR OF MRS. MARY E. VAN LENNEP, ONLY DAUGHTER OF THE REV. JOEL HAWES, by Louisa F. Hawes, pp. 84-320 passim. Hartford: Belknap & Hammersley, 1847. 5th ed. 1849.

> 1841-1844. Journal of missionary to Turkey; religi-ous reflections, emotions, weather; some notes on domestic and local affairs in Hartford, Connecticut; sickness, preparation for missionary career, mar-riage, voyage to Turkey and missionary work there.

WILKES, CHARLES, 1798-1877   2696

Meany, Edmond S., ed. "Diary of Wilkes in the North-west." WASHINGTON HISTORICAL QUARTERLY 16 (1925): 49-61, 137-145, 206-223, 290-301; 17 (1926):43-65, 129-144, 223-229.

> May-Aug 1841. Naval exploration diary which became the basis of his five-volume NARRATIVE OF THE UNITED STATES EXPLORING EXPEDITION; entry of the Strait of Juan de Fuca and explorations in the Northwest; very good descriptions of places and Indians.

WILLIAMS, JOSEPH, b. 1777   2697

NARRATIVE OF A TOUR FROM THE STATE OF INDIANA TO THE OREGON TERRITORY. Cincinnati: Printed for the author, 1843. Reprint. In TO THE ROCKIES AND OREGON, edited by LeRoy R. Hafen and Ann W. Hafen, pp. 199-287.

NARRATIVE OF A TOUR FROM THE STATE OF INDIANA TO THE OREGON TERRITORY. Introduction by James C. Bell, Jr. New York: Cadmus Book Shop, 1921. 95 pp. Reprint. Fairfield, Wash.: Ye Galleon Press, 1977. 62 pp.

> 1841-1842. Journey from Ripley County, Indiana, to Oregon Territory with an early wagon train, then from Oregon to the Southwest; accidents and incidents, especially of a sordid kind; notes on Indians and settlers, scenery, natural history, estimates of farming possibilities.

1842

ANON.   2698

JOURNAL OF A CRUISE TO THE PACIFIC OCEAN, 1842-1844, IN THE FRIGATE UNITED STATES, WITH NOTES ON HERMAN MELVILLE. Edited by Charles R. Anderson, watercolors from the Journal of William H. Meyers. Durham, N.C.: Duke University Press, 1937. 143 pp. Journal, pp. 21-67. Reprint. New York: AMS Press, 1966.

> 1842-1844. Clerk's journal of a cruise in the Pacific; routine descriptions of voyage; notes on South America, Mexico, Hawaii; important because Herman Melville was also on this cruise.

BOLDUC, JEAN BAPTISTE ZACHARIE, 1818-1889   2699

MISSION OF THE COLUMBIA. Edited and translated by Edward J. Kowrach. Fairfield, Wash.: Ye Galleon Press, 1979. 147 pp.

> 1842-1844. Journal of scholarly Catholic priest sent from Quebec to Cowlitz River Mission near the Columbia; life at sea during voyage from Boston around South America; manners and customs of Hawaiians; arrival at Vancouver, Washington, with trip up the Cowlitz to the mission; missionary trip in 1844 to Whidbey and Vancouver islands; eruption of Mount St. Helens, March, 1843.

BOLLAERT, WILLIAM, 1807-1876   2700

WILLIAM BOLLAERT'S TEXAS. Edited by W. Eugene Hollon and Ruth Lapham Butler. Norman: University of Oklahoma Press, 1956. 423 pp.

1842–1844. Young English adventurer's travels throughout the Republic of Texas, perhaps to speculate in land and to encourage English settlement; comments on scenes, people, business, politics, skirmishes with Santa Anna; an important and interesting picture of turbulent life in Texas just before annexation.

BROWNE, JOHN ROSS, 1821–1875   2701

J. ROSS BROWNE: HIS LETTERS, JOURNALS AND WRITINGS. Edited by Lina Fergusson Browne. Albuquerque: University of New Mexico Press, 1969. 419 pp. Journal extracts, pp. 3–41.

1842–1843. Private journal of an inveterate traveler and writer; account of his service on a whaler to the Indian Ocean, upon which he based ETCHINGS OF A WHALING CRUISE, said to have influenced Melville's MOBY DICK; few details of whaling itself, but much of author's disillusionment with his adventure.

CANFIELD, ISRAEL, 1808–1850   2702

Day, James M., ed. "Israel Canfield on the Mier Expedition." TEXAS MILITARY HISTORY 3 (1963):165–199.

1842–1844. Capture of Ewen Cameron's company and forced march into Mexico; treatment of Texas prisoners by Mexicans, with many deaths en route and at Perote Prison; the infamous "bean lottery" and resulting executions; diarist's eventual release; full descriptions, reactions and opinions.

CHASE, SAMUEL WORCESTER, b. 1811   2703

Extracts in SHIPBUILDING DAYS IN CASCO BAY, 1727–1890; BEING FOOTNOTES TO THE HISTORY OF MAINE, by William H. Rowe, pp. 172–186. Yarmouth, Maine, 1929.

1842–1845. Whaling journal kept by first mate of the ARAB; whale hunt, hardships, places visited, etc.; interesting account.

CRAWFORD, MEDOREM, 1819–1891   2704

"Journal of Medorem Crawford." OREGON HISTORICAL SOCIETY PUBLICATIONS 1, pt. 1 (1897):5–28. Reprint. Fairfield, Wash.: Ye Galleon Press, 1967. 26 pp.

Mar–Oct 1842. Overland journey from New York to Oregon via St. Louis, with Elijah White's party; mainly statistical.

FREMONT, JOHN CHARLES, 1813–1890   2705

REPORT OF THE EXPLORING EXPEDITION TO THE ROCKY MOUNTAINS IN THE YEAR 1842 AND TO OREGON AND NORTH CALIFORNIA IN THE YEARS 1843-'44. United States. 28th Congress. 2d Session. Senate. Executive Document 174. Washington, D.C.: Gales and Seaton, 1845. 294 pp. Frequently reprinted as NARRATIVE OF THE EXPLORING EXPEDITION TO THE ROCKY MOUNTAINS IN THE YEAR 1842 AND TO OREGON AND NORTH CALIFORNIA IN THE YEARS 1843-'44.

MEMOIRS OF MY LIFE, INCLUDING THE NARRATIVE FIVE JOURNEYS OF WESTERN EXPLORATION, DURING THE YEARS 1842, 1843-4, 1845-6-7, 1853-4. Chicago: Belford, Clarke, 1887. Journal, vol. 1.

NARRATIVE OF EXPLORATION AND ADVENTURE. Edited by Allan Nevins. New York: Longman, Green, 1956. 532 pp.

THE EXPEDITIONS OF JOHN CHARLES FREMONT. Edited by Donald Jackson and Mary Lee Spence. Urbana:

University of Illinois Press, 1970. 2 vols. Journal, vol. 1.

1842–1844. Journal of first hazardous exploration and report of country along Kansas River from St. Louis to Fort Laramie, through Wyoming following North Platte River to Sweetwater and through South Pass; second expedition from Salt Lake to Fort Vancouver, Klamath Falls, Sutter's Fort and return to Utah Lake.

GLASSCOCK, JAMES A., 1816–1876   2706

Day, James M., ed. "Diary of James A. Glasscock, Mier Man." TEXANA 1 (1963):85–119, 225–238.

1842–1844. Account by a member of ill-fated Mier Expedition; capture by Mexicans, march through Mexico, escape and recapture, executions of men selected by "bean lottery"; life in Perote Prison; rations, deaths, tasks, rumors, treatment, entertainment, hopes for release, etc.

GULICK, JOHN THOMAS, 1832–1923   2707

EVOLUTIONIST AND MISSIONARY, JOHN THOMAS GULICK, PORTRAYED THROUGH DOCUMENTS AND DISCUSSIONS. By Addison Gulick. Chicago: University of Chicago Press, 1932. 555 pp. passim.

1842–1912. Biography which quotes generously from journals of distinguished missionary, biologist and religious thinker; mission boyhood in Hawaii, travels in Oregon and gold rush California, studies at Williams College and Union Theological Seminary; missionary work in Japan and China under American Board of Commissioners for Foreign Missions; favorable reaction to Darwin's theories and pursuit of his own evolutionary studies.

HUTCHINSON, ANDERSON, 1798–1853   2708

Winkler, E.W., ed. "The Bexar and Dawson Prisoners." TEXAS HISTORICAL ASSOCIATION QUARTERLY 13 (1909–1910):292–324.

Sep 1842–Jun 1843. Prison diary; capture by Mexican forces at Bexar, travel to Mexico and imprisonment at Perote Prison; return by boat to United States; brief factual entries.

JONES, HENRY BOSWELL, 1797–1882   2709

THE DIARY OF HENRY BOSWELL JONES OF BROWNSBURG. Edited by Charles W. Turner. Verona, Va.: McClure Press, 1979. 126 pp.

1842–1871. Plantation diary; farming, social and family life at Whitehall Plantation near Brownsburg, Rockbridge County, Virginia; management of farm, planting, experimenting with deep plowing and lime, harvesting, threshing, milling, expenses, building and maintaining road; record of sabbath school, preaching and other Presbyterian activities; family affairs, health, visiting; interest in and support for school and education; a good picture of plantation life.

KOHN, ABRAHAM, 1819–1871   2710

Vossen, Abram. "A Jewish Peddler's Diary." AMERICAN JEWISH ARCHIVES 3 (June 1951):81–111.

In MEMOIRS OF AMERICAN JEWS, 1775–1865, by Jacob R. Marcus, vol. 2, pp. 1–20. New York: KTAV Publishing House, 1974.

1842–1843. Young Jewish immigrant's diary; sad farewells to family; journey on foot across Germany; from Bremen to New York as steerage passenger on board ATLANTA; work as itinerant peddler in New England, with long soliloquy on the sorry lot of immigrant peddlers; comments on towns and inhabitants; great faith in God and efforts to keep Jewish observances; an articulate and interesting diary.

M'COY, JOHN, 1782–1859   2711

In JOHN M'COY, HIS LIFE AND HIS DIARIES, by Elizabeth Hayward, pp. 143–463. New York: American Historical Co., 1948.

1842–1859. Personal diary, kept late in life, of a dedicated Baptist layman and founder of Indiana Baptist Convention, Indiana Bible Society, Franklin College and other institutions; managing as a widower, daily activities, visiting children, attending church services, illness, reflections on old age.

MCCUTCHAN, JOSEPH D., 1823–1853   2712

THE MIER EXPEDITION DIARY: A TEXAS PRISONER'S ACCOUNT. Edited by Joseph M. Nancy. The Elma Dill Russell Spencer Foundation Series, no. 8. Austin: University of Texas Press, 1978. 246 pp.

1842. A nineteen-year-old soldier's account of the unauthorized invasion of Mexico; defeat by Mexicans; forced march and imprisonment in Mexico; return home.

PREBLE, GEORGE HENRY, 1816–1885   2713

"Diary of a Canoe Expedition into the Everglades and Interior of Southern Florida in 1842." UNITED SERVICE 8 (April 1883):358–376.

Feb–Apr 1842. Account of canoe expedition across the Everglades, around Lake Okeechobee and up and down the connecting rivers and lakes; stages, topography, natural history, some personal adventures and comments.

PREUSS, CHARLES, 1803–1854   2714

EXPLORING WITH FREMONT; THE PRIVATE DIARIES OF CHARLES PREUSS, CARTOGRAPHER FOR JOHN C. FREMONT. Translated and edited by Erwin B. and Elisabeth K. Gudde. American Exploration and Travel Series, 26. Norman: University of Oklahoma Press, 1958. 162 pp.

1842–1843, 1848. Private diaries of German-born cartographer and artist for Fremont on his first, second and fourth expeditions; methodical attention to assigned tasks; notes on Kit Carson; comments on Indians; complaints about hardships, about Fremont and other colleagues; a spontaneous and unguarded diary of considerable geographical and historical importance, especially for light it sheds on Fremont's disastrous fourth expedition.

SCOTT, JAMES LEANDER   2715

A JOURNAL OF A MISSIONARY TOUR THROUGH PENNSYLVANIA, OHIO, INDIANA, ILLINOIS, IOWA, WISCONSIN AND MICHIGAN. Providence: The author, 1843. 203 pp. Reprint. Ann Arbor, Mich.: University Microfilms, 1966.

Jan–Jul 1842. Journal of Seventh-Day Baptist missionary; travels throughout Pennsylvania and much of the Midwest; zeal to combat Roman Catholicism brought by emigrants from Ireland and southern Germany; descriptions of scenery, climate, immigration prospects, religious conditions; poetical quotations.

SMITH, ELIZA ROXEY SNOW, 1804–1887   2716

Ursenbach, Maureen, ed. "Eliza R. Snow's Nauvoo Journal." BRIGHAM YOUNG UNIVERSITY STUDIES 15 (1975):391–416.

1842–1844. Diary kept at Nauvoo, Illinois, by prominent Mormon poet, plural wife of Joseph Smith; interaction with family and friends; persecution of Joseph Smith; many of her poems.

"Pioneer Diary of Eliza R. Snow." IMPROVEMENT ERA 46 (1943):142–143, 186–191, 208–209, 251–253, 272–273, 316–317, 334–335, 356–357, 398, 434–435, 466–467, 506–507, 509, 533, 571, 573, 598–599, 626, 664, 754–755, 783; 47 (1944):24–25, 55, 88–89, 113–114, 116, 152–153, 184–185, 218, 239–241.

1846–1849. Diary kept by widow of Joseph Smith and wife of Brigham Young; Mormon migration from Nauvoo to Salt Lake; incidents on the trail, group organization and governance; life in camp and at Winter Quarters; Indian encounters; settling in the Salt Lake valley; poems and hymns of diarist.

SPOFFORD, PAUL NELSON   2717

Moore, Samuel T., ed. "Journal of Paul Nelson Spofford." MICHIGAN HISTORY 29 (1945):327–334.

Aug–Sep 1842. Very brief extracts of New York merchant's trip to western New York, Chicago and Detroit.

Jun–Aug 1848. Another trip to Michigan; brief notes on agriculture, terrain, people he met, including Henry L. Ellsworth and Louis Agassiz.

TRUEHEART, JAMES L., 1815–1882   2718

THE PEROTE PRISONERS, BEING THE DIARY OF JAMES L. TRUEHEART. Introduction by Frederick C. Chabot. San Antonio: Naylor, 1934. 344 pp.

1842–1844. Prison diary; capture by Mexicans at Bexar; journey through Mexico and imprisonment at Perote; notes of hardships, general descriptions, lively characterizations and shrewd observations; highly interesting.

WALKER, SAMUEL HAMILTON   2719

SAMUEL H. WALKER'S ACCOUNT OF THE MIER EXPEDITION. Edited by Marilyn M. Sibley. Austin: Texas State Historical Association, 1978. 110 pp.

May–Sep 1842. Account of unauthorized Texas expedition against the town of Mier in Mexico; defeat and capture of Texans; forced march involving much suffering; escapes and recaptures; eventual execution of one-tenth of Texans; diarist's escape.

ZAGOSKIN, LAVRENTII ALEKSEEVICH, 1808–1890   2720

LIEUTENANT ZAGOSKIN'S TRAVELS IN RUSSIAN AMERICA, 1842–1844; THE FIRST ETHNOGRAPHIC AND GEOGRAPHIC INVESTIGATIONS IN THE YUKON AND KUSKOKWIM VALLEYS OF ALASKA. Edited by Henry N. Michael. Arctic Institute of North America, Anthropology of the North: Translations from Russian Sources, no. 7. Toronto: Published for the Arctic Institute of North America by University of Toronto Press, 1967. 358 pp.

1842–1844. Russian explorations into interior of Alaska for information valuable to fur trade; travel by dog sled and canoe; geographic discoveries and ethnographic contributions; notes on trading, festivals, customs of inhabitants as related through an interpreter.

1843

ALCOTT, ANNA BRONSON, b. 1831　　2721

In BRONSON ALCOTT'S FRUITLANDS, compiled by Clara E. Sears, pp. 86–105. Boston: Houghton Mifflin, 1915. Reprint. Philadelphia: Porcupine Press, 1975.

Jun–Sep 1843. Brief childhood diary of Louisa May Alcott's sister and Bronson Alcott's daughter, kept at Fruitlands, Alcott's short-lived cooperative vegetarian community.

ALCOTT, LOUISA MAY, 1832–1888　　2722

LOUISA MAY ALCOTT, HER LIFE, LETTERS, AND JOURNALS. Edited by Ednah D. Cheney. Boston: Roberts Brothers, 1889. 404 pp. passim. Reprint. Boston: Little, Brown, 1900; 1928.

1843–1886 (copious extracts, with gaps). Early diary kept at Fruitlands; family life, chores, lessons, evidence of the atmosphere of Fruitlands and philosophy of Bronson Alcott; reading, school, personal, domestic and social affairs in and around Boston and Concord; many notes on her writing and literary friendships.

Extracts in BRONSON ALCOTT'S FRUITLANDS, compiled by Clara E. Sears, pp. 106–113. Boston: Houghton Mifflin, 1915. Reprint. Philadelphia: Porcupine Press, 1975.

Extracts in SMALL VOICES, by Josef and Dorothy Berger, pp. 108–110.

TRANSCENDENTAL WILD OATS AND EXCERPTS FROM THE FRUITLANDS DIARY. Introduction by William H. Harrison. Harvard, Mass.: Harvard Common Press, 1975? 43 pp.

1843.

BOARDMAN, JOHN, 1824–1883　　2723

"The Journal of John Boardman: An Overland Journey from Kansas to Oregon in 1843." UTAH HISTORICAL QUARTERLY 2 (1929):99–121.

May–Nov 1843. Travel from Shawnee Mission, Kansas, to Oregon, via Laramie, Fort Hall, Fort Boise, Vancouver; brief matter-of-fact notes on the route, Indians, missionaries, scenery, buffalo.

BOONE, NATHAN, 1782–1857　　2724

In MARCHES OF THE DRAGOONS IN THE MISSISSIPPI VALLEY, by Louis Pelzer, pp. 189–237. Iowa City: State Historical Society of Iowa, 1917.

Fessler, W. Julian, ed. "Captain Nathan Boone's Journal." CHRONICLES OF OKLAHOMA 7 (1929):58–105.

May–Jul 1843. Account kept by Daniel Boone's son of dragoon expedition from Fort Gibson over the southwestern prairies; notes on Indians, buffalo hunting, preparation of buffalo meat; historical and topographical items.

BRIDGE, HORATIO, 1806–1893　　2725

JOURNAL OF AN AFRICAN CRUISER. Edited by Nathaniel Hawthorne. New York and London: Wiley and Putnam, 1845. 179 pp. Reprint. New York: G.P. Putnam, 1853; London: Dawsons; Detroit: Negro History Press, 1968.

1843–1844. United States Navy officer's journal of travel to Africa; notes on the Canary Islands, Liberia, Sierra Leone, etc., along the west coast; observations of African customs, colonization, slave vessels and slave trade.

BURNETT, PETER H.　　2726

In A HISTORY OF OREGON, GEOGRAPHICAL AND POLITICAL, by George Wilkes, pp. 63–113. New York: W.H. Colyer, 1845.

May–Nov 1843. Overland trip from Independence, Missouri, to the mouth of the Columbia; stops en route at Whitman Mission and with Dr. John McLoughlin at Fort Vancouver.

COOKE, PHILIP ST. GEORGE, 1809–1895　　2727

Connelley, William E., ed. "A Journal of the Santa Fe Trail." MISSISSIPPI VALLEY HISTORICAL REVIEW 12 (1925–1926):72–98, 227–255.

May–Jul 1843. Official military journal; record kept by colonel with a detachment of United States Dragoons assigned to protect traders on the Santa Fe Trail; patrolling from Missouri to the Mexican border.

In EXPLORING SOUTHWESTERN TRAILS, 1846–1854, edited by R.P. Bieber, pp. 65–240. Glendale, Calif.: Arthur H. Clark, 1938.

Oct 1846–Jan 1847. March from Santa Fe to San Diego in command of the Mormon Battalion.

CROCKER, ALVAH, 1801–1874　　2728

Extracts in LIFE AND TIMES OF ALVAH CROCKER, by William B. Wheelwright, pp. 29–36. Boston: Privately printed, 1923.

1843–1845. Brief reports of activities connected with Fitchburg, Massachusetts, and with Vermont and Massachusetts railroads; travels and surveys; religious notes.

ELDREDGE, JOSEPH C.　　2729

"Eldredge's Report on His Expedition to the Comanches." WEST TEXAS HISTORICAL ASSOCIATION YEAR BOOK 4 (1928):114–139.

May–Aug 1843. Report to Sam Houston by the general superintendent of Indian affairs for the Republic of Texas; meeting with Comanches to form friendly relations for government of Texas.

FIELDING, JOSEPH, b. 1797　　2730

Ehat, Andrew F., ed. "'They Might Have Known That He Was Not a Fallen Prophet': The Nauvoo Journal of Joseph Fielding." BRIGHAM YOUNG UNIVERSITY STUDIES 19 (1979):133–166.

1843–1846. Account of the Mormons' struggles at Nauvoo, Illinois, by one of the early leaders of the church; building of the temple at Nauvoo, persecution of Mormons, martyrdom of Joseph Smith, tensions within the church; a valuable contemporary account of the Mormons under the leadership of Joseph and Hyrum Smith, Fielding's brother-in-law.

GREEN, THOMAS JEFFERSON, 1801–1863　　2731

JOURNAL OF THE TEXIAN EXPEDITION AGAINST MIER. New York: Harper & Brothers, 1845. 487 pp. Reprint. Austin, Tex.: Steck Co., 1935. Journal, pp. 112–235.

Jan–Mar 1843. Officer's narrative of ill-fated Mier Expedition; prisoners' march to Matamoros and on to Perote Prison near Mexico City; events along the way, treatment by Mexican captors; encounters with runaway slaves from Texas.

HADLEY, JAMES, 1821–1872   2732

DIARY (1843–1852) OF JAMES HADLEY, TUTOR AND PRO-
FESSOR OF GREEK IN YALE COLLEGE, 1845–1872. Edited
by Laura H. Moseley. New Haven: Yale University
Press, 1951. 334 pp.

    1843–1852. Professor's diary, begun while "resident
graduate" in mathematics and private tutor at Yale
and continued while assistant professor of Greek
language and literature; daily routines of class
preparation, academic affairs, examinations, correspondence and callers; religious reflections,
local events, people and weather, books purchased.

HARRIS, EDWARD, 1799–1863   2733

UP THE MISSOURI WITH AUDUBON: THE JOURNAL OF
EDWARD HARRIS. Edited by John F. McDermott. Ameri-
can Exploration and Travel, 15. Norman: University of
Oklahoma Press, 1951. 222 pp.

    Mar–Dec 1843. Amateur naturalist's journal; notes
of Audubon patron, a gentleman farmer from New
Jersey, who accompanied Audubon up the Missouri
on the OMEGA to Fort Clark; informed descriptions
of birds and animals observed or caught; notes on
hunting, fur trade activities and life around the
fort, Indians and buffalo hunts.

HECKER, ISAAC THOMAS, 1819–1888   2734

In THE LIFE OF FATHER HECKER, by Walter Elliott,
pp. 61–193 passim. New York: Columbus Press, 1891.
2d ed. Introduced by John Ireland. New York: Columbus Press, 1894. 4th ed., 1898.

    1843–1845. Diary of a young man later to become
Catholic priest and missionary; early part kept at
Brook Farm and Fruitlands; religious interests,
spiritual disquiet and struggles; life in Concord;
notes on the various influences on his religious
life.

Extract in BRONSON ALCOTT'S FRUITLANDS, compiled by
Clara E. Sears, pp. 75–85. Boston: Houghton Mifflin,
1915.

    Jul–Aug 1843. Diarist's religious quest at Fruit-
lands; mainly his reactions to Bronson Alcott's
teaching and philosophy.

JACKSON, REBECCA COX, 1795–1871   2735

GIFTS OF POWER: THE WRITINGS OF REBECCA JACKSON,
BLACK VISIONARY, SHAKER ELDRESS. Edited by Jean M.
Humez. Amherst: University of Massachusetts Press,
1981. 368 pp.

    1843–1864. Autobiography and journal of black
Shaker eldress and mystic in Pennsylvania; from
1830–1843, autobiographical narrative probably
based on journal notes; from 1843–1864, specifically
dated passages containing descriptions of visions.

JOHNSON, OVERTON   2736

ROUTE ACROSS THE ROCKY MOUNTAINS. By Overton
Johnson and William H. Winter. Lafayette, Ind.: J.B.
Semans, Printer, 1846. 152 pp. Reprint. Preface and
notes by Carl L. Cannon. Princeton, N.J.: Princeton
University Press, 1932.

"Route across the Rocky Mountains with a Description
of Oregon and California." OREGON HISTORICAL QUAR-
TERLY 7 (1906):62–104, 163–210, 291–327.

    1843–1845. Conventional travel book written up from
notes; people, places, customs, sights.

LAWRENCE, AMOS ADAMS, 1814–1886   2737

In LIFE OF AMOS A. LAWRENCE, WITH EXTRACTS FROM
HIS DIARY AND CORRESPONDENCE, by William Lawrence,
pp. 50–273 passim. Boston and New York: Houghton,
Mifflin, 1888.

    1843–1883. Business diary; scattered extracts cover-
ing business life in Boston, work as treasurer of
Harvard, news of war, personal affairs.

MACREADY, WILLIAM CHARLES, 1793–1873   2738

THE DIARIES OF WILLIAM CHARLES MACREADY, 1833–
1851. Edited by William Toynbee. London: Chapman
and Hall, 1912. 2 vols. Reprint. New York: B. Blom,
1969. American diaries, vol. 2, pp. 222–276.

THE JOURNAL OF WILLIAM CHARLES MACREADY, 1832–
1851. Abridged and edited by J.C. Trewin. London:
Longmans, 1967. 315 pp. American journal, pp. 203–
219. Reprint. Carbondale: Southern Illinois University
Press, 1970.

    1843–1844. English actor's travel diary of rehears-
als, performances and theatrical matters while
playing in New York, Boston, Charleston, Mobile
and New Orleans; criticism of American actors.

MALLORY, JAMES, 1807–1877   2739

Stewart, Edgar A., ed. "The Journal of James Mal-
lory." ALABAMA REVIEW 14 (1961):219–232.

    1843–1877. Extracts from personal journal of Ala-
bama planter; benefits of antebellum railroad
development; stresses of Civil War and Reconstruction; the renewal of Atlanta; various Fourth of
July celebrations over a thirty year period; comments on the nature of Negroes; evidence of the
author's growing alienation.

MAXWELL, JAMES DARWIN, 1815–1892   2740

Reed, Doris M., ed. "Journal of James Darwin Maxwell." INDIANA MAGAZINE OF HISTORY 46 (1950):73–81.

    Oct–Nov 1843. Account of young man's trip from
Bloomington, Indiana, by way of Niagara Falls
and New York City to Philadelphia where he was to
study at Jefferson Medical College; travel by canal
boat, railroad and steamer; impressions of eastern
sights and inhabitants; some information on
medical education of the period.

NESMITH, JAMES W., b. 1820   2741

"Diary of the Emigration of 1843." OREGON HISTORICAL
QUARTERLY 7 (1906):329–359.

    May–Oct 1843. Overland journey from Independence,
Missouri, to Oregon with Marcus Whitman's party;
notes on hunting.

NEWBY, WILLIAM T., 1820–1884   2742

Winton, Harry N.M., ed. "William T. Newby's Diary of
the Emigration of 1843." OREGON HISTORICAL QUAR-
TERLY 40 (1939):219–242.

    May–Nov 1843, Feb 1845. Journey from Dadeville,
Missouri, to Independence and from there to Oregon
City; brief notes of travel, distances, some
descriptions; many interesting spellings.

PARRISH, EDWARD EVANS, 1791–1874   2743

"Crossing the Plains in 1844." OREGON PIONEER ASSO-
CIATION TRANSACTIONS OF THE 16TH ANNUAL REUNION
(1888):82–122.

AMERICAN DIARIES, Vol. 1

1843-1845. Clergyman's diary; journey through Ohio, Kentucky and Missouri, then overland to Oregon; notes on Indians, hunting, sights, etc.

PATTON, WILLIAM, 1796-1856   2744

"Journal of a Visit to the Indian Missions, Missouri Conference." MISSOURI HISTORICAL SOCIETY BULLETIN 10 (1954):167-180.

Apr-May 1843. Journey on horseback of three Methodist ministers to the Indian missions in Kansas Territory; description and evaluation of efforts to Christianize and "civilize" various Indian tribes which had been resettled west of the Mississippi.

PREBLE, HARRIET, 1795-1854   2745

In MEMOIR OF THE LIFE OF HARRIET PREBLE; CONTAINING PORTIONS OF HER CORRESPONDENCE, JOURNAL AND OTHER WRITINGS, LITERARY AND RELIGIOUS, by R.H. Lee, pp. 275-283, 321-327, 387-405. New York: G.P. Putnam, 1856.

1843-1845, 1853-1854. Journal extracts, mainly religious musings, of an invalid, a proponent of women's education, who carried on a lively intellectual life through correspondence with Prescott, Lafayette and Ticknor.

PYNE, PERCY RIVINGTON, 1820-1895   2746

Parsons, John E., ed. "The 'Grand Tour' to Niagara in 1843: A Diary." NEW YORK HISTORICAL SOCIETY QUARTERLY 46 (1962):383-421.

Jul 1843. Description of a trip by steamboat up the Hudson River to Troy and then by rail to Niagara Falls; return through Canada to New York City; details of travel, accommodations and sights along the way.

READING, PIERSON BARTON, 1816-1869   2747

Bekeart, Philip P., ed. "Journal of Pierson Barton Reading in His Journey of One Hundred Twenty-Three Days across the Rocky Mountains." SOCIETY OF CALIFORNIA PIONEERS QUARTERLY 7 (1930):148-198.

May-Dec 1843. Journey from Westport, Missouri, to Monterey, California; account of route, hardships, organization of emigrant party; visit to Sutter's estates; trip down the Sacramento River to San Francisco; brief account of voyage to Monterey.

SALTER, WILLIAM, d. 1910   2748

Jordan, Philip D., ed. "My Ministry in Iowa." ANNALS OF IOWA, 3d ser. 19 (1933-1935):539-553, 592-613; 20 (1935-1937):26-49. Reprint. 24 (1943):7-102.

1843-1846. Missionary journal of Congregational minister; work in Jackson County, Iowa, and adjoining country; observations of the frontier and pioneers; support for education; opposition to slavery and liquor; good frontier material.

ANNALS OF IOWA, 3d ser. 17 (1930):466-469.

Jan-Dec 1846. Almanac diary kept at Maquoketa and Burlington, Iowa; brief notes of weather, clerical visits, etc.

SIRE, JOSEPH A.   2749

"Journal of a Steamboat Voyage from St. Louis to Fort Union." In THE AMERICAN FUR TRADE OF THE FAR WEST, by Hiram Chittenden, vol. 2, pp. 984-1003. New York: F.P. Harper, 1902; Press of the Pioneers, 1935;

R.R. Wilson, 1936; Stanford, Calif.: Academic Reprints, 1954.

Apr-Jun 1843. Steamboat captain's journal of trip up the Missouri on the OMEGA, with Audubon on board; such hourly hazards as sand bars, perverse currents and bad weather; cutting or buying wood; a few notes on passengers. Translated from the French.

SUBLETTE, WILLIAM LEWIS, 1799?-1845   2750

Dale, Harrison C., ed. "A Fragmentary Journal of William L. Sublette." MISSISSIPPI VALLEY HISTORICAL REVIEW 6 (1919-1920):99-110.

May-Jun 1843. Fur trader's journal; account of a hunting trip in the Rockies with Sir William Drummond Stewart.

SYLVESTER, AVERY   2751

"Voyages of the PALLAS and CHENAMUS." OREGON HISTORICAL QUARTERLY 34 (1933):259-272, 359-371.

1843-1846. Extracts from ship captain's diaries; four voyages of the brigs PALLAS and CHENAMUS between Oahu and Oregon; notes on Indians, settlers, trading, country, etc.

TALBOT, THEODORE, d. 1862   2752

THE JOURNALS OF THEODORE TALBOT. Edited by Charles H. Carey. Portland, Oreg.: Metropolitan Press, 1931. 153 pp.

Apr-Oct 1843. Journal, kept for his mother, of Fremont's expedition to map the country from Missouri to the Oregon coast; exploration of Oregon Territory; full descriptions of scenery.

1848-1852. Travels with the first military company in Oregon; voyage to Oregon, service during gold rush period; notes on desertions.

TIBBETTS, JOHN C. 1798-1862   2753

Tibbetts, Emma L., ed. "Journal of Captain John C. Tibbetts of the Brig GULNARE." NEW ENGLAND QUARTERLY 11 (1938):154-165.

Jul-Aug 1843. Voyage of the GULNARE from Antwerp to New York; details of sailing, interesting observations on passengers; philosophizing and piety; poems; an excellent self-portrait of an actively religious Yankee seaman.

WHIPPLE, HENRY BENJAMIN, 1822-1901   2754

BISHOP WHIPPLE'S SOUTHERN DIARY. Edited by Lester B. Shippee. Minneapolis: Plenum, 1937. 208 pp. Reprint. New York: Da Capo, 1965.

Oct 1843-May 1844. Diary of travels through Florida, Georgia, Mississippi, Louisiana, up the Mississippi to St. Louis, up the Ohio, overland through Ohio, Pennsylvania, Delaware, Virginia, Maryland; acute observations and comments on social and religious conditions and slavery; long and very interesting entries.

YOUNG, JOHN EDWARD, 1824-1904   2755

Hamil, Mrs. Frederick L., ed. "From Central Illinois to the Shenandoah Valley in 1843." ILLINOIS HISTORICAL SOCIETY JOURNAL 25 (1932-1933):167-189.

Sep 1843-Jan 1844. Account of horseback journey; descriptions of farming and crops in Illinois, Indiana, Kentucky, Ohio, West Virginia and Virginia.

253

1844

ANON. 2756

Rutland, Robert, ed. "A Journal of the First Dragoons in the Iowa Territory." IOWA JOURNAL OF HISTORY 51 (1953):57-78.

Aug 1844. Campaign under Captain James Allen to exhibit military force to the unsubdued Sioux Indians; marching and encampments along the Des Moines River; notes on terrain and buffalo hunting; few Sioux encountered.

ALLEN, JAMES, 1806-1846 2757

UNITED STATES CONGRESS HOUSE EXECUTIVE DOCUMENT no. 168, 29th Congress, 1st Session, 1845.

1844. Account kept by captain of the First United States Dragoons of a march into Indian country in Iowa and South Dakota.

Van der Zee, Jacob, ed. "Captain James Allen's Dragoon Expedition from Fort Des Moines, Territory of Iowa." IOWA JOURNAL OF HISTORY AND POLITICS 11 (1913):68-108.

1844. Extracts relating to Iowa.

Stevenson, C. Stanley, ed. "Expeditions into Dakota." SOUTH DAKOTA HISTORICAL COLLECTIONS 9 (1918):347-368.

1844. Extracts relating to South Dakota.

ANDERSON, EDWARD CLIFFORD, 1815-1883 2758

FLORIDA TERRITORY IN 1844: THE DIARY OF MASTER EDWARD C. ANDERSON. Edited by W. Stanley Hoole. University, Ala.: University of Alabama Press, 1977. 105 pp.

Mar-Dec 1844. Carefully detailed description by a naval officer aboard the GENERAL TAYLOR off the Florida coast with side trips to historical sites; names, titles and duties of each man on board.

CONFEDERATE FOREIGN AGENT: THE EUROPEAN DIARY OF MAJOR EDWARD C. ANDERSON. Edited by W. Stanley Hoole. University, Ala.: Confederate Publishing Co., 1976. 161 pp.

May 1861-Mar 1862. Diary of Confederate officer dispatched to England to purchase arms and ships and to investigate the conduct of a colleague, Caleb Huse; much travel throughout England, financial details, humorous cloak and dagger incidents; notes on Charles Francis Adams and James Dunwody Bulloch; return to Savannah on the steamer FINGAL.

BAXTER, HENRY 2759

Baxter, Frances. "Rafting on the Alleghany and Ohio." PENNSYLVANIA MAGAZINE OF HISTORY AND BIOGRAPHY 51 (1927):27-78, 143-171, 207-243.

Apr-Nov 1844. Lumberman's diary; rafting lumber on the Allegheny and Ohio rivers and selling it; full daily narrative of his work and personal life; accounts of towns, industries and social life; comments on reading and religion; a very good diary.

BLANCHARD, ELIZABETH HOWELL, 1800-1846 2760

Robbins, William A., ed. "Journal of a Trip from Illinois Back to Long Island in 1844." LONG ISLAND HISTORICAL SOCIETY QUARTERLY 3 (1941):3-13, 42-53, 77-83, 107-115; 4 (1942):3-15.

May-Oct 1844. Account of a trip back home in attempt to recover health; travel by stagecoach to St. Louis, then by steamboat up the Ohio to Pittsburgh, by canal boat and railroad to Philadelphia; description of fellow-travellers; stops in St. Louis, Cincinnati, Philadelphia; sojourn in New York City and Long Island, visiting friends and relatives; return home.

BRYANT, HENRY, 1820-1867 2761

HENRY BRYANT, M.D.; A BIOGRAPHY. Compiled by William Sohier Bryant. New York: Craftsman Press, 1952. 273 pp. Diary, pp. 53-121.

Feb-Jul 1844. Letter-diary, kept for his father, of a young Boston doctor completing his medical education at Hospital Beaujon in Paris; medical studies, comments on his professors, hospital work; sights of Paris; a lively social life and his own serious illness.

CARLETON, JAMES HENRY, 1814-1873 2762

"First Logbook." SPIRIT OF THE TIMES, 9 November 1844 to 12 April 1845. Published anonymously.

"Second Logbook of Second Expedition." SPIRIT OF THE TIMES, 27 December 1845 to 30 May 1846. Published anonymously.

THE PRAIRIE LOGBOOKS: DRAGOON CAMPAIGNS TO THE PAWNEE VILLAGES IN 1844, AND TO THE ROCKY MOUNTAINS IN 1845. Edited by Louis Pelzer. Chicago: The Caxton Club, 1943. 295 pp.

Aug 1844-Jun 1845. Officer's detailed account of the movements of the First United States Dragoons through the Great Plains; life in camp and on the march; dress, equipment, procedures and tactics of soldiers; valuable notes on Indians, especially Pawnees and Dakotas, including their councils; buffalo and other wildlife; keen interest in emigrants bound for Oregon; literary style.

"Of an Excursion to the Ruins of Abó, Quarra, and Gran Quivira, in New Mexico." SMITHSONIAN INSTITUTION ANNUAL REPORT (1854):296-316.

Dec 1853. Military exploration journal; archaeological descriptions.

CLYMAN, JAMES, 1792-1881 2763

Camp, Charles L. "James Clyman, His Diaries and Reminiscences." CALIFORNIA HISTORICAL SOCIETY QUARTERLY 4 (1925):307-360; 5 (1926):48-84, 110-138, 255-282, 378-401.

JAMES CLYMAN, AMERICAN FRONTIERSMAN. 1792-1881; THE ADVENTURES OF A TRAPPER AND COVERED WAGON EMIGRANT AS TOLD IN HIS OWN REMINISCENCES AND DIARIES. Edited by Charles L. Camp. California Historical Society Special Publications, no. 3. San Francisco: California Historical Society, 1928. 247 pp. Diary, pp. 59-235. Reprint. Portland, Oreg.: Champoeg Press, 352 pp. 1960.

1844-1846. Journey from Independence, Missouri, to Oregon along the Oregon Trail to Willamette Valley, from there to Napa Valley; travels in California; return to Missouri; a simple straightforward diary with some literary allusions; interesting for the lore of plains and mountains, written with good humor and common sense; some interesting spellings and words.

Korns, J. Roderic, ed. "The Journal of James Clyman." UTAH HISTORICAL QUARTERLY 19 (1951):21-42. Diary, pp. 28-42.

May-Jun 1846.

CALIFORNIA HISTORICAL SOCIETY QUARTERLY 6 (1927): 64–65.

JAMES CLYMAN, AMERICAN FRONTIERSMAN. Edited by Charles L. Camp, pp. 242–243.

Jan–Dec 1871. Farming diary; brief notes concerning his daily occupations and farming.

GARY, GEORGE, 1793–1855　　　　2764

Carey, Charles H., ed. "Diary of Rev. George Gary." OREGON HISTORICAL QUARTERLY 24 (1923):68–105, 153–185, 269–333, 386–433.

1844–1848. Missionary travel journal; voyage from New York to Oregon via Honolulu; missionary work; notes on people, places, sermons, etc.; return to New York.

HARRIS, N. SAYRE　　　　2765

JOURNAL OF A TOUR IN THE "INDIAN TERRITORY." By the Protestant Episcopal Church in the U.S.A. Board of Missions Domestic Committee Secretary. New York: Daniel Dana, Jr., 1844. 74 pp.

Extracts in "Journal of a Tour in the Indian Territory." CHRONICLES OF OKLAHOMA 10 (1932):219–256.

Mar 1844. Missionary travel journal; from New Orleans by steamer up Mississippi via Forts Smith, Gibson and Scott, the Shawnee Mission and Fort Leavenworth to Fort Towson; inspection of missionary posts in Indian Territory among Choctaws, Seminoles, Creeks, Cherokees, Osages, etc.; valuable comments and criticisms on work of missions and much general and social matter; an interesting journal.

HEWITT, S.C.　　　　2766

Foner, Philip S. "Journal of an Early Labor Organizer." LABOR HISTORY 10 (1969):205–227.

Jul–Aug 1844. Journal of lecture tour through Massachusetts, Rhode Island and eastern Connecticut to organize local units of New England Workingman's Association; convincing groups to send delegates to a convention in September in support of ten hour working day; details of meetings in each city.

IVES, WILLIAM, 1817?–1874?　　　　2767

Gilchrist, Marie, E., ed. "A Michigan Surveyor." INLAND SEAS 21 (1965):313–321.

Aug–Oct 1844. Brief account of surveying expedition on Upper Peninsula of Michigan during which vast deposits of iron ore were incidentally discovered; mostly surveying notations and weather reports.

JACOBS, ZINA DIANTHA HUNTINGTON, 1821–1901　　　　2768

Beecher, Maureen U., ed. "'All Things Move in Order in the City': The Nauvoo Diary of Zina Diantha Huntington Jacobs." BRIGHAM YOUNG UNIVERSITY STUDIES 19 (1979):285–320.

1844–1845. Diary kept at Nauvoo, Illinois, by future church leader and wife of Brigham Young; daily life, family and friends; struggles of the Mormons and martyrdom of Joseph and Hyrum Smith.

KOCH, ALBRECHT KARL　　　　2769

JOURNEY THROUGH A PART OF THE UNITED STATES OF AMERICA IN THE YEARS 1844 TO 1846. Translated and edited by Ernst A. Stadler. Carbondale: Southern Illinois University Press, 1972. 177 pp.

1844–1846. Travel diary of German paleontologist seeking fossil remains in eastern and southern United States, particularly of a sea serpent called Zeuglodon or Hydrarchos; travel by stagecoach, train, Mississippi river boat and on foot collecting fossils, making geological and botanical observations; comments on people and customs.

LEWIS, GEORGE　　　　2770

IMPRESSIONS OF AMERICA AND THE AMERICAN CHURCHES, FROM THE JOURNAL OF THE REV. G. LEWIS. Edinburgh: W.P. Kennedy, 1845. 432 pp. Reprint. New York: Negro Universities Press, 1968.

1844. American travel journal of Scottish Free Church minister; steamer voyage, storms and seasickness; visits to plantations, conversations with slaves and masters, visits to churches of many denominations, both black and white; full of names, facts and statistics on church membership, missions, salaries of clergy, education and revivals; an intelligent, conscientious journal of the reportorial type, but with considerable charm.

LINCOLN, SETH F.　　　　2771

"Excerpts from the Journal of Seth F. Lincoln, Boatsteerer on the EMIGRANT." In "THERE SHE BLOWS" A NARRATIVE OF A WHALING VOYAGE, by Ben-Ezra S. Ely, edited by Curtis Dahl, pp. 179–206. Middletown, Conn.: Published for the Marine Historical Association by Wesleyan University Press, 1971.

Nov 1844–Jan 1845. Brief, routine notes of whaling; sightings of ships and whales; weather; work of all kinds related to whaling.

MCLANE, LOUIS, 1819–1905　　　　2772

THE PRIVATE JOURNAL OF LOUIS MCLANE, U.S.N. Edited by Jay Monaghan. Los Angeles: Published for the Santa Barbara Historical Society by Dawson's Bookshop, 1971. 120 pp.

1844–1848. Officer's adventures at sea aboard the LEVANT and the COLUMBUS; stops in Chile, Peru, the Marquesas, Society and Hawaiian Islands, California, Mexico and Panama; news of narrowly averted war with England over the settlement of Oregon Territory; Mexican War and land service under John C. Fremont in California; highly descriptive, lively and opinionated record of a varied military career.

MARTIN, WILLIAM, 1765–1846　　　　2773

Extract in FAMILY HISTORY, compiled by Lucy Henderson Horton, p. 137. Franklin, Tenn.: Press of the News, 1922.

Apr 1844. Brief political diary kept during attendance at Whig Convention; nomination of Henry Clay.

MOORE, GEORGE, 1806–1876　　　　2774

JOURNAL OF A VOYAGE ACROSS THE ATLANTIC: WITH NOTES ON CANADA & THE UNITED STATES. London: Printed for private circulation, 1845. 96 pp.

Aug–Nov 1844. Englishman's travel diary; voyage from Great Britain to New York; notes on New York, Baltimore, Washington, Niagara and return; towns, scenery, etc.

NICHOLSON, ASENATH HATCH   2775

IRELAND'S WELCOME TO THE STRANGER; OR AN EXCUR-
SION THROUGH IRELAND, IN 1844 & 1845, FOR THE
PURPOSE OF PERSONALLY INVESTIGATING THE CONDITION
OF THE POOR. New York: Baker and Scribner, 1847.
456 pp. passim.
THE BIBLE IN IRELAND (IRELAND'S WELCOME TO THE
STRANGER). Edited by Alfred T. Sheppard. New York:
John Day, 1927. 272 pp.

> 1844-1845. New York woman's journey through
> Ireland just before the onset of the Great Potato
> Famine; travels mainly on foot, visiting impover-
> ished peasants, enjoying their tales and dances,
> inquiring about their way of life and reading to
> them from the Bible; attempts at arousing land-
> owners and clergy, both Protestant and Catholic,
> to help alleviate poverty; temperance work; visits
> to schools and institutions; fascinating picture of
> Irish life at that time; partly narrative.

PARKS, WILLIAM JUSTICE, 1799-1873   2776

A DIARY-LETTER WRITTEN FROM THE METHODIST GEN-
ERAL CONFERENCE OF 1844. Edited by Franklin Nutting
Parker. Atlanta: The Library, Emory University, 1944.
24 pp.

> May-Jun 1844. Description by Georgia Methodist
> clergyman of efforts of New England delegates to
> unseat a slave-owning Georgia bishop, James
> Osgood Andrew, who owned only one slave, a child
> willed to him to raise; some of the proceedings
> against Andrew and subsequent debate during the
> momentous 1844 Conference which split the Methodist
> Church along North-South lines.

RANNEY, TIMOTHY E., b. 1815   2777

Ranney, Charles R., ed. "Letters and a Journal by
Timothy E. Ranney and Charlotte T. Ranney." VERMONT
QUARTERLY 21 (1953):118-127, 200-210. Journal, pp.
204-208.

> May-Jun 1844. Newly ordained minister's travel
> journal within a letter to his parents; trip from
> Albany to Louisville with his bride on way to
> service as missionary to the Indians under the
> American Board of Commissioners for Foreign Mis-
> sions; description of slow boat trip on the Erie
> Canal, a few excursions along the way.

STOUT, HOSEA, 1810-1889   2778

ON THE MORMON FRONTIER; THE DIARY OF HOSEA
STOUT. Edited by Juanita Brooks. Salt Lake City:
University of Utah Press, 1964. 2 vols.

> 1844-1861. Extensive and important Mormon diary;
> persecutions in Nauvoo, Illinois, where diarist was
> chief of police; journey of 1846-1848 and details of
> organization, problems and discipline of emigrants;
> encampment at Winter Quarters; leadership in Utah
> as a member of the territorial legislature and
> records of its deliberations; an unsuccessful
> mission to China, where he preached to Eng-
> lish-speaking community; return, short stay in
> Wyoming, establishment of legal practice in Utah
> with cases well chronicled in diary; service in
> Mormon military during hostilities between Mormons
> and federal troops; notes of family life in a large
> polygamous home interspersed with details of
> public affairs.

TUCKER, CHARLES F.   2779

Extracts in "THERE SHE BLOWS" A NARRATIVE OF A
WHALING VOYAGE, by Ben-Ezra S. Ely, edited by
Curtis Dahl, pp. 153-178. Middletown, Conn.: Published for the Marine Historical Association by Wesleyan University Press, 1971.

> Nov 1844-Aug? 1845. Whaling diary kept by cooper
> on board the EMIGRANT; routine tasks; dangers
> and disasters mentioned matter-of-factly.

WALLIS, MARY DAVIS COOK   2780

LIFE IN FEEJEE OR, FIVE YEARS AMONG CANNIBALS, by
a lady. Boston: W. Heath, 1851. 422 pp. Reprint.
Ridgewood, N.J.: Gregg Press, 1967.

> 1844-1849. Effusive diary of life among the inhabi-
> tants and missionaries on the Fiji Islands; customs
> and religion; conversions to Christianity; descrip-
> tions of ship travel.

WHARTON, CLIFTON, d. 1847   2781

"The Expedition of Major Clifton Wharton in 1844."
KANSAS HISTORICAL SOCIETY COLLECTIONS 16 (1923-
1925):272-305.

> Aug-Sep 1844. March of the First United States
> Dragoons from Fort Leavenworth to the Pawnee
> villages on the Platte River, from there to country
> of the Oto, Potawatomi, Iowa and Sauk on the
> Missouri River; return to Fort Leavenworth; notes
> on country and councils with Indians; literary
> style.

WOOTEN, HARDY VICKERS   2782

Jones, Virginia K., ed. "A Great Day for the Whigs of
Alabama." ALABAMA HISTORICAL QUARTERLY 25 (1963):
254-261.

> Feb-Oct 1844. Lowndesboro, Alabama, doctor's ac-
> tivities on behalf of Whig party; participation in
> Whig convention at Montgomery.

NAME INDEX

Name Index

Chirikov, Alexei Ilich, **307**
Chislacasliche, 177
Cholmley, Robert, 469
Chouteau, Auguste, **678**
Christie, Thomas, 258
Chubbuck, Emily. See Judson, Emily Chubbuck
Church, D. W., **1713**
Churchman, George, **1318**
Clap, Caleb, **1003**
Clark, George Rogers, **1004**, 1192
Clark, John, **2188**
Clark, John Alonzo, **2543**
Clark, Joseph, **1645**
Clark, Joseph, 1751–1813, **1117**
Clark, Laura Downs, **2047**
Clark, Thomas, **619**
Clark, William, **1575**, 1750
Clark, William Joseph, **1762**
Clarke, Aletta, **1467**
Clarke, C. H., **2435**
Clarke, James Freeman, **2436**
Clarkson, Matthew, **734**
Clasen, Lowrens, 166
Claus, William, **1831**
Clawson, Lawrence, 192
Clay, Henry, 1879, 2415, 2441, 2772
Claybrooke, Thomas W., **2375**
Clayton, William, **2652**
Cleaveland, John, **317**
Cleaveland, Moses, **1626**
Cleaves, Benjamin, **357**
Cleland, John, **2437**
Clerc, Laurent, **1993**
Clerke, Charles, **1180**
Clermont-Crevecoeur, Jean François Louis, comte de, **1281**
Cleveland, Moses C., **2337**
Cleveland, William, **1694**
Clewell, Christian, 685
Clifford, Anna Rawle, **1319**
Clinton, Charles, **250**
Clinton, Cornelia, **1435**
Clinton, George, **534**, 1435
Clinton, George W., **2230**
Clinton, Sir Henry, 1107, 1173, **1282**, 1323
Clinton, James, 1221
Clitherall, James, **1005**
Clopper, Edward Nicholas, **2246**, 2247
Clopper, Joseph Chambers, **2247**
Closen, Ludwig, baron von, **1283**
Clough, Abner, **378**
Clough, Gibson, **620**
Clubb, Stephen, **1818**
Clyman, James, **2763**
Cobb, David, **1320**
Cobb, Elisha, **570**
Cobb, Eunice Parsons, **2544**
Cobb, Samuel, **571**
Cobbett, William, **2015**
Cobden, Richard, **2468**
Coburn, Mary. See Dewees, Mary Coburn
Cocking, Matthew, **800**
Coffin, Ebenezer, **1994**
Coffin, Lucretia. See Mott, Lucretia Coffin
Coffin, Paul, **647**
Cogan, John, **206**
Coggeshall, George, **2115**
Cogswell, Mason Fitch, **1436**
Cohen, Myer M., **2503**
Coit, Mehetabel Chandler, **77**
Coke, Thomas, **1376**

Colbert, William, **1865**
Colbraith, William, **1118**
Colby, John, **1850**
Cole, Thomas, **2266**
Coleman, Ann Raney Thomas, **2376**
Coleridge, Samuel Taylor, **1987**
Colhoun, James E., **2164**
Collette, Elizabeth Van Horne, **1819**
Collier, Sir George, **1006**
Collin, Nicholas, **778**
Collins, Daniel Lake, **2313**
Collins, Stephen, **2141**
Colnett, James, **1468**
Columbus, Christopher, **1**
Colvocoresses, George Musalas, **2587**
Combe, George. See Coombe, George
Comer, John, **207**
Comfort, Elwood, **2653**
Comly, John, **1695**
Comly, Rebecca, **1646**
Conant, Augustus Hammond, **2504**
Concha, Fernando de la, **1450**
Condict, Jemima, **801**
Condict, Lewis, **1607**
Congreve, William, 2170
Conneau, Theophilus, **1832**
Connell, Sarah. See Ayer, Sarah Connell
Connor, James, 492
Connor, Thomas, 1774
Connor, Timothy, **1119**
Constant, Silas, **1359**
Cook, James, 615, 1171, 1177, **1181**, 1183, 1196, 1203, 1211, 1217, 1270, 1428, 1442
Cook, Mary Davis. See Wallis, Mary Davis Cook
Cooke, Amos Starr, **2625**
Cooke, John, **1576**
Cooke, Middlecott, **280**
Cooke, Philip St. George, 2683, **2727**
Cooke, Silas, **1007**
Coombe, George, **2588**
Cooper, Hanna. See Woolson, Hanna Cooper Pomeroy
Cooper, James Fenimore, **2267**, 2645
Cooper, Samuel, **446**
Cooper, William, **171**
Coote, Richard, **120**
Cope, Thomas Pym, **1696**
Copland, Charles, **1451**
Corbett, Ichabod, **1008**
Corcoran, John, **2248**
Cordero, Antonio, **1403**
Cornelius, Elias, **1120**
Cornplanter, Seneca chief, 1806
Cornwallis, Charles, 1st marquis, 1282
Corse, James, **253**
Corser, David, **1664**
Cortlandt, Burgomaster, 43
Costanso, Miguel, **763**
Cotten, John, **787**
Cotton, John, **1969**
Cotton, Josiah, **102**
Covell, Lemuel, **1743**
Covington, Leven, **2294**
Cowan, John, **1121**
Cowdery, Jonathan, **1744**
Cowdin, Thomas, **1377**
Cowdrey, Nathaniel, **1284**
Cowles, Julia, **1647**
Cox, Caleb, **2048**
Cox, Rebecca. See Jackson, Rebecca Cox

Cozine, John C., **2268**
Crabbe (or Crabb), Thomas, **1970**
Craft, Benjamin, 1706–1746, **358**
Craft, Benjamin, 1738–1823, **894**
Craft, Eleazer, **1122**
Craft, James, **753**
Crafts, Samuel, **1728**, 1734
Cram, Jacob, **1833**
Cranch, Elizabeth, **1404**
Crane, Benjamin, 157
Crawford, Medorem, **2704**
Crawford, William Harris, **1919**
Crespi, Juan, 762, **764**, 779
Cresson, Caleb, **1506**
Cresswell, Nicholas, **840**
Crocker, Alvah, **2728**
Crockett, David, **2505**
Croghan, George, **428**, 654, 698, 736, 861
Cromot DuBourg, Marie François Joseph Maxime, baron, 1312, **1321**, 1334
Crosby, Jesse W., **2626**
Cross, James. See Corse, James
Cross, Ralph, **1123**
Cross, Stephen, **515**
Crosswell, Harry, **2116**
Crowningshield, Benjamin, **1124**
Crowninshield, Clara, **2469**
Crowninshield, John, **1648**
Cruger, Henry, **895**
Cruger, John Harris, **1229**
Cuming, Sir Alexander, **254**
Cuerno Verde, Comanche warrior, 835
Curler, Arent van, 15
Curot, Michel, **1745**
Curtis, Holbrook, **1834**
Curtis, Philip, **318**
Curtis, William Edmund, **2654**
Curwen, Samuel, **359**
Cushing, Daniel Lewis, **1897**
Cushing, Deborah H. See Porter, Deborah H. Cushing
Cushing, John, **379**
Custis, Nellie, **1677**
Custis, Martha Dandridge. See Washington, Martha Dandridge Custis
Cuthbertson, John, **429**
Cutler, Benjamin Clarke, **2049**
Cutler, Ephraim, **1851**
Cutler, George Younglove, **2099**
Cutler, Manasseh, **722**
Cutler, Samuel, **1009**
Cutter, Ammi Ruhamah, **516**
Cutting, Nathaniel, **1525**

D

D'Abbadie, Jean-Jacques-Blaise. See Abbabie, Jean-Jacques-Blaise d'
Dall, Caroline Wells Healy, **2680**
Dallas, George Mifflin, **2545**
Dana, Richard Henry, **2438**, 2479
Danckaerts, Jasper. See Dankers, Jasper
Dandridge, Martha. See Washington, Martha Dandridge Custis
Danford, Jacob, **896**
Danforth, Joshua, **1010**
Danforth, Samuel, **28**

Dankers, Jasper, **67**
Darling, Jonathan, **535**
Darlington, William, **1949**
Darnell, Elias, **1898**
Darrell, John Harvey, **2165**
D'Artaguiette, Diron, **208**
Daubeny, Charles Giles Bridle, **2546**
David, George, **2405**
Davidson, James D., **2506**
Davidson, Margaret Miller, **2406**
Davies, Samuel, **447**
Davis, Hannah, **2314**
Davis, John, **1322**
Davis, John Russell, **1697**
Davis, Joseph, **2209**
Davis, Mary Elizabeth Morayne, **2507**
Davis, Moses, **1011**
Davis, Samuel, **1469**
Davis, William Hervey, 2507
Davy, William, **1577**
Davydov, Gavriil Ivanovich, **1729**
Dawson, James William, **2508**
Day, Jeremiah, **1452**
Dayton, Maria Annis Tomlinson, **2547**
Deaderick, David Anderson, **2210**
Dean, Thomas, **2016**
Deane, Samuel, **665**
Deane, Silas, **841**
De Angelis, Pascal Charles Joseph. See Angelis, Pascal Charles Joseph de
Dearborn, Henry, **897**
Dearborn, Henry Alexander, **2589**
Deas, Edward, **2470**
De Beauchamps, **380**
De Boishebert, Charles Deschamps, **395**
De Brahm, **1285**
Defoe, Jules, **1470**
De Hart, Abigail. See Mayo, Abigail De Hart
De Hooges, Antony, **24**
De Krafft, John Charles Philip, **1012**
De la croix, Armand Charles Augustin, duc de Castries. See Castries, Armand Charles Augustin de la Croix, duc de
Delafield, Joseph, **2017**
De la Harpe, Benard. See Harpe, Benard de la
De la Mothe, 478
De Lancey, Oliver, **1323**
De la Sagra, Ramón, **2471**
Delassus, Carlos Dehault, **2509**
De León, Alonso, **78**
De Lery, Joseph Gaspard Chaussegros, 289, **456**
De Léry, Joseph Gaspard Chaussegros, 289, **456**
Delisle, Legardeur, **209**
Dellius, **94**
De los Rios, Domingo de Terán. See Terán de los Rios, Domingo de
Demere, Raymond, **1125**
Deming, Sarah Winslow, **898**
De Montreuil, Chevalier, **477**
De Mun, Jules, **1971**
Dennis, Joseph, **1182**
Denny, Ebenezer, **1324**
Derby, Edward George Geoffrey Smith Stanley, 14th earl of, **2211**
De Smet, Pierre Jean. See Smet, Pierre Jean de

Des Ursins, **187**
De Tocqueville, Alexis. See Tocqueville, Alexis de
Deux-Ponts, Guillaume, comte de, **1286**
De Vaudreuil, M., **478**
Devereux, John William, **1679**
De Villiers, Neyon, **457**
De Vries, David Peterson. See Vries, David Pietersz de
Dewees, Mary Coburn, **1437**
Dewey, John, **1013**
Dewey, Russell, **1014**
De Wolfe, Mary Soley, 2628
De Wolfe family, **2628**
Dexter, Joseph, **2604**
Dexter, Samuel, **193**
Diaz, Juan, **842**
Dibble, Ebenezer, **621**
D'Iberville, Pierre Le Moyne. See Le Moyne d'Iberville, Pierre
Dick, Elizabeth. See Lindsay, Elizabeth Dick
Dickens, Charles 2170, 2644
Dickinson, Jonathan, **109**
Dickinson, Rebecca, **1438**
Dickinson, Timothy, **1578**
Dickson, Sir Alexander, **1950**
Diefenbach, Heinrich, **1730**
Digby, William, **1015**
Dillwyn, William, **802**
Dingane (or Dingaan), Zulu chief, **2467**
Dinwiddie, Robert, **406**
Dixon, Jeremiah, **701**
Dobbin, William, **2189**
Dodge, Henry, **2409**, **2439**, **2460**, **2472**
Dodge, Nathaniel Brown, **1016**
Doehla, Johann Conrad, **1325**
Domett, Alfred, **2407**
Dominquez, Francisco Atanasio, **1088**
Don Lorenzo, Picuries chief, **141**
Donelson, John, **1230**
Donelson, Rachel. See Jackson, Rachel Donelson
Donop, Carl Emil Kurt von, 1012
Doolittle, Benjamin, **325**
Dorr, Moses, **572**
Doty, James Duane, **2100**
Dougherty, Peter, **2590**
Douglas, David, **2190**
Douglas, Sir James, **2655**
Douglas, William, **1471**
Douglass, David Bates, **2018**, 2092
Dow, Lorenzo, **1579**
Dow, Peggy, **1920**
Downs, Laura. See Clark, Laura Downs
Drake, Sylvia, **2117**
Drinker, Elizabeth Sandwith, **573**
Drips, Andrew, 2430
Drowne, Solomon, **1287**
Du Bourg, Marie François Joseph Maxime, baron Cromot. See Cromot Du Bourg, Marie François Joseph Maxime, baron
Duden, Gottfried, 2412, 2525
Dudley, Paul, **297**
Duffield, George, **2269**
Duffin, Robert, **1453**
Dufour, Jean Jacques, **1627**
Dulles, Joseph Heatly, **1951**
Dummer, Jeremiah, **146**
Dunbar, Asa, **818**

Dunbar, John, 2429, **2440**
Dunbar, William, **1763**
Duncan, Elizabeth Caldwell, **2191**
Duncan, Henry, **1017**
Duncan, James, **1326**
Duncan, Joseph, **2295**
Dunlap, William, **1420**
Dunlop, Captain, **76**
Du Pont de Nemours, Victor Marie, **1714**
Duran, Narciso, **2019**
Du Roi, Augustus Wilhelm, **1018**
Du Ru, Paul, **126**
Duyckinck, Evert, 2591
Duyckinck, George Long, **2591**
Dwight, Margaret Van Horn. See Bell, Margaret Van Horn Dwight
Dwight, Nathaniel, **479**
Dwight, Timothy, **1612**
Dwinnell, Joseph Porter, **2548**
Dyer, John, **699**

E

Earle, Caleb, 1839
Earle, Pliny, **2315**
Early, John, **1820**
Easton, Peter, **14**
Eaton, William, **1731**
Ecuyer, S., 442
Edes, Peter, **899**
Edgar, Thomas, **1183**
Edgeworth, Maria, **1987**
Eduardo, Miguel Antonio, **1019**
Edwards, Esther. See Burr, Esther Edwards
Edwards, Jonathan, 190, **210**, 306
Edwards, Philip Leget, **2549**
Edwards, Timothy, **163**
Eells, Cushing, 2616
Eells, Myra Fairbanks, **2592**
Eggleston, Dick Hardaway, **2316**
Egmont, John Perceval, 1st earl of **255**
Eixarch, Thomas, **900**
Eld, George, **1231**
Eldredge, Joseph C., **2729**
Eldridge, Charles William, **2408**
Eliot, Jacob, **213**
Eliot, John, **25**
Ellery, William, **1126**, 1166
Ellice, Jane, **2593**
Ellicott, Andrew, 1605, **1628**
Ellicott, Joseph, **1715**
Elliot, James, **1544**
Ellis, Ira J., **2070**
Ellis, William, **1952**
Ellsworth, Henry Leavitt, 1748, **2377**, 2391, 2717
Elmer, Ebenezer, **1020**
Elson, Thomas, **2231**
Ely, Ezra Stiles, **1873**
Emerson, Daniel, **901**
Emerson, John, 1707-1774, **326**
Emerson, John, 1745-1826, **1680**
Emerson, John Smith, **2338**
Emerson, Joseph, **360**
Emerson, Ralph Waldo, 361, **2071**, 2075, 2226, 2301, 2385, 2577, 2628
Emerson, Ursula Sophia Newell, **2339**
Emerson, William, **709**

SUBJECT INDEX

Subject Index

Subject Index

Cayuga, 407, 458
Cayuse, 2529
Cherokee, 231, 242, 254, 304,
   593, 667, 1656, 1690, 2038,
   2061, 2118, 2162, 2183, 2258,
   2306, 2523, 2564, 2631, 2765
Chickasaw, 289, 437, 1678,
   1794, 2077, 2043, 2510
Chilkotin, 1836
Chippewa, 666, 1508, 1644,
   2092, 2215, 2343, 2363, 2367,
   2520, 2555, 2574, 2590
Choctaw, 380, 437, 1402, 1535,
   1794, 2066, 2308, 2765
Clallam, 2270
Comanche, 191, 835, 1454,
   1455, 1829, 2428, 2487, 2729
Creek, 232, 242, 264, 436,
   795, 1497, 1584, 1631, 1816,
   1937, 1943, 1952, 2091, 2211,
   2258, 2470, 2474, 2765
Crow, 1792, 2453
Dakota, 1942, 2092, 2520,
   2756, 2762
Delaware, 685, 741, 979
Five Nations. See Iroquois Con-
   federacy
Flathead. See Salish
Fox, 1942, 1947
Gila, 1297, 1403, 1450
Gros Ventre, 1718, 2434
Haida, 2182
Hidatsa, 1659
Hopi, 96, 835
Housatonic, 268
Huron, 1710, 1802, 1831, 1906
Iowa, 2781
Iroquois, 15, 711, 1279, 2537
Iroquois Confederacy, 94, 101,
   106, 110, 166, 376, 711,
   970, 1516, 2589
Kiowa, 2460
Lower Creek, 255
Mandan, 1575, 1659, 1718,
   2434, 2448
Menominee, 2328
Miami, 442, 715, 889, 1768
Mingo, 979
Minisink, 602
Mohave, 2260
Mohawk, 155, 229
Mohican. See Mohegan
Mohegan, 685
Moqui. See Hopi
Navaho, 2179
Nez Percé, 2182, 2489, 2611,
   2640
Nootka, 1522, 1749
Norridgewock, 452
Ohio, 428, 708
Ojibwa. See Chippewa
Oneida, 711, 1414
Onondaga, 94, 121, 123, 125,
   128, 129, 373, 398, 407,
   458, 1249
Osage, 1803, 2424, 2765
Oto, 2414, 2781
Ottowa, 1831, 2584
Pawnee, 198, 1430, 2428, 2429,
   2440, 2460, 2762
Paunch, 1718
Picuries, 96, 141
Piegan, 2203
Potawatomi, 1885, 2502, 2570,
   2581, 2600, 2607, 2781
Puan, 666, 1942

Quabaug, 79
Quebec, 846
Salish, 1718, 2182, 2512
Sauk, 1942, 1947, 2781
Seminole, 2523, 2561, 2643,
   2765
Seneca, 192, 197, 711, 1689,
   1806, 2123, 2584, 2589
Shawnee, 523, 806, 1575, 2449
Shoshoni, 1718, 2182
Siksika, 2182
Sioux. See Dakota
Six Nations. See Iroquois
   Confederacy
Snake. See Shoshoni
Spokan, 2616
Stockbridge, 2387
Taovaya, 1454
Tawakoni, 1430
Tejas. See Caddo
Tuscarora, 156, 680, 2433, 2589
Ute, 191, 835
Wichita, 2460
Winnebago, 2328, 2379
Wisconsin, 524
Wyandot. See Huron
Yamparika, 1829
Yokuts, 2072
Yuma, 415, 779, 900
Zuni, 96
warfare, 170, 190, 378, 390, 453,
   495, 497, 512, 540, 702, 712,
   786, 787, 848, 854, 962, 1230,
   1267, 1391, 1544, 1574, 1590,
   1886, 1902, 2304, 2485, 2488
   Battle of Fallen Timbers, 1566,
      1567, 1603
   Tippecanoe campaign, 1870,
      1885
   See also Indians, Expeditions
      against; names of individ-
      ual wars; names of individ-
      ual wars under Military
      diaries
Indians, 1849, 1911, 2087, 2097,
   2691, 2714
   Christian, 762, 2061
   resettlement, 754, 809
   Expeditions against, 136, 156,
      191, 227, 233, 235, 236, 523,
      667, 685, 708, 712, 779, 835,
      839, 1105, 1249, 1306, 1391,
      1403, 1450, 1483, 1490, 1504,
      1514, 1538, 1540, 1565, 1566,
      1567, 1571, 1575, 1594, 1893,
      1937, 2179, 2270, 2622
   by place
      Arizona, 104, 2174
      Alaska, 307, 682, 1460, 1729,
         2220, 2231, 2720
      Arkansas, 185, 1559
      California, 2, 9, 10, 73, 104,
         762, 763, 771, 779, 842,
         862, 1841, 2019, 2072, 2158,
         2174, 2220, 2236
      Canada, 1587
      Central states, 2635, 2641,
         2642, 2697, 2716, 2723, 2724,
         2743
      Connecticut, 117, 1414
      Delaware, 159
   Florida, 3, 4, 5, 97, 100,
      109, 177, 212, 1746
   Georgia, 1816
      Great Lakes region, 431

Great Plains, 198, 1748, 2361,
   2391
Illinois, 2402
Indiana, 1725, 2129
Kansas, 1430, 2388, 2744
Kentucky, 1121, 1540, 1565
Louisiana, 122, 697
Maine, 240, 1105
Massachusetts, 63, 114, 190,
   269, 295
Mexico, 189
Michigan, 2522
Minnesota, 2031, 2164
Mississippi Valley, 733, 735,
   2074
Missouri River region, 2053,
   2096
New England, 20, 25, 804,
   1753, 1761
New Hampshire, 378
New Jersey, 295
New Mexico, 6, 8, 96, 172,
   191, 2114
New York, 11, 17, 295, 687,
   746, 1645
North Carolina, 127
Ohio, 419, 428, 442, 591, 685,
   828, 1424, 1459, 1504, 1544,
   1603, 1917, 2129, 2522
Ohio River region, 979, 1172,
   1197, 2008
Oklahoma, 2377
Old Northwest, 1543, 1544,
   1566, 1567, 1571, 1594, 1658,
   2100
Oregon, 1539, 2236, 2426, 2751
Pacific coast, 764, 891, 962,
   1412
Pacific Northwest coast, 764,
   860, 891, 1180, 1181, 1203,
   1416, 1428, 1433, 1440, 1493,
   1498, 1519, 1522, 1523, 1526,
   1532, 1570, 1692, 1866, 2297
Pennsylvania, 155, 295, 442,
   511, 513, 530, 584, 591,
   599, 604, 651, 685, 1423,
   1544, 1605, 2129
Rocky Mountains, 2318, 2627
South, 815, 2137
South Carolina, 242, 436
Snake River region, 2197
Southwest, 141, 739, 740, 835,
   847, 1088, 1297, 1430, 1829,
   2223
Texas, 56, 93, 95, 147, 172,
   175, 178, 182, 201, 751,
   2259, 2582, 2622, 2648
Vermont, 839
Washington, 1539, 2398, 2425
Western states, 2364, 2397,
   2495, 2697, 2723, 2743
Wisconsin, 524, 2402, 2551
Indigo, 294
Industry. See Business and industry
Innkeepers, 2060
Inns and taverns, 169, 640, 676,
   690, 724, 766, 814, 838, 885,
   1022, 1029, 1074, 1126, 1133,
   1172, 1251, 1280, 1346, 1358,
   1360, 1375, 1425, 1457, 1495,
   1502, 1547, 1605, 1606, 1612,
   1670, 1686, 1697, 1732, 1766,
   1777, 1780, 1783, 1786, 1819,
   846, 1851, 1857, 1862, 1869,
   1880, 1884, 1925, 1954, 1974,

Subject Index

GEOGRAPHIC INDEX

Geographic Index